AN INTRODUCTION TO THE PROFESSION OF SOCIAL WORK: BECOMING A CHANGE AGENT

An Introduction to the Profession of Social Work

Becoming a Change Agent

Third Edition

Elizabeth A. Segal
Arizona State University

Karen E. Gerdes
Arizona State University

Sue Steiner
California State University Chico

BROOKS/COLE
CENGAGE Learning™

Australia • Brazil • Canada • Mexico • Singapore • Spain
United Kingdom • United States

BROOKS/COLE
CENGAGE Learning™

An Introduction to the Profession of Social Work: Becoming a Change Agent, Third Edition
Elizabeth A. Segal, Karen E. Gerdes, and Sue Steiner

Acquisitions Editor: Seth Dobrin

Assistant Editor: Allison Bowie

Editorial Assistant: Rachel McDonald

Technology Project Manager: Andrew Keay

Senior Marketing Manager: Trent Whatcott

Marketing Assistant: Darlene Macanan

Senior Marketing Communications Manager: Tami Strang

Project Manager, Editorial Production: Christy Krueger

Creative Director: Rob Hugel

Senior Art Director: Caryl Gorska

Print Buyer: Linda Hsu

Permissions Editor, Text: Margaret Chamberlain-Gaston

Permissions Editor, Images: Dean Dauphinais

Photo Researcher: Nina Smith

Production Service: Pre-Press PMG

Copy Editor: Carol A. Loomis

Cover Designer: Irene MorrisTami

Cover Image: Photodisc/Getty Images

Compositor: Pre-Press PMG

For product information and technology assistance, contact us at **Cengage Learning Customer & Sales Support, 1-800-354-9706.**

For permission to use material from this text or product, submit all requests online at **www.cengage.com/permissions**

Further permissions questions can be e-mailed to **permissionrequest@cengage.com**

Library of Congress Control Number: 2008943184

ISBN-13: 978-0-495-60170-8

ISBN-10: 0-495-60170-5

Brooks/Cole
10 Davis Drive
Belmont, CA, 94002-3098
USA

Cengage Learning is a leading provider of customized learning solutions with office locations around the globe, including Singapore, the United Kingdom, Australia, Mexico, Brazil, and Japan. Locate your local office at **www.cengage.com/international.**

Cengage Learning products are represented in Canada by Nelson Education, Ltd.

To learn more about Brooks/Cole, visit **www.cengage.com/brookscole.**

Purchase any of our products at your local college store or at our preferred online store **www.ichapters.com.**

Printed in Canada
1 2 3 4 5 6 7 13 12 11 10 09

CONTENTS

PREFACE

The start of the twenty-first century has brought with it significant challenges that affect people's lives. Many Americans struggle against poverty, oppression, and violence. Millions live without adequate wages, health care, food, or education. The threat of terrorism has required us to make our lives safer without turning to hate, bigotry, or repression. Social workers are called on to address these challenges. Social work educators must recruit a new generation of practitioners and prepare them to help individuals, families, and communities develop and expand the strengths they need to address their problems. Workers are faced with these challenges during a time of extraordinary technological advances that benefit many people but leave some far behind. The process of introducing students to the changing and demanding world often begins in social work classes.

Introductory social work courses attract a variety of students. Most are drawn to the profession because they want to help people. *An Introduction to the Profession of Social Work: Becoming a Change Agent* provides a foundation of knowledge about social work practice that prepares students for future social work classes and more advanced study. This book also introduces students to the process of becoming change agents. Although wanting to help people is critical for anyone working in human services, there is much more to becoming a professional social worker. The book provides students with information about the breadth of social work practice and what it means to be a social worker, helping them determine whether social work is a good fit for them. Therefore, the book is designed to encourage knowledge building and self-exploration, both of which are essential to developing good social work practice.

An Introduction to the Profession of Social Work: Becoming a Change Agent, like many other textbooks, informs students about what it means to be a professional social worker. Unlike some other books, it also instills interest and enthusiasm in students about pursuing a social work career and encourages students to take an active role in changing social conditions for the better. The chapters include detailed first-person stories by social work practitioners, who describe daily work in their areas of expertise and highlight cases that illustrate their work. The stories show the many sides of social work practice. The chapters also include "More About..." and "Point of View" boxes with additional detail and differing points of view on topics of interest. Each chapter includes a box featuring an ethics dilemma and an exercise in how to become a change agent and concludes with a section on how to put into practice the concepts presented.

This Third Edition includes a new Chapter 15, titled Crisis, Trauma, and Disasters. The past 10 years have included a number of national and international events, including the terrorist attacks on 9/11 and Hurricane Katrina, that have brought to the forefront of social work services the unpredictability of our world. Crises, traumas, and disasters cut across all areas of social work practice. We thought that including a chapter devoted to these issues would provide the necessary information for teaching today's social work students. We have also rearranged the chapters to flow from general information that all social workers need (Chapters 1 through 4) to more specific topics covering ways to intervene with specific populations in specific settings for social work practice (Chapters 5 through 12). The last three chapters cover issues that cross all populations and settings. We have found that chapter order varies by instructor, so we encourage use of the chapters to follow the order that best suits you.

Pedagogically, the book includes several aids to learning and teaching. Besides the boxed material, the book features challenging but uplifting case examples. Some of them remind us why we do this type of work; others end less positively and make us wonder how to make a difference. The stories give students a very real picture of social work practice and help them better understand what it is like to be a social worker. Each chapter is followed by a conclusion and a list of key terms. Each term is set in bold type in the chapter and is also defined in the glossary at the end of the textbook.

The book is a combination textbook and workbook. Brief questions are interspersed throughout the chapters to encourage students to engage more deeply with the material. At the end of each chapter are questions that can be used for full-class or small-group discussions or on examinations. The questions are based on the material presented in the chapter; they encourage students to obtain additional information and explore their thoughts about important issues. The chapters end with exercises that are designed as group or individual assignments. Many are experiential and emphasize self-exploration as well as a review of the material presented in the chapter. At the end of the course, each student will have a compendium of exercises that help to put into practice the material presented in the book. We have deliberately included more exercises than can be done in the available time in order to provide choice and flexibility. Instructors and students can choose which exercises to complete, or individuals or groups can work on different exercises and report back to the class on their findings. The exercises can be used to stimulate discussions or can be semester-long assignments. The discussion questions, change agent activities, exercises, and stories challenge students to explore the concepts introduced in the text and relate them to their own interests.

This book was developed from our combined years of practice experience and teaching of introductory social work courses. We are appreciative of all the assistance we received from colleagues, especially those who helped write some of the chapters, and from the professional social workers who shared their experiences. We are also grateful to our students who, over the years, have let us know what does and does not work in the classroom. In particular, we thank the students who reviewed chapters and provided valuable insights from the perspective of the target audience. We are appreciative of the feedback of the reviewers: Kimberley M. Zittel-Palamara, Buffalo State College; Raymie Wayne, Saint Joseph College; Lyanne Trumbull, George Mason University; Justin C. Perry, Cleveland State University; Julia Hastings, University of California, Berkeley; Amanda Reiman, University of California, Berkeley; and Saundra Weller, George Mason University. We tried to address all their suggestions and incorporate their valuable input.

Although we have incorporated much of the advice and direction we received, an introductory textbook cannot thoroughly cover all the topics important to all social workers. Therefore, the responsibility for the content and design of this book rests solely with the authors. We hope that students and instructors alike will find *An Introduction to the Profession of Social Work: Becoming a Change Agent* useful, informative, and engaging.

Liz Segal
Karen Gerdes
Sue Steiner

WHAT IS SOCIAL WORK?

CHAPTER 1

Heinle Division of Cengage Learning

Jane is a 32-year-old single mother with a 5-year-old son and an 8-year-old daughter. She has supported her family by working 30 hours a week at a small local grocery store. Her job performance was excellent, but because of a decline in business, she was laid off. Now she needs to find a way to support her family. Her low-income neighborhood has very few businesses, and most of her neighbors subsist on small amounts of earned income and public social service programs.

Jane contacts her local family service agency for advice and direction. "My neighbor said I should come here. I just lost my job, I have two young kids to support, my rent is due next week, and I don't know what to do. Can you help me?"

If Jane came to you, what would you do?

This book will help you identify the resources available to Jane. You will learn about the skills that the professional social workers at the family social service agency will draw on to help Jane and her family. Social work is not only about Jane and her lost job. It is also about neighborhoods and communities. It is about the childhood experiences that have contributed to Jane's identity and concerns. It is about government and public policies. This book is a guide to understanding how social workers fit into all these different areas.

Once you have learned about the resources and skills needed by a professional social worker, you will be better prepared to decide whether a career in social work would suit you. You will be ready to decide on your next step in pursuing a career in this ever-changing and diverse field.

This chapter provides an overview of the field of social work. It defines concepts and terms that are the basis of understanding what social workers do. The structures in which services are provided and how social work is a part of social change efforts are also presented. Throughout the chapter and throughout the book, you will explore what it means to be a social worker and whether a career in social work is right for you.

SOCIAL WORK AS A PROFESSION

Social work is such a broad field that its definition is complicated. Many different definitions of social work have evolved over time. Most of them include two aspects: helping individuals fit better into their environments, typically known as **micro practice**, and changing the environment so that it works better for individuals, referred to as **macro practice.**

Social work has been described as the profession that helps society work better for people and helps people function better within society (Bartlett, 1970). Many professions participate in improving society and helping individuals and families improve their social functioning. For example, police officers protect people and improve safety, lawyers contribute to protecting people's civil rights, and doctors strive to save lives and keep people healthy. People who are not professionals also help others. Neighbors watch each other's children or prepare meals when someone is sick. Volunteers visit the elderly or serve as big sisters or big brothers. All these efforts are concerned with improving social functioning. How is the profession of social work unique?

Almost 30 years ago, social work scholar Carol Meyer commented on the difficulty of defining social work and its purpose because

> social work has always addressed the commonplace stuff of which lay people are the real experts—people's daily lives. The other [reason it is difficult to define] is that social workers, being sensitive to self-determination, have been ambivalent about permitting themselves to be expert about what they know." (1981, p. 73)

Although social workers help people, they also believe strongly in **self-determination,** or a person's right to decide what is best for herself or himself. Therefore, there are numerous ways that social workers participate in people's lives. As a result, definitions of social work have been broad and often vague. Furthermore, social workers strive to help people and improve society in ways that overlap with other professions.

Nevertheless, social work is distinct among the helping professions. The unique contribution of social work practice is "the focus on both the person and the environment; this duality and the interaction between them constitutes the special purview of the profession and makes it distinct from other helping professions" (Gibelman, 1999, p. 300). In other words, social workers make a commitment through professional training to help people and to improve society as they also give special attention to the interactions between people and between people and their surroundings.

A psychologist or counselor would likely focus only on Jane's anxiety and depression as a result of losing her job. Although a social worker can also help Jane deal with anxiety and depression, the assistance would not stop there. The social worker would also connect Jane with local, state, and federal resources, including Temporary Assistance for Needy Families, food stamps, job training, and educational programs. In addition, if Jane were unable to get access to a needed resource, such as quality day care, or if the resource were unavailable in the community, her social worker would advocate for providing the resource and might help create it by advocating for new social policies and programs. Instead of working only from their offices and waiting for clients to come to them, social workers are out in the field trying to change societal structures so that fewer people like Jane will need help.

THE HISTORY OF THE SOCIAL WORK PROFESSION

People helping others in need is not new. For thousands of years, friends have helped bring in the harvest and care for farm animals or have watched other people's children. But paying people a salary to help others in need is relatively new. Although professions such as medicine date back thousands of years, the profession of social work is relatively young—dating back a little over a hundred years.

The history of the social work profession is intertwined with the history of social welfare policy in the United States, which is covered in more detail in Chapter 22. Social welfare policies have been publicly enacted since the colonial period (the 1600s), but professional social work did not emerge until the Progressive Era in the late 1800s. During the early 1800s, most people lived in small communities, and farming was the primary livelihood. By the end of the century, a tremendous influx of immigrants contributed to the explosive growth of cities, where factories engaged in the large-scale production of goods. With so many more people living in crowded cities, far away from ancestral homelands and extended families, and working in factories for low wages, social need grew. Local communities could no longer meet the needs of people, and poverty-related social problems increased. Two attempts to respond to social need that developed during the latter part of the 1800s were the Charity Organization Societies and the Settlement Movement. The profession of social work traces its history to the actions and principles of these two organizations.

Charity Organization Societies   The first **Charity Organization Society (COS)** was established in Buffalo, New York, in 1877 as an organized effort to eliminate poverty (Erickson, 1987). Its goal was to discover what caused poverty among individuals, eliminate the causes, and thereby rid society of poverty. In accordance with the sentiments of the time, scientific techniques were used to investigate social problems and organize helping efforts.

The focus of COS was on the individual and reflected the belief that poverty was a character defect. By rehabilitating individuals, COS participants believed, poverty would be eliminated. These principles gave rise to the use of friendly visitors, at first volunteers and later paid professionals trained to guide people to change behaviors that contributed to poverty and to become productive, healthy adults. Friendly visiting was regarded as a better alternative than charity because it used scientific investigation to determine need and to organize the giving of relief (Brieland, 1995).

Leadership in COS was exemplified by Mary Richmond, who began her social work career as a friendly visitor in Baltimore in 1891 and spent years as an administrator in several COS agencies. Richmond was a key figure in the nationwide COS movement and in the early development of the profession. She wrote *Social Diagnosis*, published in 1917, which was the first social work practice book to present professional ways to identify clients' problems. Richmond strongly advocated for the development of professional curricula for training social workers. Her efforts contributed to the development of the first school of professional training, the New York School of Applied Philanthropy, which later became the Columbia University School of Social Work (see "More About ... Mary Richmond").

In spite of the good intentions of COS workers, changing the behavior of poor people was not enough to solve the social problems of the period. Major social and

BOX 1.1   MORE ABOUT ... MARY RICHMOND

Mary E. Richmond (1861–1928) was a contemporary of Jane Addams and an influential leader in the U.S. charity organization movement. Ms. Richmond was orphaned at a young age and was largely self-educated. Her charity work was consistent with the social gospel movement of the time. And while she initially performed acts of charity as a means of self-support, she eventually turned charity work into a valid, organized profession. A century later her legacy continues to echo in social work and welfare reform (Agnew, 2003).

economic systems were in disarray. The Settlement Movement evolved in response to the greater social need.

Settlement Movement   The **Settlement Movement** began in this country in 1887 with the opening of the Neighborhood Guild settlement in New York City. The second settlement, Hull House, was opened in Chicago in 1889. Hull House was directed by Jane Addams, possibly the best-known historic figure in the social work profession (see "More About … Jane Addams").

The Settlement Movement was based on the belief that in order to help poor people, workers had to live within the community and provide services from their dwelling or settlement. The philosophy of the movement was that an individual's well-being was directly linked to external surroundings. Most settlement houses were located in poor neighborhoods, and much of the workers' efforts involved helping immigrants adjust to life in the United States. The ultimate goal was to shrink the gap between people who were poor and people of the wealthier classes. Therefore, to help individuals, settlement workers focused on changing the

---

BOX 1.2 | MORE ABOUT … JANE ADDAMS

Jane Addams was born in 1860 to a middle-class family in Illinois. Her early life was one of economic and social comfort. Her father was a well-respected businessman who had served in the Illinois House and was a good friend of Abraham Lincoln. Jane was greatly influenced by her father, and he helped shape her political views. College educated and well traveled, Jane was deeply struck by the social experiment of Toynbee Hall in London, a residence where university students could learn firsthand about the plight of poor people and work in the neighborhood to improve conditions. Jane realized the potential for this kind of work and brought the idea to Chicago, where she founded the Hull House settlement in 1889.

Jane Addams lived at Hull House for over thirty years. During those years, she fought tirelessly for social change and created numerous social programs to benefit the residents of the surrounding neighborhood. In its first year, 50,000 people came to the house, then occupied by two residents. Within ten years, there were twenty-five resident workers and a large volunteer network. The services and programs developed at Jane Addams's Hull House included the first organized kindergarten, an employment bureau, adult education classes, a library, social clubs, and the first public playground. Legislative advocacy was also an integral part of her efforts, and she was instrumental in the passage of legislation that limited child labor, created the first juvenile court in the nation, and expanded public education.

Until World War I, Jane Addams was immensely popular, with tremendous national recognition for her work and her prolific writings about her experiences at Hull House. Her firm belief in the destructiveness of war led her to assert herself as a pacifist and oppose the nation's involvement in World War I. This position cost her much public support, and her views became less central to American values. By the 1930s, with the economic upheaval of the Great Depression, Jane Addams's message for world peace and social reform returned to national favor. In 1931 she won the Nobel Peace Prize. She spent her last years writing and continuing to work for social change. She died in 1935.

Source: Segal, 1995.

environment by advocating for better neighborhood services, public health programs, and employment conditions.

In spite of the shared goal of improving people's lives, the Settlement Movement and Charity Organization Societies had serious disagreements about how to work with people and communities.

> The settlers defined problems environmentally and engaged in social melioration. The charity workers, for the most part, defined problems as personal deficiencies and emphasized the need for moral uplift to achieve social betterment…. The conflict continued and left the new profession with a legacy of struggle between those who seek to change people and those who seek to change environment. (Germain & Hartman, 1980, p. 329)

Nevertheless, the contributions of the Charity Organization Societies and the Settlement Movement are the foundation of professional social work today. COS's friendly visitors were trained to focus on individuals and families, as well as on organized ways to coordinate the provision of social services and to determine individual need. Early training of settlement workers included a focus on individuals as active participants in their surroundings, work with groups and communities, emphasis on social reform and political action, and acknowledgement of the strengths of different immigrant groups. Today's social work combines elements of both the Charity Organization Societies and the Settlement Movement.

WHO ARE SOCIAL WORKERS?

Professional social workers hold social work degrees from accredited undergraduate or graduate programs. Postbaccalaureate social work (BSW) and postgraduate social work (MSW) programs are accredited by the **Council on Social Work Education (CSWE)** on the basis of whether they meet the criteria discussed below. Students in CSWE-accredited programs are trained in values, ethics, and a variety of intervention techniques to work with individuals, families, small groups, communities, and organizations in order to solve problems and create change.

On graduation from an accredited social work program, social workers must comply with state licensing or certification requirements. Most states distinguish among three levels of social work: (1) BSW, (2) postgraduate (MSW), and (3) two years' postgraduate (MSW) clinical practice. Applicants must pass the examination appropriate to their level of practice. For clinical licensure, they must also complete at least two years of post-MSW practice experience under the supervision of a licensed clinical social worker.

MSW- and BSW-level social workers provide direct services to individuals, families, and small groups. They also conduct research into social problems and their solutions, engage in policy analysis and legislative advocacy, administer programs, and organize people to fight for social change. To effectively address problems, social workers must help individuals and families function better and at the same time work to change societal conditions that limit individual and family functioning. For example, a woman like Jane who has recently lost her job can benefit from job training and help with interviewing skills so that she can more easily get a new job. She and others like her can also be helped by social advocacy efforts to develop new jobs in low-income areas and by legislative efforts to provide health coverage for the unemployed and working poor.

In addition to BSW and MSW degrees, there are also two types of doctoral-level social work degrees. Students interested in pursing a doctorate in social work can either get a Doctor of Social Work (DSW) degree or a Doctor of Philosophy (PhD) degree, depending on the school they attend. While the DSW was the original social work doctoral degree, the PhD has become more common over the years. The course work is generally the same in DSW and PhD programs, though there are recent efforts to make the DSW more of an advanced practice degree and the PhD more of a research-focused degree. Social workers holding doctoral degrees generally work as social work educators, researchers, administrators, or policy analysts.

The desire to help others and change social conditions does not earn a person professional status as a social worker. The desire must be combined with a strong knowledge and skills base developed in one of the more than 200 graduate and 480 undergraduate programs accredited by the council (CSWE, 2008). Even though other human service practitioners are sometimes referred to as social workers, if they have not completed an accredited social work program and met licensure or certification requirements, they are not professional social workers.

Professional social workers are represented by the **National Association of Social Workers (NASW)**. NASW has over 152,000 members, almost 80 percent of whom are women. Forty percent are employed in mental health–related positions. Eight percent are employed in the health sector, 8 percent in child welfare, and 6 percent in schools. Eighty-seven percent of the members are white, 5 percent are African American, 2 percent are Latino, 2 percent are Asian and 1 percent are First Nations people (this term, which refers to the people also called Native Americans, is discussed later in the chapter). In terms of education, 90 percent of NASW members have MSW degrees; 6 percent have doctorates; and 3 percent have BSW degrees. The average NASW member has practiced social work for 16 years and earns on average $45,000 annually (NASW, 2008a; NASW, 2003).

Few careers rival social work for the diversity and wealth of opportunities offered to practitioners. The Bureau of Labor Statistics (2008) estimates that social work employment is projected to grow much faster than average for the next 10 years. Social workers operate in a variety of settings, including public and private mental health centers, community centers, courts, prisons, schools, public welfare offices, hospitals, nursing homes, businesses, and child welfare offices. They address drug and alcohol abuse, mental and physical illness, poverty, violence, lack of community power, family conflicts, workplace tensions, discrimination, oppression, and inadequate housing, among other problems (see "More About … Social Work"). Social work is one of the fastest growing careers in the United States.

SOCIAL WORK EDUCATION

The social work profession's unique integration of knowledge from a number of disciplines with the profession's own skills, values, ethics, and knowledge can be seen in the content of social work education. Accredited BSW programs include relevant material from biology and from other social sciences. Most require students to take economics, political science, human biology, philosophy, psychology, and

BOX 1.3   MORE ABOUT ... SOCIAL WORK

What people *think* they know about social work is often a myth.

Myth Most social workers work for the government.

Fact

- Fewer than 3 percent of all professional social workers work for the federal government.
- About a third of all professional social workers are employed by federal, state, and local governments combined.

Myth For therapy you need a psychologist or psychiatrist.

Fact

- Professional social workers are the nation's most numerous providers of mental health and therapy services. Professional social workers are often the only mental health care providers serving residents of many poor, rural counties.
- Social work is designated as one of the four core mental health professions under federal legislation that established the National Institute of Mental Health.

Myth Most social workers are employed in public welfare or child welfare.

Fact

- About one-quarter of all child welfare cases are handled by professional social workers.
- About 1 percent of NASW members work in public assistance.
- Professional social workers practice in many settings: family services agencies, mental health centers, schools, hospitals, corporations, courts, police departments, prisons, public and private agencies, and private practice.
- More than 200 professional social workers hold elective office, including one U.S. senator and four representatives during the 106th Congress.

Myth Social service employees, caseworkers, and volunteers are "social workers."

Fact

- A social worker is a trained professional who has a bachelor's, master's, or doctoral degree in social work.
- All states license or otherwise regulate social work practice.
- A social service employee, caseworker, or volunteer community worker is not a "social worker" unless she or he has a social work degree.

Source: naswdc.org website.

sociology courses. This material is combined with social work–specific courses in human behavior and the social environment, research, practice, and social policy.

In addition, students in accredited BSW programs complete a minimum of 400 hours of field practicum, while MSW students complete a minimum of 900 hours. In the field practicum course, students are assigned to a social service–related agency or organization under the supervision of a social work practitioner. Field practicum organizations include child welfare agencies, schools, hospitals, mental health agencies, senior centers, homeless and battered women's shelters, and juvenile and adult probation programs, among others. (See "More About ... Social Work Education Criteria").

The educational criteria for the BSW and MSW degrees constitute a progression. The BSW degree provides a foundation, and the MSW degree provides advanced training in an area of specialized practice. In many social work programs, a BSW

BOX 1.4 | **MORE ABOUT ... SOCIAL WORK EDUCATION CRITERIA**

The criteria for social work education are outlined by the Council of Social Work Education in its "Educational Policy and Accreditation Standards." All schools that wish to be accredited must follow the guidelines. Every eight years programs conduct self-studies and submit a comprehensive written portfolio to the CSWE accreditation board. As part of the accreditation process, a team of social work educators reviews the school and provides a report to the accreditation board. The report and self-study documents are then reviewed, and a determination is made whether to grant accredited status. This process ensures uniform standards for training social workers. No matter where you choose to study, as long as it is in a CSWE-accredited program, your curriculum will reflect the standards and values of the profession.

BOX 1.5 | **WHAT DO YOU THINK?**

What are the differences between a BSW and an MSW degree? What is the difference in emphasis between the two degrees? How might the different training affect the type of job a BSW graduate might do compared with an MSW graduate?

degree that was completed within the previous five years counts toward an MSW degree. Such programs are referred to as advanced standing, because they give BSW graduates the opportunity to begin their MSW program at an advanced level and complete the degree in less time.

Many two-year colleges offer social or human service programs in which students can earn preprofessional degrees. These programs provide important foundation knowledge and skills that can lay the groundwork for a BSW degree. Students with degrees from two-year programs can work in most areas of social services. The positions are typically entry level, and they provide excellent work experience should the preprofessional choose to pursue a BSW degree. Many students who complete two-year degrees transfer into accredited BSW programs.

CENTRAL CONCEPTS AND THEORIES

Part of what defines a profession is a shared vision, typically referred to as a mission. The primary mission of social work, according to the membership of NASW, is

> to enhance human well-being and help meet the basic human needs of all people, with particular attention to the needs and empowerment of people who are vulnerable, oppressed, and living in poverty. A historic and defining feature of social work is the profession's focus on individual well-being in a social context and the well-being of society. Fundamental to social work is attention to the environmental forces that create, contribute to, and address problems in living. (NASW, 2008b, p. 1)

PERSON IN ENVIRONMENT

Several aspects of the mission make the profession unique. One is the focus on the "needs and empowerment of people who are vulnerable, oppressed, and living in poverty." The profession has a clear commitment to working with members of society who are often left behind or left out. A second unique characteristic is the fact that individuals' problems are addressed in combination with the social context. Social workers realize that they must pay attention to the environment in which people live, and they work to change the environment so that it functions more effectively for individuals, families, and communities. This dual view is known as the **person-in-environment** perspective (Karls & Wandrei, 1994).

The importance of understanding problems and directing change efforts at both the individual and environmental levels is central to good social work practice. Which approach social workers use depends on where they see problems originating. If all change efforts are directed at individuals, social workers see the causes of people's problems as being inside themselves. If they focus only on the environment, they believe that the problems begin outside the individual.

Although it is true that some problems lie exclusively within individuals and others are purely environmental, most problems have multiple causes. Some causes are individual, whereas others are societal or structural in nature. If social workers do not address both individual and environmental causes, they will not be able to effectively solve problems. For example, to help someone who is depressed, a counselor might immediately engage in therapy and prescribe antidepressant drugs. Although these are certainly viable approaches, the person-in-environment concept dictates also considering whether something in the person's environment is contributing to or even causing the depression. If the person lived in poverty, for example, the everyday struggle to survive might result in depression. Therefore, interventions aimed at reducing poverty would also be appropriate ways to alleviate the individual's depression.

THEORETICAL BASIS FOR SOCIAL WORK PRACTICE

Social work practice is based on a number of theories developed in a variety of fields. A theory is "a systematic set of interrelated statements intended to explain some aspect of social life or enrich our sense of how people conduct and find meaning in their daily lives" (Rubin & Babbie, 2007, p. 41). In other words, a theory attempts to explain why something is the way it is. Theories can explain social relationships; for example, some theories explain why people develop biases against members of other groups. Theories can also make predictions about the likely outcomes of people's efforts. For example, many types of therapies are based on the theory that people's understanding of what happened to them during childhood leads to improved functioning as adults. A theory must be testable, meaning that research can be conducted to see whether it is accurate.

Theories alone do not create change, but social workers apply various theories in practice settings to create desired change. They use theoretical frameworks to help determine which theories to apply. A theoretical framework combines theories, beliefs, and assumptions about how change happens to guide work. The framework gives social workers a basis from which to view situations and provides guidance about how to respond to situations.

Most of the theories used by social workers today developed from a central theoretical framework, the **general systems theory** developed by biologist Ludwig von Bertalanffy (1971). Von Bertalanffy described the functioning of living systems, including the human body. Scientists have long realized that the systems within the human body are connected to each other. The failure of one human system often affects the functioning of other systems and of the body as a whole. Since its development, von Bertalanffy's framework has been applied to systems in many fields, including social work.

A system is a group of separate but interrelated units, or elements, that form an identifiable whole. Each of the parts in a system interacts with other parts in some way, and the various parts are dependent on each other to create the larger whole. The various parts of a system affect and are affected by one another. Social workers are most interested in social systems—the interactions and interdependence among people that together make up society. Interacting groups can be as varied as a family, residents of a group home, employees in a business, and residents in a neighborhood.

Jane's family is the point of focus for the social worker's micro interventions. Figure 1.1, Jane's System, illustrates that Jane's family system contains the subsystems of Jane, her son, and her daughter. The family is itself a subsystem within the neighborhood system or social environment. The focal system interacts with and is affected by all the subsystems in the social environment of the neighborhood, including the families of Jane's neighbors, the local school, and the family service agency. The neighborhood is a subsystem within an even larger social environment, the public social service system. If Jane is participating in such social service programs as Temporary Assistance for Needy Families (TANF) and Medicaid, those national programs are part of her social system.

The focal system is determined by the social worker's point of focus. If the social worker's macro intervention is focused on encouraging the passage of legislation that will make it easier for women like Jane to get unemployment insurance, then the unemployment insurance program is the focal system. If the social worker is developing an after-school program that could benefit Jane's children, the school is the focal system.

Changes in the focal system or in a related subsystem or social environment will affect the systems and subsystems it interacts with. For example, if Jane completes a job-training program at the local family service agency and secures new employment, her children will be affected by her new job and the additional income. The children's school will be affected by any positive or negative changes in the children. Likewise, any change in the school system will affect the children, which in turn will affect their mother.

Because of the fluidity and mutuality of the relationships between systems and subsystems, systems theory explains a person's behavior in terms of circular or mutual causality. In other words, Jane influences her environment, and Jane's environment influences her. Closely related to mutual causality is the concept of wholeness: "Every part of a system is so related to its fellow parts that a change in one part will cause a change in all of them and in the total system" (Watzlawick, Bavelas, & Jackson, 1967, p. 123).

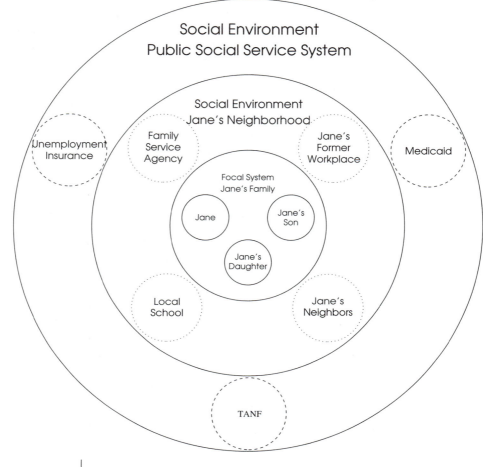

FIGURE 1.1 | Jane's System

All systems have boundaries, which makes it possible to distinguish the parts that belong in the system from those that do not belong. The boundaries of some systems are very clear; for example, the physical boundary of a human being—the skin—clearly separates that person from other people. Boundaries of social systems are often less clear. For example, the boundaries of Jane's family might depend on the situation. If a social worker were working with Jane's daughter, who was struggling in school, the relevant system members might include only Jane and her son. Yet if Jane's family were trying to care for an aging grandparent, relevant system members might include Jane's parents, siblings, aunts, uncles, and cousins as well.

Using a systems perspective means looking at people in relation to all the systems in their environment that affect them. For example, a 77-year-old woman asks a social worker in a senior center for help. She lives alone, and she is concerned about her physical abilities and financial situation. The systems perspective dictates first gaining an understanding of all the elements that make up the woman's social system. A social worker would assess her physical and mental health, her financial situation, her support system, and her living situation. He or she would also explore the larger systems in the woman's life: the area in which she lives, the social services with which she may interact, and whether she is connected to a religious institution. Without examining the entire system, areas for effective intervention might be missed.

The **ecological systems framework** builds on general systems theory. It goes beyond looking at the systems that make up a client's sphere to focus on the intersection of client systems and the larger environmental context. The ecological framework rests on the life model which views people and their environments as reacting to and changing in response to each other (Germain & Gitterman, 1980). This view requires an understanding of the nature of interactions and transactions between people and their surroundings. The focus is on the interface, which is what happens between people and the environment.

For example, as a result of Jane's job loss and her residence in a neighborhood with few employment opportunities, her life is out of balance, and the environment is not supportive of her needs. The ecological life model emphasizes examining the fit (or lack of fit) between Jane and her environment. The intervention goals become trying to help Jane adapt to this situation and changing the environment to be more supportive. One of the concerns about this approach is that adaptation is much more manageable, so environmental change is often ignored. However, adherence to the full ecological perspective includes addressing both the fit of the client to the environment, and the extent of support from the environment.

The **strengths perspective** is a third framework used to guide social work practice. This perspective dictates building on clients' strengths to create positive change. It is the opposite of frameworks that encourage social workers to approach clients from a deficit or problem base. "Social work, like so many other helping professions, has constructed much of its theory and practice around the supposition that clients become clients because they have deficits, problems, pathologies, and diseases; that they are, in some critical way, flawed or weak" (Saleebey, 1992, p. 3). The problem-based orientation of social work is not surprising, given that social workers help solve so many problems. But although problems cannot be ignored, the strengths perspective asserts that a problem-based approach is not the most effective way to help clients change and grow. Focusing primarily on problems can reinforce the negative views that clients may have of themselves and their communities.

The strengths perspective suggests that all individuals, groups, and communities have strengths that often go unnoticed and unappreciated by the individuals, groups, and communities themselves, as well as by the outside world. The strengths perspective means recognizing the strengths that are inherent in individuals, groups, and communities, and using these strengths as building blocks for change. According to Saleebey,

> A strengths perspective assumes that when people's positive capacities are supported, they are more likely to act on their strengths. Thus, a belief in people's inherent capacity for growth and well-being requires an intense attention to people's

own resources: their talents, experiences, and aspirations. Through this active attention, the probability for positive growth is significantly enhanced. (1992, p. 25)

When social workers first go into a neighborhood to begin bringing the residents together to work for change—a process called community organizing—they often begin by noting all the things that are wrong. They might note run-down houses, gangs, abandoned cars, and a lack of needed services. Approaching the area with a strengths perspective, social workers might instead start by creating an asset map of the area, pointing out all of its strengths. They might note two active neighborhood associations, a well-attended community center, several religious institutions, and residents who themselves have innumerable strengths. Although the problems cannot be ignored, they do not have to be the first and only thing to receive social work attention.

Focusing on client strengths is one way to achieve the guiding principle of client **empowerment.** Academics, politicians, and other people use the term *empowerment* to describe very different things. In relation to social work practice, it means helping clients gain power over their lives (Lee, 2001). Mondros and Wilson describe empowerment as "a psychological state—a sense of competence, control, and entitlement—that allows one to pursue concrete activities aimed at becoming powerful" (1994, p. 5). To be empowered, people must believe that they are capable of doing things for themselves, gaining increased control over their lives, and influencing events and situations that affect their lives. Many people served by social workers often feel relatively powerless. They have little control over their own lives and even less over outside events that affect them. Approaching social work practice from an empowerment perspective means finding ways to help clients take control by making their own decisions and determining the best course of action for themselves.

The **diversity perspective** is a theoretical framework that emphasizes the incredible diversity of social workers and their clients. Social workers and the people with whom they work come from a wide range of ethnic, racial, cultural, and religious backgrounds; are of different ages, genders, sexual orientations, and classes; and have different physical and mental abilities. Social workers must understand cultural differences to work effectively with diverse client populations. This means understanding themselves and their biases, as well as knowing a great deal about those with whom they are working. It also means understanding the dynamics of oppression and discrimination. Social work with diverse populations requires practitioners to be sensitive to differences between people and to develop interventions that are appropriate for specific client groups. The topics of oppression, discrimination, and work with diverse populations are discussed throughout the book and are covered in detail in Chapters 3 and 6.

BOX 1.6   **WHAT DO YOU THINK?**

Identify a friend or family member who is struggling with a problem. What strengths might help this person overcome the problem? What strengths are inherent in his or her personality? Does this person have family or friends to turn to for support or assistance? How has this person dealt with adversity in the past? Can he or she draw on those past efforts to help now?

To guide effective social work practice with diverse populations, NASW developed the **Standards for Cultural Competence in Social Work Practice** (NASW, 2001). Cultural competence refers to the behaviors, knowledge, skills, and attitudes that allow social workers to respond effectively across cultures. The 10 standards aim to provide clear guidelines about what is necessary to achieve cultural competence. They include practicing in accordance with social work values and ethics, development of self-awareness about issues of diversity, development of cross-cultural knowledge and skills, a focus on empowerment and advocacy and the encouragement of cross-cultural leadership. Box 1.7 outlines the 10 standards.

BOX 1.7 | **MORE ABOUT ... NASW STANDARDS FOR CULTURAL COMPETENCE IN SOCIAL WORK PRACTICE**

Standard 1 – Ethics and Values
Social workers shall function in accordance with the values, ethics, and standards of the profession, recognizing how personal and professional values may conflict with or accommodate the needs of diverse clients.

Standard 2 – Self-Awareness
Social workers shall seek to develop an understanding of their own personal and cultural values and beliefs as one way of appreciating the importance of multicultural identities in the lives of people.

Standard 3 – Cross-Cultural Knowledge
Social workers shall have and continue to develop specialized knowledge and understanding about the history, traditions, values, family systems, and artistic expressions of major client groups that they serve.

Standard 4 – Cross-Cultural Skills
Social workers shall use appropriate methodological approaches, skills, and techniques that reflect the workers' understanding of the role of culture in the helping process.

Standard 5 – Service Delivery
Social workers shall be knowledgeable about and skillful in the use of services available in the community and broader society and be able to make appropriate referrals for their diverse clients.

Standard 6 – Empowerment and Advocacy
Social workers shall be aware of the effect of social policies and programs on diverse client populations, advocating for and with clients whenever appropriate.

Standard 7 – Diverse Workforce
Social workers shall support and advocate for recruitment, admissions and hiring, and retention efforts in social work programs and agencies that ensure diversity within the profession.

Standard 8 – Professional Education
Social workers shall advocate for and participate in educational and training programs that help advance cultural competence within the profession.

Standard 9 – Language Diversity
Social workers shall seek to provide or advocate for the provision of information, referrals, andservices in the language appropriate to the client, which may include use of interpreters.

Standard 10 – Cross-Cultural Leadership
Social workers shall be able to communicate information about diverse client groups toother professionals.

Prepared by the NASW National Committee on Racial and Ethnic Diversity.

Adopted by the NASW Board of Directors June 23, 2001.

THE POWER OF LANGUAGE

Language is extremely powerful. Words reveal values, attitudes, and beliefs about other people. They can harm and degrade, or they can demonstrate respect and support. Because language not only expresses people's thoughts but also shapes them, it is important to make careful word choices. Using certain terms can offend others and therefore hinder open communication. Using the wrong term can send a message that the speaker is not intending to send. Fear of using the wrong words and offending others can keep people from developing relationships with members of other groups. An open discussion of language can help build bridges between groups.

Debate over language has been a central component of a number of civil rights struggles in the United States. Activists in the women's movement worked to teach people about the importance of saying *woman* rather than *girl* or *babe*. African American civil rights activists pointed out that adult males are *men*, not *boys*. Referring to adult females as *girls* and to adult African American men as *boys* communicates attitudes and values that members of these groups are inferior to and less important than adult women or adult white men. The appropriate use or the misuse of words by social workers can convey powerful attitudes and values.

A variety of words refer to the diverse groups that make up U.S. society, and it is often challenging to decide which to use. Some of the challenge comes from not knowing enough about the group. Lack of agreement between outsiders and members of the group about which term is best increases the difficulty. Also, terminology changes over time. Following is an explanation of why the authors of this book have chosen to use certain terms.

People who are members of oppressed groups are often referred to as *minorities*. One problem with this term is that not all oppressed populations make up less than half the population. In particular, women make up more than 50 percent of the population. Additionally, the word *minority* often implies "less than," which can reinforce the misconception that members of oppressed populations are somehow inferior to other groups. Other terms that can be used to refer to ways that people fit into the societal structure include *oppressed* and *oppressor* groups and *dominant* and *subordinate* or *nondominant* groups. Members of dominant groups have control over many societal resources and a strong influence on societal norms. The words *oppressed*, *dominant*, *subordinate*, and *nondominant* are used throughout this book.

The term *minority* is also used to describe the many populations whose skin color is not "white." When referring to these groups collectively, we prefer to use *people of color* and whenever possible to refer to the specific population. For example, instead of using *minority* to mean African American, we prefer to be clear and use *African American*. We do not use the term *nonwhite* because it is Eurocentric; that is, it places the dominant population at the center and defines people of color on the basis of how they differ.

Just as we use *African American* to refer to people of African decent, we use *Asian American* and *Pacific Islander* to refer to people whose heritage is from an

Asian country or a Pacific island respectively. We refer to people whose ancestry is from South and Central America and other Spanish-speaking areas as *Latino/a*. Some within the Latino/a community prefer to use *Hispanic*, which is most often used by the Census Bureau and other government entities. The term *Hispanic* was coined by Europeans, and it excludes people from non-Spanish-speaking countries in Spanish-speaking regions, such as Brazil, a Portuguese-speaking nation.

The terms *Native American* and *American Indian* are commonly used to refer to the Indigenous Peoples of North America. Even though these are the most commonly used terms, both are misleading and inaccurate. *Indian* blurs the distinction between Indigenous Peoples and people from India, and in fact the term is based on Christopher Columbus's mistaken belief that he had arrived in India. *Native American* can refer to anyone who was born in North, Central, or South America. There is great diversity among indigenous nations and tribes in the United States, and tribal members use a number of terms to refer to themselves. We use *First Nations* (Yellow Bird, 1999). Since the Indigenous Peoples were the first populations to settle North America, the term is accurate. We also use *Indigenous Peoples*, an internationally accepted term describing the descendants of the original inhabitants of a land.

We use the word *disability* rather than *handicap* throughout the book. A handicap is an obstacle in someone's path; *disability* refers to a way in which a person's body functions differently than the norm. We attempt to use people-first language throughout the book when referring to people with disabilities—language that refers to what a person has, not what he or she is. Saying "disabled person" suggests that the disability is the individual's primary characteristic. If we instead say "person with a disability," we are acknowledging that the disability is just one aspect of the total person, not all that he or she is.

We use the term *sexual orientation* rather than *sexual preference*. *Sexual preference* suggests that people decide to be heterosexual, bisexual, or homosexual. Research has demonstrated that sexuality is not a choice, but is rather a deeply imbedded part of who a person is (see Chapter 6). We also use the words *gay* and *lesbian* rather than *homosexual*. *Homosexual* is a clinical term that has negative connotations. *Gay* and *lesbian* tend to have more positive connotations. The inclusive term is *lesbian, gay, bisexual, transgender*, abbreviated as LGBT. Sometimes you will see the abbreviation LGBTQ, with the *Q* standing for "queer" or "questioning." Adding *Q* is typically done by researchers, who favor adding *queer*, which often reflects the category of queer studies, and by youth organizations and advocates, who acknowledge that sexual orientation is fluid and that many people are not sure of their sexual identity and may be questioning. Abbreviations change over time. You may see variations such as LGBTQ or GLBT. In this text we follow the major advocacy groups and use the abbreviation LGBT to include all the groups mentioned in this section.

No one knows the correct term to use in every instance, or how another person will interpret the word. Furthermore, terms and their meanings change over time. It is imperative to understand the importance of terminology, particularly in relation to diversity. See the debate over terminology in "Point of View … People-First Language."

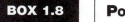

POINT OF VIEW

PEOPLE-FIRST LANGUAGE—YES!

Who are "the handicapped," … "the "disabled"?
Society's myths tell us they are

- People who "suffer" from the "tragedy" of "birth defects"
- Paraplegic "heroes" "struggling" to become "normal"
- "Victims" of diseases "fighting" to regain their lives
- Categorically, "the disabled, the retarded, the autistic, the blind, the deaf, the learning disabled," and more

Who are they really?

They are moms and dads and sons and daughters … employees and employers … scientists (Stephen Hawking) … friends and neighbors … movie stars (Marlee Matlin) … leaders and followers … students and teachers … they are … people. They are people. They are people first.

Are you myopic or do you wear glasses?

Are you cancerous or do you have cancer?

Are you freckled or do you have freckles?

Are you handicapped/disabled or do you have a disability?

People-first language describes what a person *has*, not what a person *is!* People-first language puts the person before the disability.

"Handicapped," "disabled," or "people with disabilities": Which description is more accurate?

Using "the handicapped," and even "the disabled," usually evokes negative feelings (sadness, pity, fear, and more) and creates a negative stereotypical perception that people with disabilities are all alike. All people who have brown hair are not alike. All people who have disabilities are not alike. Many people who have disabilities would never think of themselves as "handicapped."

Using people-first language is a crucial issue.

If people with disabilities are to be included in all aspects of our communities—in the very ordinary, very wonderful, very typical activities most people take for granted—then they must talk about themselves in the very ordinary, very wonderful, very typical language other people use about themselves.

- Children with disabilities are children first. The only labels they need are their names! Parents must not talk about their children in the clinical terms used by medical practitioners. A disability label is simply a medical diagnosis!
- Adults with disabilities are adults first. The only labels they need are their names! They must not talk about themselves the way service providers talk about them.

My son Benjamin is 11 years old. He loves the Lone Ranger, ice cream, and playing on the computer. He has blonde hair, blue eyes, and cerebral palsy. His disability is only one small part of his life. For many people with disabilities, their medical diagnoses define who they are!

When I introduce myself to people I don't tell them I'll never be a prima ballerina. Like others, I focus on my strengths, the things I do well, not on what I can't do. Don't you do the same?

I don't say, "My son can't write with a pencil." I say, "My son uses a computer to do his school work." I don't say, "My son doesn't walk." I say, "My son uses a walker and a wheelchair." And Benjamin isn't "wheelchair bound." He's free when he uses it—free to go when and where he wants to go!

People-first language can change how people feel about themselves. People-first language can change how society views and treats people with disabilities.

Benjamin goes ballistic when he hears "handicapped."

I hope when he's grown, labels will be extinct.

People first language is right. Just do it—*now!*

Source: Retrieved August 25, 2001, from www.caeyc .homestead.com/teacherhowimportantislang~main.html.

PEOPLE-FIRST LANGUAGE—NO!

Saying "person with autism" suggests that the autism can be separated from the person. But this is not the case. I can be separated from things that are not part of me, and I am still the same person. I am usually a "person with a purple shirt," but I could also be a "person with a blue shirt" one day and a "person with a yellow shirt" the next day, and I would still be

| BOX 1.8 | POINT OF VIEW *continued* |

the same person, because my clothing is not part of me. But autism *is* part of me. Autism is hardwired into the ways my brain works. I am autistic because I *cannot* be separated from how my brain works.

Saying "person with autism" suggests that even if autism is part of the person, it isn't a very important part. Characteristics that are recognized as central to a person's identity are appropriately stated as adjectives and may even be used as nouns to describe people: We talk about "male" and "female" people, and even about "men" and "women" and "boys" and "girls," not about "people with maleness" and "people with femaleness." We describe people's cultural and religious identifications in terms such as "Russian" or "Catholic," not as "person with Russianity" or "person with Catholicism." We describe important aspects of people's social roles in terms such as *"parent"* or *"worker,"* not as "person with offspring" or "person who has a job." We describe important aspects of people's personalities in terms such as *"generous"* or *"outgoing,"* not as "person with generosity" or "person with extroversion." Yet autism goes deeper than culture and learned belief systems. It affects how we relate to others and how we find our place in society. It even affects how we relate to our own bodies. If I did not have an autistic brain, the person that I am would not exist. I am

autistic because autism is an *essential* feature of me as a person.

Saying "person with autism" suggests that autism is something *bad*—so bad that it isn't even consistent with being a person. Nobody objects to using adjectives to refer to characteristics of a person that are considered positive or neutral. We talk about left-handed people, not "people with left-handedness," and about athletic or musical people, not about "people with athleticism" or "people with musicality." We might call someone a "blue-eyed person" or a "person with blue eyes," and nobody objects to either descriptor. It is only when someone has decided that the characteristic being referred to is *negative* that suddenly people want to separate it from the person. I know that autism is not a terrible thing and that it does not make me any less a person. If other people have trouble remembering that autism doesn't make me any less a person, then that's *their* problem, not mine. Let them find a way to remind themselves that I'm a person, without trying to define an essential feature of my personhood as something bad. I am autistic because I *accept and value* myself the way I am.

Source: Retrieved August 25, 2001, from http://members.ncbi.com/_XMCM/jimsinclair/person_first:htm. Copyright © 1999 Jim Sinclair.

| BOX 1.9 | WHAT DO YOU THINK? |

As the essays in "Point of View … People-First Language" demonstrate, there is disagreement about the best language to use to describe members of various populations. Disagreement exists among people who are themselves members of these populations, as well as those on the outside.

List the central points each author makes in support of her or his position. Where does there seem to be the greatest disagreement? Given the disagreement among people in this community, how might you decide what language to use in working with its members?

VALUES AND ETHICS

Numerous values and ethical principles influence people's behavior. Values are beliefs or assumptions about what is important or what is right. They guide decisions about how to act in various situations. For example, a person who values helping other people may decide to do volunteer work at a hospital. Ethics are based on values, and they prescribe the behavior a person should engage in to express his or her values. The value of volunteering, for example, might lead an organization to require a certain amount of volunteer work from its members.

Certain shared values and ethical principles guide the profession of social work. If a person does not agree with these principles, she or he might not be an effective social worker and should consider another career. The primary values and ethics central to social work appear in the NASW Code of Ethics (NASW, 2008b), which is reprinted in Appendix A of this book. Each value is the foundation of an ethical principle that guides professional practice. The key social work values and ethics are as follows:

- *Service: Social workers' primary goal is to help people in need and to address social problems.* Social workers' primary value is a commitment to service. Social workers intervene by using direct counseling, linking people to programs and resources, and advocating to change neighborhoods and communities. The purpose of service is to make changes that support people and contribute to improving their lives.
- *Social justice: Social workers challenge social injustice.* Social work as a profession is unique in its commitment to social justice—the level of fairness that exists in society. Working for social justice means striving to create a society in which all people, regardless of race, ethnicity, religion, gender, sexual orientation, economic status, age, or physical or mental ability, have the same basic rights and opportunities and can develop to their fullest potential.
- *Dignity and worth of the person: Social workers respect the inherent dignity and worth of the person.* Respect for each person's uniqueness and individuality is another key ethical principle for social workers. Social workers support cultural and ethnic diversity as well as the right of each client to express his or her own identity. Social workers must balance the rights of the individual with the interests of society in a socially responsible way.
- *Importance of human relationships: Social workers recognize the central importance of human relationships.* Change happens both within and between people. Therefore, human relationships are central to social work practice. Social workers are committed to working with all forms of relationships on the individual, family, group, organization, and community levels.
- *Integrity: Social workers behave in a trustworthy manner.* To be a social work professional means adhering to the standards of behavior required by the profession. A key standard is integrity, which requires workers to act honestly in all endeavors and participate responsibly in their surroundings.
- *Competence: Social workers practice within their areas of competence and develop and enhance their professional expertise.* After being trained and working as certified professionals, all social workers must strive to further develop their areas of expertise and increase their understanding of people's strengths, problems, and needs. This is a lifelong professional pursuit. It ensures that the social worker's knowledge base is current and meaningful, improving effectiveness in solving today's social problems.

Together, these values and ethical principles constitute the foundation on which social workers practice. All professional social workers are expected to adhere to them. Wanting to help people is an important ingredient in good social work practice, but it must be supported by a commitment to social justice and individual worth, along with integrity and competence. This combination of values and ethics makes social work unique among the helping professions.

In day-to-day practice, determining the right and best thing to do is not always easy. Consider the experience of a professional social worker related in "From the Field… Herman's Rights or Worker Safety?" This social worker was caught between the value of serving a client in need, Herman, and following her agency's safety procedures, which dictated not visiting a household in which the worker might be in direct danger. Herman's loaded gun was a possible danger; yet without visits, Herman would not receive much-needed meals. The choices—providing needed services or protecting a worker's safety—were in direct opposition. To do one meant not doing the other. This presents an ethical dilemma for the social worker.

BOX 1.10 | **ETHICAL PRACTICE … HELPING CLIENTS**

Early in the chapter Jane's situation is discussed: "I just lost my job, I have two young kids to support, my rent is due next week, and I don't know what to do. Can you help me?"

What if Jane asked you to loan her the money for her rent and told you she would pay you back in a couple of months? Jane is very persuasive, and it is clearly not her fault that she may be evicted if she does not pay her rent. Is it okay to loan or give a client money? Is it important in this situation? What would you do?

BOX 1.11 | **FROM THE FIELD … HERMAN'S RIGHTS OR WORKER SAFETY?**
Kathy Bailey, MSW

Herman lived in a small house in a poorer section of the city. I say *house* only because it is the most common term for a residence, not because it is representative of the dwelling in which he resided. It reminded me of the shantytown pictures of the Depression era. Herman had lived in this place for many years and had no intention or desire to move anywhere else. Everyone in the area knew him, and although they did not necessarily come to visit, they kept an eye on his place. I had been contacted to do an intake assessment to determine eligibility for home-delivered meals. During the intake I learned that Herman had lost a thumb during the attack on Pearl Harbor. It struck me at the time that a World War II veteran

injured in the line of duty should have had a pension that supported a better lifestyle. Why he came to be where he was I don't know.

While going through the intake process, Herman showed me a stack of police report reference cards. There must have been at least fifty cards that represented each time he had called the police and filed a report of a break-in attempt or some other suspicious activity. Herman had a few small, as he described them, bullet holes in his plywood door panels. He said these were left over from previous break-in attempts. Herman kept a gun next to him. Although I am not knowledgeable about guns, I believe it was his service weapon. Or maybe he told me that. Anyway,

BOX 1.11   **FROM THE FIELD ... HERMAN'S RIGHTS OR WORKER SAFETY?**
continued

Herman kept it handy. He appeared to have a reason to protect himself.

I authorized the meals, and a volunteer who worked for the senior center delivered them daily. Herman developed a relationship with the meal delivery aide and looked forward to the visits. The service was provided for several months and all seemed well until a casual comment by the delivery aide to the director of the senior center changed Herman's world.

The delivery aide happened to mention to the center director that Herman kept a gun next to him. The aide did not say that she had been threatened or that she was fearful, but merely that the gun was there. The director immediately forbade the aide from delivering any meals to the house unless Herman got rid of his gun, citing liability and safety reasons. The aide protested, but to no avail.

As the case manager, I was contacted to intervene. I spoke with Herman after I failed to change the mind of the senior center director. Herman was unwilling to give up or even hide his gun. He maintained, and I agree, that it was his right to have it. Nevertheless, the senior center stopped his meals. Appeals to the local Area Agency on Aging, which funded the meals, were denied on the basis of liability. I kept Herman on the caseload, trying to get him to go the senior center for meals. Two months later, Herman shot himself in the head. He died at home.

Seniors are vulnerable and isolated in our society. Could Herman's death have been prevented? I believe so. Just a little give and take—a little less focus on legality and regulation, and a little more focus on what the client needed—would have made a difference. I mourn Herman to this day and keep him in the forefront of my mind as a reminder that the system can just as easily condemn as it can relieve.

BOX 1.12   **WHAT DO YOU THINK?**

What are your feelings about the story of Herman? What might you tell the social worker? Is there anything that you think could have been done differently?

SOCIAL WORK CAREERS

As you have seen, social workers work in a wide variety of practice settings. Brief descriptions of some of the major areas of employment are presented here. Much of the rest of the book will look more closely at these settings.

CHILD WELFARE

Children are among society's most vulnerable members. They often have neither voice nor choice in how the world treats them. Child welfare social workers help protect children and ensure their well-being through efforts to support and strengthen families.

The most common and traditional child welfare role is in child protective services (CPS). Every state has a system designed to protect children from all forms of abuse and neglect. For example, Illinois has a Department of Children and Families Services (DCFS), Arizona puts child welfare under the Department of Economic

Security (DES), Texas has a Department of Family and Protective Services (DFPS), and in Massachusetts child protection falls under the Department of Social Services (DSS). The common goal of child welfare workers in all such programs is to ensure that no child is subjected to physical or mental abuse or is harmed or neglected by caretakers or other adults. In addition to protection, child welfare workers are involved in securing safe living environments for children who have been abused or neglected, a process that often includes foster care or adoption. Chapter 11 covers social work with children.

PEOPLE WHO ARE OLDER

Longer life expectancy is a major fact of contemporary society. Social workers have always worked directly with people as they age. The increasing population of older people means that this area is expanding.

Social workers in the field of aging specialize in issues related to maturity, health and medicine, end of life, and family relations and support. These professionals may work in specialized settings such as skilled-nursing facilities, rehabilitation centers, or senior centers, or they may concentrate on older clients in hospitals or mental health facilities, or at area agencies on aging offices. Chapter 8 presents an in-depth look at social work practice with people who are older.

HEALTH CARE/MEDICAL SOCIAL WORK

Social workers, like doctors and nurses, play an important role in health care settings. Medical social workers serve in hospitals, care facilities, hospices, and public health departments. In hospitals and care facilities, they may counsel patients and their families and are responsible for discharge planning, which includes ensuring that patients have needed support services when they leave the medical facility to return home or to go to another care facility. Medical social workers also serve as liaisons between doctors and patients, advocate for patient needs, and conduct training programs for medical personnel. Some social workers are employed by public health agencies, where they develop, implement, and evaluate prevention programs. Still others provide grief counseling in hospice settings. Social work in health care settings is presented in Chapter 9.

MENTAL HEALTH

Many social workers specialize in providing mental health services. In fact, professional social workers make up the country's largest group of mental health service providers (NASW, 2008a). Although their role is similar to that of other professionals, such as psychologists, their particular emphasis is on the person in his or her environment.

Mental health social workers help people through individual, family, and group counseling. Although mental health interventions take place in many fields of practice, mental health social workers can primarily be found in community mental health agencies, in hospitals, and in private practice. The goal of mental health social workers is to help people overcome or cope with mental disorders, such as depression or schizophrenia, or to address emotional problems, such as grief over the death of a loved one. The ultimate goal is to help all such individuals lead full and productive lives. Chapter 10 presents mental health social work in detail.

SCHOOL SOCIAL WORK

Teachers ensure that children are mastering the academic material presented in school. Unfortunately, many children come to school with problems that hinder their ability to learn effectively and socialize in healthy ways. These problems go beyond what a teacher has been trained to handle or has the time to address.

School social workers are employed by school systems to intervene with children who have emotional or social needs or both beyond the school situation. School social workers provide individual and group counseling for students, work with families, and intervene to create healthier communities that better support student and family needs. They also help administrators and teachers find ways to foster students' academic and social growth. Chapter 11 deals with school social work.

CRIMINAL JUSTICE

Social workers fill a variety of roles in both the juvenile and adult criminal justice systems. They are involved in juvenile and adult probation and parole. They work in juvenile and adult institutions (prisons and jails), group homes, halfway houses, and prevention programs. Some police departments hire social workers who go out on calls to help crime victims and calm tense family situations. Social workers are also involved in victim assistance programs, where they provide counseling to victims and help them through the complicated criminal justice system. Social work practice in criminal justice is covered in Chapter 14.

EMPLOYMENT/OCCUPATIONAL SOCIAL WORK

Many factors, both internal and external to the workplace, affect people's ability to do their jobs effectively. Problems within the workplace, such as intergroup conflict, unequal treatment of employees, or substance abuse, can have a negative effect on employee morale, satisfaction, and productivity. Employees who are struggling with external problems, such as marital difficulties or alcohol or drug abuse, often bring their struggles into the workplace. This can hinder their ability to successfully complete work tasks. Occupational social workers provide counseling for employees who are struggling with personal problems. They also advise employers on personnel issues, provide training on diversity and other issues, and refer employees to appropriate outside resources. Chapter 12 details the roles of social workers in places of employment.

PUBLIC WELFARE

Although relatively few professional social workers are employed in the public welfare field today, this type of work has been associated with social work since its inception. Public welfare provides assistance to economically deprived individuals and families. Unfortunately, work in this field often focuses on eligibility—determining whether a person is poor enough to receive public assistance. However, social workers' participation in public welfare can go beyond determining eligibility and involve helping poor clients become economically self-sufficient through job training, education, financial planning, and linkage to community resources. The impact of poverty and the role of social work in addressing this problem are discussed in Chapter 4.

SUBSTANCE ABUSE AND ADDICTIONS

Social workers encounter people who have drug and alcohol problems in many different settings. Substance abuse is a factor in most social work practice arenas, including child abuse and neglect, domestic violence, schools, poverty, juvenile delinquency, aging, the workplace, criminal justice, and the mental health area. Social workers provide individual, family, and group counseling for people struggling with drug and alcohol problems. They are involved in case management, conducting research into effective treatments for substance abuse, and shaping policies aimed at treatment and prevention of drug and alcohol abuse. Social workers can also be found advocating for better prevention programs, jobs, and housing for people with drug and alcohol problems. This issue is covered in Chapter 13.

COMMUNITY ORGANIZATION

Many communities struggle with a variety of challenges, such as crime, lack of affordable housing, intergroup tensions, inadequate transportation, and lack of jobs. Social workers help communities come together to build on their strengths, using the power of numbers to decrease isolation and address community-wide problems. They help community members understand their needs and develop new resources to address them.

The aim of community organizers is to promote change in the systems and environments that keep community members from being able to lead full and productive lives. Social workers can be found in community action agencies, community centers, neighborhood associations, and a variety of social change organizations. Community organization is a mode of social practice and is covered in more detail in Chapter 5.

POLICY PRACTICE

Legislation passed at the local, state, and federal levels often has a major effect on the practice of social work. Legislation can determine how much money is available for social services and programs, as well as who receives benefits and how much they get. Elected and appointed officials can also be involved in determining whether and where shelters can open, whether or how severely someone can be punished for a crime, and many other issues that affect people's lives.

Social workers are involved in advocacy work aimed at influencing policymakers to make changes in social policy. They are employed by individual legislators, nonprofit advocacy groups, and legislative bodies. Their work may include conducting research, writing legislation, or lobbying on issues of concern to the profession. Policy practice not only is a specialized social work role, but can and should also be a part of all social work positions.

MANAGEMENT/ADMINISTRATION

Although most social workers are involved in the direct provision of services, some are responsible for the management and administration of social service agencies and organizations. Social work administrators are typically responsible for the efficient and effective delivery of social services. They are involved in personnel management (including hiring, firing, and evaluating employees), budgeting, fundraising, and working with boards of directors and community representatives. Social work administration is typically a more advanced role, employing social workers who have a number of years of practice experience. Working as a social service administrator is one of the specialized practice domains of the profession.

INTERNATIONAL SOCIAL WORK

Our global society means that social well-being does not stop with the borders of the United States. What happens in other nations impacts people living in this country, indirectly and sometimes directly. Work with refugee resettlement and immigration are two areas that require an understanding of international social concerns. A small number of social workers specialize in international issues and the relevance to social work practice in the United States. In addition, the education and training of social workers now occurs in most countries throughout the world. Many methods of practice are shared across nations, with North American models being very influential. This has meant that social workers trained in the United States can often work effectively in other countries, and vice versa.

These are the major areas of employment for social workers. They are also employed in numerous other settings that directly or indirectly support social well-being.

IS SOCIAL WORK FOR YOU?

Social work is an exciting and rewarding career, providing practitioners with diverse tasks and opportunities. It is not, however, the right career for everyone. Most social workers enter the profession at least in part because they want to help people, to make things better. In addition, social workers should be able to effectively engage with people from various communities.

PERSONAL CHARACTERISTICS SUITED TO SOCIAL WORK PRACTICE

In addition to broad knowledge and skills, a number of personal characteristics make a person well suited for social work. Skills and knowledge can be learned, but personal characteristics are not easily taught, and changing them takes work. Following are some of the personal characteristics that make a person well suited to social work practice.

- *Commitment to self-awareness:* People who do not know themselves—who are unaware of their own values, assumptions, beliefs, strengths, and weaknesses—are unlikely to be able to effectively help others. Social workers must be willing to engage in self-reflection and do the hard work necessary to get to know themselves. Part of self-awareness is understanding one's own personal problems and biases, and addressing them so that they do not interfere in work with others.

- *Trust in people:* A central value in social work is client self-determination (discussed in more detail in Chapter 5). Briefly, self-determination means believing that people know what is best for them and that they should determine their own paths. To be able to give clients room to make their own decisions, social workers must have basic trust in other people, belief that the social worker does not always know what is right, and confidence that clients are in the best position to make informed decisions about their lives.

- *Positive outlook:* Creating positive change often requires a long and difficult struggle. Social workers must have a strong, positive mindset—a belief that change is possible and that things can get better.

- *Respect for diversity:* Social workers deal with many different types of people. They must believe that diversity is positive and that it makes society stronger. This perspective allows them to respect differences and to adapt their actions to accommodate diverse populations.

- *Creativity:* Many of the problems with which social workers struggle, including poverty, substance abuse, violence, and oppression, are large and complex. Effective social work practice requires finding new ways to look at challenges and creative approaches to problem solving.

- *Open mind:* There is rarely, if ever, only one right path to take. No one always has the right answer. Social workers must keep their minds open, be willing to listen to other points of view, and change their thinking and actions when appropriate.

- *Empathy:* When helping people, identifying what they feel and learning about their life experiences are important. Being aware of other people's struggles makes it possible to develop empathy, the understanding of another person's life as if one lived it. Viewing people's lives from their perspective makes a social worker less likely to pass judgment, be biased, or make harsh assessments. Good social work practice requires the development and use of empathy.

- *Compassion:* Having empathy leads to understanding the conditions of other people's lives and can arouse feelings of concern or compassion and the desire to help alleviate pain and suffering. The desire to improve the well-being of individuals and society is one of the driving forces behind social work practice.

- *Flexibility, willingness to receive feedback, and willingness to change:* Given that there is no single right approach to problem solving, social workers must be flexible in their efforts to create change. When an intervention does not work well, the worker must be willing to try a different one. Similarly, when someone questions or challenges a social worker, that worker needs to hear the feedback and remain open to changing her or his approach.

- *Curiosity and openness to lifelong learning:* No one leaves undergraduate or graduate social work education knowing all that is required to be an effective social worker. Effective social work practice requires openness to new ideas and information, and commitment to continue learning throughout one's career.

- *Patience:* Creating change, whether in individuals, communities, or organizations, takes time, often a lot of time. Social workers need to be able to persist over the long haul, actively working for change while being patient and understanding that true change does not usually come quickly.
- *Healthy skepticism:* One of the most powerful words is *why*. When people ask why, it means that they do not just accept that everything must be the way it is now. People who ask why are able to think critically and question the way things are. This is a crucial first step toward creating change.

Do you possess some or all of these characteristics? Few people, if any, have all these strengths or have them as thoroughly as they may like. However, being successful as a social worker means making a commitment to develop these qualities.

SOCIAL WORKERS AS CHANGE AGENTS

The *Social Work Dictionary* defines **change agent** as "a social worker or other helping professional or a group of helpers whose purpose is to facilitate improvement" (Barker, 2003, p. 64). Although this definition seems simple, the task can be very difficult. People typically come to social workers' attention after years of set behaviors. Social problems are large scale and deeply entrenched. Trying to facilitate change, and do so in ways that improve people's lives, is the foundation of social work practice, hence the reason they are often called change agents and why this book focuses on that role. Being a change agent can be controversial. Do you help individuals change, and perhaps adapt to their social surroundings? Or do you change social surroundings to adapt to people's needs? These questions will appear in numerous discussions throughout this book. And sometimes social workers make choices about where to focus the change, and those choices are sometimes based on what can readily be done rather than what may be the best alternative. For example, you may work with a family in crisis due to the murder of a parent. The family may live in a neighborhood that is dangerous, and that dangerous environment contributed to the parent's death. If the neighborhood is dangerous to one family, it is likely to be dangerous to all the residents. So the optimal change is to improve the neighborhood. But that change may require a long struggle to improve living conditions, including economic growth and police protection, which is often beyond what you can do as a professional working with one family to overcome the trauma of a parent's murder. So instead, you focus on helping the family to grieve and possibly move to a safer neighborhood.

Making a choice such as this can feel as though you are not living up to your role as a change agent. There is no way to resolve this tension between changing society and helping the individual. That is why the NASW Code of Ethics stresses both social responsibility and serving those in need. Sometimes doing one shortchanges the other. This dilemma is a major part of being a social worker. Throughout the book we will raise ways that you can be a change agent and engage in systems or large-scale change as well as change in the lives of individuals and families. It is important to be aware of the options you have to become a change agent at different levels and to reflect on what you can do to best serve individuals, families, groups, and the larger community.

BOX 1.13	BECOMING A CHANGE AGENT

In August 2005, Hurricane Katrina hit New Orleans and the surrounding area resulting in devastation to the city, particularly the low-lying areas disproportionately populated by low-income people. News of the natural disaster captivated the nation and brought attention to the aftermath and the needs of the people who had lived in that area of the Gulf Coast. Two years later, assessments of the situation take two very different sides. According to the government, progress toward rebuilding is being made, with billions of federal dollars in assistance helping (FEMA, 2007). Media reports suggest that New Orleans is "barely limping along" (Brinkley, 2007) with many areas lying vacant and with little accomplished in the poorer neighborhoods (Gruenwald, 2007).

Some of the difference in assessment lies in what is being done and for whom. Are the federal funds being used to rebuild or simply to keep people in temporary housing? Are projects being undertaken to improve flood control or only to build on higher ground? Are business areas being helped, but poorer neighborhoods ignored? These are some of the questions asked about the progress after Katrina.

Analyzing the situation: Try to learn more about the situation in New Orleans today. How do people on different sides of the situation explain what has happened? Is there a difference based on income? Based on race?

What can social workers do? Given your analysis, what might social workers do to address the situation in New Orleans? What can be done on the individual level? The community level? The government level? Which is more important, helping the individuals affected by the storm or rebuilding the levees and infrastructure so future flooding will be contained?

What can you do? What is one step you can take now, alone or working with others, to improve the living situation in New Orleans? Is there something you can do close to home to make a difference? Is there a situation with similar concerns that you are aware of in your community? If so, what can you do to help change the situation?

One of the goals of this book is to help you better understand what social workers do, so that you can make an informed choice about pursuing a career as a professional social worker. The introductory course allows you to take a closer look at yourself to determine if social work is the career you want. In addition, volunteering in a human services agency can help you see if social work suits you.

This chapter ends with a process to help you decide whether social work is for you. We hope that you continue to be self-reflective as you read the rest of the book. The better you know yourself, the better you will be able to determine whether you want to be a social worker and the better social worker you will be if you make that choice.

BOX 1.14	WHAT DO YOU THINK?

Can you see yourself in social work? Try to look several years into the future. What type of work do you see yourself doing? Can you picture an agency or organization you would like to be working for? Do you know what types of people you might be working with, and what types of problems you might be trying to address?

CHOOSING SOCIAL WORK AS A CAREER

When choosing a career, there are many things to consider. Following are questions to ask yourself when deciding whether social work is right for you:

- What types of things make you happy? Are these consistent with the work you see yourself doing as a social worker?
- What people and events in your past have influenced your interest in social work? Consider experiences with your family and friends, interactions with social service professionals, and so on.
- Why do you want to be a social worker? How would being a social worker add to your satisfaction and happiness?
- What are your life goals? When you look into the future, what do you think you will need to be happy? How do these needs fit with a career in social work? Considering how much money social workers earn, the respect and prestige they receive, the hours they work, and so on, will being a social worker bring you the financial security you want? Will it allow you the time and financial resources to do the things you want to do? Will you need to support a family, and if so, can you support a family as a social worker? Will the profession allow you to be as creative or self-expressive as you want to be?

Keep these questions in mind as you read the rest of this book. Let them serve as a guide as you explore the profession of social work.

CONCLUSION

The profession of social work provides a wide variety of occupational opportunities working with diverse people. An undergraduate BSW degree prepares a social worker for general helping positions, and the MSW degree allows the worker to serve as an advanced specialist.

Social workers comply with professional values and ethics that guide them in the application of skills and techniques designed to improve the well-being of people and society. This book provides an introduction to the full array of professional social work roles and serves as a foundation for further study.

Key Terms

change agent, (p. 28)

Charity Organization Society (COS), (p. 4)

Council on Social Work Education (CSWE), (p. 6)

diversity perspective, (p. 14)

ecological systems framework, (p. 13)

empowerment, (p. 14)

general systems theory, (p. 11)

macro practice, (p. 2)

micro practice, (p. 2)

National Association of Social Workers (NASW), (p. 7)

person-in-environment perspective, (p. 10)

Settlement Movement, (p. 5)

self-determination, (p. 3)

Standards for Cultural Competence in Social Work Practice, (p. 15)

strengths perspective, (p. 13)

Questions for Discussion

1. How does social work differ from the work of other professions? What makes social work unique?
2. How do Charity Organization Societies differ from the Settlement Movement? Choose one of the practice settings described in the chapter. What activities might you engage in that reflect COS principles? What activities might you engage in that reflect the principles of the Settlement Movement?
3. What are the differences between a BSW degree and an MSW degree?
4. What is the person-in-environment perspective? If you were hired as a hospital social worker, how might this perspective guide your work?
5. Choose one of the primary values and ethics outlined in the NASW Code of Ethics. Put it into your own words, and explain how it influences social work practice.

Change Agent Exercise

Spend a few days reading your local newspaper. Make a list of problems discussed in the newspaper that affect members of your local community or the larger national or international community. The problems should be ones that negatively affect the lives of some members of the community. Choose one of these problems, one that you care about. Write a few paragraphs offering ideas about how you and others in the community could work together to help create a solution or a partial solution to the problem.

Chapter Exercises

1. **Language**
   Review the section on language in the chapter. Without identifying yourself, record your answers to these questions.

   Are there terms used that you are not comfortable with? If so, list them.

   What terms might be more comfortable for you? Why?

   Get into groups of four. Without identifying who wrote each answer, go over and discuss the responses of group members about terms they were comfortable or not comfortable with.

2. **Compatibility with the Social Work Profession**
   The following questions are designed to help you assess your compatibility with social work. There are no right or wrong answers. Consider each question

carefully, answer it honestly, and use your answers in deciding whether to be a social worker.

a.   I am willing to look at my own behaviors and consider how I interact with other people.

1	2	3	4	5	6
ALMOST ALWAYS					RARELY

b.   I trust other people.

1	2	3	4	5	6
ALMOST ALWAYS					RARELY

c.   I believe that change for the better is possible.

1	2	3	4	5	6
ALMOST ALWAYS					RARELY

d.   I am open to listen to the points of view of others.

1	2	3	4	5	6
ALMOST ALWAYS					RARELY

e.   I am aware of how other people feel.

1	2	3	4	5	6
ALMOST ALWAYS					RARELY

f.   I am flexible and willing to change

1	2	3	4	5	6
ALMOST ALWAYS					RARELY

g.   I am patient with other people.

1	2	3	4	5	6
ALMOST ALWAYS					RARELY

Consider the answers you gave. Answer the following questions:

Did you give yourself any scores of 5 or 6?

If so, do you think those areas might present difficulties for you as a social worker?

What about any scores of 3 or 4?

Do you think a score of 3 or 4 indicates an area you need to strengthen?

3. **Volunteer Experience Assessment**

Volunteering in a social service agency can provide valuable knowledge and give you firsthand experience helping people. This exercise can help you assess whether a volunteer position is useful for you.

   a. Is the volunteer position teaching you new skills?

      Yes   No

      Why?

   b. Does the position bring out your best abilities?

      Yes   No

      Why?

   c. Does the work give you a chance to try out your own ideas?

      Yes   No

      Why?

   d. Is the position interesting nearly all of the time, interesting most of the time but with some dull stretches, or pretty dull and monotonous most of the time?

      Monotonous   Dull stretches   Interesting

      Why?

   e. Would you recommend this position to a friend?

      Yes   No

      Why?

4. **Beliefs about Diversity**

Circle the number that most closely reflects your beliefs about each question.

   a. I like people who are different from myself.

1	2	3	4	5	6
ALMOST ALWAYS					RARELY

   b. I can be comfortable with all kinds of people.

1	2	3	4	5	6
ALMOST ALWAYS					RARELY

   c. I find meeting new people to be worthwhile.

1	2	3	4	5	6
ALMOST ALWAYS					RARELY

d. I can enjoy being with people whose values are different from mine.

1	2	3	4	5	6
ALMOST ALWAYS					RARELY

Consider the answers you gave. Answer the following questions:

Did you give yourself any scores of 5 or 6?

If so, do you think those areas might present difficulties for you as a social worker?

Do you think areas in which you gave yourself a score of 3 or 4 might need to be strengthened?

5. **Social Work Values**

Some of the social work values that are of special significance when working with children and families are discussed in the section on Values and Ethics. Review the following case, paying special attention to the issues related to professional values and ethics, and answer the questions that follow:

You are a social worker at a local family service agency. One day when you are picking up your third grader at school, his classmate Julie tells you that she wants to talk to you because your son told her that you help families. Julie says that her father recently lost his job and has been hitting her mother a lot. She is worried about her mother and her baby sister, who are alone with him while Julie is at school. Julie says that her father has never hit the children but that they are often scared and upset. She asks you what she can do, but begs you not to talk to anyone else about what is going on in her home.

What social work values are relevant in this case?

How might you help Julie?

How is this case complicated by the fact that it is not officially your case but, instead, a situation you have come across in your personal life? Are you still held to social work values and ethics when you are not at work?

How might you take action, but also protect Julie's identity?

References

Agnew, E. N. (2003). *From charity to social work: Mary E. Richmond and the creation of an American profession*. Chicago: University of Illinois Press.

Bartlett, H. M. (1970). *The common base of social work practice*. New York: National Association of Social Workers.

Brieland, D. (1995). Social work practice: History and evolution. *Encyclopedia of Social Work*, Vol. 3 (19th ed.) (pp. 2247–2257). Silver Spring, MD: National Association of Social Workers.

Brinkley, D. (2007, August 26). Reckless abandonment. *Washington Post*, p. B1.

Bureau of Labor Statistics, U.S. Department of Labor. (2006–2007). Social Workers. *Occupational Outlook Handbook*. Retrieved February 29, 2008, from http://www.bls.gov/oco/ocos060.htm.

CSWE. (2008). Council on Social Work Education website. Retrieved March 23, 2008, from http://portal.cswe.org/Membership/MemberDirectorySearch.aspx.

Erickson, A. G. (1987). Family services. *Encyclopedia of Social Work*, Vol. 1 (18th ed.) (pp. 589–593). Silver Spring, MD: National Association of Social Workers.

FEMA. (2007). *Families recovering … communities rebuilding*. FEMA Gulf Coast Recovery Office.

Germain, C., & Gitterman, A. (1980). *The life model of social work practice*. New York: Columbia University Press.

Germain, C. B., & Hartman, A. (1980). People and ideas in the history of social work practice. *Social Casework, 61,* 323–331.

Gibelman, M. (1999). The search for identity: Defining social work—Past, present, future. *Social Work, 44,* 298–310.

Gruenwald, M. (2007, August 13). The threatening storm. *Time, 170,* 7.

Karls, J. M., & Wandrei, K. E. (1994). *The PIE manual*. Washington, DC: NASW Press.

Lee, J. A. B. (2001). *The empowerment approach to social work practice*. New York: Columbia University Press.

Meyer, C. H. (1981). Social work purpose: Status by choice or coercion? *Social Work, 26,* 69–75.

Mondros, J. B., & Wilson, S. M. (1994). *Organizing for power and empowerment*. New York: Columbia University Press.

NASW. (2001). *NASW Standards for Cultural Competence in Social Work Practice*. Washington, DC: Author.

NASW. (2003). *Practice Research Network*, PRN, 2.1 & 2.2.

NASW. (2008a). National Association of Social Workers website. Retrieved on March 23, 2008, from http://www.socialworkers.org/pressroom/features/general/nasw.asp.

NASW. (2008b). *NASW Code of Ethics*. Washington, DC: Author.

Rubin, A., & Babbie, E. (2007). *Research methods for social work* (6th ed.). Belmont, CA: Wadsworth Publishing.

Saleebey, D. (1992). *The strengths perspective in social work*. New York: Longman Press.

Segal, E. A. (1995). Jane Addams. In Magill, F. N. (ed.), *Great lives from history: American women* (pp. 21–25). Pasadena, CA: Salem Press.

Von Bertalanffy, L. (1971). *General systems theory*. New York: Braziller.

Watzlawick, P., Bavelas, J. M., & Jackson, D. D. (1967). *Pragmatics of human communication*. New York: W. W. Norton.

Yellow Bird, M. (1999). What we want to be called: Indigenous peoples' perspectives on racial and ethnic labels. *American Indian Quarterly*, 23, 2, 1–22.

THE SOCIAL WELFARE SYSTEM

CHAPTER **2**

Heinle Division of Cengage Learning

Any person or family can experience problems. A worker may lose a job and not have enough money to pay the mortgage. An aging person who lives alone may no longer be able to take care of things at home without assistance. When personal resources are inadequate or problems are too overwhelming, people turn to outside sources for help. That help can come from family members, friends, religious institutions, local organizations, or the city, state, tribal, or federal governments.

The collection of programs, resources, and services available to help people is referred to as the **social welfare system.** Social welfare addresses the well-being of people in society. Social welfare services are created through public laws and policies that are established by federal and state legislatures, local municipalities, and courts. These laws and public policies are developed in response to large-scale social needs (Segal, 2007). For example, because some people cannot afford to buy enough food to feed their families, public policies have created food assistance programs such as the Food Stamp Program, which is discussed in more detail later in this chapter and in Chapter 4

The term *welfare* is often perceived in a negative way as referring to something given by the government to people who may need help but may also take advantage of the system while receiving it. In this view, welfare consists of programs that provide assistance to poor people; it does not involve the many other social welfare services that are more broadly available, such as Social Security. The negative perception of welfare does a disservice to all the programs and resources that help people in need.

As you read this book, you will gain greater understanding of and insight into the array of social welfare programs that exist in our society and the complex variety of values and assumptions that are part of those programs. You will then be able to form your own opinions about the importance of and need for each social welfare program, and whether each organized public service is appropriately designed to enhance the social well-being of members of our society.

Although people refer to it as a system, the provision of social services in this country is not an organized system. The social welfare network, rather than being a single, cohesive, monolithic unit, is made up of a variety of organizations and agencies, as well as different levels of government. Public providers of social services can be under the direct supervision and auspices of the federal, state, local, or tribal government. Funding comes through the government, financed by taxes paid by individuals and businesses.

Private agencies and organizations are not directly under the supervision or control of a government body. Private providers can be either nonprofit organizations or for profit. That is, some companies that provide services such as mental health or medical care are structured to earn profits and are even listed on the stock exchange.

Although private social service agencies are not part of local, state, federal, or tribal governments, they often work in partnership with government agencies. The partnerships are typically built around contracts for services. This means that the private agencies are reimbursed for qualified services they provide to people who meet government criteria for eligibility. For example, a low-income person may be treated for depression at a private mental health facility, but the federal government pays the bill because the person qualifies for public assistance benefits and the mental health facility is certified and approved by government agencies.

Agencies and organizations related to religious denominations also serve social welfare needs. Religious organizations have a long history of involvement in the provision of social services. Starting in the 1600s, local churches or parishes were often involved in the collection and distribution of resources. Since then, religious groups have played an integral part in the provision of U.S. social welfare services. Catholic Charities, Jewish Family Services, Lutheran Social Services, and the Salvation Army are but a few of the religion-affiliated organizations that provide social welfare services.

The delivery of social welfare services has developed incrementally over decades. This means that small changes have been made over time and have evolved into the larger social welfare system of today. However, this slow evolution has caused the system to become fragmented and difficult to completely understand. Social workers often work within social welfare programs or refer people to them.

This book provides an introductory overview of the resources and services that are available through the social welfare system. It will take further study and years of social work experience to understand the system thoroughly. Because the system is constantly changing in order to adapt to shifts in social needs and social problems, social workers must continue to learn about available services and resources.

HOW THE SOCIAL WELFARE SYSTEM HELPS PEOPLE

The social welfare system helps support people preventively—before there is a problem—and responsively—when a problem is already present. Some social welfare historians refer to these two approaches to providing services as *institutional* and *residual* (Wilensky & Lebeaux, 1965).

Institutional social welfare services are in place to prevent problems. They are proactive and provide benefits or services to people before problems arise. Social Security, the national program that most people pay into during their working years, is available to people when they age. It guarantees a monthly payment to help keep people out of poverty. Even if people are wealthy and do not need Social Security benefits, if they paid in while working they receive monthly payments. Everyone who paid in during his or her working years is entitled to, or guaranteed, benefits. The preventive aspect of this program is that it provides a minimum income to keep people in retirement from falling below the poverty line.

Another example of an institutional resource is a tax benefit, such as the exemption for children on federal income tax forms. The exemption means that a specified amount is deducted (subtracted from a person's taxable income) for each dependent child. This benefit provides all parents with a small break in taxes, not because there is immediate need but because lawmakers recognize that raising children is costly. The tax break helps defray the cost of child rearing, therefore helping to prevent poverty. As with Social Security, even if a family does not need financial help, they benefit from the exemption. One last example of an institutional social welfare service is public education. All youngsters from 5 to 18 years of age are guaranteed a place in a public school, regardless of family income or resources.

Residual services, on the other hand, come into play only after there is an identifiable problem. Residual services are designed to address only the identified problem. For example, if a single-parent family is too poor to pay for even basic needs, certain programs can provide monthly cash assistance or credit to purchase food or help pay rent. These programs are available only when all other resources are lacking and when there is a documented need. This is a reactive approach to helping people. *Reactive* means that the response comes after the problem or need is identified.

The majority of social welfare services in this country are residual. There is a strong preference among policymakers and most taxpayers to pay for services only for identifiable problems and visible needs. It is more difficult to convince people to commit resources to prevent things that have not yet happened and may never happen.

An example helps explain why this is the case. Two students in an algebra class are told on the first day that they can hire a tutor to help them. Should they wait to see if they can understand the material on their own and save money by not hiring the tutor? Should they go ahead and hire the tutor, hoping that the money spent will improve their performance in the class? Should they wait to see whether they are definitely having trouble and hire the tutor if they are? Suppose one student hires the tutor, the other does not, and in the end they get the same grade. Did the first student waste the money?

These questions are difficult to answer in advance. So, too, is it difficult to determine what resources or programs to provide before knowing whether there is a problem and how severe the problem is. For example, should all young people receive counseling about child development and parenting before they have children of their own? Or should only those parents who have trouble parenting be required to attend training? The advantage to waiting is that there are typically fewer people to serve and resources are not wasted on people who do not need service. However, we usually discover that a person is having trouble being a parent when his or her child is already hurt or neglected. Although the residual approach uses resources more sparingly, it can also result in problems that are more severe and, therefore, more harmful.

Preventive institutional services cover everybody, whether there is a problem or not. For example, a person who owns a car pays for car insurance. If the person has an accident, she or he can draw on the insurance to help cover expenses. If a driver was certain that she or he would not have an accident, would the driver be willing to pay the insurance premiums? This is the principle of institutional services. All people contribute, whether they eventually need the services or not. Of course, not all social problems can be anticipated. Our social welfare system will continue to reflect a mix of residual and institutional responses to need.

BOX 2.1 | **WHAT DO YOU THINK?**

Would you rather pay more taxes to build enough housing so that no one will ever be homeless or pay lower taxes, wait to see who becomes homeless, and then try to find housing for them? Why?

THE HISTORY OF U.S. SOCIAL WELFARE

Today's social welfare system reflects four centuries of responses to social need. Several major historical events and trends have influenced the development of social welfare policy and systems since the earliest European colonists arrived in this country. U.S. social welfare history can be divided into nine key periods, which are outlined in Table 2.1.

COLONIAL PERIOD

The earliest social welfare policy in this country came from England with the colonists. When early settlers experienced illness, deprivation, or death, their new communities were immediately confronted by social need. Colonists recognized the necessity of community support beyond a person's immediate family.

The first social welfare policy to be widely implemented in this country was an English system based on the **Elizabethan Poor Laws.** Until the 1600s, the needs of the poor were the responsibility of feudal landowners in England. Under the feudal system, many people who needed help did not receive it. As England became more urban, rulers saw the need for assistance to poor people who did not "belong" to a landowner. This new sense of public responsibility for the poor resulted in the Elizabethan Poor Laws, formally adopted in England in 1601, which outlined the public's responsibility for the poor. The primary principles of the Elizabethan Poor Laws were as follows:

- The poor were categorized as either worthy or unworthy to receive aid.
- The worthy poor included widows, orphans, the elderly, and people with disabilities.
- The unworthy poor included able-bodied single adults and unmarried women with children born out of wedlock.
- Aid for the poor first came from families, and only when the family absolutely could not provide economic support, did public authorities step in.
- Legal residency in the community was necessary to be eligible for assistance.
- Assistance was temporary and only for emergencies. The ultimate goal was for each recipient to gain employment or marry someone who was employed (Axinn & Stern, 2004).

TABLE 2.1 | THE DEVELOPMENT OF SOCIAL WELFARE POLICY IN THE UNITED STATES

Time Period	Key Social Welfare Response
Colonial period, 1690–1800	Elizabethan Poor Laws
Pre–Civil War period, 1801–1860	Residential institutions
Civil War and postwar period, 1861–1874	First federal intervention
Progressive Era, 1875–1925	Birth of social work profession
Great Depression and New Deal, 1926–1940	Social insurance and public assistance
World War II and after, 1941–1959	GI Bill
Social reform period, 1960–1975	War on Poverty
Retrenchment period, 1976–2000	Cutbacks and local control
New millennium, 2001–present	Terrorism, war, and financial struggles

In terms of overall resources, colonial America was a land of abundant resources. Everything was considered available for the taking. The fact that Indigenous Peoples lived here and used resources prior to the arrival of Europeans was generally discounted. Indigenous Peoples were at best ignored and at worst viewed as impediments to the growth of the new nation and pushed from their tribal lands (Nabokov, 1991). They were not considered worthy of social welfare services. This early relationship of displacement set a foundation for relations with Indigenous Peoples that has persisted for hundreds of years.

Values Reflecting the Colonial Period   The principles espoused in the Elizabethan Poor Laws guide our system of public assistance to this day. The determination of who is deserving of assistance depends primarily on whether the person is capable of working. Americans still prefer to assist people we know or who live near us. The family is the primary source of economic support, and only when a family does not or cannot provide, do we encourage public involvement. We also wait for need to arise, and provide aid on a case-by-case basis. The influence of the Elizabethan Poor Laws has resulted in our residual approach to social welfare services.

The values and beliefs that support the current approach to social welfare focus on the individual and rarely consider how the larger society might affect individual needs. This emphasis also grew out of the Elizabethan Poor Laws. Like the English in Elizabethan times, we tend to value individual effort and achievement. When someone is poor or incapable of working, we generally place the blame for the situation on that individual.

The sense that this is a nation of abundant resources also persists as part of our value system. Most immigrants to this country left from areas that were, by comparison, crowded and had limited resources. The American sense of far-reaching lands and limitless natural resources laid the foundation for a sense of national wealth. It fostered the perception that a person who works hard can achieve anything. The converse is also held to be true: If a person does not have enough, it must be because he or she did not work hard and take advantage of the limitless opportunities and resources.

Pre–Civil War Period

After the colonial period, a distinct American identity began to develop among European immigrants and their descendents. The era prior to the Civil War (from about 1801 to 1860) was characterized by growing social problems. Cities were beginning to expand with an influx of European immigrants. Most arrived with few or no resources. Communities could not afford adequate care for social needs, and they sought new ways to deal with poverty and social problems.

The prevailing social welfare response was the creation of residential institutions—often referred to as indoor relief—by local governments and private relief groups (Leiby, 1978). These institutions included almshouses for the poor, asylums for people with mental health problems, and orphanages for children without parents or, more typically, whose parents could not afford to care for them. The institutions were believed to be the best way to alleviate social problems. Their purpose was to rehabilitate people by setting an example of the proper or healthy way of living (Rothman, 1971). The reality of institutional life was vastly different. Rehabilitation efforts were rare. Instead, most institutions became places to warehouse the poor and the severely mentally ill.

Values Reflecting the Pre–Civil War Period   Most social welfare institutions of the pre–Civil War period were substandard and lacked any real rehabilitation or treatment. Although today's institutions seem different, the ideas that underlie them are relatively unchanged. The idea of placing people with the same problems or concerns in a single residence is seen as an efficient way to serve those in need because it allows them to share resources. Some examples of current social welfare institutions are group homes, halfway houses, and residential treatment facilities.

THE CIVIL WAR AND POST–CIVIL WAR PERIOD

By the 1860s social and economic differences between the North and the South had led the United States into the Civil War. Broadly speaking, the southern states adhered to slavery, whereas the northern states insisted on abolishing it. The economy of the industrialized North—based on increasing numbers of urban workers, the development of railroads, and growth in manufacturing—did not need slavery to prosper. The large-scale agriculture of the South depended on the inexpensive labor of slaves. As the North became more prosperous and economic growth in the South became more uncertain, differences between the two areas produced social unrest. The Civil War began in 1861 and ended four years later.

The Civil War resulted in tremendous economic and social change. The devastation and upheaval caused by the war contributed to a national realization that some social concerns were well beyond the reach of families and local communities. During the Reconstruction period after the war, the federal government tried to aid displaced families and make reparations for losses incurred in the war. As part of Reconstruction, the Freedman's Bureau became the first federal social service program (Jansson, 2009). Launched in 1865, its goals were to provide temporary assistance to newly freed slaves, help reunite families, provide medical care and food rations, and make property available. The Civil War and this program were the first organized federal efforts to ensure social justice. Chapter 3 discusses the concept of social justice in more detail.

Values Reflecting the Civil War and Post–Civil War Period   Although the Freedman's Bureau lasted only until the country had recovered from the war, it firmly established federal intervention on behalf of people in need. No longer were families and localities seen as the only resources against poverty and other social problems. Since Reconstruction, policymakers have introduced, and the public has supported, numerous plans and programs that rely on federal intervention for people's social well-being.

The Civil War brought an official end to slavery, but racism was deeply embedded in American society. The dehumanizing view of Africans and African Americans held by many white people did not disappear. Being freed did not give the former slaves access to education and employment, legal rights, and civil rights. Although some former slaves were able to overcome the oppressive legacy of slavery, the vast majority continued to live and work on land owned by white south-erners who controlled their livelihoods. The white majority did not welcome African American citizens, who were theoretically free, into their economic and social world. The result of this segregation was another hundred years of subverted civil rights and further entrenchment of the racial disparity between African Americans and whites in this country.

THE PROGRESSIVE ERA

The decades following the Civil War were years of rapid economic growth and so-cial change. The period from about 1875 to 1925 is referred to as the Progressive Era. Characterized by economic and social transformations, this period saw major changes in social welfare and the birth of the profession of social work.

The turn of the nineteenth century was a time of significant economic change, with particularly rapid industrialization. Mass manufacturing, the expansion of railroads across the nation, and cheap labor (ensured by rising immigration and re-location to the North of former slaves) radically changed the typical American's way of life. Fewer people earned their livelihoods directly from agriculture. Increas-ing numbers of workers labored in industry, producing such items as clothing and steel. Work in manufacturing was very different from work in the agricultural sec-tor, where people were closer to the creation and distribution of the products of their labor. Manufacturing jobs were totally unregulated and very dangerous, and placed workers at the mercy of factory owners.

In addition, there was a huge influx of immigrants and a large-scale movement toward urbanization. These changes contributed to crowded living conditions, which in turn resulted in poor health, and to overall poverty for many people. The gap between the rich and the poor increased, and reformers called for increased social intervention.

The tremendous social, economic, and political changes of the Progressive Era gave rise to new ways to address societal problems, including the birth of the social work profession. As discussed in the first chapter and later in this chapter, the Pro-gressive Era was the time when the Charity Organization Societies and the Settlement Movement evolved. Together these nongovernmental movements served as the foun-dation for the social work profession.

Values Reflecting the Progressive Era   The Progressive Era was the first time in U.S. history that the rights of workers were at the forefront of debate. The beliefs that workplaces should be safe and that laborers were entitled to protection be-came accepted social values. Acceptance by native-born Americans of immigrants and of increasing diversity also increased.

Possibly the most significant social value that influenced social welfare services during this period was an awareness of the influence of environmental or structural factors on an individual's life. For the first time, many social problems came to be seen as consequences of imbalances in the social and economic structure of the na-tion. It followed that socioeconomic structures had to be changed if people's lives were to improve. A new pattern of social values and beliefs evolved, including an unprecedented awareness of the need for social responsibility.

During the economic upturn following World War I, the commitment to social responsibility waned and the belief in individual responsibility for social well-being reemerged. The pendulum seemed to swing from a strong belief in social responsibility during economic upheaval to emphasis on individual responsibility when the economy was strong. The same pattern persists today. When more people (particularly middle-class people) are affected by an economic downturn, they tend to believe that there are structural reasons for their poverty. Surely, they reason, the many hard-working people who have lost their jobs cannot all be at fault. On the other hand, when the economy is strong and jobs are plentiful, it is easier to explain the plight of poor people by blaming individuals. Chapter 4 discusses the way entrenched structural obstacles can keep people in poverty.

THE GREAT DEPRESSION AND THE NEW DEAL

From colonial times through the 1920s, social services were provided by private agencies, communities, and local government, with some intervention at state levels. Other than the brief foray into social services following the Civil War, the federal government did not provide social services. The Great Depression of the 1930s changed that permanently.

The Great Depression was the most significant economic downturn in U.S. history. At least one out of four workers was unemployed, and a large proportion of those still working were underemployed, earning too little to support themselves and their families. Hundreds of people waited in line outside banks to withdraw their life savings, only to discover that the institutions were bankrupt and their money gone.

Economic ups and downs have traditionally been seen as normal aspects of the U.S. economy. The balance between production and consumption has not always been perfect. Simply stated, sometimes manufacturers produce too much too quickly and have a surplus of products. To attract buyers, they drop prices, and to ensure that they will make a profit, they lay off some workers and minimize other costs of production. Eventually, fewer new products are made, and consumers begin to compete to get them. Prices go up, profits increase, and manufacturers rehire workers and increase production. If too many products are produced, the cycle begins again. Though an oversimplification, this general principle of the balance between supply and demand drives our economy.

During the Great Depression, the imbalance between supply and demand was so great that it destroyed social well-being on an immense scale. The scope of problems and social need overwhelmed existing state, local, and private agencies and programs. One of the outcomes of this severe economic imbalance was the permanent involvement of the federal government in both the provision of social services and the regulation of the economy.

The social and economic reforms introduced in response to the Great Depression were called the New Deal, reflecting President Franklin D. Roosevelt's pledge that he would develop a new approach to provide relief from the devastation. One principle behind his program was the idea that federal economic relief could be used as a stopgap measure to alleviate unemployment and economic slowdown. Another was that major public investment was required to address poverty

(Schwartz, 1993). Thus, the New Deal consisted of immediate relief efforts coupled with the creation of long-term programs, all supported by the federal government.

The goal of the New Deal programs was to first respond with immediate financial relief and short-term employment, then follow up by investing public funds to promote long-term employment. Immediate efforts included the distribution of funds through the Federal Emergency Relief Administration and job placement through the Civil Works Administration, both established in 1933. With an eye toward more organized and permanent solutions, these efforts were folded into the Works Progress Administration in 1935. The Social Security Act was enacted simultaneously (Axinn & Stern, 2004).

The **Social Security Act of 1935** provided long-term protections through a federal program of social insurance and public assistance. It was the first comprehensive federal effort to ensure economic security and address poverty. Social insurance is what we refer to today as Social Security. Part of each worker's earnings is paid into this system and matched by an employer contribution. Workers collect benefits when they leave their jobs due to retirement or disability. The amount a worker receives is determined primarily by work history. In contrast, public assistance provides cash to poor individuals or families through general tax dollars and bases benefits on economic need. (These programs are discussed in Chapter 4.) Although Social Security programs have undergone numerous changes since 1935, they remain the backbone of our country's federal social welfare efforts.

Federal policies designed to maintain economic stability were also instituted in response to the Great Depression. These include monitoring financial markets through the Securities and Exchange Commission and safeguarding personal savings through the creation of the Federal Deposit Insurance Corporation. These innovations in government regulation of the marketplace have remained in place.

Values Reflecting the Great Depression and the New Deal   The Great Depression made many Americans reconsider how larger social and economic conditions contribute to people's economic distress. The focus on structural reasons for poverty led to the creation of numerous social welfare programs designed to provide a variety of services. Although changes have been made to these programs and policies over the years, Americans continue to believe that the federal government should help correct steep imbalances in economic and social well-being.

For example, suppose a major employer closes a manufacturing plant because the cost of production is cheaper in another country, putting hundreds of laborers out of work. In the residual approach, each person would be regarded as an individual case. The institutional approach, on the other hand, considers the large-scale factors that led to the layoffs, such as a broad economic downturn or the availability of cheaper labor abroad. This approach focuses on anticipating and dealing with such problems through public policy. Programs that stress community economic development or job creation are efforts to approach problems through structural change. Such measures were originally used to mitigate the devastating impact of the Great Depression. Many of the programs instituted during the 1930s, including Social Security and public assistance, remain our strongest social welfare programs.

WORLD WAR II AND THE POSTWAR ECONOMY

Although the New Deal programs of the 1930s and 1940s created public economic and social service support in response to the Great Depression, the advent of World War II forced the nation to focus its economic and social resources on war. The war effort sharply increased employment as people joined the military and went to work in war-related industries. The federal government became even more involved in the economy as it managed the war effort. Annual federal expenditures quadrupled from the late 1930s to the late 1940s (Berkowitz & McQuaid, 1988).

Following the war, federal legislation had a profound effect on returning soldiers. The Servicemen's Readjustment Act of 1944, known as the GI Bill, funded education, training, employment services, and home and business loans to help returning soldiers adapt to civilian life (Axinn & Stern, 2004). Although the program was originally viewed as a modest effort to support readjustment, millions of people took full advantage of its benefits. As a result, people who might never have been able to afford an education, employment training, or home ownership were supported in those activities by the federal government.

By the 1950s the nation had turned its focus to economic and social development. Private well-being became the primary goal of many Americans. Although the New Deal and efforts such as the GI Bill established the role of the federal government as a major provider of social welfare services, the primary emphasis of the 1950s was on individual responsibility.

Values Reflecting World War II and the Postwar Economy   The war had a major effect on the nation's social framework. During the war years, so many men were serving overseas and so many war-related products were needed that many women entered the workforce, taking nontraditional jobs. Social roles changed with military necessity. African Americans and Indigenous Peoples played critical roles in combat. Military personnel were exposed to diverse cultures abroad, as well as to the customs and mores of other soldiers and communities. Soldiers stationed away from home made social connections that encouraged some to relocate after the war. The vast mobilization created the foundation for geographic mobility that is now part of modern life.

Young men returning from overseas were seen as heroes and therefore worthy of national support. Thus, the GI Bill garnered lavish support. Veteran status was a reflection of honor and evidence of self-sacrificing service to country.

The generation that came of age during the 1950s lived in a society that focused on family and individual achievement. The federal government emphasized the importance of home life by subsidizing home ownership and transportation that enabled people to move out of the cities and settle in newly developed suburban areas (Ehrenreich, 1985). The residential pattern we call suburbia was born.

The relocation of millions of families to the suburbs had several unanticipated consequences. One was the fragmentation of extended families. Prior to the 1950s, many people lived with or very near their larger extended families, so family members were available to provide various kinds of assistance and support. By contrast, nuclear families living in the suburbs were often far from their relatives. Similarly, the move to suburbia pulled people from their traditional and ethnic communities, reducing the community connection for many people.

THE SOCIAL REFORM YEARS

The nation's cultural focus on the individual began to shift in the 1960s. Although the federal government remained involved in helping people through social welfare policies and programs developed during the New Deal and following the war, there were gaping holes in the support. The biggest gap was in medical care. Two groups in particular suffered from lack of health care: the elderly and the poor. Advocates had been trying for decades to get the federal government to help people in need pay for health care, but it was not until 1965 that Medicaid (health coverage for low-income people) and Medicare (health coverage for senior citizens) were passed into law. The addition of these two programs to the Social Security Act completed the country's package of support under social insurance and public assistance.

The 1960s was also the decade of major legislative advances in civil rights. Although the Civil War had paved the way for racial equality, many individuals and communities never complied with either the letter or the intent of the laws. Two major bills—the **Civil Rights Act,** passed in 1964, and the **Voting Rights Act,** passed in 1965—prohibited segregation, discrimination, and measures denying people of color the right to vote. The effect of these policies is explored in Chapters 3 and 6.

The other major effort of the 1960s was the **War on Poverty.** Despite the postwar economic prosperity of the 1950s, the wealth did not reach all Americans. A compelling description of poverty in the United States, Michael Harrington's *The Other America*, was published in 1962 and helped alert policymakers to the fact that many people were living in desperate economic deprivation. The War on Poverty was a series of policies and programs under the Economic Opportunity Act of 1964 intended to fight poverty throughout the United States (Axinn & Stern, 2004). These efforts demonstrated a renewed emphasis on social justice and the fair distribution of resources and opportunities. The programs included job training, employment incentives, and community action. Other poverty-fighting programs included the Food Stamp Program and Head Start (a preschool education program for low-income children).

Values Reflecting the Social Reform Years   The key value reflected in the public policy efforts of the 1960s was social responsibility. While individual well-being had been a central value in the 1950s, the pendulum was now swinging toward larger social structures. This perspective, most prominently reflected in the civil rights movement, also undergirded the antiwar, feminist, and gay rights movements that flourished during the next decade. "Question authority," a common slogan of the time, sums up the prevailing value. Although Americans had followed this iconoclastic perspective during various eras in the past, it conflicted dramatically with the mainstream values of the previous 20 years. The result was friction between the generation that came to power during the 1950s and younger people who became politically active during the 1960s.

THE RETRENCHMENT YEARS

Although the goals of the 1960s War on Poverty were worthy, the program did not eradicate poverty, and by the 1980s there was a backlash against antipoverty programs. Partly as a result of frustration that so many people were still impoverished after so much effort, many Americans began to reconsider their support for government-funded assistance projects.

Ronald Reagan was elected president in 1980 on a platform of decreasing the federal government's role in social welfare and turning responsibility back to local entities, with the expectation that private groups would contribute social services as well. The return of control of social services from the federal to the local level was known as **devolution.** Its result was a diminished role for the federal government in antipoverty programs and increased variation among programs.

The most significant changes came during the 1990s with the movement for welfare reform. Welfare reform legislation passed in 1996 replaced the public assistance program called Aid to Families with Dependent Children (AFDC) with the Temporary Assistance for Needy Families (TANF) program. AFDC, the primary cash support program for poor women and their children, had been established under the Social Security Act of 1935 (these changes are detailed in Chapter 4).

In general, the result of welfare reform in the 1990s was to limit the total number of years that a family can receive public assistance, place more stringent work requirements on parents, and devolve program control and design to states. These changes represent a strong retrenchment from federal responsibility for social welfare.

Values Reflecting the Retrenchment Years   The values of the Elizabethan Poor Laws were evident in the social policies of the 1980s and 1990s. These policies reflected the belief that the family, not the public, should be primarily responsible for social care. External aid should be limited and should go to those who are most worthy, meaning those who cannot work for socially valid reasons.

Although earlier generations considered single women raising children alone to be worthy, primarily because their single parenthood was due to the death of a spouse, that attitude changed by the end of the twentieth century because recipients were generally unmarried mothers. In addition, changes in public policy during the 1980s and 1990s reflected the belief that state and local governments were better suited than the federal government to develop and control social services.

SOCIAL WELFARE IN THE NEW MILLENNIUM—TERRORISM, WAR, AND FINANCIAL STRUGGLES

The new century opened with a defining event, the terrorist attack on the World Trade Center and the subsequent death of almost 3,000 Americans on American soil. The terrorist attacks of September 11, 2001, led to a shift from the devolution of government social services. Although President George W. Bush had campaigned on a platform of devolution and privatization of social services, the destruction and loss of life drew the federal government deeply into the provision and funding of social services. The federal response included aid to individuals, cities, and even the airline industry. Military personnel were used to provide security and support.

Airport security was transferred from the private sector to the federal government through the creation of the Transportation Security Administration. This response was clearly essential to recovery, but it was contrary to the position of turning social services over to local government and private agencies.

Efforts to deal with terrorism were cited as the reasons for the invasion of Iraq in 2003 and the prolonged U.S. military engagement in Iraq and Afghanistan. Through 2007, the cost of these efforts had topped $700 billion (Congressional Research Service, 2008). By 2008, more than 4,000 U.S. military personnel had died and tens of thousands of Iraqi soldiers, militants, and citizens.

Since the 2001 attack, the U.S. economy has gone through two economic downturns, the recession of 2001 and the mortgage-related financial woes of 2007 and 2008. Economists and historians will debate the impact of the war for years to come, but the fact that the U.S. economy has floundered and incurred greater national debt will impact social welfare services. Already states are feeling the decline in tax revenues, and their losses lead to increased requests for the federal government to step in and cover costs for social services. The impact of the economic downturn of 2007 and 2008 will leave many people without sufficient employment and income, and this will produce needs for health care coverage and immediate services such as rent and food assistance. Moreover, the future years of this new millennium will be centered on responding to financial hardship and fallout from the many years of prolonged military engagement in the Middle East.

Values Influencing the New Millennium   Although we are only a decade into the new century, events and policy decisions will impact the country for years to come. What will the effect on the social work profession be? Of course, the answers to these questions will take years to emerge. Historically, our nation has

---

BOX 2.2	**BECOMING A CHANGE AGENT**

Historic and ongoing events can significantly impact the social well-being of individuals and communities. In March of 2003, the United States initiated war in Iraq. It has involved hundreds of thousands of U.S. soldiers directly and many more thousands of families and friends. Indirectly, it has involved all Americans. Five years into the war, over 4,000 soldiers had been killed and another 40,000 injured, many of them seriously and permanently.

Analyzing the situation:
Try to learn more about the impact of the Iraq war today. How do people on different sides of the situation explain what has happened? Has there been an impact on the social work profession? Has there been

an increase in social service needs of veterans and their families?

What can social workers do?
Given you analysis, should social workers take a position about the war? Should they get involved with the issue? Why or why not? What are some ways they could express support or dissent? In keeping with the NASW Code of Ethics, what actions should social workers take in regard to the war?

What can you do?
Is there something you could do close to home to make a difference?

BOX 2.3 | **WHAT DO YOU THINK?**

Given the growth in social welfare needs in this country, do you think that there are currently enough social services to help people have high-quality lives? Why?

moved back and forth between periods of individual accountability and social responsibility (Schlesinger, 1986). The retrenchment years reflected a period of individual focus. If the cycle continues, the next decades may bring social welfare policies and programs that reflect the values of social responsibility and social justice. Social welfare developments of the new millennium have included some major social expansions, such as coverage of prescription drugs for some Medicare recipients. However, the early years of this century have been dominated by security concerns prompted by 9/11 and the war in Iraq. With billions of dollars spent on the war, and the subsequent deficit in the federal budget, a focus on expanding social services appears unlikely. The problems of the economic downturn of 2007–2008 and the Iraq war will need to be addressed. Chapter 15 addresses one of the early impacts on social services, the trauma experienced by soldiers fighting in Iraq. This is just one outcome, and social policies will certainly need to address this crisis and others that stem from the economic and social fallout of these early years of the new millennium.

THE HISTORY OF THE SOCIAL WORK PROFESSION

Although professional social work did not appear until a little more than a hundred years ago, the social welfare policies and programs of the past helped shape the field. Social work's founding year was 1898, when formal training of social workers was initiated. The New York School of Philanthropy (which is now the Columbia University School of Social Work in New York City) opened that year at the urging of Mary Richmond—the leading voice of the Charity Organization Societies—and others involved in efforts to establish charity work as a profession (Popple, 1995). Within 20 years, there were almost 20 schools of social work in the United States (Brieland, 1995).

The social work profession grew out of conflict and uncertainty about social workers' unique role in society. As discussed in Chapter 1, the Charity Organization Societies and the Settlement Movement disagreed about the best way to work with people and communities. The two groups struggled over whether to focus on personal deficiencies, the emphasis of the COS, or environmental problems, the emphasis of the Settlement Movement. Part of the philosophical difference between the two movements was how best to empower people. COS workers did not view empowerment as a critical concern of personal change, whereas Settlement workers strove to empower people and communities to demand social change. This struggle has continued to color social work. In spite of the differences, the two movements made major contributions to the procedures and skills of the social work profession (see Chapter 1).

Outside criticism of the developing profession came early. In 1915 Dr. Abraham Flexner, a leading authority on graduate professional education representing the General Education Board, addressed the question "Is Social Work a Profession?" in a paper delivered to the National Conference on Social Welfare. His conclusion was that social work was not a profession because it lacked a unique methodology: "Lacking its own 'technique which is communicable by an educational process,' social work was no profession" (Trattner, 1999, p. 257). Flexner's criticism propelled the profession to define its role, trying to determine what makes social work unique and developing formal intervention strategies.

Mary Richmond wrote *Social Diagnosis,* the first book to address professional social work practice, in 1917. A guide for the beginning caseworker, the book outlined ways to diagnose and assess need, and it greatly influenced the new profession. Mary Richmond's work codified the emphasis on casework in the tradition of focusing on the individual (Popple, 1995).

Porter R. Lee, the president of the National Conference of Social Work, outlined the struggle in a slightly different way. In his 1929 presidential address, Lee depicted the conflict between cause and function as inherent in professional social work. Lee felt that the social worker of his day was "meeting more exacting demands for performance, assuming a more specific type of responsibility, meeting with fair success more intricate and elusive problems" (Lee, 1929, p. 12). Because of these growing demands, the professional social worker needed to embrace a more functional role by focusing on organization, techniques, efficiency, standards, and accountability. The challenge as Lee saw it was to find a way to balance cause (the belief in ideology) and function (the administration of that belief). In the end, Lee thought, although those with a cause might sway the beliefs of people, it should be the professional social worker's role "to administer a routine functional responsibility in the spirit of the servant in a cause" (p. 20).

Bertha Capen Reynolds, who in recent years has been embraced as the inspiration for a progressive social work movement, embodies the personal cost of the struggle for social work's professional identity. Trained in the psychoanalytic tradition with emphasis on the individual, she questioned the effectiveness of that form of practice. As a result of her criticism of mainstream social work practice during the 1930s, she was removed from her professional position at Smith College School of Social Work in 1938 (Freedberg, 1986). Reynolds's beliefs demonstrated the "fundamental conflict in the definition of social work: the professional individualized approach to human beings in trouble comes up against the intractable fact of a social service that ultimately is dependent upon the resources of the larger community" (Freedberg, 1986, p. 105). Reynolds's push for social action kept her at odds with the then-mainstream professional shift toward individual casework.

In 1951 the National Council on Social Work Education launched a project to define what social work was. The task was difficult. "Any attempt to define the scope and functions of social work must grapple with many formidable obstacles, the most insurmountable of which is the absence of criteria that can be used to identify a professional social worker" (cited in Brieland, 1977, p. 342). The task force summarized the state of the profession as undefinable and not yet professional: "There is not yet enough of an analysis of social work practice to identify the major functions of positions that should be classified as professional" (cited in Brieland, 1977, p. 342).

The debate about purpose has continued to the present. In the 1980s Frumkin and O'Connor (1985), social work academics, viewed social work as "adrift" and "failing to maintain a core identity." They contended that the profession had abandoned working with both clients and the environment; and in place of that dual focus, social work leaders had "called for the establishment of a psychologically oriented view of social work practice stressing intrapsychic and interpersonal dynamics and intervention strategies aimed principally at influencing changes in individual behavior, family or group dynamics" (p. 14).

More recently, the social work educators Specht and Courtney (1994) argued that social work was not simply struggling to find its identity, but that the profession had also abandoned its mission. This was strong criticism. They maintained that the historical mission of social work—to deal with social problems—had been overtaken by a move to embrace psychotherapy and focus totally on individual change.

> The concern of psychotherapy is with helping people to deal with feelings, perceptions, and emotions that prevent them from performing their normal life tasks because of impairment or insufficient development of emotional and cognitive functions that are intimately related to the self. Social Workers help people make use of and develop community and social resources to build connections with others and reduce alienation and isolation; psychotherapists help people to alter, reconstruct, and improve the self. (p. 26)

Specht and Courtney held that "the popular psychotherapies have diverted social work from its original mission and vision of the perfectibility of society" (p. 27). They claimed that there is no place for psychotherapy in social work, that "it is not possible to integrate the practice of individual psychotherapy with the practice of communally based systems of social care" (p. 170). Their conclusion was that psychotherapy "is an unsuitable mode of intervention for social work" (p. 172).

The argument continues today. In a national study of career intentions of graduate social work students, it was found that a majority of the students planned to enter private practice but the educational programs do not teach skills needed for private practice careers (Green et al., 2007). The authors call for a remediation of the disconnect between graduate education's commitment to teach about agency-based practice with a broader social mission and students' desires to pursue individual work through private practice.

The historical struggle to identify the uniqueness and importance of the social work profession is not new. Ehrenreich (1985) argued that the historic tension between individual and societal change is based in values and assumptions.

> On the one hand, there are those theories that emphasize the problems of the individual and see casework as the solution. On the other hand, there are the theories that emphasize the problems of society and see social reform as the solution. These theories are more readily understood as the ideologies and battle cries of particular groups within and outside the profession, struggling for power in the profession, than as exclusively true, well-validated (or even capable of being validated) theories of human behavior. (p. 227)

The development of professional social work has been marked by debate about the purpose and values of the field. Ehrenreich's view is that human behavior is governed by both individual and social contributions, and he suggests that the profession should look at both. This combined emphasis on micro- and macrointer-ventions is the foundation of this book.

MAJOR SOCIAL WELFARE PROGRAMS

Not every social problem is addressed in the same way, and therefore resources are distributed in different forms. Most social welfare programs use one of three forms of packaging and delivering assistance or benefits to those who need them: cash assistance, in-kind benefits, and entitlements.

Cash assistance is the provision of resources through financial transfers. Al-though most of us associate the word *welfare* with a check given to a needy person by the government, *cash assistance* is the correct term for the transfer of money from the government to a person in need. Cash assistance is typically provided after the level of financial need has been determined. On the basis of the level of a person or family's need, the number of people in the family, and the provisions of the program, a set amount is determined, and a monthly check is provided. Although the intent of cash assistance is to supply basic needs, the recipient deter-mines exactly how to spend the money. Most cash assistance is provided through federal programs, although some states also have such programs.

In-kind benefits are aid in the form of tangible items. Unlike cash, which can be used at the discretion of the recipient, in-kind benefits can be used only for spec-ified services. For example, housing assistance can take the form of vouchers to be used in place of rent or of reductions in rent for specialized housing units. Medical assistance is usually delivered through special clinics or doctors billing the govern-ment directly for services provided. Food stamps are coupons or vouchers or credit that can be exchanged in grocery stores for food.

Entitlements can be delivered as cash assistance or as in-kind benefits. In the case of entitlements, people are guaranteed help if they meet certain criteria. Once a person is eligible to receive a benefit, there is no time limit to the receipt of that benefit. For example, the largest and best-known entitlement program is Social Security. People who pay into the system during their working years qualify for benefits when they retire, typically at age 65. They are then entitled to receive Social Security benefits for the rest of their lives. A person who begins receiving benefits at 65 and lives to 95 will receive Social Security for 30 years—possibly more than the number of years she or he paid in. A more detailed discussion of Social Security appears in Chapter 8.

Another way to distinguish social welfare programs is as public assistance pro-grams and social insurance programs. **Public assistance programs** are designed to alleviate poverty. They are means-tested programs, meaning that people must be poor to qualify for benefits. In general, these programs carry a great deal of stigma, in part because recipients have not worked for the benefits, and some people feel that recipients are getting something for nothing. Examples of public assistance programs include Temporary Assistance for Needy Families, Medicaid, the Food Stamp Program, and public housing.

Social insurance programs aim to prevent poverty rather than alleviate it. Workers and employers pay into these programs, and the benefits are available regardless of income level. Social Security, Medicare, unemployment insurance, and workers compensation are social insurance programs. These programs have less of a stigma attached to them than public assistance programs do, in large part because they are universal programs, available to all.

Private services are offered by nongovernmental groups. These agencies or organizations can be either nonprofit or for profit, and they can provide services directly or on behalf of the government. For example, a private health maintenance organization may provide health care services for individuals who elect to use its services and for people who are referred from government programs to use its services. Services provided from referral are often called contracted services; the federal or state government contracts with the HMO to provide direct health care services to people who are eligible according to the public policies that oversee health services. The government pays for those services directly to the HMO.

Table 2.2 describes and categorizes the major social welfare programs, and a brief description of each follows. Many of these programs are discussed in more detail later in the book, but this list will help you become familiar with the major social services available in the United States.

CASH ASSISTANCE PROGRAMS

Old Age Survivors Disability Insurance (OASDI) is the full name of the federal program we commonly refer to as Social Security. It was first developed as part of the Social Security Act of 1935. Today it is the nation's largest social insurance program. It pays benefits to the people who paid in while they were working and currently covers most employees. OASDI provides benefits when a covered worker

TABLE 2.2 | MAJOR SOCIAL WELFARE PROGRAMS

Social Insurance	
Cash Assistance Programs	**In-Kind Benefit Programs**
Old Age Survivors Disability Insurance	Medicare
Unemployment Insurance	Veterans Health Services
Workers Compensation	

Public Assistance	
Cash Assistance Programs	**In-Kind Benefit Programs**
Temporary Assistance for Needy Families	Medicaid
Supplemental Security Income (SSI)	Food Stamp
General Assistance	Public Housing
	Supplemental Food Program for Women, Infants, and Children (WIC)
	School Breakfast and Lunch

retires or becomes disabled, and it also covers the surviving spouse or children under 18 years of a covered worker. Each employee contributes a percentage of his or her wages (6.2 percent on wages up to $106,800 in 2009), and the employer matches that amount. The program determines benefits according to the duration of past employment and earnings.

Also part of the 1935 Social Security Act, the unemployment insurance program provides temporary assistance to people who have involuntarily lost their jobs. Although the federal government sets the general regulations, each state develops and administers this social insurance program. A tax on the employer finances unemployment insurance; paying the tax entitles the employer to receive tax credit. Coverage varies from state to state, but generally a person terminated from a job is eligible to receive a portion of former wages for a period of time while actively looking for new employment.

Should an employee be hurt on the job, she or he may qualify for workers compensation. This program provides supplemental wages while a person is unable to work. The Social Security Act initiated workers compensation, and taxes paid by employers and collected by state governments fund it. Although federal law mandates the program, state governments run it.

Temporary Assistance for Needy Families (TANF) was established in 1996 to replace the Aid to Families with Dependent Children program. This federal public assistance cash support program was designed to provide monthly cash benefits for poor families. In order to be eligible, a family must fall below an income level set by each state. Primarily designed for families with incapacity, death, or the continued absence of a parent, the program also covers some two-parent families. Although the federal government provides some funding and general administrative guidelines, states must also contribute and in turn are responsible for the development and administration of the TANF program. Eligible families can receive benefits up to two years at a time for a maximum of five years. Adults must be involved in efforts to achieve employment while receiving benefits.

Supplemental Security Income (SSI) is an income-tested federal program that provides cash assistance for an elderly person or for a person with a disability whose income is below the poverty line.

Some states offer cash assistance to single able-bodied men and women under 65 years of age who are poor. These state public assistance programs are typically referred to as general assistance or general relief.

IN-KIND BENEFIT PROGRAMS

In 1965, the Social Security Act was expanded to include federal medical insurance under the Medicare program. Medicare provides health coverage for individuals who are eligible to receive OASDI benefits. Basic coverage includes the costs of inpatient hospital services and related services after a patient leaves the hospital. Participants can choose to pay for supplementary coverage, which helps pay for physician services, diagnostic tests, and other specified medical care. As with OASDI, workers contribute a percentage of wages (1.45 percent on all wages in 2009), and the employer matches that amount.

Any person who completes military service is eligible to receive medical care through Department of Veterans Affairs health facilities. A veteran is eligible for veterans' health services throughout his or her lifetime.

As part of the 1965 expansion of the Social Security Act, federal medical assistance for people in poverty was created under the Medicaid program. The states receive federal matching funds to cover the cost of medical care for low-income individuals. Although Medicaid is a federal program, states have a significant role in developing and administering it. Medicaid is typically available to TANF and SSI recipients and covers physician, hospital, laboratory, home health, and skilled nursing care. Medicaid payments are made directly to the provider of services. Each state designs and administers its program in keeping with federal standards.

The federal Food Stamp Program helps low-income individuals and households purchase food. Although different forms of food aid have been provided by the government since the Great Depression, the current program was enacted in 1964. It provides coupons or credit through a card redeemable for groceries at retail stores. The use of coupons or cards allows recipients discretion in choosing what food items to buy, but they may not be used to purchase alcoholic beverages, tobacco, paper goods, toiletries, or ready-to-eat foods.

There are two major types of in-kind government support to help low-income people with housing: public housing and Section 8 housing. Public housing properties are residential units in federally built complexes administered by local authorities. Eligible poor families or elderly persons pay minimal rent for such apartments. Section 8 housing involves government vouchers given to low-income families to supplement their rent. Privately owned apartments are officially designated by local housing authorities as Section 8 residences and are available to voucher recipients. Although the mandate for housing aid comes from federal public policy, administration is often local. In recent years, some localities have contracted with private agencies to oversee the day-to-day operations of housing properties.

The Supplemental Food Program for Women, Infants, and Children (WIC) is a federal program that provides nutrition and health assistance to low-income pregnant and new mothers, infants, and children up to the age of five years. The program includes vouchers that can be redeemed for nutritious foods such as milk and eggs and for educational programs. Children from low-income families can receive breakfasts or lunches at participating schools through federal School Breakfast and Lunch Programs.

As you expand your social work experience, you will encounter numerous other programs. Among these federal, state, tribal, and local efforts are programs to help victims of violence, promote literacy, house people who are homeless, and subsidize the cost of medications.

VALUES AND SOCIAL WELFARE

As mentioned earlier, many values and beliefs helped shape organized responses to social need. Many of society's values conflict with professional social work values and beliefs, making the development of new policies, programs, and practice by social workers a complicated challenge.

SHOULD WE CHANGE THE PERSON OR THE SYSTEM?

The economic upheavals that have occurred throughout American history have fueled the debate about whether professional social service providers should focus efforts on changing people or changing their surroundings. Today the profession holds that both are necessary. However, doing both, particularly system change, can be overwhelming. For example, trying to bring more and better paying jobs to Jane's neighborhood (Jane was discussed in Chapter 1) is a major structural effort, whereas helping Jane finish her education may seem easier. Both approaches are important, and focusing on one effort without the other will leave the problem unsolved. Until social workers can effect change at both levels, Jane and others like her will continue to live with unmet needs.

ARE RECIPIENTS WORTHY OR UNWORTHY?

Deciding whether people are worthy or unworthy of assistance dates back to the Elizabethan Poor Laws. The Poor Laws outlined the specific groups worthy of support: widows, orphans, the elderly, and people with physical disabilities. The criterion that determined this designation was whether a needy person's circumstances were the result of controllable events or of circumstances beyond that person's control. Becoming a widow, an orphan, or an elderly person was not a consequence of a personal decision. People who were perceived to have made bad choices that resulted in their need for assistance were considered unworthy. Therefore, an able-bodied adult without a job was perceived to have done or not done something that resulted in lack of employment. For example, Jane's unemployment could be viewed as a consequence of her lack of preparation for the job market or her single parenthood, making her, according to this point of view, unworthy of assistance.

The debate is still raging today. The issue of providing public assistance to poor single mothers is a perennial topic. Determining an individual's worthiness ignores social conditions, such as lack of employment opportunities for young women or high divorce rates, which contribute to people's circumstances. This view also ignores the fact that, regardless of the reason for a young mother's poverty, her children are not responsible for their mother's decisions, but they are nonetheless growing up poor and disadvantaged. Many scholars have demonstrated that our narrow definition of what constitutes personal choice ignores many social and economic conditions that affect people's lives and penalize children (Abramovitz, 1996; Edin & Lein, 1997; Miller, 1992; Sidel, 1986).

RELIGIOUS VALUES OR SEPARATION OF CHURCH AND STATE

Social welfare and the social work profession itself are laced with values that stem from religious beliefs and organizations. Charity Organization Societies drew many of their early principles and workers from the organized Christian religions of the 1800s. Today, some programs, such as the Salvation Army's valuable work with people who are homeless, directly involve religious denominations in the services provided.

Shortly after he became president in 2001, George W. Bush called for the allocation of public money to fund faith-based organizations to deliver social services. Under law, these organizations were not eligible to receive public funds because their mission and purpose were entirely based in religion. Faith-based organizations differ from private organizations affiliated with religions that are nondenominational in service delivery, such as Catholic Charities.

Many people believe that funding religious organizations is a direct violation of the constitutional separation of religion and the state. Critics worry that an organization that takes a strong religious position will not be able to put that aside when helping people in need and that public funds should not be used to preach a religious position.

Some of the people who represent faith-based organizations are opposed to receiving government support. They argue that government funding would mean that the government could dictate rules and regulations attached to that funding. If religious organizations were controlled by governmental dictates, this would potentially violate the Constitution's protection of religion from government interference. Therefore, although religious organizations have historically played a role in the provision of social services, whether that role will expand in future years as part of the faith-based initiative remains to be seen.

Spirituality, the search for meaning beyond the individual self, is sometimes separate from organized religion. People who value spirituality consider responsibility for the well-being of others to be central to their beliefs. This perspective parallels social work's values of social justice and collective responsibility. Therefore, the values of the social work profession, although separate from organized religion, do have connections to the spiritual and religious belief systems of our society.

IMPARTIAL PROFESSIONAL OR ADVOCATE

One of the professional roles of social work is to advocate for clients. For example, a social worker might need to advocate for counseling services for a child in a school. However, social work practitioners are required to be impartial, not to impose their own values on clients. Instead, they should help clients (or in the child's case, the family) become empowered to advocate for themselves. Social workers must strike a balance between knowing when to speak up and advocate on behalf of clients and when it is best to let them step forward and find their own voices.

HELPING PEOPLE WE KNOW OR HELPING STRANGERS

Almost every day, television and newspaper stories report on people in need. Often, numerous strangers respond to such stories by donating time, money, and other resources. Yet getting support for social programs can be difficult.

| BOX 2.4 | ETHICAL PRACTICE ... ABORTION |

Consider your personal beliefs about abortion. Are your beliefs related to your religious beliefs? Have your experiences as part of an organized religion affected how you view the issue of abortion? Can you separate your personal values and religious beliefs from the public, secular laws that currently make abortion a legal right for women? How does a social worker reconcile her or his religious beliefs that may conflict with public laws?

BOX 2.5 | **WHAT DO YOU THINK?**

After the terrorist attacks on the World Trade Center in New York City and the Pentagon on September 11, 2001, there was an outpouring of donations from all over the United States. Why was the response so quick and so strong? Did you feel compelled to make a donation? Why? How did this response differ from the way people respond to a person who is homeless who is asking for help on a street corner?

Typically, people are more likely to help those they know rather than those they do not know. Social programs seem to be bureaucratic and impersonal, and the general public does not know who receives what from which service. But when they read about a family with a seriously ill child, for example, they feel as though they know the people involved. The familiarity and personal connection make them more inclined to help.

Like so many approaches to social welfare, this tendency dates back to the Elizabethan Poor Laws. Colonial settlers refused to help those who were not from their community, whom they saw as strangers not deserving of support. This deeply rooted value, coupled with the American focus on individual responsibility, makes promoting public social welfare programs difficult.

CRISIS OR ONGOING NEED

Americans have a strong history of responding to crisis, of taking a residual approach. U.S. social welfare policy is less likely to take on problems that require long-term solutions. As a result, advocates often try to define a cause as a crisis rather than as an ongoing problem.

For example, not until 1987 did the federal government take an organized approach to fighting AIDS, even though the disease had been identified years before. Only after AIDS reached a critical point and could be called the AIDS crisis was there a government response. Today, although AIDS continues to be a social problem, people do not view it as a crisis in need of immediate attention, and the social response has diminished.

The conflict between crisis and ongoing need deeply affects social welfare policies and services. Although the crisis response is vital, it is important to serve those who have long-term needs and try to solve social problems to which there are no easy, quick answers.

CONCLUSION

Conflicting values create tension for the professional social worker. However, each ideological approach has an appropriate place at one time or another. Any one approach is not necessarily better or more correct than another. What is important is to be aware that social work practice is deeply affected by the values and beliefs of members of society, of clients, of social workers, and of the profession as a whole. One overriding value is the commitment to social and economic justice. Your responsibility is to learn and understand the historical implications of these values and reflect on how you and your clients are affected by these values and your own beliefs as you maintain the commitment to social and economic justice.

Key Terms

cash assistance, (p. 54)

Civil Rights Act, (p. 48)

devolution, (p. 49)

Elizabethan Poor Laws, (p. 41)

entitlements, (p. 54)

in-kind benefits, (p. 54)

institutional, (p. 39)

public assistance programs, (p. 54)

residual, (p. 39)

social insurance programs, (p. 54)

Social Security Act of 1935, (p. 46)

social welfare system, (p. 38)

Voting Rights Act, (p. 48)

War on Poverty, (p. 48)

Questions for Discussion

1. Explain the institutional and residual approaches to social welfare. How are these approaches different? Which approach best provides for people's well-being? Do different problems lend themselves to different approaches?

2. Choose a period of history discussed in the chapter. What events were significant in shaping the social welfare policies and programs of that time? What values were reflected?

3. Do you think that the distinction between worthy and unworthy is still a part of our social welfare programs and policies? If so, in what ways?

4. Why was the Progressive Era important to the development of the social work profession?

5. What are the different forms of social welfare services? In what situations would you recommend one form or another, and why?

6. Identify a value of social welfare in this country, and explain how it relates to social work practice.

Change Agent Exercise

Take the problem you wrote about in Chapter 1 (or if you did not do the exercise in Chapter 1, choose a problem that you care about that negatively affects members of your community) and try to find some historic facts about efforts to solve the problem in your community or elsewhere. Have any laws been passed that address the problem? (For example, the Americans with Disabilities Act was passed to address the problem of discrimination against people with disabilities.) Have any groups been organized to address the problem? (For example, Mothers Against Drunk Driving was formed to address the problem of people driving under the influence of alcohol.) Are there any public or private social welfare programs that offer services, goods, or cash to people who are experiencing the problem? (For example, food banks provide emergency food to address the problem of hunger.)

Chapter Exercises

1. **Social History Interview**
   Interview someone over the age of 65. Provide a description of your interview and the answers to the following questions:
   Does he or she use social services today?

   Does he or she think social services have changed over the past 50 years?

   If so, in what ways?

2. **Compare**
   Compare the Settlement Movement and the Charity Organization Societies. What forms of intervention were used by social workers involved in each setting? How are those interventions used by social workers today?

3. **Social Work and Psychotherapy**
   What are some of the competing values and beliefs about the type of interventions and practices social workers should use? Consider the debate about whether social workers should perform psychotherapy. List three reasons why psychotherapy should be used by social workers and three reasons why it should not. Which set of reasons seems more convincing to you? Why?

   Get into groups with your classmates and share your reasons. Try to reach a consensus about whether social workers should use psychotherapy as a practice option.

4. **Social Work Values**
   In groups of four, choose a set of competing values presented in the chapter. Divide into pairs, and each pair choose one value within the set. Identify and list how beliefs associated with this value shape social work practice. Compare your lists, and try to reach a consensus on which value would best serve social work practice.

5. **Media and Popular Values**
   Choose a book or movie that you feel reflects mainstream American values. List the values that you notice in the book or movie. Discuss how the book or movie communicates those values. Are they consistent with social work values? Why? The book or movie is

   I chose it because:

   Values:

   Discussion:

References

Abramovitz, M. (1996). *Regulating the lives of women: Social welfare policy from colonial times to the present* (rev. ed.). Boston: South End Press.

Axinn, J., & Stern, M. (2004). *Social welfare: A history of the American response to need* (6th ed.). Boston: Allyn & Bacon.

Berkowitz, E., & McQuaid, K. (1988). *Creating the welfare state* (2d ed.). New York: Praeger.

Brieland, D. (1977). Historical overview. *Social Work, 22,* 341–346.

Brieland, D. (1995). Social work practice: History and evolution. *Encyclopedia of Social Work,* Vol. 3 (pp. 2247–2258). Silver Spring, MD: National Association of Social Workers.

Congressional Research Service. (2008). *The cost of Iraq, Afghanistan, and other global war on terror operations since 9/11.* Washington, DC: Author.

Edin, K., & Lein, L. (1997). *Making ends meet: How single mothers survive welfare and low-wage work.* New York: Russell Sage Foundation.

Ehrenreich, J. H. (1985). *The altruistic imagination: A history of social work and social policy in the United States.* Ithaca, NY: Cornell University Press.

Freedberg, S. (1986). Religion, profession, and politics: Bertha Capen Reynolds' challenge to social work. *Smith College Studies in Social Work, 56,* 95–110.

Frumkin, M., & O'Connor, G. (1985). Where has the profession gone? Social work's search for identity. *Urban and Social Change Review, 18,* 1, 13–18.

Green, R. G., Baskind, F. R., Mustian, B. E., Reed, L. N., & Taylor, H. R. (2007). Professional education and private practice: Is there a disconnect? *Social Work, 52,* 151–159.

Jansson, B. S. (2009). *The reluctant welfare state* (6th ed.). Belmont, CA: Brooks/Cole.

Lee, P. R. (1929). *Social work: Cause and function presidential address.* Washington, DC: National Conference on Social Welfare. Leiby, J. (1978). *A history of social welfare and social work in the United States.* New York: Columbia University Press.

Miller, D. C. (1992). *Women and social welfare: A feminist analysis.* New York: Praeger.

Nabokov, P. (ed.). (1991). *Native American testimony.* New York: Penguin.

Popple, P. R. (1995). Social work profession: History. *Encyclopedia of Social Work,* Vol. 3 (pp. 2282–2292). Silver Spring, MD: National Association of Social Workers.

Rothman, D. J. (1971). *The discovery of the asylum: Social order and disorder in the new republic.* Boston: Little, Brown.

Schlesinger, A. M., Jr. (1986). *The cycles of American history.* Boston: Houghton Mifflin.

Schwarz, J. A. (1993). *The New Dealers: Power politics in the age of Roosevelt.* New York: Random House.

Segal, E. A. (2007). *Social welfare policy and social programs: A values perspective.* Belmont, CA: Brooks/Cole.

Sidel, R. (1986). *Women and children last: The plight of poor women in affluent America.* New York: Penguin Books.

Specht, H., & Courtney, M. E. (1994). *Unfaithful angels: How social work has abandoned its mission.* New York: Free Press.

Trattner, W. I. (1999). *From poor law to welfare state: A history of social welfare in America* (6th ed.). New York: Free Press.

Wilensky, H. I., & Lebeaux, C. N. (1965). *Industrial society and social welfare.* New York: Free Press.

SOCIAL JUSTICE AND CIVIL RIGHTS

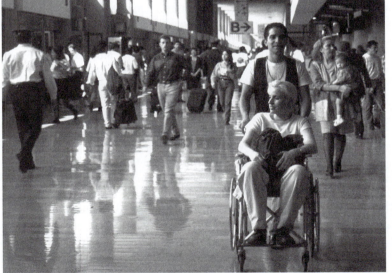

Heinle Division of Cengage Learning

On August 29, 2005, a category 5 hurricane named Katrina, made landfall on the Gulf Coast of the United States. In New Orleans, where much of the devastation occurred, images of people trapped on rooftops calling for help, wading through chest-deep water, or crammed into a sports stadium struggling to survive without adequate food and water, shared a common characteristic. Almost all of those in New Orleans hit hardest by Katrina were poor and African American. While natural disasters can happen anywhere and affect all types of people, the aftermath of Hurricane Katrina made many Americans question issues of social justice. Many questioned whether those in power would have reacted more quickly providing desperately needed assistance if those hardest hit were white or wealthier. People experiencing this tragedy, and those watching around the country and around the world, were reminded of the United States' struggle with injustice in the forms of racism and classism. Many called for measures to increase social justice.

On Februay 12, 2008, 15-year-old Lawrence King was shot in the head at school by a classmate because he was openly gay and sometimes dressed in girl's clothing. Ten years earlier, in 1998, Matthew Shepard, a 21-year-old gay man, was kidnapped, beaten, tied to a fence, and left to die. Afterward, the two assailants made antigay remarks to their girlfriends. That same year, three white men in Jasper, Texas, chained an African American man named James Byrd, Jr. to a truck and dragged him to his death. In July 1999, a 21-year-old member of a white supremecist group went on a three-day rampage shooting African Americans, Jewish Americans and a Korean student, leaving three dead and nine wounded. In October 1995 a white man attacked a Filipino man in San Francisco. The attacker yelled "Death to all minorities!" In Massachusetts in 1994, a serial batterer sexually assaulted four women. He called the women whores, bitches, and sluts. Following the terrorist attack in New York City in September 2001, a white man stormed out of a local bar in Mesa, Arizona, and shot and killed an East Indian gas station owner, claiming he thought the victim was Muslim and deserved to die.

These examples of criminal behavior all share a commonality: They are **hate crimes**. Hate crimes occur when people are victimized because of their race, ethnicity, religion, sexual orientation, ability, or gender. Hate crimes are not the only injustices that plague our society. In addition to the 7,722 hate crimes recorded in 2006 (Federal Bureau of Investigation, 2006), poverty, employment and housing discrimination, infant mortality, and racial inequality are sadly familiar features of American life. The wealth in the United States is clearly not shared. People living in the top 1 percent of households earn 40 percent of all income (Economic Policy Institute, 2005). Americans considered middle class saw their incomes remain almost stagnant over the past 30 years, while those in the top 1 percent of earners saw an increase of 450 percent (Eisenbrey, 2007). Almost 13 million children (more than 17 percent of children) live in poverty and 47 million people are uninsured (DeNavas-Walt, Proctor, & Smith, 2007). In addition, the African American infant mortality rate of 14 deaths per 1,000 live births is more than twice as high as that of whites (U.S. Bureau of the Census, 2007a).

Although some progress has been made after years of working for social change, people are still mistreated because of their membership in various groups. For simply being who they are, many people are refused jobs, housing, and access to public accommodations, and they experience fear and violence. There is a tremendous gap between the rich and the poor, and far too many children go to bed hungry. Whereas other chapters address many of these issues in more detail, we raise them in this chapter because they are all related to social justice.

WHAT IS SOCIAL JUSTICE?

Envision a society in which all members feel physically, emotionally, and psychologically safe; resources are distributed equitably, jobs are available for all who want them, all people have the same basic rights and opportunities, and all are able to develop to their fullest potential. This describes a society with true social justice.

Most of the issues social workers confront are directly or indirectly related to injustice. If we hope to solve the problems that affect the lives of so many in society, we need to understand not only the concept of social justice, but also the causes of injustice.

Justice means fairness, and **social justice** refers to the level of fairness that exists in human relationships. Injustice has been described as

> coercively established and maintained inequalities, discrimination, and dehumanizing, development-inhibiting conditions of living (e.g., slavery, serfdom, and exploitative wage labor; unemployment, poverty, starvation, and homelessness; inadequate health care and education), imposed by dominant social groups, classes, and peoples upon dominated and exploited groups, classes and people. (Gil, 1998, p. 10)

This definition states that inequalities and conditions that limit people's abilities to develop are established and maintained coercively. In other words, many limitations, such as poverty, unemployment, and inadequate education, are placed on people by conditions that exist outside of themselves. For example, although some people choose not to work, many others are forced into unemployment by a lack of jobs, inadequate transportation, and a lack of affordable child care.

According to Gil's definition, the conditions that limit people's chances are imposed by dominant social groups and classes. This suggests that certain groups in society have more power than other groups and that they can dictate the conditions under which the others must live. It also means that certain groups in society have less power and are dominated and exploited by those with more power. In American society people with money who are predominantly male, white, Protestant, heterosexual, able-bodied young to middle-aged adults tend to make up the dominant groups with power. We explore the privilege of these dominant groups in this chapter as we discuss social justice in American society.

Social justice and civil rights are important because many of the issues that confront the majority of social work clients, including poverty, unemployment, homelessness, hunger, inadequate health care, and unequal and inadequate education, exist due to injustices in the social, political, and economic systems. Because injustice is established coercively by others, we must look beyond the individual for causes and solutions.

SOCIAL WORK'S MANDATE FOR SOCIAL JUSTICE

To effectively address problems of the magnitude described above, it is essential for social workers to be involved in fighting for social justice. The Preamble to the *National Association of Social Workers Code of Ethics* (2008), which was introduced in Chapter 1, requires social workers to address issues of social justice.

> Social workers promote social justice and social change with and on behalf of clients. "Clients" is used inclusively to refer to individuals, families, groups, organizations, and communities. Social workers are sensitive to cultural and ethnic diversity and strive to end discrimination, oppression, poverty, and other forms of social injustice. (p. 1)

Social justice is one of the six core values listed in the Preamble, with the attached ethical principle that "social workers challenge social injustice." The passage continues:

> Social workers pursue social change, particularly with and on behalf of vulnerable and oppressed individuals and groups of people. Social workers' social change efforts are focused primarily on issues of poverty, unemployment, discrimination, and other forms of social injustice. These activities seek to promote sensitivity to and knowledge about oppression and cultural and ethnic diversity. Social workers strive to ensure access to needed information, services, and resources; equality of opportunity; and meaningful participation in decision making for all people. (p. 3)

The Council on Social Work Education's *Educational Policy and Accreditation Standards* (2008) shape and monitor the curriculum of social work programs. The standards outline the importance of social justice to social workers:

> The purpose of the social work profession is to promote human well-being by strengthening opportunities, resources, and capacities of people and to create policies and provide services to prevent and address conditions that limit human rights and the quality of life. Acknowledging a global perspective, the social work profession strives to eliminate poverty, discrimination, and oppression. Guided by the person and environment construct, respect for human diversity, and knowledge based on scientific inquiry, the profession aims to promote social and economic justice. (p. 1)

It is not enough for social workers to work with individuals to help them live with and adapt to injustice or to lessen the effects of injustice on individuals. Social workers must also work to change the unjust and oppressive conditions in society that limit people's ability to live self-determined, satisfying lives.

BARRIERS TO SOCIAL JUSTICE

To achieve a more just and equal society, it is necessary to first understand the barriers that stand in the way of social justice. Many barriers are related to the way people treat each other and the way societal institutions treat groups of people. These barriers include prejudice, discrimination, and oppression.

Prejudice is an attitude. It involves judging or disliking groups and individuals based on myths and misconceptions. People can be prejudiced without acting on their feelings. For example, a prejudiced person might be afraid of members of a certain group and not want them to move in next door. But he or she would not do anything to prevent members of this group from buying the house.

Discrimination is an action. Discriminating against people involves treating them differently, usually by denying them something, based on their membership in a group. Examples of discrimination abound. A landlord may refuse to rent to an Indigenous Person. A qualified woman may be turned down for a job because she is over fifty years old. In some stores, all African American customers may be followed by a security guard whereas white clients are not routinely watched.

Oppression is systematic and pervasive mistreatment of people based on their membership in a certain group. Oppression can include differential treatment that is built into institutions and systems as well as instances of violence. It restricts people's opportunities, life chances, beliefs in what they can be, and self-determination (Bell, 1997). The situation of a poor, young African American boy is an example of oppression. He lives in a neighborhood characterized by violence and decay. He goes to a school that has inadequate funding, where he receives a poor education and thus has less chance than a wealthier white child to go to college and get a job that pays well. He is often harassed by police solely on the basis of the color of his skin. This young man's mistreatment is systematic and pervasive. He is experiencing oppression.

A single individual can be prejudiced or discriminate against others, but for oppression to occur the mistreatment must be institutionalized, or built into the social system in some way. Oppression does not require overt discrimination. Instead, a lack of attention to creating societal structures that meet the needs of diverse populations can result in oppressive situations. For example, when a woman who uses a wheelchair wants to apply for a job, she discovers a steep stairway at the entrance to the business. She finally finds a freight elevator at the back of the building, but the buttons are too high for her to reach. Even after someone else pushes the button, she can't make her way into the office because the doorway is too narrow to accommodate her wheelchair. Exhausted, demoralized, and not feeling welcome, she leaves without applying for the job. (See "More About … Oppression and Violence").

The example above demonstrates **institutional discrimination,** which occurs when discrimination is built into the norms and institutions in society and is enforced by those in power. Institutional discrimination exists in the educational, health, political, social, legal, and economic systems. In fact, few areas of Americans' economic and social lives are free of institutional discrimination. It so thoroughly permeates societal institutions that people often do not recognize that it is there. Instead, Americans frequently accept the many forms of institutional discrimination as just the way things are.

For example, it is well known that public schools serving predominantly low-income children and children of color have far fewer resources than schools serving wealthier and white children and thus provide a lower standard of education. Many people do not see that institutional discrimination built into the system of public school funding limits many children's chances to succeed. They fail to recognize the inequity involved in funding schools from property tax receipts, which provide more money in rich neighborhoods than in poor neighborhoods. People also do not see individual teachers and administrators acting in a discriminatory way. Thus, they blame the problem of undereducated children on the children and their families, rather than on the unjust system of funding public schools. "What Do You Think?" (below) lists additional examples of the pervasiveness of institutional discrimination in American society.

BOX 3.1 | MORE ABOUT ... OPPRESSION AND VIOLENCE

There is a strong relationship between oppression and violence. Dominant groups often use violence or the threat of violence to retain their supremacy. For example, they can call out the police and military when members of oppressed groups threaten them. They can also use violence directly to keep nondominant groups "in their place." Lynching, gay bashing, vandalizing synagogues, burning black churches, and rape have all been used to remind members of oppressed groups of their status.

Members of oppressed groups sometimes respond to unjust treatment with violence. For example, an uprising took place in Los Angeles in 1993 among members of the African American community following the acquittal of white police officers for beating an African American motorist, and gay men and lesbians rioted in 1969 after a police raid on a gay bar in New York City. When people can no longer tolerate injustice, they strike out at the world around them. Often their actions do more harm to themselves than to the oppressor, such as when rioters burn their own neighborhoods. It is important to remember that reactions to injustice and oppression are often more emotional than rational. People who have reached the breaking point are "inflamed and enraged," and "mad, angry,

and bitter" (Bies & Tripp, 1996, p. 254). The intensity of the emotion pushes them to act, sometimes without thinking about the consequences.

When most people think of violence, individual violence against people or property—such as murder, rape, and gang violence—comes to mind. This is only a small part of the violence that takes place in society (Van Soest & Bryant, 1993). Violence that is not as easy to see or identify includes institutional violence, which takes place, for example, when a large number of low-wage workers are fired while top management and stockholders are reaping the benefits of record profits. It also includes cultural violence, such as the many ways that dominant groups deny and destroy the cultures of oppressed groups. Poverty, hunger, homelessness, racism, sexism, heterosexism, classism, ableism, ageism, and anti-Semitism are all forms of violence.

Many people believe that members of oppressed groups start the cycle of violence. However, members of oppressed groups are responding to cultural and institutional violence with individual violence. Although violence may not be the best response to violence, it is an understandable response. To stop the violence in society, institutional and cultural violence, as well as individual violence, must be addressed.

Oppression has been based on differences in race, sex, sexual orientation, economic status, physical or mental ability, age, and religion. Individuals may experience multiple forms of oppression. For example, an Asian American woman may be excluded or harmed on the basis of both her race and her sex. This makes oppression a multifaceted and complex social condition.

Racism is the systematic mistreatment of people based on race. Racism is institutionalized, and it is perpetrated by members of groups who have power or control over society and its institutions. Groups experiencing racism in the United States include African Americans, Indigenous Peoples, Latinos, and Asian Americans. There is a long history of racism in the United States. Some examples are the genocide and forced relocation of Indigenous Peoples; the enslavement of Africans; the practice of importing workers from other countries for difficult, dangerous, and low-paying jobs, including Africans in the 1700s, Chinese in the 1850s, and Mexican

BOX 3.2	WHAT DO YOU THINK?

Do you think that the following are examples of institutional discrimination? Why?

- Children from affluent families attend schools with better facilities, equipment, and books and better-paid, better-trained teachers than do children from poorer families.
- White people, heterosexuals, and the able bodied see themselves portrayed frequently and in a positive light on television, in magazines, and in the movies.
- Schoolchildren learn more about the achievements of white male historic figures than about the contributions of people of color and women.
- Lesbians and gay men are forced out of the military and are denied insurance benefits for their partners by most employers.
- In many cities African Americans are randomly pulled over by police and questioned and searched without cause. This practice is known as racial profiling.
- Banks employ redlining, which is the refusal to make loans to people in areas with high concentrations of certain racial groups.
- Healthy people are forced to retire at age 65.
- A qualified woman is not hired to do a demanding job because the employer thinks she might want to have children, which is perceived to limit her ability to give her full attention to her work.
- Latinos are rounded up by local police who are looking for illegal immigrants.
- Insurance companies refuse to sell health insurance to anyone living in a certain zip code because many gay men live in the area and the risk of HIV infection is perceived to be high.

Can you think of other examples of institutional discrimination?

farm workers today; the expulsion of Mexican American citizens during the Great Depression; the internment of Japanese Americans during World War II; and the unequal treatment of African Americans that was legal until the mid-1960s.

As a result of pervasive racism, many people of color experience extreme poverty, infant mortality, unemployment, and violence, and their level of educational attainment is lower than that of members of the dominant population. Racism is frequently based on a belief in the inherent superiority of one race over another. This belief in superiority is so ingrained in society that racism is perpetuated by a generally accepted, unconscious attitude that presumes a white cultural norm.

Sexism is oppression that grows out of the belief that men are superior to women. Inequality has long been supported by belief in "natural" and inherent differences between the sexes. Women, considered the weaker sex, have been seen as unable to fulfill certain roles and have been expected to serve as the primary caregivers for children and other family members.

Two social conditions—the gender gap and the feminization of poverty—have resulted from sexism. The gender gap is the difference between men's earnings and women's earnings. In 2005, for example, among year-round full-time workers, a woman earned 77 cents for every dollar earned by a man (DeNavas-Walt, Proctor, & Smith, 2007). The term *feminization of poverty* refers to the fact that many more women than men live in poverty. Women are also more likely to be the targets of other forms of injustice, including domestic violence, rape, and sexual harassment.

Homophobia is a fear of homosexuality or a fear of lesbians and gay men. **Heterosexism** is the institutionalized bias directed at gay men, lesbians, bisexuals, and people

BOX 3.3	**BECOMING A CHANGE AGENT**

In September 2006, several African American students at Jena High School in the small town of Jena, Louisiana, asked the principal for permission to sit under a tree where only white students gathered. The next day three nooses were found hanging from the tree. Three white students were suspended for hanging the nooses in the tree. Racial tensions continued to build at the school, and in December 2006, a 22-year-old white man attacked a 17-year-old African American Jena High student with a bottle at a private party. The white attacker was charged with simple battery and sentenced to probation. Around the same time, a white high school student pulled a gun on a group of African American students in a parking lot and had the gun wrested away from him. After these incidents, six African American students beat up a white student, stating that they attacked him after he used racial slurs. The white student claimed he did nothing to provoke the attack. The white student was treated at the hospital and went home the same day. The six African American students, who later came to be known as the Jena Six, were arrested and charged as adults with attempted murder and conspiracy to commit murder. They faced sentences of up to 22 years in prison.

Many African Americans in Jena felt that the African American students received much harsher punishment than the white people involved in the case. People outside of the area began to find out about the case via the Internet, after which it was picked up by the national media. In September 2007, outrage at what was seen as unjust treatment and racism, encouraged up to 20,000 protestors from around the country to descend on Jena, Louisiana. The case encouraged the continuation of a national dialogue and action by many individuals, begun after Hurricane Katrina, to address issues of racism.

Analyzing the Situation

- Try to learn more information about the Jena Six case by conducting an Internet search. How do people on different sides of the case explain what happened?
- What is wrong with hanging nooses from a tree? Why was the fact that it was nooses so inflammatory? Was it a prank, a hate crime, or something else? What do you think should have happened to the students who hung the nooses?
- Does the treatment that the various people involved in the case seem equal or fair to you? If not, can you think of explanations other than racism that might explain the different treatment that the whites and African Americans involved in this case received?
- Looking at the Explanations of Social Injustice in this chapter, which do you think might best explain what happened in Jena?

What Can Social Workers Do?

Given your analysis, what might social workers do to address the causes of this situation and prevent it from happening again in the future? What interventions could you suggest at the individual level? The community level? The institutional level, such as the schools or courts? The policy level, for example changes in local, state, or federal legislation?

What Can You Do?

What one step might you take now, alone or working with others, to reduce racism or another type of oppression? What are the barriers that might keep you from taking this step? What could you do to reduce those barriers?

who are transgendered. As with other types of oppression, heterosexism is seen in such acts as discrimination in housing and employment, which means that gay people are denied access solely on the basis of their sexual orientation. Homophobia is also seen in acts of violence in the form of gay bashing. Examples of institutionalized antigay bias include the exclusion of lesbians and gay men from the military and the refusal of most states to let lesbians and gay men marry and openly adopt children. As a result of homophobia, heterosexuals frequently view all aspects of gay peoples' lives in relation to their sexuality. Today lesbians and gay men make up one of the few oppressed groups that still lack federal civil rights protection against discrimination.

Classism describes the institutional and cultural attitudes and behaviors that stigmatize the poor and place a higher value on wealthier people. The economic system creates and supports excessive inequality and does not meet basic human needs of poorer people. Classist attitudes hold that the poor are less capable and less industrious than those who have more resources and that they are responsible for their own poverty. Americans rarely discuss class, and the term is often misunderstood. *Class* refers to more than just income; it also includes social status and power. People are perceived to be lower class and are treated differently, not only because of how much money they have but also because of how they talk, what they wear, where they live, and the type and extent of education they have attained.

Ableism is the oppression of people with disabilities. Like other oppression, it is systematic, pervasive, and institutionalized. Ableism is based on the presumption that perfect physical and mental health is the normal state. However, few people are in perfect physical condition their entire lives, so nearly everyone is a person with a disability at some time in her or his life. About 51.2 million Americans are estimated to have some type of disability (U.S. Bureau of the Census, 2007b). This number is expected to increase as the percentage of the population that is elderly continues to increase. Some disabilities are visible, probably the most obvious being the need to use a wheelchair, but most are invisible. A person with an invisible disability may encounter other people's impatience when he or she does not behave in the expected way.

Ageism is the belief in the superiority of youth over age and the systematic oppression of people because they are older. Discrimination based on age can happen to people of different ages in different situations. Ageism can cause extreme economic hardship. Older people are often driven out of jobs by forced retirement or find it hard to get jobs because employers do not want to hire them. Older people are also often denied choices about how to live their lives as a result of the assumption that to be old is to be frail and incapable of making decisions. Americans' quest for youth takes its toll on the elderly, and jokes, greeting cards, and the mass media constantly remind them that there's nothing worse than getting old.

Anti-Semitism, or the systematic discrimination against or oppression of Jews, is the most frequently addressed oppression based on religious belief. In many Christian countries, Jewish people have often been seen as "the other." They have been excluded from many areas of life and frequently have been targets of hate and violence. The Holocaust, the planned annihilation of Jewish people by Adolf Hitler and his Nazi movement in Germany during the 1930s and 1940s, demonstrated the horror of systematic oppression based on religion. Under the official policies of Nazi Germany, 6 million Jews were killed.

Anti-Semitism is not the only type of bias based on religion that occurs in the United States. Other religious groups, including Muslims and Hindus, have also experienced discrimination and oppression based on their religion and culture. Members of these and other religious groups are often assumed to be Christian and are expected to celebrate Christian holidays. They must take days off from work or school in order to celebrate their own holidays. Some face harassment if they dress, celebrate, and worship in ways that are foreign to members of the mainstream population. Acts of terrorism carried out by Muslim fringe groups have spurred anti-Islamic sentiments and actions in recent years, increasing the incidence and impact of hate crimes.

Privilege is another important concept to understand when thinking about oppression. People who are members of mainstream or dominant groups have certain privileges built into their lives (Adams, Bell, & Griffin, 1997). Whether they consciously take advantage of the privileges or not, they still benefit from them. For example, men have the privilege of being able to walk alone at night without fear of sexual assault. White people have the privilege of seeing themselves reflected positively in the media on an ongoing basis. Heterosexuals have the privilege of being able to marry. Having privilege means that, in general, members of dominant groups have an easier time economically and socially in American society (see "From the Field…Doing My Civic Duty").

Another way to look at privilege is that it helps maintain oppression. People who are members of dominant groups gain from the existence of oppression. Dominant group members benefit from having advantages over other groups; thus, they have less of an incentive to dismantle oppressive systems. Because members of the dominant society have been the ones in power, their views, beliefs, and concerns have shaped the development of the institutions that exist in American society. They developed the health care, mental health, and education systems with the needs of their dominant society as the driving force. For example, treatments offered in the mainstream U.S. health care system have generally been ones that are preferred by people of European descent. People from other cultures find it hard to access treatments they would prefer in mainstream health centers. Modes of healing that are not sanctioned by the mainstream are also rarely covered by insurance. If we don't honestly discuss and address privilege, it will be difficult to dismantle oppression.

BOX 3.4　**FROM THE FIELD … DOING MY CIVIC DUTY**
by Keith M. Kilty, Ph.D.

In September 2001 I was summoned to serve on a jury and was picked as a prospective juror for the trial of a young black man facing two charges, one of which was sexual battery. I am still stunned by what happened in that courtroom.

Before the bailiff led the panel of prospective jurors into the room, she organized us into three lines. The first group of twelve people sat in the jury box. A second group was seated in the first row of the audience part of the courtroom, and I was in the third group, which sat behind them. There were twenty-five or twenty-six of us altogether.

After we were all seated, I looked around the room and noticed that, with the exception of the defendant, everyone was white. That included all of us on the jury panel, the judge, the prosecution team, the defense attorney, the bailiff, and the court reporter. A few other people were in the room from time to time, and they, too, were white.

After the judge asked the twelve people in the jury box to tell a little about themselves, she turned the process over to the prosecution and then to the defense. Not once did the prosecution raise any concerns about the fact that the defendant was a

| BOX 3.4 | FROM THE FIELD … DOING MY CIVIC DUTY *continued* |

black man who would be facing an all-white jury. The defense attorney did raise race as an issue with some members of the jury pool, asking them about their ability to make a fair and impartial decision based on the merits of the case. Both prosecution and defense, without going into much detail, made it clear that the case would likely hinge on the testimony of a single accuser, a white woman.

As the afternoon wore on, some members of the jury pool were excused by peremptory challenges. Eventually, twelve white jurors were seated. Two alternates would be chosen as well. Since I was next in line, I was told to sit in one of the two remaining chairs in the jury box, and the judge asked me the same questions she had asked the others and told me to say a little about myself. I did so, and then I told the judge that I could not in good conscience sit on an all-white jury trying a black man accused of the sexual assault of a white woman.

As a professor of social work who teaches courses on minority issues, I am familiar with racial matters in the United States. I understand the significance of race as a social force, what racism is, how it is manifested as an institutional force, and how it differs from prejudice. In response to questions from the prosecutor and especially from the defense attorney, I tried to explain what these issues and concepts mean and how they could factor into the jury's decision.

The judge didn't seem to be paying much attention to my answers. Even though I insisted that I could be fair and impartial in making a decision based on the facts that would be presented, the prosecution clearly did not want me on the jury and issued a peremptory challenge. The judge excused me.

I walked out of that courtroom in a state of shock and disbelief and anger. How was it possible on September 6, 2001, in a courtroom in the United States, that a black man charged with sexual assault on a white woman would have to face a jury of twelve white people? For decades, allegations of rape of white women were used to justify lynching black men throughout this country, including here in the North.

It was a clear instance of institutional racism. I'm sure that most of the people in that courtroom believe that they are not prejudiced, but institutional racism and discrimination can occur without people being prejudiced. They can occur without people intending for them to occur or even being conscious that they are occurring. When racist consequences are part of institutional laws, customs, or practices, the institution is racist. It does not matter whether the individuals who carry out those practices have racist intentions.

How could the judge allow this to happen in her courtroom? She did not say a single word that showed concern about whether the defendant could receive a fair and impartial hearing. How could the prosecution not raise a concern? Don't they care whether justice was served? Why didn't others speak up, including some of the other members of the jury panel?

The defendant might have been guilty. I don't know, and I'll never know. But he could not receive a fair and impartial hearing in that courtroom. Even if he were acquitted, there would always be a cloud over the verdict. If he were convicted, many people would believe that the jury was influenced by racial beliefs about black men and sex. The defendant would not be tried by a jury of his peers—a jury that would reflect this community.

What worries me most is whether this kind of thing occurs often. Hardly anyone in the courtroom seemed to care, which suggests that the situation is not unusual. I would like to think that American society has changed. But I see no difference between what happened in that courtroom in September and the Jim Crow segregation I saw as a child in the 1950s and 1960s. I grew up in the North, where racism was perhaps more subtle than in the South, but I grew up in a racist society. What I saw in that courtroom tells me that not much has changed.

EXPLANATIONS OF SOCIAL INJUSTICE

The mere fact that we are a diverse society does not explain the existence of prejudice, discrimination, oppression, and other types of social injustice. There are a number of theories that strive to explain why these conditions exist.

BIOLOGICAL DETERMINISM

Since the settlement of North America by Europeans, innate biological characteristics have been used to explain and justify the mistreatment of various groups of people. The argument was made that slavery was acceptable because Africans were inherently less capable, less intelligent, and less human than white people. Indigenous Peoples were seen as savages who deserved to be forced off their land, robbed of their culture, and killed. Women have been kept out of jobs and paid less money on the basis of the belief that they are biologically inferior to men. Supporters of the belief that social and economic status is biologically determined stress that individuals and groups do well economically and socially because of innate biological characteristics.

Although the belief in biological determinism is no longer widespread, it has not completely disappeared. In 1994 a best seller entitled *The Bell Curve: Intelligence and Class Structure in American Life* (Hernstein & Murray) rekindled the debate about the biological inferiority of certain groups. The authors asserted that economic inequality is due to the genetic inferiority of some groups, which dooms them to failure. Blaming all inequality on genetics, the book dismissed generations of social and environmental inequalities between groups, such as inadequate nutrition, prenatal care, health care, and access to education.

The research on which they based *The Bell Curve* has been widely criticized. A number of authors identified the flaws in the research and demonstrated that economic and social success depend more on social circumstances than on innate intelligence (Fischer et al., 1996; Gould, 1994; Knapp et al., 1996). The belief that success is predetermined by innate intelligence is incompatible with the social work values that people are shaped by their environment and are capable of change.

THE SOCIALIZATION PROCESS

A common explanation for prejudice and discrimination is that people learn through observation. When children see their parents, teachers, friends, and the media treat people differently, they begin to see biased attitudes and behaviors as normal. For example, when a child's parents socialize only with other members of their own racial group, a child accepts this as the norm. Similarly, when children see stereotypical representations of members of various groups on television and in the movies, they begin to accept these stereotypes as reality.

PSYCHOLOGICAL PERSPECTIVES

Several psychological reasons are cited as bases for social injustice. Prejudice and discrimination are often explained by fear of difference. People are afraid of what they do not know and do not understand. Thus, people who lack contact with others who are different from them will be afraid of the others, and that will translate into differential treatment.

Scapegoating provides another explanation for prejudice and discrimination. When some people experience problems and become frustrated and angry, they look for someone else to blame. Members of oppressed populations are often easy to scapegoat because they lack the power to effectively defend themselves.

Another psychological explanation of prejudice and discrimination is projection. A person may have traits that she or he does not like or cannot accept. By projecting these unwanted traits onto other people and blaming them for having the characteristics, some individuals feel that they can distance themselves from the traits. An example is people who are fanatically antihomosexual out of a fear of homosexual feelings in themselves.

SOCIOLOGICAL PERSPECTIVES

Scarce resources and self-interest can also help explain discrimination and oppression. Conflict theorists state that because there are limited resources, there will be inter-group competition for these resources. This competition can create hostility (Levine & Campbell, 1972). When there is not enough of a resource to go around and people feel that their security is threatened, they often look for someone to blame. People begin to believe that the only way they can get ahead is at someone else's expense.

Often, economic insecurity fuels bias against oppressed groups. In a tight job market, people who are unemployed or underemployed may blame members of other groups for taking their jobs. For example, native-born Americans have often feared that immigrants were taking away "American" jobs. Fear, anxiety, and fighting can erupt between groups in such cases. As groups fight with one another, they are not looking for the real causes of economic problems.

A functionalist perspective suggests that discrimination and oppression serve a variety of purposes in society. Even though they have a negative effect on oppressed people, prejudice and discrimination can build cohesiveness and solidarity among groups. Politically, the people in power can benefit from oppression because they can blame problems on various oppressed groups. This is a form of systematic or institutionalized scapegoating, and it keeps the focus of people's anger off of those in power. Similarly, when oppressed groups are fighting each other, people are less likely to join together to fight those in power.

Oppression and discrimination can also aid the economy in general and employers more specifically. Oppressed people are often an inexpensive source of labor. For example, women traditionally make less money than men, and employers can hire them for lower wages, thus keeping costs down. This means that it is in employers' best interest to have a divided society containing a number of oppressed groups. However, even if oppression benefits some in society, it is also extremely problematic in that oppressive conditions deny millions of people the opportunity to be full participants in society.

MODELS OF INTERGROUP RELATIONS

Because American society is so diverse, Americans need to find ways to structure society to address the differences so that people can live together better. A number of theories suggest ways that different groups within society should relate to each other.

For many years, the prevailing attitude was that the various groups in society should be blended together in a melting pot. The idea was that with exposure to the mass media and a common educational system, newcomers to the United States would eventually lose their cultural uniqueness and become "Americans." All Americans would share beliefs, customs, values, and a language. But in spite of close contact between groups and a common public educational experience, the expected melting of cultures has not occurred.

The melting pot ideal rests on the belief in a unique American culture distinct from other cultures. In reality, all groups were supposed to aspire to an Anglo-European culture. In other words, the historically dominant white, Anglo-Saxon Protestants would be able to retain their culture, but all other groups were to give up theirs and adopt the dominant culture.

The melting pot ideal was based on an inaccurate belief that the white, Anglo-Saxon Protestant culture, values, and norms were the best ones for all people. It underestimated the importance of culture as a source of strength and community for many people. Members of other groups were often unwilling to abandon their cultures. Additionally, many of those who were part of the white, Anglo-Saxon Protestant mainstream were unwilling to accept other groups, no matter how hard they tried to assimilate.

An alternative to the melting pot is **cultural pluralism**. If the melting pot model creates a stew in which all ingredients blend into a single taste, cultural pluralism creates a salad in which each item remains distinct, yet complements the whole. According to the cultural pluralism model, people retain their unique cultural characteristics while they mix socially and economically with other groups. People can live and work together, yet each group is valued for its unique contribution to society. In this model people can be proud of their cultural heritage, retain their own language, and continue to observe their traditions. They draw on their cultural heritage to create strong communities and increase self-awareness and self-respect.

A third model for intergroup relations is **separatism**. This means that groups live in the same country, but do things as separately as possible. To the degree possible, each group develops its own social and economic institutions. At various times in this country's history, white Americans have called for segregating African Americans and other people of color rather than allowing them access to white neighborhoods and other institutions. Such a separatist society means further excluding members of oppressed groups from mainstream systems and institutions. Separatism by dominant groups is often fueled by prejudice and discrimination. On the other hand, members of nondominant groups have at times made decisions to live as separately as possible from dominant culture. Their desire to separate is usually a response to being left out of mainstream society, of not feeling safe, and of seeing little chance of social and economic success if they remain within the dominant culture.

Although separatism can offer members of oppressed groups relief from fear of rejection, violence, and being outsiders, it can also cause problems. A person can belong to more than one oppressed group, and such a person would have to choose one group over the others. For example, a lesbian of color who might choose to live in a women-only community would lose connection with her community of color. Separatism also makes it hard for different oppressed groups to find common ground on areas of mutual concern. This makes creating coalitions for change very difficult.

OVERCOMING SOCIAL INJUSTICE

Social workers and others have long recognized and acknowledged the inequity and injustice that exist in American society and have worked to create a more socially just society. Many approaches have been tried. Although change can be slow and the United States has a long way to go to a truly just society, it has made tremendous progress in many areas. The following section examines the remedies and interventions that have been and are being tried to address many of the wrongs that continue to plague society. Chapter 66 explores social work direct practice in relation to diversity.

CIVIL RIGHTS

Civil rights are the rights to which people are entitled because they are members of society. They afford people legal protection from discrimination and oppression. Throughout American history, oppressed groups have been denied equal access to political, social, and economic institutions. For example, for many years, only white men could vote. Employers could legally refuse to hire a person because he or she had a disability, was Latino, or was Jewish, among other reasons. African Americans were forced to sit in the back of buses, attend separate schools, and use "colored only" drinking fountains.

The list of discriminatory practices is long, and members of all of the oppressed groups discussed in this chapter have been denied some rights. Members of oppressed groups have spent years organizing and fighting to gain civil rights protections, and the battle is still being waged. When people's civil rights are protected, society becomes more socially just.

PROTECTION FROM DISCRIMINATION

Over the years there have been a number of significant efforts to legislate protection from discrimination in the United States. Most of these efforts have come after significant pressure was brought to bear on legislators by members of oppressed groups and their supporters.

The **Fourteenth Amendment** to the Constitution, which became law after the Civil War in 1868, offered early civil rights protection to U.S. citizens. According to this amendment, no state may "deny to any person within its jurisdiction the equal protection of the law." Even after slavery was outlawed and the South defeated in the Civil War, it was clear that African Americans, particularly those in the southern states, would not be afforded civil rights and protection from discrimination without intervention by the federal government. At first the effects of the Fourteenth Amendment were limited because the federal government was unwilling to take on the long and difficult task of forcing change in southern society (Segal & Brzuzy, 1998).

The **Fifteenth Amendment**, enacted into law in 1870, gave all men, regardless of race or color, the right to vote. For almost a hundred years after its passage, most African American men were kept from voting by discriminatory practices such as poll taxes and literacy tests. Voting by women was deliberately excluded from the Fifteenth Amendment. The **Nineteenth Amendment**, which guarantees women the vote, was first introduced in 1878 and, after years of organizing and advocacy work, became law in 1920.

One of the most important steps taken toward achievement of civil rights in the United States was passage of the **Civil Rights Act of 1964**. The act was in large part a result of work by Dr. Martin Luther King Jr. and other activists in the civil rights movement of the 1950s and 1960s. It outlawed discrimination or segregation in public accommodations and employment on the basis of race, color, sex, religion, or national origin as well as unfair or differential treatment of people of color in voter registration (Dye, 1992). Additionally, the Civil Rights Act gave the federal government the right to enforce antidiscrimination laws and punish people who broke them, and it gave individuals the right to sue those who discriminated. The **Civil Rights Act of 1968** added protection against discrimination in housing.

In 1967 Congress passed the **Age Discrimination in Employment Act (ADEA)**. This act protects employees who are 40 years old or over from being treated differently at work on the basis of their age. The law, which applies to companies with 15 or more employees, is designed to eliminate the practice of terminating older employees based on stereotypes that older people are slower, harder to train, more out of touch with technology, and less adaptable to change than their younger counterparts. Since 1967 laws have been passed that give older people protection in other areas, including education (Age Discrimination Act of 1975) and benefits (Older Workers Benefit Protection Act of 1990).

Several oppressed groups were not protected against discrimination in the civil rights legislation passed in the 1960s. These groups continued to advocate for equal legal protection. The **Americans with Disabilities Act** of 1990 (ADA), the result of many years of organizing and lobbying by disability activists, provides comprehensive civil rights protections for people with disabilities. It outlaws discrimination against people with disabilities in public accommodations, employment, transportation, and public services. The ADA requires "reasonable accommodation" for people with disabilities in workplaces and public facilities (Perritt, 1990).

Lesbians, gay men, bisexuals, and transgender individuals (LGBT) still have no federal protection from discrimination, although some states and municipalities have enacted antidiscrimination legislation on their behalf. As of early 2008, 13 states prohibit discrimination on the basis of both sexual orientation and gender identity, and another 7 states prohibit discrimination on the basis of sexual orientation alone. In most jurisdictions, however, LGBT individuals can be fired from jobs, evicted from housing, and refused services in public accommodations on the basis of their sexual orientation. Activists around the country have fought and continue to organize and advocate for civil rights protection for the LGBT community. Some of the most heated battles are over the right to serve openly in the military, the right to equal access to health and other partner benefits, and the right to marry. LGBT activists have been fighting for passage of the federal **Employment Non-Discrimination Act (ENDA)**, which would prohibit employers from using sexual orientation as the basis for employment decisions such as hiring, firing, promotion, and compensation. The first bill voted on by Congress that would offer protections from discrimination based on sexual orientation, ENDA was defeated in the Senate by one vote in 1996. Advocates continue to introduce ENDA in Congress in the hope that it will someday be passed and thereby ensure that civil rights are not denied on the basis of sexual orientation and gender identity.

AFFIRMATIVE ACTION

Despite antidiscrimination legislation, discrimination still occurs in the United States, and there are wide economic and social gaps between groups. **Affirmative action** programs are an additional strategy to help address past inequities in employment and education based on race and sex. In the late 1960s both the federal government and the courts required some employers and educational institutions to address discrimination in employment and education by taking affirmative action. This meant that the organizations were to come up with plans to diversify their workforces and student bodies and to establish timetables for the achievement of the plans.

Affirmative action programs aim to increase the number of women and people of color in jobs and schools. The idea is that groups that have more resources should provide something to groups that have fewer resources. Many people think that affirmative action means preferential treatment and quotas. The original purpose of affirmative action programs was not, however, to set quotas. Instead, the policies were designed to require institutions

> to develop plans enabling them to go beyond business as usual and search for qualified people in places where they did not ordinarily conduct their searches or their business.... The idea of affirmative action is not to force people into positions for which they are unqualified but to encourage institutions to develop realistic criteria for the enterprise at hand and then to find a reasonable diverse mix of people qualified to be engaged in it. (Wilkins, 1995, p. 3)

In spite of many years of antidiscrimination legislation and prior to the institution of affirmative action programs, women and people of color were almost completely shut out of many fields in many parts of the country. The implementation of affirmative action programs helped correct years of exclusion. For example, in 1979 women made up 4 percent of entry-level officers in the San Francisco Police Department; after the institution of an affirmative action plan, women made up 14.5 percent of the entry-level class in 1985. Affirmative action programs in the San Francisco Fire Department increased the number of African Americans in officer positions from 7 to 31, Latino officers from 12 to 55, and Asian American officers from 0 to 10. In a Louisiana aluminum plant, only people with prior craft experience were hired before 1974. African Americans had long been excluded from craft unions, which explained why only 5 of 273 skilled craft workers at the plant were African American. An affirmative action agreement instituted by the plant and the union established new training programs and required 50 percent of all new trainees to be African American (White House, 1998). There are many other success stories.

Affirmative action has been increasingly challenged in recent years. Critics argue that past discrimination is not reason enough to give preferential treatment today. They label affirmative action as reverse discrimination against dominant groups, and they argue that any type of discrimination is wrong. In their view, affirmative action means hiring unqualified people and lowering standards in schools and on the job; they say that it results in members of target groups believing that they cannot succeed on their own merits. However, the goal of affirmative action is to broaden the scope of training and access; this actually increases the pool of available skilled workers.

Voters in California, Michigan, and Washington approved laws to ban the use of affirmative action by government entities, and similar measures have been proposed in other states. The Board of Regents of the University of California system voted to end the use of affirmative action in admissions to all of its campuses in keeping with California law. Results were seen almost immediately. In the year following enactment, there was a 57 percent decrease in the number of nondominant students admitted to University of California at Berkeley and a 36 percent drop at University of California at Los Angeles (Matosantos & Chiu, 1998). At the University of California Law School, there was virtually no difference in the average grades or LSAT scores between students who were admitted in 1996 and those admitted in 1997 (the former went from 3.72 to 3.74, and the latter rose one point). However, there was a 76 percent drop in admissions of African American students and a 46 percent drop in admissions of Latino students in just that one year (American Civil Liberties Union, 1998).

In June of 2003, the U.S. Supreme Court handed down two rulings on affirmative action, one striking down an affirmative action admissions policy and the other allowing the use of affirmative action to increase campus diversity. The Court ruled that universities that use a point system for admissions cannot award points to an applicant simply for being a member of an underrepresented group, as was the policy for undergraduate admissions at the University of Michigan. In another case involving admissions at the University of Michigan Law School, the Court ruled that race could be an admission criterion if used in a broader, more flexible way with the aim of promoting campus diversity (Cohen, 2003). The latter decision opened the door for universities to continue to employ affirmative action policies if done correctly.

SOCIAL WORK ROLES IN FIGHTING SOCIAL INJUSTICE

Social workers can be involved in fighting social injustice in many ways (see "More About ... Social Work's Commitment to Social Justice"). These include involvement in organizing members of oppressed communities to help change the balance of power between oppressed and oppressor groups and legislative advocacy to develop and encourage the passage and implementation of legislation that protects the rights of all people and lessens the social and economic gaps between dominant and nondominant groups. Professional social workers can work to empower clients to take more control over their lives. This can involve

- Helping clients find and meet with others in similar circumstances so that they can work together to solve problems
- Ensuring that clients know agency policies, including grievance policies, so that they can advocate for their rights
- Teaching clients when threats or disruptions might be effective in getting their needs met
- Supporting clients decisions about what is right for their lives

| BOX 3.5 | MORE ABOUT ... SOCIAL WORK'S COMMITMENT TO SOCIAL JUSTICE |

The mandate for professional social workers to promote social justice and fight discrimination is clear. The National Association of Social Workers' Code of Ethics states:

> The social worker should act to prevent and eliminate discrimination against any person or group on the basis of race, color, sex, sexual orientation, age, religion, national origin, marital status, political belief, mental or physical handicap, or any other preference or personal characteristic, condition, or status. (Section 6.04(d))
> The social worker should advocate changes in policy and legislation to improve social conditions and to promote social justice. (Section 6.04(a).)

Social workers must also try to find ways to bridge gaps between oppressed groups that have common concerns and that could benefit by overcoming barriers and working together. This can be done by mediating community conflicts that keep members of communities from working with each other and by starting programs to bring together groups to explore differences and commonalties and learn to work together.

Social workers need to be involved in addressing all forms of oppression. Allowing one type of oppression to continue justifies all types of oppression.

> The tendency for inequalities to intensify in societies, once they are initiated on a small scale, has important implications for social workers and others who advocate reductions rather than elimination of inequalities: as long as inequalities, at any level, are considered legitimate and are being enforced by governments, competitive interactions focused on restructuring inequalities tend to continue among individuals, social groups, and classes, and a genuine sense of community and solidarity is unlikely to evolve. (Gil, 1998, p. 26)

| BOX 3.6 | ETHICAL PRACTICE ... SOCIAL JUSTICE |

Part of the NASW Code of Ethics calls for social justice. Define social justice in your own words. What does social justice mean to you? Is it something you feel strongly about? Why do you think it is a critical part of the social work profession? Should it be? Why?

SOCIAL JUSTICE AND CIVIL RIGHTS IN THE TWENTY-FIRST CENTURY

At the time of this writing, history is being made during the presidential elections. For the first time in U.S. history, the two remaining candidates in the Democratic primaries were from underrepresented groups, one being a woman, the other an African American. The very fact that both were taken seriously as presidential candidates speaks to how far we have come as a nation in terms of racism and sexism. Furthermore, the Republican party embraced a woman vice presidential candidate for the first time in its history. In the end, the first African-American was elected as President of the United States, a remarkable accomplishment and further step toward social justice.

However, the fact that both gender and race were constantly being discussed in the race and that polls showed that a sizable minority of potential voters would not vote for one or the other due to race or gender, speaks to how much further we have to go.

Fear of terrorism in the post-9/11 era has contributed a number of challenges to improving social justice and civil rights both in the United States and abroad. When people are afraid, they tend to want to curb rights and freedoms, rather than expand them. The USA Patriot Act, which was passed in 2001, has been criticized by many for infringing on civil liberties. Critics argue that it allows the government to spy on citizens without the oversight that had previously been required. Critics also complain that the act and recent federal government actions abuse the rights of noncitizens, including allowing long detentions of immigrants and new deportation guidelines. Looking internationally, human rights advocates suggest that Bush administration policy developed in 2002–2003, supported harsh interrogation techniques and resulted in torture at prisons in Iraq, at the U.S. military base in Guantanamo Bay, Cuba, and elsewhere. Polls suggest that many Americans are concerned about dangers that Muslims might pose and believe that there should be greater scrutiny of them as a group. In a 2007 Newsweek poll, 52 percent of respondents supported wiretapping mosques (Newsweek, 2007). All of these fear-motivated actions and beliefs potentially have an eroding effect on human and civil rights.

CONCLUSION

The future holds many challenges and many opportunities. The conditions in New Orleans and the slow government response and the Jena Six situation (discussed in Box 3.3 Becoming a Change Agent) left many concerned about the still pervasive racism in the United States. Affirmative action and human rights internationally and in the United States are under attack. Government offices responsible for investigating and prosecuting cases of discrimination are underfunded. If the current trends of cutting back on programs that promote equality continue, much ground will be lost, and American society will be less just.

As members of a profession that is committed to social justice, social workers must become involved in efforts to preserve and expand equality for members of all oppressed groups. Instead of accepting society as it is, social workers need a vision of what society should be. Fighting oppression and injustice is central to the social work role.

Key Terms

ableism, (p. 73)

affirmative action, (p. 81)

Age Discrimination in Employment Act
(ADEA), (p. 80)

ageism, (p. 73)

Americans with Disabilities Act,
   (p. 80)

anti-Semitism, (p. 73)

civil rights, (p. 79)

Civil Rights Act of 1964, (p. 80)

Civil Rights Act of 1968, (p. 80)

classism, (p. 73)

cultural pluralism, (p. 78)

discrimination, (p. 69)

Employment Non-Discrimination
  Act (ENDA), (p. 80)
Fifteenth Amendment, (p. 79)
Fourteenth Amendment, (p. 79)
hate crimes, (p. 66)
heterosexism, (p. 71)
homophobia, (p. 71)
institutional discrimination, (p. 69)
Nineteenth Amendment, (p. 80)

oppression, (p. 69)
prejudice, (p. 68)
privilege, (p. 74)
racism, (p. 70)
separatism, (p. 78)
sexism, (p. 71)
social justice, (p. 67)

Questions for Discussion

1. Discuss ways that you have privilege and ways that you lack privilege on the basis of your race, ethnicity, gender, sexual orientation, age, physical or mental ability, or class. How has your experience with privilege affected your life?
2. Which of the theories explaining prejudice, discrimination, and oppression makes the most sense to you? Describe the theory in your own words, and explain why you believe it is correct. Discuss whether and how the theory is compatible with social work values.
3. Briefly describe the three models of intergroup relations. List pros and cons of each model for reducing intergroup tensions in the United States.
4. Why might members of nondominant groups prefer to live as separately as possible from mainstream society? Should social workers support this goal? Why or why not?
5. How should social workers respond to institutional and cultural violence (described in the box More About ... Oppression and Violence) in society?

Change Agent Exercise

Conduct research using the telephone book, Internet, and library to find out what groups or organizations in your community are working to improve civil rights for one or more populations. For example, is there a local human rights commission? Is there a group working for the rights of the Latino community, for the rights of women, for the rights of seniors, or for the rights of the LGBT community? Is there an organization whose aim is to fight racism? If people have a discrimination complaint, where would they take it? Make a list of all the groups and organizations you find. Choose one of the organizations and try to find out more about them by looking at their website if they have one or by calling them to ask a few questions. What is the group trying to accomplish? How does it go about improving civil rights? Ask yourself whether this is work you might be interested in doing in the future.

Chapter Exercises

1. **Discrimination and Oppression in the Media**
   Find an article in a newspaper or newsmagazine that provides an example of discrimination and another article that provides an example of oppression.

Write a paragraph describing why you believe the articles represent cases of discrimination and oppression.

2. **The Debate over Affirmative Action**

   Should affirmative action be part of the college admissions processes? Develop your own answer to this question.

   - Research arguments on both sides of the issue.
   - Discuss why this is a controversial issue by focusing on the following questions:

     Is there adequate evidence to resolve the issue?
     Is the evidence contradictory?
     Are there definitions that are in dispute?
     What are the underlying values on both sides of the argument?

   - What is your personal interest in this issue? How does it affect your life?
   - Brainstorm a list of arguments that support one side. List and explain the strongest arguments.
   - Brainstorm a list of arguments that support the other side. List and explain the strongest arguments.
   - After reviewing the arguments on both sides, what gaps in evidence can you identify? What do you still need to know in order to choose one side or the other? Where might you find that information?
   - After considering everything, which side of the argument do you most identify with? What specifically convinces you that this is the right side?

3. **Explaining Justice**

   Describe what social, economic, and cultural justice mean to you. Describe what a socially, economically, and culturally just society would look like. How would such a society differ from U.S. society? Meet with others in your class to compare your answers. Is there general agreement about what justice is and how a just society would look?

4. **Social Justice Visit**

   Visit an organization that is working to increase social or economic justice. Describe what the organization does, and explain how its work contributes to the struggle for justice. How is the organization funded? Is it difficult for the organization to get funding for this type of work? Does funding limit the type of work that the organization can do? If so, how?

Making Society More Just

List and describe at least five concrete ways that social conditions could change to make the United States a more just society.

How can social workers become involved to encourage these changes?

References

Adams, M., Bell, L. A., & Griffin, P. (eds.). (1997). *Teaching for diversity and social justice.* New York: Routledge.

American Civil Liberties Union. (1998). *What would our nation's schools be like without affirmative action?* http://www.aclu.org/congress/affexedu.html.

Baker, G. (1998). Further rise in household income. *Financial Times*, *9*, 23, 3.

Bell, L. A. (1997). Theoretical foundations for social justice education. In M. Adams, L. A. Bell, & P. Griffin (eds.), *Teaching for diversity and social justice* (pp. 1–29). New York: Routledge.

Bies, R. J., & Tripp, T. M. (1996). Beyond mistrust: Getting even and the need for revenge. In R. Kramer & T. R. Tyler (eds.), *Trust in organizations*. Thousand Oaks, CA: Sage Publications.

Cohen, J. S. (2003). Diversity wins in U-M court rulings. *Detroit News*, June 24, p. 1a.

Council on Social Work Education. (2008). *Educational policy and accreditation standards.* Alexandria, VA: Author.

DeNavas-Walt, C., Proctor, B. D., & Smith, J. (2007). *Income, poverty, and health insurance coverage in the United States: 2006.* Current Population Reports, P60-233. Washington, DC: U.S. Census Bureau.

Dye, T. R. (1992). *Understanding public policy* (7th ed.). Englewood Cliffs, NJ: Prentice Hall.

Economic Policy Institute. (2005). *The state of working America 2004/2005.* Washington, DC: Author.

Eisenbrey, R. (2007) Labor day marks bad news for laborers. *Salt Lake Tribune*, September 1, Opinion page.

Federal Bureau of Investigation. (2006). *The uniform crime report.* Washington, DC: Author.

Fischer, C. S., Hout, M., Jankowski, M. S., Lucas, S. R., Swidler, A., & Voss, K. (1996). *Inequality by design: Cracking the bell curve myth.* Princeton, NJ: Princeton University Press.

Gil, D. C. (1998). *Confronting injustice and oppression: Concepts and strategies for social workers.* New York: Columbia University Press.

Gould, S. J. (1994). Curveball. *New Yorker, 28*, 139–149.

Hernstein, R. J., & Murray, C. (1994). *The bell curve.* New York: Free Press.

Knapp, P., Kronick, J. C., Marks, R. W., & Vosburgh, M. G. (1996). *The assault on equality.* Westport, CT: Praeger.

Levine, R. A., & Campbell, D. T. (1972) *Ethnocentrism: Theories of conflict, ethnic attitudes, and group behavior.* New York: Wiley.

Matosantos, A. J., & Chiu, M. C. (1998). *Opportunities lost: The state of public sector affirmative action in the post Proposition 209 California.* San Francisco, CA: Chinese for Affirmative Action & Equal Rights Advocates.

National Association of Social Workers. (2008). *National Association of Social Workers code of ethics.* Washington, DC: Author.

Newsweek. (2007). Polling.com website. http://www.pollingreport.com/terror.htm.

Perritt, H. H. (1990). *Americans with Disabilities Act handbook.* New York: Wiley.

Segal, E. A. (2007). *Social welfare policy and programs: A values perspective.* Belmont, CA: Brooks/Cole.

Segal, E. A, & Brzuzy, S. (1998). *Social welfare policy, programs, and practice.* Itasca, IL: F.E. Peacock Publishers.

U.S. Bureau of the Census. (2007a). *Statistical abstract of the United States: 2008* (127th ed.). Washington, DC: U.S. Department of Commerce.

U.S. Bureau of the Census. (2007b). *Facts for Features Americans with Disabilities Act: July 26, 2007.* Washington, DC: U.S. Department of Commerce.

U.S. Government. (1990). Americans with Disabilities Act of 1990. P.L. 101-336. Washington, DC: U.S. Government Printing Office.

Van Soest, D., & Bryant, S. (1993). Reconceptualizing violence for social work: The urban dilemma. Paper presented at NASW Annual Conference, November.

White House. (1998). *Affirmative action: History and rationale.* www.whitehouse.gov.

Wilkins, R. (1995). Racism has its privileges. *Poverty and Race, 4*, 3, 3–5.

POVERTY AND ECONOMIC DISPARITY

CHAPTER **4**

E. A. Segal

The United States is the most technologically and economically advanced nation in the world. Almost every home has indoor plumbing and at least one television, and most have telephones. If you are a typical American, you sleep in a warm bed under a secure roof and awaken to an ample breakfast. You have a job or are going to school, and you travel there on well-constructed roads or public transportation. A nearby airport has regularly scheduled service to hundreds of cities, and interstate highways link all parts of the nation. If you run short of cash, automatic bank machines are everywhere. So are modern grocery stores that stock an enormous variety of foods. You have the skills to use these conveniences because you had access to a free education in a public school.

Economic resources make these conveniences accessible. In this country you are surrounded by many technological advances, but you must have enough money to take advantage of them. If you do not, automatic banking is meaningless, indoor plumbing may not work properly, there is no telephone, you cannot get to the grocery store because you cannot afford a car, and air travel is far too expensive.

This chapter covers the extent and effect of poverty in the United States as well as the social welfare programs designed to respond to economic deprivation. It presents the roles of social workers in serving people who are poor and the ways social workers can advocate for improved economic conditions and supports.

DEFINING POVERTY

Who is poor in the United States? If you are a student struggling to get by while attending college on student loans and part-time employment, are you poor? If you have a 40-hour-a-week job that pays minimum wage, are you poor? If you live in the least expensive house in an expensive neighborhood, are you poorer than your neighbors? If you visit a shelter for people who are homeless, are you rich in comparison to the people there?

Defining poverty is complicated. Personal and social values play a major part in deciding who is poor. What may feel like impoverishment to one person may be adequate for someone else. Setting a definite dollar amount for poverty may seem logical and straightforward, but it too involves values and opinions that vary among people. Generally, there are two ways to view poverty: an absolute approach, and a relative approach.

Absolute poverty uses a dollar value that is firmly set; anyone who earns less than that amount is officially categorized as poor. For example, suppose that the poverty line is set at the absolute level of $35,000. Walter and his wife Barbara together earn $35,450. Kathy and her husband Gregoire earn $34,600. By the absolute poverty standard, Walter and Barbara are not in poverty, and Kathy and Gregoire are in poverty. Does the additional $850 make Walter and Barbara significantly better off than Kathy and Gregoire? With a definite cutoff, there is a clear definition of who is and who is not poor, regardless of their needs or personal circumstances.

Relative poverty uses comparisons to determine who is poor and who is not. For example, the median price for a home in 2006 was $222,000 (U.S. Bureau of the Census, 2007). Using a relative standard, any family that owns a house worth

BOX 4.1 | **WHAT DO YOU THINK?**

Are there possessions that you consider necessities but that other people may view as nonessential? Why might they think that? What would you say to help them understand how important these items are to you?

---

less than $222,000 is below the midpoint and therefore could be considered relatively poor. A relative scale begins with agreement about the level of economic resources the average person should have and then uses that standard to determine who has enough and who does not.

An absolute line, once it is set, is easier to use than a changeable relative comparison. It is difficult to get people to agree about what things are necessities and what things are extras. A person who has little income while he or she is attending college may be poor temporarily, but education and the attainment of a college degree may provide a wealth of future opportunities. A television may seem like a luxury, but for a poor elderly person who has no family or transportation, the entertainment and information on television can be essential to well-being.

THE OFFICIAL DEFINITION OF POVERTY

The definition of poverty used by federal and state governments is an absolute measure. It is important because it is often used to determine eligibility for social service programs. The measure is referred to as the **poverty threshold** or the poverty line.

Many assumptions went into developing the poverty threshold. The Social Security Administration (SSA), which at the time was responsible for overseeing social service programs designed to address the problem of poverty, set the line in 1963. The SSA tried to determine the minimum amount of income a family would need in order to maintain itself. Although there was an attempt to be objective and scientific, the SSA director responsible for the definition stated that "the standard itself is admittedly arbitrary, but not unreasonable. It is based essentially on the amount of income remaining after allowance for an adequate diet at minimum cost" (Orshansky, 1965, p. 4).

Today, the poverty threshold is set by the Census Bureau and is used for statistical purposes. For administrative purposes, particularly to determine eligibility for income support programs, the Department of Health and Human Services sets **poverty guidelines** based on the Census Bureau thresholds (U.S. Department of Health and Human Services, 2008). The guidelines do not reflect differences in the cost of living from state to state in the contiguous United States.

In 1963 the threshold for a family of four was set at $3,100. It has been adjusted for inflation over the years. In 2008 the poverty guideline was $21,200 for a family of four (see Table 13.1). Because it is adjusted for inflation, this amount has the same purchasing power as $3,100 did in 1963 (Institute for Research on Poverty, 1998).

TABLE 4.1 | THE 2008 POVERTY GUIDELINES

Size of Family	48 Contiguous States & D.C.	Alaska	Hawaii
1	$10,400	$13,000	$11,960
2	$14,000	$17,500	$16,100
3	$17,600	$22,000	$20,240
4	$21,200	$26,500	$24,380
For each additional person add	$3,600	$4,500	$4,140

Source: U.S. Department of Health and Human Services, 2008.

The poverty threshold is controversial. Some people argue that the threshold takes only income into account and does not include benefits such as medical care or food vouchers; by leaving out these benefits, those living in poverty may be over-estimated. Others argue that the threshold is too low because it is based on a minimum amount needed for survival, not a balanced way of life. For example, the threshold reflects the cost of feeding people a minimal emergency diet over a short period of time, not a diet for growth and development over prolonged periods. It does not take the cost of feeding growing children into account. It assumes that ingredients are purchased in bulk quantities, that people know how to use basic supplies to cook balanced meals, and that adults have time to do all the food preparation from scratch. Regardless of these differences of opinion, the absolute standard is the only official measure of poverty that has been consistently used to determine the extent of poverty and to establish guidelines for program eligibility.

WHO IS POOR IN AMERICA?

According to the Bureau of the Census, using the poverty threshold, 37.3 million people, or 12.5 percent of the population, were in poverty in 2007 (DeNavas-Walt, Proctor, & Smith, 2008). Table 4.2 shows some key statistics about the people officially counted as poor in this country. According to the data, one out of every eight people is officially counted as living in poverty. People living in poverty are more likely to be children and to reside in families with only one adult, who is a woman.

TABLE 4.2 | 2007 POVERTY STATISTICS

	Number	Percent
Persons below poverty threshold	37.3 million	12.5%
Children under 18 below poverty threshold	13.3 million	18.0%
Married-couple families below poverty threshold	2.8 million	4.9%
Single female-headed households below poverty threshold	4.1 million	28.3%
Single male-headed households below poverty threshold	0.7 million	13.6%

Source: DeNavas-Walt, Proctor, & Smith, 2008.

TABLE 4.3	AVERAGE PERCENTAGES OF PERSONS IN POVERTY	
Date	Children	All Persons
1960s	20.84%	17.47%
1970s	15.69%	11.81%
1980s	20.46%	13.84%
1990s	20.62%	13.75%
2000–2006	17.1%	12.2%

Source: Based on data from Dalaker & Naifeh, 1998; Rawlings, 2000; Dalaker, 2001; and DeNavas-Walt, Proctor, & Smith, 2007.

These demographics are cited as evidence for two social trends, the juvenilization of poverty and the feminization of poverty.

The term **juvenilization of poverty** describes the tendency for children to be disproportionately represented in the ranks of those who are poor (Segal, 1991; Wilson, 1985). Even when poverty rates have been high, the poverty rates for children have been higher. Table 4.3 compares the average percentage of children under 18 in poverty with the average percentage of all people. A smaller percentage of people were in poverty during the 1970s, and the proportion increased during the 1980s and 1990s. Over these four decades, the rate of poverty for children has consistently been higher than the rate of poverty for the overall population. One major social concern is that almost one child in six spends time living in poverty. As explored in this chapter, poverty is related to numerous social conditions that are detrimental to people's health and development. This is particularly true for the children who are disproportionately represented among those who are poor.

The **feminization of poverty** refers to the fact that poverty is more likely to happen to women than to men (Pearce, 1978). On average, women earn less than men; in 2007 the median income of women who worked full-time throughout the year was 78 percent of the income of men (DeNavas-Walt, Proctor, & Smith, 2008). Therefore, there is a greater likelihood that women who are raising children alone will be poor. Because raising children requires additional resources, a household with children is likely to be poorer than a household without any children. Because young children typically have young parents whose incomes are lower than those of people whose careers are established, young families are also at greater risk of living in poverty.

THE CAUSES OF POVERTY

Addressing the problem of poverty would be easier if there were consensus about the causes of poverty. There appears to be no single cause but, rather, numerous perspectives. Some theories focus on the individual, and others look at structural reasons for poverty. Many of the theories are controversial and contradictory.

For example, one long-standing belief called the **culture of poverty** contends that people learn to be poor from growing up in impoverished areas. Although the environment is certainly powerful, this theory does not explain how some people who grow up poor become economically self-sufficient. Another theory cites the functionality of poverty, indicating that poverty plays an important role in the economic structure and that there is little incentive to rid the nation of it. According to this theory, maintaining a pool of people who are poor means that workers are always available for less-desirable and lower-paying but necessary jobs. This theory maintains that poverty keeps wages from increasing too much too fast. Most views are also laden with values about worthiness and deservedness.

VALUES AND BLAMING THE VICTIM

Discussions of poverty in the United States have focused on the individual who is poor and on social values (see Chapter 2). People who are poor are viewed as being responsible for their poverty. For example, since colonial times the determination of whether a woman who is poor is deserving of help has depended on whether she has embraced the family ethic by marrying and how willing she is to work if able (Abramovitz, 1996). Poverty, particularly for unmarried women with children, carries a major social stigma: The poor person is not participating in society in the right way. The responsibility for poverty is placed on the individual, and society does not have to change economic conditions.

In 1971 William Ryan first used the term *blaming the victim* to describe the assignment of responsibility to the person who is poor.

> The generic process of Blaming the Victim is applied to almost every American problem. The miserable health care of the poor is explained away on the grounds that the victim has poor motivation and lacks health information. The problems of slum housing are traced to the characteristics of tenants who are labeled as "Southern rural immigrants" not yet "acculturated" to life in the big city. The "multiproblem" poor, it is claimed, suffer the psychological effects of impoverishment, the "culture of poverty," and the deviant value system of the lower classes; consequently, though unwittingly, they cause their own troubles. From such a viewpoint, the obvious fact that poverty is primarily an absence of money is easily overlooked or set aside. (Ryan, 1976, pp. 5–6)

Ryan argues that this is how Americans accept a society that rewards some people with good jobs, safe homes, and two-parent families while others do not receive benefits. If poverty is the fault of each poor person, then others do not need to examine the way income is earned or consider whether all people have the opportunity to acquire wealth. All efforts at fighting poverty are aimed at the individual rather than at changing the economic structure. The system's role never gets addressed, and systemic inequality continues generation after generation.

In addition, social stigma and blame enter deeply into the personal being of people who are poor. Poor people internalize this blame from a very young age, and this factor can be a challenge for social workers who try to help people move out of poverty (see Box 4.2, "From the Field … The Faces of Poverty"). The challenge is how to address internalized blame (see Box 4.3, "What Do You Think?").

A woman whose husband left her with two children to raise points out the fallacy of blaming the victim.

> I would like to be able to go to school to earn enough to provide for myself and my children. Things have just been crazy. I don't sit around eating bon-bons, but I don't

BOX 4.2   # FROM THE FIELD ... THE FACES OF POVERTY
Georgia Ackerman, MSW

Navigating a social service delivery system can be disheartening for any individual or family in need of outside assistance. For families living in poverty, it can sometimes be nearly impossible. I initially learned this in a social work class, but I experienced it firsthand as a social work case manager at an elementary school.

The school is located in an extremely impoverished community that has little hope of economic revitalization. There are no industries or big employers in the area, and jobs are few. Most residents commute to jobs in the service industry, such as cleaning or landscaping. The community is on "the wrong side of the tracks," and outsiders see high crime rates and gang activity. Yet, the kindergartners through fifth graders come to school, eat breakfast, play on the playground, and spend the day learning until the last bell rings and they return home.

My responsibilities include keeping the clothing bank stocked with donated school uniforms, coats, undergarments, and even baby clothes for younger siblings. I help the school nurse follow up with home visits to students when there is an extended illness. Many of the families have no phone; we cannot call. Children lack adequate dental care, so I solicit dentists for help. There are no backpacks for students to carry papers and notebooks home; I work with a department store manager to apply for programs that donate these. I intervene when children are sent to the principal's office for misbehaving. I spend time with the parents. I do a little of everything and never have a boring day.

Parents are frequently overwhelmed and afraid to apply for any type of assistance—food stamps, financial assistance, housing, and so on. The forms are cumbersome and confusing. The assistance offices are frequently stigmatizing. Many of the parents work; they are too proud to "take welfare." They do their best to make ends meet.

Many parents have come to the United States illegally, seeking work. They fear deportation. The children rarely speak of this unless I have passed rigorous tests of trust. Usually, I find out after spending time in their homes. These families do not meet eligibility requirements for many of the state's social service programs, and few apply when eligible. I spend time reassuring families about accepting help and "jumping through the hoops."

At Thanksgiving canned food and turkeys are collected to be distributed throughout the neighborhood. I take giant boxes of food to homes that have no running water, refrigerators, freezers, or even can openers. Children talk to me through locked doors and tell me that their parents are at work and that I can't come in. I leave notes. I return at a better time. I listen to stories when the moms, dads, grandmas, or aunties have time and energy to visit with me. Usually we find a neighbor who will store the ridiculously big turkeys. We laugh about this. Most of the parents know that I am no miracle worker and have no magic wand. Yet most seem to get the message that I care. We discuss how to improve social services and get rid of the "red tape." We talk about what their children will be when they grow up.

Each time I am amazed at their tenacity, kindhearted humor, wisdom, and strength. I receive a monthly paycheck, but I am also paid in crooked milk mustache smiles of children, crayon portraits, awkward hugs from exhausted teachers, and kind notes from parents who know I did my best because I care about their children.

BOX 4.3   # WHAT DO YOU THINK?

Do you think more can be done to help people living in poverty? What should we do on the national level? The community level? The individual level?

know how I would be able to *think* long enough to get a homework paper done. Unless someone helps, I don't know how I can manage this. I don't own any clothes; I've got three or four shirts, another pair of jeans and sneakers, and that is it. There is not enough money to get myself more clothes. There is not even enough to go to the Salvation Army and get things! So how am I supposed to go to work and look like someone even wants to hire me? People think we are too stupid or we really enjoy this life that we find ourselves in. Maybe they should put themselves in our position and realize that if we could, we would be somewhere else, believe me! (Walker, 1996, p. 27)

EMPLOYMENT AND INCOME LEVELS

Staying out of poverty requires adequate employment and income. Simply having a job does not guarantee immunity from poverty. The way income is distributed across the population affects poverty.

Jobs   Work is a key component of participation in society. Americans expect adults to work and to financially support themselves and their dependents. Employment is not only a means of support for many people; it also defines who they are. For example, a medical doctor may view his or her work as a commitment to heal people, treat their illnesses, and respond to their physical health needs. For people in poverty, the attempt to achieve adequate employment is therefore a struggle for both an adequate income and an identity in society.

For many people, employment is not available or adequate. In March 2008, 5.1 percent of adults were officially counted as **unemployed**, meaning that they were physically able to work but could not find employment (U.S. Department of Labor, 2008). That translated into 7.8 million people, many of whom care for families.

Even when more people are employed, economic well-being does not necessarily improve. For example, child poverty endured during the long economic boom of the 1990s. Between 1993 and 1996 the proportion of poor young children who lived with parents who were employed increased by 16 percent (National Center for Children in Poverty, 1998, p. 3). In 1996, after years of economic growth, almost half of all young children lived either at or near the poverty level. Worker productivity grew by 33 percent between 1995 and 2005, yet wages increased by less than 9 percent (Mishel, Bernstein, & Allegretto, 2007). While worker productivity overall increased, incomes of those working at the low end of the workforce did not. These statistics demonstrate that overall economic growth does not lift all people out of poverty, particularly families with small children.

One reason that economic well-being does not always increase when more people are employed is that many people are **underemployed** or **working poor**—their jobs do not pay enough to meet basic living expenses. The federal government sets a minimum wage, the lowest amount an employer can legally pay an employee. Although a handful of jobs are exempt, the vast majority are covered by minimum wage legislation. In 2008 the minimum wage was $6.55 per hour. If someone worked 40 hours a week for 52 weeks a year at minimum wage, her or his total annual income would be $13,624 before taxes or Social Security withholding, which is below the poverty threshold for a family of two. When taking inflation into account, the minimum wage was actually 26 percent lower in 2005 than it was in 1967 (Mishel, Bernstein, & Allegretto, 2007). Increasing the minimum wage is controversial because employers want to pay the smallest amount possible in order to maximize profits.

Income Distribution   Income is not evenly distributed across households, and over the past several decades the differences between those at the top and those at the bottom have increased. As Table 4.4 shows, people in the top fifth of the income scale account for more than half of all household income, while those in the bottom fifth earn less than 4 percent. The disparity between those at the top and those at the bottom is the worst it has been since the Great Depression of the 1930s. Over the last 30 years, the share of income at the bottom has decreased more than 17 percent and the share of income at the top has increased by 15 percent.

The difference between the top and the bottom is even more evident when income is examined. Table 4.5 lists the dollar income by groups, with the amounts held constant to account for inflation. In 1980 the top fifth of households earned more than 10 times more income on average than did the bottom fifth. By 2006 that had grown to almost 15 times more. Over the last 25 years, the real dollars earned by people in the highest fifth increased by 55 percent, compared with a 12 percent increase for those in the bottom fifth.

TABLE 4.4 | PERCENT DISTRIBUTION OF HOUSEHOLD AGGREGATE INCOME

	2006	2003	2000	1990	1980	1970
Highest 20%	50.5	49.8	49.6	46.6	43.7	43.3
Fourth 20%	22.9	23.4	23.0	24.0	24.9	24.5
Third 20%	14.5	14.8	14.8	15.9	16.9	17.4
Second 20%	8.6	8.7	8.9	9.6	10.3	10.8
Lowest 20%	3.4	3.4	3.6	3.9	4.3	4.1

Source: U.S. Bureau of the Census, 2001; DeNavas-Walt, Proctor, & Smith, 2007.

TABLE 4.5 | MEAN HOUSEHOLD INCOME BY QUINTILE

	Mean Household Income (income held in constant 2006 dollars)			
	2006	2000	1990	1980
Highest 20%	168,170	166,571	130,309	108,322
Fourth 20%	78,329	76,868	67,148	60,754
Third 20%	48,223	49,447	44,536	41,238
Second 20%	11,352	11,892	10,716	10,041
Lowest 20%	9,996	10,849	9,819	9,479

Source: DeNavas-Walt, Proctor, & Smith, 2007.

The difference in income is even more extreme between those at the very top and those at the bottom. The average income of the top 1 percent of people was $1,022,400 in 2003, compared to $51,900 for the middle fifth of earners (Mishel, Bernstein, & Allegretto, 2007). Since the 1980s income growth has benefited top earners. This is contrary to policy changes in the 1980s that were based on the trickle-down theory. Proponents of this theory contended that tax cuts given to those at the top would make more money flow down to those at the bottom. Government assistance for those at the bottom was cut when tax cuts were provided for those at the top. The result has been a greater gap between the top and the bottom, furthering economic disparity.

RACE

Other factors affect income and wealth in the United States. One of the most significant is race. The median income—the midpoint of all earners—was $52,423 for white households, $31,969 for African American households, and $37,781 for Latino families in 2006 (DeNavas-Walt, Proctor, & Smith, 2007). Therefore, families of color earned less than two-thirds of what white families earned. All types of white households had much higher income than the same types of African American and Latino families. Employment rates of people of color have also been lower than those of the white population. For example, in 2008 when the unemployment rate was 4.4 percent for whites, it was 8.8 percent for African Americans and 6.5 percent for Latinos (U.S. Department of Labor, 2008).

Several factors are likely contributors to the link between poverty and race. As discussed in Chapter 3, prejudice and discrimination can limit a person's opportunities. For example, slavery completely kept African Americans out of the mainstream economic structure for hundreds of years. Indigenous Peoples were also excluded from full participation. Table 4.6 illustrates the relationship between poverty and race. As stated above, the median household income for whites is higher than for African Americans and for Latino households. Finding ways to change the negative relationship between income and race presents another challenge to professional social workers.

THE COSTS OF POVERTY

Poverty has a personal cost. Growing up in poverty can hinder children's educational achievement and sense of self. Impoverished areas tend to have more crime than more affluent areas. For adults, poverty contributes to depression, anger, and low self-esteem. Ameliorating these costs continues to be a social welfare concern.

TABLE 4.6 | POVERTY BY RACE, 2006

	White	African American	Latino
Families below poverty	8.5%	23.1%	19.5%
Female-headed families below poverty	26.5%	39.1%	36.9%

Source: DeNaves-Walt, Proctor, & Smith, 2007.

HOMELESSNESS AND HOUSING

Homelessness is not a new problem. However, in part because of an economic downturn in the early 1980s, the number of people—especially the number of children and families—who are homeless appears to have increased dramatically. For example, in New York City, there was a 500 percent increase in the population of homeless families between the early 1980s and the early 1990s (Institute for Children and Poverty, 1998a). Three and a half million people are estimated to be homeless each year (National Coalition for the Homeless, 2007), whereas more than 36 million people experience severe food shortages in their homes (National Student Campaign against Hunger and Homelessness, 2005).

Homelessness is not only a problem in large urban centers. People without permanent residences are found in rural and suburban communities as well. The condition of being homeless is not easily overcome. For example, in a national study of homeless families, at least 40 percent returned to shelters two or more times (Institute for Children and Poverty, 1998b). Many people who leave the shelters cannot secure permanent residences.

One contributor to homelessness is the lack of affordable housing. In many cities over the past 20 years cheaper single rooms and small apartments have disappeared, and new, costly developments have taken their place. For example, just west of Chicago's downtown, entire blocks of buildings in which low-income people rented rooms have been torn down and replaced with expensive high-rises. Those who favor this kind of urban renewal contend that it enhances the city, but housing advocates point out that it has resulted in fewer affordable residential units where poor people can live and has contributed to increases in homelessness.

The increase in homelessness during the 1980s gave rise to public awareness about the problem and prompted passage of the Stewart B. McKinney Homeless Assistance Act. The act was designed to provide resources and services to address the problem of homelessness. However, programs have not kept pace with the increase in homelessness. In 2007 the U.S. Conference of Mayors reported increases in requests for emergency shelter and food assistance in most major U.S. cities, indicating an increase in the number of people who are homeless.

Homelessness is an extreme consequence of poverty, and people who are homeless require additional services and sensitivity. Employment and adequate income are critical needs of all people in poverty, but people who are homeless face additional barriers. For example, a homeless individual cannot provide an address and phone number at which a prospective employer can reach him or her. He or she does not have clothes to wear to an interview and to work, or a place to store such clothing if it is available.

Providing social services for young people who are homeless is a special challenge. Typically young people leave troubled homes or are thrown out because families cannot handle their behavior. Although youth homelessness is a problem of poverty, it is even more a problem of unmet social support and mental health needs.

CASE EXAMPLE: Noel has a learning disability and attention deficit disorder and was beaten and placed in foster care when he was a child. His parents threw him out when he was 18, and he lived on the streets for several months. He was able to join a residential program that helped him find a good job and a safe place to live. His experience has left him deeply wounded, and he tries to understand what he did to deserve being left on his own without any resources (Wilson, 1998).

CASE EXAMPLE: Joyce, who is 16, constantly stayed out of school, often lost control of her temper, and did not get along with her mother. Sexually abused as a child by her now-absent father, Joyce is angry and suspicious of adults. Tired of fighting with her mother, she left home to stay with some other young people in an abandoned apartment near a college campus. Joyce panhandled for money, but could not collect much. She does not want to sell herself for sex, but feels that doing so might be better than returning to her mother's home.

Outreach workers for agencies that provide homeless youth with food, clothing, shelter, and other services find that they are fearful and hesitant to trust. "The minute they wake up out here, someone wants something from them. They want them to do a drug run or they want them for sex. It's hard for [the youth] to believe we don't want anything from them" (Bland, 1998, p. A8). Social intervention, which is difficult with adults who are homeless, is even more difficult with youth.

PERSONAL COSTS

Most social workers come face to face with the problem of poverty on the personal level. Whether poverty is the cause of personal problems or personal deficiencies lead to poverty, there is a relationship between the two. Intervening to alleviate these problems is one of the challenges of social work practice.

Poverty is related to inadequate health, substandard housing, low educational achievement, drug use, and dangerous living situations. For young people, it leaves deep scars and often a great deal of self-blame. After interviewing low-income children, Weinger concluded that the uncertainty, worry, and stress of living with minimal resources "suggest that anxiety and depression are likely outcomes of poverty" (2000, p. 115).

Living in poverty requires coping skills and adaptation to a negative life experience. Some individuals cope by engaging in violence, crime, and drug use and by rejecting the systems that they cannot gain access to, such as the economic system (Ambert, 1998). Schools in poor neighborhoods have inferior resources and overcrowded classrooms, and criminal activity makes the neighborhoods dangerous. The consequences of living in poverty are shorter life spans, inferior education, poor health, hunger, and lack of opportunity. Research on long-term effects of poverty suggests that raising the incomes of poor families improves the cognitive development of children and seems to improve their participation in the labor market as adults (Duncan & Brooks-Gunn, 1997). These outcomes are compelling reasons for improving the lives of people who live in poverty.

THE ROLES OF SOCIAL WORKERS

Social workers pursue social change, particularly with and on behalf of vulnerable and oppressed individuals and groups of people. Social workers' social change efforts are focused primarily on issues of poverty, unemployment, discrimination, and other forms of social injustice.

Part of social workers' professional commitment is to work to eliminate economic inequality and poverty. Few professional social workers are found in public assistance offices, but most social work settings serve low-income individuals and families. To tackle the problem of poverty, social workers need sufficient knowledge of existing social welfare programs and of how to link people to those services. They have to understand the psychosocial conditions related to poverty and develop individual interventions to alleviate them. Finally, social workers need to advocate for social and economic change to create a more economically just society. Box 4.4, "Becoming a Change Agent," poses the dilemma of addressing personal needs versus structural change.

SOCIAL WELFARE PROGRAMS

As discussed in Chapter 2, assistance to people who live in poverty has ebbed and flowed since colonial times, depending on changing social and economic conditions. The strongest national efforts to assist the poor have come in social welfare programs targeted to serve them. Individual intervention has been focused on treating the related psychosocial conditions. On the local level, grassroots advocacy efforts have been effective. All these approaches involve social workers.

The two major types of public assistance are in-kind benefits and cash assistance programs (see Chapter 2). Programs that provide in-kind benefits give people commodities or coupons that they can exchange for commodities. Examples of in-kind services are treatment at public health care clinics, housing subsidies, and food stamps. Cash assistance programs provide monthly payments that recipients use as needed. The two major national cash assistance programs are Supplemental Security Income and Temporary Assistance for Needy Families.

Supplemental Security Income   The **Supplemental Security Income (SSI)** program provides cash assistance for people who are poor and are 65 or older, or blind or disabled. The program was originally created as part of the Social Security Act in 1935 and was actually three separate programs—one each for older people, people who were blind, and people who were disabled—administered as federal-state partnerships. Cash assistance for the three groups was consolidated into the current SSI program in 1972. The legislation also created uniform federal eligibility requirements and benefit levels. The SSI program is funded by general tax revenues.

SSI uses the Department of Health and Human Services poverty guidelines (discussed at the beginning of this chapter) to determine whether a person over 65 is in poverty and is eligible for cash assistance. Benefit amounts are adjusted on the basis of other income the person receives. The definition of disability used by the program mirrors that used for the Social Security Disability Insurance program and covers people of any age with disabilities who are below poverty guidelines but are not eligible to receive benefits under the social insurance part of the Social Security program. The maximum benefit for a person without any other income was $603 per month in 2006. In 2005, 7.3 million people received federal payments through the SSI program with an average monthly payment of $440 (Social Security Administration, 2007).

BOX 4.4 | BECOMING A CHANGE AGENT

According to the U.S. Department of Agriculture (Nord, Andrews, & Carlson, 2007), in 2006 10.9 percent of U.S. households experienced food insecurity at some time during the year. This means that about 12.6 million U.S. households did not have access to enough food to lead active and healthy lives. As a nation we often address hunger by providing food for people in need. People line up at food banks and soup kitchens, some once in a while and others nearly all the time, to get help to overcome hunger. The need for food assistance is constant, and it gets worse during difficult economic times. Food banks find themselves running out of food before they run out of demand for it. Mark Winne (2007) spent many years in the food bank industry in Connecticut. His experiences made him begin to question whether giving out food is a good method to deal with hunger. He is concerned that it creates a codependency where clients come to depend on food handouts rather than developing other ways to get food and where workers want to continue to give food. Giving food makes people feel that they are doing good, and they have little incentive to question or change the ever-growing food-giving industry. Winne asks the question, "What would happen if the collective energy that went into soliciting and distributing food were put into ending hunger and poverty instead?" (p. 25). Hunger is a worldwide problem. Estimates are that more than 850 million people suffer from chronic malnutrition, and those numbers are likely to rise (Chandler, 2008). At the time of this writing, dramatic increases in the cost of food are threatening the lives of millions of people around the world. Therefore, how we address hunger is a worldwide question. The U.S. government and many other governments and private groups provide food to hungry people worldwide. But some in the international relief field question the continued provision of food rather than on helping communities become more self-sufficient. Some groups are trying broader approaches to eradicating hunger. You will be asked to find out about one of them below.

Analyzing the Situation

- Do some research to find out more about the causes of hunger in the United States. Is there a shortage of food or are there other causes?
- Looking at the causes of poverty, how do you think these relate to the causes you found for hunger?
- Try to find out how much money is spent every year to provide emergency food for people nationally and in your state. How many volunteer hours go into providing emergency food?
- Go to the website for the Hunger Project (www.thp.org). Watch one of their videos and read about their approach to eradicating hunger. Does this approach fit with social work values and ethics? If so, how specifically? Is it an approach that you think would work well in the United States?

What Can Social Workers Do?

Given your analysis, what might social workers do to address the causes of hunger? Are there better ways that the money and volunteer hours could be utilized to reduce or end hunger in the United States? What interventions could you suggest at the individual level? The community level? The policy level, for example changes in local, state, or federal legislation?

What Can You Do?

What one step might you take now, alone or working with others, to reduce hunger? What are the barriers that might keep you from taking this step? What could you do to reduce those barriers?

Temporary Assistance for Needy Families   The Temporary Assistance for Needy Families (TANF) program evolved out of 1996 policy changes to the Aid to Families with Dependent Children (AFDC) program. AFDC, which started as part of the 1935 Social Security Act, provided guaranteed cash assistance to any family that was poor for as long as the family qualified. Under TANF, on the other hand, poor families with children still qualify, but the entire family is eligible to receive benefits

TABLE 4.7	STATE VARIABILITY IN TANF

States with Lifetime Limit under Five Years Time Limit

Arkansas	24 months
Connecticut	21 months
Florida	48 months
Georgia	48 months
Idaho	24 months
Indiana	24 months
Utah	36 months

Source: State Policy Documentation Project, 2002.

for no more than 24 consecutive months and a lifetime total of five years. All adult participants must spend 20 hours per week in a job or job-related activity. Under AFDC, a mother with a child under three—in some states, under six—could stay home to care for the child. That choice is no longer available.

Although AFDC was federally mandated, it was state run, so there was program variability across states. The movement of programs from the federal level to the state level is referred to as **devolution of services.** As a result of devolution, there is even greater variability among TANF programs in the different states (State Policy Documentation Project, 2002). Table 4.7 lists other examples of state variability with the TANF program.

The Personal Responsibility and Work Opportunity Reconciliation Act (PRWORA, P.L. 104-193), which created TANF in 1996, also made a major administrative change in funding. Prior to TANF, the federal government matched the amount that states spent (using a formula that took state populations and extent of need into account). Because there were no time limits on AFDC, all eligible people were served, and there was no cap on federal matching funds. TANF is funded through an annual federal block grant, a set amount of money. If a state runs out of funds, no more benefits will be paid until the next year's funding becomes available. States may choose to use their own funds to continue the program, but they receive no additional federal support during the year.

The typical TANF family consists of one female adult and two young children, although almost half have only one child. Fifty-seven percent of recipients are white, 35 percent black, and 20 percent of Hispanic origin (which means they can be identified as black or white) (U.S. Bureau of the Census, 2007). On average, families receive $370 a month, which provides an annual income of $4,440 (U.S. Department of Health and Human Services, 2007). Most TANF families receive food stamps, and almost all are eligible for medical assistance under Medicaid. Fifty-two percent of TANF recipients lived in families with at least one person in the labor force (U.S. Department of Health and Human Services, 2007). In spite of work efforts, these families remained poor and eligible for TANF.

Early analysis of the effect of PRWORA and TANF suggested progress and also raised concerns. The number of people receiving cash assistance dropped significantly between 1993 and 2005, from 14.1 million to 5.1 million (U.S. Department of Health and Human Services, 2007). The caseload rate has held steady since.

Because the decline came during economic growth, it may have been that the decrease in caseloads was a result of the booming economy. Another possibility is that the tighter eligibility criteria enacted under welfare reform allowed fewer families to qualify, in spite of very low-incomes. One concern is that the number of families with no adult recipient increased. The proportion of families in which only the children received benefits increased from 15 percent in 1992 to more than 45 percent in 2005 (U.S. Department of Health and Human Services, 2007). This dramatic rise suggests that families either completed the 24-month period, with the result that adults were ineligible to receive benefits, or that parents were being sanctioned and removed for failure to comply with the new work requirements.

The impact of TANF after the first 10 years has been mixed. As cited earlier, the caseload numbers have declined. Advocates of the 1996 welfare reform regard this as a positive outcome and proof that the changes instituted were successful. However, more detailed research reveals some disturbing data. There has been a large drop in the portion of families eligible for TANF who are being served. Prior to the creation of TANF, 80 percent of the families poor enough to qualify participated in the federal cash assistance program. By 2002 that portion had dropped to 48 percent. This means that "the caseload decline during the first decade of welfare reform reflects a decline in the extent to which TANF programs serve families that are poor enough to qualify, rather than to a reduction in the number of families who are poor enough to qualify for aid" (Center on Budget and Policy Priorities, 2006, p. 2).

Only five states—California, Indiana, Maine, Maryland, and Rhode Island—continue to provide benefits to children after the five-year time limit has been reached (State Policy Documentation Project, 2002). What may be happening is that stricter program criteria are leading to reduced caseloads, while poverty remains constant. Fewer poor families are finding assistance through the TANF program, and they are still poor. This is particularly critical for the children who constitute the majority of TANF recipients.

> Overall, there is reason to be concerned about families living in poverty.
> Despite the large caseload reduction, the national poverty rate has fallen rather little. Many who have left welfare for work remain poor and continue to depend on Food Stamps, Medicaid, and other government assistance; some have left welfare and remain poor, but do not receive the Food Stamp or Medicaid benefits to which they remain entitled. The extent of economic hardship remains high, because, given their human capital and personal characteristics, many former, as well as current, welfare recipients have limited earning prospects in a labor market that increasingly demands higher skills. Thus, despite promising early results with respect to declining caseloads and increasing work effort, much uncertainty exists about the long-run prospects for escaping poverty of both [welfare] stayers and leavers. (Danziger, 2000)

Results of studies following people who left TANF for employment are not encouraging. In Wisconsin "the majority of households who have left welfare have earnings well below the poverty line several years afterward, even in a state that has an extremely strong economy and that has invested heavily in health and child care" (Hotz, Mullin, & Scholz, 2002, p. 54). Most recipients of TANF who left the program and were able to find jobs did see some improvement in their incomes, but it tended to be limited with significant periods of joblessness (Center on Budget and Policy Priorities, 2006).

If TANF is successful in helping people who are poor make the transition to work and economic independence, the program will be an excellent resource for social workers. If TANF takes on a punitive role and fails when the economy weakens and if more people are in need of cash assistance, social workers will need to identify the program's weaknesses, speak out for change, and work to ameliorate the devastating impact of poverty on people.

Food Stamp Program   Original government food support programs, dating back to the 1930s, provided commodities to people who were poor. They originated as an agricultural support effort in which the government purchased food that growers could not sell and gave the food to people in need. Today's **Food Stamp Program** is still run by the Department of Agriculture.

Over time the program's emphasis shifted from supporting growers to supporting low-income people. The Food Stamp Act of 1964, passed as part of the War on Poverty, provides credit that can be used for food at commercial grocery stores. Eligibility is set by the federal government and is standard across the nation. The program is funded through general tax revenues. In 2006, 26.7 million people participated in the Food Stamp Program, and the average monthly value of credit was about $94.05 per person (U.S. Bureau of the Census, 2007). This was a 55 percent increase in the numbers served since 2000. The assessment of TANF over the years may be reflected in the Food Stamp Program. While numbers of people served by TANF decreased, poverty and economic need did not, as reflected in the consistency of the poverty rate and increased participation in the Food Stamp Program.

PSYCHOSOCIAL INTERVENTIONS

Living in poverty is stressful. There is constant worry about paying for rent, food, and transportation and whether the money will last the month. Parents try to provide for children who need new shoes or want a toy or a chance to see a movie. They must balance the cost of child care with their need for paid employment. People who are poor often blame themselves for the condition and feel incompetent and incapable. Fear accompanies poverty—fear of living in a dangerous neighborhood and fear of what will happen next. People in poverty typically feel out of control, that none of the things they have tried have helped change their economic conditions. Poverty leads to negative mental health and contributes to depression and low self-esteem (Link & Phelan, 1995; McCloyd & Wilson, 1990).

Several intervention techniques can be applied when working with people who are in poverty. Focusing on people's strengths and abilities can be a positive way to approach those who are in need (Saleebey, 2006). According to Segal and Stromwall (2000), a number of intervention methods at the individual, group, and community levels that are based on the strengths perspective are helpful when working with people in poverty.

Individual-level work should involve solution-focused interventions that emphasize what can be done rather than analyze problems. The goal is to help clients identify actions they have used in the past that have been helpful and to develop new ways to deal with problems. By focusing on prior successes, people feel better about themselves and begin to feel empowered to make changes.

Social workers can also help people improve their employability. For some people that means finding resources to support employment, such as child care, transportation, or affordable clothing. It may mean helping other people complete high school or college or get work training. Research demonstrates that education can increase income of public assistance recipients. "Earnings of welfare recipients who find jobs typically are higher for those who had a high school diploma at the time of enrollment [in a work program] than those who did not have a diploma" (Parrott, 1998).

Group-level interventions include encouraging people to participate in mutual aid or self-help groups. Involvement in groups helps people feel connected and decreases their feelings of isolation as they struggle to make ends meet. Groups can help people stop blaming themselves and instead begin to see the larger context of poverty in U.S. society. Another intervention is to focus on people's natural helping networks—family, friends, or religious groups. Social workers can help people find support and become natural supporters themselves.

Although intervention with individuals and in groups can help alleviate negative personal and family conditions related to poverty, it does not change the structural factors that contribute to income inequality. Social workers must also address these larger-scale structural factors. For example, even during a time of significant economic growth and low unemployment, poverty increased among people who were employed. The Conference Board (2000), a coalition of major business executives, concluded that since the mid-1970s long-term economic growth has not improved the economic well-being of full-time workers. Contrary to expectations, the poverty of full-time workers was higher at the end of the twentieth century than it was during the recession that preceded the economic boom of the 1990s. Therefore, individual intervention without structural change is not sufficient in dealing with poverty. Community-level interventions that stress advocacy and political change enhance personal interventions and can achieve social change.

ADVOCACY

Political advocacy calls for knowledge of the public policy process, how legislators create policy, and where in that process intervention can take place. Social workers are trained to listen, identify needs, and help people to find ways to meet those needs. These same skills can be used to analyze policy and advocate for change to improve economic conditions.

Emphasizing strengths can be effective on the community level. Identifying and building on a community's assets can be a positive way to address poverty (Kretzmann & McKnight, 1993). For example, a social worker can get to know the people living in a neighborhood and meet the community's informal leaders. These informal leaders meet with public officials about the community's needs. Communities may have resources to offer employers, such as many young workers. Programs that offer property tax benefits can encourage businesses to locate in the area. Poor communities can advocate for businesses to relocate. Such advocacy is most effective when the community organizes from within and natural leaders come

| BOX 4.5 | ETHICAL PRACTICE ... SELF-SUFFICIENCY OR NEGLECT? |

While working for child protective services, you get a call from a neighbor of the Johnson family. She tells you that the three Johnson children, ages 15, 13, and 9, come home after school to an empty house and that the children have no adult supervision until Mrs. Johnson gets home from work about 8:00 at night. When you go meet the family you learn that the oldest child makes dinner for the others and keeps an eye on them. Mrs. Johnson tells you that her husband left a year ago and she was on public assistance until several months ago when she found this job. She stresses that she wants to be a role model for her children and support the family by working. After months of looking, this job was the only one she could find that would support the children. The children seem to accept the situation and be healthy. Would you report this as a case of neglect?

forward. Identifying the community's strengths can be part of the social worker's community-level intervention.

CONCLUSION

Poverty is firmly entrenched in the economic system. Even after the longest economic expansion in modern history, millions of adults and children lived with incomes well below the poverty line. Current social programs provide a modicum of assistance, just enough to cover the most essential needs. Society is reluctant to do more.

Without changes in the social and economic structures, there are not enough opportunities for everyone. If lack of education inhibits a person's ability to earn a good income, it is necessary to find ways to improve that person's access to education or ability to learn. If working full-time still leaves a person in poverty or without health care, wages and benefit coverage need to be increased. If a person is willing to work full-time, employment policies should reward that effort with enough earnings so that he or she can live above the poverty threshold. Creating such opportunities is a major challenge for society and for social workers.

Key Terms

absolute poverty, (p. 90)

culture of poverty, (p. 93)

devolution of services, (p. 103)

feminization of poverty, (p. 93)

Food Stamp Program, (p. 105)

juvenilization of poverty, (p. 93)

poverty guidelines, (p. 91)

poverty threshold, (p. 91)

relative poverty, (p. 90)

Supplemental Security Income (SSI), (p. 101)

Temporary Assistance for Needy Families (TANF), (p. 102)

underemployed, (p. 96)

unemployed, (p. 96)

working poor, (p. 96)

Questions for Discussion

1. Discuss the differences between a relative and an absolute definition of poverty. What are the advantages and disadvantages of each?
2. Discuss how the U.S. poverty threshold was originally determined. Does this method seem reasonable? Does the 2008 poverty threshold of $21,200 for a family of four seem reasonable? Why?
3. What is meant by the juvenilization of poverty? The feminization of poverty? Why is it important to understand these concepts?
4. Discuss the distribution of income across households in the United States. Is income evenly distributed? What are some of the consequences of the current income distribution?
5. Describe the basic social welfare programs that are in place to assist the poor. Describe the primary differences between AFDC and TANF. Were the changes made in 1996 desirable? Why or why not?
6. What role should social workers play in relation to poverty?

Change Agent Exercise

People who are homeless often have difficulty finding a place to stay during the daytime, as most shelters are only open at night. They also have limited resources for making arrangements for job searches and interviews (e.g., no money for transportation or no telephone). What are the rules about homelessness in your community? Can homeless people sit outside? Can they stay in public places such as libraries or post offices or government offices? Where can they use bathrooms during the day? What do they do when the weather is poor? Find out about the rules and regulations regarding loitering and homelessness in your community. Do these laws seem fair and reasonable? If not, what can you do to improve the situation? Try to brainstorm actions that you and your classmates can take to improve the day-to-day conditions for people who are homeless in your community.

Chapter Exercises

1. **What Is Poverty?**
   Working alone, take 10 minutes to identify the basic essentials a person needs to live in our society. Then pair up with a classmate and compare lists. Take 10 minutes to develop a shared list. Now share it with another pair. Can the four of you agree on the basic essentials required for a minimum standard of living?

   Is this discussion difficult? Why or why not?

2. **Social Welfare Programs**
   Identify and explain three social welfare programs designed to address poverty. Answer the following questions for each program:

   Who is eligible for the program?

   What is provided by the program?

   What is the goal of the program?

   Do you think the program is adequate? Why or why not?

3. **Employment Opportunities**

   Apply for or get information about an entry-level job in your community. Ask the prospective employer about wages and benefits, particularly health insurance coverage.

   What is the salary, and which benefits are provided for a one-year period? Is this enough to support a family?

   What health coverage is provided for the employee? For family members?

   What are the job requirements? Who would fit those requirements, and who would not?

   Is this job a viable alternative to public assistance? Why or why not?

   Do you think that gender or race might play a part in this employment opportunity?

   Who is the manager? Who are the entry-level employees? Do they differ? If so, how?

4. **Site Visit**

   Find a local public assistance office. Alone, enter the office and sit in the waiting room for an hour. What did you observe?

   How was the room arranged?

   How did people interact?

   What was the gender, racial, and age composition of the people waiting and of the people working in the office?

   How did this waiting room compare to other waiting rooms you have been in, such as doctor's offices, financial aid centers, or other places of business or service?

5. **Personal Budget**

   Fill out the following budget form:

   Minimum Personal Monthly Budget

   Family size _____

   Rent or Mortgage _____

   Utilities

       Electricity _____

       Gas _____

       Water _____

       Other _____

   Total Utilities _____

   Food _____

   Transportation _____

   Health Care/Health Insurance _____

   Clothing _____

   Furniture/Housewares _____

   Pet Care _____

   Other _____ _____

   Entertainment (movies, restaurants, travel, CDs, books, etc.) _____

   TOTAL MONTHLY BUDGET _____

How does your total monthly budget compare with the federal poverty level? How does it compare with the levels of eligibility for and the benefits from current public assistance programs?

How do your minimum needs compare with those of people living in poverty?

References

Abramovitz, M. (1996). *Regulating the lives of women* (rev. ed.). Boston: South End Press.

Administration for Children and Families. (2000). *Characteristics and financial circumstances of TANF recipients fiscal year 1999*. Washington, DC: U.S. Department of Health and Human Services.

Ambert, A. M. (1998). *The web of poverty: Psychosocial perspectives*. Binghamton, NY: Haworth Press.

Bland, K. (1998). Street kids get lifeline. *Arizona Republic*, October 22, pp. A1, A8, A9.

Center for Law and Social Policy. (1998, August). HHS issues first TANF report. *CLASP Update*. Washington, DC: Author. Center for Law and Social Policy. (2000, September). Welfare at four: Administration and welfare to work partnership take stock. *CLASP Update*. Washington, DC: Author.

Center for Law and Social Policy. (2002, January). Welfare caseloads are up in most states. *CLASP Update*. Washington, DC: Author.

Center on Budget and Policy Priorities. (2006). *TANF at 10: Program results are more mixed than often understood*. Washington, DC: Author.

Chandler, J. (2008). We fill our tanks while they can't fill their stomachs. *Sidney Morning Herald*, April 18, 2008, p. 26.

Conference Board. (2000). *Does a rising tide lift all boats?* Washington, DC: Author.

Dalaker, J. (2001). *Poverty in the United States: 2000*. Current Population Reports, Series P60-214. Washington, DC: U.S. Government Printing Office.

Dalaker, J., & Naifeh, M. (1998). *Poverty in the United States: 1997*. Current Population Reports, Series P60-201. Washington, DC: U.S. Government Printing Office.

DeNavas-Walt, C., Proctor, B. D., & Smith, J. (2007). *Income, poverty, and health insurance coverage in the United States: 2006*. Current Population Reports, P60-233. Washington, DC: U.S. Census Bureau.

DeNavas-Walt, C., Proctor, B. D., & Smith, J. C. (2008). *Income, poverty, and health insurance coverage in the United States: 2007*. Current Population Reports, P60-235. Washington, DC: U.S. Census Bureau.

Danziger, S. (2000). Approaching the limit: Early lessons from welfare reform. Paper prepared for Rural Dimensions of Welfare Reform Conference, Joint Center for Poverty Research, Chicago, IL.

Duncan, G. J., & Brooks-Gunn, J. (1997). Income effects across the life span: Integration and interpretation. In Duncan, G. J., & Brooks-Gunn, J. (eds.), *Consequences of growing up poor*. New York: Russell Sage Foundation.

Hotz, V. J., Mullin, C. H., & Scholz, J. K. (2002). Welfare reform, employment, and advancement. *Focus*, 22, 1, 51–55.

Institute for Children and Poverty. (1998a). *The cycle of family homelessness*. New York: Author.

Institute for Children and Poverty. (1998b). *Ten cities: A snapshot of family homelessness across America*. New York: Author.

Institute for Research on Poverty. (1998). Revising the poverty measure. *Focus, 19*, 2, 1–6.

Kogan, R., Greenstein, R., & Friedman, J. (2002). *The new CBO projections: What do they tell us?* Washington, DC: Center on Budget and Policy Priorities.

Kretzmann, J. P., & McKnight, J. L. (1993). *Building communities from the inside out: A path toward mobilizing a community's assets*. Evanston, IL: Northwestern University Center for Urban Affairs and Poverty Research.

Lamison-White, L. (1997). *Poverty in the United States: 1996*. Current Population Reports, Series P60-198. Washington, DC: U.S. Government Printing Office.

Link, B. G., & Phelan, J. (1995). Social conditions as fundamental causes of disease. *Journal of Health and Social Behavior* (extra issue), 80–94.

McCloyd, V. C., & Wilson, L. (1990). Maternal behavior, social support, and economic conditions as a predictor of distress in children. In McCloyd, V. C., & Flanagan, C. A. (eds.), *Economic stress: Effects on family life and child development* (pp. 49–70). San Francisco: Jossey-Bass.

Mishel, L., Bernstein, J., & Allegretto, S. (2007). *The state of working America 2006/2007*. Ithaca, NY: Economic Policy Institute, Cornell University Press. 6.

National Center for Children in Poverty. (1998). Child poverty rates remain high despite booming U.S. economy. *News and Issues, 8*, 1, 3.

National Coalition for the Homeless. (2007). *How many people experience homelessness?* Washington, DC: Author.

Orshansky, M. (1965). Counting the poor: Another look at the poverty profile. *Social Security Bulletin, 28*, 1, 3–29.

National Student Campaign against Hunger and Homelessness. (2005). *Communities in crisis: A survey of hunger and homelessness in America*. Amherst, MA: Author.

Nord, M., Andrews, M., & Carlson, S. (2007). *Household Food Security in the United States, 2006*. Washington, DC: U.S. Department of Agriculture.

Parrott, S. (1998). *Welfare recipients who find jobs: What do we know about their employment and earnings?* Washington, DC: Center on Budget and Policy Priorities.

Pearce, D. (1978). The feminization of poverty: Women, work, and welfare. *Urban and Social Change Review, 11*, 1-2, 28–36.

Rawlings, L. (2000). *Poverty and income trends: 1998*. Washington, DC: Center on Budget and Policy Priorities.

Ryan, W. (1976). *Blaming the victim* (rev. ed.). New York: Vintage Books.

Saleebey, D. (2006). *The strengths perspective in social work practice* (4th ed.). Boston: Pearson/Allyn & Bacon.

Segal, E. A. (1991). The juvenilization of poverty in the 1980s. *Social Work, 36*, 5, 454–457.

Segal, E. A., & Stromwall, L. K. (2000). Social work practice issues related to poverty and homelessness. In Allen-Meares, P., & Garvin, C. *Handbook of direct practice in social work: Future directions and guidelines*. pp. 519–532. Thousand Oaks, CA: Sage Publications.

Shapiro, I., Greenstein, R., & Primus, W. (2000, September 4). *An analysis of new IRS income data*. Washington, DC: Center on Budget and Policy Priorities.

Social Security Administration. (2007). *Annual statistical supplement 2006*. Washington, DC: Author.

State Policy Documentation Project. (2002). *TANF*. Washington, DC: Center for Law and Social Policy & Center on Budget and Policy Priorities.

U.S. Bureau of the Census. (1997). *Money income in the United States: 1996*. Current Population Reports, P60-197. Washington, DC: U.S. Government Printing Office.

U.S. Bureau of the Census. (1998a). *Measuring 50 years of economic change*. Current Population Reports, P60-203. Washington, DC: U.S. Government Printing Office.

U.S. Bureau of the Census. (1998b). *Money income in the United States: 1997*. Current Population Reports, P60-200. Washington, DC: U.S. Government Printing Office.

U.S. Bureau of the Census. (1999). *Statistical abstract of the United States* (119th ed.). Washington, DC: U.S. Department of Commerce.

U.S. Bureau of the Census. (2001). *Money income in the United States: 2000*. Current Population Reports, P60-213. Washington, DC: U.S. Government Printing Office.

U.S. Bureau of the Census. (2007). *Statistical abstract of the United States: 2008* (127th ed.). Washington, DC: U.S. Department of Commerce.

U.S. Conference of Mayors. (2007). *Survey of hunger and homelessness*. Washington, DC: Author.

U.S. Department of Health and Human Services. (2000). *Trends in the well-being of America's children and youth 1999*. Washington, DC: Author.

U.S. Department of Health and Human Services. (2007). *Indicators of welfare dependence: Annual report to Congress*. Washington, DC: Author.

U.S. Department of Health and Human Services. (2008, January 23). The 2008 HHS poverty guidelines. *Federal Register, 73*, 15, 3971–3972.

U.S. Department of Labor. (2008). Employment situation summary. Washington, DC: Author. Available at http://www.bls.gov/news.release/empsit.nr0.htm.

Walker, L. (1996). If we could, we would be someplace else. In Dujon, D., & Withorn, A. (eds.), *For crying out loud: Women's poverty in the United States* (pp. 23—27). Boston: South End Press.

Weinger, S. (2000). Children's perceptions of class difference: Worries and self-perceptions. *Journal of Poverty, 4*, 3, 99–118.

Wilson, G. (1985). The juvenilization of poverty. *Public Administration Review, 45*, 880–884.

Wilson, S. (1998). HomeBase Youth Services a lifeline for homeless teen. *Arizona Republic*, December 23, p. A2.

Winne, M. (2007). Canned compassion: Holiday handouts do help, but they feed an endless cycle. *Washington Post National Weekly Edition, 25*, 6, 25.

Ziliak, J. P. (2002). Social policy and the macroeconomy: What drives welfare caseloads? *Focus, 22*, 1, 29–34.

MODES OF INTERVENTION

Social workers use a broad spectrum of approaches when working with people. The techniques can be general or highly specialized. Some interventions require additional training beyond the BSW degree, and others require training beyond the MSW degree. A major task of social work training is learning to assess what services are needed and appropriate and then either provide those services or refer clients to practitioners who can provide specialized interventions.

In addition to the broad array of interventions that are part of the professional repertoire, there are different levels of services. Social workers intervene with individuals, families, groups, communities, organizations, and make their views known in the policy arena. Learning to assess clients and social systems and use those assessments to determine what interventions may be most beneficial is a lifetime process. Social work education is designed to provide practitioners with the foundation necessary to carry out these functions. This chapter provides an overview of the most commonly used social work interventions.

Consider Jane and her family from Chapter 1. Jane went to see a social worker after losing her job. She told the social worker in the family service agency that she was worried that her children were angry with her and were acting out. She was also concerned that her children were not covered by health insurance. The social worker approached Jane's situation at every possible level. First, she arranged counseling for Jane and her children at the family service agency. She then referred Jane to social work professionals in other agencies. One of them helped Jane get health insurance for her children. Social workers in another agency provided Jane with job training. Jane and her children never actually met a number of the social workers helping them. These unseen professionals included social workers advocating in the legislative arena for health coverage for the working poor as well as community social workers who were organizing Jane's neighbors to fight to improve local schools and secure funding for after-school programs.

This wide range of social service involvement is typically referred to as **generalist social work practice**. The generalist social work practitioner possesses a broad range of training and uses his or her skills to guide and coordinate services for clients (see "More About … Generalist Social Work Practice").

Social workers obtaining a BSW degree are usually trained as generalist practitioners. This means they have the skills and knowledge to intervene on a variety of practice levels, in many practice settings, for a wide range of social problems. Most MSW programs use generalist practice as a foundation for the acquisition of more advanced and specialized skills.

BOX 5.1 | **MORE ABOUT … GENERALIST SOCIAL WORK PRACTICE**

"A *generalist approach* requires that the social worker assess the situation with the client and decide which systems are the appropriate *units of attention*, or focus of the work, for the change effort. As the units of attention may include an individual, a family, a small group, an agency or organization, a community, or the transactions among these, the generalist approach emphasizes knowledge that can be applied to a variety of systems." (Johnson & Yanca, 2001, p. 1)

Within the generalist framework, social work can be divided into micro and macro practice. In **micro practice** social workers help individuals, families, and small groups function better within the larger environment. For example, there are a number of micro practice interventions that social workers might be able to use to help Jane function better as an individual. They might help her develop job skills so that she can find better-paying employment. They might also provide counseling to help Jane overcome low self-esteem or encourage her to understand how her childhood has shaped her adult life. Social workers might also provide family counseling to Jane and her children to improve communication and relationships within the family.

Macro practice means working to change the larger environment in ways that benefit individuals and families. When doing macro practice, social workers intervene in communities, organizations, and the legislative arena to effect social change. There are a number of changes in the social environment that would benefit Jane and her family. For example, social workers could help Jane and her neighbors organize a neighborhood association to press for improvements in the local public school or to pressure banks or government agencies to provide low-interest small-business loans or seed money to start new businesses in the area. Social workers might also work to improve service delivery in a local agency used by Jane and her family.

For purposes of explanation, it is helpful to distinguish between micro- and macro practice. However, the distinction between the two levels of practice is often a false one, and the boundaries between them are blurred. To be effective, social workers must be able to use both micro and macro interventions to address the needs and concerns of their clients. Few problems have only individual solutions. Social workers must usually work on an individual and family level while at the same time addressing structural concerns. For example, helping Jane improve her job skills will not change the fact that there are few jobs available in her neighborhood. If there are no jobs nearby and no transportation to take her to a job, even strong job skills will not ensure that Jane can get a job. Effective social work involves helping Jane improve her employability as an individual and also helping change the environment so that there will be jobs available.

Social work interventions can include a wide array of approaches with different theories and emphases. Some approaches are more commonly used than others, and new ones emerge over time. Students may be trained to use one or several approaches, depending on the perspectives of their instructors, their schools, and later their supervisors. The varied approaches allow social work practitioners to

| **BOX 5.2** | **MORE ABOUT ... LEVELS OF PRACTICE** |

In the text we discuss micro and macro levels of practice. Some in the field add a third level, mezzo practice. *Micro* means small, referring to work with individuals or families. *Macro* means large, referring to work with larger systems, usually communities or organizations. *Mezzo* refers to a middle level of practice, which for many in the field means work with small groups. In this text, small-group practice is included as a part of micro practice. However, given that some social workers use the term *mezzo,* it is good to be aware of it.

choose from a variety of skills and techniques to find the intervention that best fits the person in his or her environment.

This chapter highlights a number of the most frequently used interventions. Although intervention happens at many levels, in order to best identify the various approaches, they are divided according to three general practice levels: individuals and families, groups, and communities. Social work practice often involves working on two or all three levels, and practitioners need to be comfortable working with people on all levels.

SOCIAL WORK WITH INDIVIDUALS AND FAMILIES

An individual is often the focus of social work intervention. Over the 100 years of professional social work, numerous approaches have evolved. Many of them originated in other disciplines and grew out of various theories of human behavior. A case example helps demonstrate the variety of approaches and steps social workers use to provide services.

CASE EXAMPLE: Michael is a 38-year-old, gay, white male. Although HIV-positive for years, he had been fairly healthy. However, over the past year he has developed more health problems and is now HIV-symptomatic. Michael had been employed as a retail store manager, but frequent absences this past year made him take a position in the store as an hourly clerk, and his employer no longer paid for his health insurance coverage. At first Michael used his savings to pay the portion of the premiums previously paid by his employer, but his savings were exhausted. His health is deteriorating. When he was hospitalized with pneumonia, one of the nurses recommended support services. In the past, Michael preferred to rely on himself, his friends, and his family, but he realizes that he needs additional help. Thus, Michael has come to the HIV/AIDS Social Service Center.

All social work practice begins with some form of assessment. **Assessment** can be defined as determining what the presenting concerns are, who is involved, details of the person's environment, and personal history and background. The social worker gathers data from the client and from the systems that affect the client (Hepworth, Rooney, Rooney, Strom-Gottfried, & Larson, 2005). For example, if the client is a child, a full assessment may involve gathering information from the child, the family, the school, the child's doctor, and other professionals. A generalist social work practitioner is often the person who gathers information to develop the initial or baseline assessment of individual clients.

One form of this assessment is **intake**. The intake is an initial assessment that usually includes gathering data about the client, getting a preliminary perspective on the problem, and informing the client about what services are available and the conditions of those services, such as fees and appointment procedures (Barker, 1999). These data make it possible for the intake worker to determine eligibility, identify the problem, and determine the next step.

Assessment makes use of the skills of conducting effective interviews, engaging the client in the process, and analyzing the information collected. Often, the assessment process involves bringing the intake information to a clinical team or supervisor for further assessment. From the assessment, the provision of services is determined and a course of intervention or treatment is designed.

Figure 5.1 is a sample intake form for Michael. In this case, the intake specialist is recommending that Michael be seen by a case manager and be assessed for further services. In the meantime, the intake specialist has referred Michael to other resources for financial assistance and health care.

The actual delivery of services is a major part of social work practice. Delivery can take place through information and referral, through the creation of network linkages, and through the provision of direct services. Social workers play active roles in all three areas of service delivery.

INFORMATION AND REFERRAL

Social workers often provide services through **information and referral (I & R)**. The overall goal of information and referral is to enhance a client's access to service by improving awareness and knowledge of services and reducing barriers to them (Haynes, 1997). Often, social services are specialized or are offered as parts of larger systems, and are thus difficult to locate. Without specialized knowledge, and particularly when they are in crisis, clients are at a loss to identify needed services.

For example, suppose one of your parents is suddenly hospitalized for emergency heart surgery. Although the hospital and medical staff handle the immediate medical emergency and in-hospital care following surgery, what will you do about after-hospital care? Do you know how to find home health care if your parent is not ready to care for himself or herself? What if the recovery period is long and physical therapy is needed? Can you find an intermediary care facility if your parent needs more care than can be provided at home? A medical social worker can help you cope with the emergency and can provide information on services and refer you to agencies and specialists.

Social workers also help people overcome barriers or obstacles to receiving services. Some social workers are bilingual and can work with people whose first language is not English. Social workers can arrange for transportation to medical appointments or for a child with a disability to attend a special school. Some barriers to service can be physical or legal. For example, agency services may be available only during the day, and people who work may have trouble accessing them. Social workers can lobby for extended evening hours or make special arrangements for after-hour interventions. An agency may mistakenly withhold services from a person who is undocumented, an infraction of a legal right to access. A social worker can advocate for services and ensure that the person's legal right is upheld.

These efforts are part of reducing barriers to service and fulfilling the role of information and referral. In order for I & R to be helpful, the social worker must know about the breadth of services available, must have advocacy skills, and must be able to assess problems and needs.

In Michael's case, the intake worker would make several referrals in addition to providing information. She would refer Michael to his local public assistance office so that he could apply for financial aid, and she would make a preliminary determination of whether he is eligible for health and disability services. On the basis of his employment history, she may instead refer him to the local Social

Name: Michael Allen Crane
DOB: June 28, 1965
Phone: (h) 555-5555   (w) 555-3333
Home Address: 1234 W. Pinewood Avenue
Living Arrangements: Lives alone in a rental apartment
Ethnicity: Caucasian
Gender: Male
Language: English
Referral Source: Nurse at Memorial Hospital

MEDICAL BACKGROUND

Doctor: Primary care physician—Janet L. Goodson, MD
Insurance Carrier: Health Network HMO; client is paying premiums.
Year of Diagnosis: 2000
HIV Stage: Symptomatic
Medications: Antiviral/transcriptase inhibitors and protease inhibitors
Current Health Concerns: Reports loss of appetite, nausea, fatigue
Hospitalizations: Recent bout of pneumonia, hospitalized for 6 days

FINANCIAL SITUATION

Income per Month: $650, part-time employment
Benefits Assistance: None

HOUSING

Lives alone in a one bedroom apartment, monthly rent is $600 plus utilities

TRANSPORTATION

Owns a 2002 car with 72,000 miles on it. Runs well, but needs new tires and
some general maintenance.

BEHAVIORAL HEALTH

Client reports feeling depressed; states does not have alcohol or drug-use problem.

SUPPORTS

Client relies on friends and family. Has a sister who lives near and is helpful
and supportive.

INTAKE SPECIALIST ASSESSMENT

Referred to case management?
Yes, client could benefit from more in-depth assessment for medical care and
mental health care.

Other referrals made
Client is in need of financial assistance and health care coverage. Referred client to
office for Social Security disability insurance and Supplemental Security Income for
financial assistance and medical assistance.

FIGURE 5.1 | Intake Form for HIV/AIDS Social Service Center

Security office to apply for disability insurance coverage. As an intake worker at an agency specializing in HIV/AIDS services, she would have information about clinical trials at local hospitals that might provide Michael with health care and medications. She might direct him to a group home where he could pay much lower rent and receive support with daily living. The intake specialist would also have detailed written information to share with Michael so that he could learn more about services and his illness. All these efforts are examples of I & R.

NETWORK LINKAGES

Knowledge about the breadth of services is a critical component of providing **network linkages**. People may receive services from multiple social service systems. The social worker can act as the link between the systems.

For example, children's problems often require the involvement of many social service systems. Consider a child who is caught vandalizing school property by security personnel. A police officer may be called, possibly leading to involvement of the juvenile justice system. The child may be assessed as having severe emotional disturbances, and the community mental health agency becomes involved. A school social worker may also be involved, since the child is a student at the school. In this case, three systems—juvenile justice, school, and mental health—are all involved with one child. Social workers are trained to work in and with multiple systems. This training helps them ensure that there is neither a duplication of services nor a gap in service.

The efforts of the intake specialist begin the process of network linkage for Michael. She may call a staff person at one of the agencies to which she referred him. She may recommend that he see a person with specialized skills. The network linkages will continue as Michael progresses in the social service system at the HIV/AIDS Social Service Center.

DIRECT SERVICES

Social workers are key personnel in the provision of **direct services**. They may counsel a person for depression, provide transportation, help make arrangements for home health care, serve as an advocate for a child, assist a victim of crime, or provide crisis intervention on a suicide hotline. Social workers are the direct providers of service in behavioral health agencies, hospitals, schools, domestic violence shelters, residential treatment centers for children, homeless shelters, day treatment centers for seniors, group homes for people with developmental disabilities, drug abuse treatment centers, hospices, wellness and prevention centers, and countless other social service settings.

The range of social work roles in the direct provision of services is as varied as the range of social services available. In 2006, 595,000 social workers were employed. Social work employment is expected to grow much faster than the national average for other professions. Half of social workers are employed in health care and social assistance industries, and about 30 percent work for state and local government agencies (Summary Report, 2008).

The most common forms of direct social work services provided on the individual level are case management and therapeutic interventions. Case management offers more general services, and therapeutic interventions tend to be more highly specialized.

CASE MANAGEMENT

One of the direct practice roles that a social worker most frequently fills is that of case manager. **Case management** is

> a series of actions and a process to assure that clients and human services systems receive a service, treatment, care, and opportunities to which they are entitled.... It is a set of logical steps and a process of interaction within a service network which assure that a client receives needed services in a supportive, effective, efficient, and cost effective manner. (Weil & Karls, 1985, p. 2)

Rather than providing a specific service, such as alcohol counseling, a case manager coordinates a program of services and refers clients to appropriate places where they can receive these services. The case manager also follows up with the client, ensuring both continuity and coordination of the services that are provided. Over time, a case manager can develop a good rapport with and a deeper knowledge of the client and his or her concerns. With this understanding, the case manager can serve as an advocate for the client while providing linkages with other service providers.

One of the key provisions of case management is to view the client from the person-in-environment perspective. The case manager is uniquely positioned to follow the individual's needs in the context of his or her home, work, and community environments and help to facilitate linkages across those systems. Case management strategies include outreach and engagement, assessment of needs, planning for service or treatment, linkages to resources and referrals, and service delivery monitoring (Stoesen, 2008). The components of case management fit social work well, making it a significant part of practice.

CASE EXAMPLE: Following intake at the family service center, Michael is assigned to a case manager. She refers Michael to a range of appropriate services and coordinates them. She conducts an in-depth assessment of his social, psychological, and health needs, and together they create a care plan that outlines the goals and objectives of a service plan. She helps Michael with the referrals he received through the intake process and is an integral part of the network linkages of the services he needs. The case manager meets with Michael regularly and periodically checks in with his other service providers. She serves as an ongoing resource and support to Michael while he remains a client of the HIV/AIDS Social Service Center. Through regular meetings and follow-up, she determines whether he needs additional services or more specialized care.

Therapeutic Interventions   Therapeutic direct services provide specialized care beyond the domain of case management. The goal of providing therapeutic services on an individual basis is to restore or enhance mental well-being. The earliest form of therapeutic intervention was social casework, which can be traced back to Mary Richmond's work in the early 1900s as codified in her book *Social Diagnosis* (discussed in Chapter 1). Over the years, social casework has evolved to include numerous approaches and techniques.

The ecological systems framework is the foundation for therapeutic interventions with individuals. A metaphor helps explain the relationship between this overarching framework and the theories of practice and models of intervention with individuals. Imagine a large and leafy tree (see Figure 5.2). The tree is embedded in rich soil.

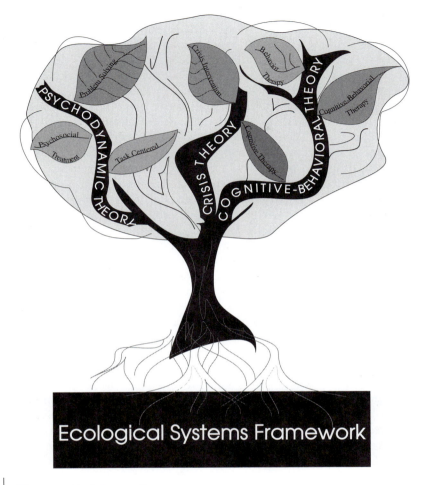

Ecological Systems Framework

FIGURE 5.2 | Therapeutic Interventions

The soil represents the ecological systems framework. The tree consists of several large limbs with branches. The limbs are social work practice theories that have grown out from the tree. Many social work practice theories have been adapted from other helping professions such as psychology and grafted onto the tree. Both the homegrown and grafted theories have become a part of social work practice during the last hundred years.

Psychodynamic-Based Approaches   By the early twentieth century, the ideas of Sigmund Freud had emerged as a dominant theory of human behavior and were influential among social workers. Freud's theories of human behavior were adopted by others and eventually evolved into psychodynamic theory.

The components of pyschodynamic theory that influenced early social work practice established that people's behaviors were purposeful and determined and that some of those determinants were unconscious. These two fundamental beliefs changed the direction of social work practice. Social workers were no longer limited to working only with people living in poverty, as in the early 1900s; their domain grew to include all people.

The modern practice of psychosocial treatment was influenced by Anna Freud, Sigmund's daughter (1946), and by Erik Erikson (1950). Both made significant contributions to the understanding of ego psychology. Building on the works of Mary Richmond, Anna Freud, and Erik Erikson, Florence Hollis's *Casework: A Psychosocial Therapy* (1964) became the social work profession's guide to psychosocial treatment. (A second edition was prepared by Woods and Hollis, 1990.)

According to psychodynamic theory, interacting genetic, biological, and socio-cultural factors explain the cognitive and emotional processes, both conscious and unconscious, that motivate human behavior. This theory is the basis of many casework interventions. The branches that grow off the psychodynamic limb are models of intervention that flow logically from the theory. They include psychosocial treatment, the problem-solving method, and task-centered casework. All three are used in social work practice with individuals and families.

Psychosocial treatment emphasizes the internal determinants of people's behavior, focusing on early life experiences and childhood memories. Psychological symptoms such as depression and anxiety are viewed as adaptive attempts to uncover and resolve internal conflicts. The goal of the social worker is to help clients overcome conflicts that are barriers to self-fulfillment. The key to effective treatment is the social worker's positive, nonpossessive, and empathic regard for the client. Within the safety of the client-worker relationship, clients can discover the underlying conscious and unconscious motivations for their behavior. With this understanding, they can better understand their feelings and the ways, both positive and negative, they have coped with those feelings. Exploring their feelings and patterns of responses allows them to resolve internal conflicts so as to achieve improved mental health and improved relationships with others.

One of the criticisms of psychosocial treatment is that it does not pay enough attention to external conflicts or the influences of social systems. For example, a psychosocial approach would probably not be effective in assisting Jane (see Chapter 1) because her situation requires more focus on external conflicts or problems with social systems, rather than internal conflicts.

During the 1950s Helen Harris Perlman (1957) developed the **problem-solving method** of intervention. Her goal was to move away from the psychosocial focus on early childhood experiences and memories and to make social work practice more pragmatic and more focused on the present moment (Turner & Jaco, 1996). Today, most BSW programs prepare graduates for generalist or practical casework positions and include courses on values and ethics, diversity, promotion of social justice, social welfare policy, human behavior, and research methods (Summary Report, 2008).

Two fundamental assumptions underlie the problem-solving method. The first is that client problems do not represent weakness and failure on the part of the client, but are instead a natural part of life and the process of human growth and change (Compton & Galaway, 1994, p. 44). The second assumption is that if clients cannot solve their problems, it is because they lack the knowledge or resources to effectively do so (Turner & Jaco, 1996). As is the case with psychosocial treatment, the client-worker relationship is critical to the problem-solving method. The relationship is collaborative and provides the client with a source of encouragement and the safety needed to initiate creative problem solving.

The problem-solving model would probably be very effective in assisting Jane and her family. However, clients who do not need to deal with immediate problems in daily living but would rather resolve issues from the past may not find the problem-solving method effective.

In the late 1960s **task-centered social work** evolved out of the discovery that shortened treatment periods were more effective in problem solving than the long-term treatments associated with psychosocial therapy. Thus, Reid and Epstein (1972), who were influenced by Perlman's problem-solving model, developed task-centered social work with time limits in mind. The basic characteristics of task-centered casework are that it is short term, the focus is on client-acknowledged problems, and sessions are highly structured into specific activities. Because task-centered casework is brief and focuses on the presenting problem, the emphasis is on identifying a problem rather than identifying the underlying cause. Once the problem is identified, the desired outcome or change is then identified. Determining tasks to overcome obstacles and achieve the desired outcome is the goal of this approach.

Crisis Theory and Crisis Intervention   A crisis is a situation in which a person's normal coping mechanisms are inadequate or are not working. The person becomes immobilized by feelings of helplessness, confusion, anxiety, depression, and anger. **Crisis intervention**, which is based on crisis theory, is a short-term model of social work practice that is designed to assist victims and survivors to return to their precrisis level of functioning. Crisis intervention is a primary social work intervention and is provided in almost every social work setting.

Crisis theorists have suggested that a crisis is a normal, time-limited reaction to a situational or developmental life stressor such as death, divorce, retirement, or physical illness (Parad & Parad, 1990). Overcoming the crisis is perceived as part of the maturation process and as necessary to developing healthy self-esteem. Recent crisis theorists have focused on reactions to and consequences of such catastrophic or traumatic crises as war, rape, natural disaster, and workplace and school violence (Ell, 1996). Chapter 15 provides more detail on these areas of social work practice.

The critical components of effective crisis intervention include assistance that is provided as quickly as possible, brief treatment periods with a focus on practical information and tangible support, the goal of reducing symptoms, and efforts to mobilize the client's social support networks (Ell, 1996). In some cases, clients may need to be referred for longer-term psychosocial treatment. For example, a client diagnosed with post–traumatic stress disorder (PTSD) as a result of the crisis may need both medication and long-term therapy.

COGNITIVE-BEHAVIORAL THEORIES AND THERAPIES

Although Sigmund Freud was not the only theorist developing explanations of human behavior in the early twentieth century, social workers were not as interested in other theorists' efforts. One important theory was developed by Ivan Pavlov, a Russian chemist and physiologist, who discovered the conditioned reflex or response while doing experiments on the digestive process of dogs. The conditioned reflex is a learned reflex, in contrast to an innate reflex such as pulling one's hand away from a hot flame. Pavlov's finding later became a critical component of behavioral psychology.

John Watson, an American psychologist, was a critic of Freud's theories of human behavior and was fascinated by Pavlov's discovery of the conditioned response. He undertook a series of studies on the behaviors of children and developed a set of ideas that came to be known as behaviorism, a branch of psychology (Watson, 1914). During the 1950s behaviorism was further developed by B. F. Skinner (1953). Behaviorism took the focus off Freud's unconscious motives and instinctual drives and argued that maladaptive behaviors are learned and can therefore be unlearned (Barker, 1999). While early life experiences are not ignored, behavior therapies are more present centered and forward looking than psychosocial therapies.

During the 1960s and 1970s the cognitive theory of human behavior began to evolve and become increasingly dominant in the fields of psychology and social work. Cognitive theory is based on the belief that how and what a person thinks determine or contribute to how the person feels and behaves. Maladaptive behaviors can be explained by irrational or distorted thinking that results from misperceptions and misinterpretations of the environment (Payne, 2004).

Cognitive and behavior theories have been combined in several different types of **cognitive-behavioral therapies** or interventions. In these approaches, the behavioral aspects of treatment are designed to weaken connections between habitual reactions (fear, depression, rage, or self-defeating behaviors) and troublesome situations and also to calm the mind and body so the person can think more clearly and make better decisions. The cognitive aspects teach about thinking patterns and how to change patterns that are based on distorted or irrational beliefs. Cognitive-behavioral therapies have been the subject of a great deal of social work research and have been shown to be effective in treating depression, anxiety, relationship problems, social phobias, eating disorders, and post–traumatic stress disorder. As a result, cognitive-behavioral therapies are commonly used in clinical social work practice (Ledley, Marx, & Heimberg, 2007).

Family Intervention   Intervention with families can be viewed as an extension of individual work, as a form of group work, or as a form of practice separate from both. While all three views have support, we view family work as an extension of individual casework practice as well as a bridge to group work. Often, families become involved in treatment as an outgrowth of an individual's course of intervention. For example, a woman who is seeing a social worker to help her address anxious feelings may agree with the worker that including her family would be beneficial.

To effectively work with a family, a social work practitioner needs knowledge and skills drawn from individual and group interventions (see "From the Field ... Using Multiple Skills"). Unlike formal groups, which are discussed in the next section, families are natural groups with lifetime relationships that are structured through legal, biological, or intimate bonds. The purpose of family social work is to focus on the family as the unit of service in order to help improve the health and well-being of all family members.

BOX 5.3	**FROM THE FIELD … USING PRACTICE SKILLS**
	Mary Palacios, MSW, PhD

I had been working in a private, not-for-profit child welfare agency for two years, when I decided to pursue a PhD in social work. In order to put myself through school, I took a position as a crisis intervention counselor with a private for-profit agency in my university town. The agency had a contract with Child Protective Services (CPS) in a southern state to provide intensive family preservation services (IFPS) in rural areas of the state. The primary goals of IFPS services are to protect children by maintaining and strengthening family bonds, to stabilize crisis situations, to increase the skills of the parents, to help families connect with needed resources, and to prevent unnecessary out-of-home placements. I would receive a referral from the agency director and then I would have six weeks to work with the family in their home. I was expected to visit them at least twice a week, sometimes as many as three or four times a week depending on the situation.

The very first case I received would require me to draw on all of my knowledge and practice experience to help the family achieve a positive outcome. The family had been referred due to an allegation of sexual abuse. My first goal was to assess whether the children were in a dangerous situation; that is, did they need to be removed from the home or was the situation safe enough to proceed with in-home services. CPS had already made the determination that there was no evidence of sexual abuse; however, they believed the family was in crisis primarily because of the allegation but also because they had limited resources. The family consisted of a grandfather, a grandmother, and three biological granddaughters. The three girls were 8, 10, and 11 years old. One of the girls was developmentally delayed. She was mildly retarded and had physical problems as well. The grand parents were in their late sixties. The girls had been living with their grandparents for two years. They were removed from their biological mother's home because she had a substance abuse problem and had been neglecting the girls. The family was referred to our agency because the biological mother alleged that her father was sexually molesting the girls, "the same way he had molested me when I was young."

I interviewed each girl. Then, I interviewed the grandparents one at a time. I also interviewed the court-appointed guardian ad litem for the girls and the girls' biological mother. The girls and their grandparents all denied that any sexual abuse had occurred, and they denied that there was any ongoing sexual abuse. The guardian ad litem believed the girls were living in a chaotic situation, but she did not see any evidence of sexual abuse. The grandparents alleged that their biological daughter had made the sexual abuse claim to seek revenge and to disrupt their family. They believed she was still struggling with a crack addiction.

Based on the initial evidence, I made the determination that it was best for the girls to remain in their grandparents' home while the family received IFPS services. However, I was still gravely concerned because of several red flags that I identified in the family dynamic. Since the grandmother was the primary financial provider, the grandfather was the primary caregiver for the children (he did not work). Despite the fact that grandmother worked, she had several serious health problems, including severe back pain that caused her to remain in her bedroom, lying down most of the time when she was home. Grandfather slept on the couch at night so as not to disturb the sleep of his wife and vice versa. Therefore, the grandfather had ample opportunity to be alone with the girls, and he and his wife, based on their own account, had stopped all sexual relations between them two years earlier because of her ill health. The girls all had serious self-esteem issues. The oldest girl was self-mutilating using whatever sharp objects she could find. The developmentally delayed daughter had some inappropriate sexual behaviors in public and occasionally made sexually inappropriate comments. *Despite* these red flags, I viewed the grandparents as very gregarious personalities who were openly and appropriately affectionate with their granddaughters. They were very likeable people. The trailer they lived in was always a mess, and it was clear that the family was barely making it from month to month even with the extra support from the state, but the family had many "stories" to explain why they "had never been able to catch a break."

The family was aligned against the biological mother. The girls claimed they hated their mother and didn't want to see her. The grandparents never had a kind word to say about their daughter. I made a classic mistake in the first three weeks of my work with the family. Instead of maintaining a

BOX 5.3 | **FROM THE FIELD ... USING PRACTICE SKILLS** *continued*

neutral position, I was surprised that without even being aware of it, I had begun to "align" with the family position that they were "victims" of the biological mother and other parties and circumstances as well. Looking back, and writing this now, it is embarrassing that at the time I did not realize what I was doing. I was so eager to help the family, and I did by referring the girls for individual therapy and by helping them to identify resources (i.e., food stamps, clothing, etc.) that eased the stress on the family, that I allowed myself to become the family's advocate rather than their IFPS counselor. Social workers often assume the role of advocate; however, in a family system as chaotic as this one was, it was more appropriate and most important for me to remain objective and stay focused on whether or not this was a safe situation for the girls.

When my six weeks expired, I approached my supervisor about a six-week extension. We were occasionally allowed to extend our services if we could document that the family was still in crisis and the children were still at risk. The extension was necessary because I had allowed myself to be "hooked" into the family story very early on, that they were all victims–for many different reasons. I did not empower the girls or the family during the first three weeks of service, and soon discovered that some of the things the family had been telling me were not verifiable and in some cases were flat out false. My supervisor agreed to give me six more weeks to work with the family and determine if the girls could remain in the home. It was very difficult to switch from an "advocate" role in which the

family viewed me as "being on their side" back to the objective IFPS counselor role. It confused the family that I was now asking them more tough questions instead of just listening to their many stories about how "evil" the biological mother was and how so many of their problems could be attributed to her actions.

Eventually, I recommended that the girls be placed in a foster home. While there was no physical evidence of sexual abuse, the chaotic family situation was contributing to the girls' low self-esteem and self-destructive behaviors. The girls continued to maintain that they were never sexually abused by their grandfather, but several years later I discovered that the girls had in fact admitted that two of them had been sexually abused by him. I was relieved to know that I had recommended they be removed from the situation and grateful that I had learned a very important lesson—when working with family systems my role was to remain objective, professional, and empathic. My role was not to be their "friend" which ultimately only reinforced and validated their victim mentality and their rationalizations for the chaos in their lives. Working with a family system is very different from working with an individual client because the dynamics are much more complex. I found the work of IFPS very challenging and rewarding, and I am grateful that while I made mistakes, I was able to "right the ship" and stay on course. The ultimate lesson for me was that when dealing with chaotic family systems it is critical to remain in the role of an outside observer, otherwise, you may be "sucked in" to the family dynamic without even realizing that it is happening.

Family social workers typically intervene with families in their homes or communities and focus their interventions on concrete needs and improving daily living. This differs from family therapy, which is a specialized type of clinical practice. Family therapy approaches tend to be insight oriented, focus on interpersonal behaviors, and explore unresolved conflicts and multigenerational issues. Models of family therapy include psychodynamic, functional, experiential, strategic, and cognitive-behavioral, all of which have an established body of literature and theoretical foundation. The current focus of family therapy includes topics such as family resiliency, alternative forms of family life today, gender, culture, and ethnic considerations (Goldenberg & Goldenberg, 2007).

E-Therapy   The preponderance of Internet connections and social service–related websites have led to the development of **e-therapy**, or cybertherapy—therapy or support delivered electronically (Finn, 2002). There has been increasing interest in e-therapy, likely due to improvements in technology, affordability of technology, and increasing comfort with technology for communication (Bischoff, 2004). About 500 to 1,000 therapists were estimated to be on line in 2000, providing counseling and therapy to over 10,000 clients (Kicklighter, 2000). Determining exact numbers is difficult. It is estimated that between 5,000 and 25,000 e-mail messages are sent a day in on-line counseling sessions (Finn, 2002). At this point, e-therapy primarily consists of the exchange of written communications through asynchronous e-mail messages or of live chat sessions with a therapist (Rochlen, Zack, & Speyer, 2004). Web-camera technology and videoconferencing are becoming more readily available and affordable, and visual and voice contact between the therapist and the client may soon replace written exchanges.

The benefits of e-therapy include the elimination of access, time, and transportation barriers. Some people, especially those with verbal communication difficulties, are less inhibited and more effective at communicating on the Internet (Finn, 2001). Because people can receive help easily and anonymously on line, people who might not otherwise seek treatment may be willing to use on-line services (Banach & Bernat, 2000).

However, the limitations, potential harm, and ethical and legal issues surrounding e-therapy are daunting. For example, how can a couple in need of professional intervention find a licensed e-therapist with the appropriate experience and skills for couples counseling? How well can an on-line therapist perform an assessment of the couple without the benefit of verbal and visual cues? What effect will their typing abilities have on the therapy process? Are there contingency plans in case of technology failures? How does the therapist protect the clients' privacy and security on line? Since electronic mail can become part of a permanent record on a computer's hard drive, how can the therapist protect e-mail communications? How does the therapist know who and where the client really is? These and many other questions about e-therapy have not yet been fully answered (Heinlen, Welfel, Richmond, & Rak, 2003).

To date, few studies examining the effectiveness of e-therapy with individuals and families have been conducted. Of those that have, most have found on-line therapy to be effective in reducing symptoms and improving intimate partner relationships (Rachlen, Zack, & Speyer, 2004). Over time, e-therapy may become an effective social work intervention method, or at least a supplement to face-to-face interactions, but it is too early to tell whether computer-mediated therapy is here to stay or is only a passing fad. For now, social work practitioners who want to practice e-therapy need to concentrate on producing research that can help identify the type of clients who could benefit from it and in what types of situations it is most appropriate.

ETHICAL CHALLENGES IN WORKING WITH INDIVIDUALS AND FAMILIES

In working with individuals and families, the social work practitioner is faced with numerous ethical challenges. The Code of Ethics requires social workers to follow procedures to guarantee confidentiality, ensure informed consent, and provide services that are helpful and do no harm. Sometimes those requirements are difficult to meet. For example, what if a client confides that she is planning to commit suicide? Do you keep that between you and the client and not warn others? Or what if a client confides that he is aware of a child who has been physically abused? If you are confident of the veracity, you are required to report such knowledge to protect the child.

When social workers guarantee confidentiality, they do so with some limits, and those limits are to safeguard the client and other people. A social worker is required by legal decree to divulge information in a court of law. Although confidentiality is part of social workers' conduct, it has limits, and clients need to understand these limits.

There are other ethical dilemmas. One of the strongest criticisms of individual practice is that it strives to change the individual rather than the social environment. Critics argue that it provides symptom relief and does not solve social problems. For example, should a social worker try to help a person deal with personal stress that results from poverty or should the social worker try to end poverty? The demands of individual work often take precedence over working to change the environment. Ethically, social workers have a mandate to concern themselves with both.

Ethical good conduct is also the foundation of being aware of one's own practice limitations. In this section we have briefly described numerous modes of intervention that require extensive training. Insight-oriented therapies rely on sophisticated understandings of psychology and human behavior and hours of specialized supervised instruction. Although BSW and MSW programs provide quality training and education, additional postgraduate training is essential for advanced clinical interventions. Social workers have an ethical obligation to practice within their abilities and not to try techniques in which they are not fully trained.

SOCIAL WORK WITH GROUPS

Group membership is part of most people's lives. Children are socialized early in life to participate in groups. Some groups are informal; others have rules, regulations, and membership criteria.

Social work practice often relies on groups to provide services and assist people in their day-to-day living. These groups tend to be formal and are created for a specific purpose. Formal groups can provide opportunities for socialization, can serve numerous clients simultaneously, and can expand insight as people reflect on their

| BOX 5.4 | ETHICAL PRACTICE ... DOING TWO THINGS AT ONCE? |

According to the Code of Ethics (see Appendix A) a social worker's primary goal is to help people in need. The code also tells us that social workers are supposed to "challenge social injustice." Can you describe ways in which you would primarily work with individual clients, but at the same time address social problems and challenge social injustice? Can you do both?

interactions with others. Therefore, part of social work training involves understanding the functions and processes of various kinds of groups and learning to work with them.

One way to categorize groups is by their purpose. Groups differ according to their goals—the reasons people join together. Although formal groups are usually formed for a specified purpose, that purpose can change over time. Groups can also fulfill more than one objective and thus have more than one purpose. In general, the purposes of social work groups are socialization, education, therapeutic, or performance of tasks.

SOCIALIZATION

The purpose of **socialization groups** is to help participants "learn social skills and socially accepted behavior patterns so they can function effectively in the community" (Toseland & Rivas, 2001, p. 27). These groups are usually centered around program activities in which interpersonal skills are emphasized. Socialization groups can also help reduce social isolation by bringing people together for a shared purpose, as singles groups and senior center recreation groups do.

Socialization groups can include a variety of activities ranging from informal recreation to skill building for a specific purpose. For example, a community center youth group that meets after school might have recreation as its expressed purpose. However, while the young people are participating in recreation activities, they are also being guided by group leaders to learn how to interact with peers, mediate differences, and cooperate.

EDUCATIONAL GROUPS

Many professionals are involved in using groups to help people learn new information and skills. Social workers use **educational groups** to impart information and train people in needed skills. Training, workshops, and self-help groups are the major forms of educational groups.

Training Groups All sorts of life skills can be taught through group training. Examples include job skills and foster-parenting skills. Training groups typically last for a predetermined number of sessions. They use learning materials that are prepared specifically to impart information about the topic. The group leader is knowledgeable and serves as the teacher. Because participants share the goal of learning the material, participants may develop ongoing relationships.

Workshops The workshop format is similar to a training group in that it is centered around learning a specific skill or topic and is led by a trained leader. Workshops tend to last over a shorter period of time than education groups, usually one or two sessions. Participants usually come expressly to learn the information and do not develop ongoing relationships.

Self-Help Self-help groups have become popular over the past twenty years. Their goal is to bring together people who share a specific need, problem, or concern so as to provide social and emotional support. Guidance in behavior is also a goal of self-help groups. Alcoholics Anonymous is one of the best-known self-help efforts. All members of the group identify themselves as recovering alcoholics, and participants take turns in leadership roles and act as mentors to one another.

The guiding principle of these groups is that participants share a personal involvement in the concern and usually eschew professional leadership in favor of lay leadership. While social workers do not usually have a professional role in self-help groups, they are an important part of the social service network of resources. It is useful for social workers to be aware of the services available through self-help groups in order to refer clients to them.

THERAPEUTIC GROUPS

Groups that share the purpose of psychological intervention to address internal concerns are called **therapeutic groups**. Group therapy stresses interventions that help people "who have emotional disorders or social maladjustment problems by bringing together two or more individuals under the direction of a social worker or other professional therapist" (Barker, 1999, p. 203). Therapeutic group work requires specialized training in therapy and group process as well as skill in facilitating people's interactions to develop insight and socially desirable behaviors. There are three basic types of therapeutic groups: psychotherapy, counseling, and support groups.

Psychotherapy Groups   The goal of a psychotherapy group is to "help individual group members remediate in-depth psychological problems. Group members have acute or chronic mental or emotional disorders that evidence marked distress, impairment in functioning, or both" (Corey & Corey, 2002, p. 15). Psychotherapy groups are typically used in conjunction with inpatient or outpatient treatment of people with severe mental illness.

The group becomes the forum for analyzing maladaptive social behaviors that are exhibited by participants. Group members assist the leader by observing behaviors and trying to intervene to help each person express deep feelings, gain insight, and alleviate emotional distress. The hoped-for outcome is for participants to develop socially positive behaviors. The group serves as the context for members to practice those behaviors with the goal of using them in everyday life. The role of the group leader is to use psychotherapeutic skills in a group context. This involves a fluidity between guiding individuals and facilitating a group as a trained psychotherapist.

Counseling Groups   Although both use therapeutic interventions, counseling groups differ from psychotherapy groups in that they emphasize overcoming the problems of daily living, not addressing major personality changes or severe psychological and behavioral disorders (Corey & Corey, 2002). An example of a counseling group is a group for children of divorced parents. The children discuss their feelings about their parents' divorces and examine how to successfully reestablish their daily routines. The goal is positive adaptation to the divorce by exploring all the feelings that the child may have. Another example is a women's group for survivors of sexual abuse. The purpose of the group is to explore the effect of past sexual abuse on their current lives and improve their lives through better insight and empowerment.

Support Groups   The underlying goal of most groups is to support the individual in a collective of other people. Support groups specialize in this. Although these groups involve the expression of feelings and improving daily living, their primary goal is to support people through a difficult time. Support groups are typically used with people who are in crisis and need help in facing it. There are crisis support groups for people surviving the death of a spouse or family member, dealing with divorce, and facing a severe illness. For example, although parents who have lost a child may benefit from individual treatment for grief and depression, they may also find solace and comfort among others who understand their feelings from firsthand experience. Such a support group can be an excellent resource for parents trying to find ways to manage the crisis.

TASK-CENTERED GROUPS

Groups that are concerned with organizational and social change fall into the category of **task-centered groups**. People are often involved in task-centered groups in their places of employment, as members of organizations, in community and political organizing, and in raising social awareness. Sometimes social workers serve as professional leaders, while at other times social workers are active members of task-centered groups. The most common task-centered groups are committees, work teams, and groups effecting social change.

Committees   Most volunteer organizations, whether social, religious, or political in purpose, use committees to accomplish goals, offer activities, and provide services. For example, a religious organization may have a membership and recruitment committee responsible for bringing in new members and tracking current ones; a fundraising committee responsible for raising money; and a social activities committee for planning outings and events. People join the organization because they share goals and values, and they volunteer to participate on the committees to ensure that the work of the organization is accomplished. In some organizations paid professionals lead the committees. Places of employment also use committees, but all members are paid employees, so these groups tend to operate more like work teams.

Work Teams   As a condition of employment, social workers may be required to participate in groups to provide services or accomplish organizational tasks. For example, a mental health agency may ask for volunteers or assign workers to a team to develop a questionnaire to poll clients about their satisfaction with services. This team meets during regular business hours, uses agency resources, and is part of workers' paid employment. Even if involvement is an additional assignment and members must spend their own time on it, the requirement that they participate is part of their workload. Hence, this task-centered group is a work team.

Social Action Groups   Group social action is often used to achieve social change. Social action groups, also referred to as grassroots efforts, are often used by community organizers. Therefore, the roles of group worker and community organizer intersect in social change groups.

The goal of social change groups is to organize local constituencies so that people "see themselves as powerful, that changes must occur on significant substantive

BOX 5.5	WHAT DO YOU THINK?

What kind of problems or concerns would you rather discuss in a group than individually with a social worker? Why? Are there types of groups that feel more useful to you? Which ones, and why? When and under what circumstances might you refer a friend to participate in a group?

issues, and that power must be redistributed" (Mondros & Wilson, 1994, p. 229). While the organizer is active in maintaining the group, he or she works behind the scenes. The members make decisions, speak publicly, choose strategies, and chair meetings. The organizer serves as a facilitator of the group process, helping to ensure that the members can achieve the goal of social change through their own efforts and empowerment.

ETHICAL CHALLENGES IN WORKING WITH GROUPS

Confidentiality is the biggest ethical challenge in working with groups. To what extent are people free to discuss information shared during sessions outside the group? If one of the purposes of the group is for members to share intimate feelings and past experiences, how should that information be handled by participants? When groups meet in public settings, as when a support group for recovering drug users meets in a community center where recreation groups also meet, it is difficult to guarantee confidentiality.

Group workers have an obligation to discuss confidentiality with group members and to help the group define what should remain confidential (Pollio, Brower, & Galinsky, 2000). While the social worker leading a group can never guarantee that each group member will abide by the rules set by the group, it is the social worker's ethical responsibility to ensure that the group discusses confidentiality and develops guidelines.

Another ethical challenge for group workers is to determine when to interact with group participants on an individual level. Sometimes group members seek out the professional for private intervention. Some groups can tolerate this, and others cannot. Individual attention may raise anxiety among group members and be seen as preferential treatment. It is important for group workers to set the boundaries of interaction with all the group members. The rules of the group need to be clarified from the beginning.

Safety is critical for group success. Participants need to know that they are free to share sensitive and personal information without having to deal with negative responses to their feelings. This requires cultural sensitivity. At the same time, participants should not be allowed to share feelings that express prejudice or are hurtful to another member. Group workers cannot always ensure appropriate sharing, but setting rules of conduct with the group from the beginning and providing guidelines to create a safe environment are important.

COMMUNITY PRACTICE

The term *community practice* encompasses a number of different methods, all of which are focused on creating change in the social environment. These methods include organizing, planning, development, and change (Weil, 2004). **Community organizing** is the process of bringing people together to work for needed change. **Community planning** involves collecting data, analyzing a situation, and developing strategies to move from a problem to a solution. **Community development** is the process of helping individuals improve the conditions of their lives by increased involvement in the social and economic conditions of their communities. **Community change** is the desired outcome, whether it means adding needed services, shifting the balance of power from the haves to the have-nots, reducing isolation, or developing and implementing more effective policies. Community practitioners are involved in recruiting community members, identifying community strengths and problems, planning change efforts, developing strategies and tactics needed to carry out change efforts, raising needed resources, and evaluating their efforts.

Communities can be made up of groups of people with common characteristics or interests or of people living in the same geographic area. Weil and Gamble (1995) suggest the following reasons for social work involvement in community practice:

1. Improving the quality of life for community residents
2. Advocating for a community of interest, for a specific issue, for the establishment of political and social rights, and for additional resources
3. Increasing participation, building grassroots leadership, and strengthening communities socially and economically
4. Establishing or improving needed services
5. Developing better integrated and coordinated services locally, nationally, and internationally
6. Building political power, improving access and opportunity for marginalized people, and increasing their participation
7. Fighting for social justice to increase equality and opportunity across race, class, gender, and other lines

Although most social work practitioners concentrate on interventions with individuals and small groups, the problems that social workers confront cannot be adequately addressed by this type of work alone. To begin to solve the immense problems that confront us, such as poverty, homelessness, oppression, hunger, child abuse, and domestic violence, to name just a few, social workers must engage community members in social change efforts. Without this step, the problems society faces will continue to worsen and the suffering of social work clients will continue to increase. Consider the reasons for organizing as described in "More About ... The Goals of Organizing." By focusing on changing the social environment, community practice brings hope to those who are locked out of the mainstream of society and thus works toward ensuring social justice.

| BOX 5.6 | MORE ABOUT ... THE GOALS OF ORGANIZING |

Somewhere in the deep south, on the road that runs from New Orleans to Atlanta, an 80 year old woman is living alone in a shack by the roadside. If you are driving along that road, you can sometimes see her going painfully along in the long grass beside the highway. She is looking for the drink bottles the motorists throw out the windows of their cars as they go past at 70 miles an hour. Tomorrow a child will come by her shack to collect the bottles and bring them to the grocery downtown and will bring the 5 cents a bottle she gets back to the old woman to buy food.

Or if you were walking the dirt streets of a town not far from there, you might have seen a child playing in the road. He is throwing his toy into the air, chasing it, picking it up and throwing it again. You come closer. It is a dead bird.

Make no mistake. Organizing is not just about strategies, about analyses, about tactics. Organizing is about people, about the old woman with her drink bottles and the child with his dead bird. Organizing is about the 'welfare cheats' the 'deadbeats' the 'punks'—everyone else this society locks out and shuts in.

What would she or he say, that famous poor person the 'leaders' of this country so often talk about, and so rarely talk with, if given the chance to speak?

That I needed a home, and you gave me food stamps.

That I needed a job, and you got me on welfare.

That my family was sick, and you gave us your used clothes.

That I needed my pride and dignity as a human being, and you gave me surplus beans.

Let us not forget, when we talk of violence, that the death of a young mother in childbirth is violent, that the slow starvation of the mind and body of a child is violent. Let us not forget that hunger is violent, that pain is violent, that oppression is violent, that early death is violent. And that death of hope is the most violent of all.

The organizer brings hope to the people.

Source: Kahn, 1994, pp. 131–132.

ROLES

Social work practitioners take on a variety of roles when working with communities. These roles include community organizer, community planner, advocate, researcher/evaluator, fundraiser, and trainer/teacher.

Community organizers bring people in a community together to work toward some type of social change. They work with existing groups or help form new groups that utilize the strengths or assets of community members to create needed change.

Community planners work with communities, agencies, or government entities to understand problems and develop appropriate plans of action.

Social workers at all levels of practice are involved in **advocacy**. Advocacy means pleading the cause of another or, put more simply, speaking up and supporting what one believes in. At the community level, social workers are generally involved in advocating for funds and services with and for community members. They are also involved in legislative advocacy for changes in laws or policies.

Conducting research as a community practitioner means facilitating the research or evaluation effort. The researcher involves all those who are affected by the concern, program, or need using principles of democratic participation. Rather than serving as an outside expert, the community researcher provides guidance to meet the goals of finding information and effecting change. This approach is referred to as action research or critical action research (Stringer, 2007). Through the research process, the subjects of the research are also often participants and are involved in data collection, analysis, and reporting findings. The most vital component of community action research is that the findings lead to community change.

Community social workers are often involved in raising money to support community change efforts. They conduct research and write grants to receive money from government sources and private and corporate foundations. Organizing and implementing grassroots fundraising efforts, including raffles, concerts, and sales events, are also common activities at the community practice level.

Social workers have skills that can help community members more effectively work together to create change. They are often involved in helping community members learn to recruit, strategize, work with the media, raise resources, and join together in coalitions.

MODELS OF COMMUNITY PRACTICE

Practitioners can use a number of approaches or models to create community change (Homan, 2007; Weil & Gamble, 1995). A model gives practitioners a framework that guides them in determining how best to approach a situation within a specific community. It provides guidelines about the roles practitioners should take, how power comes into play in the change effort, the target of the change effort, who becomes involved in creating change, and the types of issues that are addressed. The common thread that joins all of the models is that each is aimed at creating community-level change.

Neighborhood and Community Organizing   When people hear the term *community practice,* they often think of community organizing. Neighborhood and community organizing is the process of bringing members of a geographic community together to create power in numbers. Practitioners organize residents to act on their own behalf, developing local control and empowerment. This type of organizing has an external and an internal focus. The external focus is on accomplishing specific tasks, whereas the internal focus is on helping members build their capacity for future organizing efforts.

Group goals can vary widely. They may include improving neighborhood safety by adding streetlights, stop signs, or increased police patrols. Some groups lobby to change local, state, or national policies, whereas others fight for new services for their communities. The internal focus of neighborhood and community organizing is on helping members develop the knowledge base and skills necessary to be effective in their external pursuits. This means working with residents to develop their skills in the areas of leadership, problem analysis, planning, resource development, strategic analysis, and evaluation. Social work roles in this model include organizer, teacher, facilitator, and coach.

Functional Organizing   Functional organizing is similar to neighborhood and community organizing, but the focus is on recruiting people with similar interests or concerns rather than on recruiting people in the same geographic location. The aim is still to bring like-minded people together to shift the balance of power and advocate for needed change. Examples of functional communities include people concerned about the environment, treatment of children, health care for the poor, domestic violence, and discrimination based on race, ethnicity, gender, sexual orientation, class, age, or mental or physical ability.

As in neighborhood and community organizing, the aim in functional organizing is on creating external change and building internal capacity. Organizing efforts focus on advocating for a specific issue or population and are often aimed at policy change, service development, and community education. Practitioner roles include organizer, teacher, advocate, and facilitator.

Community Social and Economic Development   Community social and economic development strives to empower and improve the lives of low-income, marginalized, and oppressed people by bringing residents together to become more involved in the social and economic lives of their communities. The goals of this model include improving education, leadership, and political skills within the community and improving the economic health of a community. The latter is achieved by enlisting the support of government entities, banks, foundations, and developers to invest in the community. This approach differs from other economic development approaches in that the community members are involved in each step of the process. Community members assess their community, determine what its needs are, develop a plan for change, and help with the implementation of the plan.

Community social and economic development efforts focus on housing development, job training, business development, and such support services as child care, education, and transportation. Practitioner roles include planner, teacher, manager, promoter, and negotiator.

Social Planning   Social planning is a rational problem-solving process in which planners look at communities and available resources and create plans to develop, expand, coordinate, and implement services. The social planning process takes place at the local and regional levels. Social planning has traditionally been conducted by outside experts. These experts study the community and make recommendations about needed changes, often with little or no input from community members.

While planning is still often done in this manner, community groups are increasingly demanding involvement. They are tired of outsiders coming in and telling them what is right for their community. Thus, community groups are gaining access to the planning process nationwide. Social work roles in the social planning process include planner, researcher, manager, proposal writer, and negotiator.

Program Development and Community Liaison   The purpose of program development is the creation of a new service or expansion of an existing service or program to meet community needs. The process involves conducting a needs assessment, planning new services specifically designed to meet community needs, and implementing and evaluating those services. To be effective, the program development process should include input from all those who will be affected by the new program. This includes current clients, potential clients, agency staff, community leaders, and community residents. Practitioner roles include planner, proposal writer, mediator, facilitator, and liaison with the community.

Political and Social Action   The political and social action model focuses on helping citizens gain political power and a voice in the decision-making process. The aim of this model is to increase social justice by pressuring political and corporate leaders to replace harmful policies or practices with ones that benefit disadvantaged and low-income groups. The model attempts to increase participatory democracy by engaging citizens who have traditionally been left out of the process. It also tries to "challenge inequalities that limit opportunities, confront decision makers who have ignored community needs, dispute unjust decisions, and empower people through strengthening their belief in their own efficacy and developing their skills to change unjust conditions" (Weil & Gamble, 1995, p. 587).

Public and elected officials and corporate leaders are often the targets of political and social action campaigns. These include efforts to stop corporations from polluting the air and water in low-income communities, to increase funding for education or social services, to pass legislation to require stiffer penalties for hate crimes, and to elect a legislator who supports progressive causes to replace one who supports policies that harm low-income and marginalized groups. Practitioner roles include advocate, organizer, educator, and researcher.

Coalition Building   Coalitions are formed when separate groups come together to work collectively on an issue of concern. Joining a coalition allows groups to increase their power base and available resources while at the same time maintaining their autonomy. Most groups do not have the number of people or the resources necessary to create large-scale change on an issue. However, when a number of groups join together, their combined membership is large enough and strong enough to influence policy and demand additional resources.

Coalitions usually focus on a single issue and are often time limited. They may join together to support or oppose a specific piece of legislation or to address a common problem. For example, a neighborhood may be targeted as the location of a new factory. Different groups may come together to oppose it—the PTA because the factory will be built near a school, an environmental rights group because members are concerned that the factory will emit pollutants, or a labor group because the factory owners are against unionization.

Coalitions present a number of interesting challenges to community practitioners. Groups that join together may agree on one issue, yet disagree on many others. There may be tensions over who gets to make decisions, who speaks for the group, how resources are divided, and what direction the coalition should take. Social work practitioners often take on the roles of mediator and negotiator to help keep coalitions together. A practitioner may also act as a spokesperson and teacher.

Whichever approach practitioners decide to use, to be effective in community practice they must have a strong understanding of the population with whom they are working and of their own biases, strengths, and challenges. They must also have good interpersonal and critical thinking skills, and a lot of patience, persistence, and passion.

ETHICAL CHALLENGES IN WORKING WITH COMMUNITIES

Community practitioners face a number of unique ethical challenges. Some of the biggest challenges come in the form of the process or product debate. As mentioned earlier, many efforts to create social change focus on both internal capacity building (process goals) and external task accomplishment (product goals). Process goals involve working with group members to help them improve their skills and become increasingly self-sufficient. Achieving these goals takes time, and tension can result from trying to build the capacity of members and trying also to achieve an external goal.

Social work values stress the importance of client self-determination. This suggests the importance of process goals, which help community members develop skills that let them take more control over their lives. Yet communities often have limited time available to address an issue of great concern. For example, a city council is planning to close a neighborhood elementary school that predominantly serves low-income students of color. Residents believe that sending their children to schools elsewhere in the city will be harmful. Action needs to be taken quickly, for the school is scheduled to be closed in less than two months. The organizer can put together a protest event and notify the media and the public in a short period of time. This would meet the product goal. Meeting the process goal requires the residents to themselves take on many or all of the tasks so that they will learn skills to increase their self-determination and continue the work in the future. However, because they have not done these tasks before, it will likely take the residents much longer to accomplish them, possibly threatening the product goal.

Community practitioners need to find ways to balance both the process and the product goals of a group. This can be done by addressing process goals as a first priority when a group is formed. Social workers can conduct training sessions to pass on the skills needed to do effective community work, spend time on leadership development, and address internal group conflicts as they arise. If these issues are addressed early and consistently, group members are prepared to take on necessary roles when the need arises.

A second ethical challenge common in community work is the conflict between individual and community rights and responsibilities. Although the community practitioner values the autonomy and rights of an individual resident based on the values of self-determination and freedom, individual autonomy sometimes threatens the rights of others in the community. For example, a resident who likes to collect things has a house and yard filled with belongings that he treasures, but his neighbors see his belongings as junk. Neighbors worry that the house and yard are a fire hazard and that they make the street look less desirable, therefore lowering the property value of their houses.

Differences over whose rights take precedence come up frequently in community practice settings. Practitioners must have strong mediation and negotiation skills to help people reach a compromise in such situations. If compromise cannot be reached, they must also be able to consider the ethical questions involved and critically weigh the two sides against the backdrop of the social work Code of Ethics. Using the principle of the most good for the most people can be one helpful way to reach a decision in many situations.

INTERNATIONAL SOCIAL WORK

Social workers have drawn on the knowledge and practice of others across international boundaries since the earliest days of the profession. Jane Addams was inspired by what she saw at Toynbee Hall in England and used their work to guide her in the development of the settlement residence of Hull House in Chicago in the 1800s. Social workers today see clients from all over the world due to immigration and the United States long serving as a refuge for people fleeing dangerous conditions in their countries of origin. The Council on Social Work Education emphasizes a global perspective in its Educational Policy and Accreditation Standards (CSWE, 2008).

Interest in the global context of social work practice has grown in recent years. Schools of social work are allowing students to do fieldwork overseas, sponsoring international study tours, conducting research internationally, and promoting cross-border collaborations (Leggett, 2008). The reality of our global culture is that today's social worker needs to expand his or her cultural awareness and sensitivity. When working with someone from a different culture, there are numerous factors to consider. Those details are discussed in Chapter 6. Being an international social worker includes more than the understanding of an individual's culture. It emphasizes learning about social welfare conditions in other parts of the world and what those conditions might mean for conditions here in the United States.

CONCLUSION

This chapter provides an overview of the multiplicity of interventions that social workers use. It is important to remember that while we discussed each separately for educational purposes, the modes of intervention are dynamic and fluid. Social workers blend approaches and levels of intervention depending on the need and situation. A social worker may be identified as a micropractitioner but still interact with groups and work toward change on the community level. A community organizer's work involves groups and individuals, so he or she needs the skills appropriate for those levels of intervention. Your social work training will include numerous approaches to practice on all levels. The experience of training and specializing in one area of practice does not always dictate the direction that social workers take over time. Consider the practice blend faced by the social worker in "From the Field ... Social Work Takes Many Forms of Practice." Integration of practice across the individual, group, and community levels is in the box "Becoming a Change Agent." You are asked to test your understanding of the connection between the various social work modes of practice.

BOX 5.7	FROM THE FIELD ... SOCIAL WORK TAKES MANY FORMS OF PRACTICE
	Diane McEachern, LCSW

Upon graduation from my MSW program I accepted a position as a school social worker in remote western Alaska. Shortly after arriving in Bethel, Alaska, I decided that I needed to move out to a rural village and immerse myself in the culture of the region rather than remain based in Bethel. I was determined to break away from a relationship with villages in which I was the "expert" who flies in every week or two, sees children within the school and then leaves. I wanted my work to have a deeper connection and relevance in terms of community organizing and cross-cultural collaboration. With Jane Addams on my shoulder, I made the move to a small village. My, at times breathtaking, break from conventional social work practice began.

My first three years in western Alaska were spent living in Kwethluk (pop. 650), a small Yup'ik Eskimo village. At the time I was their school social worker. While I did travel to other assigned villages, more time was spent with Kwethluk. Working with children K–12 within the school building quickly became unsatisfying. I knew that children essentially bring their family and their community with them to school every day. Taking to heart that realization, I began to extend my social work practice out of the school and into the community focusing first on families. I sat at many kitchen tables eating dried fish dipped in seal oil listening to parents tell me about their children. One of the first questions I would ask a parent was, "What would you like the school to always remember about your child?" I would also ask the parent to share with me a story from when their child was a baby. Parents' primary experience when hearing from the school was when their child was misbehaving. These two simple questions brought a noticeable relaxation and many times tender and culturally rich stories. Whenever parents grew angry with the school system or fearful of my role as an "outside" social worker, I would merely respond, "Tell me more; I want to understand better." I absorbed these conversations and worked them through my mind and work experiences with the intention of broadening my

understanding of not just cultural considerations but also the kinds of inevitable cultural changes that have been, at times, devastating to villages. Through ongoing dialogue with parents and extended families, a natural pathway developed for me to follow which led to working more closely with Kwethluk's own providers of social services.

I distinctly remember the day I walked to the end of the village where the small blue ramshackle Kwethluk social services building was. I walked in and there were a few people in their offices. They greeted me politely but remained somewhat cool and distant. I explained who I was and asked if we could all meet sometime to talk. I heartily suggested the day and time for us to meet, to which they cordially agreed. The next week on the day and time of the meeting I sat in the small blue building proud of the snacks I had remembered to bring but eating them alone. No one came. I was later told that they were in shock that the school social worker had actually come to their offices. That had never happened before and they had no idea how to interact with me. Yet the roles they played in their community were critical partners to my role. One was the community suicide prevention counselor, another was the youth outreach counselor and a third was the village alcohol education counselor. Within this particular school district of twenty-four K–12 village schools, we were about to create a collaborative cross-cultural work life that had not been tried anywhere else in the region.

We began a slow process of building rapport and trust with one another. Over time we decided we wanted to form a Kwethluk-based mental health collaborative team. We began outreach to those people in the village who could join our team. Two community health aides were selected by their peers to join the mental health team. An Elder joined the team as well. The village police officer agreed to periodically join if invited when we needed his expertise. After almost three years of deliberate but steady work, the Kwethluk mental health team consisted of 10 members who met regularly.

My autonomy had eventually given way to an alignment of my work with these key practitioners.

As our group grew we discussed often my role with the team in order to reduce any tendencies for dependency or disempowerment. Essentially, I asked them to design my skills, training and degrees to fit their needs. My stance was that those areas of my professional life did not belong solely to me but could be molded by them to best fit their needs. These discussions were vibrant and enlightening to all of us. One of the team members spoke about his surprise at both the idea and the real experience of my involvement being that of joining rather than ordering them or otherwise depositing information and expecting them to comply. Those meetings were full of good humor and teasing, a sure sign of connection with Yup'ik people. I remember one time when I was late for our weekly meeting. They called up to the school and insisted, "Where are you? We're all here!" I jokingly asked if I could get away with some "Yup'ik time" and they laughed and said that, in fact, no I could not because I was not Yup'ik. I was Western and as such I needed to maintain punctuality a standard they in turn were not as wedded to. When I arrived to the meeting one of the men with false seriousness and in front of everyone began to gently inform me of why I was not Yup'ik and would never be Yup'ik. Everyone found this incredibly funny and enjoyed my red face and helpless smile. It was an interesting and fresh insight to me that no one wanted me to be Yup'ik. They had good reason to want me to be the Westerner that I am.

Alaska ranks near or at the top in per capita rates of domestic violence, child sexual abuse and suicide in the nation. Tribal communities throughout Alaska have the highest rates within the state. Kwethluk's mental health team realized they needed to find a way to have what would be difficult discussions about these sensitive social issues. In a small rural native community it would be uncomfortable and inappropriate for people to talk openly about such sensitive topics. Without doubt the individual team members had all been impacted by these tragic kinds of events as well. Discussions would have to be done with great care and mindfulness of the historical and cultural context before moving slowly into planning how to work with the community. Our meetings together thus blended my social work clinical skills with those of an educator.

When we discussed my role at the meetings, they were clear that it was important for me to continue to facilitate the meetings. The team also wanted an education process and I needed to, at times, take the role of a teacher. As an "outsider" I could get away with bringing tough issues to the team for discussions. Our agreement was that if I would be willing to find a way to initiate dialogue they would participate in discussing what many found both frightening and shameful. They appreciated that as a Westerner, I could be more "blunt" and within the context and purpose of our meetings, this characteristic was valued. I realized that my "outsider" status was useful to them and they found a way to put it to work.

Reflecting on those first yeas, what I notice most was my plunge into an empowerment model of work within the community and the necessity to blend my skills as a social worker and an educator. I was not supervised in this nor was I guided in any way by the school district. As a matter of fact when I began making ties to the community leadership in another village that school's principal (who like most school personnel are from the lower 48) told me, "Remember who signs your paycheck ... the school district not the village." I met this attitude from outside school officials continually, and methodically worked out diplomatic strategies in order to follow my belief that 1:1 work with children within the school building was disjointed at best and woefully inadequate without links to family and community. The team in Kwethluk continued to guide me in this outreach and I carried that to my other assigned villages.

BOX 5.8 | BECOMING A CHANGE AGENT

The "Becoming a Change Agent" box in Chapter 1 discusses Hurricane Katrina. The hurricane caused all of New Orleans's levees to fail, resulting in massive flooding. The storm, combined with an inadequate government response, shattered hundreds of thousands of lives. It is estimated that as many as 150,000 mostly low-income people were in New Orleans when Katrina hit. At least 1,100 people were killed from the hurricane and subsequent flooding. Some argue that the death toll from Katrina continues to grow as medical and other types of services are still inadequate and people are dying from lack of appropriate services. Thousands of people lost their homes and all of their possessions. Additionally, people who survived Katrina have been experiencing high rates of mental health problems. Addressing the challenges that arose before, during, and after the hurricane has required use of all levels of social work skills. There has been tremendous need at the individual, family, small group, community, and policy levels.

Analyzing the Situation

Conduct research to find out how social workers and others have been involved in creating change at the individual, family, small group, community, and policy levels. Do you get a sense of whether most of the social work efforts have been at the micro or macro level or has it been split somewhat evenly? Which types of interventions have seemed most useful? Given limited resources, how do you think the money and time should have been spent in the post-Katrina period?

What Can Social Workers Do?

Given your analysis and your understanding of social work roles from this chapter, what might social workers do to prevent the tremendous suffering that resulted from Katrina from happening again? What interventions could you suggest at the individual level? The community level? The policy level, for example changes in local, state, or federal legislation?

What Can You Do?

What one step might you take now, alone or working with others, to help those still suffering from the aftermath of Katrina or to assist in preventing this level of suffering from happening somewhere else? What are the barriers?

Key Terms

advocacy, (p. 134)

assessment, (p. 116)

case management, (p. 120)

cognitive-behavioral therapies, (p. 124)

community change, (p. 133)

community development, (p. 133)

community organizing, (p. 133)

community planning, (p. 133)

crisis intervention, (p. 123)

direct services, (p. 119)

educational groups, (p. 129)

e-therapy, (p. 127)

generalist social work practice, (p. 114)

information and referral (I & R), (p. 117)

intake, (p. 116)

macro practice, (p. 115)

micro practice, (p. 115)

network linkages, (p. 119)

problem-solving method, (p. 122)

psychosocial treatment, (p. 122)

socialization groups, (p. 129)

task-centered groups, (p. 131)

task-centered social work, (p. 123)

therapeutic groups, (p. 130)

Questions for Discussion

1. Social work practice is often classified as either micro or macro. Explain what is meant by *micro practice* and *macro practice* and why addressing both micro and macro issues is essential to effective social work practice.
2. Compare two of the numerous theories that provide a foundation for social work interventions with individuals.
3. Social work practitioners play a variety of roles when working with communities. Provide examples of the types of activities engaged in by an advocate, an organizer, and a researcher/evaluator.
4. Describe an ethical challenge that might occur in (a) practice with individuals and families, (b) practice with groups, and (c) practice with communities.
5. Compare educational groups and therapeutic groups in terms of their purpose, size, leadership, role of the social worker, and outcome.

Change Agent Exercise

Looking at the problem you chose in Chapter 1, list possible approaches to solving the problem that a social worker might take. Try to come up with approaches at the micro level (working with individuals and families), mezzo level (working with small groups), and macro level (working with communities or creating legislative change). From what you already know and can find out from the Internet or talking to people involved in addressing the problem, are there attempts to solve the problem at all three levels in your community?

Chapter Exercises

1. **Providing Information and Referral**
   Locate an agency in your community that provides information and referral services, and answer the following questions about it:
   - How do people know about the agency?
   - Does the agency provide a directory of local services?
   - If the agency has a directory, does it include listings for organizations and groups that address problems in both micro and macro ways? If not, why do you think the directory does not include the missing information?
   - What strategies do you think the organization could employ to let more people know about its services?

2. **Contemporary Issues Journal**
   Find at least one current newspaper article that relates to material from this chapter.
   What is the article?
   Why did you choose it?
   Discuss how the article relates to the course material, what questions it brings up, what else you would like to know about the topic, and how you might find out the information.

3. **Understanding Systems Theory**

Your cousin, who is taking a sociology class, mentions that he does not understand what systems theory is. He wants to be a social worker, and you think it is important for him to understand the concept. Explain systems theory to your cousin, and tell him why systems theory provides an important foundation for social work practice. Meet with a classmate and compare your answers.

4. **Macropractice Ethics Exercise**

Complete the following either on your own or in small groups:

You are a social worker at a community center. You have spent the past eight months working with local residents to organize a neighborhood association. People are beginning to trust you and each other enough to be willing to work together on some of the hard issues that are challenging residents, and a project to clean up the area is under way. You begin to receive complaints about a man who has a lot of junk in his yard. Residents tell you that they are concerned about health hazards and the possibility that property values in the area will fall.

Your first step is to visit the man. His house is very run down and filled with stuff. You find out that the man is a widower with no family in the area. He collects and repairs old items and then tries to sell them. He has not sold much lately, so a lot of the items are in his yard. When you tell him about the complaints, he replies that he has been in the area more than sixty years, has never bothered anyone, and needs all this stuff to make a living.

List all the possible responses you can think of to address this dilemma. What are the pros and cons of each response?

What social work values are in conflict in the situation, and how can the Code of Ethics guide your decision?

5. **Generalist Social Work Dialogue**

You are having a conversation with two classmates. One believes that counseling people with problems is the only role that social workers should have. The other believes that organizing communities and engaging in legislative advocacy to create social change is the right role for social workers. Explain the concept of generalist social work practice to them. Tell them what you think the best role is for social work practitioners. List your responses. Meet with several classmates to compare responses and discuss the ideal role or roles for social work practitioners.

References

Banach, M., & Bernat, F. P. (2000). Liability and the Internet: Risks and recommendations for social work practice. *Journal of Technology in Human Services, 17,* 2/3, 153–171.

Barker, R. L. (1999). *The social work dictionary* (4th ed.). Washington, DC: NASW Press.

Bischoff, R. J. (2004). Considerations in the use of telecommunications as a primary treatment medium: The application of behavioral health to marriage and family therapy. *American Journal of Family Therapy, 32,* 173–187.

Compton, B., & Galaway, B. (1994). *Social work processes.* Pacific Grove, CA: Brooks/Cole.

Corey, M. S., & Corey, G. (2002). *Groups: Process and practice* (6th ed.). Pacific Grove, CA: Brooks/Cole.

CSWE. (2008). *Educational Policy and Accreditation Standards*. Alexandria, VA: Author.

Ell, K. (1996). Crisis theory and social work practice. In Turner, F. J. (ed.), *Social work treatment*. New York: Free Press.

Erickson, E. (1950). *Childhood and society*. London: Hogarth Press.

Finn, J. (2001). Ethics and liability issues in online human service practice. Paper presented at NASW-ARIZONA Annual Conference, October 4–5.

Finn, J. (2002). MSW Students Perceptions of the Efficacy and Ethics of Internet-Based Therapy. *Journal of Social Work Education, 38,* 3, 403–419

Freud, A. (1946). *The ego and mechanisms of defense*. New York: International Universities Press.

Glasser, W. (1965). *Reality therapy*. New York: Harper & Row.

Goldenberg H. & Goldenberg, I. (2007). *Family therapy: An overview*. Florence, KY: Brooks Cole.

Haynes, K. S. (1997). Information and referral services. In *Encyclopedia of social work* (19th ed.) (pp. 1464–1469). Washington, DC: National Association of Social Workers.

Heinlen, K. T., Welfel, E. R., Richmond, E. N., & Rak, C. F. (2003). The scope of Web counseling: A survey of services and compliance with NBCC standards for the ethical practice of Web counseling. *Journal of Counseling Development, 81,* 61–69.

Hepworth, D., Rooney, R. H., Rooney, G. D., Strom-Gottfried, K., & Larson, J. A. (2005). *Direct social work practice: Theory and skills*. Belmont, CA: Wadsworth Publishing.

Hollis, F. (1964). *Casework: A psychosocial therapy*. New York: Random House.

Homan, M. (2007). *Promoting community change: Making it happen in the real world*. Belmont, CA: Brooks/Cole.

Johnson, L. C., & Yanca, S. J. (2001). *Social work practice: A generalist approach* (7th ed.). Needham Heights, MA: Allyn & Bacon.

Kahn, S. (1994). *How people get power*. Washington, DC: NASW Press.

Kicklighter, K. (2000). www.sigmundreud.net; Psychotherapy has gone online—and critics say that's depressing. *Atlanta Journal Constitution*, July 25, p. lC.

Ledley, D. R., Marx, B. P., & Heimberg, R. G. (2007). *Making cognitive-behavioral therapy work: Clinical process for new practitioners*. New York: Guilford Press.

Leggett, K. (2008). Making a world of difference. *International Educator*, March/April, pp. 42–49.

Mondros, J. B., & Wilson, S. M. (1994). *Organizing for power and empowerment*. New York: Columbia University Press.

Parad, H. J., & Parad, L. G. (1990). Crisis intervention: An introductory overview. In Parad, H. J., & Parad, L. G. (eds.), *Crisis intervention book 2: The practitioners sourcebook for brief therapy*. Milwaukee, WI: Family Services of America.

Payne, M. (2004). *Modern social work theory* (3rd ed.). Chicago, ILL: Lyceum Books.

Perlman, H. H. (1957). *Social casework: A problem-solving process*. Chicago, ILL: University of Chicago Press.

Pollio, D. E., Brower, A. M., & Galinsky, M. J. (2000). Change in groups. In Allen-Meares, P., & Garvin, C. (eds.), *The handbook of social work direct practice* (pp. 281–300). Thousand Oaks, CA: Sage Publications.

Reid, W. J., & Epstein, L. (1972). *Task-centered casework*. New York: Columbia University Press.

Richmond, M. (1917). *Social diagnosis*. New York: Russell Sage Foundation.

Rochlen, A. B., Zack, J. S., & Speyer, C. (2004). Online Therapy: Review of Relevant Definitions, Debates, and Current Empirical Support. *Journal of Clinical Psychology, 60,* 3, 269–283.

Skinner, B. F. (1953). *Science and human behavior*. New York: Macmillan.

Stringer, E. T. (2007). *Action research* (3d ed.). Thousand Oaks, CA: Sage Publications.

Stoesen, L. (2008). Teaming up for case management. *NASW News, 53,* 4, 4.

Summary Report (2008). 21-1021.00 *Child, family, and school social workers.* http://online.onetcenter.org/link/summary/21-1021.00.

Toseland, R. W., & Rivas, R. F. (2001). *An introduction to group work practice.* (4th ed.). Boston: Allyn Bacon.

Turner, J., & Jaco, R. M. (1996). Problem-solving theory and social work treatment. In Turner, F. J. (ed.), *Social work treatment*. New York: Free Press.

Watson, J. B. (1914). *Behavior: An introduction to comparative psychology*. New York: Henry Holt.

Weil, M. (2004). *The handbook of community practice*. Thousand Oaks, CA: Sage Publications.

Weil, M., & Gamble, D. (1995). Community practice models. *Encyclopedia of social work* (19th ed.) (pp. 577–594). Washington, DC: National Association of Social Workers.

Weil, M., & Karls, J. (eds.). (1985). *Case management in human service practice*. San Francisco: Jossey-Bass.

Woods, M., & Hollis, F. (1990). *Casework: A psychological process* (2d ed.). New York: Random House.

WORKING WITH DIVERSE POPULATIONS

CHAPTER 6

Co-authored by Lynn Holley, Ph.D.

Heile Division of Cengage Learning

Every person is a member of multiple social groups. A social group is a "group of people who share a range of physical, cultural, or social characteristics within one of the categories of social identity" (Griffin, 1997, p. 70). People have many different characteristics, including gender, race, ethnicity, religion, ability, sexual orientation, social class, age, and national origin, as well as from the unique experiences they have had in the course of their lives. Membership groups often share ideologies, values, and behaviors that are shaped by their cultures and experiences. Social group memberships affect people's values, worldviews, attitudes, behaviors, and experiences.

An individual may identify strongly by gender, by ethnic background, or by religion. In other words, the individual is claiming a social identity. For example, a Catholic Latino man may be a member of a number of social groups—Catholic by religion, Mexican American or Chicano by ethnicity, and male by gender. He may live in a predominantly Latino community and be very involved in his church. Thus he considers his race or his ethnicity and religion to be the most significant characteristics of his day-to-day living, without giving much thought to gender. His religion and ethnic groups are important parts of his social identity, whereas his gender is not. People often pay attention to the social identities that differentiate them from most other people around them. For example, a white woman who had grown up poor and made her way into the position of chief executive officer of a large corporation might find herself in a situation where there are no other women or people of her socioeconomic background in management positions. She may not often notice her race as a social identity because she lives and works among people who are white, but gender and social class may be strong social identities for her.

Membership groups and social identity are important considerations when working with people. Social workers need to consider how they are influenced by their own social group memberships, how the people with whom they work identify themselves, what it means to each person to be part of a membership group, and how it feels to be excluded. Providing relevant and meaningful support to so many different people makes social work practice a challenge. What separates social workers from other helpers is the social workers' mandate to consider and respect all differences among the people with whom they work.

This chapter explores the importance of membership groups when working with people. It also looks at the diversity-related competencies that social workers need in order to be effective professionals.

SOCIAL CONSTRUCTION OF DIFFERENCES

People tend to attribute various characteristics to groups, believing, for example, that "all men are …" or "all women are…." These views are shared with others through language, stories, and interpretations. Although people see these images and beliefs as reality, they are actually socially constructed. **Social construction** takes place when the people who have power in a society define a group's characteristics and determine the group's value. Their perceptions of their own and other social groups are accepted by the larger society.

Americans tend to think of differences between social groups as facts of nature. For example, the anthropologist Jonathan Marks has discussed the historic designation of race as a "category of nature" (1994, p. 32), when in reality "the racial categories with which we have become so familiar are the result of our imposing arbitrary cultural boundaries in order to partition gradual biological variation" (p. 34). On the basis of new scientific knowledge from mapping the human genetic structure, the biological differences in race are not genetically discrete (Smedley & Smedley, 2005). In other words, society has constructed the concept of race, has created a finite number of racial categories based on certain physical characteristics, and has agreed that these socially constructed categories are biologically rather than culturally determined. Social construction means that people give meaning and values to the physical attribute of skin color. Are people substantially different because of skin color, or has a difference been socially created? How much "color" makes a person a member of a particular "race"? While the example above focuses on the social construction of race, the same is true of other characteristics that distinguish people from each other, including gender, sexual orientation, and class. Social construction theory contends that people create differences with ideas and values and that the differences are not based on physiological realities.

In the area of "race," as with many other socially constructed differences, the United States has a long history of determining that some "races" are more desirable than others. For instance, using the assumption that whites were superior to people of color, the U.S. government developed many policies to exclude people of color. These included denying people of color the rights to become naturalized citizens, to vote, to marry whites, and to own land. Employers who accepted this faulty assumption often paid lower wages to people of color or refused to hire them at all. People of color were prevented from moving into certain residential areas and were openly discriminated against in other ways. These overtly racist practices are now illegal, although some still occur.

Gender is also a social construction. That is, most of the differences attributed to sex are really the result of socially defined gender roles (Schmookler & Bursik, 2007). The culture has valued the characteristics attributed to males more than those attributed to females. For instance, auto mechanics (traditionally male) are generally paid more than child-care workers (traditionally female), although caring for children requires at least as many skills as repairing automobiles.

The dominant culture also has constructed sexual orientation as an important difference among individuals. Heterosexuality has been designated as "natural" and thus superior to homosexuality, which is perceived to be "unnatural" or deviant (Richardson, 2007).

One final example of a socially constructed difference is social class. The economic system has created and sustains distinctive class divisions, which are often viewed by people as inevitable. This social construction results in an unequal distribution of resources and power, with people who have more money and power considered to be superior to those who have less (Reay, 2007).

Social differences that today seem "normal" may change over time because they are socially constructed. For example, 100 years ago it was not socially acceptable for women to wear pants or to make investments in their own name because those were male-only privileges, yet today both are the norm. Until recent years, the perception was that a gay man was effeminate, but "manly" men have been publicly identified as gay (the actor Rock Hudson is an early example and the football player Esera Tuaolo is a more recent example). The supposed inferiority of Africans was socially constructed by whites, and this social construction was used as a justification for slavery and later for legally maintaining racial segregation. As a result of the enormous power of whites' social construction of African Americans as inferior, it took decades for activists to succeed in winning passage of civil rights legislation. The lesson is that commonly held beliefs about social groups are socially constructed and tend to reflect the dominant way of thinking, but they may be inaccurate and are subject to change.

DIVERSITY IN THE UNITED STATES

The constellation of communities and membership groups in the United States is tremendous. More than 300 million people reside in the United States. That number is expected to grow by more than 40 percent by 2050. Table 6.1 illustrates some of the racial and gender diversity and its projected growth.

The United States is a nation of various racial and ethnic groups. **Race** is considered an umbrella term that generally includes multiple **ethnic groups**, which are groups that share common cultural patterns or national origins. People who are descendants of Spanish-speaking ancestors are often racially grouped as Latino. There are Latino groups that strongly identify as Chicanos, Puerto Ricans, Cubans, or one of dozens of other ethnic groups, each with distinct and unique cultural characteristics. Thus, what is perceived as one group is often a collection of multiple ethnic groups with different cultural patterns and backgrounds.

Although 80 percent of the current U.S. population is categorized as white or Anglo, that percentage will be changing. As of 50 years ago the population was 90 percent white, but 50 years from now less than 75 percent of the population is expected to be categorized as white. The portion of the population that is of Latino origin is expected to double over the next 50 years, as well as the number of people who identify as Asian American. Although the English language will continue to dominate, other languages such as Spanish will most likely become more common. By 2008, the populations in four states (Hawaii, New Mexico, California, and Texas) and the District of Columbia were made up of more nonwhite or nondominant people than those who identify as white, from 52 to 75 percent (U.S. Bureau of the Census, 2008).

TABLE 6.1 | UNITED STATES POPULATION (IN THOUSANDS)

	2005	Projected for 2050	Percent Change
Total population	296,940	419,854	+41.4%
Gender			
Male	145,974	206,477	+41.4%
Female	150,534	213,377	+41.7%
Race			
White	237,885	302,626	+27.2%
Black	37,905	61,361	+61.9%
Hispanic	42,872	102,560	+139.2%
Asian	12,757	33,430	+162.1%

Source: U.S. Bureau of the Census, 2007.

TABLE 6.2 | POPULATION CHANGE BY AGE IN THE UNITED STATES

	Projected for 2050
Under 5 years	+46.1%
5–19 years	+32.2%
20–44 years	+25.8%
45–64 years	+49.1%
65–84 years	+113.8%
85 and over	+388.9%

Source: U.S. Bureau of the Census, 2004.

Age is another characteristic that will shift over the next 50 years. As Table 6.2 shows, the age of the population is increasing. Today, only 6 percent of the population is 75 years of age or older. In 50 years, the proportion will almost double, to over 11 percent. One out of three people will be 55 years or older by 2050. The portion of the population that is in their eighties will be four times as great as today by the year 2050. The aging of the population will place new demands on the social welfare system.

Until the past 20 years, sexual orientation was not regarded as a significant part of the diversity of the nation. However, the gay rights movement and subsequent public discussion about sexual orientation have brought to light the existence of a significant portion of the population who identify as lesbian, gay, bisexual, or transgender (LGBT). An accurate count of the number of LGBT people in this country does not exist. Studies estimate that anywhere from 1 to over 10 percent of the population may be gay or lesbian or have "exhibited some form of same gender sexuality based on their desire, sexual activity, or self-definition" (Lipkin, 1999, p. 8). The most commonly held estimate, based on the famous Kinsey report on sexuality (Kinsey, Pomeroy, & Martin, 1948; Kinsey, Pomeroy, Martin, & Gebhart, 1953), is that one in ten people is gay or lesbian (Hildago, Peterson, & Woodman, 1985).

Almost 40 million Americans live with some form of physical disability (U.S. Bureau of the Census, 2007). Disability can include a temporary injury that makes a person unable to work, a severe mental illness, and physical limitations of daily-living skills that may or may not allow a person to be employed. One of eight people has limited activity due to a chronic condition (U.S. Bureau of the Census, 2007). Regardless of the exact number, a sizable number of people with physical, developmental, or other limitations need to be recognized as members of distinct groups within social work practice. Advancing medical capabilities and longer life expectancies mean that more people will spend part of their lives with physical or cognitive disabilities, creating a greater need for services for and sensitivities to people living with disabilities.

In addition to variation in gender, race, ethnicity, sexual orientation, and physical ability, Americans have numerous religious affiliations, ideological beliefs, political affinities, mental and developmental abilities, national origins, and social ranks. There is no one typical American, although all have a place in the nation's social, economic, and political makeup. This vast diversity of people presents a challenge to social work practitioners as they strive to provide meaningful and relevant service.

HISTORICAL BACKGROUND

The diversity of the United States came about as the result of numerous forces and historical events. Some of the forces were positive, and some were negative; some of the events happened by design, and others were unanticipated. Vast numbers of people representing hundreds of cultures and identities found a home in the United States, creating the nation's vast diversity.

EXPLORATION AND COLONIZATION

Americans are proud that the United States came about through the courage and persistence of explorers. For example, Columbus Day honors the man credited with discovering this land for Europeans. Lewis and Clark are esteemed for exploring the Northwest Passage. The drive to explore the vast continent paved the way for settlement and population growth. Settlers followed the explorers, creating communities that reflected their behaviors, beliefs, and values.

The land that is now the United States was home to many nations before Columbus "discovered" it. The **colonization** of these First Nations was supported by the U.S. and the state governments, which passed laws that allowed, encouraged, or mandated forcing the indigenous peoples from their homes to provide land for white settlers. Entire nations were uprooted and moved to desolate lands, where they were often forced to live among other nations without any recognition of the vast cultural differences among them. Oppression, discrimination, and prejudice based on race also involved massacres by whites and decimation of native cultures. Children were forced to attend boarding schools where they had to forsake their cultures, including their religions, spiritual traditions, and languages, and learn to behave according to the dominant European-American culture.

FORCED RELOCATION AND ENSLAVEMENT

Not only were the First Nations forcibly relocated to unwanted and barely habitable land, but upward of a million Africans were ripped from their homes and families and shipped against their will to the American continent to be enslaved. Prior to the American Revolution, an estimated 1 million people of African descent were enslaved, making up almost 20 percent of the population in the American colonies. Enslaved women, men, and children endured tremendous brutality and were kept powerless by laws that shaped every facet of their lives. This included the loss of control over personal relationships and of economic freedom and the outlawing of the rights to gain access to education, to own land, and to vote and participate as citizens.

The impetus for the institution of slavery was primarily economic. Agriculture, particularly the cultivation and harvesting of tobacco and cotton, required numerous workers who could endure severe working conditions. Enslaving people of African descent provided a cheap source of labor. Slave laws were reinforced with race laws, thereby socially constructing an economic system that benefited the white landowners who controlled most of the wealth. By the time slavery was repealed in

1863, many generations had passed and people of African descent were far removed from their lands and cultures of origin.

EXPANSION INTO MEXICO

Believing that the United States was destined to extend westward across the continent (an ideology termed manifest destiny), white settlers continued to take lands from indigenous peoples as they migrated into what are now the states of Texas, New Mexico, Arizona, California, Utah, and Nevada in the Southwest. During the 1800s these areas were part of Mexico. In 1845, the government declared that Texas was part of the United States, which led to what U.S. history books call the Mexican-American War. At the conclusion of the war in 1848, the Treaty of Guadalupe Hidalgo ceded these territories to the United States (Day, 2006). Mexican citizens residing there were granted U.S. citizenship and the right to maintain their lands and cultures, but most lost their lands when these provisions were not enforced.

IMMIGRATION

From the time Europeans first settled on the American continent until 1965, most voluntary **immigration** was from Europe. Each migrating group experienced difficulties arising from leaving their homes, traveling to a new land, and adjusting to a new life. Some northern and western European immigrants, such as people from England and France, were immediately welcomed to the United States, while others, such as immigrants from Ireland and Italy, were not. In part this was due to economics. Native-born workers feared that poor Irish and Italian immigrants would work for less money and thus take away their jobs. These newer immigrants tended to be Catholic, whereas most prior immigrants from Europe were Protestant, and anti-Catholic prejudice and discrimination were widespread.

Some northern and western European immigrants were also initially considered inferior by people already settled here. Most of them assimilated (were absorbed into the existing culture) within a few generations. Once one generation settled into their new lives, newer immigrants from the same area were able to move into established ethnic enclaves where they felt more comfortable because others spoke their native languages and followed the same customs.

Immigrants from Asia, southern and eastern Europe, and the Pacific Islands often experienced racism and exclusion based on ethnic, religious, and class biases. In the early 1900s laws restricted immigration from certain nations and denied citizenship to some immigrant groups. Immigration quotas, for example, were based on the percentage of each group that already lived in the United States, so that the ethnic composition of the United States would not be altered by immigration.

The Immigration and Nationality Act of 1965 (P.L. 89-236) was an attempt to replace the quota system that had dominated immigration patterns. Enactment led to increased immigration from Latin America, Asia, and eastern and southern Europe. By 1977 about three-quarters of the people migrating to the United States were from Asia, Latin America, and the Caribbean. Immigration continues to increase, and it is anticipated that one out of four Americans will either be an immigrant or the child of an immigrant by 2040 (Padilla, 1997).

REFUGEE STATUS

Americans also prize their country's reputation as a haven for persecuted people. Some of the earliest colonists immigrated so that they could practice their religion freely. Many different groups have made the United States their destination in order to escape religious persecution and political conflicts. However, it was not until the 1950s that **refugees**, particularly those fleeing communist countries, were given special treatment.

By law, refugees are people who are fleeing persecution from countries that the U.S. government considers to be oppressing certain groups of people. For example, as a consequence of U.S. military intervention in Vietnam and other Southeast Asian countries, large numbers of immigrants were categorized as refugees after 1975. Their migration to the United States was the most rapid in American history. Passage of the Refugee Act of 1980 (P.L. 96-212), which gave legal status to people fleeing dangerous conditions such as armed conflict or natural disasters, provided more social services for the resettlement of refugees.

UNDOCUMENTED OR UNAUTHORIZED IMMIGRANTS

Recent debate has centered on the topic of people residing in the United States without proper authorization. The terms often used to refer to these more than 10 million people are *illegal immigrants* or *illegal aliens*. Language is powerful, as discussed in Chapter 1. Those who work with undocumented people find the term *alien* to be offensive, as if the lack of documentation makes a person less than human (think about the use of the term *alien*, typically used to describe a creature from another planet). Therefore, the use of the terms *undocumented* or *unauthorized* are preferable from a social work perspective that discourages labels that are pejorative or carry negative imagery. As will be discussed in Chapter 14, living in the United States without legal documentation is a civil infraction and, as such, is not legally considered a criminal act but a contractual violation. The vast majority of undocumented people come to the United States for economic reasons. Immigrants tend to be poor with countries of origin in Latin America. These characteristics have brought race, class, and ethnicity issues into the immigration debate, and the ramifications of increased immigration have become important issues for social workers.

IMPLICATIONS FOR SOCIAL WORK PRACTICE

As discussed in Chapter 1, part of social workers' professional mandate is to respect and appreciate diversity within and among those served. In the Council on Social Work Education's 2008 *Educational Policy and Accreditation Standards*, a primary purpose of social work education is to engage diversity and difference in practice and understand the dimensions of diversity—age, class, color, culture, disability, ethnicity, gender, gender identity and expression, immigration status, political ideology, race, religion, sex, and sexual orientation (p. 5). In order to accomplish that goal, social workers must develop practice skills that are responsive to the diversity of their clients.

Influence of History   Historic events provide an important context for understanding current concerns of nondominant groups. The colonization of indigenous peoples has resulted in a continued struggle to enforce their rights as sovereign nations (as assured by treaties), to maintain or regain their cultures, and to fight racism. Therefore, when working with indigenous people, the social worker needs to understand the history of oppression and current racism and its effect on contemporary communities (Weaver, 1998). Similarly, African Americans' long endurance of oppression, racism, discrimination, and prejudice, as well as their current experiences of social injustice based on race, contribute to the outlook, experiences, opportunities, and behaviors of African American clients and must be given attention in the practice realm. It is also important to recognize the enduring effects of such historic events as displacement and colonization, in addition to current experiences of racism, in the lives of Mexican Americans.

Refugees may have been traumatized by their experiences in their homelands and stressed by the need to adapt to a new environment. Often refugees have also faced racism in the United States. People who work with refugees emphasize the need to understand the pressures of living in a new place and to build on the strengths of peoples' cultures, values, and social supports (Padilla, 1997). Increased restrictions on undocumented people have caused growing fear of contact with authorities. For social workers, this has meant that connecting immigrants to social services and government resources has become much more difficult. This calls for new sensitivities about immigration and legal status.

Barriers to Service   Research suggests that social services, particularly mental health services, are underutilized by people of color because of geographic distances, language barriers, and cultural values (Lecca, Quervalu, Nunes, & Gonzales, 1998; Smedley, Stith, & Nelson, 2002). Some people of color avoid seeking services from agencies staffed primarily by European Americans because of negative experiences with members of this group. That is, if people of color have reason to assume that most whites are racist, they will be reluctant to approach whites for services unless no other options are available.

In spite of such underutilization, the needs of people of color are at least as significant as the needs of the majority population. Indeed, because people of color must deal with racism, they may experience issues not faced by whites. A challenge for practitioners is to bridge the gap between service providers and the people from diverse cultures who need services but are reluctant to use them (see "From the Field ... Cultural Divide").

Religious beliefs can also be a barrier to seeking service. A woman may be taught by her religion that a wife must be obedient to her husband. If there are marital problems or violence in the home, she may be reluctant to get help because she perceives going outside the family as not being obedient.

Rules and regulations may discourage people from using social services. Even today, some medical facilities such as hospitals allow only family members to visit seriously ill patients. This presents a problem for gay and lesbian couples,

BOX 6.1   FROM THE FIELD ... CULTURAL DIVIDE
Lilly Perez-Freerks, MSW

During my second year of graduate study in social work, my internship placement involved community action efforts in a low-income, primarily Latino neighborhood. The organizational effort was centered around the local elementary school through their welcome center. The administration of one school requested assistance in recruiting Latino parents as volunteers. It was unclear why the numerous Latino parents did not support the school through volunteerism.

I met with the staff community worker to discuss strategies to mobilize Latino parents to participate in neighborhood organizing efforts and to volunteer time at the elementary school. The community outreach worker and I were both Latina women, and both of us desired to empower the Latino parents by unifying their voices to effect social change.

As time went on, I became more confused about why the parents would not attend neighborhood meetings or participate in PTA meetings and after-school activities. They seemed willing to donate time to the welcome center in exchange for food boxes and school uniforms for their children. Yet it remained a challenge to engage them as volunteers in the school.

My efforts to participate in the neighborhood partnership meetings seemed futile. I attended several meetings, feeling invisible. Rarely did any of the meeting participants make eye contact with me or give me any hint of recognition. The school vice principal did not address me by name or welcome me in any meaningful way. I began to wonder if my race had anything to do with this, as the meetings were attended mostly by Caucasians and business leaders. I even wondered if my attire of jeans and T-shirt projected a negative image. I later ruled out clothing as a factor; professional attire elicited no more of a welcome.

I shared my experiences and frustration with the community worker at lunch one day. She became very quiet, then said that she might understand the exclusion. She began to talk about the time when Latino parents were excited about assisting the teachers and helping the children learn. They told the community worker that they did not feel welcome in the classrooms and that they felt that they were in the way. When the community worker shared this with the vice principal, she was told that the Latino parents did not have to work in the classrooms; there were other needs on the campus that these parents could help with. Specifically, the Latino parents could pick up trash on the campus or clean the bathrooms.

Shock and anger led to rage. I could not speak. I felt like I was suffocating. We sat in silence, not knowing what to say. Eventually I was able to say in Spanish, "To clean bathrooms, I can stay at home and do that." My lunch companion laughed and responded in Spanish, "That's just what the parents say."

Minutes later we were asked to meet with the vice principal to review the welcome center activities. As we entered the office, I noticed a pale blue crystal apple on her desk. I reintroduced myself to the vice principal and sat down. As the women spoke of upcoming projects, I reflected on the symbolism of that glass apple. My rage resurfaced as I fought the urge to hurt this blond-haired, blue-eyed woman who was acting as my peoples' oppressor. Her face is imprinted on my mind. I can still see the pale blue crystal apple on the mahogany desk. That glass apple may have once symbolized knowledge, but it will forever symbolize ignorance to me.

BOX 6.2   WHAT DO YOU THINK?

How did school personnel view the "fit" of the Latino families in their school? What interventions would you recommend to deal with this situation?

who are not officially regarded as spouses or family and may be denied access to their partners.

These examples point to the need to understand historical, political, and administrative factors that can impede social service delivery to diverse social groups. They demonstrate the importance of the ecological perspective in diversity practice.

CULTURAL COMPETENCY

Understanding how and why people are different is the foundation for social work practice with diverse populations. To be effective with different clients, groups, and communities, social workers must build on that foundation to develop skills and competencies that reflect a true understanding of diversity.

MULTICULTURALISM

Culture is based on the behaviors and beliefs characteristic of a particular group. This does not mean that every single person belonging to a group has all the characteristics or beliefs attributed to the culture, but rather that many of the characteristics are shared by the members of the group. The historical evolution of immigration to the United States has resulted in a collection of diverse cultures.

Multiculturalism is regarded as the ideology that society should recognize and include equally all different cultures (Sue, 2006). This concept emphasizes that multiculturalism promotes people's differences and counters ethnocentrism—the belief that one's own culture is the central way of viewing the world and that other cultures are inferior. Because social work practitioners work with many people who have various cultural backgrounds and membership in numerous identity groups, they need to develop skills that help them navigate cultural differences. The ability to work with different cultures effectively is often referred to as cultural competence.

In social work practice, **cultural competence** is the worker's ability to understand individuals and families of different cultures and to use that understanding as a basis for intervention and practice. In order to be a culturally competent social worker, one must understand the effect of culture on the person in environment—what an individual's culture means to him or her in all his or her systems.

Culturally competent practice goes beyond understanding diversity. It includes awareness of the effect of oppression and discrimination on peoples' lives: "To be culturally competent, one must understand the historical oppression of ethnic minorities, the similarities and differences among people of color, the practice principles of

---

| **BOX 6.3** | **WHAT DO YOU THINK?** |

Some people think that all people are members of ethnic groups. Other people feel that being part of the dominant culture—being white, Anglo-Saxon, and Protestant—means that a person does not have an ethnic identity. What do you think about these opposing beliefs? Do you agree with each of them? Why or why not?

ethnic sensitivity and cultural awareness, and the practice emphasis on cultural diversity" (Lum, 2000, p. 22). These same understandings are required for working effectively with members of other subordinated groups, such as women, LGBT people, and people with disabilities, among others. For example, a client who is indigenous may be struggling with a life-threatening illness such as cancer. The culturally competent social worker will not only recommend medical options from Western medicine, but will also assist the client in considering whether to make use of indigenous healers or practices.

ECOLOGICAL FRAMEWORK

The ecological framework for practice provides a strong foundation for social workers to integrate cultural sensitivity and multiculturalism. By understanding that all people are in constant interaction with all aspects of their environments, the social worker can recognize cultural and experiential differences. Such awareness helps the worker develop "an attitude of respect for the client's experiences and lifestyle, an appreciation of the client's right of self-determination, knowledge about the client's group's life, skill in helping and knowledge of human behavior" (Appleby, 2001, p. 10). This understanding is gained in the context of the client's unique life experiences.

The ecological framework helps social workers recognize the influence of environmental factors on people's lives. These factors may include racism, sexism, classism, heterosexism, ableism, ageism, and religious oppression that limit members of oppressed groups from reaching their full potential. Once social workers recognize the effects of oppression on their clients' lives, they seek interventions that address social structures in addition to helping clients deal with the detrimental effects of these structures. Thus, the ecological framework, with its emphasis on a person's fit in her or his environment, provides a strong theoretical foundation for social work practice that is culturally competent.

A number of models based on the ecological framework promote ethnic-sensitive practice, culturally diverse practice, multicultural practice, and diversity practice. These approaches all require social workers to become aware of their own values and cultures, learn about other groups' cultures, and develop skills for working with people from different cultures (Williams, 2006). In addition to a focus on cultural differences, some practice models also emphasize the need to learn about environmental factors that have negative effects on the lives of people. Empowerment practice (Gutiérrez, DeLois, & GlenMaye, 1995; Simon, 1994) and ethno-conscious practice (Gutiérrez, 1992) include strategies for effecting social change in addition to providing culturally competent social services. Both approaches should be grounded in a strengths perspective (see Chapter 1). Social work practitioners must identify the positive elements of each person's culture and build on those strengths.

EMPOWERMENT PRACTICE

Many authors assert that social work practice with oppressed populations should have client empowerment as a goal. When clients are empowered, they have control (power) over their environment, which makes it possible for them to improve their lives (Everett, Homestead, & Drisko, 2007). The goal of empowerment is to increase the abilities of individuals, families, and communities to get what they need; influence how others think, act, or believe; and influence how resources are distributed (Gutiérrez et al., 1995).

The strengths perspective is critical to cultural competency. The rich and varied backgrounds and identities of clients make it necessary to explore the social networks and cultural practices in which people find meaning. A social worker who is unfamiliar with such practices should ask the client to identify all the resources in his or her personal environment. These resources may involve the immediate family, extended family, friends, community, religion, work, or other social networks. The resources, which reflect the unique culture of the individual, can be tapped to improve the level of the client's functioning.

ACHIEVING CULTURAL COMPETENCY

History and theory help teach how to be a culturally competent social worker. However, specific steps can be taken to enhance cultural competency. They include understanding oneself and understanding the differences among cultures.

Awareness of Self

A competent social worker must develop a strong awareness of self. This component of effective practice is particularly critical in encounters between people who are members of different social groups. Whether working across ethnic, gender, sexual orientation, religious, social class, or other differences, the culturally competent social worker must constantly reflect on ways in which her or his culture affects practice. Selected aspects of the self that are influenced by culture and about which social workers must have knowledge include

- The way problems are defined (For example, is the source of the problems attributed to individual thoughts or behaviors? If so, are problems viewed as being related to spiritual, physical, cognitive, or emotional sources? Is the source of problems attributed to environmental factors?)
- Preferred problem-solving styles (For example, does one attempt to solve problems without outside assistance? Does one turn to certain family members, friends, religious leaders, government agencies, or professionals?)
- Body language
- Speaking style, including comfort with silence
- Which characteristics are viewed as strengths and which are viewed as weaknesses
- Attitudes and beliefs about others' values and behaviors (For example, are values that differ from one's own considered immoral or simply different?)
- Spirituality and the role religion plays in life
- Relative value placed on individualism, familism, and communitarism
- Relative comfort with certain topics (For example, are religious and spiritual beliefs private, or are they to be shared? Is it acceptable to talk about sexual practices?)

- Orientation to time (For example, what is the relative value placed on past, present, and future? Does time flow, pass, or fly?)
- Who and what are entitled to respect, and how respect is demonstrated
- One's own internalized racism, sexism, classism, and heterosexism; how much a person believes the negative and positive social constructs about his or her life (For example, does a woman social worker accept that women are to be subordinate to men? Does a heterosexual social worker accept that heterosexuals are "normal" and "healthy," whereas LGBT people are not?)

In addition, particularly when working cross-culturally, social workers need to reflect on the ways in which each of these aspects will be perceived by those with whom they work, and consider changing their attitudes, knowledge, and behaviors in order to practice more effectively.

UNDERSTANDING CULTURAL DIFFERENCES

In addition to awareness of self, the key skills needed to develop culturally competent practice are communication, openness to differences, and genuine interest in learning about those differences. Developing strong practice skills requires understanding all real-world phenomena, and cultural differences are very much a part of that reality:

> One's practice knowledge and skills, grounded in the practice model, are an extension of real world knowledge and skills. Practice wisdom becomes possible when one's practice model corresponds to true states of affairs in the real world. (DeRoos, 1990, pp. 284–285)

Nothing could be more real world than the life experiences of clients and of social workers. For clients who differ from the worker in culture, background, ethnicity, and other ways, good social work practice requires learning about the reality of the clients' lives. This is a key ingredient in cultural competence.

Part of culturally competent practice is to understand that values vary among individuals and that variations may be influenced by a person's identity or membership group experience. There are a number of general values to consider when working with diverse populations. A culturally proficient social worker examines the way people view time, accomplishments, relationships, and human behavior and considers how a person's cultural background may influence those values (see "More About ... Core Values for Working with Diverse Populations"). For example, a person who perceives that a focus on the present is valuable may perceive that people who expend energy planning and saving for the future are failing to enjoy life. Conversely, if a person's view of time is that future planning is important, she or he may regard one who focuses on today as being lazy or unable to delay gratification.

It is important for a social worker to strive to understand how his or her own and others' cultures influence values and to interpret people's behavior in light of their culture. Culturally competent practice requires social work practitioners to become knowledgeable about different groups and their cultures, to be self-reflective—that is, to think about their own actions, beliefs, biases, and values in relation to others—and to make use of their self-reflective insight in their practice (Weaver, 1998).

| BOX 6.4 | MORE ABOUT ... CORE VALUES FOR WORKING WITH DIVERSE POPULATIONS |

1. *How is time perceived?* There are three common responses: past, present, and future. Some people believe that the past is most important because people learn from history, whereas others believe the present moment is everything and you should not worry about tomorrow. Others plan for the future by sacrificing today for a better tomorrow.

2. *What measures human activity?* The three value-orientation responses are being, being and becoming, and doing. *Being* means it is enough to just be; *being and becoming* emphasizes that our purpose is to develop our inner selves. *Doing* means to be active; by working hard one's efforts will be rewarded.

3. *Social relations focus on how human relationships are defined.* The three responses are lineal, collateral, and individualistic. Lineal relationships are vertical and involve leaders and followers. Collateral relationships emphasize that people should consult with friends and families when problems are presented. An individualistic orientation promotes the importance of individual autonomy and the belief that people control their own destinies.

4. *The people-to-nature relationship asks what is the relationship of human beings to nature.* The responses can be subjugation to nature, harmony with nature, or mastery over nature. In subjugation to nature, life is dependent on external forces such as God, fate, or genetics. In harmony with nature, people and nature coexist in harmony. The third response, mastery of nature, is the belief that the human challenge is to conquer and control nature.

5. *Is human nature good or evil?* Possible answers are good, evil, neutral, or mixed good and evil.

Source: Lecca et al., 1998, p. 34.

STAGES OF CULTURAL UNDERSTANDING

A model developed by the Child and Adolescent Service System Program Technical Assistance Center views cultural competency as a continuum consisting of six stages (Cross, Bazron, Dennis, & Isaacs, 1989; cited in Lecca et al., 1998). On this scale, the lowest level is cultural destructiveness, and the highest is cultural proficiency. The six stages are as follows:

1. *Cultural destructiveness:* The worker holds attitudes, policies, and practices that destroy cultures.
2. *Cultural incapacity:* The worker believes in the superiority of dominant groups, does not support nondominant groups, and engages in discriminatory behaviors.
3. *Cultural blindness:* The worker believes that there are no differences between people, that they are all the same; this tends to reflect a belief that the dominant culture is universal. A nonableist term for this concept is *cultural evasiveness.*
4. *Cultural precompetence:* The worker begins to respect other cultures and demonstrates this respect through one or two actions, followed by a sense that he or she has done enough.

| BOX 6.5 | WHAT DO YOU THINK? |

Review "From the Field...Cultural Divide," and consider which stage of cultural understanding describes the vice principal. How could you help her become more culturally competent and move toward cultural proficiency?

| BOX 6.6 | ETHICAL PRACTICE ... RACISM |

You have been working as a case manager with Terry, an older adult, for a number of months. The two of you have developed a good working relationship. He is recovering from a stroke and you notice that he has been making good progress during your weekly visits. On one of those visits, Terry makes several racial slurs complaining about people living in his neighborhood. What should you do?

5. *Cultural competence:* The worker accepts and respects differences, continuously expands cultural knowledge and resources, and actively pursues engagement with nondominant clients and coworkers.
6. *Cultural proficiency:* The worker esteems other cultures, engages in research and outreach to build cultural knowledge, and specializes in culturally competent practice.

It should be noted that becoming culturally competent and developing cultural understanding does not happen quickly or easily. Becoming a culturally competent social worker and citizen is an ongoing process that can take a lifetime and requires continual effort, learning, and self-examination.

Chapter 3 discussed ways that prejudice, discrimination, and oppression contribute to social injustice. These three forms of injustice are used to marginalize people who are not part of the dominant culture. Supporting diversity decreases prejudice, discrimination, and oppression. The lowest levels on the scale—cultural destructiveness and cultural incapacity—are ways that people and institutions perpetuate discrimination against and oppression of people based on their cultural identities. At the other end of the continuum, cultural competence and cultural proficiency embrace and nurture the differences between groups. By achieving cultural proficiency, a social worker helps create a socially just society. This effort is part of the social work mandate. Thus, culturally competent social work practice not only follows the principles of the profession, but also contributes to the eradication of prejudice, discrimination, and oppression.

EMERGING ISSUES

Most social problems disproportionately affect people of color, those who live in poverty, women, and other nondominant groups. For example, on average, women earn less than men; the average income of people of color is lower than that of whites; and members of nondominant racial and ethnic groups are disproportionately victimized by crime. Over the past several decades, progress has been made toward greater social justice and civil rights. The Civil Rights Act of 1964 legally opened doors for people of color, and the Americans with Disabilities Act of 1990 secured rights for people with disabilities. Women have greater access to employment opportunities and have moved closer to economic parity with men. However, numerous areas of social injustice continue to require social work attention. This section discusses some of them.

CIVIL RIGHTS FOR LGBT PEOPLE

Lesbian, gay, bisexual, and transgender (LGBT) people lack specific civil rights protections. A person who is—or is perceived to be—lesbian, gay, bisexual, or transgender can be evicted from an apartment or fired from a job on the basis of his or her perceived sexual orientation. Legislative reform has been pursued, for the most part to no avail. For example, the Employment Non-Discrimination Act (ENDA) has been introduced in Congress numerous times, but it has not yet become law. Progress was made in 2007 when the U.S. House of Representatives did pass ENDA. Although it languished in the Senate, many advocates after years of no support were heartened by the progress in the House. Some cities, organizations, and businesses are extending civil rights protections to LGBT people. Nearly 90 percent of the *Fortune* 500 corporations have nondiscrimination policies that include sexual orientation and over 50 percent provide domestic partner health insurance benefits to their employees (Human Rights Campaign Foundation, 2008a). However, the issue of marriage has become very contentious. The state of Vermont recognizes civil unions of gay and lesbian couples, and in 2004 the Massachusetts Supreme Court ruled that the state must legally permit same-sex marriage. In 2008, the California Supreme Court followed suit ruling that outlawing same-sex marriage is unconstitutional. Although acceptance has been growing, there has also been tremendous resistance. As of 2008, 33 states had passed laws that prohibit gay marriages (Human Rights Campaign Foundation, 2008b). This issue will continue to be at the forefront of civil rights debates in the years to come. The debate regarding protection from discrimination and rights for LGBT people is examined in the box "Becoming a Change Agent."

BOX 6.7	BECOMING A CHANGE AGENT

As has been stated throughout this chapter, social workers support diversity and in general support the inclusion of diverse groups in various settings, such as schools. Social workers also advocate for the development of programs to make schools safe for all students. However, whether school is a safe place may depend on one's social group membership. On February 8, 2008, 15-year-old Lawrence King was shot and killed by a classmate. King was openly gay and sometimes wore makeup or what some considered feminine clothes to school. The 15-year-old who shot Larry King reportedly did so because of King's sexual orientation and was charged with committing a hate crime.

Many LGBT youth or those who are perceived as being LGBT are subjected to violence at school.

BOX 6.7	**BECOMING A CHANGE AGENT** *continued*

According to the Gay, Lesbian, Straight Education Network's (GLSEN) 2005 Climate Survey, more than a third of students reported physical harassment at school because of their sexual orientation and almost a fifth of the students reported being physically assaulted because of their sexual orientation (Kosciw & Diaz, 2006). A school climate of harassment and violence prompted the opening of a LGBT high school in New York City. After some controversy, the Harvey Milk School opened in September 2003. Supporters say the school provides a safe place where students who were or could be harassed or injured at other schools can get an education. Opponents argue that the school is not necessary or that it promotes segregation and is a step backward in the effort for equality for LGBT people.

Analyze the Situation

Conduct research on bullying, harassment, and violence against LBGT students and on the Harvey Milk School. What are the arguments for and against having a school for LGBT students? Do you believe that it provides a needed environment where LGBT students can safely get an education or do you agree with opponents that it is unnecessary or even harmful? Does the creation of a separate school for LGBT students go against social work efforts at inclusion and acceptance of diverse groups? Why did you reach this conclusion?

What Can Social Workers Do?

What can social workers do to reduce bullying and other violence and help all kids feel safe at school? What can they do at the individual, family, small-group, community, institutional, and policy levels?

What can you do?

What one step could you take now, either working on your own or with others, to reduce violence and bullying against LGBT students in the schools?

MULTIETHNIC OR TRANSRACIAL ADOPTIONS

Multiethnic or transracial adoption, the permanent placement of children of one ethnicity or race with parents of a different ethnicity or race, is very controversial among social work practitioners. Almost all such adoptions have involved children from non-dominant groups who have been adopted by dominant-culture—white—families. Supporters argue that there are not enough homes for all the children in need of permanent placements. To limit the number of adoptions because parents of the same races and ethnicities cannot be found is detrimental to the well-being of children in need. Placing children in good, safe homes, they contend, is better than keeping them in foster care and group residences. Those who oppose this practice feel strongly that permanently placing a child with parents of a different ethnicity or race is culturally insensitive and will cause the child to lose his or her racial and cultural identity. Opponents argue that the adoption of First Nation children by white families represents a practice used to strip the children of their culture and Americanize them. Due to greater cultural awareness in recent years, many adoptive parents try to ensure that the children learn about their cultures of origin.

REDRESS OR REPARATIONS FOR PAST SOCIAL INJUSTICES

In the last decade many people have advocated making financial **reparations** to the descendants of enslaved African Americans. Supporters of reparations point out that this nation's economic prosperity was largely a result of the labor of people who were enslaved. They note that the United States has never apologized for the practice of slavery nor adequately compensated African Americans for their exploitation. They point to the precedent set by the payment of reparations to the people of Japanese descent who were interned in camps during World War II.

People who oppose the payment of reparations note that it is not fair to expect today's taxpayers—who did not themselves enslave African Americans—to pay for the practices of non–African American ancestors. Further, they point out that no African Americans alive today were enslaved, which makes their situation different from that of the Japanese Americans who received reparations. The issue of reparations makes clear the importance of acknowledging and finding a way of making amends for historic injustices.

UNDERFUNDED SCHOOLS

School districts rely primarily on property taxes for revenue. As a result, schools in low-income communities generally have more students and receive less revenue than do schools in higher-income communities. Students in the poorer schools thus often must learn from old textbooks and poorly paid teachers in overcrowded classrooms in substandard buildings. The result is inadequate preparation for higher educational opportunities for low-income children and youth, who disproportionately are people of color. Social workers need to be interested in improving the opportunities of all children and youth, and so must identify and advocate for strategies that provide equal educational opportunities for all.

ENVIRONMENTAL JUSTICE

Some people assert that companies that pollute the air and water and discard toxic waste materials unfairly target communities populated mainly by poor people and people of color. Typically, these communities lack the resources and political power to stop corporations from engaging in environmentally dangerous actions that may also be health hazards. Some residents need the jobs created by these companies, so they may favor policies to attract and retain the companies in spite of the environmental and health risks. Social workers need to seek ways to improve residents' economic opportunities without endangering their health.

ENGLISH ONLY EMPHASIS

Schools and other public agencies have become central to fights over language and cultural pluralism. For example, **bilingual education** programs allow children to learn course material in their native languages while they develop skills in a second language, usually English. Some schools also feature programs that allow native English speakers to become bilingual in a different language. Many states are passing laws banning such programs. Opponents of bilingual education advocate English-immersion programs in which non-English speakers are required to focus on learning English for a short time, and then are placed in regular classrooms.

Some people support English immersion because they believe that it best prepares students for success in the United States. Others oppose it because students who do not speak English as their first language struggle when immersed in English-only classrooms and fall behind in their education. Other educators support bilingual education because they see bilingualism as an asset and a group's language as a vital component of the culture. Some states have outlawed the use of other languages when conducting official business. These efforts at ensuring that English is the one and only language spoken in the United States demonstrate the conflict between the cultures of the dominant group and newly arrived immigrant groups.

NEW RESEARCH ON HUMAN DIVERSITY AND GENETIC MAKEUP

Some of the most heinous acts of oppression have been based on the belief that biological differences between races and ethnic groups warrant discrimination and even annihilation. The belief in the biological superiority of the "white race" was used to institutionalize slavery, to exterminate Jewish people in Nazi Germany, and to strip indigenous peoples of rights and force their relocation to reservations, among many other acts of persecution. Biological arguments are still used to justify the oppression of women, LGBT people, people with disabilities, people who are poor, and others perceived to be inferior to those with power.

For the most part, those who believe in biological determinism point to differences in the way people live as proof of the accuracy of their beliefs. Critics, including the profession of social work, question using people's lives as evidence because all life experiences are, at least in part, different as a consequence of social interactions and constructions. That is the foundation of the ecological framework.

The Human Genome Project, a large-scale scientific effort to catalog the biological composition of human beings, may answer the question of whether human differences are based on biology or environment. Data from this extensive research effort indicate that people are 99.9 percent exactly the same genetically. In fact, "race itself has no genetic basis. No genes, either by themselves or in concert with others, were able to predict which race each person had claimed to be" (Weiss, 2001, p. 7). Although there is not a genetic basis for racial differences, the social conditions accompanying race matter (Smedley & Smedley, 2005). Employment, education, and civic involvement opportunities, as well as health care treatment, are all influenced by race and therefore demand social work attention.

CONCLUSION

People are different in many ways. It is not possible to understand, know, or anticipate all the differences that people consider important in their lives. However, it is possible to develop awareness and ways to understand, accept, and celebrate those differences. People can and should appreciate the positive contributions that the full array of human diversity brings to the culture. Furthermore, social workers need to work to ensure that all people, regardless of their differences, are treated with dignity and social justice.

Key Terms

bilingual education, (p. 165)

colonization, (p. 152)

cultural competence, (p. 157)

ethnic groups, (p. 150)

immigration, (p. 153)

multiculturalism, (p. 157)

multiethnic or transracial adoption, (p. 164)

race, (p. 150)

refugees, (p. 154)

reparations, (p. 164)

social construction, (p. 148)

Questions for Discussion

1. Define social identity, social construction, and multiculturalism.
2. Why is it critical for social workers to identify environmental factors that disproportionately affect people of color and other nondominant groups?
3. Compare cultural destructiveness, cultural incapacity, cultural blindness, cultural precompetence, cultural competence, and cultural proficiency.
4. In empowerment practice, at which four levels do social workers try to effect change?
5. Explain the differences among prejudice, discrimination, and oppression. Give an example of each.

Change Agent Exercise

To solve social problems is it often necessary to bring diverse groups together to work for change. Assume that you wanted to try to encourage the state legislature to pass a bill that would help solve the problem you examined in Chapters 1 to 3 (or another problem you choose that negatively affects people in your community). Brainstorm a list of groups, agencies, and organizations that you think could be involved in a coalition to work for the bill's passage. Why do you think each group would be interested in supporting the bill? Can you think of any potential challenges members of these groups might have in working together? How might any of the challenges be addressed by a culturally competent social worker?

Chapter Exercises

1. **Creating Metaphors**

   Metaphors compare two things. For example, Eating a mint is like a breath of fresh air and Writing a research paper is like pulling teeth.

   Use of metaphors allows us to view familiar things in a new way and to connect with things with which we may not be familiar. Creating metaphors challenges us to develop insights into a variety of areas of our lives. Completing the following metaphors can help you gain a deeper understanding about how you might feel about working with a variety of types of people and in a number of different practice settings.

   Working on your own, complete each of the following metaphors. Try to avoid censoring your answers. Write the first thing that comes to mind.

Working with poor people would be like

Working with Asian Americans would be like

Working with sex offenders would be like

Working with children would be like

Working with African Americans would be like

Working in a school would be like

Working with older people would be like

Working with people who are blind would be like

Working with European Americans would be like

Working with lesbians would be like

Working with batterers would be like

Working with mentally ill people would be like

Working with homeless people would be like

Working with Latinos would be like

Working with physically ill people would be like

Working with people who are dying would be like

Working with people who are deaf would be like

Working with people who have been victims of crimes would be like

Working in a hospital would be like

Reread and think about your answers. Do you think any of your metaphors reflect anger, fear, excitement, or other strong feelings?

How might your feelings hinder or enhance your ability to work with members of that group?

2. **Social Identity**

Each person has a social identity. List your social identities.

Is one most important? Why?

Consider other identities that are not your own. Visit a social activity, public gathering, or other group activity in which the majority of people are from a social identity different from your own. Afterward, answer the following questions:

How did you feel being different?

Were there activities or comments that made you aware of being in the numerical minority?

Did you feel welcome? Comfortable? Out of place? Why?

3. **Diversity Issues**

Select one of the following topics:

Civil rights for people who are lesbian, gay, bisexual or transgender

Multiethnic and transracial adoptions

Reparations for the enslavement of African and African American people

Bilingual education

Worker visas for undocumented immigrants

Once you have selected your topic, research the pros and cons of the issue. List the opinions and arguments on both sides of the issue. Identify which opinions or arguments are supported by facts, and which ones are not.

MY TOPIC IS:

PROS:

CONS:

OPINIONS AND ARGUMENTS FOR:

OPINIONS AND ARGUMENTS AGAINST:

Explain your position on the issue you have researched.

4. **Diversity Interview**

    Identify someone with a different ethnic or cultural background than your own. Interview the person on his or her own turf. Ask the following questions:

    What constitutes a stressful situation or problem in your family?

    How do individuals in your family respond to or cope with problematic situations?

    Describe any support systems in your family (intrafamilial systems).

    How would your family respond to the prospect of going into family therapy? What are the prevailing attitudes in your family about seeking help?

    What family values and behaviors are influenced by your ethnic/cultural heritage? How are they influenced?

    Who in your family experience influenced your social identity?

    Describe the traditions or rituals that your family celebrates.

    Describe the accepted roles for men and women in your family.

    What signs of your social identity (e.g., art, books, toys, clothing, language, or foods) are in your home?

    Describe any prejudice or discrimination you have experienced.

    Have you been taught to respond to prejudice or discrimination when you experience it or observe it? If so, how?

    What are your family's attitudes about education, work, family time, leisure, upward mobility, physical appearance, politics, expressing emotions, marital intimacy, and children expressing their feelings?

    What social policy role has your ethnic or cultural group played in this country?

    After you have completed the interview, answer the following questions:

    What was hardest about doing the interview?

    What was easiest about doing the interview?

    What did you learn about yourself while doing the interview?

    What did you learn about the person you were interviewing?

5. **Policy Analysis**

Select one of the following topics covered in the chapter:

Colonization

Forced relocation and enslavement

Expansion into Mexico

Immigration

Refugee status

Identify a U.S. government policy that has had an effect on the topic area you selected. It can be a current policy (or law) or one that has been changed or rejected (repealed). Analyze the policy using social work values and ethics. Determine whether social work values and ethics are supported by the policy, and explain.

References

Appleby, G. A. (2001). Framework for practice with diverse and oppressed clients. In Appleby, G. A., Colon, E., & Hamilton, J. (eds.), *Diversity, oppression, and social functioning*. Boston: Allyn & Bacon.

Cross, T. L., Bazron, B. J., Dennis, K. W., & Isaacs, M. R. (1989). *Towards a culturally competent system of care*. Washington, DC: Georgetown University Child Development Center, Technical Assistance Center.

DeRoos, Y. S. (1990). The development of practice wisdom through human problem-solving processes. *Social Service Review, 64,* 276–287.

Day, P. J. (2006). *A new history of social welfare.* (5th ed.). Boston: Allyn & Bacon.

Everett, J. E., Homstead, K., & Drisko, J. (2007). Frontline worker perceptions of the empowerment process in community-based agencies. *Social Work, 52,* 2, 161–170.

Griffin, P. (1997). Introductory module for the single issue courses. In Adams, M., Bell, L. A., & Griffin, P. (eds.), *Teaching for diversity and social justice: A sourcebook* (pp. 61–79). New York: Routledge.

Gutiérrez, L. M. (1992). Empowering ethnic minorities in the twenty-first century: The role of human service organizations. In Hasenfeld, Y. (ed.), *Human services as complex organizations* (pp. 301–319). Newbury Park, CA: Sage Publications.

Gutiérrez, L. M., DeLois, K. A., & GlenMaye. L. (1995). Understanding empowerment practice: Building on practitioner-based knowledge. *Families in Society, 76,* 534–542.

Hasenfeld, Y. (1992). Power in social work practice. In Hasenfeld, Y. (ed.), *Human services as complex organizations* (pp. 259–275). Newbury Park, CA: Sage Publications.

Hildalgo, H., Peterson, T. L., & Woodman, N. J. (eds.). (1985). *Lesbian and gay issues: A resource manual for social workers.* Silver Spring, MD: NASW.

Human Rights Campaign Foundation. (2008a). *GLBT equality at the Fortune 500.* Washington, DC: Author.

Human Rights Campaign Foundation. (2008b). *Statewide marriage laws.* Washington, DC: Author.

Kinsey, A. C., Pomeroy, W. B., & Martin, C. E. (1948). *Sexual behavior in the human male*. Philadelphia: W. B. Saunders.

Kinsey, A. C., Pomeroy, W. B., Martin, C. E., & Gebhart, P. H. (1953). *Sexual behavior in the human female*. Philadelphia: W. B. Saunders.

Kosciw, J. G., and Diaz, E. M. (2006). *The 2005 National School Climate Survey: The Experiences of Lesbian, Gay, Bisexual and Transgendered Youth in our Nation's Schools*. New York: Gay, Lesbian, Straight Education Network.

Lecca, P. J., Quervalu, I., Nunes, J. V., & Gonzales, H. F. (1998). *Cultural competency in health, social, and human services: Directions for the twenty-first century*. New York: Garland Publishing.

Lipkin, A. (1999). *Understanding homosexuality, changing schools*. Boulder, CO: Westview Press.

Lum, D. (2000). *Social work practice and people of color* (4th ed.). Belmont, CA: Brooks/ Cole.

Marks, J. (1994). Black, white, other. *Natural History*, December, pp. 32–35.

Padilla, Y. C. (1997). Immigrant policy: Issues for social work practice. *Social Work, 42*, 595–606.

Reay, D. (2007). Education and social class. *Sociology Review, 17*, 2, 2–5.

Richardson, D. (2007). Patterned fluidities: (Re)Imagining the relationship between gender and sexuality. *Sociology, 41*, 3, 457–474.

Schmookler, T., & Bursik, K. (2007). The value of monogamy in emerging adulthood: A gendered perspective. *Journal of Social and Personal Relationships, 24*, 6, 819–835.

Simon, B. L. (1994). *The empowerment tradition in American social work*. New York: Columbia University Press.

Smedley, A., & Smedley, B. D. (2005). Races as biology is fiction, racism as social problem is real. *American Psychologist, 60*, 1, 16–26.

Smedley, S. B., Stith, A. Y., and Nelson, A. R. (eds.). (2002). *Unequal treatment: Confronting racial and ethnic disparities in health care*. Washington, DC: Institute of Medicine.

Sue, D. W. (2006). *Multicultural social work practice*. Hoboken, NJ: John Wiley.

U.S. Bureau of the Census. (2004). *U.S. interim projections by age, race, and Hispanic origin*. http://www.census.gov/ipc/www/usinterimproj/. Washington, DC: Author.

U.S. Bureau of the Census. (2007). *Statistical abstract of the United States* (127 th. ed.). Washington, DC: Author.

U.S. Bureau of the Census. (2008). *U.S. Hispanic population surpasses 45 million, now 15 percent of total*. Washington, DC: Author.

Weaver, H. N. (1998). Indigenous people in a multicultural society: Unique issues for human services. *Social Work, 43*, 203–211.

Weiss, R. (2001). Breaking the human code. *Washington Post National Weekly Edition, 18*, 7, 6–7.

Williams, C. C. (2006). The epistemology of cultural competence. *Families in Society, 87*, 2, 209–220.

CHILD WELFARE: WORKING WITH CHILDREN AND THEIR FAMILIES

CHAPTER 7

Co-authored by Cynthia Lietz, Ph.D.

Heinle Division of Cengage Learning

People often say that today's children are the future of our nation and children are our greatest resource. While these sentiments may suggest Americans value every child and support the well-being of all children, they do not translate into the health, safety, and overall well-being for all of America's children.

More than thirteen million children (18 percent) live in poverty in the United States (DeNavas-Walt, Proctor, & Smith, 2008). One-third of the children in this country live in homes where no parent has full-time, year round employment (Casey, 2006). This is very troubling because poverty has a negative and long-lasting effect on children (Eamon, 2000). More than 8 million children, or about 11 percent, do not have health insurance coverage, and many more do not receive regular medical care (DeNavas-Walt, et al., 2007). In 2006, 3.3 million child abuse reports were made to state agencies and over 900,000 children were confirmed to have been victims of maltreatment (Administration for Children and Families, 2006). In 2006, 513,000 children, the majority of them under 11 years of age, were in foster care (Administration for Children and Families, 2006). Millions of children suffer from emotional and behavioral disorders and many of them do not receive treatment for these problems (Children's Defense Fund, 2004). Suicide is the second leading cause of death for teens, but homicide is the third leading cause of death for children aged 5 to 14 (Casey, 2006). These and other statistics cause many people to ask, what should be done about such significant and far-reaching problems? Who will advocate for this vulnerable population?

Although the statistics may be discouraging, they can be used to raise awareness and demonstrate the needs of children in the United States. Prior to the regular collection of data related to children, it was easy to overlook problems affecting youth. Children are unable to advocate for their own needs. Data on the current status of children in the United States provide social workers with the information they need to advocate on individual, community, and national levels for the well-being of children and their families. This knowledge frames interventions and makes it possible to work with children to improve their day-to-day living. Children are our future, and we are theirs.

THE IMPORTANCE OF THEORY

Regardless of the role a social worker maintains while intervening with children and families, such work must be based on sound social work theory. The history of child welfare practice clearly indicates that early work with children involved diverse and often opposing methods for effecting change. For example, children whose parents could not or would not care for them were placed in orphanages in some cases and with substitute families in others. Similarly, there was controversy over how to handle problems of delinquency such as running away, theft, or violence. Some people advocated separating children from their families so as to eliminate the negative

| BOX 7.1 | WHAT DO YOU THINK? |

Do you believe that the United States is a society that values children? Why?

effect of the family, whereas others believed that delinquent children needed a loving family environment in which to grow. Opposing theories continue to be debated. Should punitive measures be used to teach children how to behave, or will rehabilitation and retraining alter behavior?

Without theory that directs practice, social work would involve contradictory interventions based on opinion and anecdotal experience rather than consistent intervention established through research and collaboration. Therefore, a solid understanding of the theories that relate to work with children and families is required of social workers intervening in the lives of children and families.

THEORIES OF CHILD DEVELOPMENT

Many of the terms used when discussing social work practice with children are common ones, while others are unique to professionals. The first period of life is generally referred to as **childhood**. Legally, childhood is defined as a stage of life that begins at birth and ends at age 18. In the United States anyone under the age of 18 is considered to be legally dependent and is classified as a child.

The growth period of childhood involves several developmental stages. Understanding a child's social, cognitive, physical, and emotional development helps social workers understand what services are needed to best enhance the child's well-being. Theories of development are discussed later in this section.

Children in the United States are defined as being **vulnerable** to oppression and discrimination. In social work vulnerable populations are considered to need special attention and advocacy. One of the cardinal values in social work is that social workers seek social justice by creating opportunities to overcome vulnerability.

Why are children so vulnerable? Children look to others to recognize their needs (Chafel, 1993). They must rely on people outside of their population, namely adults, to make their needs known to decision makers. For example, an infant failing to receive good medical care cannot make her concerns known. A seven-year-old is unlikely to tell the school principal that he is not receiving special education services to which he is entitled. Because their cognitive and social functioning is not fully developed, children are reliant on people outside of their population to advocate for their needs. This dependence has led social workers to identify the population as vulnerable and to determine that children as a group are in need of advocacy on many levels.

A **family** is a system of individuals who are interrelated and have significant relationships (Goldenberg & Goldenberg, 2004). Although many families are related through heredity, that is not true of all families. Significant relationships that are not biological play an important role in a child's life and must be recognized and embraced (Crosson-Tower, 1998). A family may be made up of a father, a mother, and three siblings; of a grandmother and her five grandchildren; of a lesbian or gay couple raising a child; of an unmarried couple raising a child from a previous marriage; or of two adults and no children. All these systems are families. The members of each system are interrelated. In the case of children, families typically include the children's primary caregivers. It is important to understand and accept this extended view of the term *family*. Social workers often intervene on behalf of children through involvement with their families. A more rigid definition of *family* could cause social workers to miss valuable resources when working with a child.

Additional definitions suggest that family systems exist to serve certain functions. For example, when a child is part of a family, one of the family's functions is to care for, support, and nurture that child. Social workers who specialize with children and families often intervene when the family does not or cannot provide care, support, and nurturance.

ECOLOGICAL APPROACH

As discussed earlier in this text, the ecological approach provides a framework for social workers to assess a client within the context of his or her environment. As it relates to children, this approach requires social workers to develop a broad understanding of a child and his or her situation. First, the social worker must identify the systems that affect the child's life. Systems that are commonly part of a child's environment include families, schools, peer groups, and neighborhoods. The larger systems affecting a child may include public policies, the surrounding community, and even changes in the federal system that result in resources or barriers for children. Second, the social worker must consider the interaction between the child and these systems; hence the application of person-in-environment, or the ecological framework. By considering such factors, a social worker is able to identify all areas for intervention, not just those at the individual level.

Consider an eight-year-old boy who has been arrested for theft. Simply assessing this client at an individual level may lead a professional to intervene by counseling the boy in order to improve his problem-solving and self-control skills. However, further investigation under the ecological approach shows that the boy is the oldest of five children in a single-parent home. His mother has recently been laid off from her job, and her oldest son feels responsible to help provide for his younger siblings. In fact, his arrest occurred as a result of stealing some basic food items from a grocery store for his younger siblings. In this case, the initial assessment on the individual level would have led the social worker to build skills that were likely not really at issue. The ecological approach helped the social worker identify the cause of the boy's behavior as the financial stressors in the family, not impulsiveness or lack of self-control. Intervention that stems out of this ecological assessment may involve referring this family to local financial support services, rather than simply focusing on the behavior of the child as an isolated phenomenon (see "More About... Systems and Children").

BOX 7.2 | **MORE ABOUT ... SYSTEMS AND CHILDREN**

Often, when we think about systems and children, we think of social services, schools, and families. Many other groups and activities are central in children's lives. Examples include Boys and Girls Clubs, 4-H clubs, church choirs, religious youth groups, tribal youth groups, and even gangs. Social workers need to consider the effect of these systems on the children with whom they work.

HUMAN DEVELOPMENT

In addition to assessing a client and his or her interaction with the environment, it is also important to understand theories about how human beings develop throughout their lives. Although there is variance in the way that children develop, it has been shown that growth is continuous and orderly, and that development follows fairly predictable patterns. These patterns have been studied and organized into categories that can help social workers assess the current level of functioning of a client. Human development theories describe stages and the tasks that are expected to be accomplished at each stage. Using these theories and development milestones as guidelines for determining whether a child is maturing appropriately, a social worker can assess whether a client is in need of intervention.

Although the stages are helpful guides, each person is unique and may not exactly match the descriptions. Also, many of the development characteristics that have been identified are linked to dominant cultures and fail to take into account cultural diversity and the norms of nondominant populations. For example, in many cultures children sleep with their parents for a significant part of their childhood. While sharing a room or a bed can be an economic necessity, there is also a strong cultural belief in the value of such closeness. The dominant American culture emphasizes individuality, and babies are expected to sleep in separate beds and often in their own rooms from birth. To some cultures, this seems cold and distant and would not be considered nurturing. Taking into account cultural differences is an important part of utilizing developmental theories appropriately.

Prenatal   The prenatal stage of development is the time during which a fetus develops within the mother's womb prior to birth. Development during this stage is assessed medically; prenatal care allows a physician to monitor growth, heartbeat, and organ development. Prenatal medical care typically emphasizes healthy living for the mother, which allows for healthy development of the fetus. It is a way for medical professionals to detect early problems, such as genetic disorders, symptoms related to drug or alcohol use, or transmission of a virus from mother to child. Good preventive health care can improve pregnancy outcomes and the physical well-being of newborns.

Infancy   Infancy is the first three years of a child's life. In this stage children's development of attachment relationships is seen in their recognition of and interaction with their primary caregivers and other significant people (Zastrow & Kirst-Ashman, 2007). In addition, skills of coordination such as locomotor and sensorimotor skills are being developed. Language development begins as babbling sounds turn into more purposeful patterns and eventually into recognizable words. Problems can occur at this stage when a child lacks a healthy attachment to a caregiver, when there is no recognizable progression in language development, and when physical development is not progressing (Allen-Meares, 1995)

Preschool Years   From ages three to five, children continue physical development as seen in gains in height and weight. Language becomes more complex; sentences become longer; and there is increased questioning and desire for understanding.

Peer relations are being formed, and issues related to asserting self and resolving conflict are of increased significance. Problems can involve a lack of social reaction, failure to imitate others, refusal to eat, refusal to talk, withdrawn behavior, poor muscle control, or failure to follow simple instructions (Allen-Meares, 1995).

Middle Childhood   Middle childhood extends from age 6 to 12 and includes a child's years in primary school. During this time, cognitive abilities are increasing rapidly; that is, skills in memory, conceptual thinking, deductive reasoning, and problem solving are developing (Allen-Meares, 1995). Significant relationships expand to include not only parents and family, but also peers, teachers, and extended family. Some of the problems seen during this development stage include psychosomatic complaints, anxiety disorders such as obsessive-compulsive reactions and phobias, mood issues including depression, behavior problems such as noncompliance, and educational issues such as learning disabilities (Zastrow & Kirst-Ashman, 2007).

Adolescence   Children ages 13 to 18 are adolescents. They typically attend junior high school and high school. In general, adolescence is assessed in terms of physical, social, cognitive, emotional, and moral development. Physical development is marked by growth spurts, hormone changes due to the increased activity of the pituitary gland, and maturation of the reproductive system. Cognitive changes include the ability to master complex processes such as abstract thinking and complex problem solving. Socially, teens seek acceptance from a peer group and begin to separate from their parents and families. Emotionally, they are learning to express and to manage emotions more effectively, and moral development is evidenced by the ability to recognize standards and behave in ways that comply with them (Allen-Meares, 1995).

Problems during this stage can include anxious reactions to the changes and pressures of adolescence, and experimentation, including drug abuse, alcohol abuse, at-risk sexual behaviors, and delinquency. Other common problems include eating disorders, problems in school, dropping out of school, running away, depression, pregnancy, conflict with the family, noncompliance with authority, and violent reactions (Zastrow & Kirst-Ashman, 2007).

OTHER THEORIES

In addition to the ecological approach and the stages of childhood development, other theories related to children and families inform social work practice. For example, Jean Piaget presented a theory of **cognitive development** that described the stages that children must go through in order to progress to higher levels of thinking. His basic premise was that cognitive processes start out basic and concrete in infancy and become more abstract and complicated with moral development (Piaget, 1965).

Social learning theory is based on the idea that behavior is learned through socialization (Bandura, 1977). Within this context, the theory derives a variety of behavioral methods such as modeling and positive reinforcement for bringing about learned behaviors. Parent training programs and residential and group-home settings for children make use of the methods of social learning theory.

Erik Erikson's **psychosocial theory** states that children progress through clear stages of development. In this theory, human development is presented as a series of psychosocial crises. Ideally, people prepare themselves for the next stage of development by resolving each crisis. Failing to resolve a crisis can lead to problems in later stages (Erikson, 1968).

Theories of development and human behavior, coupled with the person-in-environment framework of social work, are the basis for practice with children and families. These theories serve as the context for determining which intervention strategies are appropriate in a given situation.

THE CHILD WELFARE SYSTEM

The child welfare system is a loosely formed network of federal and state mandates that promote the welfare of all children and facilitate permanency by providing services to prevent the unnecessary separation of children from their families, to restore children to their families if they have been separated, and to place children in adoptive homes when reunification is not possible. The child welfare system includes social work services such as child protection, foster care, and adoption. Child welfare services are part of a larger interactive system that includes juvenile justice and family court services, mental and public health services, schools, and income maintenance programs.

HISTORICAL BACKGROUND

Some of the first recorded efforts to manage troubled youth came in the early 1800s as communities struggled to deal with dependent, delinquent, or neglected children (Lindsey, 1994). In those days, troubled children were placed in orphan asylums or reformatories to provide structure and discipline to correct for the negative effect of the family or community. The strategy at that time was that separating a child from her or his family and community was the best way to address delinquency and child maltreatment.

In the late 1800s and early 1900s, such efforts were criticized due to poor living conditions in orphan asylums. A growing concern also emerged regarding whether children can be socialized and integrated into society when they are raised in institutions. In response, new theories of intervention were developed. One solution, called placing out, arranged for children to live with substitute families. Many consider placing out as the origin of what we now know as foster care (Petr, 1998). As the debate over institutional care versus in-home care intensified, social workers began to develop a practice specialization in the care of children and families. The development of this specialization occurred in conjunction with the professionalization of social work in the early 1900s.

At the same time, public policies were beginning to focus on issues relevant to children and families. In 1912 the U.S. Children's Bureau was created. This federal office was responsible for monitoring the condition and treatment of children in the nation. In 1921 the Child Welfare League of America, a private organization concerned with ensuring the well-being of children, was established (Axinn & Stern, 2008). In addition, the concept of assistance to mothers was introduced.

At this time, juvenile court systems were also developed. Prior to their creation, the judicial system treated youth like adults, with no consideration for their age.

BOX 7.3	POINT OF VIEW

The decision about whether to try a youth accused of breaking the law as an adult or in juvenile court, where sentences are typically not as harsh or as long, is extremely controversial. A 15-year-old who is tried and convicted of murder in an adult court may be sentenced to life imprisonment or even the death penalty. In a juvenile court, this same youth would likely be sentenced to juvenile detention with the intent of providing rehabilitation and returning him or her to society on adulthood (18 years of age). Which approach seems best? Why?

Child welfare advocates successfully lobbied for special treatment of young people in the legal system. For the first time in American history, there seemed to be recognition of the unique needs of children and families by policymakers as well as by professionals working with this population (see "Point of View" box above).

By the middle of the 1900s, investigation of the institutions that were designed to care for children often revealed improper and dangerous conditions. This led to a shift in philosophy away from removing children from family environments and toward supporting family environments and keeping children at home. Thus, the 1940s and 1950s saw a reduction in the use of institutional care and an increase in the use of foster care (Crosson-Tower, 1998). Theories focusing on keeping families together were being formulated, and social workers were becoming more involved in advocating for the best interests of children (Hess McCartt, McGowans, & Botsko, 2000). Child welfare was being further defined. Theories about the causes of and solutions to problems affecting children were formulated, and the friendly visits practiced by Charity Organization Society workers (see Chapter 1) were replaced by assessment and counseling.

As the profession moved further into the twentieth century, family preservation and home-based placements became accepted as the best practice for most child welfare needs (Lindsey, 1994). Intervention with children and families expanded to include counseling methods such as individual, family, and group work. More recently, these interventions were enhanced through the concept of wraparound services, a strengths-based response to child welfare that uses formal and informal services that are community based. In addition, family group decision making was also adopted by many states as a way of supporting the idea that families can contribute to decision making in child welfare (Mather, Lager, & Harris, 2007). Advocacy on behalf of children has become increasingly important to the profession, as social workers are more involved in policymaking regarding issues facing children and families. Social workers also started working in the schools.

CHILD WELFARE

Broadly defined, **child welfare** includes the activities, programs, interventions, or policies that are intended to improve the overall well-being of children (Pecora, Whittaker, & Maluccio, 1992). In this text, the term is used to describe the private and public systems put in place to serve the needs of children. One of the most significant parts of the child welfare system is the protection of children who are at risk of maltreatment. The legal definition of child **maltreatment** is:

> The physical or mental injury, sexual abuse, or exploitation, negligent treatment, or maltreatment of a child by a person who is responsible for the child's welfare, under circumstances which indicate that the child's health or welfare is harmed or threatened thereby, as determined in accordance with [federal] regulations. (P.L. 100-294, Section 14 [4])

Should a child be maltreated or if there is a concern that maltreatment is a possibility, specialized agencies and workers become involved in the child's life. These units are known as child protective service agencies.

Child Protective Services (CPS)   The term *child protective services (CPS)* is typically used to refer to the state system, department, or agency responsible for the investigation of allegations of abuse or neglect, the protection of children at risk of abuse or neglect, service delivery, and the placement of children who have been maltreated. Social workers serve as CPS intake workers, caseworkers, supervisors, and administrators. Although child protective services workers are involved in assessing maltreatment, they are also involved in numerous other services for children and families.

When a family cannot care for a child or is legally found to have mistreated a child, CPS workers rely on services that temporarily take the place of the family. **Foster care** is the major social welfare program to care for children outside of their families. The idea is for a child to be placed in a foster home while his or her family receives services to overcome problems. The ultimate goal is for the child to return home.

This goal is implemented through **permanency planning**. To provide stability for children in foster care, social workers follow federal guidelines. The first choice should be to return a child home. If that fails, the second choice is **adoption**, which involves legally moving a child to an adoptive family. If a child is not adopted, foster care becomes the long-term solution.

A stronger commitment to keeping families together has developed over the past 20 years. When children cannot be kept in their homes, the goal is to keep the separation as short as possible. CPS and private child welfare agencies offer prevention and support services. **Family preservation services** are "activities that alleviate crises that might lead to out-of-home placements of children" (Administration on Children, Youth and Families, 2001, pp. 2–3). The purpose of family preservation is to provide support so that crises can be averted; if crises do occur, families are helped to cope and stay together.

The role of CPS workers can be extremely difficult and controversial. Information on abuse and neglect cases must be collected with enough detail to make a well-founded decision, but the decision also must be made in a timely manner. Many CPS workers have large caseloads, and sometimes must make assessments within minutes. It can be extremely complicated to know what is in the best interest of a child, and evidence (what can be seen) and information (what a third-party report states) may not always corroborate. Public scrutiny is often greatest in the child welfare domain as cases of severe child abuse and neglect attract news coverage. This can add to the stress of the job. CPS is a challenging field, yet a critical place for trained social workers.

JUVENILE JUSTICE

Each state also maintains a juvenile justice system that handles delinquency, juvenile detention, probation programs, juvenile court proceedings, and case management. Local and state governments use the system to deal with legal issues related to children, such as crime, violence, and running away. It is also the legal forum where decisions about removing children from their homes in cases of abuse or neglect are made. Because of its involvement in abuse and neglect cases, the juvenile justice system is considered to be part of the child welfare system.

THE ROLES OF SOCIAL WORKERS

As the needs of children became further identified and clarified in the twentieth century, social work took the lead in intervening with children and their families. Today social workers play three main roles when working with children and their families: case management, direct practice, and advocacy and policy building.

CASE MANAGEMENT

Although social workers utilize case management with many populations, it is especially useful with children and families. Case management with children includes assessing a child's problems and needs and determining what steps are necessary to provide services for the child and his or her family. This may include contacts with other service providers. Case managers may need to advocate for a child to obtain services despite barriers in the process. Case management is involved when a social worker tries to find low-income housing for a family in need, works with a foster family to provide counseling services for a child placed in the home, and works in a hospital to help a family find aftercare services for a child.

DIRECT PRACTICE

Direct practice with children and their families can be varied depending on clients' needs and the environment in which a social worker is based. Generally, direct practice involves face-to-face contact with children and family members to form a therapeutic relationship and work through issues (Hepworth, Rooney, Rooney, Strom-Gottfried, & Larsen, 2006). Relationships may be formed for only one day, as in the case of a crisis intervention specialist, or for a longer period of time, such as with a therapist at a behavioral health center.

The direct practice interventions outlined in Chapter 5 are often used with children. Clinical social workers may use psychodynamic therapy or cognitive behavioral techniques. Because children may not have the verbal skills or insight that adults have, psychodynamic therapies are adapted for use with them. Examples include using dolls to enact behaviors or having children draw pictures to show their feelings. In general, social workers in child welfare utilize interviewing skills to assess a child's needs, develop a case plan with the child and family, and work together to ensure positive relations within the family system. "From the Field…Learning from a Child" describes the use of direct practice with a child.

BOX 7.4   ## FROM THE FIELD ... LEARNING FROM A CHILD
JoAnn Del-Colle, MSW

As a counselor of sexually abused children, I have often felt wonderment at the way each child knows his or her own truth, what is needed for healing, and what is needed to move forward. I have often seen one of the basic tenets of social work, that the client is the expert, come to life, and I have realized that every person, no matter his or her age or life situation has something to teach me.

The first time I met 10-year-old Tia, she barely spoke, and instead spent her session exploring and organizing all the objects in my office. During the intake, Tia's mother told me that Tia was very concerned about contracting a deadly disease and that she had begun engaging in repetitive behaviors such as checking doors and windows throughout the night to make sure they were locked. Tia no longer wanted to visit her biological father on the weekend.

From the time she was five until she was seven, Tia had been sexually abused by her half-brother, who was eight years older than Tia. She received short-term counseling to address the abuse. Tia's half-brother had court-ordered counseling. Eventually he left the state and joined the navy. This brother left the military and moved back to Arizona six months prior to Tia's counseling intake.

When Tia disclosed the abuse, her parents were still married, though significantly different religious beliefs and the biological father's alcohol abuse caused conflict. After the disclosure, Tia's parents divorced. Tia's father had not remarried; her mother had remarried and now had a six-month-old baby. The new marriage was also conflict filled.

Initially, Tia's parents were focused on changing the presenting behaviors. Though I empathized with their concern, I felt it important to begin by understanding the purpose and message of Tia's actions without judging them. Since fear and control appeared to be concerns, I encouraged Tia to set her own therapeutic pace as well as to choose her own therapeutic activities.

Tia told me that she needed to do something to get ready to talk about her feelings. She asked if she could peel the orange that was on my desk. When she had done so, she split the orange in half and asked me to join her in a snack. This gesture of coming together marked the start of every session that followed. Tia knew she needed something to create a sense of entry into the session.

As Tia began to express her feelings and thoughts in art, structured therapeutic exercises, and a sand tray, her problematic behaviors became more frequent. New behaviors emerged, including wanting several showers a day, repeated hand washing, and fear of blood. Though Tia's parents became concerned and fretful, I stayed the therapeutic course, encouraging Tia to put words to her feelings, thoughts, and activities. It was not always easy to reassure her parents that she would be okay. To be honest, there were times when I had to work hard to maintain faith in the therapeutic process. There were successes and missteps as Tia's behaviors ebbed and flowed. At one point, Tia's parents requested a consult with a child psychiatrist. The psychiatrist supported my approach of allowing Tia to set her own course in treatment without medication.

Over time, it became apparent that, in addition to experiencing tension in her family relationships, Tia was feeling ambivalent about the return of her half-brother to Arizona. One of her greatest fears was that the sexual abuse had placed a dark spot on her life and that she would be unlikely to experience "Paradise" in the next life. Tia's mother had raised her to believe that life on Earth was an indicator of life after death. Tia lived in constant fear that she was doomed. Her repeated thoughts of catching a deadly disease and her ritualistic behaviors reflected this fear and were related to her attempts to control her environment and her feelings. Tia's pain and confusion needed to be heard.

Though counseling was at times painful, confusing, and frightening, Tia and I developed a close therapeutic relationship. In time her need to straighten everything in my office gave way to other activities and conversations. As Tia's emotional issues were addressed, Tia's presenting behaviors decreased, and her parents were willing to look at their own roles and influences on Tia's feelings, perceptions, and mastery of the sexual abuse. I felt satisfied with my efforts to focus on Tia's process rather than on her behaviors. Tia had been encouraged and supported in her efforts to tell her story in her own unique way.

After nearly a year of weekly sessions, Tia was doing well. Yet every time Tia and I talked about ending treatment, new issues arose. It was apparent that Tia was feeling ambivalent about ending treatment. I began scheduling appointments farther and

| BOX 7.4 | FROM THE FIELD ... LEARNING FROM A CHILD *continued* |

farther apart in the hope of fostering closure, but new problematic behaviors continued to surface. What was I not hearing? What was I missing?

After several attempts to schedule a final session, I asked Tia, "What do you need in order to be okay with ending counseling?" Without missing a beat, Tia said she wanted to give something to me before she stopped counseling. After talking about this idea, Tia said that she wanted to write a counseling book for other children to read during their first counseling visit. Tia explained that the book would be her way of helping other kids not be so scared. Until then, I had not fully realized how important it was for Tia to leave something concrete behind. Tia truly was her own expert in knowing what she needed to do in order to let go and move on.

Tia wrote and illustrated a book depicting the process of counseling. Once the book was completed, Tia was ready to let go. I have never forgotten Tia and how much she taught me about the circular nature of counseling. In these days of managed care and brief interventions, social workers must never forget to make space and time for our clients' inner voices and wisdom to be heard. In taking the time to listen to the wisdom of those I have helped, I have learned the most about myself not only as professional, but also as a human being on a journey of my own.

| BOX 7.5 | WHAT DO YOU THINK? |

How did the social worker develop her assessment of Tia? Did the social worker identify Tia's strengths? Did she use Tia's strengths in therapy sessions? What skills can you identify that the social worker used with Tia? What do you think the social worker learned from Tia?

ADVOCACY AND POLICY BUILDING

Advocacy in child welfare is "acting on behalf of children to assure protection of their basic rights and needs" (Chafel & Condit, 1993, p. 276). It may include seeking services to address the needs of a child. It may involve identifying areas in which policies fail to meet the basic needs of children and recommending the expansion of current policies or creation of new ones (Mallucio & Anderson, 2000). Advocacy may involve collateral contacts with an organization that is intervening with a child so as to bring attention to a need that is not being addressed (Woods & Hollis, 1990). Advocacy can occur on the local, state, or national level. It is a critical part of working with children and families because it does what children cannot do for themselves—identify a need and bring it to the attention of decision makers.

There are many ways a social worker can affect policymaking. One of the easiest and most common is to vote for candidates in general elections and for policy referendums in state and local elections. Because children cannot vote, adults must do so on their behalf. Lobbying public officials by means of telephone calls, letters, and visits is often an effective way to inform decision makers about an issue. Social workers can organize grassroots campaigns in which many people, including children, participate. Groups such as the Children's Defense Fund and the Child Welfare League advocate for policy changes on behalf of children.

THE INTERVENTION PROCESS

As outlined in Chapter 5, the term *intervention* refers to the actions taken by a client and a social worker to effect change in an area of the client's life. In many cases, a client is referred to a social worker to deal with a particular problem. The social worker often engages in a problem-solving process that includes engaging the client, assessing the problem area and situation, developing a list of potential solutions, coming up with an action plan, and supporting the client in implementing the plan. The social worker encourages the client to take ownership of and responsibility for the change process. Such efforts support the social work value of self-determination and emphasize the strengths perspective.

When social workers intervene with children and families, the process can be somewhat different. For example, children rarely bring themselves to the attention of a social worker; most do not receive services because they have identified a problem in their lives but rather because someone else has decided that they need help. Also, self-determination can be difficult with children. By virtue of their age and abilities, children cannot be empowered the same way adults can. This brings about unique considerations that can affect all stages of intervention with children and families.

REFERRAL

Children and families are often referred to social workers by other professionals such as teachers, police officers, and health care professionals. In this context, a **referral** is an appeal or, in some cases, a demand that social work services be provided.

CASE EXAMPLE A: Thirteen-year-old Lyn was recently sent to meet with Roger, the school social worker. Lyn has always been quiet in class, but her teachers have known her to be a good student who is conscientious about her studies and seems to get along well with classmates. However, Lyn's math teacher has noticed that Lyn has been absent or tardy several times in the past month and that she has come to class unprepared and seems to have lost interest in school. Last week, the math teacher observed Lyn sitting alone during recess and became concerned about these sudden changes in Lyn's behavior. The teacher contacted the school social worker, who called Lyn in for a meeting.

CASE EXAMPLE B: The Jones family was recently referred to a family service agency after allegations of abuse were investigated by Child Protective Services. The youngest son, a five-year-old boy named Jaime, had been taken to the doctor for an ear infection when the doctor noticed bruising on the child's neck. When Jaime's mother was asked about the bruises, she explained that she is a single mother raising five boys on her own and that she has to be strict to keep them in line. Sometimes she pinches their shoulders when they are misbehaving in public. The Child Protective Services worker who completed an assessment felt that the children were not at immediate risk of harm and therefore did not need to be removed from their mother. However, the worker did recommend parenting education and support for the mother. The Jones family was referred to the local family service agency for family counseling and for parent training for the mother. Here the family meets with another social work professional.

CASE EXAMPLE C: Kate is a social worker at a county hospital. A psychiatric nurse from the adolescent unit has asked Kate to help with the problem of insurance companies denying continued stay for adolescents admitted for suicide attempts and other self-injurious behaviors. The staff and many families were concerned that the children were being released without being stabilized; this increased the potential for future harm. In addition, the decreased time frame made it difficult to set up aftercare services to support the clients and their families. Kate must assess the policies on discharging youth.

These cases are just a few examples of the kinds of situations encountered by social workers who work with children and families. None of the clients initiated or requested social work services. These kinds of mandated or non-client-driven referrals are common in child and family services.

In such cases, the social worker must be respectful and understanding of the client and the client's view of the situation. For example, the social worker who counsels Ms. Jones and her sons must be open to hearing and understanding the perspective of each family member. Lyn's social worker must be patient, for Lyn may initially be uncomfortable meeting with him. Clients may not understand the referral or the purpose of social work intervention, so the social worker needs to explain. Gathering clear data from the referral source and from other systems is important as well. It is difficult to intervene effectively with a child or family without understanding the point of view of the referral source.

ASSESSMENT AND ENGAGEMENT

Collecting information from the referral source, the client, and related systems such as schools leads social workers to the next stage of intervention—the assessment. **Assessment** involves gathering data from a client and from the systems affecting the client, such as the family, the school counselor, and the probation officer (Hepworth et al., 2006). These data are analyzed to determine which issues are problematic for the client.

Assessment is critical because it sets up the goals and intervention plans for the client (Kayser & Lyon, 2000). Therefore, the social worker must be thorough to gather all relevant data and keep an open mind when analyzing the information.

CASE EXAMPLE A: When Roger, the school social worker, met with Lyn the first time, he already had some information for his assessment. He knew that Lyn was a good student and was usually responsible about her studies. In the past month, she seemed to have lost interest in school and to have withdrawn from her peers. Roger used the first meeting to assess whether Lyn was in need of intervention.

At this first meeting, Lyn was initially quiet and made no eye contact with Roger. When Roger asked about a poem she wrote that had been published in the school yearbook, she seemed to show some excitement. Roger then used his interviewing skills to discuss Lyn's current situation and the concerns that her math teacher had identified. Lyn told him that her grandparents moved back to China a month earlier. She cried when she explained that her grandfather had taken an interest in her education. He drove her to school each day and helped her with homework each afternoon. Her parents worked long hours, and she is an only child, so she was often home alone. Further questioning elicited the information that Lyn was having trouble sleeping since her grandparents moved away and was having difficulty getting up in the morning.

Roger asked Lyn if he could contact her parents to discuss the situation with them. She was initially hesitant, but Roger's support and encouragement seemed to ease her tension, and she gave him permission to call her mother that night. Roger's conversation with Lyn's mother, along with the interview with Lyn and her teacher's observations, all led Roger to his assessment of this case.

Three skills are critical in the assessment stage. First, the social worker must have effective interviewing skills to draw out information (Shulman, 2006). The school social worker asked Lyn questions that brought clarification of the issues observed by the teacher. He discovered that Lyn was having trouble sleeping, was feeling lonely, and was not as motivated in school. In addition, he uncovered some potential causes of these symptoms when Lyn mentioned that her problems began when her grandparents moved back to China. Asking clear and discerning questions, listening carefully, providing empathic and supportive responses, and presenting questions and information in a way that is appropriate to the client are essential parts of assessment (Shulman, 2006).

Secondly, a social worker must use engagement skills to connect with a client and draw the client into the intervention process (Hepworth et al., 2006). Engagement involves building a therapeutic connection with a client so that he or she feels involved in the problem-solving processes. This is especially significant because, as discussed earlier, many children and families do not initiate the work. In the case example, Lyn was initially quiet when she met with Roger. She may have been confused by the meeting and may not have understood its purpose. Roger's effort to connect with Lyn by discussing her poem is an example of the use of engagement skills; he was able to decrease her discomfort by discussing a topic of interest.

Finally, analyzing the information collected for the assessment is critical. For example, if the social worker had received information from the teacher, from Lyn, and from her mother that was consistent, but had failed to understand or interpret it correctly, the assessment would be faulty. Being able to draw conclusions that are sound and consistent with the information presented brings about intervention plans that are accurate and useful.

DETERMINING INTERVENTION STRATEGIES

The third stage of intervention involves using the assessment to generate possible solutions or interventions (Hepworth et al., 2006). In the case of children and families, the social worker may spend time exploring the solutions identified by all the family members. The family and worker can then collaborate by discussing each potential solution, evaluating which ones are best, and then determining which plan is best.

CASE EXAMPLE C: The nurse from the adolescent mental health unit was concerned about the premature discharge of suicidal adolescents as well as the lack of immediate follow-up care. Kate's assessment led her to investigate the county's policies on continued stays for adolescents who present with self-injurious symptoms. In addition, she decided to make a collateral contact with local outpatient counseling agencies to advocate for new policies allowing clients with symptoms to begin outpatient aftercare counseling services within 48 hours of discharge. In this case, the social worker was not intervening with a particular child or family, but instead was intervening at the system level to ultimately affect many children and families. Her assessment led her to an intervention plan that included advocacy and policymaking.

The problem presented by the nurse could have brought a variety of responses. Kate's assessment was that policy-level intervention would be the most effective way to address the problem.

When generating and evaluating potential intervention, it is important to consider all levels of intervention. Sometimes individual intervention is best. At other times system intervention is best, such as looking at the family-system influences in Lyn's case or the case of the Jones family. At times macro intervention that involves advocacy and policymaking will provide the best possible outcome.

PLANNING AND IMPLEMENTATION

Once the possible strategies have been evaluated and interventions have been identified, it is time to come up with a plan and put it into action. This involves working closely with clients to plan how to proceed with the interventions that have been selected.

> **CASE EXAMPLE B:** Child welfare social workers often respond by implementing a treatment plan that seeks to lower a family's risk of abuse or neglect (Pecora et al., 1992). In the Jones case, the social worker and Ms. Jones agreed that the family was under a lot of stress. Ms. Jones was willing to learn parenting techniques that would not involve physical punishment. As a result, the social worker and Ms. Jones agreed that family counseling and parent training would be appropriate interventions. The social worker found a family service agency near the Jones's home and asked Ms. Jones to initiate services within two weeks. The social worker followed up with Ms. Jones and learned that the family had their first appointment at the agency within one week.

Social workers are often involved in making referrals to other agencies to provide services for children and families. Making sure that a client has access to service is part of the social worker's job, as is following up in a supportive way. In other situations, planning and implementation may not require referral. For example, family counselors may provide parenting education, help a family improve communication, or advocate for a child. In any case, planning and implementation must engage the client in the intervention process.

TERMINATION

The final stage of the problem-solving model is known as termination. **Termination** is the process by which social workers and clients complete their work together. It is an important part of the intervention process because it determines how clients will remember the work that was completed. In a healthy termination the client and social worker feel good about their work together and agree that it is time to complete what they began. Endings that are abrupt and occur without preparation can damage the therapeutic relationship established between client and worker and may negatively impact positive gains (Compton, Galaway & Cournoyer, 2005).

> **CASE EXAMPLE B:** Ms. Jones became an active participant in the counseling she received from her family service agency social worker. She formed a positive working relationship with and learned to trust the social worker, even sharing information that she had never told anyone else. At the end of the tenth session, the social worker informed Ms. Jones that they had completed the maximum number of sessions allowed by the mental health system and that the counseling had to be discontinued. Imagine

Ms. Jones's disappointment when she lost a service she appreciated. Imagine her feelings about the abrupt end of a relationship with someone she trusted.

Endings occur in social work for many reasons. Most terminations occur when clients and social workers agree that their work is complete. However, forced endings such as the one in the case of Ms. Jones are also common. Services financed by a managed care insurance plan can end due to lack of authorization. If the social worker is aware of the limitations, he or she should explain them to the client at the beginning. Personal situations bring endings as well. A social worker may leave a position, or a client may relocate. In all cases, social workers should recognize the importance of endings and do all they can to make them comfortable and positive for clients.

In summary, important general strategies when working with children include collecting information from both the child and others who are significant in the child's life. The social worker must be aware of the developmental abilities of the child and adjust interventions accordingly. Specifically, child welfare workers need to understand the milestones of child development and be aware of the indicators and consequences of abuse and neglect (Crosson-Tower, 1998). Perhaps most important, although children are young, they should be treated with respect and dignity and included in the planning and decision making for the intervention process.

VALUES AND ETHICS

Social work values and ethics guide all work (see Chapter 1). When working with children and families, certain values are of particular interest. These include respect for the dignity and uniqueness of the individual, respect for self-determination, and respect for confidentiality.

RESPECT FOR THE DIGNITY AND UNIQUENESS OF THE INDIVIDUAL

A central value of the social work profession is the focus on embracing and supporting diversity. The profession recognizes that human experience is varied. Social workers must both respect and appreciate the uniqueness that each person brings to an interaction. This is especially significant in the case of children and families. A social worker should try to accept, value, and enjoy differences in family situations rather than requiring families to conform to what is seen as traditional or mainstream in society (Allen-Meares & Garvin, 2000). For example, the social worker should ask a child to identify the key people in his or her life and allow the child to define family.

The respect given to families should also be given to children. Recent studies have identified the trauma experienced by children and teenagers as a result of discrimination (Miliora, 2000) and have questioned the effect of being marginalized through racism on a child's development (Fisher, Wallace, & Fenton, 2000). Social workers must become knowledgeable about the effects of discrimination on child well-being and must be comfortable working with children from a variety of ethnic, racial, and cultural backgrounds. Because social workers commonly work with children from backgrounds different from their own, they need to become especially sensitive to and respectful of differences. Children and families should be treated in ways that model acceptance, not judgment.

RESPECT FOR SELF-DETERMINATION

Another social work value that is important in relation to children and families is **self-determination**—respect for a client's own choices (discussed earlier). Many problems present in our society stem from lack of access to resources or opportunities, which inhibits people from achieving their goals. Therefore, social workers seek to increase the opportunities for children and families so that they will have more choices in their efforts to address problems.

The emphasis on self-determination reflects the strengths perspective. By encouraging an individual, even a child, to focus on his or her own choices for behavior and treatment, the social worker emphasizes the person's resources and skills and encourages building on them. However, the goal of self-determination is complicated in working with children and families. As discussed earlier, children are often referred or mandated into treatment, and they may not perceive a problem or desire change. It is possible to work at achieving the goals of the referral source while overlooking the choices of the child. For example, when parents bring a child in for counseling due to a lack of compliance with parental authority, it is challenging to meet their goal while also supporting the child's right to self-determination. In addition, different family members often have different perspectives and varying goals. Negotiating the self-determination of each individual in a family system is difficult, yet essential.

RESPECT FOR CONFIDENTIALITY

Another important value in the field of social work, confidentiality, can also be complicated when working with children and families. Social workers sometimes hear about the physical or sexual abuse of a child. As state mandated reporters of abuse, they are required to break confidentiality for the purpose of keeping a child safe, regardless of the wishes of the child (Pecora et al., 1992; Zastrow & Kirst-Ashman, 1990). In such a situation, the social worker must make it clear to the child that safety overrides not telling and that telling is in the child's best interest, even if it seems like a betrayal of trust. The social worker must continue to work with the child to protect him or her and build a trusting relationship. The social worker strives to help the child understand his or her rights, including the right not to be violated by an adult.

Maintaining confidentiality is also complicated when parents want to know all of the details of social workers' sessions with their children. Parents generally want to protect and remain informed about their children, but children need to feel that they can talk openly with social workers. In some cases, a social worker does need to inform the parents, as when a client is suicidal or is being abused; in both such cases, the social worker is mandated to inform others as well, such as Child Protective Services in the case of abuse. The issue of teenage pregnancy and abortion is another area of difficulty for social workers pledged to keep confidentiality. There is no mandate for disclosure unless the young person is in danger or a victim of abuse, but there are laws in most states that a minor cannot have an abortion without

BOX 7.6	ETHICAL PRACTICE ... CHILD WELFARE

The child protective services agency in your state is underfunded. There are too few caseworkers to respond to reported cases of abuse or neglect in a timely fashion. You believe this puts children at increased risk. Do you have an ethical obligation to do something to address this problem? What can you do?

parental permission. Social workers who work with teenagers must know the law regarding the rights for termination of a pregnancy and be sensitive to the wishes of both children and their parents. It can be difficult to navigate between the confidences of a child and what is in his or her best interest to disclose to parents. To the extent possible, much of what is discussed by children can and should remain confidential. Children need a safe place to express themselves. Respecting a child's right to confidentiality helps create that sense of safety. However, parents' rights and needs to know about the well-being of their children must also be respected.

CRITICAL ISSUES FACING CHILDREN AND FAMILIES

A number of areas critical to children and families present challenges to social workers, program planners, and policymakers. This section will cover several of them, including child maltreatment, foster care, substance abuse, sexual behavior, delinquency, divorce, and poverty.

CHILD MALTREATMENT

One serious issue that continues to confront children and families today is child maltreatment. The effects of child maltreatment reach beyond physical damage (Corcoran, 2000); children who endure maltreatment also develop other social and psychological problems that often affect them well into adulthood. The costs of this problem are significant and long lasting.

Child maltreatment encompasses all of the ways children are hurt by the people who are expected to care for them. This may include physical abuse, sexual abuse, emotional abuse, or neglect. Maltreatment can occur in the context of the child's home or outside of the home in the child's neighborhood or school or in the home of a relative or friend.

Social workers often work with children who have been abused and neglected. A teacher who overhears a child talk about being hit by his stepmother refers the child to the school social worker. A social worker in a hospital setting is called in to consult when a doctor questions the possibility of sexual abuse. A child may disclose abuse to a family counselor during a session. Social workers who work in child protective services assess and manage cases of maltreatment every day. Whether through education programs, advocating for policies that value the rights of children, or participating in programs that assess and treat children, social workers play a significant role in the problem of child maltreatment. The investigation and determination of maltreatment is often complex. The box "Becoming a Change Agent," presents the complexities of a highly publicized case of child maltreatment.

BOX 7.7   BECOMING A CHANGE AGENT

On April 3, 2008, police raided a compound in Eldorado, Texas. A polygamist sect lived in the compound. The raid was prompted by an anonymous phone call to a family violence center by a 16-year-old girl who reported being forced into an underage marriage to a 50-year-old man, who she claimed beat and raped her. She said she had given birth at age 15. Texas law states that girls under 16 cannot marry, even with parental consent. Authorities removed 463 children between the ages of 6 months and 17 years of age, from the compound. The children were placed in foster homes around the state while their cases were being investigated. This became one of the largest child welfare cases in history.

The case raises a number of challenging questions. The local authorities knew about the group and accusations of underage marriage and sexual abuse for a number of years. They did not intervene until the anonymous phone call. Some authorities stated that they did not intervene because the group's practices were based on their religious beliefs and we all have the right to religious freedom; they did not want to violate their civil rights. Originally, officials only suspected abuse of girls living at the compound. They stated that they also removed male children "because they were being groomed to become adult perpetrators in the sect" (Roberts and Castro, 2008). Later concerns were raised that some of the boys might also have been victims of physical and sexual abuse.

Analyzing the Situation

- Go back and look at news stories about this case. Why did the authorities decide to remove all of the girls from the compound, rather than only those they suspected had been victims of abuse? What is the practice of child protective services in your area in regard to removing children from the home? If abuse is suspected, do they only remove the specific child who they believe has been abused or all children in the home? Why do you think they do it this way?
- Where do the bounds of religious freedom end and the responsibilities of the state to protect children begin?
- Some civil libertarians were concerned about the reasoning that it was right to take the boys from the home because they were learning practices that might lead them to be abusers. What do you think about this?

What Can Social Workers Do?

Given your analysis, what might social workers do to address the needs of abused children in more traditional cases involving individual families or in larger cases such as the one reported above? What interventions could you suggest at the individual level? The community level? The institutional level? And the policy level?

What Can You Do?

What one step might you take now, alone or working with others, to prevent abuse or neglect of children in your community? What are the barriers that might keep you from taking this step? What could you do to reduce those barriers?

FOSTER CARE

When a child is in need of a safe place to live, foster care can be a good option. Many foster families are nurturing and supportive of the children in their care. But there are also problems with the foster care system, including too few quality placements, growing numbers of children needing care, high costs, and increasing length of time spent in foster care.

The foster care population stands at over half a million children (Administration for Children and Families, 2004). Historically, at least one-third of the children in foster care never return home (General Accounting Office, 1998). When reunification with their families is impossible, some children may not be adopted.

Often, children in foster care have been severely affected by the maltreatment they experienced, are emotionally and physically troubled, and can be difficult to manage. The challenges of needing temporary help while finding permanent solutions for children is the task of social workers in the child welfare system.

ALCOHOL AND DRUG ABUSE

Another critical issue for children and families is the presence of alcohol or drug abuse. Families and children are deeply affected by parental alcoholism and drug addiction. Since families are small, interrelated systems, having a parent who abuses alcohol or drugs leads to conflict, violence, financial stress, neglect, or emotional abuse. Additionally, research indicates that the presence of an alcohol-abusing parent results in decreased connection and difficulty expressing emotion, limiting the family's potential for healthy relationships and effective communication (Dundas, 2000).

Families are also seriously affected when a child is involved with illegal substances. Recent studies suggest that teens and even preteens continue to experiment with tobacco, alcohol, and drugs (Ashford, Lecroy, & Lortie, 2001). Such behaviors have serious consequences for these young people and their families. Heavy drug or alcohol use results in problems at school, conflicts with parents, involvement with the legal system, and negative health consequences. In addition, alcohol and drug experimentation can also lead to other risky behaviors, such as theft, driving when intoxicated, unsafe decisions related to sexuality, and other impulsive choices.

Social workers often see situations of alcohol or drug abuse by parents or children. This is especially true for school social workers, caseworkers in child welfare agencies, social workers in police departments, hospital social workers, and counselors in family service agencies. Typically, social workers refer parents and children who abuse drugs and alcohol or are affected by family members' abuse to prevention programs, outpatient counseling, group counseling, or inpatient substance abuse programs.

DECISIONS ABOUT SEXUAL BEHAVIOR

Another important issue commonly seen by social workers who intervene with children and families is impulsivity in teen sexual behavior. Because of the risks of contracting HIV/AIDS and other sexually transmitted diseases (STDs) and the risk of pregnancy, it is critical for social workers to educate teens about the dangers of unsafe sex. Current studies show that most teens engage in sexual activity (Kann, Williams, Ross, Lowry, & Graham, 2000), much of it high-risk sexual behavior that often occurs simultaneously with other risky behaviors such as alcohol and drug use. Knowledge about the consequences of sexual behaviors varies greatly. Many young people today consider anything that cannot result in pregnancy to be safe, so oral sex has gained popularity without regard for the possibility of contracting STDs. Advocacy for the use of condoms is very controversial, leaving many young people unaware or uninterested in the role of condoms in preventing the spread of STDs. The rate of STDs among adolescents is higher than in the general population. Although adolescents represent about a quarter of the sexually active population, they account for almost half of all new STDs (Centers for Disease Control and Prevention, 2007). Thus, it is essential for teens to be empowered with knowledge about their sexual choices.

Intervention involves a variety of modes and settings. Social workers often plan and implement prevention programs, including facilitating groups, using peer education strategies to train youth to speak to other teens about sexuality, and working with schools to strengthen sex education programs. In addition, many programs work with teens who are pregnant or have been diagnosed with an STD. Counseling that emphasizes young people's choices strengthens their ability to make decisions.

DELINQUENCY

Another critical issue for youth today is delinquency. The term **delinquency** refers to any behavior that is illegal and could involve a child with the juvenile justice system. The behavior may be illegal only for minors, such as running away, using alcohol, being truant, or violating curfew, or it may involve offenses that are illegal regardless of age, such as theft, assault, violence, and the use of illegal substances.

Public concern about the problem of delinquency continues to grow as a result of perceived increases in school violence and teen substance abuse. School social workers, social workers in police departments, and child and family counselors are most likely to see such problems. All of them must seek to understand and intervene with children who engage in delinquent behavior in a way that helps the children respect themselves as well as those around them.

Runaway and homeless youth often fall under the category of delinquency. Because they are minors, living on the street or in a shelter means they are unlikely to be attending school and are away from home without permission. While the youth may be seen as committing a delinquent act, there are high numbers of runaway and homeless youth who have no place to go. They may have been thrown out of their homes or fought with family members and do not think they are welcome to return. Financial destitution may have caused the family to lose housing, and the older youth are on their own. They may have been victims of violence or sexual abuse and do not consider the home to be a safe place. These reasons for delinquency among youth complicate the role that social workers play with homeless and runaway youth. Although they may be technically breaking the law, their social service needs are significant and their life on the street places them at great risk. Intervention is required beyond the determination of delinquency.

DIVORCE

Wallerstein's early work (1983) showed that divorce can have a negative effect on children who are unable to process the loss of their intact family appropriately. Other research suggests that the first year after a divorce can be traumatic for both children and adults. Social workers also commonly see clients who are affected by the stress of single parenthood and complications resulting from remarriage and blended families. Family counselors and school social workers commonly work to help children and families achieve the emotional adjustment needed in such situations.

POVERTY

Poverty is a critical problem for millions of children. It can have negative effects on their health, development, and overall well-being; economic deprivation leads to

BOX 7.8	WHAT DO YOU THINK?

What other critical issues affect children and families today? How might social workers respond to these concerns?

poorer health, dangerous living conditions, and lack of opportunities for social, economic, and educational advancement. As discussed in Chapter 4, the problems associated with poverty and programs that provide income support for families are critical areas in need of social work practice and social welfare services.

IMMIGRATION

In recent years, the tightening of immigration enforcement and new laws aimed at removing people who are undocumented has led to a rising concern among child welfare service providers. As undocumented parents are arrested and detained for deportation, their children are being left behind because the children were born in the United States and are legal citizens. Workplace raids left hundreds of children without one or both of their parents within minutes, as undocumented workers were immediately arrested and targeted for deportation. With tightened enforcement, people are no longer being released pending deportation hearings, rather they are being held in prison. For example, 38-year-old Ismael Valeriano had worked in the United States for almost 20 years and was raising his three sons who were all born in the United States. He was arrested when he went to claim his impounded car, which was being held for driving without a valid license and insurance. He was immediately arrested because he was undocumented and was held for several months until a community group could raise the bail. In the meantime, his three children ages 12, 15, and 16 were at home taking care of themselves until their grandmother could travel from out of state to care for them (Gonzalez, 2008). Their case raises concern for child welfare advocates, because no one knows how many children who are U.S. citizens themselves are being raised by undocumented parents. These children will either be left to grow up in the United States without their parents or will have to move to countries where they have never lived before. For those who work in immigrant neighborhoods and schools, the impact of the increase in arrests and laws geared to remove undocumented people is having a profound impact on the thousands of children in these immigrant families.

WORKING WITH CHILDREN AND FAMILIES FROM A STRENGTHS PERSPECTIVE

The issues facing children and families today can be daunting. Poverty, child maltreatment, substance abuse, and lack of health care are all serious concerns that social workers must address head on. At the same time, the strengths perspective in social work takes the position that problems are best addressed by identifying and embellishing the strengths of children, families, and communities (Saleebey, 2006).

While social work has a history of adopting the medical model that focuses on assessing and labeling problems, the strengths perspective requires social workers to look within the family or community for the resources needed to solve the complex problems facing children today (Blundo, 2006). A growing body of literature suggests that children and families are resilient and that strengths such as insight, appraisal, social support, and even a sense of humor can help people to cope effectively with the challenges they face (Benard, 1993; Lietz, 2006; 2007; Werner & Smith, 1992; Wolin & Wolin, 1993). Research also suggests that families who have hope can better adapt to challenges (Walsh, 2002). In the same way, a sense of hope and belief that change is possible can help social workers to move forward in their efforts to address the problems facing the children and families in their communities.

CONCLUSION

Working in the field of child and family services is both challenging and rewarding. Many problems face today's youth. Despite the fact that the United States is one of the wealthiest countries in the world, poverty continues to be problematic. Child abuse and neglect devastate children despite prevention programs, laws that mandate reporting, and the presence of a child welfare system. Teens engage in risky behaviors such as unprotected sex, experimentation with alcohol and drugs, and crime. Families dissolve as often as they remain intact, and the stresses on single-parent homes continue to challenge parents and children alike.

However, many advances have been made in the field of child and family services. Prior to the twentieth century, child welfare and concern for the rights of children simply did not exist. Not until the 1960s did social work professionals recognize the value of the family and begin working from a family-centered perspective. Knowledge about the critical issues facing children and families has advanced, and research brings new theories and knowledge to the field.

While the problems are great, so is the opportunity. As a profession that fights for the rights of those with less opportunity, social work plays a crucial role in the welfare of children. What is needed are leaders to champion the rights of children and to explore new ways to intervene with children and families.

Key Terms

adoption, (p. 181)

assessment, (p. 186)

childhood, (p. 175)

child welfare, (p. 180)

cognitive development, (p. 178)

delinquency, (p. 194)

family, (p. 175)

family preservation services, (p. 181)

foster care, (p. 181)

maltreatment, (p. 181)

permanency planning, (p. 181)

psychosocial theory, (p. 178)

referral, (p. 185)

self-determination, (p. 190)

social learning theory, (p. 178)

termination, (p. 188)

vulnerable, (p. 175)

Questions for Discussion

1. In the dominant American culture, the term *family* is often assumed to refer to a heterosexual married couple with children. What do you see as an appropriate definition of *family?* Does your definition impose any limits on social work practice?

2. A clear definition of the term *child maltreatment* was provided early in this chapter. Determining whether maltreatment has occurred is not always that easy. What factors do social workers need to consider when they assess whether an event is a case of maltreatment?

3. What does the phrase "best interest of the child" really mean? Give an example of a case in which two different social workers could interpret the "best interest of the child" differently.

4. When working with children, why is it important to be knowledgeable about stages of development?

5. Identify two critical issues other than those discussed in this chapter that greatly affect children and families, and discuss why they are significant.

Change Agent Exercise

The agency in your state that is responsible for investigating and acting on suspected cases of child maltreatment is underfunded. There are too few caseworkers to respond to reported cases of abuse and neglect in a timely fashion. You believe this puts children at increased risk. Do you have an ethical obligation to try to intervene to try to address this problem?

Chapter Exercises

1. **Children as a Vulnerable Group**
   In the field of social work what does it mean to be vulnerable? Do you see children as vulnerable? Why?

2. **Defining** *Family*
   Divide into groups, and develop a consensus definition of *family* within your group.

   The U. S. Census Bureau defines *family* as "A group of 2 or more persons related by birth, marriage, or adoption and residing together in a household." How does this definition differ from your group's?

   Share each group's definition with the other groups. What common themes are found in the definitions developed by all the groups in the class?

   If your definition were adopted by national or state agencies, how might it affect family-related social welfare policies or services provided by social welfare agencies?

3. **Understanding Child Maltreatment**
   List behaviors that you believe constitute child maltreatment (abuse or neglect).

   Give examples of ways of raising children that might be interpreted by some people as appropriate and by others as maltreatment.

4. **Ecological Assessment**

Once you are familiar with the concepts involved in an ecological assessment, review the following case and answer the questions that follow:

CASE EXAMPLE: Joey is a 12-year-old boy who is currently living in foster care with a relative. Six months ago he was removed from the care of his father after his school nurse called CPS when Joey came to school with bruises on his arm and face. Joey was placed with his maternal aunt and uncle, who live in a community about 50 minutes away from his home. According to case files from the CPS worker, Joey has lived with his father since the death of his mother two years ago. His father has struggled with alcohol abuse since his wife's death, and he becomes angry when drunk.

The service plan for the family requires Joey's father to attend weekly counseling at the local family service agency, to attend alcohol treatment meetings weekly, and to have weekly visits with Joey that are supervised by Joey's aunt and uncle. Unfortunately, conflict between Joey's foster family and his father has limited the number of visits. Joey is having difficulty adjusting to his new school, so he is meeting with the school social worker. All this information will be presented to the juvenile court at his six-month review.

Identify all the systems that affect Joey's life.

Discuss the interactions between Joey and the systems you have identified.

5. **Small-Group Exercise: Child Protective Services**

Contact the child protective service (CPS) agency that is charged with the task of assessing and treating child maltreatment in your community. Each member of your group should interview a different member of the CPS staff (preferably, the CPS staff members should have different roles in the organization) so as to best answer the following questions. Compare your information with that of the other members of your group, and answer the following questions by incorporating all of your group's information:

What is the organization's definition of maltreatment?

What is the agency's process for identifying children who need to be assessed for maltreatment?

Once maltreatment is substantiated, what is the process for providing ongoing assessment and treatment?

What role do social workers play in this process?

What policies guide the decisions made by workers at this agency?

What do staff members see as the greatest needs as they face the problem of child abuse or neglect?

6. **Family Ethics Exercise**

Complete the questions following the Case Example either on your own or in small groups.

CASE EXAMPLE: You are a counselor with a nonprofit family service agency. A couple has been coming to you for marriage counseling once a week for the past three months. The husband lost his job six months ago, and the family is struggling to make ends meet. During one session, the husband tells you that he has been receiving Supplemental Security Income (SSI) payments from the state for his aged mother who used to live with them but who moved overseas to live with his sister two years ago. You suspect that this is a case of fraud—that the couple is breaking the law and is getting money that the family is not entitled to.

Should you report this case to the Department of Social Services? Discuss the pros and cons of doing so.

PROS:
CONS:

What social work values are in conflict in the situation? How might the Code of Ethics guide you in making a decision?

Would your obligation to report the case be different if your client had robbed a bank or was planning to do so? Why? What if your client were selling drugs to minors?

References

Administration for Children and Families. (2004). *The adoption and foster care analysis and reporting system report*. Washington, DC: Department of Health and Human Services.

Administration for Children and Families (2006). *Child Maltreatment 2006*. Washington, DC: Department of Health and Human Services.

Administration on Children, Youth and Families. (2001). *Fact sheet on administration for children and families*. Washington, DC: Department of Health and Human Services.

Allen-Meares, P. (1995). *Social work with children and adolescents*. New York: Longman.

Allen-Meares, P., & Garvin, C. (2000). *The handbook of social work direct practice*. Thousand Oaks, CA: Sage Publications.

Ashford, J., Lecroy, C., & Lortie, K. (2001). *Human behavior in the social environment*. Belmont, CA.: Wadsworth.

Axinn, J., & Stern, M. J. (2008). *Social welfare: A history of the American response to need* (7th ed.). Boston: Allyn and Bacon.

Bandura, A. (1977). *Social learning theory*. Englewood Cliffs, NJ: Prentice Hall.

Benard, B. (1993). Fostering resiliency in kids. *Educational Leadership*, 51, 3, 44–48.

Blundo, R. (2006). Shifting our habits of mind: Learning to practice from a strengths perspective. In D. Saleebey (Ed.) *The Strengths Perspective in Social Work Practice* (4th ed., pp. 25–45). Boston: Allyn & Bacon.

Casey Foundation. (2006). *2006 Kids Count Data Book*. Baltimore, MD: Annie E. Casey Foundation.

Centers for Disease Control and Prevention. (2007). *STD surveillance 2006: Adolescents and young adults*. Atlanta, GA: Author.

Chafel, J. A. (1993). *Child poverty and public policy*. Washington DC: Urban Institute.

Chafel, J. A., & Condit, K. (1993). Advocacy for children in poverty. In Chafel, J. (ed.), *Child poverty and public policy* (pp. 273–302). Washington DC: Urban Institute.

Children's Defense Fund. (2004). *The state of America's children 2004*. Washington, DC: Author.

Compton, B., Galaway, B., & Cournoyer, B. (2005). *Social Work Processes* (7th ed.). Belmont, CA: Brooks/Cole.

Corcoran, J. (2000). *Evidence-based social work practice with families: A lifespan approach*. New York: Springer.

Crosson-Tower, C. (1998). *Exploring child welfare: A practice perspective*. Needham Heights, MA: Allyn & Bacon.

DeNavas-Walt, C., Proctor, B. D., & Smith, J. (2008). *Income, poverty, and health insurance coverage in the United States: 2007*. Washington, DC: U.S. Census Bureau.

Dundas, I. (2000). Cognitive/affective distancing as a coping strategy of children of parents with a drinking problem. *Alcoholism Treatment Quarterly*, 18, 4, 85–98.

Eamon, M. K. (2000). Structural model of the effects of poverty on externalizing and internalizing behaviors of four- to five-year-old children. *Social Work Research*, 24, 3, 143–154.

Erikson, E. H. (1968). *Identity, youth, and crisis*. New York: W. W. Norton.

Fisher, C., Wallace, S., & Fenton, R. (2000). Discrimination distress during adolescence. *Journal of Youth & Adolescence*, 29, 6, 679–695.

General Accounting Office. (1998). *Foster care: Implementation of the Multiethnic Placement Act poses difficult challenges*. GAO/HEHS-98-204. Washington, DC: Author.

Goldenberg, I. & Goldenberg, H. (2004). *Family Therapy: An Overview* (6th ed.). Pacific Grove, CA: Thomson & Brooks/Cole.

Gonzalez, D. (2008, February 17). U.S. immigration law drives husband, wife apart. *Arizona Republic*, p. A1, A 18.

Hepworth, D., Rooney, R., Rooney, G. D., Strom-Gottfried, K., & Larsen, J. (2006). *Direct social work practice: Theory and skills* (6th ed.). Belmont, CA: Brooks/Cole.

Hess McCartt, P., McGowans, B., & Botsko, M. (2000). A preventive services program model for preserving and supporting families over time. *Child Welfare*, 1, 227–263.

Kann, L., Williams, B., Ross, J., Lowry, R., & Graham, J. (2000). Youth risk behavior surveillance. *Journal of School Health*, 70, 7, 271–285.

Kayser, J. A., & Lyon, M. A. (2000). Teaching social workers to use psychological assessment data. *Child Welfare League of America*, 26, 197–222.

Kilpatrick, A., & Holland, T. (1999). *Working with families: An integrative model by level of need*. Boston: Allyn & Bacon.

Lietz, C. (2006). Uncovering stories of family resilience: A mixed methods study of resilient families, part 1. *Families in Society*, 87, 4, 575–582.

Lietz, C. (2007). Uncovering stories of family resilience: A mixed methods study of resilient families, part 2. *Families in Society*, 88, 1, 147–155.

Lindsey, D. (1994). *The welfare of children*. New York: Oxford University Press.

Mallucio, A., & Anderson, G. (2000). Future challenges and opportunities in child welfare. *Child Welfare*, 1, 3–9.

Mather, J., Lager, P. & Harris, N. (2007). *Child Welfare: Policies and Best Practices*. Belmont, CA: Thomson Brooks/Cole.

Miliora, M. (2000). Beyond empathetic failures: Cultural racism as narcissistic trauma and disenchantment of grandiosity. *Clinical Social Work Journal*, 28, 1, 43–54.

Pecora, P., Whittaker, J., & Maluccio, A. (1992). *The child welfare challenge*. New York: Aldine De Gruyter.

Petr, C. (1998). *Social work with children and their families*. New York: Oxford University Press.

Piaget, J. (1965). *The moral judgment of the child*. New York: Free Press.

Roberts, M., & Castro, A. (2008). Officials probing possible abuse of boys in polygamous sect. *San Francisco Examiner Website*. http://www.examiner.com/printa-1369488~Officials_probing_possible_abuse_of_boys_in_polygamous_sect.html.

Saleebey, D. 2006. (Ed.) *The strengths perspective in social work practice*. 4th edition. Boston: Pearson/Allyn & Bacon.

Shulman, L. (2006). *The Skills of Helping Individuals, Families, Groups and Communities* (5th ed.). Belmont, CA: Thomson & Brooks/Cole.

Walsh, F. (2002). A family resilience framework: Innovative practice applications. *Family Relations, 51*, 2, 130–137.

Wallerstein, J. S. (1983). Children of divorce: The psychological tasks of the child. *American Journal of Orthopsychiatry, 53*, 2, 230–243.

Werner, E., & Smith, R. (1992). *Overcoming the odds*. Ithaca, NY: Cornell University Press.

Wolin, S., & Wolin, S. (1993). *The resilience self: How survivors of troubled families rise above adversity*. New York: Villard.

Woods, M., & Hollis, F. (1990). *Casework: A psychosocial therapy*. New York: McGraw Hill.

Zastrow, C., & Kirst-Ashman, K. (2007). *Understanding human behavior and the social environment* (7th ed.). Belmont, CA.: Wadsworth.

Gerontology: Working with People Who Are Older

CHAPTER 8

Co-authored by Kathleen Bailey, MSW

Heinle Division of Cengage Learning

Seventy-year-old Tresca and 74-year-old James Brady have been married for 45 years. Both are active and healthy. Mr. Brady works part-time as a consultant, and Mrs. Brady volunteers one day a week at a center for pregnant teens. They have 11 grandchildren with whom they spend much time, often caring for the youngest when his parents are at work. They have a beautiful home and are financially independent. Their one complaint about being older is that U.S. culture portrays older people as sexless and weak or as "greedy geezers" who do not want to pay taxes for school improvements.

Thomas Wayne is 72 years old and is a patient in the geriatric unit of a veteran's hospital. Complications from diabetes resulted in the amputation of Mr. Wayne's right leg. His liver is damaged from a lifelong struggle with alcoholism. He has no living relatives and has been homeless for several years. Mr. Wayne does not know where he will go when he is discharged from the hospital. He can no longer function without considerable help.

Conchita Alvarez is 82 years old and has been diagnosed with Alzheimer's disease. For more than 40 years, her favorite activity was cooking. She had never left the house without turning off the oven—until yesterday. Ms. Alvarez is forgetful and gets confused easily. She gets most upset when people think she knows things that she does not, that she just cannot remember any more. Ms. Alvarez lives with her 60-year-old daughter, who worries that she can no longer safely care for her mother.

Barbara and Sam Howe, ages 80 and 81, have lived independently in the home they owned for 30 years. Barbara is suffering from Parkinson's disease and is no longer able to drive or prepare meals and requires some assistance with basic activities of daily living (bathing, dressing, etc.). Sam is finding it difficult to provide for all of their needs, so they have decided to move into a continuing care retirement community (CCR) where help such as meals, housekeeping, and medication management are available on-site. The community offers three advancing levels of service: independent apartments, assisted living apartments, and a skilled nursing facility that will be able to provide for increasing needs they may have as they get older. Although Sam and Barbara do not want to leave their home, their children live out of state and they feel this is the best option to prevent more moves in the future.

Bob Williams, age 68, was a corporate law specialist at a large accounting firm until he was recently fired by the new CEO, Mr. Johnson, who is 37 years old. Mr. Johnson told Mr. Williams that he was "over the hill" and that the company needed "young blood."

More than 37 million people (12.4 percent of the population) in the United States are over the age of 65 (U.S. Bureau of the Census, 2007). The vast majority of them are economically independent (median worth of $108,885), active (12.4 million exercise regularly), and healthy, and 81 percent live in their own homes. Millions have part-time or full-time jobs or volunteer their time to important causes. Some are helping raise their grandchildren (U.S. Bureau of the Census, 2005).

However, individuals over 65 are affected by ageist attitudes, and some are directly discriminated against. **Ageism** is prejudice against people based solely on age. The term is sometimes used about young people, but it is generally associated with older people. Prejudice and rejection, as discussed in Chapters 3 and 6, are based largely on misconceptions and myths (see "More About … Age Discrimination").

| ## MORE ABOUT ... AGE DISCRIMINATION

Joe Moore was the widely acclaimed offensive line coach for Notre Dame University's football team. Just before Christmas 1996, when he was 66 years old, Joe was fired by the new head coach, 43-year-old Bob Davie. Davie allegedly made derogatory age-related comments when he fired

Moore. Moore filed a lawsuit alleging that he was the victim of age discrimination. In 1999 a jury found in Moore's favor, and Notre Dame agreed to pay his legal fees, which amounted to $85,000.

Sources: Van Duch, 1998; Lieberman, 2001.

The social work profession is committed to preventing and fighting ageism, negative stereotypes, myths, and negative practices that affect older people. A minority of older people, such as Conchita Alvarez and Thomas Wayne, are in need of more direct social work interventions. They may live in poverty or be homeless, suffer from depression, be victims of elder abuse, or have health-related problems and diseases associated with aging.

Gerontological social work—social work practice with people who are older—is a specialized area that requires extensive knowledge and a unique set of skills. **Gerontology** is the study of the biological, psychological, and social aspects of aging. The goal of gerontological social workers is to promote and advance older clients' social, emotional, and physical well-being so that they can live more independent and satisfying lives.

HUMAN DEVELOPMENT WITHIN THE SOCIAL CONTEXT

When a social worker enters an older person's life, the problems may seem overwhelming. Gerontological social workers use an ecological approach (see Chapter 1) to examine the context of an older client's life. They analyze the dynamics between client and family, client and neighborhood, client and social supports, client and medical supports, and client and other systems. Extensive specialized knowledge is required to work effectively with clients who are older. Four major knowledge categories are relevant: (1) biological and physiological aspects of aging; (2) cognitive processes and emotional/psychological development; (3) sociological aspects of aging; and, (4) legal, political, and economic aspects of aging.

BIOLOGICAL AND PHYSIOLOGICAL ASPECTS OF AGING

Social workers need to have a basic understanding of the effect of aging on the body's systems in order to help older clients like Thomas Wayne, the 72-year-old veteran with health problems and no place to live, and Conchita Alvarez, the 82-year-old woman who has Alzheimer's disease. Mr. Wayne and Ms. Alvarez need help to establish daily routines and to monitor and control symptoms so as to avoid medical crises. This requires a basic knowledge of the functions of human physiology, including the circulatory, endocrine, respiratory, musculoskeletal, gastrointestinal, urinary, nervous, digestive, and reproductive systems. Normal aging of the body's systems need not diminish a person's quality of life. Knowledge of the way aging does affect the body's systems helps social workers assist elderly clients in modifying their lifestyles and homes so they can continue to enjoy satisfying and productive lives.

Social workers must have knowledge about the physical and mental impairments that are related to chronic illness as well as normal changes that may occur in the senses (sight, hearing, touch, taste, and smell) and sleep patterns as a person ages (Hooyman & Kiyak, 2007). Social workers can help people adapt to these changes so that their daily activities are not drastically altered. It may be as simple as pointing out the availability of large-print books or books on audiotape to a client who has weakened eyesight or of telephone amplifiers for a client who has a hearing deficit. For older people who have difficulty sleeping and are at risk for dependency on sleeping pills, the social worker can suggest using relaxation techniques, abstaining from certain foods and drinks, taking daily walks, and avoiding afternoon naps.

In addition, gerontological social workers need to be aware of commonly used medications and of advances in pharmacology. Eighty-seven percent of individuals age 65 or over take a prescription drug on a regular basis. Of those who say they are currently taking prescription drugs regularly, they report taking on average four prescription drugs daily (AARP, 2005). Social workers need to be aware of the side effects of commonly used medications and of potentially harmful interactions between prescription and over-the-counter drugs. In some cases, clients may be taking several drugs prescribed by different doctors, each of whom may not be aware of the other prescriptions. An adverse drug event (ADE), more commonly called a drug reaction, could lead to a hospitalization or, in the extreme, a loss of independence for this group. With a basic knowledge of medications, social workers can help monitor a person's prescriptions.

COGNITIVE PROCESS AND EMOTIONAL/PSYCHOLOGICAL DEVELOPMENT

When older people retire, as James and Tresca Brady have, they must restructure their time, build relationships outside of work, and develop new identities not linked to their jobs. Elders who are able to accomplish these tasks are more likely to have satisfying postretirement years. On the basis of theories of personality development, gerontological social workers can help clients navigate stressful life events such as retirement, widowhood, physical decline, residential relocation, loss, and approaching death.

Gerontological social workers also need to know about factors that affect learning, intelligence, and memory as people age. The inability to learn or perform new tasks, impairment of intelligence, and memory loss are not necessarily synonymous with aging. Many life and environmental factors interact to affect cognitive processes. For example, anxiety in late life has been found to be a risk factor for disability (Lenze, et al., 2001). Anxiety can adversely impact well-being and recovery and hasten decline in the elderly.

SOCIOLOGICAL ASPECTS OF AGING

As a victim of ageism, Bob Williams, who was fired from his job at a large accounting firm, knows firsthand how society's expectations for a 68-year-old man can be limiting and shortsighted. To be effective advocates for clients like Mr. Williams, gerontological social workers need to understand social roles and expectations—for example, marital roles, grandparenthood, and sexual behavior—and how they change as people age.

Activity theory (Westerberg, 2004) and disengagement theory (Chen, 2003) examine role changes among the elderly. Activity theory proposes that the more active a person is, the more satisfied that person will be during his or her golden years. Disengagement theory, by contrast, asserts that to withdraw and become more introspective as one grows older is normal and healthy. Both behaviors can be found in people as they age.

LEGAL, ECONOMIC, AND POLITICAL ASPECTS

Bob Williams was a victim of age discrimination. Thomas Wayne wants to die with dignity. How can a social worker help Mr. Williams and Mr. Wayne with their problems? To be effective advocates, gerontological social workers need to be well informed about important legal issues, court cases, legislation, and economic policies that affect and protect the rights of the elderly. Issues include age discrimination, guardianship and conservatorship, living wills, power of attorney for health care, and Social Security and pension benefits.

Gerontological social workers in medical facilities need to be aware of the legal rights of chronically and terminally ill older people. One study reported that doctors honor patients' treatment options and choices only about half the time (Legal Counsel for the Elderly, 2008). The medical system is designed to deemphasize patients' wishes unless patients aggressively advocate or someone else advocates for them. It is important for an elderly person to name an agent (i.e., a like-minded friend or family member) who can make health care decisions when the patient can no longer do it himself or herself. In the absence of a legally executed health care directive (power of attorney or living will), the patient who is incapacitated is at risk for receiving treatments he or she otherwise would not have authorized.

To be assertive and well-informed advocates, gerontological social workers need to master this extensive knowledge base. They must understand and be able to work within the political system to promote the rights of people who are older, the legal system to enforce the rights of older people, and the medical system to protect their rights.

SOCIAL WORK PRACTICE WITH PEOPLE WHO ARE OLDER

As the population ages and people live longer, there is greater need for professional social workers. Although people of all ages have medical, economic, and social needs, these concerns become specialized as people get older. What are some of the unique dimensions of gerontological social work?

HISTORICAL BACKGROUND

Although social workers have been employed in health care settings since 1905, the profession paid little attention to practice with older people until 1945 (Lowy, 1985). That year the first professional organization, the Gerontological Society of

America, was established to promote age-related issues. Today it is a multidisciplinary organization of physicians, biologists, social workers, psychologists, and others that focuses on research and practice issues with older people. Two years later, in 1947, the National Conference of Social Workers highlighted a paper by social worker Rose McHugh on practice with people who are older. McHugh emphasized the dignity and uniqueness of older clients (Lowy, 1985). In 1958 the Council on Social Work Education, with support from the Ford Foundation, presented the Seminar on Aging in Aspen, Colorado. This was the first time social work educators discussed how to assess the social service needs of older clients and how to build a curriculum that prepared students to work with them (Lowy, 1985).

The federal government began to recognize the needs and contributions of older people in 1960 when it established the National Council on Aging. The first White House Conference on Aging was held in 1961 and led to a 1963 speech by President John F. Kennedy entitled "The Elderly Citizens of Our Nation." In this speech Kennedy promoted housing, employment, and health care policies that would benefit people who are older.

The momentum from the 1961 White House Conference and Kennedy's 1963 speech led to the passage of several significant pieces of legislation. The Economic Opportunity Act of 1964 (EOA) funded community-based social services, including services for the elderly. The 1965 **Older Americans Act (OAA)** established the federal Administration on Aging (AOA), and statewide **Area Agencies on Aging (AAA)**, both of which were designed to coordinate and fund social services for older people. Unfortunately, both the EOA and OAA were and remain seriously underfunded. However, the federal government recognized the health care needs of people who are older with the establishment of the Medicare and Medicaid programs in 1965.

The 1960s also saw a dramatic increase in the number of skilled nursing facilities. Many nursing homes hired social workers to provide services for residents and their families. For the first time, social workers were beginning to adjust their practice knowledge and skills to the unique needs of older clients (Holosko & Holosko, 1996).

A second White House Conference on Aging in 1971 identified ways to make life more rewarding for older people. The attendees concluded that the elderly should have adequate incomes, appropriate living arrangements, and independence and dignity. On the basis of conference recommendations, the federal Department of Housing and Urban Development (HUD) worked to provide better housing for people who are older. One HUD project included building rent-controlled apartments for older people on fixed incomes. These apartment complexes were modest, safe, and more attractive than most federally subsidized housing. In 1974 Supplemental Security Income (SSI) was added to the public assistance package provided by the federal government. SSI provides income for older people living in poverty.

During the 1980s the American Association of Retired Persons (AARP) became more visible and lobbied to increase and maintain gains made by and for older people. AARP is a nonprofit, nonpartisan organization dedicated to helping older Americans achieve lives of independence, dignity, and purpose. With a membership of over 30 million, it is the most powerful organization of senior citizens. AARP's focus on quality-of-life issues and monetary benefits helped change society's perception of older people as poor, sick, or needy. AARP continues to increase awareness about the productivity of older people by highlighting their contributions to society.

Gerontological social work became an established field of practice in the 1980s. Social workers' need for research-based information led to the establishment of the *Journal of Gerontological Social Work* in 1980. By 1989 almost half the schools of social work with master's programs began offering a concentration or specialization in gerontological social work.

Unfortunately, during the same period, federal funding for social services to older clients was systematically reduced, and proposed cuts to Social Security overshadowed critical issues such as ageism, elder abuse, long-term health care, and the need to combat negative stereotyping of seniors (Cox & Parsons, 1993). The third White House Conference on Aging in 1981 sought to address several of these critical issues. Since little changed, the conference was widely viewed as unsuccessful. In 1995 the fourth White House Conference on Aging, despite high expectations, resulted in only one major message to Congress: Save Social Security and Medicare (Elder Law Issues, 1995).

In 2003, Congress enacted the **Medicare Prescription Drug Improvement and Modernization Act (MMA)** which was initiated in January 2006. This legislation provides prescription drug benefits for Medicare eligible seniors by implementing a Part D benefit where members enroll with private companies to obtain prescription medications. Provision in the legislation does not allow the federal government to negotiate drug prices with the drug companies, a controversial position. Although the legislation did provide some relief for many seniors, it has been widely criticized for its complicated enrollment process and the variable coverage gaps that exist. The MMA is discussed further in Chapter 9.

In 2005, the fifth White House Conference on Aging was held. Among the top ten resolutions sent to Congress, was a new emphasis on ensuring that older Americans have transportation options that will contribute to continuing independence and mobility, promoting new models of noninstitutional long-term care, and improving the recognition, assessment, and treatment of mental illness and depression in the elderly (White House Conference on Aging, 2005). This conference also held a degree of scandal, when George W. Bush became the first president to refuse to address it.

Today, gerontological social workers are employed in hospitals and medical centers, Adult Protective Services, veterans services, adult day care centers, private geriatric care agencies, family service organizations, hospices, and at the macro level in Area Agencies on Aging. Gerontological social workers continue to advocate for older people. Currently, advocacy groups are pressing for a universal health care plan that would cover the costs of long-term health care and for increasing the support of informal caregivers.

CURRENT CONTEXT

Older people, according to the U.S. Census Bureau, are persons 65 years old and over. They are often categorized in three groups: the young-old (ages 65–74 years); the old-old (ages 75–84 years); and the oldest-old (ages 85 years and over). One in every eight Americans, or 12.4 percent of the population, is old. This segment of the population includes almost 22 million women and 16 million men (U.S. Bureau of the Census, 2007).

During the twenty-first century, the percentage of the population that is older will increase dramatically. There are three primary reasons for the increase. First, fewer children are being born. Second, between 2010 and 2030 the baby-boom generation will begin to reach the age of 65. By 2030, the older population will more than double, and by 2050, at least 21 percent of the population will be old (U.S. Bureau of the Census, 2005). **Baby boomers**, Americans born between 1946 and 1964, make up the largest age cohort in the U.S. population. Their aging will necessitate a vast increase in health, recreation, housing, and nutrition services for people who are older, as well as increases in entitlement programs like Social Security. Third, people will continue to live longer and longer. A child born today can expect to live for almost 78 years on average, as compared to 47 years for someone born in 1900 (U.S. Bureau of the Census, 2002, 2007). Life expectancy is projected to increase to 79 years in 2010.

The oldest-old, who are also called frail older people, are projected to be the fastest-growing segment of the population in the twenty-first century (see "More About...The Population of People Who Are Older"). In 2006 there were 5.3 million people over the age of 85; in 2050 there could be as many as 21 million (U.S. Bureau of the Census, 2007). The majority of the over-85 cohort will be women. The healthy aging of the oldest-old in the twenty-first century is due to improved medical technologies such as heart bypass, hip replacement, and cataract surgery; less smoking; improved diet and nutrition; and better medications.

Only 5 percent of professional social workers are primarily employed in the practice area of aging (Practice Research Network, 2005). With the growth in our aging population, the need for gerontological social workers is increasing steadily. Most gerontological social work jobs require a master's degree in social work or a graduate degree with a certificate in gerontology. A bachelor of social work degree (BSW) does not provide the necessary skills, particularly clinical skills, to work in many settings with the elderly. However, there are BSW-level geriatric social work positions in Area Agencies on Aging, senior centers, skilled nursing facilities, and hospitals.

Services provided by gerontological social workers vary from setting to setting. Adult protective service (APS) workers investigate reported cases of elder abuse, neglect, and self-neglect (Dubble, 2006). They arrange emergency shelter and transportation for victims, and facilitate the victims' return home or to alternative long-term

---

BOX 8.2 | **MORE ABOUT ... THE GROUP OF PEOPLE WHO ARE OLDER**

In 2006 there were more than 37 million people over 65 years of age. Of them,

- 18.9 million were between the ages of 65 and 74

- 13 million were between the ages of 75 and 84
- 5.3 million were 85 and older

Source: U.S. Bureau of the Census, 2007.

living arrangements. Adult foster care (AFC), Adult Care Homes (ACH), and Assisted Living Facilities (AL) are alternatives to institutional placement for some older clients. In AFC and ACH settings there is a concerted effort to maintain a family home environment. Sizes of AFC and ACH homes can range from 1 to 20 clients. These settings are most commonly housed in private homes in the community. This differs from AL facilities that can house hundreds of clients and typically utilize apartment-like settings.

Adult day care is the provision of community-based services in a group setting. It has two purposes: (1) to help older clients maintain a certain level of independence and remain in their homes and communities and (2) to provide respite for caregivers. Many centers provide services for special populations, including people with Alzheimer's disease, AIDS, mental illness, visual impairment, or hearing loss (Rosenwald, 2007). Adult day care social workers provide case management services and facilitate different types of groups, including bereavement and grief groups, reality-orientation groups for elderly adults who are cognitively impaired, and educational or self-help groups.

Gerontological social workers in health care settings such as skilled nursing facilities, hospitals, home health care agencies, and hospice care facilities provide a variety of services. Psychosocial assessments are a critical part of social work practice in health care settings. Social workers in hospitals and hospices provide family support services, discharge planning, and death and dying counseling. Discharge planning occurs before a client is released from an inpatient medical or mental health facility, as well as a home health agency. The social worker helps the client determine where he or she will go and the type and scope of supportive care needed and links the client to community resources and family supports. Social workers in psychogeriatric settings, such as public or private mental health facilities, also conduct psychosocial assessments and provide therapy for elderly persons who are depressed or are struggling with other emotional disorders. **Psychogeriatrics** is a combination of psychiatric and mental health care and services for older people. Gerontological social workers in health care settings generally work as part of a multidisciplinary team. They collaborate with doctors, nurses, and psychologists to provide comprehensive services to clients.

Social workers make every effort to help people who are older stay in their own homes. Comprehensive assessments are used to determine the mental, physical, environmental, social, and financial condition of older clients. The findings are used to identify clients' strengths as well as the supports needed to help them remain safely independent. Networking and information and referral services are critical in helping clients and their families locate companionship services, home care aides, transportation services, meal programs, adaptive devices, and in-home nurses and therapists. Regardless of the setting, gerontological social workers usually provide case management services and act as advocates for the elderly. They also serve as liaisons to community agencies.

Finally, social workers in gerontology work as policymakers, quality improvement specialists, and administrators. Social workers in the field of aging, although focused primarily on direct care, participate in the development of new programs and policy development demonstrations and engage in multidisciplinary team efforts with the medical community to improve the overall care and wellness of our elders.

DIVERSITY

Estimates suggest that almost 40 percent of older people will be members of non-dominant groups by 2050, as compared with 17 percent today (Federal Interagency Forum on Aging-Related Statistics, 2004). The percentage of increase of Americans who are older is shown by group in Table 8.1, with Asians and Pacific Islanders and Latinos projected to have the largest increases.

The multigenerational, multiracial, multiethnic twenty-first century requires gerontological social workers to be aware of cultural and ethnic attitudes about aging, illness, family responsibility and obligation, institutionalization, and death and dying. As people age, they have strengths and resources that can aid them in the aging process. Hooyman and Kiyak (2007) highlighted inherent cultural strengths that gerontological social workers can utilize when working with diverse elderly. For example, Latino families have traditionally provided emotional support to elders, especially in rural areas. Social workers can often rely on informal supports within the Latino community to help elderly clients remain in their homes. African American elderly are more likely than whites to be members of extended families that help care for their older relatives in the home. Older people who are African American are the least likely to be admitted to skilled nursing facilities, but they have more of an honored place in their families. They thus report a greater level of satisfaction than whites.

Indigenous older people are the least likely to utilize government services. Many First Nation communities do not trust the government. Government social, medical, and health services are often miles away, and transportation is a problem. Many indigenous elders prefer traditional healing methods. Honoring and showing respect to elders is a significant part of indigenous peoples' value systems; the elderly have important roles, such as wise person, or storyteller and keeper of oral traditions.

The strengths of diverse racial and ethnic communities can be used by gerontological social workers to assist clients. In fact, people from nondominant groups who have fully assimilated into mainstream culture tend to return to their cultural and ethnic roots as they get older (Hooyman & Kiyak, 2007). This makes it even more critical for social workers to recognize and use cultural strengths.

CRITICAL PUBLIC POLICIES

The Social Security Act of 1935 was the first major legislation that included programs to aid older adults. (The development of this legislation is discussed in Chapter 2.) Old Age, Survivors, and Disability Insurance (OASDI) is the social insurance program that most people refer to as Social Security. Simply put, all working

TABLE 8.1	PROJECTED INCREASE OF OLDER PEOPLE BY 2010
Asian and Pacific Islander	40% increase
Latino	40% increase
Indigenous people	27% increase
African American	19% increase
White	32% increase

Source: U.S. Bureau of the Census, 2007.

Americans pay taxes into the system during their working years, and they and eligible family members receive monthly benefits on retirement or in the event of long-term disability.

The average Social Security benefit for a retired worker is about $1,079 per month (Social Security Administration, 2007). Social Security was never intended to be a retired person's only source of income, but rather to supplement pension funds and savings. However, for the majority of seniors, less than 15 percent of their retirement income comes from pensions (Federal Interagency Forum on Aging-Related Statistics, 2004). Nevertheless, Social Security benefits play an important role in keeping people who are older out of poverty. While 9 percent of Social Security beneficiaries lived below the poverty line in 2002, without benefits the rate would have been 48 percent, more than five times greater (Sherman and Shapiro, 2005). The majority of older people lifted from poverty due to Social Security benefits are women (Porter, Larin, & Primus, 1999).

The original legislation did not include medical coverage. In 1950 President Truman signed an amendment to the Social Security Act that provided financial help to states for some health care costs of needy older adults. In 1965 this amendment grew into Medicare and Medicaid. The basic health insurance program for all people 65 and over is **Medicare**. It is a universal, federally funded, compulsory health insurance program for older people. Medicare covers basic health services, but does not cover nursing home care costs over 100 days.

Medicare has four parts (Social Security Administration, 2007). Hospital insurance (Part A) helps pay for inpatient hospital care and certain follow-up services. Medical insurance (Part B) is optional with a monthly premium and pays for up to 80 percent of allowable doctors' services, outpatient hospital care, and other medical services. Medicare Advantage (Part C) provides an expanded set of options for the delivery of health care, typically coordinated care plans through HMOs or PPOs (which are described in more detail in Chapter 9). Prescription drugs (Part D) provides subsidized access to prescription drug insurance. Part D is also optional with the enrollee paying a premium.

Medicaid is a jointly funded (federal and state), needs-based health insurance program for individuals and families whose incomes and assets fall beneath a set amount. Medicaid covers hospital inpatient care, doctors' services, skilled nursing facility care, home health services, pharmacy services, mental health services, and long-term and short-term nursing home costs.

In 1974 the Social Security Act was amended to include **Supplemental Security Income (SSI)**. This program includes cash assistance to people who are poor and elderly or poor with disabilities. The average monthly benefit for those over 65 years is $393 (Social Security Administration Office of Policy, 2008), but the amount an older person receives depends on other income and where the person lives. Some states add money to the basic SSI rate. However, in most states SSI benefits are only 75 percent of the poverty level.

The Social Services Block Grant program provides federal funds for adult foster care and day care programs, as well as for home meals and other social services primarily for SSI recipients. The Older Americans Act of 1965 (OAA), which has been reauthorized several times, also funds social services like senior centers and nutrition programs.

Women, the primary caregivers in our society, pressed hard for passage of the **Family and Medical Leave Act** of 1993 (FMLA). The FMLA allows women and men time off from work to care for dependent parents and newborn children. The act requires covered employers to grant eligible employees up to 12 weeks of un-paid leave during any 12-month period for the birth of a child, adoption of a child, or placement of a foster child or to care for a spouse, child, or parent with a seri-ous health condition. As a result of this legislation, adult children can take unpaid leave to care for ailing parents with a guarantee that they will not lose their jobs.

Gerontological social workers need to be aggressive advocates for elder care programs. However, the inevitability of funding cutbacks requires social workers to explore new, innovative approaches to home health care. The trend is for family members to provide care in their own homes or in the homes of the elderly. To make this work, family members and caregivers need technological and medical support and plenty of respite. The concerns of family caregivers and caregiver stress are discussed later in the chapter.

THE ROLES OF SOCIAL WORKERS

The general roles of gerontological social workers include direct practice, program planning, and administration in numerous settings. Although gerontological social workers draw on the skills presented in Chapter 5, there are also specialized tech-niques and approaches to working with older people.

CURRENT PRACTICE INTERVENTIONS

> **CASE EXAMPLE:** Ida Curtis is 86 years old. She lives alone. At one time Ms. Curtis was independent. She was a secretary in a law firm for many years. She has one daughter, but they have not spoken in five years. Ms. Curtis has diabetes and linger-ing debilitating effects from a stroke a year ago. A home health care nurse visits once a week to medically assess her and fill insulin syringes. Ms. Curtis recently lost her driver's license because her eyesight is failing due to diabetes. She is devastated by the loss of her independence, and she is growing increasingly bitter and angry. The home health care nurse has made a referral to her agency's social worker.

Case management services are the treatment method of choice for older clients who live in the community and need ongoing care (Morrow-Howell, 1992). The first step is to complete a psychosocial needs assessment. Once Ms. Curtis's multiple strengths and needs are identified, her case manager will plan the appropriate inter-ventions. The social worker would link Ms. Curtis with appropriate community re-sources, such as transportation services, household care assistance, adaptive equipment providers, and medical specialists. The social worker would also try to help Ms. Curtis and her daughter reestablish communication and begin to rebuild their relationship. While providing concrete case management services, the social worker will help Ms. Curtis process issues of dependency, loss, and loneliness (Cox, Green, Hobart, & Jang, 2007).

Case management is the primary tool in social service agencies that help people who are older, like Ida Curtis, remain in their homes. It is also the primary tool used by social workers who work in long-term care facilities or nursing homes.

Long-term care is a set of health and social services (diagnostic, preventative, therapeutic, and rehabilitative) delivered over a sustained period of time at home or in a medical or nursing facility. The goals of case management include ensuring that services are appropriate to the needs of the client, improving client access to the continuum of long-term care services, supporting caregivers with counseling and information, and serving as a bridge between institutional and community-based care services (Parker & Thorsland, 2007).

Kaye (2005) identified numerous skill sets that are helpful ways to intervene with aging clients. These approaches emphasize the concept of productive aging, which builds on the strength-based orientation to social work practice. These skill sets include using empowerment strategies, knowledge of both traditional and nontraditional community resources, preventive outreach, and use of programs that are oriented toward productive aging. Examples of such programs are volunteering, civic engagement, mentoring or tutoring, retirement planning, health and wellness education and recreation. These approaches reflect the current focus on healthy and productive aging as an expected part of our lives.

Group work is also an effective intervention with clients who are older. Toseland (1995) developed a typology of five groups for older adults: (1) support groups; (2) therapy groups; (3) social, recreational, and educational groups; (4) service and advocacy groups; and (5) family caregiving groups. The focus of a therapy or support group may be reminiscence, whereas the focus of a social or recreational group for adults with dementia may be orientation to day and time of year. Social workers who facilitate groups for elderly clients may use talk therapy, physical exercise, and sing-alongs, among other techniques (MacKenzie & Beck, 1996). Many basic needs of older people, including status, identity, love, affection, usefulness, and growth through learning, can be met through group interaction (Ebenstein, 2007).

A social worker who serves older clients must be prepared to work as part of a multidisciplinary team that can include psychiatrists, doctors, nurses, physical therapists, occupational therapists, and dieticians or nutritionists. Multidisciplinary teams can be found in adult day care programs, nursing homes, home health agencies, and geriatric units in veterans' hospitals. The team members work together to develop and formalize an individual care plan. Most commonly, the social worker is the principal liaison among team members, other staff, and the caregivers or family members (Donald & Brown, 2003).

The varied roles of gerontological social workers include case manager, group facilitator, advocate, and therapist. Social work practice with the elderly is challenging. It requires exploring and articulating one's own ageist attitudes and fears, as well as a commitment to master the necessary knowledge and skills.

OLDER PEOPLE AT RISK

> **CASE EXAMPLE:** Mary Yazzie is 65 years old. She lives in a small hogan on the Navajo reservation with her daughter and two grandchildren. Mrs. Yazzie has had diabetes since she was 50. She rarely receives professional health care because the nearest doctor is 120 miles away. Her insulin injections are irregular at best. As a result, Mrs. Yazzie's kidneys are beginning to fail. To stay alive, Mary Yazzie needs regular access to a kidney dialysis machine.

CASE EXAMPLE: Leon Coles is 70. He is African American. Mr. Coles worked all his life until he had a stroke. His jobs varied, but he always earned just a little more than the minimum wage. As a result, he receives minimal Social Security benefits. The stroke severely limited his mobility. Mr. Coles lives with his wife, Louise, their daughter, and three teenage grandchildren. Louise Coles is in relatively good health and spends most of her time caring for Leon. The daughter works full-time as a legal secretary. Her salary feeds and clothes the family, but there is nothing left for her father's long-term health care needs. The family is just hanging on.

CASE EXAMPLE: Emilia Gonzalez is 85 years old and lives alone. She speaks little English. Her husband, who is deceased, was a migrant farm worker most of his life and never had Social Security or other pension coverage. Mrs. Gonzalez also worked in farm fields and was exposed to harmful pesticides. She has been diagnosed with uterine cancer, which was advanced by the time she could get access to a doctor. The prognosis is poor. Mrs. Gonzalez has no monetary resources; she relies on Medicaid to pay for her health care.

Women who are older; African American, Latino, and indigenous older people; older persons living alone; the oldest-old; and older people in rural areas are the most at risk in our society. Older people like Mary Yazzie, Leon Coles, and Emilia Gonzalez are more likely to live in poverty, have early onset of chronic health problems, and have shorter life expectancies than other Americans. Many factors account for the vulnerability of Mrs. Yazzie, Mr. Coles, and Mrs. Gonzalez. Lifelong race and gender discrimination exacerbate the difficulties of growing older. Racism and discrimination in hiring and promotion cause unemployment and underemployment, which result in lack of pensions and lower Social Security benefits. Living in prolonged poverty, language barriers, the stigma associated with needing help, geographic distance and transportation problems, lack of knowledge of services, and underutilization of available services also help account for the vulnerability of people who are older.

Although more women than men are in the young-old, old-old, and oldest-old age categories, they have only recently been included in research and political dialogue. The 1981 White House Conference on Aging was the first forum to address the concerns of women who are older and to look at breast cancer, osteoporosis, and the effects of hormone replacement therapy. The long-term effects of gender discrimination are not yet fully understood. In a society that celebrates women for their beauty and their ability to give birth, little value is placed on older women. There is evidence that the combined effects of being female and being old negatively affects women's mental health (Cummings, 2002).

The major sources of income for people who are older include Social Security, Supplemental Security Income (SSI), income from property and other assets, public and private pensions, earnings, and public assistance. Although the majority of older people have adequate income and the extent of poverty is lower than among the rest of the population, 9.4 percent, or 3.4 million, of older people live below the poverty level. Table 8.2 identifies the percentage of various groups of people who live in poverty.

Gerontological social workers need to advocate for services located in the racial or ethnic communities of people who are older. These services should be culturally

TABLE 8.2	PERCENTAGE OF OLDER PEOPLE WHO LIVE IN POVERTY
Asian and Pacific Islander	10.6%
Latino	20.4%
Indigenous people	45.0%
African American	22.7%
White	8.3%

Source: U.S. Bureau of the Census, 2007.

appropriate; for example, nutrition programs should use local foods. It is preferable for the social worker and the staff to be bicultural or bilingual. Communities that are predominantly Latino should have pertinent social service and elder care information in Spanish as well as in English. All communities should be encouraged to determine how to deliver services so that they best fit the needs of residents. Outreach services are particularly critical to ensure delivery and implementation of social services for older people in nondominant communities.

VALUES AND ETHICAL ISSUES

Gerontological social workers encounter difficult professional situations that have profound ethical aspects. Among the most difficult is the question of whether physician-assisted suicide is carefully controlled compassion for patients with painful, terminal illnesses or physician-initiated murder.

Dr. Jack Kevorkian of Michigan is well known for his efforts in the area of physician-assisted suicide. Prior to 1998, Dr. Kevorkian participated only in **passive euthanasia**, the intentional termination of one's own life with means provided by another person, such as a doctor. In other words, the patient commits suicide by taking a lethal dose of medication or using some other means obtained from another person. Dr. Kevorkian was arrested two times for providing means of death in cases of passive euthanasia.

Kevorkian's third arrest took place in 1998, and it concerned a case of **active euthanasia**. In such cases, the doctor actually administers the lethal injection or actively causes death in some other manner. Kevorkian injected a lethal dose of drugs into a patient with Lou Gehrig's disease. He was convicted of second-degree murder and of delivering a controlled substance without a license and was sentenced to 10 to 25 years in prison. His appeal and request for a new trial were denied by the Michigan Court of Appeals in November 2001. He was released from jail in June 2007.

The majority of the U.S. public favors permitting doctors to assist in the suicide of terminally ill patients (Knickerbocker, 2007). However, only one state, Oregon, has legalized physician-assisted suicide. Oregon voters approved the Death with Dignity Act in 1994 and reaffirmed it in 1997 (60 percent of voters supported it). Under the Oregon law, doctors may prescribe, but cannot administer, lethal doses of medication. There are several built-in safeguards. For example, the patient must ask for the lethal prescription several times over a period of 15 days, two doctors must certify that the patient has six months or less to live, and the patient must be of sound mind. Since 1994, 456 Oregonian patients have received the lethal pre-scriptions from doctors, and 292 Oregonians have used the medication to commit suicide (Levine, 2007). There was no correlation between elderly, poor, or minori-ties and likeliness or pressure to use the lethal medication. In fact, people with AIDS were the only group with a heightened use of physician-assisted suicide.

In 1999 Republicans in Congress, led by Senator John Ashcroft, attempted and failed to pass federal legislation to sanction doctors who participated in assisted suicides, which in effect would have nullified Oregon's Death with Dignity law. In November 2001, undaunted by public opinion and the failure of previous efforts to nullify the Oregon law, Ashcroft, who was now attorney general, announced that the Justice Department would use the federal Controlled Substance Act (CSA) against Oregon physicians who helped patients commit suicide by prescribing lethal doses of medication. The CSA was originally designed to address drug abuse and drug traffick-ing. Ashcroft's ruling would have made it possible for the Drug Enforcement Adminis-tration to revoke the prescription-writing privileges of any Oregon doctor who prescribed a lethal dose of medication. In addition, criminal charges could be filed against such doctors. In 2002 a federal judge in Oregon ruled that the attorney general lacked the authority to decide what "constitutes the legitimate practice of medicine" in Oregon. In the meantime, Oregon's Death with Dignity Act stands (see the "Point of View" box). The official position of the American Geriatrics Society regarding physician-assisted suicide and voluntary active euthanasia states:

> For patients whose quality of life and expected lifespan has become so limited as to make earlier death preferable to prolongation of life, the professional standard of care should be that of aggressive palliation of suffering and enhancement of opportunities for a meaningful life, not that of intentional termination of life. It is morally acceptable for a physician to administer a medication or forgo a treatment calculated to improve the patient's and the family's experience, knowing that this plan of care may have the unintended effect of hastening the patient's death. Good care may include the withholding or withdrawing of any medical intervention as well as the specific palliation of symptoms, even if this shortens a person's life. (American Geriatrics Society, 2007, position 1)

The recognition of current effective palliative care interventions and the con-cern about patient coercion were other critical aspects in the decision of the ethics committee to not endorse further changes in the law. Efforts to follow Oregon's lead in California and other states have failed (Knickerbocker, 2007).

Gerontological social workers need to be aware of all the legal and ethical issues surrounding physician-assisted suicide and to recognize their own feelings so as to avoid imposing their values on clients. A growing number of health care facilities have developed committees to deal with ethical concerns. These committees gener-ally consist of doctors, clergy, social workers, care providers, lawyers, and family representatives. In hospitals, nursing homes, and hospices, ethics committees often have the responsibility of deciding whether life-sustaining treatment should be with-drawn from incapacitated patients. Social workers should encourage elderly clients to have a full discussion with their doctor, family, and friends about their wishes should they become incapacitated. They should also encourage clients to have a liv-ing will that outlines their health care choices. A **living will** is a formal statement written and signed while a person is mentally competent that specifies how the

BOX 8.3   POINT OF VIEW

Committing suicide or attempting to commit suicide is not a crime, but helping another person commit suicide is a crime. Should a person who is terminally ill and in severe physical pain and who directly requests help committing suicide be allowed to receive assistance in ending his or her life?

No

> Among the people who answer no are many pro-life groups and some groups that advocate for the rights of people with disabilities and people who are older. The pro-life groups argue that euthanasia, whether passive or active, is a rejection of God's sovereignty. Rights groups of older people or of people with disabilities fear that legalized euthanasia may lead to involuntary euthanasia (of patients who do

not request assistance in dying) and the killing of anyone who may be deemed a burden to society.

Yes

> People who support passive euthanasia or active euthanasia argue that the government should not deny people the right to die on their own terms. In many cases medications have proven to be inadequate in controlling pain and maintaining quality of life, and ending one's life seems to be the only relief possible. The vast majority of those who favor physician-assisted suicide agree that euthanasia should be tightly controlled and should apply only to patients who have less than six months to live.

BOX 8.4   WHAT DO YOU THINK?

Jane Smith, age 69, is a retired schoolteacher who has suffered from bone cancer for six years. She is in constant pain and has bedsores, nausea, and impaired vision. Ms. Smith is in the terminal phase of her illness.

Orlando Cruz, also age 69, suffers from emphysema. He is connected to an oxygen tank. Mr. Cruz often feels that he is being suffocated. He takes morphine regularly to calm panic attacks. Mr. Cruz is in the terminal phase of his disease.

Should Jane Smith and Orlando Cruz be allowed to end their lives through physician-assisted suicide? What

role would a social worker play in the lives of Ms. Smith and Mr. Cruz? If Ms. Smith or Mr. Cruz asked you to help them locate a doctor who might assist them in committing suicide, what would you say or do?

Self-determination is one of the core values of social work practice. However, self-determination is limited in cases of harm to self and others. Are people who want to utilize a lethal dose of medication provided by a physician doing harm to themselves? Are physicians who provide lethal-dose prescriptions doing harm to patients?

person wishes to have his or her own death handled in the event that the person cannot participate in the decision making. Another arrangement that can be handled prior to the need is an advance directive. An **advance directive** is also a formal written statement that outlines the medical options and procedures a person may or may not want to prolong life. This document is used when the person cannot participate in the decision making due to his or her physical condition. Both these documents can help family and friends to honor a person's wishes when it is impossible to ask. However, this requires prior planning about end-of-life events, and it can be difficult for people to face this planning. Social workers can help facilitate this process.

Assisted suicide is not the only ethical dilemma gerontological social workers face. Other ethical challenges occur due to lack of adequate funding for health care. Concern about the possibility of new epidemics or pandemics has prompted policy conversations about who should receive vaccines if there is a limited supply available. Some experts believe that if there were bird flu pandemic, there would only be enough vaccine available to protect 10 percent of the U.S. population. There is general agreement that essential health care workers should be among the first to receive that vaccine. Government policy has generally been that those most at risk of dying from the disease should be next in line to receive the vaccine. This group has included older people. However, some ethicists argue that people between the ages of 13 and 40 should be the high-priority group for the vaccine instead (Emanuel & Wertheimer, 2006). Rather than placing an emphasis on reducing the death rate of the most vulnerable, these ethicists argue that it is better to protect those who will be most productive and have yet to live most of their lives. Social workers should be involved in the discussion about how age and other factors should be considered when trying to allocate scarce resources.

CRITICAL ISSUES AND EMERGING CONCERNS

The costs of medications, elder abuse and neglect, an increase in the incidence of Alzheimer's disease and dementia, the mental health of older people, and the growing number of children serving as caregivers for aging parents are some of the critical issues facing gerontological social workers in the twenty-first century. The costs, both financial and emotional, to the families and individuals affected by these critical issues can be staggering.

MEDICARE DRUG PRESCRIPTION BENEFIT

In 2002, Carol McMahon faced the same problem millions of older people faced each month—"How do I pay for my prescription drugs?" Mrs. McMahon was taking seven different prescription drugs at a monthly cost of $513. The drugs were covered by her husband's retirement package, but the company ended coverage for over 80,000 retirees (McKay & Gaynor, 2002). Like millions of other older Americans, Mrs. McMahon was scrambling to find a way to pay for her medications.

BOX 8.5   **ETHICAL PRACTICE ... HIGH COST OF CARE**

You are working in an assisted living facility for older adults. You notice a pattern that as the residents need more help from the staff, which costs the facility more money, the top administration puts pressure on you and the other social worker to recommend they be transferred to a facility that provides more comprehensive skilled nursing care. It seems clear to you that many of the residents do not yet need to be in a skilled nursing facility. You speak to your supervisor telling him that you believe the facility wants to transfer out the most costly residents to save money, even if it is not in the best interest of the residents. He confirms that this is happening, but tells you it is necessary to keep the facility open and for all of you to keep your jobs. What should you do?

Medicare, the primary source of health benefits for older people, did not cover prescription drugs, even though they are the central component of much modern medical care. Private insurance policies that offered prescription drug coverage proved to be inadequate and unreliable for most seniors. Some older Americans prefer to buy their prescription drugs from Canada via the Internet. Because of cost-containment policies, prescription drugs cost 30 to 40 percent less in Canada than in the United States. Other seniors travel to Mexico, where medications are also less expensive. Some have even moved to states that border Canada or Mexico so that they can make regular excursions across the border. The irony is that many of the drugs sold in Mexico and some in Canada are manufactured in the United States or by U.S. pharmaceutical companies.

As described earlier in the chapter, in 2003, Congress and the president agreed on a plan to include coverage for prescription medication under the Medicare program. The Medicare Prescription Drug, Improvement, and Modernization Act of 2003 (MMA) was signed into law, making it the largest expansion of benefits since the inception of the Medicare program. Among the growing concerns previously discussed, there is also concern that the program is very costly, estimated to top $635 billion for the first 10 years (Congressional Budget Office, 2008). Although costly for the nation, it has provided relief in the personal cost for prescription medications for some elderly persons.

ELDER ABUSE AND NEGLECT

CASE EXAMPLE: In 2005, Ellen Gutierrez, 84, was held prisoner in her San Francisco apartment by six gang members. The gang members were able to keep social workers at bay for several months, eating her senior meals, and dealing drugs from her home (Doyle, 2005). Just south in San Diego, a 73-year-old bank customer was repeatedly withdrawing large sums of money. An alert bank teller notified the police. The man's caregiver had persuaded his client to give him over $30,000 in cash. The caregiver also stole three pocket-watches valued at over $50,000, a car, and a big-screen television. Elder abuse cases in the San Diego area tripled between 2002 and 2005 (Heller, 2005).

The incidence of **elder abuse** is not known. Definitions of abuse are varied, state-by-state statistics are not consistent, and there is no comprehensive national data collected, but according to the best available estimates, between 1 and 2 million older people have been injured, exploited, or mistreated by someone they depend on for their care (Elder Mistreatment, 2003). According to the National Center on Elder Abuse (2008), approximately 1 in 14 incidents of abuse go unreported. Not unlike spousal abuse prior to the 1980s, elder abuse is a hidden and underreported crime. Social workers have referred to it as the secret national crisis (Beaucar, 2000). Older victims often do not report abuse or neglect because they fear that the abuser will abandon them or institutionalize them.

Elder abuse can take many forms. Physical abuse is the willful infliction of injury, forced confinement, or cruel punishment. Sexual abuse is nonconsensual sexual contact of any kind. Emotional abuse is humiliation, harassment, or social isolation of an older person. **Neglect** is the withholding of basic necessities such as food or medical attention. Financial exploitation is stealing, withholding, or mismanaging money that belongs to an older person. Self-neglect is the failure to provide for one's self or the failure to avoid physical harm or mental anguish. It may be a side effect of dementia, depression, or physical disability.

In most states, elder abuse is reported to the police or to Adult Protective Services (APS). Any elderly person who is a victim of abuse or exploitation is eligible for APS services. An APS social worker investigates allegations and can provide or refer the victim to appropriate services, including emergency shelter, transportation, meals, medical or mental health services, home health services, or help with budgeting and financial management. Many states also utilize an ombudsman to investigate complaints in nursing homes and care homes in the community. According to the National Long Term Care Ombudsman Resource Center, an **ombudsman** is an advocate for residents of nursing homes, board and care homes, and assisted living facilities. In 2003, state long term care ombudsman programs nationally investigated 20,673 complaints of abuse, gross neglect, and exploitation on behalf of nursing home and board and care residents. The most common form of abuse found was physical abuse (National Ombudsman Reporting System, 2003).

Older people who are abused or neglected are three times more likely to die from heart disease, cancer, lung disease, and accidental injuries than those who are not abused. They are also more likely to commit suicide. The typical victim is 75, widowed, female, socially isolated, dependent, and frail. More women than men are victims, mainly because women live longer. The female victim often lives with her abuser (National Center on Elder Abuse, 2008).

The perpetrator is usually a family member, perhaps a spouse, more typically an adult son or daughter. Other perpetrators include trusted adults and institutional caregivers (nurse's aides, nurses, attendants). Some perpetrators have money problems, personal problems such as alcoholism or emotional impairment, or a history of using violence to address family problems. In other cases, the family member is financially and emotionally exhausted from caregiving responsibilities and acts in ways she or he normally would not (National Center on Elder Abuse, 2008). The vulnerability of the victim, stress on the caregiver, and long-term economic hardship often combine to create a high-risk scenario for abuse. Victims are often isolated by the caregiver and are not aware of community resources that can help.

Gerontological social workers educate the general public, police, physicians, hospital and health care staff, and ambulance attendants about elder abuse and neglect. Skills often include how to recognize the signs of elder abuse and how to report it. In addition, employees of banks and other financial institutions need to be trained to identify and report incidents of financial exploitation. Social workers supported the Clinton administration's efforts to mandate state spot checks of nursing homes and stiffer penalties for noncompliance with standards (Beaucar, 2000). Spot checks are now done in most states, but many states still do not have mandatory fines for noncompliance. At the same time, states must provide money to hire more qualified staff to help prevent abuse and neglect. Social workers also support the Elder Justice Act, authored by Senators Orrin Hatch (UT-Republican) and John Breaux (LA-Democrat) and first introduced in 2003. The legislation is intended to combat elder abuse at the federal level and would establish the Elder Justice Center within the Administration on Aging Office. On March 29, 2007, the act was again introduced in the House (H.R. 1783) and Senate (S. 1070). The act is still pending legislative action. Gerontological social workers explain and promote the rights of people who are older and empower victims of abuse or neglect by helping them take control of their lives as much as possible (see "From the Field...Quality of Life").

BOX 8.6 | ### FROM THE FIELD ... QUALITY OF LIFE
Susan Appel-Brewer, MSW

Myrtle Susens was an 87-year-old Caucasian female who came to our skilled nursing facility when Jessica, her 36-year-old granddaughter, could no longer care for her. Mrs. Susens was alert, but didn't speak at all. She occasionally looked in my direction. She had senile dementia, Alzheimer's type, and a heart condition that required medication twice a day. Mrs. Susens used a wheelchair that she was unable to propel. She did not have the strength to transfer herself from her chair to her bed, and it took two nursing assistants to move her. Mrs. Susens appeared to be comfortable sitting in the wheelchair during the intake process. Staff reported that she lay in the same position while in bed. They requested immediate orders to turn her on a regular schedule to avoid ulcers. Blood tests ordered by the facility physician showed that Mrs. Susens was dehydrated and had unusual levels of barbiturates in her blood.

By the time Mrs. Susens had been in the facility for three weeks, she had gone from a catatonic state to talking in single-word answers, following us around the room with her eyes, and requiring only one person to transfer her from her bed into her wheelchair. At this point, Jessica took her home, claiming that she and her husband could not afford to pay for her grandmother to stay at the facility. Five days later, Jessica brought Mrs. Susens back and said that she simply could not take care of her.

Mrs. Susens again stayed with us for three weeks. This time she could talk in short sentences, indicate what she wanted, transfer herself to her wheelchair and back into bed with a minimum of assistance, and even take several steps with the therapist's help. Again, Jessica took her home for five days. By this time, I was seeing the pattern. The family was taking their grandmother home at the end of every month in order to continue to collect her Social Security check, which she would fingerprint so they could cash it. Then they brought her back to us.

Knowing that Mrs. Susens had no assets, I had applied for state assistance when she first came in. Long-term state assistance is a great program for indigent seniors, but it takes about three months for the paperwork to be processed and go into effect. Many nursing facilities will not accept residents like Mrs. Susens who are pending state assistance approval because of the delay in payment. She was already a patient with us, so we could keep her even if Jessica stopped paying.

At the time of the third discharge, I thought we might not get Mrs. Susens back. She was walking short distances with a walker, feeding herself, talking in short sentences, and participating in activities in the facility. She smiled and laughed, and she loved going to therapy and walking. She had gained weight and was eating solid food. Jessica and her husband seemed pleased with the progress their grandmother had made, and they said they felt confident that she could be alone for short periods of time. I arranged for additional home health care services to assist them with the adjustment and to make sure Mrs. Susens was safe.

Ten days later, Mrs. Susens was brought back. She was catatonic again and was sitting in her wheelchair making little whining noises. She was dressed in a floor-length gown, even though it was July. Jessica said she would not remove her grandmother again. She provided no information about what happened or why Mrs. Susens was in this condition.

In their initial examination, the nurses discovered that Mrs. Susens was bruised from head to toe. Heavy makeup hid her black eyes and the bruises on her face. She was immediately hospitalized, where it was determined that she had two broken ribs, a concussion, and multiple abrasions and skin tears. She had been left in a diaper and not bathed for the full ten days she had been gone. Mrs. Susens had been given an excessive dose of Valium before being

BOX 8.6 | FROM THE FIELD ... QUALITY OF LIFE *continued*

brought to our facility, and she slipped into a coma in the hospital. My next step was to call the police and Adult Protective Services. It took a number of days to locate the family. We later found out they had left town with Mrs. Susens's Social Security check.

Mrs. Susens came back to our facility under a court order, which included an order of protection so that the family could not take her out again. I reported the case to the state long-term assistance office, which can speed up the process for eligibility in emergency situations. My purpose in doing this was not to see that our bill got paid, but rather to make sure that Mrs. Susens's Social Security check would go to the state instead of her family.

Mrs. Susens remained in our facility for another six months. When she got better and could talk, she told me about Margaret, a daughter who lived in Boston. Margaret had been led to believe that Mrs. Susens's care was being provided by Jessica, who was Margaret's niece. Margaret was living on her own Social Security and had very little money, but when she found out what was going on, she scraped enough money together to fly to our area so that she could move her mother to Boston. The state ombudsperson provided us with a paid hotel room for Margaret's visit, given by an anonymous donor, and with transportation. The Area Agency on Aging

provided money for meals and for a suitcase for Mrs. Susens's things. The staff donated money to buy Mrs. Susens a plane ticket to Boston.

I worked through a nursing facility in Boston to set up home health care for Mrs. Susens in Boston. She received meals on wheels from a local hospital, and a friendly visitor from one of the local senior centers came once a week as well. For several months I called about once a week to see how Mrs. Susens was doing. She talked about all of the things she was getting to do, like going for rides in the car and walks in the rain. She was eating, gaining weight, and walking and seemed to have adjusted well to her new environment.

Then Margaret called me. She had been reading the Bible to Mrs. Susens, which she did every night before bedtime, and when she had finished a passage, she looked up to find that her mother had quietly passed away.

Although working with older people seems morbid and depressing to some, I love it. If you can make even a small difference in someone's life in his or her later years, you have been successful. We can't stop the onset of age or the coming of death; these are a part of life. But we can enhance the quality of the years a person has left; this is what I believe we did for Mrs. Susens.

ALZHEIMER'S DISEASE AND DEMENTIA

CASE EXAMPLE: An older man tells his story: "My wife was diagnosed with Alzheimer's disease. All of our dreams for our retirement years have come to an end. I take care of her now. I rarely leave the house, and when I do I cannot find a place to go where I can forget how much our lives have changed. Sometimes I feel guilty because I want to escape from it all."

Dementia is loss of intellectual and social abilities that is severe enough to interfere with daily functioning. It is not a normal part of the aging process. Rather, it is caused by an underlying condition or cerebral disease. **Alzheimer's disease** is the most common form of dementia and accounts for 60 to 80 percent of dementias (Alzheimer's Association, 2008). Symptoms vary but generally include impaired memory, thinking, and language abilities, along with personality or behavior changes. An estimated 5.2 million Americans have Alzheimer's disease. The cost of care and lost productivity due to Alzheimer's and other types of dementia is estimated at $148 billion annually in the United States (Alzheimer's Association, 2008).

Alzheimer's is usually diagnosed in people who are in their eighties. Half of all people in their nineties have some symptoms of dementia. As more and more people survive into their eighties and nineties, as many as 12 million people may be affected by Alzheimer's by 2020. There is currently no cure, but early detection and treatment can delay the disease's most difficult and expensive stages. Drugs can temporarily improve mental abilities in patients with mild cases of Alzheimer's.

On initial referral of a client with Alzheimer's disease, the social worker usually visits the client's home to establish rapport and make an initial assessment (Adams & McClendon, 2006). Effective interviewing skills are especially important. The social worker must strike a balance between focusing on and assessing the dependency level of the client and appreciating that the client is an adult. Clients with Alzheimer's disease or another form of dementia function more on an emotional level than on an intellectual level. Their world is often confusing and frightening, and they may display aggressive or disoriented behaviors. The social worker should always place these behaviors in the appropriate context.

Social workers also provide services for all types of caregivers. Caring for someone with Alzheimer's or dementia can be all consuming. When dementia becomes severe, patients may need constant supervision. As caregivers try to balance the demands of work, family, and other relationships, they often deal with feelings of guilt, anxiety, frustration, social isolation, anger, and depression.

Caregivers are also dealing with their own issues regarding the loss of the relationship with their loved one. Spouses and child caregivers must manage such personal tasks as bathing, feeding, and dressing the person with Alzheimer's and come to terms with the change in the relationship. It has been found that Alzheimer's caregivers' reports of loneliness are linked to greater reported depression and relationship deprivation in those caregivers (Beeson, Horton-Deutsch, Farran, and Neundorfer, 2000). It is critical that social workers identify and intervene with caregivers in order to enable continued wellness and ability to care for their loved one.

Social workers can help caregivers prevent burnout through the use of stress management techniques and respite care services. Caregivers need to take time for themselves, get plenty of rest, develop a support system that provides respite and encouragement, and use adult day care and support groups. Medicare and most private insurance companies do not cover care for dementia. If the patient has a co-existing medical problem such as pneumonia, Medicare may cover up to 150 days in a nursing home. Although Medicaid will pay for care for Alzheimer's disease, to be eligible for Medicaid the client must first exhaust his or her personal savings. Gerontological social workers need to advocate for long-term health care coverage for patients and their families.

MENTAL HEALTH AND DEPRESSION

Many seniors experience mental health difficulties as they age. Depression is the primary emotional disorder among people who are older, affecting as many as 2 million people who are older adults each year (National Institute of Health, 2003). Depression becomes more common as individuals begin to experience the physical, social, and psychological changes associated with aging. Although it can be treated with medications or psychotherapy, many older people refuse to seek treatment. Often they believe that they should "pick themselves up" rather than seek outside help. They may also be afraid that they will be institutionalized if they admit they need help. Depression in the elderly is one of the most under diagnosed conditions and impacts health and well-being. This is especially true in nursing homes. It is recommended that all residents be screened for depression within two weeks of admission and every six months thereafter using such tools as the Geriatric Depression Scale or Beck Depression Inventory for those without dementia or the Cornell Scale for Depression with Dementia for those who are moderately or cognitively impaired (American Geriatrics Society and American Association for Geriatric Psychiatry, 2003).

Other mental health problems that commonly develop among older people include anxiety, paranoid disorders, and substance abuse (Kindiak & Grieve, 1996). All three are often a result of the social isolation, sense of powerlessness, and progressive sensory decline that many people experience as they age (Eisdorfer, Cohen, & Veith, 1980). Mental health problems among the elderly are often overlooked or ignored by practitioners. It was found in a recent study of 35 primary physicians working in an academic medical center, a managed care group, and fee-for-service solo practice that a typical mental health discussion with an elderly patient lasted two minutes with a wide variation in physician methods in providing mental health care (Tai-Seale, McGuire, Colenda, Rosen, & Cook, 2007). Social workers can act as liaisons with client's physicians and other health providers. They can make referrals and use their psychosocial assessment skills to help advocate for care and vigilance in identifying and diagnosing mental health problems in the elderly.

It is important to maintain a cultural perspective in the practice of psychogeriatrics.

For example, groups differ in how much information they are willing to disclose. White women are more likely than white men and African American women and men to readily disclose their thoughts and feelings to a pyschogeriatric social worker (Harper et al., 2007). When working with older people from traditional backgrounds, the social worker must strive to achieve a balance between formality and informality. It is also important to dress professionally, be willing to chat, and not be in a hurry. Elderly people who are members of nondominant groups are more likely to avoid therapy, to be reluctant to disclose personal feelings, and to drop out of treatment. To avoid these problems, the social worker must be patient and culturally sensitive.

CAREGIVERS FOR AGING PARENTS

It is estimated that for persons 65 or older there are 5.8 million to 7 million caregivers providing assistance with some type of daily activity (Spector, 2000). Informal or unpaid family caregivers represent a large portion of these estimates and are predicted to continue to be the largest source of long-term care services in the United States. Long-term care family caregivers are estimated to reach 37 million caregivers by 2050, which is an increase of 85 percent from 2000 (Health and Human Services, 2003). Fifty-four percent of family caregivers are between 34 and 65 years old. These are key wage-earning years, and caregiving does have a negative effect on the financial well-being and earning power of caregivers. On average, long-distance caretakers spend 35 hours a month in care-related activities and $196 a month on care-related expenses.

Additionally, caregivers of persons over 65 tend to be older themselves. Of those caring for someone aged 65 or over, the average age of caregivers is 63 years with one-third of these caregivers in fair to poor health themselves (Administration on Aging, 2005). Caregivers also suffer emotionally from caregiving responsibilities. Studies consistently report higher levels of depressive symptoms, stress, and mental health problems among caregivers than among their noncaregiving peers (Schulz, O'Brien, Bookwals, & Fleissner, 1995). In terms of time spent caregiving, nearly half of caregivers provide fewer than eight hours of care per week, whereas nearly one in five provide more than 40 hours of care per week (AARP and National Alliance on Caregiving, 2004). Older caregivers often spend the most hours providing care whereas almost one-third (28 percent) of caregivers who provide more than 40 hours of care per week are over 65 years of age (Johns Hopkins University, 2002). It has also been found that social isolation is a particularly unfortunate outcome of a prolonged caregiving experience (Tebb & Jivanjee, 2000). An expected increase in the number of family caregivers is due in part to the baby-boom children who are now caring for their older parents. It is also a result of noncovered services under Medicare and Medicaid.

A survey by the National Family Caregivers Association (NFCA, 2001) indicated that people who identify themselves as caregivers tend to be proactive in identifying resources to assist their family members, tend not to feel isolated, believe in self-care, and tend to put the needs of their older relatives before their own health needs. Caregivers who choose to take on a caregiving role tend to feel less like victims and more empowered to take charge of the situation. The caregiver is less likely to exercise than before he or she became a caregiver and takes longer to visit a doctor for his or her own health problems.

Social workers can educate caregivers about the financial and emotional costs of caregiving, especially if they allow their loved one's illness or disability to always take first priority. Caregivers need to be encouraged to seek support from other caregivers as well as from professionals to help maintain a healthy balance in their lives. Asking for help is both a sign of strength and an acknowledgement of one's limitations (NFCA, 2001). Social workers can help caregivers identify viable alternatives to caregiving. Social workers need to advocate for better support services for family caregivers and resources to help clients safely remain in their own homes.

When to step in and make decisions for people who are aging is another concern that affects caregivers and social workers. People who are older tend to be vulnerable to financial scams and can be preyed on by unscrupulous financial service providers (see the box "Becoming a Change Agent").

GRANDPARENTS CARING FOR GRANDCHILDREN

The issue of grandparents serving as the primary caregivers for their grandchildren has begun to receive increased attention. According to the 2000 census, approximately 2.4 million grandparents had primary responsibility for their grandchildren (Simmons & Dye, 2003). Abuse, neglect, substance abuse, and parental physical and mental illness are primary reasons why grandparents step in as parents. This

BOX 8.7 | BECOMING A CHANGE AGENT

Older Americans are the population most likely to be the target of financial fraud. Ninety-two-year-old army veteran Richard Guthrie's story is a typical example (Duhigg, 2007a). Mr. Guthrie's name and phone number were put on a list by InfoUSA, a company that compiles information and sells lists, often to criminals. They marketed lists such as the Suffering Seniors list, which had the names of 4.7 million older people with cancer or Alzheimer's disease and the Elderly Opportunity Seekers list, containing 3.3 million older people wanting or needing to make money. Mr. Guthrie's name made its way onto a list after he entered several sweepstakes. Telemarketing criminals repeatedly called Mr. Guthrie and eventually encouraged him to reveal his banking information. They then proceeded to steal his life savings. When interviewed, Mr. Guthrie said, "I loved getting those calls. Since my wife passed away, I don't have many people to talk with. I didn't even know they were stealing from me until everything was gone" (p. 1). Robert Pyle is another example of an older person who found himself without his life savings (Duhigg, 2007b). At age 73 he had $500,000 in the bank and owned a home worth $650,000. By age 81, he had no savings and no home of his own and was living with his stepdaughter. After his losses he sued a mortgage broker and a bank. Mr. Pyle acknowledged that he willingly made financial decisions the caused him to lose his money and home, but claimed that he was not responsible for

those decisions because he was older and not as sharp as he had been.

Analyzing the Situation
- Conduct some research to try to find out why older people are more commonly the targets and victims of financial fraud.
- Do older people need additional protection from financial fraud because of their age? If so, who should be responsible for providing that protection?
- Should older people have less freedom to make financial decisions? Should they have less responsibility for the financial decisions they do make, because of their age?

What Can Social Workers Do?
Given your analysis what can social workers do to help protect older people from financial fraud? What can we do at the individual and family levels? What could be done at the community and policy levels?

What Can You Do?
What one step might you take now, alone or working with others, to reduce the risk of financial fraud to older people? What are the barriers that might keep you from taking this step? What could you do to reduce those barriers?

situation brings up a number of challenges. Many older adults live on a fixed income. The increased responsibility of providing for children can put a strain on family budgets. Many children coming to live with their grandparents are coming from difficult circumstances and bring a variety of problems with them. Often grandparents were expecting a quiet retirement and are not emotionally prepared for the responsibility of child rearing they thought was over for them. Additionally, health problems tend to increase as people age, making illness a more common challenge for grandparents. The added responsibility of taking care of children may increase stress and health problems for grandparents. Social workers can help families find support groups in their area or start them if none are available. They can help grandparents access financial resources and can lobby for better financial assistance and special service or housing programs that target grandparents and their grandchildren. Social workers can also provide clinical services, such as family therapy, to families who are experiencing challenges, and organize respite care so grandparents can focus on caring for themselves as well.

CONCLUSION

Social workers who choose to focus on people who are older face more daunting requirements than many of their colleagues. They must master a broad spectrum of psychological, sociological, political, and medical topics; negotiate complex and often underfunded systems of government assistance; and sometimes support their clients through experiences as difficult as dementia, physical decline, abuse, and death.

The care of people who are older has been gaining importance in the United States. One reason is the aging of the enormous demographic bulge of baby boomers, born in the decade following World War II. The strain on the Social Security system is drawing increasing attention from lawmakers and the aging population. Biomedical research continues to increase the human life span. As the average age in the population increases, gerontological social work is likely to gain influence.

Modern Western cultures tend to have an exaggerated focus on youth, as compared to traditional cultures in which older people are honored for their experience and valued for the example they provide to younger people. Social workers who choose to work with the elderly can directly improve the quality of life for individuals and also help correct the mistreatment and devaluation of all older people. This effort will not only benefit every person who reaches old age, but will also create a richer and more open society.

In 1966, at the age of 45, astronaut John Glenn became the first American to orbit Earth. In 1998 77-year-old Senator John Glenn returned to space as a crew member on the space shuttle and was honored in a ticker-tape parade on his return. He was hailed as a hero not only because of his actions but also because of his age. An aging population, whose life expectancy is longer than ever before in history, seemed ready to believe that age does not mean uselessness, that vitality and enjoyment can continue as long as life, and that older people can make powerful contributions to society. Gerontological social workers play a crucial role in strengthening and disseminating these positive attitudes. Though the job is not an easy one, it will benefit virtually every member of our society.

Key Terms

active euthanasia, (p. 217)

advance directive, (p. 219)

ageism, (p. 204)

Alzheimer's disease, (p. 224)

Area Agencies on Aging (AAA), (p. 208)

baby boomers, (p. 210)

dementia, (p. 224)

elder abuse, (p. 221)

Family and Medical Leave Act, (p. 214)

gerontology, (p. 205)

living will, (p. 218)

long-term care, (p. 215)

Medicaid, (p. 213)

Medicare, (p. 213)

Medicare Prescription Drug Improvement and Modernization Act (MMA), (p. 209)

neglect, (p. 221)

Older Americans Act (OAA), (p. 208)

ombudsman, (p. 222)

passive euthanasia, (p. 217)

psychogeriatrics, (p. 211)

Supplemental Security Income (SSI), (p. 213)

Questions for Discussion

1. What are some of the central challenges facing older people in U.S. society? How do social workers address some of these challenges?
2. What social work interventions seem to be effective with the elderly? Why is each particularly appropriate?
3. What effect is the rapid growth of the older population in the United States likely to have on public policy and social work practice?
4. Discuss some of the biological, psychological, cognitive, and economic issues that people experience as they age.
5. Describe the primary public programs that address the needs of older people in the United States.

Change Agent Exercise

AARP is a national service and advocacy organization for older people in the United States. Older Americans are a very powerful lobbying group, and AARP is involved in advocating for legislative and legal change on issues of concern to people over 50 years of age. AARP originally stood for the American Association of Retired People, however currently, Americans are staying in the workplace longer and so therefore many of AARP's members are not retired. Therefore, AARP is the branded name of the organization. Go online to AARP's website and find out if there is a local chapter in your area. Also try to find out if there are other organizations that advocate for the rights of older people in your community. If one exists, call them to see if they use volunteers and, if so, what types of things volunteers can do. Schedule a time to go to the organization's office and spend a morning, afternoon, or evening learning more about what the organization does. See if you can help out.

Chapter Exercises

1. **Site Visit**
   Visit an assisted living facility or a skilled nursing facility. Ask permission to interview two or three residents about their experiences of growing older. What do they think would improve social conditions for older people in the United States?

   Have they ever been discriminated against because of their age? If so, briefly describe what they experienced.

   What challenges do they currently face?

   Have they had any interactions with social workers? Were the experiences positive or negative?

   Analyze their answers and discuss several interventions social workers could be involved in to improve social conditions for older people.

2. **Privatization of Social Security**
   In recent years, there has been a debate about privatizing part or all of the Social Security system. Research and list the pros and cons of privatization.

   Pros of privatization:

Cons of privatization:

Articulate your position on this issue.

Meet with classmates to compare what you found. Is there agreement among you about whether privatization is good or not?

3. **Preventing Burnout (Job Exhaustion)**
   Interview (1) a social worker who works on elder abuse cases, (2) a social worker who works with Alzheimer's patients, or (3) an adult who is a caregiver of an elderly patient. Ask the following questions:

   What is the most difficult part of your job?

   What would make your job easier?

   What do you do to prevent burnout?

   What are some of the signs or symptoms that appear when you begin to feel burned out?

   If your best friend were going to take over your job, what would you tell him or her about how to succeed?

4. **Depression among the Elderly**
   Reread the paragraphs about Thomas Wayne, age 72, and Conchita Alvarez, age 82, at the beginning of the chapter. List the environmental factors that could contribute to depression.

   Discuss what social workers can do to mitigate each environmental factor.

5. **Web-Based Research**
   Search for a website that offers information about or assistance to the elderly and answer the following questions:

   Who sponsors the site?

   What types of information or assistance are offered?

   Do you think the information is valuable? If so, who would benefit from it and in what way?

   Make at least two suggestions about how the site could be improved.

References

AARP and National Alliance for Caregiving. (2004). *Caregiving in the U.S.* Washington, DC: National Alliance for Caregiving.

AARP. (2005). Retrieved May 2, 2008, from http://assets.aarp.org/rgcenter/health/rx_midlife_plus.pdf.

Adams, K. B., & McClendon, M. J. (2006). Early-stage cognitive impairment: a social work practice and research agenda. *Families in Society*, 87, 4, 590–600.

Administration on Aging. (2005). *National family caregiver support program complete resource guide.* Washington, DC: Department of Health and Human Services.

Alzheimer's Association. (2008). *Alzheimer's disease facts and figures.* Retrieved May 3, 2008, from http://www.alz.org/national/documents/report_alzfactsfigures2008.pdf.

American Geriatric Society. (2007). *Position statement: Physician assisted suicide and voluntary active euthanasia.* Retrieved May 3, 2008, from http://www.americangeriatrics. org/products/positionpapers/vae94.shtml.

American Geriatrics Society and American Association for Geriatric Psychiatry. (2003). Consensus statement on improving the quality of mental health care in U.S. nursing homes: Management of depression and behavioral symptoms associated with dementia. *Journal of the American Geriatrics Society, 51,* 1287–1298.

Austin, C. D. (1996). Case management practice with the elderly. In Holosko, M. J., & Feit, M. D. (eds.), *Social work practice with the elderly.* Toronto, CAN: Canadian Scholar's Press.

Beaucar, K. O. (2000). Elder abuse is a crisis group says. *NASW News,* January.

Beeson, R., Horton-Deutsch, S., Farran, C., and Neundorfer, M. (2000). Loneliness and depression in caregivers of persons with Alzheimer's disease or related disorders. *Issues in Mental Health Nursing, 21,* 779–806.

Chen, C. (2003). Revisiting the disengagement theory with differentials in the determinants of life satisfaction. *Social Indicators Research, 64,* 2, 209–224.

Congressional Budget Office. (2008). *The budget and economic outlook: Fiscal years 2008 to 2018.* Washington, DC: Congress of the United States.

Cox, E. O., & Parsons, R. J. (1993). *Empowerment-oriented social work practice with the elderly.* Pacific Grove, CA: Brooks/Cole.

Cox, E. O., Green, K. E., Hobart, K., & Jang, S. L. (2007). Strengthening the late-life care process: Effects of two forms of a care-receiver efficacy intervention. *Gerontologist, 47,* 3, 388–397.

Cummings, S. M. (2002). Predictors of psychological well-being among assisted-living residents. *Health and Social Work, 27,* 4, 293–302.

Donald, I. P., & Brown, H. (2003). Independent multidisciplinary review before entry into institutional care. *British Journal of Social Work, 33,* 5, 689–697.

Doyle, J. (2005). Golden years tarnished by abuse. *San Francisco Chronicle,* May 31, p. A1.

Dubble, C. (2006). A policy perspective on elder justice through APS and law enforcement collaboration. *Journal of Gerontological Social Work, 46,* 3/4, 35–55.

Duhigg, C. (2007a). Bilking the elderly, with a corporate assist. *New York Times,* May 20, p. A1.

Duhigg, C. (2007b). When shielding money clashes with elders free will. *New York Times,* December 24, p. A1.

Ebenstein, H. (2007). Caregiver support groups: Finding common ground. *Social Work with Groups, 29,* 2/3, 243–258.

Eisdorfer, C., Cohen, D., & Veith, R. (1980). The psychopathology of aging. *Current Concepts* (Kalamazoo, MI: Upjohn Company).

Elder Law Issues. (1995). White House Conference on Aging results. *Elder Law Issues, 2,* 48, 5.

Elder Mistreatment. (2003). *Abuse, neglect, and exploitation in an aging America.* Washington, DC: National Council Panel to Review Risk and Prevalence of Elder Abuse and Neglect.

Emanuel, E., & Wertheimer, A. (2006). Who should get influenza vaccine when not all can? *Science, 312,* 884–885.

Federal Interagency Forum on Aging-Related Statistics. (2004). *Older Americans 2004: Key indicators of well-being.* Washington, DC: U.S. Department of Health and Human Services.

Harper, L., Reddon, J. R., Ward, J. R., Lyle, A. M., Moorthy, T., & Brahim, A. (2007). Behavioral and psychological symptoms of dementia of psychogeriatric inpatients on admission to a psychiatric hospital. *Clinical Gerontologist*, 30, 3, 56–63.

Health and Human Services and Assistant Secretary for Planning and Evaluation. (2003). The future supply of long-term care workers in relation to the aging baby boom generation. Report to Congress. Washington, DC: U.S. Department of Health and Human Services.

Heller, J. (2005). Cases of elder abuse triple in five years. *San Diego Tribune*, May 11, pp. B-4, 6, 7.

Hooyman, N., & Kiyak, H. A. (2007). *Social gerontology: A Multidisciplinary perspective* (8th ed.). Boston: Allyn & Bacon.

Johns Hopkins University. (2002). *Partnership for Solutions. Chronic conditions: Making the case for ongoing care.* Baltimore, MD: Johns Hopkins University.

Kaye, L. W. (2005). *Perspectives on productive aging: Social work with the new aged.* Washington, DC: NASW Press.

Kindiak, D. H., & Grieve, J. L. (1996). Social work practice in community psychogeriatric programmes. In Holosko, M. J., & Feit, M. D. (eds.), *Social work practice with the elderly*. Toronto Canadian Scholars' Press.

Knickerbocker, B. (2007). Oregon takes stock of "right to die" law. *Christian Science Monitor*, March 12, p. 3.

Legal Counsel for the Elderly. (2008). *Your rights in a nursing home.* University of Alabama Law School Clinical Program. Retrieved May 13, 2008, from http://www.uaelderlaw.org/nursing.html.

Lenze, E., Rogers, J., Martire, L., Mulsant, B., Rollman, B., Dew, M., Schulz, R., & Reynolds, C. (2001). The association of late-life depression and anxiety with physical disability: A review of the literature and prospectus for future research. *American Journal of Geriatric Psychiatry*, 9, 2, 113–135.

Levine, B. (2007). Assisted-suicide study finds no bias against the vulnerable; Concerns focus on the elderly, poor, minorities. *USA Today*, October 1, p. 9D.

Lieberman, R. (2001). *Personal foul: Coach Joe Moore vs. the university of Notre Dame.* Chicago Academy Chicago.

Lowy, L. (1985). *Social work with the aging: The challenge and promise of the later years.* New York: Longman.

MacKenzie, P., & Beck, I. (1996). Social work practice with dementia patients in adult day care. In M. J. Holosko & M. D. Feit (editors), *Social work practice with the elderly.* Toronto: Canadian Scholar's Press.

McKay, J., & Gaynor, P. (2002). Broken promises. *Pittsburgh Post-Gazette*, May 24, p. F-1.

Morrow-Howell, N. (1992). Clinical case management: The hallmark of gerontological social work. *Journal of Gerontological Social Work*, 18, 3/4, 119–131.

NFCA (2001). The National Family Caregivers Association's survey of self-identified family caregivers. www.nfacares.org/pr-2001survey.html.

National Center on Elder Abuse. (2008). *Fact sheet.* Washington, DC: U.S. Department of Health & Human Services. Retrieved May 13, 2008, from http://www.ncea.aoa.gov/ncearoot/Main_Site/index.aspx.

National Institute of Health. (2003). *Older adults: Depression and suicide facts. NIH Publication No. 03-4593.* Washington, DC: Author.

National Ombudsman Reporting System. (2003). *Data tables*. Washington DC: U.S. Administration on Aging.

Parker, M. G., & Thorslund, M. (2007). Health trends in the elderly population: Getting better and getting worse. *Gerontologist, 47*, 2, 150–158.

Porter, K. H., Larin, K., & Primus, W. (1999). *Social security and poverty among the elderly: A national and state perspective*. Washington, DC: Center on Budget and Policy Priorities.

Practice Research Network. (2005). *Practice Research Network III final report*. Washington, DC: National Association of Social Workers.

Rosenwald, D. (2007). Mutual aid: Alive and well in group work. *Reflections, 13*, 1, 56–65.

Schulz, R., O'Brien, A. T., Bookwals, J., and Fleissner, K. (1995). Psychiatric and physical morbidity effects of dementia caregiving: Prevalence, correlates, and causes. *Gerontologist, 35*, 771–791.

Sherman, A., & Shapiro, I. (2005). *Social Security lifts 13 million seniors above poverty line: A state by state analysis*. Center on Budget and Policy Priorities. Washington, DC: Author.

Simmons, T., & Dye, J. L. (2003). *Grandparents living with grandchildren 2000*. Washington, DC: U.S. Bureau of the Census.

Social Security Administration. (2007). *Annual statistical supplement to the Social Security Bulletin*. Washington, DC: Author.

Social Security Administration Office of Policy. (2008). *Monthly statistical snapshot: March 2008*. Table 3. Retrieved on May 3, 2008, from http://www.ssa.gov/policy/docs/quickfacts/stat_snapshot/#table3.

Spector, W. D., Fleishman, J. A., Pezzin, L. E., & Spillman, B. C. (2000). The characteristics of long-term care users. AHRQ Publication No. 00-0049. Rockville, MD: Agency for Healthcare Research and Policy.

Tai-Seale, M., McGuire, T., Colenda, C., Rosen, D., & Cook, M. (2007). Two-minute mental health care for elderly patients: Inside primary care visits. *Journal of the American Geriatrics Society, 55*, 12, 1903–1911.

Tebb, S., & Jivanjee, P. (2000). Caregiver isolation: An ecological model. *Journal of Gerontological Social Work, 34*, 2, 51–73.

Toseland, R. W. (1995). Aging: Direct practice. *Encyclopedia of social work*. Washington, DC: NASW Press.

U.S. Bureau of the Census. (2005). *Census Bureau estimates the number of children and adults in the States and Puerto Rico*. Washington, DC: U.S. Department of Commerce.

U.S. Bureau of the Census. (2007). *2008 statistical abstract of the United States* (127th ed.). Washington, DC: U.S. Department of Commerce.

Van Duch, D. (1998). Notre Dame coach goes to the mat. *National Law Journal, 7*, 20, B01.

Westerberg, K. (2004). Workplace development and learning in elder care: The importance of a fertile soil and the trouble of project implementation. *Outlines: Critical Social Studies, 6*, 1, 61–72.

White House Conference on Aging. (2005). Report to the president and Congress, P. 25. Retrieved on May 3, 2008, from http://www.genpolicy.com/articles/whcoa_report_2005.pdf.

HEALTH CARE SERVICES

CHAPTER 9

Heinle Division of Cengage Learning

The health care system in the United States is often described as being in a state of crisis or at least in need of major reform. The concern most frequently voiced is that not everyone has access to quality and affordable health care. Unfortunately, debate about the lack of health care coverage has led to very little action. Although there have been some efforts to reform health care in the United States, the last significant reform occurred 40 years ago with the enactment of Medicare and Medicaid. During the 1990s, the Clinton administration created a task force that proposed **universal health care**, under which everyone would be covered by insurance, regardless of preexisting conditions and employment status. The task force also advocated for the development of a **single-payer plan**, in which health care would be financed by the federal government through payroll and personal taxes and administered by state governments. Economic distinctions are eliminated in a single-payer plan, and everyone receives the same quality and quantity of care, regardless of ability to pay.

By September 1994 the proposal had been killed by Congress, which claimed it resembled socialized medicine and gave too much power to the federal government, and by the insurance industry, which mounted a strong lobbying effort because it wanted little or no change in the current system. Some members of Congress said that the universal health care plan was too complicated and too expensive. Health care reform was raised again during the 2008 presidential campaign with Democratic candidates calling for different versions of universal health care. The arguments and parties opposing universal health care remained the same. The lack of health care coverage for millions of Americans is still a concern.

While the federal government has been slow to make changes in the health care system, individual states have begun to take action of their own. In April 2006, Massachusetts lawmakers enacted sweeping health care reform legislation. It was designed to achieve near-universal coverage by 2009. The Massachusetts law mandates that all residents be covered under health insurance plans (Geisel, 2006). Within weeks of Massachusetts passing its groundbreaking measure, Vermont enacted a health care reform bill that was nearly as ambitious establishing health insurance premium subsidies for low-income people, including those who were covered by employer plans. In 2008, Michigan was considering a proposed amendment to the state constitution that would require the legislature to craft universal health care coverage. In addition, they were examining ways to subsidize premiums for the low-income uninsured, as well as create an exchange through which small employers and individuals could purchase coverage on a pretax basis. In 2008 too, California was investigating the possibility of a Massachusetts-like health plan. The impact of these state programs has not been evaluated yet, but they underscore the sense of urgency many Americans feel about the current crisis.

The U.S. health care system is plagued by rising costs and declining insurance coverage. The American people agree that major reform in health care policy is long overdue. The United States is a world leader in developing new medical technologies and probing the mysteries of disease through research. People from all over the world come here for specialized medical training and high-quality health care. It is ironic that the current system does not provide high-quality care and choices for all of the nation's citizens.

HEALTH CARE IN AMERICA

Why is health care delivery one of the dominant domestic issues today? It affects all Americans.

- $571 billion was spent by the 5,800 hospitals in the United States for care, staffed by 4.8 million personnel in 2005 (U.S. Census Bureau, 2007).
- There are 16,100 nursing homes in the United States, with 1.5 million residents. (U.S. Census Bureau, 2007).
- Forty-seven million Americans lack health insurance coverage, almost 16 percent of the population (DeNavas-Walt, Proctor, & Smith, 2007).
- Employer health insurance premiums are growing at five times the rate of inflation. Health insurance premiums paid by employers and their employees increased 7.7 percent in 2006 and another 6.1 percent in 2007 (Kaiser Family Foundation, 2008).
- In 2006, Americans made more than 1 billion visits to doctors' offices, emergency rooms, and hospital outpatient departments. Ambulatory care visits have increased at three times the rate of population growth over the past decade (Centers for Disease Control and Prevention, 2008).
- One in six Americans has inadequate access to health care (National Center for Health Workforce, 2008).
- More than 46 million Americans live in areas in which there are shortages of primary care health professionals (National Center for Health Workforce, 2008).
- Medicare is projected to begin to run low on funds between 2015 and 2025 (OASDHI Board of Trustees, 2008).

During the last century, social workers were among the most vocal advocates for a universal comprehensive health care system. Besides advocating for a better health care system through legislative reform, social workers are also providers in the health care delivery system in a variety of settings and roles. This chapter introduces many of the social work settings and roles in health care practice.

DEFINING HEALTH

Health is not merely the absence of illness; it is also a "state of complete physical, mental, and social well-being" (World Health Organization, 2000a). For centuries people have regarded mental health as separate from physical health. Hence, the health care delivery system is set up separately from the mental health care delivery system. The result is that few social service delivery systems look at the whole person in the context of the interconnectedness of physical, mental, and social well-being. Reflecting that separation, this chapter presents physical health care, and Chapter 10 covers the mental health care delivery system.

It is important to note the use of the term *system* when referring to health care services. Although this term implies that there is an organized network for health care services, this is far from true. Rather, there exists a patchwork of services and providers that are accessed differently, depending on many variables including one's income, employment, and geographic location. These shortcomings are addressed throughout the chapter. Although it may seem misleading, the term *health care system* is widely used and is therefore also used in this chapter.

The U.S. health care system follows the **medical model**—the approach doctors traditionally have used. According to this model, the sickness is located in the patient and the physician or licensed expert has the authority to heal or cure it. The medical model of health care is a deficit model in that doctors' questions are designed to elicit disabilities, distress, dysfunction, and dependency. Strengths, successes, and effective coping strategies are not solicited or taken into account. Every clinical intervention is an attempt to cure a disease or sickness. There is little connection between the patient and the patient's environment (e.g., community context, social life, workplace) (Shah, 2007).

In the medical model, the role of patients in their own healing is diminished; they are rewarded for being passive. Patients learn to place complete trust in the authority of the doctor. They wait for illnesses to go away or be cured by the doctor, and they get angry if the doctor does not cure them. The doctor's main goal is to eliminate symptoms and complaints or cure the sickness. This view of health care is contrary to the social work values of emphasizing strengths and empowerment.

The twenty-first century is seeing a decreasing reliance on the traditional medical model of health care and increasing support for the wellness model. The **wellness model** places the authority and responsibility for health in each individual. It promotes a healthy lifestyle in the areas of physical, social, mental, and environmental well-being and works to create strong and healthy communities with safe and clean physical environments.

The wellness model emphasizes prevention. More than half of diseases and health risks are related to things that can be controlled. Numerous injuries and diseases could be prevented by wearing seatbelts in cars, eating nutritious foods, getting regular exercise and preventive medical checkups, avoiding smoking, practicing safer sex, and using mindfulness and relaxation techniques. The preventive aspects of the wellness model empower the patient and make him or her the doctor's partner in a comprehensive and well-coordinated plan to enhance the quality of life. The growing use of the wellness model is accompanied by increased reliance on alternative medical methods such as acupuncture and homeopathy. Americans already spend over $20 billion a year on alternative medical methods and therapies (Hetherwick, Morris, & Silliman, 2006).

The emphasis on wellness and prevention may eradicate the artificial barriers between mental and physical health. Instead, there will be as much focus on psychological disorders resulting from lifestyle, environment, substance abuse, and stress as on the treatment of physical diseases (Hetherwick et al., 2006).

THE EFFECT OF SOCIAL INEQUALITY

You won't see inequality on a medical chart or a coroner's report under cause of death. You won't see it listed among the top killers in the United States each year. All too often, however, it is social inequality that lurks behind a more immediate cause of death, be it heart disease or diabetes, accidental injury or homicide. Few of the top causes of death are "equal opportunity killers." Instead, they tend to strike poor people more than rich people, the less educated more than the highly educated, people lower on the occupational ladder more than those higher up, or people of color more than white people. (Reuss, 2001, p. 10)

The United States rations health care on the basis of socioeconomic status. There has been clear documentation for many years that poverty is hazardous to a person's mental and physical health. On average, people in lower socioeconomic groups have higher **mortality** (death) and **morbidity** (illness) rates than people in higher socioeconomic groups. People in lower socioeconomic groups have higher rates of heart disease, diabetes, arthritis, respiratory infections, epilepsy, and certain types of cancer, among other diseases (Centers for Disease Control and Prevention, 2007b). Additionally, women who live in families with incomes below $10,000 are three times more likely to die from heart disease and diabetes than are women with family incomes over $25,000 (National Women's Health Information Center, 2005).

The reasons for these disparities are complex. One explanation is lack of or inadequate health insurance. Uninsured or inadequately insured people cannot afford to see doctors when they get sick, so their health worsens. Lack of health insurance can also mean that the poor do not get medications to address their medical problems.

Most uninsured people in the United States are the working poor, that is, people who earn too much to be eligible for government assistance but too little to pay insurance premiums. Forty percent of poor workers do not receive health insurance from their employers (Rowland, 2008). For women in families, the situation is even worse. In 2007, over 85 percent of mothers without health insurance were members of working families (Rowland, 2008).

Another factor in higher mortality and morbidity rates is that poor people usually receive their health care in public settings, while those with greater resources get care in private settings. Public medical settings often require long waits for services, which can deter potential patients. Public settings also operate with fewer resources, so practitioners have less time per patient and can perform fewer tests. Other possible reasons for substandard health among the poor are that people with few resources often live in substandard and crowded housing conditions, get inadequate nutrition, have more dangerous jobs, have less education, smoke more, and have more stress in their lives (Rowland, 2008).

Women, Latinos, the less educated, people who are foreign born, and young adults are less likely to have health insurance and are at higher risk for poor health (National Women's Health Information Center, 2005). Women have traditionally been the primary health care providers and decision makers for their families. They tend to the sick, help one another in childbirth, and pass information about treatments and remedies from one generation to the next. They have also been the nation's primary health care reformers, leading advocacy efforts to improve the quality of and expand access to health care services.

Despite their traditional roles, in general women are less likely to have health insurance than men. Since many poor women cannot afford prenatal care, uninsured women are 31 percent more likely to give birth to children who require prolonged hospitalization or who die than insured women are. Uninsured women are also less likely to have regular preventive and early-intervention mammograms, resulting in a 49 percent higher risk of death from breast cancer (National Women's Health Information Center, 2005).

As a group, women of color have poorer health, use fewer health services, and have disproportionately high premature death, disease, and disability rates compared to Caucasian women. While women of color are found in all socioeconomic categories, they are more likely to have lower incomes and live in poverty than Caucasian women. The high mortality and disease rates among women of color are explained by several factors, including cultural and language barriers, low income, late diagnosis and late entrance to treatment, and an inadequate number of primary care physicians serving neighborhoods populated by women of color. Many women of color live in poor areas and have access only to hospital outpatient clinics. These clinics have a high volume of patients, and doctors there spend less time with patients and provide less preventive care. For example, 55 percent of Asian American women, 43 percent of Latinas, 37 percent of African American women, and 40 percent of indigenous women are not routinely screened for cervical cancer; and 54 percent of Asian American women, 52 percent of African American women, and 51 percent of Latinas are not routinely screened for breast cancer. Fifty-four percent of indigenous women do not routinely receive mammograms (National Women's Health Information Center, 2005).

THE U.S. HEALTH CARE SYSTEM

The health care system in the United States encompasses many types of services in a number of settings. It includes prevention, diagnosis, treatment, rehabilitation, and health maintenance services. These services are provided in public, private, for-profit, and nonprofit settings that include hospitals, private clinics, public clinics, long-term care facilities (e.g., nursing homes, assisted living facilities), hospices, rehabilitation facilities, and home health care agencies. It is an interdisciplinary system in which social workers, doctors, nurses, physical therapists, technicians, and others work together to provide care. Key points to remember while reading through the history of health care in this country is the emphasis on the medical model and the tension between that approach's emphasis on responding to illness with efforts toward finding a cure versus the wellness approach of prevention and controlling risk. The push and pull between treatment and prevention are critical aspects of health care services. This section provides an overview of the history and current status of the U.S. health care system.

HISTORICAL BACKGROUND

The first organized efforts at developing a health care system came during the mid-1800s through the public health movement (Trattner, 1999). Spurred by the filth and disease of poor, crowded urban areas, advocates urged policymakers to pass sanitation legislation. Whereas many cities established health boards to oversee sanitation, not until the 1900s did advances in knowledge about the contagion of bacterial diseases support the attempts of public health advocates to institute reforms that could positively affect people's health.

As health and medical organizations and services began to develop during the early 1900s, social work began to participate in the burgeoning movement. In 1905 the first medical social worker was hired at Massachusetts General Hospital;

ten years later more than 100 hospitals employed social workers (Dhooper, 1997). Social workers such as Jane Addams and Florence Kelley pressed employers to improve working conditions and provide health care coverage (Mizrahi, 1995).

As a result of the economic upheaval caused by the Great Depression, numerous patients could not afford medical care. This prompted doctors and hospitals to develop health insurance companies, including Blue Shield in 1933 (Sullivan, 1999). Supporters of publicly funded health insurance plans urged legislators to include health insurance in the developing social insurance system. However, crafters of the Social Security system found health insurance to be too controversial and did not include it in their proposals (Hirshfield, 1970).

By the 1950s health insurance was primarily provided as part of employment. For people with jobs and their dependents, employer-sponsored health insurance provided adequate care. Those outside the employment system had to pay for the services themselves or make use of services subsidized by charitable organizations or hospitals.

Health care coverage expanded with the growth in social welfare services during the 1960s. In 1965, thirty years after passage of the Social Security Act, **Medicare** was added to the Old Age, Survivors, Disability Insurance program (OASDI) to complete the social insurance coverage of retirees. Medicare provides health insurance coverage to people who are eligible for Social Security as well as for some in certain categories of medical need. As discussed in Chapter 2, Part A of Medicare covers inpatient hospital costs, posthospital nursing facility services, home health services, and hospice care. It is funded by payroll taxes and contributions by employees. Part B, Supplementary Medical Insurance, is a voluntary program subsidized by the federal government. People who choose to participate pay monthly premiums, an annual deductible, and copayments for services. Part B covers physician services, outpatient services, and diagnostic tests. Medicare was expanded in 2003 through the Medicare Prescription Drug, Improvement, and Modernization Act, which created Part D, a new prescription drug benefit. Medicare recipients can opt to enroll in subsidized prescription drug coverage and pay monthly premiums, an annual deductible, and copayments (Social Security Administration, 2007). The program is subsidized to cover more of the expenses for low-income Medicare recipients. There are some health care services that are not covered by Medicare, most notably long-term nursing care. This exception in coverage can be very costly to people as they age, as was discussed in more detail in Chapter 8.

The **Medicaid** program was also enacted in 1965 under the Social Security Act. Medicaid provides health coverage and medical care to people in poverty. People whose incomes are below a certain amount are eligible to receive services from physicians who agree to accept Medicaid patients, as well as from hospitals and other health care providers. Medicaid covers physician services, diagnostic tests, home health services, and long-term care. States may elect to offer additional services, including dental care and prescription drug coverage.

It was assumed that Medicaid, Medicare, and employer-provided health insurance would together cover all citizens. However, by the late 1970s evidence was mounting that many people were not covered by any form of health insurance and that the number of uninsured was growing (Sullivan, 1999). At the same time, the cost of medical care was on the rise. In response to rising costs, the Health

Maintenance Organization Act of 1973 helped start the managed care movement, which is discussed in the next section (Mizrahi, 1995).

THE CURRENT HEALTH CARE SYSTEM

Despite changes over the past 50 years, the U.S. health care system is still primarily financed through an employment-based, voluntary health insurance system. Approximately 60 percent of Americans receive health insurance through some type of private plan that is not fully or partially financed by the government, primarily through work insurance programs (DeNavas-Walt et al., 2007). A much smaller number who are not covered at work, do not work, or do not want the coverage offered by their employers purchase their own health insurance. About 27 percent participate in Medicare, Medicaid, or another government health plan.

A growing number of Americans have neither private nor public health insurance. Approximately 47 million Americans are uninsured (DeNavas-Walt et al., 2007). More than 9 million children under the age of 19—close to 90 percent of them in working families—have no health insurance (Children's Defense Fund, 2005). Of the nearly one in five people who are uninsured, two-thirds are people of color (National Center for Health Workforce, 2008). Those without health insurance pay for services, get free care at public clinics or hospitals, or go without care. The issue of lack of access to health care, including the increasing number of uninsured people, is discussed in more detail in the next section.

There are two broad types of health insurance plans: fee for service and managed care. In a traditional **fee-for-service** plan, the insured chooses a doctor and receives services, and the insurance company pays the bill. The insured often must pay part of the bill. The patient can choose any doctor and can go to specialists at will.

One of the most dramatic changes in the U.S. health care system in recent years has been the growth of managed care. The **managed care** health care delivery structure is designed to screen out unnecessary and inappropriate care and to reduce costs (Snowden, 2000). Managed care organizations require patients to use doctors and hospitals that are part of an approved network. If a patient goes out of the network, the services either are not covered or are reimbursed at a lower rate. Managed care companies also review and often limit what doctors can do. For example, doctors must frequently get preapproval before ordering tests. They may also be required to prescribe cheaper generic drugs, rather than brand-name products.

The **health maintenance organization (HMO)** is a common managed care structure. An HMO requires a client to have a **primary care** physician who is the first contact and who provides complete care. The client can visit a specialist only after getting a referral from the primary care physician. HMOs pay physicians monthly fees, and patients make copayments for office visits and prescriptions. One of the ways HMOs reduce costs is by limiting tests.

The **preferred provider organization (PPO)** is another form of managed care. PPOs encourage clients to use health care providers from an approved network of doctors and hospitals. Fees from hospitals and doctors who are not part of the network are not covered or are reimbursed at a lower rate. PPOs offer participants more choice than do HMOs.

The managed care system has become central to health care service delivery in the United States. Supporters argue that it has helped control health care costs and that, without it, even fewer people would be able to afford health insurance. Critics contend that

> Incentives are felt within the organization to solely enroll clients who are the least needy and the easiest to serve—to "cream" the population. Receiving widespread attention in the popular press is a related problem of "skimping" on care, or under treating. Consumers also complain of restrictions on their freedom of choice: Under some arrangements, they are no longer able to select their preferred provider, which may include the provider with whom they have an ongoing and successful relationship. (Snowden, 2000, p. 440; see also Krugman, 2007).

Critics also argue that managed care does not address many of the root causes of increasing health costs, including an aging population and expensive new technologies and medications. Nevertheless, managed care seems to be here to stay and will continue to affect the way that Americans receive health care.

LIMITATIONS OF THE CURRENT HEALTH CARE SYSTEM

Americans spend more money per capita on health care than citizens of other developed nations do, yet the United States lags far behind on many health statistics. The nation spends about 50 percent more per capita on health care than any other country. A World Health Organization study, which looked at expected health, life span, and infant mortality, ranked the United States thirty-seventh in overall provision of health-related services and health outcomes (World Health Organization, 2000).

As discussed earlier, one of the primary challenges facing the U.S. health care system is health insurance coverage. About 47 million people are estimated to be uninsured. Most likely to be uninsured are people who earn low wages whose employers do not provide coverage or who do not earn enough to be able to afford the premiums. Other factors associated with lack of health insurance are age, race, and educational level. Young adults 18 to 24 years of age have the lowest rate of coverage, as do Latinos and people with less education (National Center for Health Statistics, 2005).

Within a capitalist system, the economy goes through boom and bust cycles. When the economy is strong, more people are employed, so more people have health insurance coverage. However, when the economy contracts, large numbers of people lose their jobs—and their health insurance. The growing use of contract labor and temporary employment is another limitation of an employment-based insurance system. Contract and temporary workers rarely receive health insurance benefits. In fact, many employers prefer to use contract or temporary workers so

BOX 9.1   WHAT DO YOU THINK?

What health care coverage do you have? Are you satisfied with this coverage? Do you or others you know lack health care coverage? What might be the consequences of this lack of coverage?

that they do not have to provide coverage. The result is that many people move in and out of health insurance coverage, and many others have no coverage at all.

Lack of insurance means that people must choose between necessities such as health care and food. Many do not get proper medical treatment when they are sick, and others wait until their conditions have worsened before seeking treatment. On average, people without health insurance are in worse health than those with health insurance. Mortality rates are 20 percent higher for the uninsured (National Center for Health Statistics, 2005).

People without health insurance frequently go without needed care. When they reach a critical point, they often end up in emergency rooms, sicker than they need to be and requiring expensive care for a condition that would have been preventable or treated more easily earlier. Use of emergency rooms for routine care by the uninsured also places a strain on already overcrowded facilities. Many Americans are underinsured. This means that some of their health care needs are not covered. For example, people who do not have coverage for prescription drugs may be unable to afford medications that they need. The costs of health care and health insurance have been rising at a dramatic pace, about five times the rate of inflation. Total spending on health care was $2.3 trillion in 2007, or $7,600 per person. Total health care spending represented 16 percent of the gross domestic product (GDP). Health care spending is expected to increase at similar levels for the next decade reaching $4.2 trillion in 2016, or 20 percent of GDP (Poisal, 2007). Why? There are many reasons. Some of the principal expenses are in new technologies and drugs, greater demand for services by an aging population, administrative costs of insurers, hospitals, doctors, nursing homes, and so on, and the drive for profits, all contributing to higher costs (see the "Point of View" box below).

One possible solution is to follow the lead of California and 23 other states that have limited jury awards. In California awards are limited to $250,000 for pain and suffering, and insurance premiums have remained relatively low. Others argue that victims of medical malpractice deserve fair payment for their suffering. Until a solution is found, the increasing costs of malpractice insurance will add to the costs of providing health care in this country.

BOX 9.2 | **POINT OF VIEW**

One factor that contributes to rising health care costs is that the U.S. health care system is profit based. Most providers are in business to earn a profit. Often the cost of health care is higher than it would be in a not-for-profit system. For example, when a drug company creates a new drug, one of the primary motivations is to make money from it. The company patents the drug so that no one else can sell it. The company is then able to charge any price it wants to.

Many advocates argue that drugs' costs are unreasonably high and that drug companies should not be allowed to make large profits on medication to ease suffering or save lives. This argument is often heard about drugs used to treat HIV/AIDS. The drugs, which are necessary for survival, are generally extremely expensive. The drug companies counter that they must invest a large amount of money into research and development of new drugs, and many of their efforts fail. They argue that without the profit incentive, fewer new and effective drugs will be developed.

Should health care be a for-profit enterprise?

BOX 9.3   **MORE ABOUT ... THE RISING COST OF HEALTH CARE**

The cost of medical malpractice insurance has increased more than fourfold in recent years. The District of Columbia lost about 60 practicing obstetricians during 2004–2005. Doctors claim rising medical-malpractice insurance costs are driving them out of business. National Capital Reciprocal Insurance Co., the largest insurer of D.C. physicians, said premiums for many obstetricians rose from $122,323 in 2004 to $139,528 in 2005. They project that insurance premiums will increase to $235,113 by 2010 (Redding, 2005).

Some insurers have declared bankruptcy, and others have decided to stop offering medical malpractice insurance. One of the largest, the St. Paul Companies, left the business in 2001, forcing 42,000 doctors across the country to look for new coverage (Treaster, 2002). As a result of extremely high rates and difficulty finding coverage, some doctors have left places like Washington, D.C., and have set up practices in states like California that limit jury awards and have lower insurance premiums. Other doctors have stopped practicing medicine. This leaves many areas of the country without enough doctors and sometimes with no doctors in certain specializations.

Higher costs are attributable to a number of factors.

- The pressure to produce new and costly medical technologies, products (including new experimental drugs to treat cancer), and services. The United States leads the world in expensive diagnostic and therapeutic technology and procedures.
- An aging population. Medical costs increase as people age. As the 77 million baby boomers reach their senior years, costs will continue to increase dramatically.
- Sharply higher costs of prescription drugs, with an annual total of $216.7 billion (CMS Reports, 2008).
- Increasing fees for physicians and other health professionals.
- Excessive and sometimes unnecessary medical testing, often administered to protect against malpractice lawsuits.
- Rapidly rising costs of medical malpractice insurance. In many states, increases in the cost of malpractice insurance have required doctors to charge more for their services (see "More About...The Rising Cost of Health Care").
- Use of heroic measures to save lives.

Today's health care often ignores prevention, instead waiting until people are sick before the system begins to work. In general, the system is biased toward specialty care and pays inadequate attention to cost-effective primary and preventive care. This approach ends up costing much more money over time. Additional problems are caused by insurance company procedures that make payment and reimbursement for services unpredictable for consumers and providers.

THE ROLES OF SOCIAL WORKERS

In the medical model of health care, social work roles are not as clear as the roles of nurses and other health care professionals. Because they do not tend to the physical symptoms of illness, social workers may not always be considered necessary, and nurses have been replacing them as the primary providers of case management services in hospitals (NASW, 2008).

However, at least 32 percent of social workers are in the health field, and they have several roles (NASW, 2008). One is helping clients and their families move through and effectively deal with a complex system of care so that they can return home as soon as possible. A second major social work concern is advocating for universal availability and accessibility and increased effectiveness in delivery of health care services. In addition, social work's person-in-environment approach is compatible with the wellness model, which is increasingly recognized as a useful and cost-effective approach to health care.

Health care settings are collaborative interdisciplinary environments that involve social workers, physicians, psychiatrists, nurses, psychologists, nutritionists, physical and occupational therapists, and others. The most significant contribution of social workers is the person-in-environment, or holistic, perspective on patient problems and situations (NASW, 2008). As a result of this contribution, social services are an integral component in the delivery of comprehensive health care services. Social workers in the field of health care must be highly sophisticated practitioners; have the expertise to address the biopsychosocial components of health and illness; provide case management, prevention, and education services; and generate the resources needed to implement new or innovative programs of health service delivery (see "From the Field...Helping to Find the Problem"). Social work interventions can occur in acute care, ambulatory care, and long-term care settings.

| BOX 9.4 | **FROM THE FIELD ... HELPING TO FIND THE PROBLEM**
Kathryn S. Collins, MSW, Ph.D. |

The first time I met Nicholas he was 10 years old. His pediatrician called because Nick's mother had informed her that he had been suspended from school and would not be readmitted until he had been "assessed and placed on medicine to control his aggressive outbursts." The pediatrician was not sure what was going on in Nick's home and suspected that some form of abuse was making Nick act out, as she said, "horribly at school, in the neighborhood, and at home."

I expected to see a child who was out of control. Instead, I found a boy who appeared to be timid and who was rocking back and forth in a chair, cuddled next to his mother. He was chewing on the top of his T-shirt and had tears in his eyes. Lisa, his mother, looked exhausted. As they walked into the office, Lisa gently took her son's hand and told him that it would be okay.

Before Lisa sat down, she was already tearfully relating the story of Nick's life from birth as if she had been over it a hundred times. I listened intently for any history of trauma, victimization, problems at birth, illnesses, or drastic life changes. Nick sat rigid

and upright in his chair, with his hands clasped under his legs. He avoided eye contact with me at first and hung his head as if he were deeply ashamed and holding in something he did not want me to know. He would occasionally begin rocking back and forth, then stopped when he thought I was watching and became rigid again. He kept his hands clasped under his legs and tried to keep his face, neck, and shoulders from moving, almost as if he were trying to turn himself into a cement statue.

Nick was an only child. Lisa and her husband Robert were divorced when Nick was three. Lisa alleged that Robert had been drinking heavily and that they both had wanted the divorce. Nick visited his father weekly. Lisa stated that Robert was not as patient with Nick as she was. Sometimes Nick would come home visibly upset and aggressive, but he would not talk about his weekend with his father. Since the divorce, Robert had been in treatment and attended AA regularly; as far as Lisa knew, he was not drinking. Nick said that his father took him to

BOX 9.4 | **FROM THE FIELD ... HELPING TO FIND THE PROBLEM** *continued*

work sometimes, played games with him, watched him play football, and watched television and went boating and fishing with him. Nick commented that he did not think his dad liked him sometimes, but that most of the time they had fun.

As I involved Nick in the conversation, he became more relaxed. He unclasped his hands and began playing with a figurine on the table. I invited Nick and his mother to join me in a board game while they continued talking. That was when I noticed Nick's rapid eye blinking, head nodding, and occasional but repetitive shoulder shrugging. Lisa began to talk about this physical behavior. She said that over the past two years movements like these happened all of the time. His father and teachers thought that Nick was trying to get attention, but she didn't think so. Nick said, "Yeah, dad doesn't like me when I move around a lot, so I try not to do it at his house." Even though his jerky movements happened more when Nick was upset about something, it seemed to Lisa that he could not help what he was doing. Lisa said that at times Nick's arms would flail and that he made coughing noises almost as if he were possessed. Lisa could not remember a day in the past year when she did not witness these movements; they seemed to be "getting worse, and now the teachers are complaining and won't let him come back to school." When Nick realized that we were talking about his body movements, he immediately assumed his rigid, upright position, holding his body as stiffly as possible. He seemed embarrassed and again hung his head and refused to speak about the movements.

Lisa told me that Nick's behavior at home, at school, and in the neighborhood had ups and downs. He received average grades (Bs and Cs), yet always had Ds and Fs for conduct and behavior. He was in a regular fifth-grade classroom at a public elementary school and had not been detained at any grade level. His behavior was distracting and annoying his

teachers and the other children. Nick had few friends at school and in the neighborhood. He said, "All of the kids just stare at me, call me names like 'twitchy,' and say that I am weird. I hate when they say that to me because it makes me mad."

According to the principal, Nick would go several days with minor problems and without his usual continuous body movements; then he would explode and fight with other children and curse teachers, and could not be calmed down. On these days, Nick would sit in the special education room with four children with severe mental retardation until his behavior was deemed appropriate. The teachers and principal stated that Nick was a bright child who appeared remorseful about his behavior. He was willing to skip recess to help the teachers prepare for activities or clean the classroom. Over the past three months, Nick's behavior problems, according to his teachers, had escalated to the point that they would not tolerate his being in the classroom until he was evaluated and placed on medicine.

I asked Lisa if anyone had ever suggested that Nick had a neurological disorder called Tourette's syndrome. She said that she had watched a television news program about it, but discounted it because Nick's teachers never talked about its being a possibility. She recalled her grandmother's talking about a cousin who had similar body movements and was institutionalized in the early 1950s. Lisa was terrified this would happen to Nick, so she did not want to explore the issue.

Nick's behaviors and symptoms matched the American Psychiatric Association criteria for Tourette's syndrome. Using the biopsychosocial perspective allowed me to develop appropriate treatment. Through the course of treatment, Nick was able to perform better at school; interactions with his father improved; and his mother gained understanding into the physical elements of Nick's condition and could stop blaming herself for his behaviors.

ACUTE CARE

Acute care settings include hospitals and other inpatient environments. Acute care generally involves a two- or three-day stay in a hospital. Social workers can be found in almost every hospital unit, including intensive care, kidney dialysis, oncology, newborn nurseries, neonatal intensive care, pediatrics, and geriatrics.

| BOX 9.5 | **WHAT DO YOU THINK?** |

Refer to the section on the Theoretical Basis for Social Work Practice in Chapter 1. How did the social worker in "From the Field…Helping to Find the Problem" use those principles of practice in her diagnosis of Nick? What might have happened to Nick had the social worker not considered the biological origins of Nick's behaviors?

Most hospitals, particularly large urban facilities, have social workers on staff who specialize in one area or work in several different units. The functions of a social worker in a hospital unit include high-risk screening, psychosocial assessments and interventions, interdisciplinary collaboration for coordinated patient care, discharge planning, and postdischarge follow-up (Dhooper, 1997).

> **CASE EXAMPLE:** Ming is a forty-three-year-old Asian American woman who has been diagnosed with advanced breast cancer. Ming immigrated from Taiwan to the United States with her parents when she was 12 years old. She lives in Los Angeles with her husband, their two children, who are 14 and 16 years old, and her aging parents. She has been admitted to the oncology unit of a large public hospital in Los Angeles.

Ming's oncology social worker, Sarah, provided psychosocial services to Ming and her family after they received the devastating diagnosis of cancer. In her role as educator, Sarah increased the family's awareness of the psychosocial effects of cancer. Sarah's first task was to complete a **psychosocial assessment**, which required her to investigate Ming's psychological struggles as well as the external social challenges faced by Ming and her family. For example, when Ming was first told she had cancer, she experienced great personal stress (psychological) and isolated herself from friends and family members (social) until she was able to cope (psychological) with the diagnosis.

Sarah's psychosocial assessment included Ming's current and historic coping mechanisms and life circumstances in addition to the physical, emotional, and social changes Ming was experiencing. Sarah discovered that Ming's primary worry was caring for her aging parents. Sarah referred Ming's husband to several community support programs, including meals-on-wheels, adult day care, and transportation services, to help manage Ming's parents' needs. What seemed like a simple information and referral task to Sarah made a great difference to Ming's peace of mind.

Before Ming was discharged from the hospital after her first round of chemotherapy, Sarah arranged for Ming to begin attending a breast cancer support group that Sarah facilitates. She also referred Ming's family members to a family support group. **Discharge planning** is one of the critical roles of social workers in acute care settings. It involves helping patients make the transition out of the acute care facility. The social worker assesses medical needs following acute care, determines informal and formal supports available to the patient, and develops a continuum-of-care plan so that all services needed to promote healing and well-being are available (NASW, 2008).

> **CASE EXAMPLE:** Sam is 85 years old and currently in the geriatrics unit of the Salt Lake City Veteran's Hospital. A World War II veteran, he has limited mobility as a result of a stroke he suffered five years ago. He is currently in the hospital because he had a mild heart attack. Sam shows the early signs of senile dementia.

Debbie, Sam's social worker, has been making arrangements for his discharge from the hospital. He will not be able to return home because of the level of in-home medical services he requires. Sam has no family, so Debbie is identifying long-term care facilities that can accommodate his medical needs and will accept Medicaid. Because Sam is a veteran, he can take advantage of resources provided through the Department of Veterans Affairs (VA). Debbie arranges for Sam to move to a skilled nursing facility under Medicaid and ensures that additional medical care will be provided through the VA. In the skilled nursing facility, Sam will receive physical therapy to help regain mobility, occupational therapy to improve his daily living activities such as bathing and dressing, and ongoing medical supervision.

AMBULATORY CARE

Ambulatory care includes outpatient services, education, counseling, and community outreach. Coordinating patient care through case management and crisis intervention counseling are the predominant roles of social workers in ambulatory care settings such as public health clinics, hospital outpatient clinics, emergency rooms, urgent care centers, primary care physician offices, and prison health centers. The goal of the case manager is to coordinate, integrate, and manage an array of services that effectively and efficiently address the health and social service needs of the client.

Social workers serve in numerous other ambulatory health-related environments. Social workers who specialize in maternal and child health, for example, are found in hospitals, homes for pregnant teenagers, and public health clinics. They also work in family planning clinics as counselors and educators.

Prevention services and education are often promoted by health care workers in outpatient or community settings. These professionals bring health care information and practices into the community, rather than making them available within medical facilities.

LONG-TERM CARE

Long-term care (LTC) is medical care within a residential setting. It is provided to individuals who are unable to care for themselves but who do not need the intensive services provided in a hospital. LTC can be provided through home health care or in outside facilities such as nursing homes. Levels of care range from complete care to limited services such as provision of meals and help dressing or bathing.

Long-term care settings include nursing homes, rehabilitative facilities, assisted living residences, hospice care facilities, and patients' homes. Generally, services are provided in the least restrictive environment. Residents are urged to maintain autonomy and make their own decisions, and physical, social, and psychological functioning are maximized. Social work services in long-term care settings focus on both chronic physical conditions and emotional well-being (Kinosian, Stallard, & Wieland, 2007).

Because long-term residences are typically used by older people, knowledge about chronic conditions can help the social worker recognize the progression of disease. Many residents of long-term facilities have decreased ability to care for themselves and have likely experienced major life changes such as widowhood or retirement, so attention should be paid to their mental health.

In recent years, there has been a trend toward promoting positive long-term care options. **Nursing homes**, also referred to as skilled nursing facilities, are residential health care facilities that provide medical care similar to that provided in a hospital, although not as intensive. They often serve as a stepping-stone for people, particularly older people, between the hospital and return home or a move to a less medically oriented setting.

Assisted living facilities, which first were built more than 25 ago, are gaining in popularity. Designed to emulate retirement living, these facilities promote social activities, congregate dining, and recreational opportunities. New assisted living facilities have living rooms, television rooms, and private dining areas that residents can reserve. These facilities differ from retirement communities in that they offer a continuum of medical care and assistance with daily living tasks. Often there are medical personnel on staff. Residents can receive assistance with bathing, dressing, and upkeep of their small individual rooms or apartments. Meals are served in dining rooms to promote socialization. Assisted living facilities are much less restrictive than nursing homes, but more structured and medically equipped than people's own homes. However, they are expensive, and the costs are not covered by health insurance.

Hospice provides services for people with terminal illnesses who are expected to die within six months. The services are offered in the person's home or in inpatient hospice facilities. The hospice movement calls on specialized skills in counseling related to grief and dying. Hospice social workers typically work in interdisciplinary teams to help dying patients and their family members and friends prepare for natural death.

The perspective in hospice work is different from that of the medical model. The social worker does not encourage medical interventions or prolonging life, but rather helps people accept the dying process, prepare to say good-bye, and reconcile differences if needed and serves as a mediator between the dying person and the people who are part of the patient's dying process (Munn & Zimmerman, 2006; Callanan & Kelley, 1992).

DEVELOPMENTAL DISABILITIES

CASE EXAMPLE: Richard and Dawn Kelso brought their 10-year-old son, Steven, to a hospital in December 1999 and departed, leaving him in the emergency room. Steven has cerebral palsy, uses a wheelchair, and can breathe and eat only through a tube. The Kelsos did not have prior criminal records and had never been accused of abuse or neglect. Mrs. Kelso said that she was exhausted and frustrated with the system, and that she did not know what else to do. The Kelsos were charged with abandonment and sentenced to probation. Steven has remained under state care in a health facility, where his parents visit him under supervision (Peterson, 2000).

Raising a child with severe disabilities is demanding and stressful. It can tax a family to the breaking point. Respite care and home health care services are not always available or affordable. Some states currently refuse to use Medicaid dollars to pay for in-home services, and sometimes the only option is a specialized nursing home. The fact that Steven is in a medical setting indicates that he needs very specialized care.

A **developmental disability** is a severe, chronic disability that is attributable to a mental or physical impairment that manifests itself before age 22 years and is likely to continue indefinitely. The disability results in substantial limitations in three or more areas of major life activity, such as self-care, learning, mobility, economic self-sufficiency, and capacity for independent living. Mental retardation, autism, cerebral palsy, epilepsy, and Down syndrome are common developmental disabilities.

The causes of developmental disabilities vary. Mental retardation can result from numerous factors, including genetic abnormalities, malnutrition, premature birth, exposure to toxic agents, and social deprivation. Cerebral palsy is usually caused by a brain injury that occurs before or during birth. Down syndrome is caused by chromosomal abnormalities. Epilepsy is often caused by lesions on the brain. The cause of autism is still unknown. Environmental factors, such as poverty, can also cause or contribute to developmental disabilities. For example, poor women are less likely to receive prenatal care and more likely to be malnourished during pregnancy than more affluent women. Both of these factors can cause or contribute to a child's mental retardation. Approximately two out of every hundred Americans—nearly 4.5 million people—have developmental disabilities (Administration on Developmental Disabilities, 2008). Some are as serious as Steven's; others are less so.

Social workers serve as case managers, coordinating services to ensure that clients' needs are met. They advocate for clients' rights within the maze of programs and services, and also for the development and implementation of well-funded client-centered programs that meet the needs of diverse client groups. Social workers investigate claims of abuse and neglect by caregivers, educate parents and other providers about available resources, and work in programs that train and employ people with developmental disabilities. Social workers are also involved in preventing developmental disabilities through efforts to reduce poverty and improve prenatal care.

PUBLIC HEALTH POLICIES

Stories like the ones that follow received a lot of press attention during the early 1990s and may be partly responsible for the movement in favor of universal health care. Although that effort was not successful, advocates did manage to win a few small victories.

CASE EXAMPLE: In 1990 Frank was employed in a small manufacturing company outside of Los Angeles. Due to cutbacks, he was one of 50 workers who lost their jobs and their health insurance. Frank was unemployed for only two months, but during that time his three-year-old daughter Maria was diagnosed with leukemia. When Frank found another job, the health insurance carrier refused to cover Maria's preexisting health problem. The family tried to find medical care for Maria, but they were not eligible for Medicaid once Frank started working. Maria died in 1993.

CASE EXAMPLE: Nancy had her baby in a "drive-through delivery" in the hospital. Her HMO's "concurrent utilization review person" (a nurse who goes from floor to floor to make sure covered patients do not get too much in the way of care) cut off Nancy's coverage, against the attending doctor's advice, within 15 hours of the delivery. Nancy suffered no serious complications as a result of her early release. Thousands of other women were not so lucky. Many mothers and newborn children suffered from hemorrhaging, infections, and other complications after being the victims of reckless discharge.

CASE EXAMPLE: In 1997 Veronica had a mastectomy. Her insurance policy covered the mastectomy (many don't), but the insurance company categorized breast reconstruction as cosmetic surgery and refused to cover it. Veronica went into debt in order to have the breast reconstruction surgery.

Partly in response to growing gaps in health care coverage, The Family and Medical Leave Act (FMLA) was passed in February 1993. FMLA requires public agencies, including state, local, and federal employers, local schools, and private-sector employers with 50 or more employees, to grant family leave and temporary medical leave under certain circumstances. An eligible employee must be granted up to 12 workweeks of unpaid leave during any 12-month period

- For the birth and care of the employee's newborn child
- For placement with the employee of a child for adoption or foster care
- To care for an immediate family member (spouse, child, or parent) with a serious health condition
- When the employee is unable to work because of a serious health condition

On return from FMLA leave, the employee must be restored to his or her original job or to a job with equivalent pay, benefits, and other terms and conditions of employment (P.L. 103-3). Although people who cannot afford to take unpaid leave are not helped by FMLA, it is a start.

Limited health insurance protection for millions of working Americans and their families was instituted with passage of the Health Insurance Portability and Accountability Act of 1996 (HIPAA). This act increased many people's ability to maintain continuous health coverage when they change jobs by guaranteeing a continuation of eligibility for equivalent coverage and limiting the use of some preexisting conditions. Frank's daughter Maria would have received better medical care had HIPAA been in place when Frank lost his job. HIPAA does not require employers to pay for health coverage, so the cost, which can be very high, is borne by the former employee. HIPAA does not apply to workers in all places of employment, and it does not permit people to keep the same health coverage when they change jobs.

Two important amendments were made to HIPAA. As a result of the first, the Newborn and Mother's Health Protection Act of 1996 (NMHPA), health insurance plans may not automatically restrict benefits for a hospital stay in connection with childbirth to less than 48 hours following vaginal delivery or 96 hours following a cesarean section unless a doctor determines that the mother or newborn child is ready for discharge. Had Nancy been covered by NMHPA, she would not have been discharged from the hospital early.

The second amendment, the Women's Health Care and Cancer Rights Act of 1998 (WHCRA), provides protections to patients who choose to have breast reconstruction in connection with a mastectomy. WHCRA does not require plans to pay for a mastectomy, but health plans that cover mastectomies are subject to WHCRA protections. Veronica would have benefited from WHCRA.

HIPAA, NMHPA, and WHCRA do not advance the cause of universal health care, and they help only people who already have health coverage. None of them addresses the needs of the uninsured. About 20 percent of the uninsured (versus 3 percent of those with coverage) say their usual source of care is the emergency room (Kaiser Family Foundation, 2006). As noted earlier, emergency room care is always more expensive. The costs of caring for the uninsured are passed along in higher hospital rates for the insured, which result in higher health insurance premiums. Social workers must advocate for up-front funding for universal primary and preventive care.

Another shortcoming in our health insurance programs was the lack of coverage for prescription medications for seniors under Medicare. For many elderly persons, the cost of their prescriptions came entirely out of their own expenses, in some cases running hundreds and hundreds of dollars a month. As mentioned under the discussion of the history of health care coverage in the United States, in 2003 Congress and the president enacted the Medicare Prescription Drug, Improvement, and Modernization Act with provisions to provide funds for prescription drug coverage. The program officially started in 2006 with the provision of prescription drug insurance coverage through private agencies, overseen by Medicare administration. The formula for benefits is extremely complicated and is targeted to cover people with low incomes. Early analysis of the legislation suggests that in order to reach a compromise and appease all sides of the issue, the program is complicated, does not cover all medication costs, and will be expensive to administer. Estimates place the cost of the program to be $635 billion over the first 10 years (Congressional Budget Office, 2008). In spite of these limitations, the program begins to address one of the many shortfalls in our health care system.

SOCIAL WORK VALUES AND ETHICS IN HEALTH CARE SETTINGS

Social work in health care settings is fraught with ethical challenges. This is particularly true in an era of managed care, high costs, and profit-driven medical care. Like all members of the profession, health care social workers are expected to promote the dignity and worth of each person, believe that everyone can reach full potential, and make self-determination and the right to be fully informed the core of all treatment. Rehr, Rosenberg, and Blumenfield stress the following additional values for health care social workers:

- Health care is a universal right.
- All people should be guaranteed access to services.
- Consumers should be able to choose care.
- Care is a mutual and informed partnership between the consumer and his or her provider.
- Confidentiality should be guaranteed.
- Care is based on a biopsychosocial framework. (1998, pp. 25–26)

Those working in health care settings face ethical issues related to end-of-life situations. Personal values about the important issues of life and death can come into conflict with professional values. Should treatment be withheld if it is painful and the person may not live longer as a result? Should people who are in a great deal of pain and have little or no chance of long-term survival be able to end their lives? Should doctors be allowed to help? How much pain is too much pain? Who should decide whether a patient should receive further treatment or be allowed to die with dignity? How can compassion for the dying be balanced with safeguards so that people cannot take advantage of end-of-life situations?

CASE EXAMPLE: In 1995, Terri Schiavo was reduced to a vegetative state. She apparently suffered cardiac arrest due to a vitamin deficiency brought on by bulimia, though her autopsy could not definitively prove it. Robert and Mary Schindler, Terri's parents, accused her husband, Michael Schiavo, of strangling her, though the courts and medical personnel rejected that claim.

On March 31, 2005, Terri Schiavo finally died, after a 10-year, scorching legal battle between her husband and her parents. In the end, Michael won a court order that allowed the hospital to stop Terri's food and water. She died 13 days later. The family's bitter legal battle divided America and reached the highest levels of our government. The medical establishment firmly sided with Michael Schiavo and his belief that Terri was brain dead and beyond rehabilitation. He also reported that Terri and he had discussed end-of-life issues and she did not want to be kept alive under such conditions. However, there was no living will or written document stating Terri's wishes. The majority of Americans, according to public opinion polls taken at the time, believed that it was Michael Schiavo's right to decide the fate of his wife. However, then governor of Florida Jeb Bush and many conservative Republicans in the U.S. Senate and House of Representatives supported legislation that asked a federal court to reconsider its decision and reinsert a feeding tube days before Terri's death. The attempt by government officials to intervene in a private family matter was interpreted by most Americans as overreaching and inappropriate. The Schindler's never accepted that Terri was indeed brain dead. However, medical experts reported that she was and an autopsy after her death proved that she had in fact been brain dead. Questions: What would you have done if you were Michael Schiavo? What is the potential role of social workers in this case? Why were most Americans against the efforts of government officials to intervene? Do you agree that the governor and legislators were overreaching?

Social workers are often in the difficult position of helping people determine what constitutes a dignified death and how people should be treated at the end of their lives. This issue is directly related to the social work values of promoting the dignity and worth of each individual, self-determination, and respect for and preservation of life. About half of all hospitalized patients experience moderate to severe pain in the last days of their lives (Field & Behrman, 2002). Although they are able to treat pain effectively, many doctors do not do so because they fear that the patient will become addicted to drugs or they are not trained in pain management. Regulations on how much medication can be given for pain vary from state to state, and many doctors limit pain medication to avoid regulatory scrutiny.

Physician-assisted suicide (discussed in Chapter 8) presents ethical concerns for the medical social worker. If a patient is unable to speak for himself or herself, when should medical treatment or the provision of nutrition and hydration through a feeding tube be withheld? Who should make the decision? Increasing numbers of people are preparing for end-of-life situations by communicating their wishes in living wills and medical powers of attorney. A living will specifies which life-prolonging treatments a person does and does not want. A medical power of attorney is used to appoint a person to make medical decisions for an individual who is no longer able to make them for himself or herself.

Some states do not allow family members to decide to end life-sustaining treatments. In states where family members are permitted to make such decisions, situations can become quite complicated if they disagree about what the patient would have wanted. Social workers can encourage individuals to address difficult end-of-life issues in advance, so that the dying person's wishes are more likely to be honored. Advance directives, living wills, and durable health power of attorney forms can all be done in advance and help family and friends make health care choices for a person if he or she cannot do so. Social workers are also involved in lobbying for policies that respect the wishes of the dying and their families. However, it can be a difficult balance between the authority of the medical professionals and the wishes of patients. To what extent do patients have the right of self-determination to decide on treatments or even the refusal of treatments and to what extent do medical professionals know best and can insist on treatments? Health care social workers can serve as brokers between patients and medical professionals.

CRITICAL ISSUES

Not only do people live longer as a result of advances in health care, but people who in previous generations would not have survived are also living full lives. Many need supplemental services and accommodation to perform daily tasks. Their needs as well as the health needs of people with chronic health conditions such as HIV and AIDS present an increasing challenge to social workers.

DISABILITY

CASE EXAMPLE: Casey Martin was a teammate of Tiger Woods on the Stanford University golf team that won the 1994 NCAA championship. Martin has a circulatory disorder that has weakened his right leg, and he needs to use a golf cart in order to play 18 holes. According to PGA tour rules, professional golfers cannot use carts, and the PGA refused to make an exception for Martin. He sued the PGA under the Americans with Disabilities Act. A federal court in Oregon agreed that Casey should be allowed to use a cart, as did the California appeals court. Martin joined the PGA tour (*Buffalo News*, 2001).

According to the Americans with Disabilities Act (ADA), the term **disability** is used when a person has a physical or mental impairment that substantially limits one or more major life activities, the individual has a record of such an impairment, or the person is regarded as having such an impairment. In 2008, lawmakers were considering a bill to broaden the reach of the ADA. It now applies only to conditions that substantially limit a major life activity, but draft legislation would drop that qualifier. The new bill would apply the law to all ailments, mental and physical, even when controlled by medication or treatment.

More than 49 million Americans (15.7 percent of the population) have disabilities (Brault, 2008). Nearly half of them are of an employable age, and 78 percent of those who are employable say that they want to work, but only one-third of those of employable age are employed (American Association of People with Disabilities, 2008). Social workers advocate for persons with disabilities so that they will be free from abuse, neglect, and discrimination and have access to education, health care, housing, jobs, and other services.

As discussed in Chapter 3, the Americans with Disabilities Act, which Casey Martin and others have used to protect their rights, was signed into law in 1990. The ADA is intended to make American society more accessible to people with disabilities by requiring reasonable accommodations. This means making existing facilities used by employees readily accessible to and usable by persons with disabilities; restructuring jobs and modifying work schedules; acquiring or modifying equipment or devices, examinations, training materials, or policies; and providing qualified readers and interpreters (Equal Employment Opportunity Commission, 2000; see also "More About…The Americans with Disabilities Act"). Many advocates for people with disabilities fought long and hard to win these provisions, and they continue to fight to have them properly enforced.

BOX 9.6 | **MORE ABOUT … THE AMERICANS WITH DISABILITIES ACT**

The ADA is divided into five titles.

1. *Employment (Title I):* The provisions in ADA Title I require employers of 15 employees or more to provide reasonable accommodations to protect the rights of individuals with disabilities in all aspects of employment. For example, office space and workstations must be wheelchair accessible.

   Title I protects only qualified individuals with disabilities. A qualified individual is a person who meets legitimate skill, experience, education, or other requirements of an employment position and can perform the essential functions of the position.

2. *Public services (Title II):* Public services, including restrooms, must be accessible to people with disabilities. Individuals with disabilities cannot be denied access to public transportation services. Buses, trains, and other public vehicles must be modified to be accessible and safe for individuals with disabilities.

3. *Public accommodations (Title III):* Restaurants, hotels, grocery stores, retail stores, golf courses, and privately owned transportation systems must be made accessible to individuals with disabilities.

4. *Telecommunications (Title IV):* Telephone companies must provide telephone relay service to individuals who use telecommunication devices for the deaf (TTYs—teletypewriters) or similar devices.

5. *Miscellaneous (Title V):* Individuals are prohibited from coercing, threatening, or retaliating against people with disabilities or those attempting to aid people with disabilities by asserting their rights under the ADA.

HIV/AIDS

Acquired immune deficiency syndrome (AIDS) is a chronic disease that damages and destroys the immune system. To be diagnosed as having AIDS, an individual must test positive for **human immunodeficiency virus (HIV)** antibodies and must also have an opportunistic infection, an AIDS-related cancer, severe wasting or dementia, or a reduction in the number of the T cells that help provide immunity to disease.

Today, there are approximately 32.2 million people in the world living with HIV/AIDS. In the United States, there are 1.2 million people, including more than 500,000 who are black and approximately 250,000 who are Latino. Whereas African Americans make up 12 percent of the U.S. population, they account for 50 percent of the new HIV/AIDS cases (Centers for Disease Control and Prevention, 2007a).

The good news about HIV/AIDS in the United States is that starting in 1994 the number of deaths from AIDS began decreasing. By 1997 the disease had dropped from eighth to fourteenth place among the causes of death in the United States. This is due in large part to the use of protease inhibitors and reverse transcriptase inhibitors to treat patients infected with AIDS. The combination of drugs, referred to as the cocktail, has changed AIDS from a death sentence to a chronic but manageable disease (AVERT, 2007).

However, the cocktail is not a cure. At this time, the medications are very expensive. Many people with AIDS in the United States and around the world (one in four) cannot afford the antiretroviral drugs. Additionally, the cocktail must be taken following a strict regimen. If the regimen is not followed, treatment can fail and the possibility is increased for the rapid development of drug-resistant strains of the virus (Institute of Medicine, 2005). There is concern that the presence of the antiretroviral drugs is also creating a treatment optimism, a sense the HIV is treatable and thus not so serious. This can result in less concern about becoming infected or spreading the virus to others and a reduction in safer sexual and drug-using behaviors (Cohen & Hosseinipour, 2005).

The Americans with Disabilities Act applies to individuals who are HIV-positive or have AIDS. For example, a public school cannot prohibit an HIV-positive child from attending elementary school; a state-owned nursing home may not refuse a patient who has HIV/AIDS; and a county summer recreation program cannot refuse to admit the brother of someone who has AIDS.

BOX 9.7	ETHICAL PRACTICE ... CONFIDENTIALITY OR HEALTH SAFETY?

You are a case manager for a social service agency. You have a client who has been using IV drugs and wants to get into a drug treatment program. During your intake interview he tells you that he thinks he might be HIV positive, but is too afraid to go get tested. He tells you he is married and that he has an active social life outside of his marriage with other sexual partners. You are aware of the risk that if he is HIV positive he may spread the virus to his sexual partners. What should you do?

MEDICAL USE OF MARIJUANA

For decades there has been strong debate about the medicinal benefits of marijuana. The arguments are complicated by the categorization of marijuana as an illegal substance since the 1940s. A decade ago, the prestigious National Academy of Science's Institute of Medicine (1999) reviewed all major research on the use of marijuana and found "Scientific data indicate the potential therapeutic value of cannabinoid drugs, primarily THC, for pain relief, control of nausea and vomiting, and appetite stimulation" (p. 1). Their concern was that smoking the drug was dangerous, and therefore they could not recommend that form of ingestion. With advances in medicine, there are ways to administer medical marijuana that do not involve smoking, such as orally or through a vapor. Yet the use of marijuana is still very controversial. Some states allow it through prescription, and the process is highly controlled. Efforts have gone as far as the Supreme Court. In 2005 the Supreme Court sided with the federal government to outlaw marijuana as a medicine, but allowed states to continue to keep their own laws. So far, 12 states including California, Oregon, New Mexico, Vermont, and Colorado have laws that allow some form of medical use of marijuana. Supporters argue that a valuable medicine is being withheld from the public, while opponents see it as a gateway to other drugs and the public sanctioning of a now-illegal behavior. Patients looking for medical alternatives will continue to push for the medical use of marijuana and drug control advocates will continue to argue against legalization. Although a health issue, medical use of marijuana will likely be decided through the courts, legislatures, and state ballot initiatives.

DIABETES

Diabetes is a disorder of the metabolism. When a person's metabolism is in order, food that is digested produces glucose to be absorbed by cells and used by the body for energy. In people with diabetes, however, the pancreas either produces little or no insulin, or the cells do not respond appropriately to the insulin that is produced. Glucose builds up in the blood, overflows into the urine, and passes out of the body in the urine. Thus, the body loses its main source of fuel even though the blood contains large amounts of glucose (National Diabetes Information Clearinghouse, 2008). With the development of insulin outside the body, people with diabetes can be treated and live long and productive lives. However, diabetes does take a toll on the body and often complicates other health conditions. Today, most people in the United States know someone with diabetes. It is estimated that 21 million people, or almost 10 percent of the population, over 20 years of age have diabetes. Half of those people are over 60 years of age. Diabetes typically develops over time with age. This number has been growing, from 5.6 million in 1980 to 15.8 million in 2005. The numbers and proportion of the population that have diabetes are anticipated to grow and require greater medical attention and dollars. See the box "Becoming a Change Agent," which analyzes one of the leading contributors to diabetes, obesity.

The prevalence of diabetes is disproportionately distributed over the population and is correlated with several social conditions. Twelve percent of adults with

BOX 9.8   **BECOMING A CHANGE AGENT**

Headlines from around the world tell the story of a troubling health problem in industrialized countries. "Fatty food adverts must be controlled: Warning as childhood obesity soars in Ireland" reads one headline (Kelpie, 2008). A headline from Colorado paper reads, "Kaiser study: Diabetes risk rises for pregnant women, sharp increase in obesity to blame, researchers say" (Scanlon, 2008). A Scottish headline states, "World shame of Scotland the Fat; Our nation named as the most overweight on entire planet after the U.S. with one in four of all Scots now obese" (Nicolson, 2007). "Italy's obesity epidemic gives lie to dietary myth" is a headline from an Italian paper (Lakhani, 2007). People in industrialized countries around the world are getting fatter, and Americans are taking the lead. Obesity is linked to a variety of health problems including cardiovascular diseases, diabetes, cancer, and osteoarthritis. Particular concerns are being raised about childhood obesity. In the past 30 years, the childhood obesity rate has doubled for children aged 2–5 and 12–19 years old, and tripled for children 6–11 years of age (Finkelstein, Trogdon, & Trogdon, 2008). Childhood obesity increases the risk for asthma, high blood pressure, high cholesterol, diabetes, orthopedic problems, and other challenges that can last into adulthood.

Analyzing the Situation

- Conduct some research and try to answer the following questions: What is causing the obesity epidemic in the United States? Are the causes the same in other countries? Do most researchers agree on the causes? What do you see as the most significant cause for the rise in obesity in the United States and abroad?
- Why do the rates of childhood obesity seem to be going up so fast? Is the childhood obesity epidemic spread evenly among all children, or are some populations suffering from it more than others?
- Is the obesity epidemic an appropriate concern for the social work profession? Why or why not?

What Can Social Workers Do?

Given your analysis and understanding of the causes of obesity, what can social workers do to address the problem? What can they do at the individual and family levels? What can they do at the community and policy levels?

What Can You Do?

What one step might you take now, alone or working with others, to prevent or reduce obesity in your community? What are the barriers that might keep you from taking this step? What could you do to reduce those barriers?

less than a high school diploma had diabetes compared with 6 percent of adults with a bachelor's degree or higher; adults in poor and near poor families were more likely to have diabetes (Centers for Disease Control and Prevention, 2007b). In addition to education and income, diabetes disproportionately affects members of nondominant groups. Although 8.7 percent, of whites have diabetes, blacks have a rate of 13.3 percent, and Mexican Americans have a rate of 9.3 percent (National Diabetes Information Clearinghouse, 2008).

The increase in incidence and the linkage to poverty and lack of education place diabetes as a major health and social concern. In addition, it is troubling that a lack of health care, which impacts people who are poor, often means that diabetes can go undiagnosed, compromising people's health further. Therefore, understanding the indicators and symptoms of diabetes is critical for social workers.

CONCLUSION

Physical health affects all aspects of life and is intertwined with emotional and social well-being. This chapter focused on the unique social work challenges in health care settings. Understanding physical health is vital to social work practice in other arenas as well. Treatment of alcohol and drug use (Chapter 13) is part of the larger system of health care. Poverty is also intricately tied to health and well-being. Therefore, although the health care social worker deals with the physical and medical care of people, biopsychosocial needs are part of many domains of social work practice.

Key Terms

acquired immune deficiency syndrome (AIDS), (p. 257)

acute care, (p. 247)

ambulatory care, (p. 249)

assisted living facilities, (p. 250)

developmental disability, (p. 251)

disability, (p. 255)

discharge planning, (p. 248)

fee-for-service, (p. 242)

health, (p. 237)

health maintenance organization (HMO), (p. 242)

hospice, (p. 250)

human immunodeficiency virus (HIV), (p. 257)

long-term care (LTC), (p. 249)

managed care, (p. 242)

Medicaid, (p. 241)

medical model, (p. 238)

Medicare, (p. 241)

morbidity, (p. 239)

mortality, (p. 239)

nursing homes, (p. 250)

preferred provider organization (PPO), (p. 242)

primary care, (p. 242)

psychosocial assessment, (p. 248)

single-payer plan, (p. 236)

universal health care, (p. 236)

wellness model, (p. 238)

Questions for Discussion

1. What is managed care? What are some of the benefits of managed care? What are some of the disadvantages?
2. What are the key differences between the medical model of health care delivery and the wellness model?
3. What factors help explain the higher mortality and disease rates among women of color? What does this mean for social workers in the health care field?
4. Why is the infection rate of young, gay, urban African American men rising?
5. A patient in a long-term care facility informs his social worker that he no longer wants a feeding tube. Without the feeding tube in place, the patient will die within 12 days. What questions should the social worker ask the patient? What ethical and legal considerations should the social worker and the medical staff face before deciding whether to grant the patient's request? How should the patient's family be involved?

Change Agent Exercise

Eating well is an essential component to good health. Although many people experience hunger and malnutrition around the world and in the United States, experts agree that these are not problems caused by not having enough food for everyone. Hunger and malnutrition are often due to an individual's lack of money. Such a person cannot afford to buy food in general and nutritious food specifically. Conduct some research to find out the estimated levels of hunger and malnutrition in your community. How many people rely on food banks or food stamps to eat? Working with others in your class, plan and organize a food drive on your campus or in other locations in your community to collect food for a local food bank.

Chapter Exercises

1. **Health Care Letter to the President**
   Write a letter to the president of the United States expressing your views about the fact that millions of people have no health insurance. Explain the problem of uninsured persons as you understand it, and suggest an appropriate response. Use data to support your position.

2. **Health Care Rationing**
   The state legislature has limited funds for its Medicaid program. Legislators must choose between a funding increase for prenatal care and funding organ transplants for Medicaid recipients. The cost of 30 organ transplants is approximately the same as the cost of providing prenatal care to 1,500 women. If you were a state legislator, what information would you need to make a decision?
   What are the most important factors to consider?

3. **Physician-Assisted Suicide**
   Should physician-assisted suicide be legal for patients who have less than six months to live? What about patients who have debilitating chronic pain or other conditions that may not be terminal but have destroyed their quality of life?
   - Describe why physician-assisted suicide is a controversial issue. The following questions may be helpful:
     - Is there adequate evidence to resolve the issue?
     - Is the current evidence contradictory?
     - What are the underlying values on each side of the issue?
   - Examine your personal beliefs. Does physician-assisted suicide affect your life? If so, how? What are your personal experiences, if any, in relation to this issue?
   - Choose one side of the issue. Brainstorm a list of the arguments that support it. List and explain the strongest arguments in favor of the position you have chosen.
   - Do the same for the other side of the issue.
   - After looking at the arguments on both sides, what gaps are there in the available information? What would you need to know to help convince you? Where might you find this information?

- After reviewing all the available information, which side do you support? What specifically convinces you that this is the right side? Is this the same or a different position than you had before researching the topic?

4. **Ethical Issues Case Study and Role-Play**

CASE EXAMPLE: Mr. Roberto Gonzalez was recently admitted to the hospital. He is 74 years old and has been married to his wife, Evie, for 45 years. They are both practicing Catholics. Roberto and Evie immigrated to Miami from Cuba over 30 years ago with their three children. The Gonzalez children are now grown: Roberto Jr. is 43, Rosa is 41, and Tomas is 36. They have families of their own.

Mr. Gonzalez has been struggling with a variety of medical problems for the past nine years, and his current condition is critical. Dr. Garcia has recommended a liver transplant. The transplant has less than a 50 percent chance of success, but Dr. Garcia has indicated it is Mr. Gonzalez's only hope for long-term survival.

Mr. Gonzalez is tired of the pain and tired of fighting. He tells Dr. Garcia that he prefers to let nature take its course and to not have the transplant. Mrs. Gonzalez is not ready to let go. She called the social worker, Jorge Lopez, and asks for his assistance in convincing Mr. Gonzalez to have the surgery. Roberto Jr. supports his father's position. Rosa wants her father to keep fighting. Tomas is ambivalent.

Mr. Lopez calls a family meeting to discuss the issue.

Assign the roles (Mr. Gonzalez, Mrs. Gonzalez, Dr. Garcia, Jorge Lopez, Roberto Jr., Rosa, and Tomas) and role-play the family meeting. After the role-play, address the following ethical issues:

What are the major ethical considerations in this case?

Ultimately, who has the decision-making authority?

What should the role of the social worker be? Facilitator? Advocate?

5. **HIV/AIDS**

Using the library or the Internet, find current information by a reliable source about the AIDS epidemic. On the basis of the data you find, answer the following questions:

Since the Centers on Disease Control began collecting data on AIDS cases, how many total cases have been reported in the United States?

What percentage of these total cases were in women?

Which ethnic group is at greatest risk of contracting HIV? Why do you think this might be so?

What was your source of information? How do you know it is a reliable source?

What are the implications of the findings presented in this report for social work practice?

Get into small groups. Compare the information you found with others in your class. If there was a difference in what you found, how might you decide which data is most accurate?

References

Administration on Developmental Disabilities (ADD). (2000). *ADD fact sheet*. Retrieved on January 22, 2000, from http://www.acf.dhhs.gov/programs/add/Factsheet.htm.

American Association of People with Disabilities. (2008). *Fact sheet*. Washington, DC: American Association of People with Disabilities.

AVERT. (2007). *AIDS treatment targets and success*. West Sussex, UK: Averting AIDS and HIV.

Blumenfield, S., Bennett, C., & Rehr, H. (1998). Discharge planning a key function. In Rehr, H., Rosenberg, G., & Blumenfield, S. (eds.), *Creative social work in health care: Clients, the community, and your organization* (pp. 89–93). New York: Springer Publishing Company.

Brault, C. (2008). Disability status and the characteristics of people in group quarters: *A brief analysis of disability prevalence among the civilian noninstitutionalized and total populations in the American community survey*. Washington, DC: U.S. Census Bureau.

Buffalo News. (2001). It's about hitting the ball. *Buffalo News*, February 4, p. B2.

Callanan, M., & Kelley, P. (1992). *Final gifts: Understanding the special awareness, needs, and communications of the dying*. New York: Bantam Books.

Centers for Disease Control and Prevention. (2007a). *HIV/AIDS surveillance report, 17*, 1–46. Atlanta, GA: U.S. Department of Health and Human Services.

Centers for Disease Control and Prevention. (2007b). *Summary health statistics for US adults: National Health Interview Survey, 2006*. Atlanta, GA: U.S. Department of Health and Human Services.

Centers for Disease Control and Prevention. (2008). Outpatient U.S. medical care visits exceeds 1 billion. Retrieved on May 12, 2008, from http://www.cdc.gov/nchs/pressroom/06facts/outpatient.htm.

Children's Defense Fund. (2005). General health facts: Uninsured children. Retrieved on June 25, 2005, from http://www.childrensdefensefund.org/hs_tp_genfacts.php.

CMS Reports. (2008). *U.S. health care spending growth accelerated only slightly in 2006*. Washington, DC: CMS Office of Public Affairs.

Cohen, M. S., & Hosseinipour, M. C. (2005). HIV treatment meets prevention: Antiretroviral therapy as prophylaxis. In Mayer, K. H., & Pizer, H. F. (eds.), *The AIDS pandemic: Impact on science and society* (pp. 137–161). San Diego, CA: Elsevier Academic Press.

Congressional Budget Office. (2008). *The budget and economic outlook: Fiscal years 2008 to 2018*. Washington, DC: Congress of the United States.

DeNavas-Walt, C., Proctor, B. D., & Smith, J. (2007). *Income, poverty, and health insurance coverage in the United States: 2006*. Current Population Reports, pp. 60–233. Washington, DC: U.S. Census Bureau.

Dhooper, S. S. (1997). *Social work in health care in the 21st century*. Thousand Oaks, CA: Sage.

Equal Employment Opportunity Commission. (2000). *Facts about the Americans with Disabilities Act*. Washington, DC: Author.

Estes, R. J. (1984). *Health care and the social services: Social work practice in health care*. St Louis, MO: W.H. Green.

Falk, I. S. (1941). Medical care. *Social work year book*. New York: Russell Sage Foundation.

Field, M. J., & Behrman, R. E. (2002). *When children die: Improving palliative and end-of-life care for children and their families*. Washington, DC: Institute of Medicine.

Finkelstein, E., Trogdon, J., & Trogdon, J. (2008). Public health interventions for addressing childhood overweight: Analysis of the business case. *American Journal of Public Health, 9,* 3, 411–415.

Franks, P., Clancy, C. M., & Gold, M. R. (1993). Health insurance and mortality: Evidence from a national cohort. *Journal of the American Medical Association, 270,* 6, 737–741.

Geisel, J. (2006). State sparks blaze of reform. *Business Insurance*, May 29, p. 11.

Hetherwick, M., Morris, K., & Silliman, M. (2006). Perceived knowledge, attitudes, and practices of California registered dietitians regarding dietary supplements. *Journal of the American Dietetic Association, 106,* 3, 438–442.

Hirshfield, D. (1970). *The lost reform 1932–1943.* Cambridge, MA: Harvard University Press.

Institute of Medicine. (1999). *Marijuana and medicine: Assessing the science base.* Washington, DC: National Academy Press.

Institute of Medicine. (2005). *Scaling up treatment for the global AIDS pandemic: Challenges and opportunities.* Washington, DC: National Academy Press.

Kaiser Family Foundation. (2000). *Health insurance coverage and access to care among Latinos.* Washington, DC: Kaiser Family Foundation.

Kaiser Family Foundation. (2006). *The uninsured: A primer, key facts about Americans without health insurance.* Washington, D.C.: Kaiser Family Foundation.

Kaiser Family Foundation. (2008). *Employer health benefits: Summary of findings 2008.* Washington, D.C.: The Henry J. Kaiser Family Foundation and Health Research & Educational Trust.

Kelpie, C. (2008). Fatty food adverts must be controlled: Warning as childhood obesity soars in Ireland. *Daily Mirror*, January 25, p. 16.

Kinosian, B., Stallard, E., & Wieland, D. (2007). Projected use of long-term-care services by enrolled veterans. *Gerontologist, 47,* 3, 356–364.

Krugman, P. (2007). First, do less harm. *New York Times*, January 5, p. A17.

Lakhani, N. (2007). Italy's obesity epidemic gives lie to dietary myth. *Independent on Sunday*, December 16, p. 20.

Mizrahi, T. (1995). Health care: Reform initiatives. *Encyclopedia of Social Work* (pp. 1185–1198). Washington, DC: NASW Press.

Munn, J. C., & Zimmerman, S. (2006). A good death for residents of long-term care: family members speak. *Journal of Social Work in the End of Life and Palliative Care, 2,* 3, 45–59.

NASW. (2008). *Issue fact sheet: Health.* Washington, D.C.: National Association of Social Workers. Retrieved on May 12, 2008, from http://www.socialworkers.org/pressroom/features/issue/health.asp.

National Center for Health Statistics. (2005). *Health, United States Annual Report.* Washington, D.C.: Department of Health and Human Services.

National Center for Health Workforce. (2008). *Health workforce analysis and forecasting tools.* Retrieved on May 12, 2008, from http://www.hhs.gov/news/facts/index.html.

National Diabetes Information Clearinghouse. (2008). *Diabetes overview.* Washington, DC: National Institute of Health.

National Women's Health Information Center. (2005). Retrieved on June 25, 2005, from http://www.4woman.gov/media/statistics.htm.

Nicolson, S. (2007). World shame of Scotland the Fat; Our nation named as the most over-weight on entire planet after the U.S. with one in four of all Scots now obese. *Daily Mail*, September 26, p. 1.

OASDHI Board of Trustees. (2008). *Annual Report*. Washington, DC: Author.

Peterson, J. (2000). Parents who abandoned disabled son get probation in plea deal. *New York Times*, March 4, p. A9.

Poisal, J. A. (2007). Health spending projections through 2016: Modest changes obscure part D's impact. *Health Affairs*, February 21, pp. 242–253.

Redding, R. (2005). Rising cost of malpractice insurance pushes doctor out of the city. *Washington Times*, May 14. p. 5.

Rehr, H., Rosenberg, G., & Blumenfield, S. (1998). Clinical interventions and social work roles and functions. In Rehr, H., Rosenberg, G., & Blumenfield, S. (eds.), *Creative social work in health care: Clients, the community, and your organization* (pp. 21–40). New York: Springer.

Reuss, A. (2001). Cause of death: Inequality. *Dollars and Sense Magazine*, May/June, p. 10.

Rowland, D. (2008). *Health care affordability and the uninsured*. Testimony before the Congress of the United States House of Representatives Committee on Ways and Means Health Subcommittee, April 15.

Scanlon, B. (2008). Kaiser study: Diabetes risk rises for pregnant women. Sharp increase in obesity to blame, researchers say. *Rocky Mountain News*, April 28, p. 15.

Shah P. (2007). The medical model is dead--long live the medical model. *British Journal of Psychiatry, 191*, 375–377.

Snowden, L. R. (2000). The new world of practice in physical and mental health: Comorbidity, cultural competence, and managed care. In Allen-Meares, P., & Garvin, C. (eds.), *The handbook of social work direct practice* (pp. 437–450). Thousand Oaks, CA: Sage Publications.

Social Security Administration. (2007). *Annual statistical supplement to the Social Security Bulletin*. Washington, DC: Author.

Sullivan, K. (1999). *Making sense of the health care reform debate*. Mankato, MN: Minnesota COACT and the COACT Education Foundation.

Trattner, W. I. (1999). *From poor law to welfare state: A history of social welfare in America* (6th ed.). New York: Free Press.

Treaster, J. B. (2002). Doctors face a big jump in insurance. *New York Times*, March 22, p. B1.

U.S. Census Bureau. (2007). *Statistical abstract of the United States* (127th ed.). Washington, DC: U.S. Department of Commerce.

World Health Organization. (2000a). Definition of health. Retrieved on January 2001, from http://www.who.int/aboutwho/en/definition.

World Health Organization. (2000b). *World health report 2000*. Washington, DC: Author.

MENTAL HEALTH SERVICES

CHAPTER 10

Co-authored by Layne K. Stromwall, Ph.D.

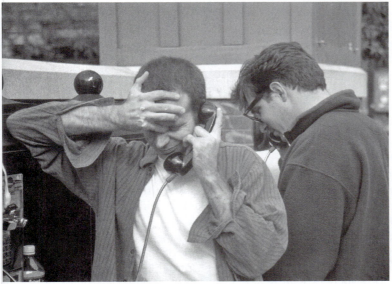

Heinle Division of Cengage Learning

Mental illness affects the lives of millions of people. Although some struggle with their own mental illnesses, others cope with the illnesses of friends and families.

- Mental illnesses are more common than cancer, diabetes, or heart disease. Twenty-five percent of all Americans meet the criteria for having a mental illness (Kornblum, 2008; WHO World Mental Health Survey Consortium, 2004). Serious mental disorders affect an estimated 6 percent of the adult population, or approximately 1 in 17 people. Less than half receive treatment (Kessler et al., 2005).
- About 20 percent of children and adolescents have experienced mental disorders, and 12 percent of those have serious emotional disturbances. Children of depressed parents are three times more likely to suffer from depression and anxiety than the children of mentally healthy parents. Only about one-third of children who need it receive mental health services (Arons & Bornemann, 2000; Hochman, 2006).
- An estimated 33 percent of the homeless suffer with severe mental illness (Kornblum, 2008).
- Nearly half of all people with one mental disorder also meet the criteria for a second disorder (Kessler et al., 2005).
- The effectiveness of a variety of treatments for the array of mental and behavioral disorders has been well documented. In fact, treatments improve symptoms and quality of life for 70 to 90 percent of people with a serious mental illness (Kornblum, 2008).
- Social workers provide most of the country's mental health services. According to government sources, 60 percent of mental health professionals are clinically trained social workers, compared to 10 percent of psychiatrists, 23 percent of psychologists, and 5 percent of psychiatric nurses (NASW, 2008).

Despite evidence that one in four U.S. adults experiences mental illness (e.g., depression, anxiety, eating disorders, or substance abuse) at some point, researchers still consider the figure an underestimate. They acknowledge that many people remain reluctant to tell surveyors about their mental health history, mainly because of the stigma attached to mental diseases (WHO World Mental Health Survey Consortium, 2004).

Social workers now play a key role in providing mental health services by promoting emotional well-being, advocating for parity of mental illness services with physical illness services, and helping to develop affordable and accessible treatment methods and interventions to help people recover from mental disorders (National Association of Social Workers, 1997). Social workers constitute the largest group of mental health professionals in the United States (SAMHSA, 2005). Almost half of all professional social workers identify mental health as their primary or secondary practice area (National Association of Social Workers, 2005). Social workers are committed to making mental health care and the prevention of mental disorders a national priority.

It is an exciting time to be a social worker in the field of mental health. Ongoing scientific discoveries about the functioning of the brain are increasing understanding of effective treatment, creating an atmosphere of hope and the possibility of recovery for even the most serious mental disorders. Social workers play an important part in researching and delivering these new **evidence-based practice** models. Evidence-based practice is a process used to choose and evaluate the most effective treatment available.

MENTAL HEALTH AND MENTAL ILLNESS

According to the U.S. surgeon general (1999), **mental health** is the successful performance of mental function, resulting in productive activities, fulfilling relationships with other people, and providing the ability to adapt to change and cope with adversity. The term **mental illness** refers collectively to all diagnosable **mental disorders**—health conditions characterized by alterations in thinking, mood, or behavior associated with distress or impaired functioning (American Psychiatric Association, 1994). Some of the most prevalent disorders are described in "More About...Mental Disorders."

BOX 10.1   MORE ABOUT ... MENTAL DISORDERS

Within the broad category of mental illness, many specific psychiatric conditions have been defined.

Mood disorders affect the individual's emotional state and thinking. The most common, clinical depression, is a serious medical illness with symptoms of ongoing sad mood, difficulty in concentration, sleep disturbances (inability to fall asleep and early waking), changes in appetite (either lesser or greater), changes in social behavior, and increased risk of suicide. Depression can develop in any person at any age. Although it is highly treatable with both medication and psychotherapy, it is frequently a lifelong condition in which periods of wellness alternate with recurrences of illness. Worldwide, clinical depression affects twice as many women as men. One in seven women will develop the illness at some time in her life. Women's greater vulnerability is thought to be due to a combination of biological, genetic, psychological, and social factors (Weissman et al., 1993).

Bipolar disorder was previously called manic depression. To be diagnosed with bipolar disorder, the person must have had at least one episode of depression and one episode of mania. Manic episodes often include hallucinations or delusions, which can lead to a misdiagnosis of schizophrenia.

About 1 percent of the population is affected by bipolar disorder, and it occurs equally in males and females. Psychotropic medications are effective in the treatment of bipolar disorder and can prevent recurrence of future manic episodes (NIMH, 2001).

Anxiety disorders are chronic or recurring states of tension, worry, fear, and uneasiness arising from unknown or unrecognized perceptions of danger. They include generalized anxiety disorder, acute stress disorder, obsessive-compulsive disorder, post-traumatic stress disorder, panic disorder, social phobia, specific phobia, and substance-induced anxiety disorder (Barker, 1999).

Considered the most severe type of anxiety disorder, panic disorder affects between 3 and 6 million Americans. It is twice as common in women as in men. It can appear at any age, but most often it begins in the young adult years. Feelings of terror occur with no warning. Between panic attacks, the person experiences persistent and lingering worry that another attack will begin at any minute. Panic disorder can be accompanied by other conditions like alcoholism or depression. It is treated with both medication and psychotherapy (National Institute of Mental Health, 2000).

| BOX 10.1 | **MORE ABOUT ... MENTAL DISORDERS** *continued* |

Obsessive-compulsive disorder (OCD) is characterized by anxious thoughts or rituals that the person feels she or he cannot control. The disturbing thoughts or images are called obsessions, and the rituals performed to dispel the thoughts are called compulsions. OCD can begin in childhood, adolescence, or adulthood and affects about the same number of men as women. About 1 in 50 people suffers from OCD, and researchers have located a specific genetic component. Depression, anxiety, or eating disorders may accompany OCD. A specific type of behavioral therapy called exposure and response prevention has proven effective, as has psychotropic medication (National Institute of Mental Health, 2000).

Schizophrenia is considered one of the most disabling mental disorders. Its symptoms include at least two of the following: hallucinations (hearing or sometimes seeing or smelling something that is not really there), delusions (thoughts or perceptions not related to reality), disorganized thinking or speech, inappropriate mood, flat emotions, and lack of motivation and energy. Although researchers have not yet determined what causes or can cure schizophrenia, their work has revealed that profound changes occur in the brain (Nathan, Gorman, & Salkind, 1998).

Serious emotional disturbance is a legal term that describes any diagnosable mental health problem in children under the age of 18. The condition must severely disrupt the child's ability to function socially, academically, or emotionally. If a child's condition meets these criteria, a number of services are mandated to meet his or her needs (U.S. Surgeon General, 1999).

Serious mental illness (SMI) and *serious and persistent mental illness (SMPI)* are legal terms for groups of mental disorders that interfere with social functioning sufficiently to require ongoing treatment. In many states, individuals with mental disorders must be assessed as meeting this criterion in order to qualify for public mental health services. Serious mental illnesses can include schizophrenia, bipolar disorder, and major depression, among others.

Characterizing mental health and mental illness is not as simple as these definitions might lead one to believe. For one thing, definitions of mental health and mental illness vary depending on cultural norms and social conditions. What is considered mental illness in one culture may be considered acceptable healthy behavior in another. Similarly, what was considered mental illness at one time may not be thought of the same way at a later time.

Mental health and mental illness can be viewed as being on a continuum. Few people are completely mentally healthy all the time. All have times of impaired functioning when they are less able to have fulfilling relationships, adapt to change, or cope with adversity. For example, following the death of a loved one, it is not unusual for a person to become depressed and to have a hard time meeting day-to-day demands. He or she may develop relationship problems or have difficulty at work or both. One of the challenges in the mental health field is to distinguish between problems in daily living and mental illness.

BIOLOGICAL AND PSYCHOLOGICAL FACTORS

For centuries, people have distinguished between the human mind and the human body and have regarded mental health as separate from physical health. An example of this enduring belief is found in the U.S. medical insurance system. Insurance plans generally provide full coverage for physical health problems but not for mental health problems. The U.S. surgeon general's 1999 report emphasized that mental illness and physical illness are inseparable. The "mind" is now understood by most researchers to be activities in the brain, a physical body organ. Current scientific research emphasizes that mental illness, in most cases, can be traced to physical changes in the brain. There is no real split between mind and body or between mental health and physical health.

Successfully diagnosing and treating mental disorders requires a biopsychosocial perspective that focuses on interactions between a person's social environment, medical history, past experiences (e.g., trauma, family, peers, school, larger sociocultural environment), psychological variables, and genetic factors. This complicated mix makes it necessary for mental health social workers to have a broad knowledge base that includes sociology, psychology, psychiatry, anthropology, neurobiology, pharmacology, immunology, and epidemiology. Perhaps most importantly, mental health social workers must keep up with advances in neuroscience and behavioral research that help explain the development and successful treatment of mental disorders.

From childhood to adulthood through old age there are variabilities in the diagnosis, course, and treatment of a mental disorder. For example, depression can cause a child to act out and engage in disruptive behavior, and the child can be treated for attention deficit hyperactivity disorder. As the child matures, disruptive behavior diminishes, and it is believed that the child no longer has a problem. However, the depression has not been treated, and during adolescence or young adulthood it may manifest itself in withdrawn behaviors and lead to social isolation. Early identification of the underlying depression could change the progression of the illness and lessen the possibility of later problems.

A social worker in the area of children's mental health needs to understand human development, age-appropriate behaviors, and language development in order to distinguish abnormal behavior from normal developmental stages. For example, a temper tantrum is a normal behavior in a two-year-old child. However, serious tantrums that continue past that developmental stage may indicate a problem. The tantrums may be the child's reaction to a maladaptive environment or a warning sign of a mental health problem.

As people grow older, their vision, hearing, and memory decline (Siegler, Poon, Madden, & Welsh, 1996), and their pulmonary and immune systems weaken (Miller, 1996; Carman, 1997). However, most older adults have stable intellectual functioning, continue to have the capacity for change, and are productively engaged with life. Just as children's development affects their mental health, normal adult development needs to be understood to accurately assess and treat psychiatric conditions in people who are aging.

CASE EXAMPLE: Seventy-year-old Edna Walker was widowed after 52 years of marriage. Before her husband's death, she was actively involved in life and had a part-time job. Since her husband's death, she has found it difficult to get back to normal. There are financial pressures. She is tearful most of the day. She does not sleep well, and many days she feels so tired that she stays in bed. She does not have much interest in food and has lost weight. Ms. Walker's primary care physician thinks she is suffering from depression.

Some adults 55 years and older experience mental disorders that are not a normal part of aging. These disorders include depression, Alzheimer's disease, alcohol and drug abuse, anxiety disorders, and late-life schizophrenia. It is difficult to assess and diagnose late-life mental disorders because the physical complaints or symptoms of older adults may not appear to meet the full criteria for such mood disorders as depression and anxiety (U.S. Surgeon General, 1999). In addition, family members may ignore their older relative's symptoms, believing them to be part of the aging process that cannot be changed.

Prevention efforts need to be focused in primary care settings because physicians are the first point of contact for many older adults who are experiencing mental health problems. Specialty psychosocial interventions such as grief counseling, suicide prevention services, and self-help groups need to be readily available and accessible within primary care settings. Social workers who work in non–mental health settings need to have knowledge of the symptoms of mental disorders so that they can make appropriate referrals.

SOCIAL FACTORS

Gender, culture, race, poverty, and age are important variables in correctly diagnosing and treating mental disorders. A client's problems must be seen in the context of the social environment (i.e., family, peers, colleagues, friends) and the larger physical and cultural surroundings. For example, a few mental disorders—including depression, panic disorder, and eating disorders—disproportionately affect women. Women are twice as likely to suffer from depression than men; it may be the result of biochemical differences or childhood socialization or both (*Drug Week*, 2008). Other disorders affect more men than women; men are five times more likely to develop alcoholism and antisocial personality disorders (Breslow, 2008).

Cultural interpretations of symptoms differ. A specific behavior may be considered acceptable or normal in one culture or setting and viewed as pathological in another. For example, *ataques de nervios* is a culture-bound syndrome most commonly seen in the Spanish-speaking Caribbean (Oquendo, Horwath, & Martinez, 1992). It appears suddenly after a psychosocial stressor, such as a funeral or a family fight, and is characterized by violence, a nonviolent frenzy of activity, or hallucinations that may end in convulsions or a suicide attempt. In the Spanish-speaking Caribbean, *ataques de nervios* is considered to be an acceptable way to display distress. The person's family mobilizes immediately to help alleviate the stress, and there is rarely need for medications or hospitalization.

There is a reciprocal relationship between a child's biological state and the environment. Physiological changes may result from exposure to trauma (e.g., abuse, neglect, violence, or separation from a parent) and may interfere with the child's development of the ability to deal with an adverse environment. Biological vulnerability sometimes occurs first, making some children more susceptible to problems when their environment is not nurturing. Social factors that increase biological risk include inadequate prenatal care, which can lead to prenatal damage from low birth weight; exposure to alcohol, tobacco, or illegal drugs, which can trigger or exacerbate mental disorders; exposure to toxic chemicals; and dangerous living conditions. Social work's emphasis on the person-in-environment is particularly appropriate for understanding the reciprocity between biological and social factors in promoting mental health.

THE MENTAL HEALTH CARE SYSTEM

Mental health services are provided in numerous settings and by a variety of professionals. The various public and private services are together thought of as the mental health care system. This network of services began in the early 1800s and today includes professional social workers.

HISTORICAL BACKGROUND

As long as there have been people, there has probably been mental illness. Explanations of mental illness have changed over time, and public beliefs about mental disorders have strongly influenced treatment. In the United States, according to Lin (1997), there have been five major movements in mental health since the early 1800s. These are the moral treatment movement, the mental hygiene movement, the community mental health movement, the legal advocacy movement, and the consumer movement.

During the early nineteenth century there was no organized government effort to treat mental illness. People with mental illnesses were regarded as "lunatics," and their families took care of them. The prevailing attitude was that mental illness stemmed from violations of physical, mental, and moral laws. Taking corrective action and enforcing moral behaviors was believed to cure mental illness and was initiated in hospitals. This period of moral treatment lasted until the early twentieth century.

During the 1840s, Dorothea Lynde Dix, a retired Boston teacher who is considered the founder of the mental health movement, began a crusade that would change the way people with mental disorders were viewed and treated. Dix called to attention the overcrowded, appalling, and often-abusive conditions in the institutions in which people with mental illnesses were placed (Shapiro, 1994). Her efforts brought about many reforms at both the state and federal levels, including the founding of more than thirty public and private institutions (Brandwein, 1997). Dix was not a social worker; the profession was not established until after her death in 1887. However, her life and work were embraced by early social workers, and she is considered one of the pioneers of psychiatric social work along with Elizabeth Horton, who in 1907 was the first psychiatric social worker in the New York hospital system, and others (Rossi, 1969). Dorothea Dix's work led to the mental hygiene movement.

The early twentieth century was a time of progressive public policies. Advocates of improved public health focused attention on care and treatment in mental hospitals. Recognition of the needs of people with mental illnesses led to the development of the first psychiatric units in hospitals, which moved away from punitive moral treatment to a more medical approach.

Following World War II, the mental health needs of returning veterans evoked public sympathy and understanding and changed attitudes about mental illness. Encouraged by the promise of **psychotropic drugs**, or antipsychotics, which are chemicals used to treat mental disorders, the Community Mental Health Centers Act was passed in 1963. This policy encouraged the **deinstitutionalization** of people with mental illness—the shift in the location of psychiatric care from inpatient facilities, particularly public mental hospitals, to the community. It was believed that previously institutionalized people could take psychotropic medications and live in the community while being supervised by community mental health professionals.

Even as deinstitutionalization was being implemented, the rights of people with mental illnesses became the focus of the legal advocacy movement of the 1970s. Landmark court cases ensured their rights and self-determination. Restrictions were placed on potentially harmful treatment methods, and mental illness and the attendant need for treatment were no longer justification for involuntary confinement. Placing people in institutions against their wishes, regardless of their conditions, was no longer legal (unless they were a danger to themselves or others). These legal changes were viewed as empowering to people with mental illnesses and helped prevent unnecessary involuntary confinements.

The 1980s and 1990s gave rise to the consumer movement in mental health care. A **consumer** is a person who has received or is currently receiving services for a psychiatric condition. People with mental disorders and their families became advocates for better care. Organizations such as the National Alliance on Mental Illness were created to educate the public and reduce the stigma of mental illness. Building public understanding and awareness through consumer advocacy helped bring mental illness and its treatment into mainstream medicine and social services. Most progressive mental health programs now espouse the recovery philosophy, which has developed due to consumers' advocacy for programs that give them hope for a normal life and more power and responsibility in making decisions to meet their own personal recovery goals (Ralph & Corrigan, 2005). Recovery acknowledges that many people with serious mental illness spontaneously recover and others recover and improve with proper treatment.

A significant movement not included in Lin's summary is the managed care movement. **Managed care** (see Chapter 9) describes a health care delivery system designed to eliminate unnecessary and inappropriate care in order to reduce costs (Langwell, 1992). The costs to employers of providing medical mental health insurance coverage have been rising 4 to 12 percent annually (Decamp, 2008). Mental health insurance paid for the treatment a physician recommended, and physicians tended to recommend costly inpatient treatment, especially for adolescents. The cost increase resulted in a reexamination of how insurance companies and public health insurance programs paid for treatment, and health maintenance organizations (HMOs, discussed in Chapter 9) were developed to manage costs. Rather than following all physician recommendations for care, HMOs pay only for agreed-on medically necessary treatment, and they choose the least costly alternative (Edinburg & Cottler, 1997).

THE CURRENT SYSTEM

The delivery of mental health services, although referred to as a system, is more accurately a loose network of services ranging from highly structured inpatient psychiatric units to informal support groups. Social workers can be found throughout the various mental health services. While the array of services permits diverse approaches in multiple settings, a number of limitations compromise the delivery and effectiveness of mental health interventions.

Fragmentation of the System   Social workers contend with a complex and fragmented mental health delivery system. Professionals from a number of fields receive funding from a variety of disconnected sources with little coordination. Regier et al. (1993) describe it as a de facto mental health service system because it is simply a loosely coordinated set of public (government funded or operated) and private services. The U.S. surgeon general (1999) refers to four segments within the de facto system: (1) specialty mental health services, (2) general medical/primary care services, (3) human services, and (4) voluntary support network services.

Specialty mental health services include private for-profit, private not-for-profit, and public settings. Approximately 6 percent of adults and 8 percent of children and adolescents use specialty mental health services in any year.

General/medical primary care service providers include doctors and nurses in hospitals and primary care physicians in clinics. For many people who enter the de facto mental health system, the first point of contact is through medical doctors or hospitals. Primary care physicians have been the focus of educational efforts by mental health professionals to assist them in recognizing early symptoms of mental disorders, particularly clinical depression. The most common reason for hospital admission is a biological psychiatric condition, such as bipolar disorder or schizophrenia. Almost 21 percent of all hospital beds are filled by people with mental illnesses.

The human service sector consists of social services, school-based services, counseling, vocational rehabilitation, prison-based services, and religious-based social services. This sector is by far the largest provider of children's mental health services.

The voluntary support network sector consists of self-help groups such as Alcoholics Anonymous (AA) and similar twelve-step programs; Recovery Inc., a support group for people with mental disorders; and other support groups sponsored by voluntary organizations like the National Alliance on Mental Illness and Mental Health America. The number of self-help groups has been increasing as consumers and their families recognize that social support can buffer the effects of stress. Many consumers perceive the value of activities that promote wellness and view self-help and support groups as powerful adjuncts to professional services.

Managed Care   As a result of the managed care movement, health insurance plans often give oversight of mental health services to companies with expertise in behavioral health. The goal is to reduce costs by emphasizing cheaper brief or group treatment approaches, by making sure applicants for service meet criteria, and by reviewing the medical necessity of all treatment. Incentives, in which professionals receive bonuses for providing less care, and risk-sharing contracts, in which providers agree to treat a specified number of consumers for a specified cost, are features of managed behavioral health care service delivery.

Although there is a great deal of controversy surrounding managed care, it is unlikely to vanish. Managed care benefits some consumers by reducing out-of-pocket costs and making care more accessible. Eighty-nine percent of U.S. workers have employer-sponsored health insurance with mental health coverage; 74 percent of those plans are subject to annual outpatient visit limitations, and 64 percent were subject to limitations on inpatient care. In 2000, only 75 percent had such coverage, and in 1984, only 5 percent had both. Social workers are advocating for all Americans to be able to afford and access mental health coverage (U.S. Fed News, 2008), with special emphasis on efforts to create parity, or equality, of insurance benefits for physical and mental health treatment.

Deinstitutionalization   Deinstitutionalization was prompted by the need to reduce the costs of psychiatric care, by attention to the rights of people who were involuntarily hospitalized, and by advances in evidence-based psychosocial and psychotropic drug treatment. With treatment, people are able to function in ways that were previously impossible. Between 1970 and the 1990s, the inpatient population of state and county institutions fell from 413,000 beds to below 100,000 (Grob, 2001). Despite increases in the overall population, inpatient beds have declined further, and the United States currently has a deficit of nearly 100,000 inpatient beds. This has resulted in increased homelessness, emergency room overcrowding, and use of jails and prisons as de facto psychiatric hospitals (Torrey, Entsminger, Geller, Stanley, & Jaffe, 2008).

Deinstitutionalization was implemented with little understanding of its individual and social consequences (Mechanic, 1999). The Community Mental Health Center Act was never fully funded, and insufficient housing, treatment, rehabilitation, and education services were provided for people with serious mental disorders. Deinstitutionalization is blamed for the homelessness of a large number of seriously mentally ill people and for the inability of mentally ill people and their families to secure treatment. As a result of the deinstitutionalization movement, many mental hospitals were permanently closed, leaving fewer options available for people who had difficulty benefiting from treatment offered in the community.

Criminalization   The fragmented delivery system is further complicated by the criminalization of mental health problems coupled with ineffective follow-up care after discharge from hospitals and inpatient psychiatric facilities. Twenty-four percent of people in state prisons and 21 percent of those in local jails have a recent history of a psychiatric disorder (Glaze & James, 2006). This is almost four times as many people as are receiving inpatient treatment in state mental hospitals. When individuals with mental disorders live in the community and do not receive treatment, their abnormal behavior sometimes results in arrests rather than in referral for treatment. However, the common belief that people with mental illnesses are more violent than average is not borne out by research (Swanson et al., 2006).

Community Treatment   Historically, inpatient clients have not always connected with case management services after discharge (Belcher & DeForge, 2005). Part of the problem is poor coordination between inpatient hospital settings and community mental health clinics. Also, consumers who have not proved to be a danger to themselves or others are not required to accept treatment. Some consumers choose not to accept treatment because they fear or have previously experienced the common side effects of psychotropic medication as extreme sedation, inability to think clearly, sexual difficulties, and excessive weight gain. Others do not seek treatment because the symptoms of their mental illnesses make them unduly suspicious of the treatment system. As a result, some people who have severe and persistent mental illnesses become homeless or are quickly returned to the hospital when their symptoms recur.

MULTIDISCIPLINARY ASPECTS OF MENTAL HEALTH CARE

In most mental health settings, social workers are members of teams that include colleagues from a variety of other professional disciplines. Table 10.1 lists disciplines whose members practice in mental health settings and shows their educational and professional qualifications and common professional roles. Paraprofessional workers in the mental health system include **peer counselors**, consumers who have recovered from psychiatric disorders and who now assist other consumers. Social work students often gain experience as part-time psychiatric technicians under the supervision of professionals. They are involved in a variety of tasks including providing ongoing support to consumers in residential settings, carrying out behavioral programs designed by professionals, and monitoring consumer needs in inpatient settings.

The multidisciplinary nature of mental health care is particularly notable in terms of diagnosis. The standard for identifying and categorizing symptoms into diagnosed disorders is the American Psychiatric Association's *Diagnostic and Statistical Manual of Mental Disorders*, Fourth Edition, Text Revision (2000) (**DSM-IV-TR**). This manual lists all currently recognized mental disorders, provides a detailed description of each diagnostic category, and specifies the diagnostic criteria practitioners should use

TABLE 10.1 | MORE ABOUT PROFESSIONAL DISCIPLINES IN MENTAL HEALTH SETTINGS

Discipline	Qualifications	Role
Psychiatrist	M. D. plus psychiatric residency, board certification in psychiatry	Prescribes psychotropic medication; diagnoses mental disorders
Psychologist	Doctorate (Ph.D. or Psy.D.), state licensure	Conducts psychological testing; provides psychological treatment
Social Worker	MSW/BSW; MSW plus state licensure or certification required for independent or clinical practice	Provides assessment, clinical treatment
Professional Counselor or Marriage and Family Therapist	MA/MS; state licensure	Provides psychotherapeutic treatment
Nursing: Psychiatric Nurse Practitioner	Master's degree from psychiatric nurse practitioner program; state license	Prescribes and monitors medication
Psychiatric Nurse	R. N. or B.S.N.; sometimes Master's degree	Monitors medication and medical needs; with Master's degree, provides psychotherapy

to make reliable diagnoses (Williams, 1998). The Fourth Edition was first published in 1994, and the latest text revision reflects new empirical findings and corrects errors. Another full version is expected to be published around 2010. The diagnostic categories of the DSM are used by all mental health providers and insurance companies. The "Point of View" box discusses controversies about some of the definitions.

BOX 10.2 | **POINT OF VIEW**

A diagnostic system like the DSM can be used to distinguish between mental disorders and the problems in living that all people encounter. It helps practitioners and researchers develop a better understanding of conditions and effective treatments. However, some mental health practitioners, consumers, and consumer advocates are troubled by certain aspects of the DSM. One complaint is that people in a position of power have decided whether certain behaviors are symptoms of mental illness. The result is diagnoses that some believe unfairly stigmatize behaviors seen more frequently in nondominant groups. Others argue that the DSM provides "scientific" justification for the oppression of members of marginalized groups, including women, people of color, lesbians, gay men, and poor people: "psychological 'evidence' has been invoked as a rationale for locking us up in mental hospitals and prisons, breaking up our relationships with our lovers, taking our children away, denying us jobs, and blatantly discriminating against us in law and social policy" (Kitzinger, 1997, p. 203).

Many criteria listed in the DSM are criticized as being too broad. For example, the criteria for major depressive disorder "contain an exclusion for uncomplicated bereavement (up to 2 months of symptoms after loss of a loved one are allowed as normal), but no exclusions for equally normal uncomplicated sadness reactions to other major losses such as a terminal medical diagnosis in oneself or a loved one, separation from one's spouse, the end of an intense love affair, or loss of one's job" (Wakefield, 1997, p. 637). In other words, a person who recently lost a job and has been grieving could be diagnosed with major depressive disorder.

There is also concern that the broad diagnostic criteria are often used to enforce conformity to mainstream social norms rather than to diagnose mental illness. Behaviors that might threaten dominant cultural values are stigmatized and labeled as mental illness. Individuals and groups of people can be forced into treatment or punished by being removed from society if they stray too far out of line. For example, some slaves were diagnosed as having *drapetomania*, a term coined by a Southern doctor in the 1850s as a pejorative label for an "uncontrollable urge to escape from slavery" (Hare-Mustin & Marecek, 1997, p. 106). Today the diagnostic category conduct disorder can be applied to adolescents who are acting out, even if their behavior is a reasonable response to problematic situations in their lives.

There is often disagreement about whether a behavior should be included in the DSM. Some say that inclusion is at times based on "political compromise rather than scientific consensus" (Kutchins & Kirk, 1997, p. 99). One often-cited example is the 1974 struggle over whether to remove homosexuality from the DSM. Many feel that the decisions to include and to later remove it were made on political and moral rather than scientific grounds.

Finally, some people worry that the overuse of diagnostic labels will infringe on patients' rights. Insurance companies are increasingly requiring a diagnosis from the DSM before they will reimburse for services. This puts practitioners in the position of having to give a diagnosis that may not be accurate so that a client can receive services. The label may stay with the person for his or her entire life, putting the person at risk of employment discrimination or making it difficult to get health insurance in the future. Many managed care companies use the symptoms listed in the DSM as a guideline for appropriate treatment. This can mean ignoring the environmental and social context of a patient's distress. The DSM itself "implies that psychological disorders are closely akin to physical disorders, and that they exist apart from the life situations and cultural backgrounds of those who experience them" (Hare-Mustin & Marecek, 1997, p. 107).

BOX 10.3 | **WHAT DO YOU THINK?**

Should professional organizations define mental disorders? If not, who should?

Kutchins and Kirk sum up concerns about increasing reliance on the DSM:

> There are certainly many people who are troubled and plenty of individuals and families made miserable by mental illness. DSM is intended to describe these illnesses and identify those who have them. But DSM oversteps its bounds by defining how we should think about ourselves; how we should respond to stress; how much anxiety or sadness we should feel; and when and how we should sleep, eat, and express ourselves sexually. Although people inevitably base these judgments on personal and social values, the APA tries through the DSM to extend its professional jurisdiction over daily life by arguing that its descriptions of illnesses are based on science. (1997, p. 15)

SOCIAL WORK PRACTICE IN MENTAL HEALTH SETTINGS

Social workers with expertise in mental health practice in a variety of settings, including public community mental health centers, nonprofit and for-profit provider agencies that contract to treat public mental health clients, state and county hospitals, private psychiatric hospitals, psychiatric units in general hospitals, Department of Veterans Affairs psychiatric services, and private practice settings. As a result of deinstitutionalization, inpatient psychiatric hospitals hire fewer social workers than in previous decades, but additional jobs have been created in outpatient mental health, psychiatric rehabilitation, and private clinical practice settings. As services to people with serious mental illnesses have moved into the community, social workers have expanded their roles, and opportunities will probably continue to increase during the twenty-first century (NASW, 2008).

SOCIAL WORK ROLES

Social workers play many roles in mental health settings, including case manager, advocate, administrator, and therapist. As case manager for a local public mental health system, a social worker works with people with a variety of serious mental illnesses including schizophrenia, bipolar disorder, and borderline personality disorder. The social worker spends workdays meeting with consumers to determine their strengths, goals, and needs; finding appropriate housing and vocational services that will assist them in building on their strengths; helping them find services aimed at recovery from both the mental illness and substance abuse when the consumer has a co-occurring substance abuse problem; and advocating for their needs with landlords, law enforcement personnel, and other service providers as necessary.

Case management developed in the mental health field as a response to deinstitutionalization. It was designed to ensure that consumers were connected with the services they need and received continuity of care. Social workers who are case managers view consumers in the context of their environment and monitor consumers' needs and support their personal goals as they change over time. Strengths-based case management focuses on the desires and capacities of consumers rather than on their psychopathology or deficits (Rapp & Goscha, 2006).

In addition to case management, social workers serve as advocates for people with mental illnesses. They advocate for clients and their families within the mental health system to ensure proper treatment. They also work as advocates in the policy arena, developing and promoting legislation that will help people with mental illnesses receive equitable treatment.

Clinical social workers provide individual and family counseling. They work in mental health centers, private practice, drug treatment centers, and school-based programs.

TREATMENT

Social workers use a number of evidence-based psychosocial treatment approaches to address the needs of people with mental illnesses. In evidence-based practice, the professional social worker uses research as a basis for problem solving and choice of interventions. Data on interventions are systematically collected, using measurable variables to identify techniques and outcomes. Evidence-based practice draws on this research to evaluate the effectiveness and appropriateness of interventions (Jenson & Howard, 2008). Among the evidence-based treatments are assertive community treatment, psychiatric rehabilitation, family psychoeducation, and cognitive-behavioral therapies.

Assertive community treatment (ACT) is an integrated community-based treatment approach for people with serious mental illnesses (Stein & Santos, 1998). A multidisciplinary team—composed of cross-trained psychiatry, social work, nursing, vocational rehabilitation, substance abuse staff, and a peer specialist—provides services 24 hours a day to help consumers succeed in the community.

Social workers are viewed as particularly valuable ACT team members because of their training as generalists (Stein & Santos, 1998). Besides working on an individual level with the client, they are often also responsible for working with the client's family and the community in which the client lives. Because of their person-in-environment view, social workers can help other team members understand the broad range of factors that affect a client's path to recovery.

Psychiatric (or psychosocial) rehabilitation teaches skills needed to function as normally as possible in the community. Consumers learn how to reduce the effect of their ongoing symptoms of mental illness and promote wellness and recovery. A range of social, educational, occupational, behavioral, and cognitive approaches are used (Corrigan, Mueser, Bond, Drake, & Solomon, 2008). This approach targets all life domains, including vocational, social, and familial.

Family psychoeducation has been found to reduce the recurrence of psychiatric symptoms in people diagnosed with many mental illnesses (McFarlane, 2002). It typically educates the family and the consumer about the condition, including how to deal with symptoms when they occur, and helps the family understand what the consumer is experiencing and identify early warning signs of relapse. It involves a social support component when education occurs in a group format. One of the most important aspects of family psychoeducation is forming an alliance between the family, consumer, and treatment team. Through a better understanding of the consumer's condition, family members can provide effective assistance.

A cognitive-behavioral approach helps consumers diagnosed with serious mental illnesses like major depression and bipolar disorder. Cognitive-behavioral psychotherapy is based on the premise that faulty thinking results in unwanted behavior. The consumer is taught to change his or her reaction to faulty thoughts when they occur. There is evidence that consumers diagnosed with schizophrenia and treated with psychotropic medications can use a cognitive-behavioral approach to better control lingering symptoms.

Social workers come across numerous types of mental disorders. Specialized clinical training is needed to reliably diagnose them and prescribe appropriate treatments. Table 10.2 highlights the major psychiatric disorders and identifies some of the prevalent evidence-based interventions used today.

CULTURALLY RESPONSIVE PRACTICE

During the 1960s and 1970s, community mental health programs that attempted to serve diverse groups were developed in low-income communities. However, traditional services and therapies used primarily on white middle-class clients were not always effective with people from different cultures and classes (Rogler, Malgady, Constantino, & Blumenthal, 1987). Today's mental health professionals are developing more culturally relevant services and becoming more culturally sensitive and competent. Social workers need to understand cultural beliefs about mental illness and ways of coping with it in order to understand behavior and plan interventions that meet the needs of all groups of consumers.

For example, members of some Asian American cultures believe that people should not dwell on morbid thoughts and should be taught to use willpower to avoid emotional upset (Yeung & Kam, 2006). This belief makes the use of psychosocial interventions problematic. African Americans have a higher incidence of somatization, in which mental distress is expressed in terms of physical suffering (U.S. Surgeon General, 1999). In some cultures, mental illness is viewed as a spiritual concern, and religious leaders may be the first source of help. **Culture-bound syndromes**—patterns of aberrant or problematic behavior unique to a local culture—may appear more commonly among people who are older or less acculturated. Culture-bound syndromes are not well understood within the parameters of DSM-IV diagnoses.

As discussed in Chapter 6, members of nondominant groups are less likely than members of dominant groups to seek help from human service professionals. This may be a result of lack of trust in government-operated institutions. Other reasons may include lack of affordable treatment, experience of clinician, or previous experiences of inferior or ineffective treatment (Daley, 2005).

When nondominant consumers do enter the treatment system, they may receive discriminatory care and differential diagnoses, causing them to drop out before completion (Miller, 2002). African Americans and Indigenous People are overrepresented in inpatient psychiatric units, with the exception of private psychiatric hospitals (Daley, 2005). A combination of factors may account for this, including overt discrimination (perceiving clients of color as more dangerous or more impaired), limited access to outpatient treatment approaches due to lack of availability or affordability, and differences in help-seeking behaviors such as delaying seeking help until conditions have worsened.

TABLE 10.2 | MORE ABOUT MAJOR PSYCHIATRIC DIAGNOSES AND THEIR TREATMENT

DSM-IV Diagnosis	Etiology	Prevalence	Evidence-Based Psychosocial Interventions	Evidence-Based Pharmacological Interventions
Anxiety Disorders Panic Disorder, Generalized Anxiety Disorder, Social Phobia, Obsessive-Compulsive Disorder	The development of an anxiety disorder comes from a combination of life experiences, psychological traits, and/or genetic factors. Panic disorder appears to have the strongest genetic base (U. S. Surgeon General, 1999).	It is estimated that 16% of the population has some type of anxiety disorder.	Cognitive behavioral therapy (Barlow & Cerny, 1988) Exposure and response prevention for OCD (Steketee et al., 1982)	Benzodiazepines: e.g., alprazolam (Xanax); clonazepam (Klonopin) Antidepressants: e.g., fluoxetine (Prozac); sertraline (Zoloft); paroxetine (Paxil); fluvoxamine (Luvox)
Mood Disorders Depression, Bi-polar Disorder, Dysthymia	Depressive episodes may be triggered by stressful life events. It is believed that there is a biological component. However, it is not clear if biological abnormalities cause depression. Perhaps they only correlate with depression. Research has demonstrated that chronic stress effects brain function, and depression may be the result of severe and prolonged stress (Ingram, 1998). Social, psychological, and genetic factors may act together to protect against or predispose to depression. Depression and bipolar disorder do run in families, especially in the case of bipolar disorder.	It is estimated that 7% of the population has some type of mood disorder.	Cognitive-behavioral therapy (Beck et al., 1979) Interpersonal therapy (Weissman, 1984)	Antidepressants: e.g. fluoxetine (Prozac); sertraline (Zoloft); paroxetine (Paxil) Bipolar: lithium carbonate; divalproex sodium (Depakote)

| Borderline Personality Disorder | As yet unknown, but some evidence of genetic factors, familial factors or history of childhood sexual abuse (Blum & Pfohl, 1998). | Affects about 2% of the population. | Dialectical behavior therapy (Linehan, 1993) | Sertogenic antidepressants, e.g. fluoxetine. Low doses of haloperidol, thioridazine, risperdone |
| Schizophrenia | Genetic factors seem to be prominent, as well as adverse environmental influences during early brain development (Andreasen, 1984). | Affects about 1% of the population. | Psychoeducational Multifamily Groups (McFarlane et al, 1995) Intensive case management (Solomon, 1998) Assertive Community Treatment (ACT) (Stein & Santos, 1998) Social skills training (Hogarty et al., 1991) Vocational/employment interventions (Drake et al, 1998) | Antipsychotic medications: e.g., clozapine, chlorpromazine, haloperidol, risperidone |

Ethnopyschopharmacology is a relatively new area of study that looks at the way ethnic and cultural influences affect a client's response to medication. There is some evidence that Asian Americans and Latinos with schizophrenia may require lower doses of antipsychotic medications than white Americans. These differences are believed to be due to a combination of factors, including genetics, diet, and health behaviors (Yeung & Kam, 2006).

People in the lowest socioeconomic group are about two and a half times more likely than those in the highest group to have a mental disorder (Costello, Messer, Bird, Cohen, & Reinherz, 1998). The reason for the correlation between lower income and mental disorders is still being debated. According to one view, the unremitting stress of living in poverty promotes the development of psychiatric conditions. For example, a mother who does not know how she will find shelter or food for her children may be more likely to develop an anxiety disorder or clinical depression. Another view is that people who are experiencing psychiatric disorders are less able to work to their full capacity or at all, and therefore are in a lower income group (Regier et al., 1993).

STRENGTHS PERSPECTIVE

Social workers bring a strengths perspective to the multidisciplinary field of mental health. By focusing on consumers' strengths and capabilities as well as on their symptoms, social workers can counter the **stigma,** or discredit, that occurs when the individual's diagnosis becomes an enduring label. Many consumers and professionals have united to attack the labeling that is still common in the mental health field and unthinkable in other areas. Bjorklund (1996) points out that people diagnosed with schizophrenia are called schizophrenics, but people diagnosed with cancer are never called cancerics. Social workers can help in this social justice effort by being attentive to the use of language.

A strengths perspective allows social workers to view the whole person, not just the mental illness. By assessing areas of strength, the social worker can identify ways to help. For example, a consumer who has learned to structure his or her environment in order to maintain control over psychiatric symptoms might do well in a volunteer or paid position that requires creating a structured environment, such as organizing and overseeing a waiting room or keeping careful records of donations to a nonprofit agency.

The strengths perspective can help the social worker maintain hope and appreciation for the many acts of heroism involved in day-to-day living with long-term mental illnesses. By looking for strengths, social workers can identify the many ways that consumers are already attempting to cope with their conditions and can view consumers as partners in the treatment process rather than as individuals whose deficits overwhelm their lives (see "From the Field...Working with People Living with Serious Mental Illness").

OBSTACLES TO TREATMENT

Only about half of the people with diagnosable mental disorders receive treatment in a given year (Kessler et al., 2005). Some do not seek treatment because they are afraid of being stigmatized by family, friends, or employers. They may be concerned

BOX 10.4	**FROM THE FIELD … WORKING WITH PEOPLE LIVING WITH SERIOUS MENTAL ILLNESS**

Robert Bjorklund, LICSW, MSW, MPA

After completing my graduate social work education, I was deeply committed to seeking innovative ways to enhance the lives of people living with serious mental illness. The direct practice experience I gained in both community and inpatient settings have been integral to my current position as a state mental health program administrator. I oversee the statewide implementation of an evidence-based practice model called Program of Assertive Community Treatment (PACT), which is a research-proven program providing intensive community supports for individuals living with serious mental illness. Possessing a solid clinical understanding of mental health treatment issues greatly enhances my ability to effectively implement such a major program serving up to 800 people throughout the state of Washington.

PACT teams are multidisciplinary with bachelor's- and master's-level social workers playing integral roles and interacting as equals with all team members including psychiatrists. The teams address the entire range of needs for individuals with serious mental illness through the provision of a broad range of services. The emphasis is on providing individualized and intensive outreach-oriented services, the majority of which are provided in the community. Services provided by PACT team members include mental health, chemical dependency, vocational, and housing assistance among others. Priority is given to individuals diagnosed with schizophrenia, bipolar disorder, and co-occurring substance abuse disorders among other diagnoses. These individuals have a high use of psychiatric hospitalization and crisis services, have difficulty benefiting from traditional services, and may have a high risk or history of arrest and incarceration. Without the intensive community supports provided by committed PACT team members 24 hours a day, seven days a week, most individuals would most likely be rehospitalized, incarcerated, on the streets, *or worse*! It has been gratifying for me to see, firsthand, how individuals and their families have been positively impacted and are on a path to living a far more rewarding and productive life than what their original prognosis had predicted. A highly rewarding aspect of my varied social work roles, especially in my current administrative position, is to be directly part of contributing to a statewide recovery culture in the mental health field. The concept of

recovery has been a major paradigm shift occurring across the country for over the past decade. I am proud to say I was practicing recovery well before it became an operationalized term in the mental health field. My social work education had prepared me for working from a strengths-based perspective, using people-first language, utilizing an ecological systems framework, and fostering the concepts of self-determination and empowerment—all of which *are* recovery!

One of my supplemental professional roles is providing clinical supervision to social work licensure candidates pursuing clinical licensure which allows me to stay current on mental health employment trends. Without doubt, the social work degree is preferred by the majority of public and private social service agencies. It is highly advisable that you investigate your state's specific licensing requirements well before you graduate so that you are clear on the requirements for earning your license (some states have baccalaureate-level licensure requirements whereas every state has master's-level licensure or certification requirements). Clinical licensure, although required for many direct practice positions, is increasingly required for supervisory and administrative positions. Your marketability and professional credibility are greatly enhanced by possessing a social work license. In my prior position as clinical director of a licensed community mental health agency, it was a requirement that I had my LICSW so I could supervise licensed staff, conduct assessments and mental health evaluations, and bill for Medicaid services. For far too long, individuals with serious mental illness have been viewed and treated based on their *perceived* deficiencies rather than their many unrecognized and underdeveloped strengths. Social workers are uniquely trained to build on individual and family-system strengths, thereby helping to change the unfortunate (and outdated) carryover of the medical model's shortsighted views of mental illness. Thankfully, these days, social workers have virtually limitless professional opportunities to be recovery-based change agents at all levels and areas of mental health practice. BSW and MSW candidates contemplating a mental health career would benefit from interviewing social workers to gain invaluable field-based perspectives. During my eight years as an

| BOX 10.4 | **FROM THE FIELD ... WORKING WITH PEOPLE LIVING WITH SERIOUS MENTAL ILLNESS** *continued* |

adjunct instructor at several schools of social work, I emphasized to students that their formal education does not end at graduation. Rather, the quest to develop your knowledge and sharpen your skills set is a lifelong process. The decision on which field of social work practice to follow is not something to be taken lightly. Good social workers possess self-awareness and share a genuine compassion for, and a commitment to, the people they work with. You are taking one of the many important steps to investigate if pursuing a social work career in mental health is right for you.

| BOX 10.5 | **WHAT DO YOU THINK?** |

Do you think working with people diagnosed with serious mental illnesses might interest you one day? Why?

that discrimination will result in loss of a job or removal of children from their custody. Others do not receive treatment due to the mistaken belief that their symptoms are physical rather than psychological. For example, insomnia, headaches, fatigue, or weight loss might be due to stress, depression, or anxiety. Some people do not seek treatment because they do not realize that they are suffering from mental illness.

Another major obstacle to the receipt of mental health treatment is its cost. For many of the millions of Americans with no health insurance, mental health treatment is out of financial reach. Others who do have health insurance find that it does not cover their mental health needs. Traditionally, health insurance plans have provided less coverage for treatment of mental illness than for treatment of physical illness.

State and federal lawmakers have begun to address this issue. A number of states have passed laws requiring fairer coverage for mental health conditions by health insurance providers. In 1996 Congress passed the **Mental Health Parity Act** (P.L. 104-204), which prohibits insurers from imposing lifetime and annual benefit limits on mental health services that are not imposed on physical health care. Before passage of the act, an insurance plan could cap lifetime mental health benefits at $30,000 and physical health benefits at $1,000,000. While this act was an important first step, it did not solve the problem of inadequate coverage. By March 2008, mental health parity bills had passed both houses of Congress with broad bipartisan and public support. Through the persistent efforts of legislators, advocates, patients, and family members, parity has finally become a mainstream issue. The House and the Senate have taken different approaches to this legislation. Hopefully, a mutually acceptable compromise will quickly emerge. It is time to end discrimination against people with mental illness and substance-use disorders.

The House and Senate agree that group health care plans should not be able to impose higher cost-sharing requirements for mental health care expenses than for other medical conditions, there should be no discriminatory treatment limitations for mental health care services, employers with fewer than 50 employees should be exempt from parity requirements, and the proposed legislation exempts employers from parity requirements if upgrading mental health benefits boosts costs by at least 2 percent the first year after the legislation goes into effect and 1 percent in succeeding years. However, the House bill would not preempt stronger state parity laws and the Senate bill would; and the House bill requires coverage, if medically necessary, of mental disorders that are covered by the health plan with the greatest enrollment offered to federal employees (*Business Insurance,* 2007). Some of the people most in need of mental health services are children.

CASE EXAMPLE: Sixteen-year-old Daniel has struggled to control his behavior and thinking for as long as he can remember. He was recently diagnosed with bipolar disorder and has started on a new medication that has worked for a number of people. He is hopeful, but his experience in the mental health system has been rough so far. His parents relinquished custody when he was 14 because they had exhausted their private insurance benefits and couldn't afford the hospitalization that his psychiatrist said he needed. They did not qualify for public services even though they had already incurred over $100,000 in debt to pay for his care.

A national survey of 903 American families that have children with severe mental illnesses reported many problems in finding appropriate care, particularly because of its high cost (Vitanza, Cohen, & Hall, 1999). These findings are especially devastating because the success rate for treating mental illness is very high when medication and therapy are made available. In fact, mood disorders are treated effectively with pharmacological and psychosocial treatments in outpatient settings 50 to 70 percent of the time (Kornblum, 2008). By comparison, the success rate for treatment of heart disease is only 41 to 52 percent (National Alliance for the Mentally Ill, 2000). Mental health treatment can be controversial, as discussed in the box "Becoming a Change Agent."

POLICY ISSUES

By 1996 research on mental disorders was demonstrating the biological nature of many mental illnesses, raising questions of fairness in the way insurance coverage of physical illnesses differed from the limited insurance coverage most often provided for mental illnesses. As discussed earlier, the Mental Health Parity Act of 1996 was a beginning step toward equalizing coverage of physical and mental disorders. However, the act applies only to employers who provide mental health coverage and who have 50 or more employees. Employers who can show an increased cost of 1 percent or more due to additional mental health coverage can be exempted. The act is thought to benefit the most severely mentally ill who need the most costly treatment over their lifetimes, but it does not benefit seriously mentally ill people who are unemployed or are not covered by policies of working spouses or parents. Advocates continue to fight for true parity for mental health benefits at the state and federal levels, and hopefully, the House and Senate will jointly pass new parity legislation with the new Congressional session.

BOX 10.6 | BECOMING A CHANGE AGENT

Many cities around the country have faced challenges with growing homeless populations. As was discussed earlier in this chapter, a large percentage of the homeless population have a mental illness, and deinstitutionalization of the mentally ill made a major contribution to homelessness. Additionally, many homeless, mentally ill people self medicate with drugs and alcohol. As cities have struggled to address homelessness, some have found approaches that seem to be working. Seattle is one of those cities. In 2006 Seattle opened 1811 Eastlake, a housing complex for homeless people who are also alcoholics. The majority also suffer from various types of mental illness. Most are housed there at public expense, and none are required to stop drinking prior to being given housing or to stop drinking once they are housed. The program is based on a housing first philosophy. The idea is that once people are no longer homeless, service providers can address their other problems. It is a change from the philosophy held by many housing programs which require people to stop using substances before they can receive housing and which do not allow people to drink or use other substances and remain housed. Original responses to the program in Seattle were mixed. Many residents were angry. They struggled to pay rising rents themselves and thought the $1.1 million being spent to house people who were not even required to stop drinking could be used in better ways. Concern was also raised that such an approach supported people in continuing to abuse alcohol. A study completed by the University of Washington a year after 1811 Eastlake opened, quieted some of the critics. The study found that days in jail, visits to centers to sober up, and visits to the local emergency room and clinics dropped dramatically for the residents who were now

off the street. Savings in that first year topped $2 million dollars (Vanderkam, 2008).

Analyzing the Situation

- Conduct research into the areas of mental illness, homelessness, and substance abuse. Does the research support a relationship between the three? If so, how do researchers explain the relationship?
- Try to find the policies for some of your local programs that house homeless people. Do they house people who currently have substance abuse problems? If not, what options are available for these people?
- What do you think about the housing first approach? Should the government or private organizations pay to provide housing for people who do not give up using alcohol or drugs? Why or why not?

What Can Social Workers Do?

Given your analysis and understanding of the relationship between mental illness, homelessness, and substance abuse, what can social workers do to address the problem? What can we do at the individual and family levels? What could be done at the community and policy levels?

What Can You Do?

What one step might you take now, alone or working with others, to address the needs of the substance-using, mentally ill homeless population in your community? What are the barriers that might keep you from taking this step? What could you do to reduce those barriers?

The proposed Omnibus Mental Illness Recovery Act would bring a number of important reforms. It would increase consumer and family involvement in planning, provide more equitable health care coverage, enable states to use Medicaid dollars for intensive community treatment, require changes in the way law enforcement and the courts deal with offenders who are mentally ill, and provide incentives for seriously mentally ill people to work without losing health insurance coverage.

Another proposed federal policy change focuses on increasing access to treatment that has been scientifically determined to be effective. The goal is to provide funds for localities to expand services to prevent homelessness, violence, and criminalization of people with mental illnesses. Other efforts include expanding help to families who have severely disabled children, including children with mental illnesses. Currently, parents who cannot afford treatment must give custody of the child to the state in order to obtain physical or mental health services. States would be able to offer public mental health services on a sliding fee scale to children with severe disabilities living in middle-income families that are otherwise unable to pay.

VALUES AND ETHICS

A number of ethical concerns raise questions and pose values dilemmas for social workers in mental health care. **Confidentiality** is a strongly held social work value. It requires all information to remain with the therapist and to be released only with the consent of the client. Clients can generally expect their personal information to stay private unless danger to themselves or others is involved. In some cases, social workers' strict adherence to confidentiality has meant not providing information to family members. If a family member is hospitalized due to a car accident, medical personnel keep the family informed and ask their permission to provide treatment. If a family member is hospitalized due to mental illness, no information can be provided to the family unless the consumer has given express permission. Sometimes the consumer may be too impaired to provide consent.

The managed care system has raised many ethical dilemmas for social workers, especially those working with people diagnosed with serious mental illnesses. In the managed care system, companies are paid a specified amount to provide mental health care to all people within a geographic area who need it. The company needs to stay within budget or make a profit. Money is saved when some people who need treatment do not seek it and when people are denied treatment because they are evaluated as not meeting strict eligibility criteria. Social workers' treatment recommendations may be overturned by administrators who are untrained in clinical practice. Who is responsible? The legislators who failed to allocate sufficient funds? The companies whose profit margins are paramount? The social workers who did not raise these ethical issues?

The social work value of supporting self-determination has been challenged by an emerging mental health issue. Some people with serious mental illnesses do not seek or accept treatment that could help them control symptoms. A few untreated individuals experience symptoms that provoke them to commit violent acts. In response to this problem, some states have passed assisted treatment laws, also called community treatment orders and outpatient commitment. One of the first, called Kendra's Law (New York Mental Hygiene Law § 9.60), allows courts to order certain individuals with mental illnesses to accept treatment while living in the community. The law was named in honor of Kendra Webdale, who died after being pushed into the path of a subway train by a man with severe mental illness who had a history of noncompliance with treatment.

These problems are complex. Is it better to allow individuals to choose whether to seek treatment even if they experience such severe symptoms that they are incapable of making rational decisions? Should they be allowed to

---

BOX 10.7 | **ETHICAL PRACTICE ... COST OR CARE?**

Your neighbor Sophie has been diagnosed with schizophrenia. Your state has a program that provides free care to people with an SMI who have limited financial resources. Sophie has slightly too high of an income to access the free services, yet does not have enough resources to pay for the care she needs. If she does not get help, her quality of life will clearly be diminished and she may potentially be a risk to herself. She knows that you are a social worker and that you understand how important receiving treatment is for her and you know the mental health system. She asks you to help her find a way to hide some of her income so she can receive the mental health services she needs. What should you do?

---

remain symptomatic even if their symptoms impinge on the rights of others and their behavior brings them to the attention of the criminal justice system? Should treatment be enforced, even against a person's will, when experts deem that the person needs it? Social workers in the mental health field must deal with these questions.

CONCLUSION

As the concept of **recovery** is increasingly used by consumers to describe their hopes for the future, the mental health field is increasingly open to social workers who want to partner with consumers to help them meet their personal recovery goals. When consumers seek to live normal lives within their own community, social workers can be of assistance both to individual consumers and within larger systems to educate the community.

Stigma is being addressed by consumers, families, and advocates—including social workers—who view it as the largest obstacle to improving the lives of people recovering from mental illnesses who want to live normal lives integrated within their own communities. To address this problem, broad community education efforts are underway to provide accurate information about mental illnesses, to respond to inaccuracies reported by the news media, and to address discriminatory practices (Corrigan, 2005). Social workers are active in these efforts.

Key Terms

confidentiality, (p. 289)

consumer, (p. 274)

culture-bound syndrome, (p. 281)

deinstitutionalization, (p. 274)

DSM-IV-TR, (p. 277)

ethnopyschopharmacology, (p. 284)

evidence-based practice, (p. 269)

managed care, (p. 274)

mental disorders, (p. 269)

mental health, (p. 269)

Mental Health Parity Act, (p. 286)

mental illness, (p. 269)

peer counselors, (p. 277)

psychotropic drugs, (p. 273)

recovery, (p. 290)

stigma, (p. 284)

Questions for Discussion

1. Briefly outline the five major movements in mental health care in the United States.
2. Identify and describe at least three barriers to receiving mental health care. How might workers intervene to reduce those barriers?
3. Define and give an example of a culture-bound syndrome. Why do social workers need to understand this concept?
4. Identify and describe three ways the mental health care delivery system could be improved.
5. Identify the advantages and disadvantages of managed care for people with serious mental illnesses.

Change Agent Exercise

Writing letters to legislators is an important way to influence policies that can improve lives. Go online and find several websites that offer suggestions about writing effective letters to legislators. Make of list of the suggestions that they offer, including both things they recommend doing and things they recommend not doing. Get together in small groups with your classmates and compare what you found. Using the best information you have gathered, develop an information sheet about how to write effective letters to legislators. Is there an issue relating to mental health care that you would like to write a letter about to a legislator? What might such a letter include? To whom would you address it? Why?

Chapter Exercises

1. **Mental Health Ethics**

   Complete the following on your own or in a small group:

   You are a counselor in a residential mental health facility. Two months ago, a client came in on his own to receive help. He frequently hears voices, believes that he is from another world, and believes that he has been sent here to observe your culture. He now wants to be released. He has little money and no friends or relatives. He lived on the street in the past, and he says that he wants to return to the street even though it is bitterly cold outside. You feel that he would be safer and more likely to receive help if he stayed at the residential facility, at least through the winter. What should you do?

   List every response you can think of. What are the pros and cons of each?

   What social work values come into conflict in this situation? How might the NASW Code of Ethics guide your decision?

2. **Defining Mental Illness**

   On your own or in a small group, develop a list of behaviors, beliefs, and actions that demonstrate mental illness.

   Behaviors that demonstrate mental illness:

   Beliefs that demonstrate mental illness:

Actions that demonstrate mental illness:

Is there anything on the list that might have a cultural component?

Are there things that people with a different cultural, religious, or economic background might see as normal?

3. **Diagnostic and Statistical Manual Debate**
Review the "Point of View" box on page 278, and summarize the advantages and disadvantages of using the DSM as a tool for diagnosing mental illness.

Pair up with a classmate. You and your classmate each argue one side of the issue. Use this page as a guide in your debate. Join another pair, and develop and support a position on one side or the other.

Your pair's position:

4. **Health Insurance Coverage**
Contact a major employer that provides workers with health insurance. Gather information about the coverage the employer provides for physical and mental illnesses. Is there parity between the two types of coverage?

What are the similarities?

What are the differences?

How would the mental health coverage help or hinder consumers seeking mental health services?

5. **Media Images**
Read a book or watch a movie that portrays a person with a mental illness. I chose the following book or movie _____ because:

How are people with mental illnesses portrayed?

Does the portrayal fit with what you have learned about mental illness? Why?

References

American Psychiatric Association. (1994). *Diagnostic and statistical manual of mental disorders* (4th ed.). Washington, DC: American Psychiatric Association.

American Psychiatric Association. (2000). *Diagnostic and statistical manual of mental disorders IVtr* (4th ed., text rev.). Washington, DC: American Psychiatric Association.

Arons, B. S., & Bornemann, T. H. (2000). *Center for mental health services: Overview.* Washington, DC: Center for Mental Health Services.

Barker, R. (1999). *The social work dictionary.* Baltimore, MD: Port City Press and NASW Press.

Belcher, J. R., & DeForge, B. R. (2005). The longitudinal discharge planning and treatment model. *Social Work in Mental Health, 3,* 4, 17–32.

Bjorklund, R. (1996). Psychiatric labels: Still hard to shake. *Psychiatric Services, 47,* 1329–1332.

Brandwein, R. A. (1997). Women in social policy. *Encyclopedia of Social Work, 19, 3,* 2552–2560.

Breslow, R. A. (2008). Prospective study of alcohol consumption in the United States: Quantity, frequency, and cause-specific mortality. *Alcoholism—Clinical and Experimental Research, 32,* 3, 513–523.

Business Insurance. (2007). Different takes on mental health parity. *Business Insurance,* July 23, p. 6.

Carman, M. B. (1997). The psychology of normal aging. *Psychiatric Clinics of North America, 20,* 15–24.

Corrigan, P. W. (ed.). (2005). *On the stigma of mental illness.* New York: Guilford Press.

Corrigan, P. W., Mueser, K. T., Bond, G. R., Drake, R. E., & Solomon, P. (2008). *Principles and practice of psychiatric rehabilitation: An empirical approach.* New York: Guilford Press.

Costello, E. J., Messer, S. C., Bird, H. R., Cohen, P., & Reinherz, H. Z. (1998). The prevalence of serious emotional disturbance: A re-analysis of community studies. *Journal of Child and Family Studies, 7,* 4, 411–432.

Daley, M. C. (2005). Race, managed care, and the quality of substance abuse treatment. *Administration and Policy in Mental Health, 32,* 4, 457–476.

Decamp, D. (2008). Parity of health coverage urged. *St. Petersburg Times,* March 9, p. 1B.

Drug Week. (2008). Psychosocial: Reports from G. P. Keita and colleagues advance knowledge in psychosocial. *Drug Week,* February 29, p. 807.

Edinburg, G. M., & Cottler, J. M. (1997). Managed care. *Encyclopedia of Social Work, 19,* 2, 1635–1641.

Glaze, L. E., & James, D. J. (2006, September). *Mental health problems of prison and jail inmates.* Washington, DC: U.S. Department of Justice, Office of Justice Programs, Bureau of Justice Statistics: Washington, DC.

Grob, G. N. (2001). Mental health policy in 20th century America. In Manderscheid, R. W., & Henderson, M. J. (eds.), *Mental health, United States, 2000* (Chap. 2). Washington, DC: U.S. Department of Health and Human Services Center for Mental Health Services.

Hare-Mustin, R. T., & Marecek, J. (1997). Abnormal and clinical psychology: The politics of madness. In Fox, D., & Prilleltensky, I. (eds.), *Critical psychology: An introduction.* Thousand Oaks, CA: Sage Publications.

Hochman, M. E. (2006). Children of depressed parents are more vulnerable. *Health Science,* June 5, p. C3.

Jenson, J. M., & Howard, M. O. (2008). Evidence-based practice. In Mizrachi, T., & Davis, L. E. (eds.), *Encyclopedia of Social Work* (20th ed.), (pp. 158–165). Washington, DC: NASW Press and Oxford University Press.

Kessler, R. C., Berglund, P. Chiu, W. T., Demler, O., Heeringa, S. Hiripi, E., Jim, R., Pennell, B. E., Walters, E. E., Zaslavskym, A., & Zheng, H. (2005). The U.S. national comorbidity survey replication (NCS-R): Design and field procedures. *International Journal of Methods in Psychiatric Research, 13,* 2, 69–93.

Kitzinger, C. (1997). Lesbian and gay psychology: A critical analysis. In Fox, D., & Prilleltensky, I. (eds.), *Critical psychology: An introduction.* Thousand Oaks, CA: Sage Publications.

Kornblum, J. (2008). Families often 'lost' in trauma of mental illness; Stigma, guilt, denial keep common signals in the dark. *USA TODAY,* February 5, p. 10D.

Kutchins, H., & Kirk, S. (1997). *Making us crazy: DSM—The psychiatric bible and the creation of mental disorders*. New York: Free Press.

Langwell, K. M. (1992). *The effects of managed care on use and costs of health services*. Washington DC: Congressional Budget Office.

Lin, A. M. P. (1997). Mental health overview. *Encyclopedia of Social Work, 19*, 2, 1705–1711.

McFarlane, W. (2002). *Multifamily groups in the treatment of severe psychiatric disorders*. New York: Guilford Press.

Mechanic, D. (1999). *Mental health and social policy: The emergence of managed care*. Boston: Allyn & Bacon.

Miller, A. C. (2002). Changing the face of the organization: Addressing challenges of work in multi-ethnic society. *Journal of Family Therapy, 24*, 1, 72–84.

Miller, R. A. (1996). The aging immune system: Primer and prospectus. *Science, 273*, 7–74.

Nathan, P. E., Gorman, J. M., & Salkind, N. J. (1999). *Treating mental disorders: A guide to what works*. New York: Oxford University Press.

NASW (2008). *Mental health issue fact sheet*. Washington, DC: National Association of Social Workers. Retrieved on May 5, 2008, from https://www.socialworkers.org/pressroom/features/issue/mental.asp.

National Alliance for the Mentally Ill. (2000). *Facts about mental illness*. http://www.nami.org/fact.htm.

National Association of Social Workers. (1997). *Policy statements*. Washington, DC: Author.

National Association of Social Workers. (2005). *Practice research network III final report*. Washington, DC: Author.

National Institute of Mental Health. (2000). *Anxiety disorders educational program library*. http://www.nimh.nih.gov/anxiety/library.

NIMH. (2001). *Bipolar disorder brochure*. Washington, DC: National Institute of Mental Health.

Oquendo, M., Horwath, E., & Martinez, A. (1992). *Ataques de nervios:* Proposed diagnostic criteria for a culture specific syndrome. *Culture, Medicine and Psychiatry, 16*, 367–376.

Ralph, R. O., & Corrigan, P. W. (2005). *Recovery in mental illness: Broadening our understanding of wellness*. Washington, DC: American Psychological Association.

Rapp, C. A., & Goscha, R. J. (2006). *The strengths model: Case management with people with psychiatric disabilities* (2d ed.). New York: Oxford University Press.

Regier, D. A., Narrow, W. E., Rae, D. S., Manderscheid, R. W., Locke, B. Z., & Goodwin, F. K. (1993). The de facto U.S. mental and addictive disorders system. *Archives of General Psychiatry, 50*, 85–94.

Rogler, L. H., Malgady, R. G., Constantino, G., & Blumenthal, R. (1987). What do culturally sensitive mental health services mean? The case of Hispanics. *American Psychologist, 42*, 565–570.

Rossi, A. (1969). Some pre-World War II antecedents of community mental health theory and practice. In Bindman, A. J., & Spiegel, A. D. (eds.), *Perspectives in community mental health*. Chicago: Aldine de Gruyter.

SAMHSA. (2005). *SAMHSA News*, Social workers in the mental health field. 13(1), p. 2. Washington, DC: Author.

Shapiro, J. (1994). *No pity*. New York: Random House.

Siegler, I. C., Poon, L. W., Madden, D. J., & Welsh, K. A. (1996). Psychological aspects of normal aging. In Busse, E. W., & Blazer, D. G. (eds.), *The American Psychiatric Press textbook of geriatric psychiatry*. Washington, DC: American Psychiatric Press.

Stein, L. I., & Santos, A. B. (1998). *Assertive community treatment of persons with severe mental illness*. New York: W. W. Norton.

Swanson J. W., Swartz, M. S., Van Dorn, R. A., Elbogen, E. B, Wagner, H. R., Rosenheck, R. A., Stroup, T. S., McEvoy, J. P., & Lieberman J. A. (2006). A national study of violent behavior in persons with schizophrenia.. *Archives of General Psychiatry, 63*, 5, 490–499.

Torrey, E. F, Entsminger, K, Geller, J., Stanley, J., Jaffe, D. J. (2008). *The shortage of public hospital beds for mentally ill persons*. A report by the Treatment Advocacy Center.

U.S. Fed News. (2008). *Rep. Sullivan fights for mental health parity*. Washington, DC.

U.S. General Accounting Office. (2000). *Mental Health Parity Act: Employers mental health benefits remain limited despite new federal standards*. Washington, DC: Author.

U.S. Surgeon General. (1999). *Mental health: A report of the Surgeon General*. Washington, DC: Department of Health and Human Services.

Vanderkam, L. (2008). Give them homes. *USA Today*, April 29, p. 9a.

Vitanza, S., Cohen, R., & Hall L. L. (1999). *Families on the brink: The impact of ignoring children with serious mental illness*. Washington, DC: National Alliance for the Mentally Ill and the Commonwealth Institute for Child and Family Studies, Department of Psychiatry, Virginia Commonwealth University.

Wakefield, J. C. (1997). Diagnosing DSM-IV—Part I: DSM-IV and the concept of disorder. *Behavior Research and Therapy, 35*, 7, 633–649.

Weissman, M. M., Bland, R., Joyce, P. R., Newman, S., Wells, J. E., & Wittchen, H. U. (1993). Sex differences in rates of depression: Cross-national perspectives. *Journal of Affective Disorders, 29*, 77–84.

WHO World Mental Health Survey Consortium. (2004). Prevalence, severity, and unmet need for treatment of mental disorders in the World Health Organization world mental health surveys. *Journal of the American Medical Association, 291*, 2581–2590.

Williams, J. B. W. (1998). Classification and diagnostic assessment. In Williams, J. B. W., & Ell, K. (eds.), *Advances in mental health research: Implications for practice*. Washington, DC: NASW Press.

Yeung, A., & Kam, R. (2006). Recognizing and treating depression in Asian Americans. *Psychiatric Times*, December 1. p. 10.

SCHOOL SOCIAL WORK

CHAPTER 11

Heinle Division of Cengage Learning

During the 1990s and into the first decade of this new century, it has not been uncommon for Americans to turn on the news and hear about students shooting other students at school. On February 11, 2008, a 16-year-old student in Tennessee shot and wounded a classmate in gym class. The following day, a 14-year-old student in California shot a classmate who later died. In Red Lake, Minnesota, in March 2005, a 16-year-old male with a history of depression, drug use, and suicide attempts shot and killed his grandfather and his grandfather's female companion. He then went to his school and killed seven more people before killing himself. Many people speculated that his "inspiration" was the worst school shooting in history that occurred at Columbine High School in Littleton, Colorado, in 1999. At Columbine, two male students shot and killed 12 other students and a teacher and wounded 23 others before killing themselves. In Pearl, Mississippi, in October 1997, a 16-year-old boy who was an outcast at school killed his mother, then went to school and calmly killed two classmates and wounded seven others. Two months later, a 14-year-old boy in Paducah, Kentucky, opened fire on a school prayer circle, killing three students and wounding five. In Jonesboro, Arkansas, in March 1998 two boys, ages 11 and 13, pulled the fire alarm to force students out of the building. They ran to a field behind the school, where they had hidden their guns, and opened fire, killing 5 and wounding 12. Despite these horrific acts or perhaps in part because of the steps taken in direct response to them, school violence began to decrease during the mid-1990s.

However, children across the United States, in both urban and rural areas, live in a world where they see violence all around them, on television, in their neighborhoods, in their schools, and even in their families. As a result, children are both shocked by their surroundings and becoming increasingly numb to them. To help students and parents cope and to help prevent further violence and emotional harm, schools across the nation are implementing violence awareness and prevention programs. Social workers who provide crisis counseling and support, social skills training, and treatment for students are key components of these programs. Social workers also develop and implement education and awareness programs for the community, students, and their parents.

School social work is the provision of services in educational settings by credentialed school social workers (National Association of Social Workers, 1992). School social workers use a distinct body of knowledge and a unique set of skills to enhance home-school-community collaboration. They help ensure the social functioning and success of every student. Besides school violence, social workers are involved in a host of other areas. These include, but are not limited to, liaison work between home, school, and community; assessment and testing; case management services; development of programs to prevent students from dropping out, joining gangs, or using drugs and alcohol; development of support groups for students who are dealing with death or whose parents have divorced; helping students organize to address issues that hinder their education such as bullying and discrimination; immigration concerns of nonnative students; truancy or attendance problems; child abuse and neglect; services for students with disabilities; after-school services; counseling; referrals; teacher empowerment; peer mediation; interdisciplinary teamwork (with school psychologist, school nurse, teachers); and school reform. Obviously, school social work includes a wide array of services. This chapter provides a context for these services and introduces the information basic to accepting the challenge of becoming a school social worker.

THE HISTORY OF SCHOOL SOCIAL WORK

Prior to the twentieth century, most children did not attend school. But by the early 1900s most states had passed legislation mandating school attendance. This was a significant turning point for children's rights; no longer could children be forced to work rather than attend school. As a result of mandatory attendance, schools were faced with a larger and more diverse student body, and they needed assistance to adjust to these new academic and cultural circumstances. The specialization of school social work was founded in the early 1900s to respond to this need.

School social work traces its origins to private agencies and civic organizations in Boston, New York, and Hartford in 1906 and 1907. These organizations funded visiting teachers (the name given to early school social workers) to help support immigrant and "underprivileged" children in their schools. The Rochester, New York, Board of Education introduced the first school-financed visiting teachers in 1913. Their job was to increase interaction and cooperation between students' families and the schools (Allen-Meares, 2007). One of the most notable visiting teachers, Jane Fullerton Culbert, was a founder and the first president of the National Association of Visiting Teachers and Home and School Visitors in 1919 (McCullagh, 1998).

In 1923 the Commonwealth Fund of New York financed 30 school social workers in 30 different communities (Allen-Meares, 2007). This project raised the visibility of school social work. However, school social work almost disappeared during the Great Depression of the 1930s. With unemployment at record highs, states could not afford the services performed by school social workers. By the late 1940s the country was once again economically sound, and school social work reemerged. As was true of social work practice in general during the 1940s and 1950s, school social work focused on social casework, or students' identified problems.

The identity of school social work was solidified with the founding of the American Association of School Social Workers in the 1940s. In 1955 the association became part of the larger National Association of Social Workers (NASW) (McCullagh, 1998). Other organizations exclusive to school social workers later emerged, such as the School Social Work Association of America in 1994 (Pryor, 1998).

The focus of school social work changed again during the 1960s. At this time the efforts of school social workers began to be assessed using social science research techniques. President Johnson's War on Poverty programs pushed all social services to a new level of accountability, and survey results indicated that social workers were too focused on interactions with individual students. To better serve students, school social workers needed to take more advantage of group and community work methods (Allen-Meares, 2007). As a result, school social workers began to focus on school reform and began to address the problem of inequality in educational opportunities. They also began to tackle such issues as racism and students' rights in response to racial tensions brought about by integration and busing.

School social workers became the case managers for children with disabilities after the passage of the **Education for All Handicapped Children Act** of 1975. This act mandated an education for every child, including children with disabilities. In 1990 the act was reauthorized as the Individuals with Disabilities Act (IDEA), which is discussed later in the chapter.

Throughout the 1980s school social workers emphasized coalition building and collaboration with other social service agencies and the community and focused on getting parents involved in their children's education. Parents were encouraged to participate in developing **individualized education plans** (**IEPs**) for children with disabilities and to network with other programs and services. The IEP outlines the expected level of educational performance; annual goals, including short-term objectives; specific educational services that will be provided to the child; the extent to which the child will be able to participate in regular education classes; and an evaluation process to determine how goals and objectives will be met. An IEP must be prepared for every child with a disability by a representative from the school district, the student's teacher, and the parents. The plan must be revised annually.

The passage of the Improving America's Schools Act in 1994 secured the role of school social workers as advocates and brokers of services for students with disabilities, students from nondominant groups, and students who are economically disadvantaged. In addition, school social work became a conduit for bilingual Spanish-speaking social workers. This is especially true in California, Arizona, New Mexico, Texas, and Florida, where there are large populations of monolingual Spanish-speaking families. Non-English-speaking students have been funneled into special education classrooms because language barriers resulted in misdiagnosing them. Bilingual social workers play an important role in protecting the rights of non-English-speaking students.

SCHOOL SOCIAL WORK ROLES AND SKILLS

According to Allen-Meares (2008, p. 3), school social workers serve to link the school, home, and community by providing "direct services, as well as specialized services such as mental health intervention, crisis management and intervention, and facilitating community involvement in the schools" while monitoring and evaluating the organization of school systems and policies. To achieve this goal, school social workers—like other trained social work professionals—rely on systems theory and the ecological framework to analyze the transactions between students, teachers, parents, and the school system (National Association of Social Workers, 2008).

For example, a school social worker receives a referral from a teacher indicating that a student recently began to exhibit serious behavior problems in the classroom. The social worker will investigate the teacher's, student's, and parent's perspectives of the problem as well as the perspectives of other teachers and school personnel who interact regularly with the child and perhaps the perspectives of significant classmates. Exactly what are the behaviors? When and where are they exhibited? In only one class or in all classes? Which class or classes? Are the behaviors occurring at home as well? What events recently transpired in the student's family, at school, or in an after-school activity that may help explain the sudden appearance of serious behavior problems? To take effective action, the social worker will have to do more than simply talk to the student. She or he will have to investigate the systems of which the student is a part and consult with other members of those systems.

RESPONSIBILITIES OF SCHOOL SOCIAL WORKERS

The roles of school social workers and the interventions utilized vary from state to state and from school district to school district. In some school districts, social workers are solely responsible for assessing and meeting the needs of students using special education services. Their primary function is to ensure that students with disabilities receive free and appropriate educational services in the **least restrictive environment**. Each state must provide personalized instruction with sufficient support services to permit a child with disabilities to benefit educationally from that instruction. The state must ensure a continuum of alternative placements including regular classes, special classes, home instruction, and instruction in hospitals and institutions.

In other school districts, school social workers focus entirely on providing group and individual counseling for regular education students and sometimes, when necessary, for their families. In some schools, the school social worker is part of an interdisciplinary team, sometimes referred to as the **pupil services team** (National Association of Social Workers, 1997). Teachers, school administrators, school psychologists, school nurses, parents, and perhaps a speech/hearing therapist may also be part of the team. The purpose of the team is to make an ongoing assessment of students' social, emotional, and physical needs as well as their strengths. The school social worker helps students use their strengths to meet the identified needs, and also helps them gain access to school and community resources when appropriate.

Some schools have developed family service centers on their campuses. These centers provide clothing and services ranging from family counseling to medical and dental treatment. Lack of dental services has become a serious problem for students in many low-income neighborhoods.

According to the National Association of Social Workers, school social workers are primarily advocates, consultants, and mediators (National Association of Social Workers, 2008). They advocate for the rights of all students, especially students who are socially and economically isolated and students with disabilities. Advocacy efforts take place in schools through the IEP process, in the community, and in the larger society through the promotion of state and national policies that advance and protect students' rights and improve the educational environment.

School social workers have long advocated for educational equity—less disparity between school programs in poor districts and in rich districts. Traditionally, schools have been funded solely through local property taxes. This system has provided poorer rural and inner-city districts with fewer resources for building maintenance, safety, books, special programs, and teacher salaries than their wealthier counterparts. Since 1973, lawsuits have been filed in 45 states to address this resource inequity. Studies suggest that successful lawsuits have had a large impact in decreasing the inequity between rich and poor districts (Rebell, 2008).

For example, a legislative council in Oregon has developed the Quality Education Model (QEM). The QEM uses research-based information to determine the best education practices with regard to appropriate class size, adequate professional development for teachers and instruction time for students, and appropriate access to computers and other learning supports. Schools can calculate the cost of implementing these practices on the basis of their enrollment and circumstances. QEM requires state-funding levels for schools to be based on the amount a school needs to achieve its goals, not on local property tax receipts or some other arbitrary method. It requires schools to be accountable for how they spend funds and whether they achieve their goals for student learning. Since the states that are moving away from property tax financing have not had enough time to fully develop and implement new funding methods, it remains to be seen whether the QEM and other similar models will achieve equitable funding.

School social workers act as consultants on school policy matters, such as discipline, cultural sensitivity, and child abuse and neglect (National Association of Social Workers, 2008). They consult with school boards, community members, and parent groups. School social workers trained in conflict resolution strategies can act as mediators in conflicts between parents and schools or in conflicts among students.

The funding for school social work services comes from multiple sources, including federal, state, and local governments; private donations; and grants. Most of the federal and state funds are tied to providing free and appropriate public education in the least restrictive environment for children with disabilities. As a result, more than half of all school social workers exclusively serve students with disabilities, particularly students with developmental disabilities.

WORKING WITH STUDENTS AT RISK

CASE EXAMPLE: David is eight years old. He has Down syndrome and is in a special education class 20 miles away from his home. The bus ride takes 45 minutes each way, and he is exhausted when he comes home from school. David is isolated from the other neighborhood children because he doesn't attend school with them, so he has no friends to play with. The special education class has been moved from school to school in the last three years. Each time David has had to orient himself to new surroundings. The school district keeps pushing the special education classes out of the local schools to make room for more regular classes.

CASE EXAMPLE: Luis is 10 years old. At least three times a week, he is in after-school detention for fighting or causing trouble. He is failing math and reading. The teachers are perplexed because he seems so bright, but he won't cooperate and do his work. His parents say he has no behavior problems at home. Luis's father thinks he is lazy; his mother disagrees. Luis has just been diagnosed with a learning disability.

CASE EXAMPLE: Jamika is six years old. She, her mother, and her two-year-old sister have been staying at the Salvation Army Homeless Shelter for the last two months. They will have to leave in another four weeks because of length-of-stay restrictions. Jamika's family previously lived in the other shelter in town, and now there are no more shelters to turn to. Jamika hasn't been to school in five months. She doesn't have suitable clothes, and she doesn't have transportation to the school, which is on the other side of town.

David, Luis, and Jamika are part of an ever-increasing group of schoolchildren who are at risk because they are not receiving an appropriate education in the least restrictive environment. Students who have physical, developmental, or learning disabilities and students who are living in poverty or are homeless are more likely to have negative school experiences, develop emotional or behavior problems, and never reach their full learning potential (Kid Source, 1997). Research suggests that receiving social work services at school reduced a variety of risk factors that hinder students' chances of success in school (Newsome, Anderson-Butcher, Fink, Hall, & Huffer, 2008).

Developmental disabilities, as defined by the Developmental Disabilities Assistance and Bill of Rights Act of 1990, are attributable to mental or physical impairments (or a combination) that are manifested before age 22. The impairment is likely to continue indefinitely and result in substantial limitations in major life activities such as self-care, mobility, economic self-sufficiency, and the capacity for independent living (CDC, 2008). David's social isolation is common among school-aged children who have Down syndrome. Advocates and family members who work to make the educational system more inclusive for children like David often encounter negative attitudes from school officials, as well as a plethora of local school policies that make inclusion the exception, not the rule. The laws and national public policies that can be used to protect David's interests are reviewed in the next section.

Diagnosis of autism, another type of developmental disability, has increased 10-fold in the past decade. Currently autism may affect as many as one in 150 children (Kalb, 2008). There is a great deal of debate about the causes of autism in general, as well as the cause of the increase in diagnosis. Some researchers and members of advocacy groups have suggested that there is a relationship between childhood vaccines and autism. One belief is that thimerosal, a mercury-based preservative used in some vaccines, can cause or worsen autism (Baker, 2008). Although there is still no clear answer about the cause of autism, fear of vaccines has caused some parents to stop vaccinating their children. This raises concerns about the spread of other diseases that vaccines can prevent. This issue presents a challenging dilemma for social workers trying to work with schools and parents about how to best keep their children safe.

Luis is one of the estimated 10 percent of school-age children who have learning disabilities (Altarac, 2007). A **learning disability** is characterized by a significant difference between the child's overall intelligence and his or her ability to read, write, or do mathematical calculations. Most children with learning disabilities are intelligent, but get frustrated with school because they cannot master some academic skills as quickly as the other children. Early detection and assessment is critical. If the teacher, parents, and child are unaware of the learning disability, as in Luis's case, the child may be labeled stupid, dumb, or lazy and develop low self-esteem. Some children begin to misbehave and may be labeled bad.

Once a learning disability has been diagnosed, the school social worker works closely with teachers and resource personnel to develop an effective educational plan. The social worker focuses on the student's strengths and provides opportunities for success in a supportive environment. This strategy helps the child build and maintain self-esteem (see "From the Field...Social Work Persistence").

BOX 11.1 | **FROM THE FIELD ... SOCIAL WORK PERSISTENCE**
Barbara Weigand, MSW

I had been working as a school social worker for only two days when Joyce, the school nurse, came to my office to tell me about Angie, a seven-year-old second grader who frequently missed school. When she did attend, she constantly asked for food, clothing, and a ride home. People from Angie's neighborhood had been calling to report that Angie often wandered around the neighborhood asking for food or shelter. The neighbors and the school had made numerous calls to Child Protective Services (CPS) and to the police, but so far no one had been able to get any outside agency involved.

The previous week Angie had walked into traffic on her way home from school and was almost run over by a van. The van driver brought Angie back to school because he could not find her parents. Again, the school had tried to get some outside help for Angie, but neither CPS nor the police would open a case. Ms. Graff, Angie's teacher, told me that Angie's school performance was considerably below grade level. Angie did not yet recognize letters or numbers, count, or write her name. Ms. Graff had referred her to the school psychologist for testing, writing, "Angie seems to always need my attention. She uses me for help with all of her assignments, and I don't know whether she is just lazy or whether she really can't do any of the work. She often seems so sad or unemotional. She has no friends in our classroom. She always wants to play by herself. When she does try to play with others, she gets into fights." Ms. Graff was concerned about Angie's recent behavior: "I took her home after school whenever I could last week because I was so worried about her walking into traffic again. I've tried to get food for her family, and I've found ways to get clothes and school supplies for her. But how will she go on to third grade when she is so far behind? And what if she walks into traffic again and gets hurt?"

Dr. Stevens, the school psychologist, shared everyone's concern about Angie but reported that her hands were tied because Angie had missed so much school. The special education laws required that a child be in school consistently for a certain number of consecutive days before being tested for a learning disability. Angie had never been in school for that many days.

I met with Angie the next morning. She was happy to come to my office. She talked constantly and seemed to have a hard time sitting still. We played some games together to get to know one another. When I asked her to write a story with me so that I could learn more about her, Angie dictated the following story:

> Once upon a time there was a little girl. She did not know where she was, and her name was Angie. Then she heard a call, "Help," coming from a big old forest. Then she ran and ran and then she found a bike. Then she climbed up a tree and called, "Help, help! There is a big old wolf after me!" Then she said, "Hold on—I don't see no wolf after me. Maybe I'm wrong." Then all of a sudden the wolf came rushing after her. She just kept running and running for help but she never could find anyone.

That day I took Angie home after school so that I could meet her family. Her parents shared their stories. Angie's mother, Claire, had been diagnosed with bipolar disorder at age 20. Claire stayed in bed for days and even weeks at a time. During those times she had a hard time getting Angie up and ready for school. Claire reported that she had a case manager and that their housing was provided by the state mental health system. However, she was not actively engaged in treatment or taking her medication, so the case manager had terminated services. They would soon lose their housing. Claire also reported that Pete, Angie's father, used crystal daily and that "He never comes down." Pete did not confirm or deny this statement. Both said that there had been frequent incidents of domestic violence in the home. Each reported that the other was physically abusive. The police had often been called, but both seem to be at fault and neither would press charges, so there had been no arrests.

I began working on Angie's case the next day. I started by filing another Child Protective Service report for neglect. Because of all the reports on file from the past, an investigation was conducted, but no case was opened. I also contacted Claire's case manager to see if further help could be obtained for the family. The case manager was frustrated with Claire's noncompliance and refused to talk with me.

Angie's case frustrated all of us for a long time. However, little by little, we made progress. I continued

BOX 11.1   **FROM THE FIELD ... SOCIAL WORK PERSISTENCE** *continued*

to talk with people at Child Protective Services and at the mental health agency. Finally, through contacts with people I'd known in the past, I found help in both places. A friend and colleague from the local university CPS training unit agreed to talk with the family about a voluntary placement, which would qualify the family for intensive services. To everyone's surprise, the family agreed.

Angie was placed in temporary custody while her father went into treatment and her mother was hospitalized. Angie disliked the foster home. By now it was summer vacation. The protective services training unit arranged with the mental health agency to let me see Angie several times a week during the summer so that she would feel connected to the school. We often went out for ice cream or to the park with Angie's CPS case manager, and sometimes we were joined by Mrs. Sundstrom, who would be Angie's third-grade teacher in the fall.

Meanwhile, the school had worked on Angie's attendance throughout the year. If she did not show up in the morning, someone went to her home to bring her to school. We had finally reached the required number of days, and she had qualified for testing. Dr. Stevens found that Angie had a learning disability, and she began to receive special education services. Because this

was now an active CPS case, the mental health agency approved a psychiatric exam. Her psychiatrist prescribed ritalin, which immediately helped Angie focus on both academics and peers. The school placed her with a teacher who had exceptional skills in establishing rapport with children.

Angie returned to her family just before school started in the fall. By the end of third grade, she was reading at a second-grade level. She had also made a few friends in her class, and she loved her teacher. On Angie's last day of third grade, I asked her to write another story about herself.

> This is the story of Angie. Last year she used to be a monster. Now she's just a kid. The End.

Angie's case was successful because of collaboration and relationships. My contacts with people in the child welfare and mental health systems helped me intervene on her behalf. The new professionals in Angie's family's life used their ability to establish relationships to pursue new solutions for Angie's mother and father. Most importantly, Angie's third-grade teacher had exceptional relationship skills, and she created a safe haven at school for Angie. By the end of third grade, Angie saw herself as someone quite ready to cope with all that life had dealt her.

BOX 11.2   **WHAT DO YOU THINK?**

What do you think about Angie's case? Should the social worker have done anything differently? The school social worker did not have to visit Angie during the summer and was not paid to do so. Would you have made the visit? Why?

The U.S. Department of Education has ruled that students who are diagnosed with attention deficit hyperactivity disorder are eligible for special education services and resources. **Attention deficit hyperactivity disorder (ADHD)** is identified when a child repeatedly displays distractibility, hyperactivity, and impulsivity for more than six months. Since all children display these symptoms to some extent, detailed guidelines are followed in making the diagnosis. The cause of ADHD is unknown. Some experts believe that it is caused by a chemical imbalance or malfunction in the way the brain filters information, while others consider it an inherited illness, like diabetes or high blood pressure. School social workers may need to advocate for children with ADHD because not all school districts may be aware of their responsibilities to provide services.

Attention deficit disorder (without hyperactivity; ADD) is also prevalent among school-age children, particularly girls. ADD often goes undiagnosed because the symptoms are different from those of ADHD. Parents of a child with ADD may think that their daughter or son is lazy or willful when in fact the child is not able to process information as efficiently as most people. As a result, children with ADD often lack organizational skills and have difficulty tracking things like homework. Recent research suggests that some of what is being diagnosed as ADHD may actually be coming from reducing play and the increased use of structured play over the past several decades (Diamond, Barnett, Thomas, & Munro, 2007). Many of the activities that children engage in at school and at home are much more structured than they used to be. For example, computer games provide users a structure for the situation and characters involved. They require little imagination or creativity. The loss of free play where children use their imaginations to create their own scenarios, characters, and games may be partially responsible for children having fewer executive function skills, including the ability to self-regulate. This can result in children who misbehave in class, have poor self-control, and generally lack self-discipline. Programs to improve executive function skills for children as young as preschool age have been showing success. Social workers can research programs that seem to have good potential to reduce classroom problems and advocate that schools utilize these programs.

Estimates are that about 1.35 million children experience homelessness each year in the United States (National Alliance to End Homelessness, 2007). The number of homeless children in rural areas may be even higher. Homeless families like Jamika's are often forced to move from shelter to shelter because of length-of-stay restrictions, or they may stay with relatives and friends for short periods of time. These conditions make it very difficult for the children to enroll in and regularly attend school.

KNOWLEDGE AND SKILLS

NASW identifies the following as primary skills needed by school social workers:

- The ability to strengthen the connections with home, school, and community by identifying and linking these constituents to create the best learning environment for the student
- The ability to build mutual communication and support among all participants in the school system, including parents, students, staff, and the community
- The ability to develop preventive and healing intervention programs for problems in the school system, such as sexism, heterosexism, or racism
- The ability to provide meaningful and relevant consultation and in-service programs to teachers and school administrators concerning student needs and rights, and counterproductive school policies

- The ability to provide training and support for conflict resolution programs and other student support programs, such as drug prevention, sex education, alternative suspension programs, and parent education programs (National Association of Social Workers, 1997, pp. 110–111)

Within the framework of systems theory and the ecological perspective, school social workers draw from a broad research and knowledge base that includes information from child development, education, psychology, neuroscience, communication theory, social learning theory, behavioral theory, case law, political science, and social work. The field of neuroscience has revealed that a child's brain best absorbs and processes information when the child is immersed in compelling and lifelike situations, is in a state of relaxed alertness, and has an overall sense of safety in the classroom and the school (Malchiodi, 2008). School social workers use this information to promote and encourage thematic and creative teaching (Loughran, 2005) and the use of relaxation techniques in the classroom. It also suggests that students' security and safety concerns should be a priority for school social workers (Oehlberg, 2006).

Growth and development research is important to school social workers because the public school experience spans a 12-year period for most children, from age 6 to age 18. Social workers must be familiar with the physical, motor, cognitive, moral, gender-role, and pyschosocial growth and development that normally occurs during this period (Zastrow & Kirst-Ashman, 2007; also see Chapter 7). The school social worker must also understand how the school's environment and social rules affect a student's growth and development. Of particular importance is how the school setting affects the child's sense of social acceptance and the development of self-esteem and ego identity (Pillari, 1998). This information is critical to the accurate assessment of the strengths and needs of the student.

Above all, school social workers need good intervention skills and knowledge of how to use the various approaches to social work practice outlined in Chapter 5. As described in "From the Field…Experiencing School Social Work," building relationships is critical. To do that well, the school social worker needs to feel comfortable with children and understand how to communicate and relate to them.

If it seems as though school social workers do everything, in some schools they do. Regardless of specific tasks, there is a unifying perspective and philosophy. School social work is based on the belief that every child is entitled to the best possible learning environment. School social workers contribute to the learning environment by matching the needs of students and their families with the resources available in the community and by creating new resources when the existing ones are inadequate. School social workers are employed by local school systems, school districts, county school boards, private schools, and charter schools.

Most states regulate and require certification of school social workers. Although requirements for licensing and certification vary, they generally include some combination of the following: a BSW or MSW degree, a certificate for school social work from an accredited school of social work, practicum or professional experience in a school setting, and a passing grade on a state exam. Many states require the MSW degree. "More About…School Social Work Credentials" summarizes the qualifications needed to receive the NASW school social worker specialist (SSWS) credential.

BOX 11.3 | FROM THE FIELD ... EXPERIENCING SCHOOL SOCIAL WORK
Charlie Boyse, MSW

I had the opportunity to do a field placement at an elementary school that enrolled children in kindergarten through third grade. I had never worked with children this young before, and I wasn't looking forward to it. Because I was one of few men on staff, one of my responsibilities was one-on-one relationship building with troubled male students in need of a positive male role model.

My first case, Robert, was referred to the counseling department by his second-grade teacher because of disturbing entries he made in his journal. Robert wrote about death and dying; he wrote that he wished he were dead and made many negatives remarks about himself, writing that he was stupid, unimportant, and so on. He had behavioral problems and was referred to the Responsibility Room almost daily. I had no idea how to start a relationship with Robert, and the school's counselor and social worker met with me on a regular basis to mentor and guide me through the process.

Initially, I interviewed Robert's teacher to gather information about his behavior. I then observed Robert in the classroom and on the playground. I also met with his mother to discuss his family life. Robert's father had mysteriously disappeared a year earlier. He had been involved in illegal activities and had many dangerous acquaintances, and Robert's mother suspected foul play. Robert had been close to his father and was just now coming to terms with the fact that his father might not return and might in fact be dead.

I was now ready to meet with Robert. At our initial meeting I explained that we would be meeting twice a week for a half an hour at a time to talk, play, or do whatever he wanted to do. I had Robert draw a picture of his family, and we discussed the picture. I was surprised by his openness, honesty, and directness as he discussed his father's disappearance and the probability that he was dead.

We continued to meet regularly for the rest of the school year. I was amazed by how quickly children bond to adults who give them attention and praise. I treated Robert as if he were the best kid in the world. I praised him often and honestly. Robert decided what we would do during our time together, and we usually played soccer or basketball. I asked about his life and about how things were going at school and at home. Robert's behavior improved dramatically.

We had many opportunities to discuss abandonment and death that year. Robert's teacher left on maternity leave during the second semester. She and Robert had grown close, and he was upset at her leaving. A student at the school was murdered by his father. Robert told me that he believed the father must have been angry with the boy to have murdered him. I suggested other possibilities that placed the blame on the father, not on the murdered son. Robert then spoke about how sad the boy's family must be and how the father probably didn't really mean to do it. Robert asked me if I would be sad if he were murdered. I said that I would be and that lots of people would be. We then discussed all the people who would be sad if he were murdered. I ended the conversation by saying that he would be the saddest because of all the things that he would miss seeing and doing. Robert came up with a large list of things he would miss.

By the end of the school year Robert was no longer talking about death and dying. He was no longer being sent to the Responsibility Room. His mother reported that his behavior and attitude had greatly improved. All of this was due to the fact that an adult had showed interest in him and had given him time and attention. An adult had treated him as though he was the best kid in the world, and he started to behave that way.

Here are some things I learned about building relationships with children.

- Look at the child as though he or she is the best child in the world.
- Allow her or him to direct the activity of the day.
- Show interest in his or her home life and school life.
- Clearly state your high expectations.
- Be consistent in behavior, attitude, and expectations.
- Give praise openly and honestly.
- Verbalize your feelings, and verbalize and validate the child's feelings for himself or herself.
- Allow yourself to learn from the child.

| BOX 11.4 | **WHAT DO YOU THINK?** |

What are some other ways to build relationships with young children in schools?

| BOX 11.5 | **MORE ABOUT ... SCHOOL SOCIAL WORK CREDENTIALS** |

The National Association of Social Workers offers a special credential called School Social Work Specialist. To receive the credential you must complete the following requirements:

- Graduate with an MSW degree from an accredited program.
- Work as a school social worker for two years after completing your MSW. During the two years you must be supervised by an MSW.

Your supervisor will be asked to evaluate your performance and recommend you for certification at the end of the two years.

- Obtain one reference from an MSW or doctoral-level social worker other than your supervisor.
- Renew your certification every three years. The renewal requirement is 30 hours of continuing professional education every three years.

CRITICAL PUBLIC POLICIES

School social workers and other advocates have been working to make sure that students like David and Luis are not socially segregated from other children and that students like Jamika make it to school every day. Certain public policies and laws are relevant to advocating for the rights of students like David, Luis, and Jamika. The most critical policy is the one that guarantees the right to free access to the least restrictive and most effective learning environment.

STUDENTS WITH DISABILITIES

Special education does not have to mean separate education. As noted earlier, the Education for All Handicapped Children Act of 1975, which set legal standards and requirements for education of children with disabilities, was reauthorized in 1990 as the **Individuals with Disabilities Education Act (IDEA)**. The intent of IDEA is to limit removal of children with disabilities from regular education classes or schools. IDEA's policy of **inclusion** involves making every effort to educate a child with a disability in his or her own neighborhood school and with his or her own peers. Support services are brought to the child, rather than taking the child to services in a special school. Unless the IEP stipulates a special reason to move the child, he or she should attend the regular neighborhood school or be moved to an appropriate school as close as possible to his or her home. In other words, significant efforts must be made by the school district to find an inclusive placement.

By itself, the law does not protect David's interests. If school administrators, teachers, parents, and especially school social workers do not develop a culture of inclusion, children like David are often stared at and called names and receive inadequate support services. Sometimes, the school social worker and the parents have to fight the school district to be sure each child receives a free and appropriate education.

For example, in 1994 the Sacramento City school district was challenged in court by the Holland family (*Sacramento City School District* v. *Rachel H.,* Ninth Circuit Court, 1994). Rachel Holland is moderately mentally retarded, with an IQ of 44. In 1989, when Rachel was seven, her parents asked the school district to mainstream her full-time in a regular education class. **Mainstreaming** is the act of removing a child with a disability from special education classes and placing him or her in one or more regular education classes. The school district rejected the request, instead proposing that Rachel be placed in a special education classroom for academic subjects and a regular education classroom for nonacademic activities such as art, music, and recess. The Hollands put Rachel in a private school while they battled the school district in the courts. The court eventually decided in their favor.

The judge used four questions to guide his decision.

1. *What were the educational benefits of placing Rachel in a full-time regular education program?* The judge decided that the academic benefits favored placing Rachel in a regular education classroom. Rachel's private school teacher testified that Rachel was a full member of the class, that she was doing well in math and the English and Hebrew alphabets, and that her communication skills were improving.

2. *What were the nonacademic benefits of a regular education placement?* The Hollands submitted evidence that Rachel was doing well with her social and communication skills. Her self-confidence was also high. The district's evidence showed that Rachel had been isolated from her classmates during the time she spent in special education classes.

3. *What effect might Rachel have on the teacher and other students in the regular education classroom?* The judge determined that Rachel was not disruptive or unruly in class and that she did not require a disproportionate amount of the teacher's time.

4. *What are the costs to the school associated with this placement?* The district argued that it would take $109,000 to educate Rachel full-time in a regular education classroom. The figure was based on providing a full-time aide for Rachel, plus $80,000 for schoolwide sensitivity training. The court found that the training could be provided at no cost by the California Department of Education if it was needed. The judge also felt that Rachel would not need a full-time aide.

Each child's situation, particularly the nature of the child's disability, will result in varying answers to these questions. Evidence is mounting that students with mild disabilities benefit enormously from inclusion. Students with disabilities who are included in regular education classes rank in the eightieth percentile academically, while their counterparts in special education rank in the fiftieth percentile. In addition, the students benefit from warm and caring friendships, growth in social cognition, and improvement of self-concept, and their classmates experience reduced fear of human differences, accompanied by increased comfort and awareness (Neely-Barnes, Marcenko, & Weber, 2008; Smith, 2007).

In a landmark case, Garret Frey, a student who is quadriplegic, sued his local school district because they refused to furnish a trained aide to provide extensive assistance while he was in school. Garret's case went all the way to the Supreme Court (*Frey* v. *Cedar Rapids Community School District*, 1998). In 1999 the Court ruled that the school district must provide an aide because IDEA guarantees a "free and appropriate public education" to students with disabilities (NAMI E-News, 1999).

Many children cannot afford to go to private school while their parents battle for their rights. To prevent long court battles, school social workers need to educate school districts about the requirements of IDEA, facilitate the inclusion of children with disabilities into regular education, and ensure that students are provided needed services.

POOR AND HOMELESS STUDENTS

The **Education of Homeless Children and Youth** (EHCY) program was established under the Stewart B. McKinney Homeless Assistance Act of 1987. The EHCY program provides grants to state and local educational agencies to ensure that homeless children like Jamika have access to the same free and appropriate education as other children. In 1990 the program was amended to include direct services to homeless children. In 1987, before creation of the program, over 50 percent of homeless children were not attending school. An evaluation completed in 1995 showed that over 86 percent of homeless children in districts that received funding were attending school (Anderson, 1995). The McKinney Act was reauthorized in 2002 as part of the No Child Left Behind bill.

Serious barriers to the education of homeless children remain. The EHCY program has never been fully funded by Congress. In fiscal year 2007, more than 900,000 K–12 public school students were identified as homeless, a 50 percent increase from 2003–2004 (National Association for the Education of Homeless Children, 2008). National disasters such as Hurricane Katrina have resulted in large numbers of children who qualify as homeless and could potentially receive assistance from the EHCY program. Although need for the program's services has increased, funding has not kept pace with this need. School social workers need to continue advocating for full funding of the EHCY program and increased attention to the needs of homeless students as well as preschoolers. A survey by the National Law Center on Homelessness and Poverty (1997) indicated that few if any homeless children were enrolled in preschool.

The **Elementary and Secondary Education Act** (ESEA) of 1965 was the largest source of federal assistance to poor schools, communities, and children for 30 years. President Bill Clinton reauthorized ESEA when he signed the Improving America's

Schools Act (IASA) into law in 1994. The new law supports schools in their efforts to move all children toward high academic standards. Title I, previously known as Chapter I, supports local educational agencies in helping disadvantaged students meet high academic standards by

- Improving teaching by promoting effective instruction for at-risk children and for enriched and accelerated programs
- Catalyzing sweeping changes in the poorest communities, including providing new textbooks and more support for teachers and curriculum development
- Promoting effective parental participation
- Supporting coordination with health and social services agencies
- Focusing resources on the schools with the highest percentage of students in poverty

The Migrant Education Program (MEP) is also authorized under Title I of IASA to ensure that migrant workers' children have access to the same free and appropriate public education, including public preschool education, as other children. Title IX supports local school districts' efforts to meet the educational and related cultural needs of First-Nation children so that they can achieve the same academic standards expected of all students. This legislation is critical because First-Nation students are at risk for school failure due to a 31 percent poverty rate, health problems, and high unemployment on reservations.

In 2001, President George W. Bush signed into law the **No Child Left Behind Act (NCLB)**, which requires that every child must learn to read, write, and add, subtract and multiply at grade level. Every state is required to set standards to achieve this goal, which are applied to all schools that receive Title I funding. The legislation gives school greater flexibility in how they may use federal education dollars, but it also holds them accountable for improving student achievement. Schools that are consistently low-performing would get extra federal funding to enhance outcomes. However, schools that do not improve will face the loss of federal funds and a loss of students because parents of low-income children in poor-performing schools will be able to send their children to other public schools and get federal funds for private tutoring.

In the time since its passage, NCLB has raised many concerns (Klein, 2008; Kolderie, 2008). Many believe that the law has never been properly funded, leaving struggling schools without the resources needed to improve. There are concerns that the focus on test taking is not helping students learn to think critically or creatively, as teachers must spend time just teaching to the test. The number of failing schools nationwide has been increasing. The lack of flexibility and the complexity of the legislation has also proved problematic. "The laws tangled rules have mystified and demoralized many ... schools should be rewarded for elevating achievement levels by some degree, rather than penalized for not meeting an absolute, unrealistic standard" (Fuller, 2004, p. 23). Frustrations with the legislation have run so high that some states have even considered opting out of the legislation, thus putting themselves at risk of losing their federal education funding (Zehr, 2008). While the goal of improving the education system is admirable, changes in NCLB seem needed to achieve that goal.

DIVERSITY

At the beginning of the twentieth century, 1 of every 10 students was a member of a nondominant group. By the end of the twentieth century, the number was one of every four. The ranks of Latino and Asian American students, in particular, have grown enormously due to immigration trends over the last 20 years. This dramatic change in the demographics of American communities and schools has had a profound effect on education.

The U.S. educational system has long been based on a dominant-culture, middle-class value structure. African American, Asian American, Latino, Islamic, Jewish, and First Nation students are especially vulnerable to discrimination because their cultures, values, and interaction patterns have often been discounted or rejected in the educational structure and curriculum (Freeman, 1995). As a result, students from many nondominant groups have often been overrepresented in remedial programs.

MULTICULTURAL EDUCATION

One way to address discrimination and teaching styles or curricula that ignore the cultural characteristics of students is to raise the awareness of school administrators, parents, and teachers about the benefits of **multicultural education**. This is easier said than done. Many parents and educators still think of diversity as a burden and do not realize that current curricula and teaching approaches are biased.

A 30-student public school classroom that mirrors the population of the United States would have the following make up of students: an almost even mix of girls and boys, 18 white, 5 African American, 5 Latino, 1 First Nation, and 1 second generation Asian American student (Sleeter & Grant, 2007). Our population and our public school classrooms are becoming more diverse each year. Multicultural education allows the U.S. education system to adequately and fairly teach to an increasingly diverse group of students. Multicultural education embraces and affirms diversity among students. By doing this, it challenges and rejects all forms of oppression in schools and society. It is designed to teach principles of social justice. Multicultural education allows students to develop their own identities and reach their true potential as learners. It respects individuality while promoting respect for others. In a multicultural setting, students learn to think critically about their world and take ownership of their lives. Multicultural education teaches students how to be better citizens. It empowers them to transform both themselves and society in positive ways (Dilworth, 1998).

To promote multicultural education school social workers can

1. Provide opportunities and encourage teachers, students, and parents to share their own life stories, attitudes, prejudices, and values as they relate to dealing with different ethnic groups.
2. Provide opportunities to acknowledge and appreciate the contributions of different groups.
3. Encourage teachers to select content that includes different cultural viewpoints and interpretations. Content should also reflect positive role models of different ethnic groups.

4. Provide opportunities for students to discuss issues like racism, sexism, hetero-sexism, and classism.
5. Provide students with opportunities to develop cross-cultural communication and conflict resolution skills. (Hernandez, 1989)

BILINGUAL EDUCATION AND IMMIGRATION

Bilingual education was introduced in the United States in the 1960s under the Elementary and Secondary Education Act of 1965. It had long been believed that bilingual programs produce better academic English and improved literacy (Curriel, Rosenthal, & Richek, 1986). However, the effectiveness of bilingual education has been challenged.

In 1998 California voters passed a proposition that requires public school classes to be taught in English only. Students who speak limited English were required to take a one-year English immersion class. Thus far, the courts have judged the proposition to be constitutional. To the surprise of some, the ballot initiative was widely supported by Latinos, many of whom perceive English to be key to upward mobility (Streisand, 1997). A number of other states have followed California's lead and voted on initiatives to end bilingual education. Initiatives have passed in some states, including Massachusetts and Arizona, but failed in Colorado.

August and Hakuta (1997) published a study that contradicts two key arguments often used to support bilingual education. These researchers found that teaching children to read in English, rather than their native languages, has no apparent negative consequences and that there appear to be no long-term advantages to teaching limited-English students in their native languages. These findings contradict findings of earlier studies, as well as a National Association of Social Workers (1997) policy statement that, in part, supports the use of bilingual education.

An influx of immigrants into the United States has meant an increase in the number of immigrant children in U.S. classrooms and has fueled the debate about bilingual education, as well as about immigration in general. The number of children of immigrants more than tripled from 6 percent in 1970 to almost 19 percent in 2000. One in five children in K–12 schools has at least one parent who is an immigrant. Estimates are that by 2010, roughly one-quarter of the K–12 student population will be children of immigrants (Capps et al., 2005). Many of these children grew up speaking a language other than English and face language challenges at school. Inconsistent findings among research studies and conflicting views among educators, policy makers, and the general public, leave the question of whether bilingual education is the best approach up in the air. The one thing that is certain is that as this population continues to grow, it is essential that policies and programs are developed that help these children succeed in school. School social workers are in an ideal position to conduct research and develop programs and policies to improve the likelihood of success for limited English proficient (LEP) students.

STUDENTS WHO ARE DEAF OR HARD OF HEARING

Deaf and hard of hearing students have traditionally struggled in the U.S. education system. Put another way, the U.S. education system has generally proven inadequate

BOX 11.6 | BECOMING A CHANGE AGENT

In June 2002, a group of high-achieving high school students from Wilson Charter High School in Phoenix, Arizona, traveled to a national science competition in Buffalo, New York. The group wanted to take a side trip into Canada to visit Niagara Falls. A teacher traveling with the students asked officials if the students could cross into Canada using their student ID cards. Though they never crossed the border, four Latino students were detained and questioned about their immigration status. It turned out that all four had been brought to the United States from Mexico by their undocumented parents when they were young children. The students, who became known as the Wilson Four, were in a situation shared by many other children and youth. They had grown up in the United States, the only home most of them remembered, yet they were not citizens. Estimates are that as many as 65,000 students in a similar situation graduate from high school in the United States every year (Passel, 2003). These students are not eligible for many services and forms of assistance that United States citizens can receive, including in-state college tuition and access to many types of student loans and grants. They are not able to work legally and are at risk of deportation, back to a country that most had only lived for a short time and few think of as home. Cases such as the Wilson Four prompted legislators to introduce the Development, Relief and Education for Alien Minors (DREAM) Act into the U.S. House of Representatives and Senate. If passed, the DREAM Act would allow students brought to the United States before the age of 15 who graduate high school or obtain their GED and who are of "good moral character" to enter into a path to obtain citizenship.

Analyzing the Situation

*   Research the situation of the Wilson Four. What happened in their case? Were they deported? Continue your research and learn more about children who were brought to the United States when they were young and are now caught in the dilemma described above. What challenges do they face? What options do they have?
*   Learn more about the DREAM Act. What do its supporters say? What do its opponents say? Are the arguments on one side or the other a better fit with social work values and ethics?
*   How does the situation of children brought to the United States when they are young relate to the larger debate about immigration in the United States?

What Can Social Workers Do?

Given your analysis, what might social workers do to address the needs and challenges of various parties involved in the situation described above? What interventions could you suggest at the individual level? The community level? The institutional level? And the policy level?

What Can You Do?

What one step might you take now, alone or working with others, to address the situation these students are stuck in? What are the barriers that might keep you from taking this step? What could you do to reduce those barriers?

for deaf and hard of hearing students. On average, deaf and hard of hearing students have low academic achievement in the areas of language acquisition, math and reading skills. One example of this can be seen in the fact that the majority of deaf and hard of hearing students that graduate from high school, do so reading at only a third- or fourth-grade level (Gilbertson & Ferre, 2008).

Since the first one was founded in 1817, schools for the deaf have been established around the country to better address the educational needs of deaf students. Staff at these schools have an in-depth understanding of the academic and social needs of deaf and hard of hearing students. Deaf schools also serve an important cultural role, teaching a common language, American Sign Language focusing on the history of the deaf community; and providing deaf students with deaf role models. However, the vast majority of deaf and hard of hearing students attend mainstream schools. In 2007, only about 15 percent of deaf and hard of hearing students attended a school for the deaf (Samuels, 2007). Deaf students in mainstream public schools have a variety of educational and social needs that may not be met. School social workers can help address the needs of deaf and hard of hearing students by gaining an understanding of deaf culture and of the students' educational and social needs. School social workers must be prepared to provide direct services and advocate for appropriate instruction and support for deaf and hard of hearing students. Social workers can also be involved in educating the community about the benefits of schools for the deaf and advocating for adequate funding for these institutions.

SOCIAL WORK VALUES AND ETHICS

In addition to the National Association of Social Work Code of Ethics, school social workers should be familiar with the NASW *Standards for School Social Work Services* (2002), the NASW *Standards for the Practice of Social Work with Adolescents* (1993), and the NASW policy statement on "Education of Children and Youths" (NASW, 1997). Excerpts from the *Standards for School Social Work Services* are reprinted in "More About...School Social Work Standards."

The school social work standards emphasize the social worker's obligation to identify student needs and mobilize community resources in order to maximize opportunities for students to reach their potential. This requires school social workers to become involved in school funding issues. The need to reduce class sizes, hire more teachers, and increase opportunities for tutoring and computer skills training

---

BOX 11.7 | **MORE ABOUT ... SCHOOL SOCIAL WORK STANDARDS**

NASW Standards for School Social Work Services include the following:

Standard 2: As leaders or members of interdisciplinary teams, school social workers shall work collaboratively to mobilize the resources of the local education agencies [the school] and the community to meet the needs of children and families.

Standard 6: School social workers shall be responsible for identifying individual children and target populations in need of services. They shall do so through a process of needs assessment that includes planned consultation with personnel of the local education agency, community representatives, and children and their families.

Standard 12: School social work services shall be extended to children in ways that build on the children's individual strengths and that offer them maximum opportunity to participate in the planning and direction of their own learning experiences.

Standard 13: School social workers shall empower children and their families to gain access to and effectively use formal and informal community resources.

Source: National Association of Social Workers, 1992.

is well documented. Ethically, social workers need to actively advocate and campaign for funding methods that will achieve these and other goals.

CASE EXAMPLE: Sixteen-year-old Alexandra has just discovered that she is pregnant. She asks her school social worker for information about adoption and abortion, and she mentions that she is also thinking about keeping the baby. Alexandra does not want her parents to know about the pregnancy. What should the school social worker do?

In a school setting, ethical issues and decisions related to confidentiality can be complicated. In 1974 Congress passed the Family Educational Rights and Privacy Act (FERPA), which allows parents access to their children's school records and gives them control over access to the records by other people. Although these parental rights are necessary and appropriate, they conflict with students' rights to confidentiality.

In Alexandra's case, the social worker must be certain of policies and laws pertaining to pregnancy counseling in schools, particularly when a student wants information about abortion. In some states, abortion counseling is permitted on school sites, but in many others school social workers have to refer students to community social service agencies that offer pregnancy counseling services. The law does recognize Alexandra's right to make her own decision about whether to keep the child, place the child for adoption, or have an abortion. However, in some states Alexandra's parents would have to be notified before she could have an abortion.

What standard do school social workers use to determine whether to involve parents or other adults when students like Alexandra come to them for assistance? The NASW Code of Ethics clearly states that the only time confidentiality does not apply is when "disclosure is necessary to prevent serious, foreseeable, and imminent harm to a client or other identifiable person." In Alexandra's case the decision to breech confidentiality is not clear-cut. The social worker's responsibility is much clearer when a student talks about wanting to harm another student or a teacher or mentions having suicidal thoughts. If a student says to a school social worker, "I need to tell you something, but you have to promise not to tell my parents," the school social worker must explain the limits of confidentiality before the student proceeds. School social workers are mandated by law to report child abuse and neglect to law enforcement or child protective services.

The National Association of Social Workers and the American Association on Mental Deficiency developed standards for social workers who work with persons who have developmental disabilities. These standards suggest that social workers should acquire basic knowledge about developmental disabilities and subscribe to a set of principles, for example, to help maintain clients in the least restrictive environments and to protect clients' individual rights and personal dignity. Social workers should keep pace with current research on developmental disabilities.

CHALLENGES FACING SCHOOL SOCIAL WORKERS

School social workers face several serious challenges, including school violence, teen pregnancy, sexually transmitted diseases, drug and alcohol use, and high dropout rates. Social workers can best deal with these challenges by focusing on empirically based prevention and intervention efforts. This section briefly describes the major challenges and the way social workers are currently confronting them.

VIOLENCE PREVENTION

Violent crime against students in schools fell by 50 percent between 1992 and 2002 (Devoe et al., 2004). Critics of the most recent statistics argue that violent crimes in schools are being underreported and that is what accounts for the reduction. However, many argue that the reduction in school crime can be explained by the fact that schools are doing more to reduce bullying, which can lead to serious crimes. Schools have also done more prevention, such as hiring more security guards and installing metal detectors (Anderson, 2004).

A survey of 1,200 school social workers found that those who are employed by inner-city schools are more likely than their peers to fear for their own safety (Astor, Behre, Wallace, & Fravil, 1998). Thirty-five percent of the respondents reported being physically assaulted or threatened during the previous year. Additionally, in spite of statistics that suggest that school violence has decreased in recent years, a study of school social workers found that most believe that school violence is remaining the same or increasing (Slovak, 2006). It is clear that social workers and other school personnel, as well as the general public, are concerned about school violence, in spite of the data that suggests it is on the decline.

Parent education groups, after-school recreation programs, family therapy, anti-gang programs, street-savvy mentors, and early intervention programs with infants can effectively keep children from turning to guns and violence. Studies show that school-based violence prevention programs can reduce school violence by up to 50 percent. Programs that coordinate with and utilize teachers and programs that deliver more intensive services including one-on-one attention are the most effective in reducing school violence (Wilson, Lipsey, & Derzon, 2003). Rather than focus on deficits, social workers need to build on the strengths of the community as well as the strengths of the children and families served by the school. To help build trust with teachers, parents, children, and community members, social workers should advocate, in the job market and the court system, for better opportunities for youth.

TEENAGE PREGNANCY AND DISEASE PREVENTION

Approximately 750,000 teenage girls between the ages of 15 and 19 become pregnant each year. While this may sound like a lot, the teen pregnancy rate is down by 36 percent from its highest point in 1990. Additionally, the teenage abortion rate has dropped by 50 percent from its peak in 1988 (Guttmacher Institute, 2006). In spite of these decreases, many still have concerns about teenage sexual activity and teen pregnancy. Adolescents are more sexually active than ever before. In 2002, 50 percent of high school students reported having sexual intercourse, including oral sex (Wagner, 2002). These sexually active students "lack adequate knowledge and motivation to protect themselves from the hazards of premature sexuality, including pregnancy and disease" (National Association of Social Workers, 1997, p. 110).

School social workers often advocate for comprehensive sex education in schools, including STD/HIV education.

In a comprehensive review of the research findings on programs to reduce teen pregnancy, Kirby uncovered several relevant facts.

1. Abstinence only programs do not delay the onset of intercourse.
2. Sex education programs, even those that include HIV/AIDS education and information on contraception use, do not hasten the onset of sexual activity or increase the frequency of students' sexual activity. Rather, these programs delay the onset of sexual activity, reduce the frequency of intercourse, and reduce the number of sexual partners.
3. Programs that included HIV/AIDS education increased condom use among participants.
4. Most successful sex education programs

    • Focus on reducing one or two behaviors that lead to unintended pregnancy or HIV/STD infection
    • Use methods and materials that are appropriate to the age and culture of the students
    • Employ long-term programs rather than short, time-limited programs
    • Include activities that address the social pressures related to sex
    • Teach communication, negotiation, and refusal skills
    • Select teachers or social workers who believe in the program and train them to administer the program
    • Do not provide condoms or other contraceptives without a requirement to participate in an educational program (1997, pp. 1–2)

Latino and African American teens, like white teens, have experienced a decrease in the rate of teenage pregnancy; however, they are still more likely to become pregnant than a white teenager (Guttmacher Institute, 2006). Students who live in poor areas, change residences often, and have parents who are divorced are most at risk for pregnancy and STD/HIV infection (Kirby, 1997). In poor school districts, social workers may have to lobby for the resources to provide much-needed sex education programs.

TOBACCO, ALCOHOL, AND ILLICIT DRUG PREVENTION

The use of tobacco, alcohol, and other drugs skyrocketed during much of the 1990s. Since 2000, there has been a small, steady decrease in overall usage (PRIDE Survey, 2006). However, the use of tobacco, alcohol, and other drugs is still significant among youth. More than 4,000 youth have their first cigarette every day in the United States, and 2,000 become daily smokers (American Cancer Society, 2007). In 2004–2005, 47.2 percent of junior and senior high school students reported consuming some type of alcoholic beverage in the past year. During that same time period, 22.3 percent reported use of some type of illegal drug. Among seniors in high school, more than 35 percent reported the use of an illegal drug in the past year (PRIDE Survey, 2006).

School social workers need to provide students, parents, and teachers with accurate information about the effects of drugs and help students understand and manage the pressures that can lead to their use. Appropriate interventions include stress management, assertiveness training, communication and decision-making workshops, and peer support groups. Many school social workers are involved in the Drug Abuse Resistance Education (D.A.R.E.) program. A collaborative effort between schools and local law enforcement, the program begins in the sixth grade with 17 lessons on such topics as Considering Consequences, Resistance Techniques, and Building Self-Esteem. Eighth-grade students receive 10 follow-up lessons, including Pressures from Gangs and Gang Violence. There is no current research demonstrating the effectiveness of the D.A.R.E. program. School social workers have an obligation to demonstrate the effectiveness of drug prevention programs that they promote and in which they participate.

DROPOUT PREVENTION

Estimating accurate rates for those who drop out of high school in the United States is somewhat challenging. This is due to the fact that states calculate dropout rates differently. Because the No Child Left Behind Act penalizes states with high dropout rates, it gave states an incentive to use methods to calculate rates so that dropout rates appear lower. In spite of these challenges, various research studies, groups, and agencies have gathered data on dropouts. A number of studies suggest that about 30 percent of students drop out of school before graduation (Swanson, 2008). Dropout rates differ considerably on the basis of ethnicity and where students live. Students in suburban school systems are twice as likely to graduate as their urban counterparts. Native American students have the lowest graduation rate at 49.3 percent, followed by African Americans at 53.4 percent, Latino students at 57.8 percent, white students at 76.2 percent and Asian American students at 80.2 percent. Additionally, students with disabilities (Kemp, 2006) and LGBT students (Herr, 1997) tend to drop out of school at higher rates than the general student population.

Dropping out of school can have a large impact on a person's life. Dropouts are more likely to be unemployed, earn less money when they do work, receive public assistance, and be incarcerated (Kaufman, Alt, & Chapman, 2001). The reasons students drop out of school are complex and varied. There are personal and family reasons, including poverty-created need for youth to work full-time and pregnancy. Some students drop out due to poor academic achievement. Students also drop out because they feel they don't belong or are being bullied. Research suggests that the school's culture, the general structure of high school, and how classes are taught may conflict with many students' home culture and contribute to high dropout rates (Patterson, Hale, & Stessman, 2008). Schools are generally bureaucratic, which means a hierarchical structure and a focus on accountability, control, and impersonal relationships. They have also long had the mission of helping all students assimilate into American culture. As an increasing number of immigrant children enter schools, their cultures and their desire to maintain those cultures often clash with the school culture and structure.

Dropout prevention efforts by school social workers have focused on finding ways to reduce feelings of alienation and helping students achieve a sense of belonging. Social workers have also attempted to make the school environment more relevant to students' needs. Effective strategies include peer tutoring, mentoring programs, outreach programs, cultural awareness activities, peer support groups,

BOX 11.8 | **ETHICAL PRACTICE**

You are a social worker in a high school where you run a discussion group for teens. It is a drop-in group where the kids can come and talk about whatever is on their mind. One of the youths approaches you after the group and tells you that although he promised not to say anything, he is worried about his friend Stephen. It seems Stephen has been making comments about wishing he were dead, but then he laughs about it. He asks you if he should worry about his friend? What do you recommend? What is your ethical responsibility? Does it differ from your legal responsibility? What would you do? Do you need to speak with other school personnel? Do you need to speak with Stephen's parents?

work-study programs, and service learning (Duckenfield, 1998). Service learning is a combination of community service and academic instruction designed to teach civic responsibility and commitment to the community as well as academic skills.

CONCLUSION

To effectively prepare students for the twenty-first century workplace, school social workers need to work on advocacy with school administrators, teachers, and parents. Equitable and creative funding methods for schools need to be instituted. Computer technology and telecommunications equipment need to be available to all students. Many schools, particularly in traditionally poor districts, need to be rewired to support such technology. Class size and teacher-student ratios need to be reduced.

Social workers must also be knowledgeable about the ongoing school choice debate. Some advocates strongly favor the right of parents to select the best schools for their children. Providing private schools with public money—for example through tax credits or direct subsidies—to accommodate school choice has been a hotly debated topic for the last four decades. During the 1990s the debate centered on the use of school vouchers. A school voucher is a tax-supported education stipend provided to parents who want to remove their child from public school and place the child in a religious or secular private school.

During the 1990s, due to strong opposition from teachers and labor unions and skepticism on the part of many parents, only a few public school systems offered pilot school voucher programs. In June 2002, in a 5 to 4 decision (*Simmons-Harris* v. *Zelman*), the Supreme Court ruled that the Cleveland city school district could use public money to underwrite tuition at religious schools as long as parents can choose to spend that money among a range of religious and secular schools. The Court saw no conflict with church-state separation because parents, not the state, choose children's schools. Although the ruling declared school voucher programs constitutional, it did not mandate their use, and there will probably not be an immediate push to provide school vouchers in most states.

It is no secret that some public schools are failing their students, particularly in low-income neighborhoods. However, opponents of school vouchers argue that private schools, not children who live in poverty, will reap the benefits. Teachers worry that voucher programs could cause a significant dollar drain on public schools and that private schools will likely reject children with problems and those in special education, leaving the depleted public school system to educate them. Even with school vouchers, many families living in poverty would not be able to afford to send their children to private schools. African American parents in particular are skeptical of the sudden interest of outsiders, many of whom are white, in helping African American children (Pierre, 2002).

To improve and maintain an effective public community school system with equal opportunities for all students, social workers will have to lobby hard against diverting funds to private schools. School social workers need to look at alternative solutions for school choice and create partnerships with community businesses that can provide funding for needed equipment and programs in public schools. An alternative to school vouchers is a tax credit to parents who choose to send their children to private schools.

Research evidence suggests that we know how to prevent students from turning to drugs, getting pregnant, using violence to solve problems, and dropping out of school. Why are so many mired in these situations? The short answer is lack of money. Successful school prevention programs are intensive, comprehensive, and costly in the short term. In the long term, they can save dollars and lives. School social workers need to promote and use programs and interventions that have proven track records. They must also search for creative ways to fund these programs.

Nationally standardized licensing or certification of school social workers would protect the profession from the growing numbers of uncertified personnel who perform social work tasks. Because specialized knowledge and skills are needed to be effective, it is critical that school social work responsibilities be performed by trained and certified professionals.

Key Terms

attention deficit hyperactivity disorder (ADHD), (p. 305)

developmental disabilities, (p. 303)

Education for All Handicapped Children Act, (p. 299)

Education of Homeless Children and Youth (EHCY), (p. 311)

Elementary and Secondary Education Act (ESEA), (p. 311)

inclusion, (p. 309)

individualized education plans (IEPs), (p. 300)

Individuals with Disabilities Education Act (IDEA), (p. 309)

learning disability, (p. 303)

least restrictive environment, (p. 301)

mainstreaming, (p. 310)

multicultural education, (p. 313)

No Child Left Behind Act (NCLB), (p. 312)

pupil services team, (p. 301)

school social work, (p. 298)

Questions for Discussion

1. How did the Education for All Handicapped Children Act of 1975 change the face of school social work? What significant changes were made when the act was reauthorized in 1990 as the Individuals with Disabilities Act (IDEA)?

2. What is the purpose of a pupil services team?
3. According to NASW, what five primary skills do school social workers need?
4. Should children who are homeless attend special schools for homeless children, or should they be mainstreamed into the public school system? Why? Is there a school in your area that serves homeless children?
5. Should the government provide school vouchers that allow parents to send their children to any school, public or private?

Change Agent Exercise

Find the website for your state legislature. Conduct a search on the website to find any proposed legislation that would affect your local schools. This could include bills about school vouchers, funding for schools, prayer in the schools, junk food for sale in schools, bilingual education, to name just a few. If your state legislature is not in session or you cannot find bills on the website, try to find information about school-related bills at the federal level. A good website to try is http://thomas.loc. gov. Choose a bill related to schools that interests you. Decide whether you support or oppose the bill. Write a letter to one of your legislators supporting or opposing the bill.

Chapter Exercises

1. **Mainstreaming Children with Developmental Disabilities**
   Should school-age children with disabilities be mainstreamed in regular education classes or placed in self-contained special education classes?

   Research arguments on both sides of the issue.

   Yes, school-age children with disabilities should be mainstreamed in regular classes:

   No, school-age children with disabilities should be placed in self-contained special education classes:

   Discuss the reasons the issue is controversial.

   Is there adequate evidence to resolve the issue?

   Is the evidence contradictory?

   Are there definitions (e.g., mainstream, special education) that are in dispute?

   What are the underlying values on both sides of the argument?

   Do you have a personal interest in this issue? How does it affect your life?

   Brainstorm a list of arguments that support one side. List and explain the strongest arguments.

   Brainstorm a list of arguments that support the other side. List and explain the strongest arguments.

   After reviewing the arguments on both sides, what gaps in the evidence can you identify? What do you still need to know in order to choose one side or the other? Where might you find the information?

After considering everything, which side of the argument do you most identify with? What specifically convinces you that this is the right side?

Use this exercise as a guide to have a debate with small groups of classmates.

2. **Bilingual Education**
   Research the topic of bilingual education. Interview one teacher who supports bilingual education and one teacher who does not. Ask the teachers to consider cost, available resources, benefits and disadvantages to students, and other important factors. List what you found out from both teachers.

   Supports bilingual education:

   Does not support bilingual education:

   Supplement their opinions with the facts you discovered in your research.

   Eliminate opinions that are not fact based, and use the facts to list the pros and cons of bilingual education.

   Pros:

   Cons:

   On the basis of your list, do you support bilingual education? Why?

3. **Alcohol and Illicit Drug Use Among Children Under Age 15**
   The Substance Abuse and Mental Health Services Administration (SAMHSA) maintains the Treatment Episode Data collection system (TEDS), which allows each state to report substance abuse treatment admissions by primary substance abuse according to sex, age, and race/ethnicity. Below are two data sets, one for New York (2000) and the other for Utah (1999).

   Substance Abuse Treatment Admissions by Primary Substance Abuse for Children Under the Age of 15

	Number	Percent	Alcohol	Opiates	Cocaine	Marijuana	Stimulants
UTAH	500	2.7	3.1	1.5	.3	10.3	10.7
NEW YORK	3,143	1.7	1.2	.2	.2	4.5	1.7

   Which state had the highest number of admissions?

   In which state was the highest percentage children under age 15 admitted?

   Which primary substance is the biggest problem for 15-year-olds in New York?

   Which primary substance is the biggest problem for 15-year-olds in Utah?

   What are the implications for social work prevention and treatment in each state?

   New York:

   Utah:

   Compare your answers with classmates' to see if you all interpreted the data the same way.

4. **School Social Work Activities**
   A. Sit in on a PTA meeting at a local school. What issues were discussed? How might a school social worker contribute to the group's efforts?

B. Visit a drug prevention program. What are the goals of the program? How does the program operate?

What role might a school social worker play in this program?

C. Visit a school and find out how it addresses teenage pregnancy issues. Do you think these efforts are sufficient? If yes, why? If no, what else should school personnel be doing?

5. **Safety in Schools**

Visit a local school. Have the school administrators developed an emergency response plan in case serious violence breaks out? If yes, why? If no, why not? What suggestions would you make for such a plan?

References

Allen-Meares, P. (2007). *Social work services in schools* (5th ed.). Boston: Allyn & Bacon.

Allen-Meares, P. (2008). School social work. In Mizrachi, T., and Davis, L. E. (eds.), *Encyclopedia of Social Work*, Vol. 4 (20th ed.) (pp. 3–7).

Altarac, M. (2007). Prevalence of learning disabilities among United States children with asthma and diabetes. *Annals of Epidemiology, 17,* 746–747.

American Cancer Society. (2007). *Cancer prevention and early detection, facts and figures 2007.* Atlanta, GA: American Cancer Society.

Anderson, C. (2004). Violent crime in schools cut in half over 10 years, government says. *Associated Press Report,* November 29., p. 1

Anderson, L. (1995). *An evaluation of state and local efforts to serve the educational needs of homeless children and youth.* Washington, DC: U.S. Department of Education.

Astor, R. A., Behre, W. J., Wallace, J. M., & Fravil, K. A. (1998). School social workers and school violence: Personal safety, training, and violence programs. *Social Work, 43,* 3, 193–288.

August, D., & Hakuta, K. (1997). *Improving schooling for language-minority children: A research agenda.* Washington, DC: National Research Council.

Baker, J. P. (2008). Mercury, vaccines and autism: One controversy, three histories. *American Journal of Public Health, 98,* 2, 244–253.

Capps, R., Fix, M., Murray, J., Ost, J., Passel, J. S., & Herwantoro, S. (2005). *The new demography of America's schools: Immigration and the No Child Left Behind Act.* Washington, DC: Urban Institute.

CDC. (2008). *Developmental disabilities.* Atlanta, GA: Center for Disease Control and Prevention. http://www.cdc.gov/ncbddd/dd.

Curriel, H., Rosenthal, J., & Richek, H. (1986). Impacts of bilingual education on secondary school grades, attendance, retentions, and drop-outs. *Hispanic Journal of Behavioral Sciences, 8,* 4, 357–367.

Devoe, J., Peter, K., Kaufman, P., Miller, A., Noonan, M., Snyder, X., et al. (2004). *Indicators of school crime and safety: 2004.* U.S. Departments of Education and Justice. Washington, DC: U.S. Government Printing Office.

Diamond, A., Barnett, W., Thomas, J., & Munro, S. (2007). Preschool program improves cognitive control. *Science, 318,* 5855, 1387–1388.

Dilworth, M. E. (1998). *Being responsive to cultural differences*. Thousand Oaks, CA: Corwin Press.

Duckenfield, M. (1998). *Service learning: Real dropout prevention*. Clemson, SC: National Dropout Prevention Center.

Freeman, E. M. (1995). School social work overview. In *Encyclopedia of social work* (19th ed.). Washington, DC: NASW Press.

Fuller, B. (2004). No politics left behind: Bush's education plan has flaws, but both parties can work to retool it for the long run. *Washington Post National Weekly Edition, 21,* 6, 23.

Gilbertson, D., & Ferre, S. (2008). Considerations in the identification, assessment, and intervention process for deaf and hard of hearing students with reading difficulties. *Psychology in the Schools, 45,* 104–120.

Guttmacher Institute. (2006). *U.S. teenage pregnancy statistics: Overall trends, trends by race and ethnicity, and state-by-state information*. New York: Author.

Hernandez, H. (1989). *Multicultural education: A teacher's guide to content and process*. Columbus, OH: Merrill Publishing.

Herr, K. (1997). Learning lessons from school: Homophobia, heterosexism, and the construction of failure. In *Learning lessons from school: Homophobia, heterosexism, and the construction of failure* (pp. 51–64). Binghamton, NY: Hayworth Press.

Kalb, C. (2008). Mysteries and complications. *Newsweek,* March 24., p. 15

Kaufman, P., Alt, M. N., & Chapman, C. D. (2001). *Dropout rates in the United States: 2000* (No. NCES 2002–114). Washington, DC: National Center for Education Statistics, U.S. Department of Education.

Kemp, S. (2006). Dropout policies and trends for students with and without disabilities. *Adolescence, 14*(162), pp. 235–250.

Kid Source (1997). *General information about learning disabilities*. Fact sheet number 7 (FS7).

Kirby, D. (1997). School-based programs to reduce sexual risk-taking behavior. *Children and Youth Services, 19*(5/6), pp. 415–436.

Klein, A. (2008). Bush education budget inadequate, Spellings is told. *Education Week, 27,* 26, 19.

Kolderie, T. (2008). Beyond system reform. *Education Week, 27, 27,* 36–39.

Loughran, S. B. (2005). Thematic teaching in action. *Kappa Delta Pi Record, 41,* 3, 112–117.

Malchiodi, C. A. (2008). *Creative interventions with traumatized children*. New York: Guilford Press.

McCullagh, J. G. (1998). Early school social work leaders: Women forgotten by the profession. *Social Work in Education, 20,* 1, 55–63.

NAMI E-News. (1999). *Supreme Court ruling on IDEA*. Washington, DC: National Alliance for the Mentally Ill.

National Alliance to End Homelessness. (2007). *Fact checker: Family homelessness*. Washington, DC: Author.

National Association for the Education of Homeless Children. (2008). *Legislative update: Funding for education of homeless children and youth program (FY 2008 Appropriations)*. Retrieved on April 16, 2008, from http://www.naehcy.org/update.html#ehcy_funding.

National Association of Social Workers. (1992). *Standards for school social work services.* Washington, DC: NASW Press.

National Association of Social Workers. (1997). Education of children and youths. In *NASW policy statements* (4th ed.). Washington, DC: Author.

National Association of Social Workers. (2008). *Issue fact sheet: School social work.* http://www.socialworkers.org/pressroom/features/issue/school.asp.

National Law Center on Homelessness and Poverty. (1997). *Blocks to their future: A report on the barriers to preschool education for homeless children.* Washington, DC: Author.

Neely-Barnes, S., Marcenko, M., & Weber, L. (2008). Does choice influence quality of life for people with mild intellectual disabilities? *Intellectual and Developmental Disabilities, 46,* 1, 12–26.

Newsome, W. S., Anderson-Butcher, S., Fink, J., Hall, L., & Huffer, J. (2008). The impact of school social work services on student absenteeism and risk factors related to school truancy. *School Social Work Journal, 32,* 21–38.

Oehlberg, B. E. (2006). *Reaching and teaching stressed and anxious learners in grades 4–8: Strategies for relieving distress and trauma in schools and classrooms.* Tyler, TX: Corwin Press.

Passel, J. S. (2003). *Further demographic information related to the DREAM Act.* Washington, DC: Urban Institute. http://www.nilc.org/immlawpolicy/DREAM/DREAM_Demographics.pdf.

Patterson, J., Hale, D., & Stessman, M. (2008). Cultural contradictions and school leaving: A case study of an urban high school. *High School Journal, 91,* 1–15.

Pierre, R. E. (2002). Skepticism on school vouchers: Some wariness lingers about which students, institutions would benefit. *Washington Post,* July 28, p. A1.

Pillari, V. (1998). *Human behavior in the social environment.* Pacific Grove, CA: Brooks/Cole.

PRIDE Survey. (2006). *PRIDE questionnaire report for grades 6–12: 2004/2005 national summary.* Bowling Green, KY: PRIDE Surveys.

Pryor, C. B. (1998). School social work services and their regulation. *Social Work in Education, 20,* 1, 45–53.

Rebell, M. A. (2008). Sleepless after Seattle? *Education Week, 27,* 32–33.

Samuels, C. A. (2007). Schools for deaf confront other disabilities. *Education Week, 27,* 1.

Sleeter, C. E., & Grant, C. A. (2007). *Making choices for Multicultural education: Five approaches to race, class and gender.* Hoboken, NJ: John Wiley & Sons.

Slovak, K. (2006). School social workers' perceptions of student violence and prevention programming. *School Social Work Journal, 31,* 1, 30–42.

Smith, P. (2007). Have we made any progress? Including students with intellectual disabilities in regular education classrooms. *Intellectual and Developmental Disabilities, 45,* 5, 2997–3009.

Streisand, B. (1997). Is it hasta la vista for bilingual education? *U.S. News and World Report,* November 24, pp. 36–38.

Swanson, C. B. (2008). *Cities in crisis: A special analytic report on high school graduation.* Bethesda, MD: Editorial Projects in Education Research Center.

Wagner, D. H. (2002). Our children need a real sex education. *St. Petersburg Times,* June 2, p. 1D.

Wilson, S. J., Lipsey, M. W., & Derzon, J. H. (2003). The effects of school-based intervention programs on aggressive behavior: A meta-analysis. *Journal of Consulting and Clinical Psychology, 71,* 136–149.

Zastrow, C., & Kirst-Ashman, K. (2007). *Understanding human behavior and the social environment* (7th ed.). Belmont, CA: Wadsworth Publishing.

Zehr, M. (2008). Virginia lawmakers enact measure taking aim at NCLB. *Education Week, 27,* 28, 16.

THE WORKPLACE

CHAPTER 12

Heinle Division of Cengage Learning

Work is central in most American's lives. Adults spend the majority of their waking hours on the job. People often obtain their sense of identity from the work they do; the first question asked of a new acquaintance is what he or she does for a living. Ideally, workers should have satisfying and fulfilling work experiences. They need to feel physically safe; they want an honest day's pay for an honest day's work; and they want to be free of coercion, intimidation, and discrimination.

Social workers have an important role in helping guarantee healthy working conditions and fair treatment for all people in the workplace, and in providing services that improve the social functioning and productivity of employees. They do this through the practice of **occupational social work**. Occupational social workers are placed in personnel departments and health units in companies, organizations, and agencies through **employee assistance programs** (**EAPs**). These programs are set up by employers or unions—or by outside firms that contract with employers or unions—to provide health and social services to employees and their families. Occupational social workers help people cope with job-related pressures or personal problems that affect the quality of their work and home lives. They offer direct counseling to employees whose performance is hindered by emotional or family problems or substance abuse. They advocate to reduce discrimination and sexual harassment in the workplace. They promote policies and practices that increase the minimum wage. On a most basic level, they try to create safe, alcohol-free, and drug-free workplaces.

This chapter looks at the field of occupational social work and at social work's connection to the broad area of work. It examines social workers' roles in the workplace as well as the ways social workers help people obtain meaningful employment and decent wages. It also discusses barriers to work, including institutional discrimination, and policies that address work-related issues.

THE WORLD OF WORK

Work is more than what people do outside the home to earn money. It also includes what homemakers and stay-at-home parents do for no pay. Both types of work contribute to the overall economy and to healthy societal functioning.

The term **unemployment** refers to the condition of people who want jobs but do not have paid employment. The U.S. government stipulates that people are officially unemployed only when they are available and looking for work. In November 2008, the national jobless rate rose to 6.7 percent, reflecting a count of 10.3 million unemployed people, the highest level in 15 years. (U.S. Department of Labor, 2008a). People who are not actively looking for work, and are thus not included in federal unemployment statistics, are called **discouraged workers**. **Underemployment** is the condition experienced by people who are employed, but are not working enough hours or earning adequate income to meet their financial needs, and who want or need to be working more. Thus, whereas the official numbers only reflect people who are unemployed, the total number of people in inadequate employment is far greater. In a society that stresses the moral importance of work and self-sufficiency, being unemployed can cause great stress and emotional hardship. Unemployment is correlated with an increased risk of child abuse (Jones, 1990), child neglect (Mayer, Lavergne, Tourigny, & Wright, 2007), as well as with increased levels of depression, drug and alcohol use, criminal activity, and suicide (Bluestone, 1987; Jones, 1991).

On the other hand, employment has been shown to have a positive impact on overall mental health (Wilkinson, 2007).

WORK TODAY

The world of work is continually changing. Where people work, the types of work they do, how many people are working outside the home, how people are rewarded for their work, how many hours people work, and how long people stay in the labor market are different today than in the past. In early 2008, there were approximately 146 million people in the civilian labor force (Bureau of Labor Statistics, 2008). On average, during the 1990s Americans worked longer hours than they did in the past. Beginning in 2001, the number of hours worked by the average American began to fall, primarily due to worsening economic conditions (Mishel, Bernstein, & Allegretto, 2007). This decrease in hours worked resulted in a decrease in wages earned for most families. In spite of the decrease in hours worked, Americans still work longer hours than they did in the 1970s. On average, Americans take less vacation time than workers in other industrialized countries, with the exception of New Zealand. In many countries, a minimum of three weeks vacation time is mandated. The U.S. economy experiences recurring cycles of high employment and high unemployment; unemployment fell dramatically during the mid to late 1990s, began to increase in 2001, stabilized until 2008 when it began to rise significantly. These cycles can place workers in difficult economic positions.

People in the United States are expected to work not only to support themselves and their families but also because it is "the right thing to do." American values and beliefs about work have been shaped by many factors, but none is more important than the so-called **Protestant work ethic**. Early Protestantism espoused the belief that everyone must work hard—that, in fact, not working hard was sinful. Leisure and free time were seen as essentially immoral; the harder a person worked, the better. The work ethic was also shaped by the fact that the United States was founded as a frontier nation with a shortage of labor. For the economy to function, people were needed to fill jobs, and there was little sympathy for those who were not working. People were expected to work if they wanted to eat.

The world of work changed dramatically in the late twentieth century. One primary reason is **deindustrialization**, the economic changes that have occurred as the United States has shifted from a primarily manufacturing economy to an information-based and service-based economy. Between 2000 and 2004, average annual wages declined slightly each year (Mishel et al., 2007). The exception to declining wages has been in CEO pay, which increased more than 186 percent between 1992 and 2005. In 1965, CEO pay was 24 times that of the average worker; in 2005 CEOs were earning 262 times the pay of the average worker. Today's average employee received lower wages on entering the workforce, has seen his or her wages eroded more by inflation, has less job security, and has fewer health and retirement benefits than workers during the 1980s.

In addition, the growing use of technology has created a **digital divide** among American workers. Technology-based jobs require a more educated workforce, even in entry-level jobs, resulting in a disparity between the incomes of technical workers and workers in the service sector. The digital divide disproportionately affects people of color and children who grow up in poor neighborhoods. Schools located in poor areas are often not able to purchase computers and other technology required to adequately prepare their students for college, nor are they able to prepare students for entry-level jobs in the technology sector. Research suggests that the digital divide is particularly acute for people living on tribal lands (Brescia & Daily, 2007).

Globalization—the increasing interconnection of the world's economies—has had a dramatic effect on the U.S. economy. More and more products are being manufactured abroad, where companies pay lower wages and deal with fewer costly government restrictions. U.S. companies that do not produce goods outside of the United States may be unable to compete and may go out of business. Globalization has resulted in a loss of U.S. jobs, particularly those in the higher-paying manufacturing sector. Employers use the threat of foreign competition or overseas plants to keep employees from demanding higher wages and increased benefits. Increased global competition has also resulted in new pressures on American workers to be more efficient and more productive and has increased worker stress by reducing job security.

BOX 12.1 | **BECOMING A CHANGE AGENT**

In addition to providing many challenges for U.S. workers, globalization has proved to be challenging for U.S. consumers as well. In April 2007, the Food and Drug Administration (FDA) notified consumers that 15 dogs and cats died from eating dog food made in China that contained a poison. In June 2007, the FDA put out a warning to U.S. consumers to avoid using toothpaste imported from China as it could contain a poisonous chemical. During the summer of 2007, the federal government warned consumers that millions of toys made in China were coated with a paint containing lead. In early 2008, a blood thinner called heparin, was connected to more than 81 deaths and many severe allergic reactions (Harris, 2008). The first step of the making of this heparin took place at a plant in China. China has become the world's largest producer of pharmaceutical ingredients.

Analyzing the Situation

- Conduct research to learn more about the situations described above. Can you find similar cases of products imported into the United States that have posed a threat to people's health and well-being? What factors allow or encourage the importation of tainted products?
- The economy and economic policy have a major impact on the work that social workers do. Social work texts and articles include discussion of budgets and taxes. Yet it is less common to see

discussions about issues such as free trade agreements and importing of products from abroad. Do you see the issues about importing products from China or elsewhere and the issue of free trade as related to the work that social workers do? Why?

- Read more about globalization. Who seems to benefit most from current patterns in globalization? In general, do you think it is a positive or negative trend for U.S. workers and U.S. consumers? Do you think it is a positive or negative trend for workers and consumers in other countries? Why?
- Given what you have learned, do you think continued globalization is inevitable? Are there ways that we can mitigate its negative impact on American society?

What Can Social Workers Do?

Given your analysis what can social workers to do help protect U.S. consumers from risky imports from abroad? What can we do at the individual and family levels? What could be done at the community and policy levels?

What Can You Do?

What one step might you take now, alone or working with others, to address the impact of globalization on consumers and workers? What are the barriers that might keep you from taking this step? What could you do to reduce those barriers?

Global competition, combined with other factors, has hurt American **labor unions** (Mishel et al., 2007). Union membership in the United States has fallen dramatically. The union membership rate was more than 30 percent in 1960 (Greenhouse, 2007), 20.1 percent in 1983, and down to 12.1 percent in 2007 (U.S. Department of Labor, 2008b). Workers in the public sector, primarily teachers, other school employees, police officers, and firefighters, are five times more likely to be union members than those in the private sector. Job growth is fastest in industries where unions are weakest (for example, hotels, child care, and retail), whereas job losses are greatest in sectors where unions are strongest (such as auto and steel) (Greenhouse, 2000). Layoffs and downsizing are a major reason for declining unionization.

Union members earn higher wages than their nonunion counterparts. In 2006 the average union wage was 28.1 percent higher than that of a nonunion worker (Mishel et al., 2007). This gap is even bigger when benefits are included in the examination. The total compensation package for union members was 43.7 percent higher than nonunion workers in 2006. Additionally, union members were 28.2 percent more likely to receive health benefits from their employer. Thus, globalization and stronger employer stances against unions have meant a decrease in wages, benefits, and job security for many nonunionized employees.

HUMAN DEVELOPMENT AND WORK

People cannot separate their work lives from their lives with families, neighbors, and communities. A person who is having problems with a spouse, partner, parent, or child often brings those problems into the workplace. People who live in violent neighborhoods and fear for their own or their families' safety may have a hard time being effective at work. Occupational social workers strive to find ways to address stressors inside and outside the workplace.

The occupational social worker's ability to intervene with individuals, families, small groups, organizations, and communities is essential for effective practice. For example, José's marriage recently ended, and he is depressed and having trouble at work; Tonya's panic disorder leaves her unable to concentrate for more than a few minutes at a time; Dana is frequently absent because she is being harassed by co-workers who know that she is a lesbian; Dante is a single father, and he often has to stay home because of the difficulty of finding affordable, quality child care; and Mike's entire work group is experiencing high levels of stress and lowered productivity because white male workers fear losing their jobs to recently arrived Mexican American immigrants. To address these challenges effectively, the social worker needs a knowledge of biopyschosocial factors that affect a person's work life, as well as insight into small-group dynamics and organizational behavior.

Work-related obstacles are determined in part by where a person is in the life cycle as well as his or her racial, ethnic, religious, class, ability/disability, sexual orientation, and gender status. Younger employees face a variety of unique challenges. Some are going to school and working at the same time. Others are starting families and trying to balance work and home life. In both cases, workers may need to miss work or have more flexible work schedules. Long hours on the job cut into the time workers can spend with their children, causing stress for children and parents alike.

BOX 12.2 | ## WHAT DO YOU THINK?

Many children whose parents are working longer hours are spending more time in day care. Some advocates have suggested that businesses should institute such pro-family policies as on-site day care, family leave, and flexible scheduling. Others argue that such policies would be equivalent to a subsidy for kids and would imply that "some families are more valuable than others" (Frank, 1998). Some people without children resent having to pay for the care of other people's children.

What do you think? Is the fact that children are spending more hours in day care a problem? If so, what would be a fair way to address it?

The growing number of older people in the U.S. workforce face a different set of challenges. People are staying healthy and are continuing to work longer than they might have in the past. Employees approaching retirement age may need help planning for retirement and making a successful transition to a retirement lifestyle.

Many older Americans are unable to get jobs because employers think that they are too old or that it costs too much to train people who will retire after a few years. During economic downturns, such as the one that began in late 2007, older workers are more likely to be the ones laid off, in part because companies want to reduce their health care and pension costs (Turner, 2008). When plants close or corporations merge, older workers are more likely to lose their jobs than are younger workers (Mor-Barak & Tynan, 1993). Many employers and managers are unprepared to deal with the life events that older workers face, including caring for aging spouses and the loss of partners and friends. All these factors cause increased stress for older workers, and may cause them to retire earlier than they had planned to.

To function effectively in the workplace, occupational social workers need to be familiar with small-group dynamics. Human beings are social animals with an inherent need to claim and protect their turf at work. Occupational social workers need to acknowledge this dynamic before they can respond to it and intervene appropriately. They must also understand how communication breakdowns occur in small groups and organizations in order to help avoid them. Many people choose to avoid conflicts, making it critical for coworkers to develop mechanisms for constructive feedback. Often the occupational social worker is responsible for creating effective means of communication.

Finally, occupational social workers in large organizations need a thorough knowledge of organizational behavior, especially how power is distributed in the organization. Is power centralized or decentralized? Who has the formal or legal authority and power? Who has the de facto or real power? Without the answers to these questions, the social worker will not be able to function effectively in the organization.

OCCUPATIONAL SOCIAL WORK

Social workers intervene on the micro level, helping workers adjust better to their surroundings, and on the macro level, creating programs and policies to improve work conditions. According to Googins and Godfrey, occupational social work is "a field of practice in which social workers attend to the human and social needs of the work community by designing and executing appropriate interventions to insure healthier individuals and environments" (1987, p. 5).

HISTORICAL BACKGROUND

During the late 1800s businessmen encountered new workplace challenges. As companies expanded, there was less personal contact between management and workers. Increasing numbers of women and immigrants entered the workforce. Discontented workers began to organize into unions. In an effort to appease workers, business leaders implemented policies and programs that came to be known as the welfare movement in American business (Popple, 1981). The business welfare movement was designed to make the work environment more efficient and more welcoming so that workers would not want to unionize.

Starting around 1875 employers hired welfare secretaries, the precursors to modern occupational social workers, to staff programs designed to improve moral development and assist in the socialization of women and immigrants who were new to the workplace (Popple, 1981). Welfare secretaries developed aid programs that provided food and shelter, basics that were often beyond the reach of working families. They used casework and group work methods to teach employees about hygiene and manners and to help them better fit into the American way of work. The role of welfare secretaries began to decline during the 1920s and the Great Depression.

During World War II women and African Americans entered the workforce in record numbers, primarily to replace white male workers who were fighting the war. Employers brought in social workers to help these newly hired people adjust. For example, Bertha Capen Reynolds, a social worker during World War II, developed a joint union-management industrial social work program. After the war, when returning soldiers reclaimed their jobs, the number of workplace social workers declined.

The structured field of practice called industrial or occupational social work did not fully take root until the early 1960s. Concern for the rights of workers was reflected in new worker protection laws.

- The Equal Pay Act of 1963 (EPA) protected men and women who perform substantially equal work in the same company from sex-based wage discrimination.
- Title VII of the Civil Rights Act of 1964 prohibited employment discrimination based on race, color, religion, sex, or national origin.
- The Age Discrimination Employment Act of 1967 (ADEA) protected individuals who are 40 years of age or older from job discrimination.

These laws emphasized a changing relationship between employers and employees. Now that employers had more responsibility for the well-being of personnel, many needed outside help to address the variety of problems facing employees. They often turned to social workers.

Currently, social workers serve a variety of functions within the U.S. workplace. Occupational social workers have created prevention programs, health improvement programs, and mediation programs, among others. Much can still be done to increase opportunities for all Americans in the workplace and to ensure safe, drug-free working environments.

OCCUPATIONAL SOCIAL WORK STRUCTURES

The five structures within which occupational social workers generate interventions are employee assistance programs, labor union social services, human resource management offices, community relations offices, and organizational development initiatives.

Employee Assistance Programs   Occupational social workers are most commonly found in employee assistance programs (EAPs). The number of EAPs has steadily increased since their initial development, and currently more than 75 percent of employers offer some type of EAP. Of companies offering EAP services, 35 percent report that they have increased their services to employees since the September 11th terrorist attacks (Reddin, 2007). Three out of four companies now contract with firms to provide EAP services (Spake, 2000), and more than 90 percent of *Fortune* 500 companies offer benefit packages that include such services.

Staffed largely by social workers, EAPs provide short-term therapy, substance abuse treatment, debt counseling, legal aid, and help finding such services as adult day care and child care. Studies indicate that EAP services keep employees working longer and better, reduce turnover and retraining costs, and decrease sick time and absenteeism. A number of major corporations have studied the effectiveness of their EAPs. The studies found decreases of 66 percent in absenteeism, 33 percent in health benefits, 65 percent in work-related accidents, and 30 percent in workers' compensation claims (Doehrman, 2003). (See "More About … EAPs.")

Employees can self-refer to the EAP, or supervisors can refer employees. Many organizations encourage employees to seek EAP services when they have job-related or personal problems that interfere with their work. Employees are usually assured that their visits will be kept confidential. Confidentiality is important because employees may fear that going for help will jeopardize their jobs.

A supervisory referral may be formal or informal. A supervisor who notices that an employee has been tired or seems distracted or who is aware that an employee has a personal problem might informally suggest that the employee seek assistance from the EAP staff. Formal referrals are more often made when job performance

---

BOX 12.3 | **MORE ABOUT … EAPs**

- In the most common sponsorship model, the company's owner or management establishes and financially supports the EAP.
- Some labor unions sponsor and financially support EAPs for their members.
- Labor and management can jointly sponsor and finance an EAP. This model is the least common, in part because of a general lack of cooperation between union and management. The Ford Motor Company and the

United Auto Workers (UAW) collaborated to provide social services, child care, elder care, and vocational training to Ford employees. The company considers the program to be critical in recruiting and retaining good employees.

All three models can be run by an in-house EAP or can be contracted out to an EAP provider.

Source: Googins & Godfrey, 1987.

BOX 12.4 | **ETHICAL PRACTICE ... PRIORITIZING EMPLOYEES OR EMPLOYERS?**

You work for an employee assistance program funded by a large manufacturing firm. Management of the company has instructed the EAP staff to report any employees who might be having problems that result in their being distracted on the job. The company says that they are concerned about worker safety, but you believe they are trying to improve productivity and reduce insurance costs. You believe that workers who are not productive enough will be fired. Is your responsibility to your employer or to your clients? Would you report your clients to the company?

---

has been declining over time. Supervisors are usually trained to recognize a variety of job performance problems and to document them and discuss them with the employee. If a problem continues over time, the supervisor will often refer the employee to the EAP.

Social workers are particularly valuable in the workplace because of their grounding in the person-in-environment perspective. They focus interventions not only on individual employees, but also on environmental issues that affect employees' lives (see "From the Field ... Domestic Violence Visits the Workplace"). For example, Natasha is having trouble concentrating because she is worried about her children's safety at school. One appropriate intervention might be to work to lower Natasha's anxiety. However, her concerns about her children's safety are likely grounded in reality. Thus, the social worker may help Natasha work with other concerned parents to make the school safer. Until the children's safety is assured, Natasha's concerns are unlikely to disappear.

BOX 12.5 | **FROM THE FIELD ... DOMESTIC VIOLENCE VISITS THE WORKPLACE**
Joan Allen, MSW

"I know he loves me," Mary repeated as she told her story of physical abuse. I could see the bruise on the side of her face where Ken hit her a few nights before after drinking "a few beers." Mary was positive that Ken really loved her, but what price was she paying for his love?

I first met Mary in December of my second year as an employee assistance counselor at a large university. Mary had moved to the area a year before, shortly after her parents died, and had not established a new support network. She had worked at the university for six months, just long enough to qualify for benefits from the employee assistance program. She looked older than her 45 years, and she appeared to be anxious as she glanced around the counseling room, taking in all the details, as if she were checking for an exit. I did not know it then, but this was the beginning of two-year relationship.

At first Ken treated Mary well. Then he began finding fault with her appearance and the way she spent her money. Verbal abuse quickly progressed to harsh physical contact. He'd shove her, slap her, punch her. After the abuse Ken would always be pleasant to Mary. Then the cycle would begin again. Ken drank a six-pack of beer each weeknight, and more on weekends.

Mary had been in recovery from alcohol abuse for 10 years. Finally, she could not withstand Ken's pressure to share a beer with him, and she started to drink again. Mary denied that she was in danger of beginning to drink again and said that she would just share a beer or two. I encouraged her to attend Al-Anon and pointed out the cycle of verbal and physical abuse she was subjected to. Mary was also in denial about the physical danger. She accepted some handouts

BOX 12.5   FROM THE FIELD ... DOMESTIC VIOLENCE VISITS THE WORKPLACE *continued*

on coping with stress and agreed to meet with me again.

Mary did not keep her next appointment with me. When I called her, she told me that everything was fine, that she did not want to come back to EAP, and that she did not need Al-Anon.

Six months passed before I heard about Mary again. One of her coworkers called to tell me that Mary had arrived at work with a black eye. I offered to meet with Mary. She was crying when she arrived at the office. The physical abuse had obviously intensified.

The EAP provides only short-term counseling and was not open on weekends, when most of the abuse took place. Since this was obviously a long-term problem, I offered to refer Mary for counseling at the mental health center, where services were covered by her insurance. She readily agreed to a referral for long-term counseling, and I helped Mary make an appointment for later that morning. Mary met with the counselor at the mental health clinic for two sessions, then refused to return because she resented the small copayment that her insurance company required her to pay.

Three weeks later, Mary's supervisor called, concerned because Mary kept calling in sick. I met with Mary the following day. I was disheartened to learn that her relationship with Ken had become more entrenched since our previous meeting. Not only were she and Ken co-owners of a house, but Mary's daughter Kim and her four children were living there as well. I again encouraged Mary to attend Al-Anon. I reviewed steps she could take if she had to leave her home to protect herself and her family.

A month later, Mary stopped by the EAP office unannounced and wanted to talk. "I can't stand him

for one more day. He hit me again last night, right in front of the kids. I'm going to the shelter, and I'm taking Kim and the grandbabies with me." I found a shelter with enough empty beds to accommodate two adults and four children, and Mary arranged to move there that night. But when I called the shelter the next day, I was told that Mary had changed her mind. She did not return my follow-up calls, and she did not keep her appointment with me that week.

Two weeks later I received a telephone call from Mary. Ken had held her at gunpoint for five hours, and the neighbors called the police. Ken spent the night in jail. Luckily, Kim and her children had moved out a week earlier. The police advised Mary to move out, and this time she took the advice. Mary scheduled another appointment with me, then canceled it due to a "family emergency."

The following week the new supervisor of Mary's department called to tell me that some of Mary's coworkers became fearful when Mary told them that Ken had unexpectedly appeared in the parking garage the night before. I asked the supervisor to refer Mary to me.

Now Mary was ready to file an order of protection. I saw her four more times. Her self-esteem gradually increased, and she began to have more hope for her future. Two years later she left the university for a new position. Although I felt that my therapeutic alliance with her was fragile, Mary did benefit from the counseling I provided. Women who have been abused find it difficult to trust and to form healthy relationships. My hope is that Mary learned that she can trust EAP professionals. If I did my job well, she will feel comfortable contacting the EAP at her new workplace if she needs help again.

Labor Union Social Services   Many labor unions have social service departments that hire social workers to provide services to union members.

CASE EXAMPLE: Terri is a social worker employed by a labor union in Massachusetts. In addition to developing effective programs that can benefit members, she is helping organize a coalition of union members, social service providers, and activists. The coalition is working with residents of low-income neighborhoods to develop a legislative agenda to address their needs. After deciding on the most important legislative and budget items for the year, Terri helps union members and local residents get involved in educating other residents and lobbying for passage of the bills.

Unlike EAPs, union social service departments generally focus on human resource policy issues rather than on the provision of direct services. They are often responsible for establishing and managing child-care programs, legal service programs, retiree programs, and other education and prevention programs to help members. Social workers are involved in policy development and political advocacy. They also advocate for better medical and retirement benefits and higher wages.

As union organizers, social workers help employees join together to address areas of concern and to benefit from power in numbers. When workers come together, they often realize that they have the right and the ability to obtain decent working conditions and fair pay.

Human Resource Management   Human resource (HR) management involves planning for staffing needs, recruitment, training, labor relations, compensation and benefits, and evaluation of employee performance. Human resource managers strive to develop and implement policies and programs that improve worker productivity and job satisfaction. Social workers bring a variety of skills to positions as HR managers or staff. Their knowledge about the person and the environment makes them particularly well suited to advocate for employees with personal and environmental problems. For example, as more women enter the workforce, human resource personnel are developing and implementing policies that help working mothers balance work and child rearing.

Human resource personnel also assist companies in developing and implementing policies to improve workplace functioning. They monitor and evaluate policies and programs to determine their effectiveness. Social workers are involved in finding ways to more effectively motivate employees through reward packages (salary and benefits), training programs, and services such as child care. They also help with relocation when an employee is transferred and help employees who have been laid off.

Community Relations   In addition to addressing the needs of individual employees, occupational social workers develop relationships between the organization and the larger community (Googins & Godfrey, 1987).

CASE EXAMPLE: For years, FleetBoston Financial Corporation was criticized for not investing in nearby low-income neighborhoods. In December 2000 Fleet Bank announced plans to bring computers, computer training, and Internet access to residents in those neighborhoods (Nelson, 2000).

CASE EXAMPLE: The Masco Corporation set up a corporate foundation in 1952. The foundation gives primarily to low-income housing, the arts, and cultural organizations that serve the Detroit area. The foundation gave cash and in-kind gifts totaling more than $12 million in 2006 (Begin, 2007).

Community relations programs help companies function better within their community settings. Companies can have strained relationships with their neighbors for a variety of reasons. Mergers and acquisitions, globalization, and other forces have caused many companies to shrink operations or move out of communities, taking jobs and charitable contributions with them. Some companies have tried to allay community concerns about the potential for diminished community and civic involvement by increasing their contributions. When California-based Bank of America merged with NationsBank in North Carolina, the new company announced that it would contribute $30 million more than the original company had (King & Farr, 2001).

Social workers help company management understand the community's needs, developing programs to bring the company and the community together.

CASE EXAMPLE: In Kansas City in November 1999 four white employees of an Osco Drug store suspected Demetrius Davis, an African American man, of shoplifting. They chased him and held him face down on the sidewalk, where he died of "cocaine intoxication and physical struggle" (Sanchez, 2001). Davis's death was a tragedy and a potential public relations nightmare for the company. Osco representatives, including community relations officers, quickly met with community leaders. As a result of the meeting, Osco offers more products from African American–owned companies, provides more diversity training for its employees, and hires African American contractors for store construction. The negotiated agreement benefited both the community and the company's bottom line.

Organizational Development The goal of most **organizational development** efforts is to improve organizational effectiveness and efficiency. Social workers first analyze the organization to determine what is impeding optimal performance. They then develop programs or policies to improve the situation. Occupational social workers often help with team building, intergroup conflict resolution, diversity training, leadership development, and other interventions aimed at changing organizational structure or culture.

COMMON WORKPLACE CHALLENGES

Social workers employ a variety of interventions to address workplace challenges. Three of the most common challenges are substance abuse, mental health issues, and discrimination.

SUBSTANCE ABUSE

Employee assistance programs grew out of a grassroots movement in the 1970s among recovering alcoholics who wanted to help coworkers. According to the Substance Abuse and Mental Health Services Administration, approximately 9.4 million workers reported recent illicit drug use in the past year, and 3 million full-time workers met their criteria for drug dependence or abuse (Larson, Eyerman, Foster, & Gfroerer, 2007). Roughly 10.6 million full-time workers met their criteria for alcohol dependence or abuse. Over 20 percent of EAP self-referrals and 50 to 78 percent of manager referrals are related to substance abuse and job performance issues. In fact, problem drinkers alone take a total of 51 million extra sick days and rack up $26 billion in health care costs (Teicher, 2003). Substance abuse shows up in many ways in the workplace. Some employees abuse drugs or alcohol, others try to cope with drug or alcohol use by family members or close associates, and still others sell or use drugs.

Social workers address employee substance abuse by training supervisors to recognize its signs so that they can refer employees with substance abuse problems for assistance. When an employee is referred or comes in voluntarily, occupational social workers assess the individual's situation and recommend appropriate treatment. In many cases, they refer the employee to an off-site treatment program. Social workers also provide follow-up services for employees who have completed treatment programs. Many workplaces around the country have established drug-free workplace programs, generally run through EAPs. These programs have been shown to reduce on the job accident rates and absenteeism (Wickizer, Kopjar, Franklin, & Joesch, 2004).

MENTAL HEALTH ISSUES

Depression and anxiety disorders are the nation's most pressing and costliest workplace problems (Mashberg, 2001; Vargas, 2001). Depression is estimated to cost approximately $51 billion in lost productivity and $26 billion in medical treatment annually. On average, people with depression take more sick days per year than do people with heart disease or diabetes (Turkel, 2006). One-quarter of U.S. workers reported that ongoing and excessive stress or anxiety interfered with their ability to effectively function. These symptoms are among the criteria for diagnosing an anxiety disorder, yet only 9 percent of those surveyed reported being diagnosed with such a disorder (*Drug Week*, 2006). Those experiencing extreme stress and anxiety reported that it caused a variety of problematic behaviors including avoiding people, overeating, compulsive shopping, or abuse of drugs and alcohol. The majority also reported feeling fatigued, having difficulty concentrating, and being less productive. Research over several decades indicates that stress, sick days, injuries, and substance abuse decrease and productivity increases when workers have ready access to quality mental health care (SAMHSA, 1999).

Businesses that want to increase productivity provide employees who are coping with stress, burnout, anxiety, depression, and domestic violence with EAP services that include direct counseling and referrals to outside help. Employees need to be reassured that treatment for mental health problems is effective. When the Boston University Center for Psychiatric Rehabilitation studied over 500 professionals with mental illnesses (including bipolar disorder and depression) in 1999, the researchers found that 73 percent were able to successfully work at full-time jobs (Mashberg, 2001).

Worker burnout is a growing problem for many companies, particularly when layoffs escalate and the remaining workers shoulder added responsibilities under stressful conditions. People who suffer from burnout may deny that they are mentally and physically exhausted. Often they ignore the symptoms and plunge ahead with their work, only to make errors, forget appointments, and snap at coworkers (Vaughn, 2001).

EAP social workers provide educational programs to help employees prevent burnout or at least recognize the early signs and take steps to remedy the situation.

BOX 12.6   WHAT DO YOU THINK?

Alice has been working as a project manager in a large engineering firm for nine years. She manages 12 employees and works long hours, including many weekends. Alice is usually working toward a deadline and is often under a great deal of pressure to finish a project on time. No matter how much she works, she never seems to get everything done. She can't remember the last time she took a vacation or even saw a movie. She knows that she doesn't spend enough time with her children or get enough exercise. She is irritable at work and at home. More often than not, Alice hates getting up in the morning and going to work. Alice is experiencing burnout.

Have you or anyone you know experienced work-related burnout? What do you do to reduce burnout? If Alice came to you, what would you recommend?

Early warning signs include headaches, digestive problems, sleep difficulties, and the following:

- The employee used to love work, but now finds it exhausting emotionally or physically.
- The employee is less productive than in the past.
- The employee feels increasingly cynical about work and coworkers.
- The employee is no longer interested in hobbies he or she once enjoyed.
- The employee needs more time alone than ever before.
- The employee is frequently angry and lashes out at others (Dinnocenzo & Swegan, 2001).

Remedies include regular exercise, weekend trips and long drives, regular participation in enjoyable activities outside of work, establishment of better boundaries at work, and more assertive behavior to protect one's time and space.

When layoffs occur, whether during economic downturns or when the economy is strong, surviving employees often experience the same mental health symptoms as the employees who were let go (Baker, 2001). This is known as layoff survivor sickness or survivor syndrome. Occupational social workers can help prevent survivor syndrome by helping management implement layoffs in a way that is reasonable, fair, and justifiable and by providing support services that treat laid-off employees respectfully and fairly. Social workers can also identify employees who may be at risk for survivor syndrome and provide early intervention. High-risk employees are those whose jobs were similar to the jobs of people who were laid off, who shared office space with laid-off workers, or who were more cynical and negative to begin with (Baker, 2001).

DISCRIMINATION

In addition to the direct provision of services to employees and their families, occupational social workers are involved in developing and advocating for a variety of policies that affect people's work lives, including laws prohibiting job discrimination. Antidiscrimination legislation and affirmative action policies have helped people of color, women, older workers, and people with disabilities get and keep a variety of jobs.

The Equal Employment Opportunity Commission (EEOC) is charged with enforcing laws that prohibit job discrimination. It provides oversight and coordination of all federal equal opportunity regulations, practices, and policies. In addition to the three programs mentioned earlier—Title VII of the 1964 Civil Rights Act, the Equal Pay Act of 1963 (EPA), and the Age Discrimination Employment Act of 1967 (ADEA)—three major federal laws prohibit employment discrimination.

1. Title I and Title V of the Americans with Disabilities Act (ADA) of 1990 prohibit employment discrimination against qualified individuals with disabilities in the private sector and in state and local governments.
2. Sections 501 and 505 of the Rehabilitation Act of 1973 prohibit discrimination against qualified individuals with disabilities who work in the federal government.
3. The Civil Rights Act of 1991 provides monetary damages in cases of intentional employment discrimination.

Affirmative action policies have been implemented nationwide. As discussed in Chapter 3, affirmative action calls for people of color and women to be actively recruited for consideration in employment, education, and contracting decisions. Affirmative action policies are not based on quotas, and they do not involve giving jobs to unqualified candidates. Often the policies dictate that, when there are two similarly qualified applicants, the manager should hire the woman over the man or the person of color over the Caucasian.

Affirmative action has become a critical workplace issue. During the 1990s Supreme Court decisions limited affirmative action efforts, and several states, including California, Michigan, and Texas, struck down sexual-preference and racial-preference policies. Many white men claim that affirmative action has kept them from getting jobs and promotions. One negative effect of their outcry has been the perception that women and people of color have not earned their jobs or promotions.

The evidence suggests otherwise. Overall, women and people of color still face active discrimination and are in jobs that pay a great deal less than jobs held by white men. More than 82,000 charges of job discrimination were lodged with the EEOC in 2007, and many hundreds of thousands more probably went unreported (EEOC, 2008).

Despite the continuing controversy, the diversity of the U.S. workplace is increasing and will continue to increase. The majority of new workers are women, people of color, and immigrants. The diversification of the workforce has brought an influx of creativity and fresh ideas, as well as a variety of challenges, to the workplace. Cultural and language differences can create intergroup tensions that must be confronted and resolved.

People of Color People from different racial and ethnic backgrounds often face enormous difficulties in the workplace. They are the victims of both subtle and overt discrimination and harassment from coworkers. The organizational culture—the beliefs and values that determine acceptable employee behavior—is usually based on the dominant culture and may seem foreign and unsupportive. People from nondominant cultural backgrounds are expected to conform to the dominant ways of dressing, speaking, and being while at work. Workplace training rarely acknowledges diverse learning styles, language, and rewards. Not only does this harm workers of color, but it also limits creativity and lowers morale, which is detrimental to employers as well.

CASE EXAMPLE: In December 1999 the Publix grocery chain agreed to pay $10 million to settle a class-action lawsuit contending that it discriminated against African American employees. The plaintiffs alleged that as many as 15,000 African Americans had been fired or passed over for promotion because of their race since 1993 (Albright, 2000).

In the Publix case, the exams used to help select employees were found to discriminate against African Americans. The grocery chain was ordered to hire an industrial psychologist to rewrite the tests and a mediator to referee disputed racial discrimination claims and provide diversity training to help ease tensions among workers.

CASE EXAMPLE: Imagine going to work and finding a noose at your desk. The Equal Employment Opportunity Commission (EEOC) has filed complaints against a number of employers in what have come to be called noose cases, where white employees harass African American workers by putting nooses in the workplace. In one particularly troubling case, a Texas company paid more than $1 million after white employees put a noose around the neck of an African American employee and choked him. One of the white employees in the case said that he was "just funning" (Solis, 2006).

Women   More and more women are participating in the workforce. In 2006, women made up 46.3 percent of the civilian labor force (Bureau of Labor Statistics, 2007a). Estimates are that women will outnumber men in the workforce by 2010.

CASE EXAMPLE: You put in a lot of effort to go to college and hope to benefit from your efforts when you graduate. Research suggests that men benefit much more for their efforts than do women. A study by the American Association of University Women found that one year after college graduation, women earned about 80 percent of what male graduates earned. Even worse, that proportion falls to 69 percent after 10 years (Schoeff, 2007).

CASE EXAMPLE: Discrimination complaints by pregnant workers increased 39 percent from 1992 to 2003. Marilyn Picker is an example of such a case. She told her manager at the car dealership where she worked that she was pregnant. A week later she was fired after being told that it would be unsafe for her to drive while pregnant and that driving was an essential part of the job (Armour, 2005).

Employed women are often required to fill the conflicting roles of mother, homemaker, and employee. Role stress is especially intense for women who are members of the so-called sandwich generation—women who are caring for both young children and aging parents. In addition to the challenge of trying to balance home and work lives, many female employees are subjected to harassment and discrimination at work, particularly if they have jobs not traditionally held by women. All of this adds to stress and psychological hardship and can cause emotional, relational, financial, and physical problems for women who are trying to do it all.

People with Disabilities   People with disabilities, particularly those classified as severe, are much less likely to be employed than people who report no disability. In spite of this, there are still almost 9 million Americans in the workforce who report some type of disability (U.S. Census Bureau, 2006). These disabilities include physical conditions that can be seen, such as limited motor ability that requires the use of a wheelchair or other mobile supports, and invisible conditions such as learning disabilities. Workers with disabilities face a variety of challenges in the workplace, ranging from inaccessible workspaces to coworkers' ignorance and fear.

CASE EXAMPLE: In January 2001, the U.S. Postal Service was ordered to pay more than $400,000 to Rick Byrne, a mail handler with a disability. Senior managers at a Denver facility had subjected him to an "intolerable, intimidating and offensive work environment." Byrne had a breathing disability and needed to use a portable oxygen tank at work. He had been recruited by the Postal Service as part of a program that targeted people with disabilities. Shortly after he was hired, the management at his facility arbitrarily issued a "no oxygen" policy. Byrne had to keep his portable oxygen tank in his car and walk to the parking lot several times a day to inhale oxygen. There was no evidence that the portable tank created a safety hazard, and similar devices were allowed in neighboring plants. As a direct result of the "no oxygen" policy, Byrne's health deteriorated. When he was hospitalized for oxygen deprivation, his employer docked his pay for excessive absenteeism. Five years prior to the settlement, Byrne died from health problems related to his disability. The settlement money would go to his estate (Accola, 2001).

CASE EXAMPLE: Stephen Orr was employed as a Wal-Mart pharmacist. As a diabetic, he was required to take several breaks to eat so he could avoid low blood sugar levels. He was fired from his job because he took these breaks. He filed a law suite under the ADA and lost because the court believed he was not actually disabled because his diabetes could be controlled by insulin and diet. This case shows the contradiction in how the ADA is often interpreted; people who successfully manage their diseases and disabilities receive less protection under the ADA (U.S. Newswire, 2007).

LGBT People   For decades gay activists have been trying and failing to get Congress to pass legislation protecting gays and lesbians in the workplace. LGBT people can be fired from their jobs for their sexual orientation unless they live in a state or municipality that outlaws discrimination based on sexual orientation. They have no federal protections. Early attempts focused on adding protections for lesbians and gay men to the 1964 Civil Rights Act. In the 1990s efforts began to focus on passing legislation specifically to ban employment discrimination. Efforts to pass the Employment Nondiscrimination Act (ENDA) have been ongoing.

CASE EXAMPLE: Medina Rene, a gay man who worked at the MGM Grand Hotel in Las Vegas, was subjected to crude harassment from coworkers every day for four years. They grabbed his crotch, poked him, made him look at pictures of naked men having sex, whistled and blew kisses, and called him sweetheart. Rene complained to his boss several times but received no assistance. In March 2001 a federal appeals court in California ruled that the harassment was "appalling," but that it did not violate federal law because it was based on sexual orientation. The court pointed out that same-sex harassment is prohibited by federal law only if it is motivated by sexual hostility or sexual desire, not on the basis of sexual orientation alone (Egelko, 2001).

CASE EXAMPLE: Diane Schroer spent many years of her life in the military, moving up to the rank of colonel in the Special Forces. She was highly decorated for her service in dangerous places around the world and was considered an expert on terrorism. When she retired from the military, Schroer applied for a job with a library at a federal agency as a terrorism research analyst. She also decided to finally act on her knowledge that she was transgender, transitioning from male to female. She was offered the job and, prior to starting work, met with her boss to explain that she was transgender and wanted to start the new job as a woman. The next day the job offer was rescinded with the explanation that Schroer was not a good fit. Nothing had changed about this terrorist expert's qualifications. The only thing that changed was her gender identity (Vagins & Engardio, 2007).

Because of discrimination, many LGBT people hide their sexual orientation or gender identity at work, creating stress on a daily basis. When they have problems in their personal lives, such as the breakup of a relationship or death of a partner, members of the LGBT community must attend to their jobs without the support or accommodations that would routinely be given to heterosexual employees during difficult times.

Some LGBT people find more acceptance in the workplace. Almost 90 percent of *Fortune* 500 companies prohibit discrimination on the basis of sexual orientation, and over 30 percent prohibit discrimination based on gender identity. More than 50 percent of these companies provide domestic partner benefits as well (Human Rights Campaign Foundation, 2007). However, the majority of lesbian and gay employees are still excluded from partner health and life insurance benefits and leave to care for a sick partner.

Diversity Training   White men control the vast majority of senior management positions in the U.S. workplace, but they make up an increasingly smaller percentage of new workers. The majority of new workers over the coming decade will be women, people of color, and immigrants. For businesses to thrive, employers must institute safeguards against on-the-job harassment and discrimination, as well as policies that promote and implement effective work strategies for diverse groups of people. In every work setting, maintaining high productivity requires the creation of genuine trust, communication, and teamwork.

The most effective way to develop a positive and supportive work environment is to educate people. Diversity training includes information about age issues, religion, sexual orientation, marital conflicts, the unique struggles of single parents, gender, and race. Police departments nationwide have instituted diversity training and sensitivity programs. The courts have instructed such large corporations as Georgia Power and Coca-Cola to provide diversity training to all employees. Once training is completed, the hard work begins: employees must practice and implement what they have learned. Social workers are involved in developing and implementing diversity training programs for all types of businesses and organizations.

WORK-RELATED PUBLIC POLICIES

People spend a significant amount of their time working, and employment is the way most people achieve economic success. Thus, ensuring social and economic justice is critical in the context of the workplace.

THE FAMILY AND MEDICAL LEAVE ACT

The social work profession advocated for passage of the Family and Medical Leave Act (FMLA) of 1993 (see Chapter 9). FMLA allows eligible employees to take up to 12 weeks of unpaid, job-protected leave each year for specified family and medical reasons. It is especially helpful to women who are primary caretakers of children and aging parents.

QUALITY CHILD CARE

From 1975 through 2006, the percentage of mothers who work jumped from 47 to 71 percent (Bureau of Labor Statistics, 2007b). Currently, 63 percent of working mothers have children under the age of six. More parents are working outside the home, and they are working longer hours. In most two-parent families, both adults hold jobs, and more than 10 million male and female workers are single parents. However, neither the government nor the private sector has a comprehensive plan for quality day care for employees. As a result, working parents with young children are experiencing more work-family conflict than ever before, in part because today's jobs take more time and more emotional and physical energy.

Quality child care is central to the economic well-being of families, businesses, and communities. Private-sector companies that have invested in child-care programs have reported improved employee recruitment, reduced turnover, reduced absenteeism, increased productivity, and more positive public relations (Childcare Partnership Project, 1999). This is to say nothing of the benefits of secure and positive care of future generations. Perhaps the most important social policy for which occupational social workers must advocate is the provision of comprehensive and quality child-care programs in both the government and private sector.

LIVING WAGES

When President George W. Bush persuaded Congress to cut income taxes in 2001, a journalist posed the question, "What else might we accomplish if we didn't give back $1.6 trillion in tax cuts, about half the money going to millionaires?" He answered, "We could literally end poverty in America—by making sure that work pays a living wage and that children don't pay the price when mothers work" (Kuttner, 2001). Most of the people who have exited welfare since the system was reformed in 1996 and are now working hold jobs that pay $7 to $8 an hour, but eventually lose health care coverage (Acs & Loprest, 2004). As a result, although working and off welfare, they are worse off economically.

Occupational social workers should be advocating for a national **living wage** policy. Currently, more than 120 cities and counties in the United States require contractors and recipients of city or county subsidies or contracts to pay a living wage and provide health benefits (Thompson & Chapman, 2006). The way to end poverty is clear. First, make work pay. Second, provide affordable, quality day care. And third, combine a living wage with a more generous earned-income tax credit that rewards families with paid work.

UNEMPLOYMENT INSURANCE

Unemployment insurance benefits (see Chapter 2) are intended to provide temporary financial assistance to unemployed people while they look for work. Each state administers its own unemployment insurance program on the basis of federal guidelines. State law also determines eligibility, which is based on the individual's earnings over a one-year period, the level of support, and the length of time support is offered—up to 26 weeks in most states. In the majority of states, benefits are funded by a tax imposed on employers. Three states require minimal employee contributions. Social workers can help eligible people gain access to unemployment benefits. They can also remain involved in the struggle for adequate unemployment benefits.

VALUES AND ETHICS

Occupational social work presents a number of ethical challenges. One of the most difficult is determining who the client is. Occupational social workers are usually employed by an organization, so in one sense the organization is the client. Social workers are responsible to that organization and must follow its policies and procedures. However, occupational social workers often work with individual employees, and sometimes the needs of the employee may be at odds with the policies of the employing organization. The NASW Code of Ethics clearly states that a social worker's first responsibility is to the client, but in this situation both the individual employee and the organization can be considered the client.

CASE EXAMPLE: Imagine being at work and having your telephone calls, e-mails, and other activities on the computer monitored on a continual basis. This is happening in many workplaces. Employers are using technology that can monitor all telephone calls for content and monitor computer keystrokes so everything that is typed is captured. Some are also installing video surveillance equipment in bathrooms, break rooms, and rest areas, as well as other public locations. Some employers are giving employees smart ID cards that can track an employee's location as she or he moves about the workplace. Similarly, employers are using Global Positioning System (GPS) technology in cell phones and vehicles to monitor the whereabouts of employees. There is little agreement about how much employee scrutiny is too much (EPIC, 2007).

Issues involving employees' right to privacy are increasing in the U.S. workplace. A social worker would most likely fight against a company policy that invaded employees' privacy rights. However, if the social worker was employed by the company, he or she could be penalized or even fired.

Social workers employed by organizations whose primary motive is to make a profit face additional challenges. Decisions that are good for the organization might be bad for employees.

CASE EXAMPLE: Ray Reynolds is dying at age 43 from toxins that seeped into his nerve cells during his 16 years of employment at a Texas chemical plant. The owners of the plant knew that medical problems could result from long-term exposure to the chemicals, but they lied to employees, telling them that there were no negative consequences (Ryan, 2001).

Social workers who knew about the health consequences would have had an ethical obligation to tell employees.

Some employees may be reluctant to use EAP services because they are afraid that what they say will get back to their superiors. It would be extremely unethical for an occupational social worker to breach a worker's confidentiality by making reports to his or her boss. Occupational social workers need to take extra care in educating their clients about EAP services. Employees need to know that occupational social workers are licensed professionals bound by a code of conduct and that they treat all employee and family-member information as confidential, except when disclosure is authorized by the client or required by law, as in the case of intended suicide or child abuse.

CRITICAL ISSUES

Many work-related challenges face social workers, policymakers, employers, and employees. The following section explores two that are touching the lives of increasing numbers of people—workplace violence and contingent workers.

WORKPLACE VIOLENCE

CASE EXAMPLE: During the summer of 2004, a dispute between a furniture warehouse supervisor and an employee over job performance ended in the shooting death of an employee. The supervisor pulled a handgun, later claiming he thought the employee had a gun, and shot the employee in the back of the head, then stood over him and shot him two more times (Frank, 2005).

CASE EXAMPLE: In January 2002, Barbara Kallas, a library assistant, was gunned down in the parking lot of the main library. Her husband George has pleaded not guilty by reason of insanity. He was found guilty and sentenced to 23 years in prison (Matzelle, 2004).

The number one reason for workplace violence is layoffs. There are approximately 5,500 incidents of workplace violence everyday, including robberies, assaults, and other criminal acts. In 2003, there were 631 workplace homicides, 487 shootings and 58 stabbings; 512 female victims and 119 male victims. Homicide is the third leading cause of on-the-job deaths, behind transportation and falls, but it is the fastest rising cause (*Industrial Safety and Hygiene News,* 2005; Viollis, 2005).

Workplace violence is preventable if employees know what to look for and report it. Occupational social workers can address prevention and workplace violence in a number of ways. They can train supervisors to watch for signs of stress and anger in employees. They can offer stress management programs, intergroup communication programs, and communication training for managers and employees. They can help workers who are facing unemployment find other jobs and access needed resources. They can also become involved in efforts to regulate access to guns, making it harder for potentially violent employees to obtain weapons and bring them into the workplace.

CONTINGENT WORKERS

CASE EXAMPLE: Tony Bardolino was laid off from the chemical plant where he had worked for 10 years. He believed that the economy would improve and that his old job would reappear, and he waited to be called back to work. Three years of unemployment and underemployment followed. Tony started to drink, one of his kids got in trouble with the law, and he and his wife separated. He eventually began working as an independent handyman.

According to Lillian Rubin, "True, like Tony Bardolino, many of the workers displaced by downsizing, restructuring, and corporate moves will eventually find other work. But like him also, they'll probably have to give up what little security they knew in the past. For the forty-hour-a-week steady job that pays a decent wage and provides good benefits is quickly becoming a thing of the past. Instead, as part of the new lean, clean, mean look of corporate America, we now have what the federal government and employment agencies call 'contingent' workers—a more benign name for what some labor economists refer to as 'disposable' or 'throwaway' workers" (Rubin, 1994, p. 224).

Over the past 25 years, **contingent workers**—temporary, contract, and part-time employees—have constituted an increasing portion of the U.S. labor force. It is usually not the employee who is looking for this type of work, but rather employers who are seeking more flexibility and reduced costs. Contingent workers generally make up nearly one-third of the U.S. workforce, which meant roughly 43 million people in 2005 (Cummings & Kreiss, 2008). Increasing use of contingent workers is occurring in government employment, as well as in the private sector. In 2006, the federal government spent an estimated $400 billion per year on contract workers. Many businesses have eliminated full-time, permanent jobs and use contingent workers instead. Companies hire temporary and contract employees full-time or part-time for a period of time or use independent contractors who work for more than one company. Contingent workers obviously have little job security; they are, as one author puts it, "disposable workers" (Sklar, 1995, p. 31).

Using contingent workers offers a number of benefits to companies. Contingent workers can be called in only when needed, and they cost companies less money than do permanent workers.

This growing trend is not as beneficial for the employees. Contingent workers generally work longer hours for less money than their full-time, permanent counterparts. Although some companies provide health insurance, paid vacations, paid holidays, or other benefits to contingent workers, most do not. Contingent workers' prospects for promotion are poor, and they are often penalized when it comes to Social Security and unemployment compensation. For example, most states exclude temporary workers from receiving unemployment benefits. Contract employees pay both their own and the employer's portions of Social Security withholding, while regular employees pay only their own portion. While job security has been shrinking for most employees, the situation is particularly bad for contingent workers. They are easier to fire and are thus more vulnerable to harassment, discrimination, and safety violations. If they complain, they can simply be let go (Sklar, 1995). Additionally, 5 percent of companies surveyed by the W. E. Upjohn Institute kept their temporary employees for more than one year. These long-term "permatemps" work just like full-time, permanent employees, but they receive less for their efforts (Jorgensen, 1999).

Increases in contingent work will continue to erode Americans' standard of living. Social workers can address this issue by lobbying for unemployment insurance, pensions, and health benefits for contingent workers. Increases in the minimum wage and passage of legislation to ensure that contingent workers receive the same wages as permanent workers who perform the same tasks would also prove helpful, as would providing contingent workers with the same protections against discrimination and health and safety violations that currently protect full-time, permanent employees.

CONCLUSION

Given the importance of work in people's lives and of the economy in shaping U.S. society, occupational social workers can have a major effect on individuals and the larger society. They intervene to address a variety of personal and workplace-related problems that interfere with an employee's ability to do his or her job effectively. The primary focus of occupational social work has been employee assistance programs that provide services to employees and their families.

As Googins and Godfrey have indicated, if "social work is to have a significant and lasting impact in the workplace, it will be in the area of organizational and institutional change" (1987, p. 16). Occupational social workers should pay more attention to addressing the structural causes of workplace problems. They must become increasingly involved in the development and implementation of policies at the corporate, local, state, and federal levels that improve the lives of working Americans. They must also work with management to create workplace environments that are as concerned with people as they are with profits. Issues of particular concern include fair wages, elimination of discrimination, and the development and implementation of policies that recognize the dual roles of family member and employee.

Key Terms

community relations, (p. 339)

contingent workers, (p. 350)

deindustrialization, (p. 331)

digital divide, (p. 331)

discouraged workers, (p. 330)

employee assistance programs (EAPs), (p. 330)

globalization, (p. 332)

Questions for Discussion

1. How has the shift from a manufacturing economy to a service-based economy affected the average worker?
2. What does work mean in your life? What do you look for in a job? How might the effective practice of occupational social work make your work life more productive or satisfying?
3. How do mental health issues and substance abuse manifest themselves in the workplace?
4. Why is it important for occupational social workers to help establish, develop, and nurture relationships between the organization and the surrounding community?
5. Employees are protected from sex, age, disability, and racial discrimination. Why do you think there are no federal protections for gay and lesbian workers? Should this protection exist? Why?
6. What is a living wage? Should occupational social workers promote living wage legislation and policies? Why?

Change Agent Exercise

By reading your local newspaper, watching the news, or conducting a search on a legislative website at the town, city, state, or federal level, find a bill that relates to employment, working conditions, health care benefits, domestic partner benefits, or the workplace in general. Find out if the legislative body will be discussing the bill anytime soon. If so, try to attend the session where the bill is being discussed. Either through attending the session, talking to knowledgeable people, reading the newspaper, or conducting on-line research, develop a good understanding of the bill; what it would mean for employers, employees, or companies if it passed; and whether you support or oppose it. Using this information, try to encourage two or three people that you know to call or send an e-mail to their legislator to support or oppose the bill.

Chapter Exercises

1. **Contemporary Issues Journal**
   Find at least one newspaper article that relates to occupational social work practice. Discuss how the article relates to social work in the workplace.

   What questions or concerns does it raise for you?

   What else would you like to know about the topic, and how might you find the information?

Does the article make you more or less interested in working in the field of occupational social work? Why?

2. **Ethical Concerns**

    What are the primary ethical concerns for occupational social workers?

    Choose one concern, and explain which social work values could help you successfully navigate it.

3. **Globalization**

    Some people feel that globalization is a positive trend, whereas others feel that it is harmful. Research both sides of the issue. In what ways is globalization positive, and in what ways is it negative?

    Globalization is positive because:

    Globalization is negative because:

    Is it inevitable that the process of globalization will continue? Should social workers be concerned about globalization? Why?

4. **Employee Assistance Programs**

    Identify several major employers in your community.

    Do they provide employee assistance programs? If so, what services do they offer?

    Do the programs have a full-time staff? Are they staffed by social workers?

    If there are no employee assistance programs in your community, can you think of a way in which an EAP could be added? What business, institution, or group might house it?

5. **Diversity in the Workplace**

    Choose a population that faces distinct challenges in the workplace (such as older people, women, people of color, lesbians, gay men, people with disabilities). Discuss the problems that members of this population confront at work.

    What policies or practices address these concerns?

    Can social workers contribute to making work environments more inclusive? How?

References

Accola, J. (2001). Judge orders postal service to pay $400,000 in job suit. *Rocky Mountain News,* January 24, p. 6B.

Acs, G., & Loprest, P. (2004). *Leaving welfare: Employment and well-being of families that left welfare in the post-entitlement era.* Kalamazoo, MI: W. E. Upjohn Institute for Employment Research.

Albright, M. (2000). Publix settles race bias dispute. *St. Petersburg Times,* December 30, p. 1E.

Armour, S. (2005). Pregnant workers report growing discrimination. *USA Today,* February 16, p. 1B.

Baker, B. (2001). Survivor syndrome. *Washington Post*, March 20, p. T10.

Begin, S. (2007). Tailor-made giving programs suit corporate cultures. *Crain's Detroit Business*, November 12, p. 14.

Bluestone, B. (1987). Deindustrialization and unemployment in America. In Staudohar, P. D., & Brown, H. E. (eds.), *Deindustrialization and plant closure* (pp. 6–7). Lexington, MA: D. C. Heath.

Brescia, W., & Daily, T. (2007). Economic development and technology-skill needs on American Indian reservations. *American Indian Quarterly, 31*, 23–43.

Bureau of Labor Statistics. (2007a). *Employment status of women and men in 2006*. Washington, DC: U.S. Bureau of Labor Statistics.

Bureau of Labor Statistics. (2007b). *Labor force participation rate of mothers, 1975–2006*. Washington, DC: U.S. Bureau of Labor Statistics.

Bureau of Labor Statistics. (2008). *Bureau of Labor Statistics News*, Spring, p. 1. Washington D.C.: U.S. Department of Labor.

Childcare Partnership Project. (1999). *Employer toolkit*. Washington, DC: Child Care Bureau, U.S. Department of Health and Human Services.

Cummings, K., & Kreiss, K. (2008). Contingent workers and contingent health. *Journal of the American Medical Association, 299*, 448-450.

Dinnocenzo, D. A., & Swegan, R. B. (2001). *Dot calm: The search for sanity in a wired society*. San Francisco, CA: Berrett Koehler.

Doehrman, M. (2003). Mental health issues affect the bottom line. *Colorado Springs Business Journal*, April 25, p. 1.

Drug Week. (2006). Anxiety disorders: Anxiety Disorders Association of America survey finds Americans report stress, anxiety. *Drug Week*, December 15, p. 117.

EEOC. (2008). *Charge statistics: FY 1992 through FY 2000*. Washington, DC: U.S. Equal Employment Opportunity Commission.

Egelko, B. (2001). Federal court setback for gay rights: Workplace harassment isn't illegal. *San Francisco Chronicle*, March 30, p. A9.

EPIC. (2007). *Workplace privacy*. Washington, DC: Electronic Privacy Information Center.

Frank, E. (1998). It takes a community. *Dollars and Sense, 215*, 12–13.

Googins, G., & Godfrey, J. (1987). *Occupational social work*. Englewood Cliffs, NJ: Prentice Hall.

Greenhouse, S. (2000). Growth in unions' membership in 1999 was the best in 2 decades. *New York Times*, January 20, p. A13.

Greenhouse, S. (2007). Labor union, redefined, for freelance workers. *New York Times*, January 27, p. A11.

Harris, G. (2008). U.S. identifies tainted heparin in 11 countries. *New York Times*, April 22. p. 2.

Human Rights Campaign Foundation. (2007). *GLBT Equality at the Fortune 500*. Washington, DC: Author.

Industrial Safety & Hygiene News. (2005). Workplace homicides: Fastest rising cause of on-the-job deaths. *Industrial Safety & Hygiene News, 39*, 4, 10.

Jones, L. P. (1991). Unemployment: The effect on social networks, depression, and re-employment opportunities. *Journal of Social Service Research, 15*, 1–27.

Jorgensen, H. (1999). *When good jobs go bad: Young adults and temporary work in the new economy*. Washington, DC: 2030 Center.

King, M., & Farr, S. (2001). Generous giant vows it will keep on giving. *Seattle Times*, March 22, p. A17.

Kuttner, R. (2001). Help the poor instead of the rich. *Boston Globe*, February 25, p. E7.

Larson, S. L., Eyerman, J., Foster, M. S., & Gfroerer, J. C. (2007). *Worker substance use and workplace policies and programs* (DHHS Publication No. SMA 07-4273, Analytic Series A-29). Rockville, MD: Substance Abuse and Mental Health Services Administration, Office of Applied Studies.

Mann, J. (2000). For a better brew, a pinch of social justice. *Washington Post*, October 18, C13.

Mashberg, T. (2001). Experts: Depression taking toll at work. *Boston Herald*, January 7, p. 12.

Matzelle, C. (2004). Library acts to avoid repeat of employee killing. *Plain Dealer*, June 20, p. B5.

Mayer, M., Lavergne, C., Tourigny, M., & Wright, J. (2007). Characteristics differentiating neglected children from other reported children. *Journal of Family Violence* , 22, 721–732.

Mishel, L., Bernstein, J., & Allegretto, S. (2007). *The state of working America 2006–2007*. Ithaca, NY: Cornell University Press.

Mor-Barak, M. E., & Tynan, M. (1993). Older workers and the workplace: A new challenge for occupational social work. *Social Work, 38*, 1, 45–55.

Nelson, S. B. (2000). Fleet plans free PCs to bridge tech gap; parts of Dorchester and Roxbury will be part of low-income program. *Boston Globe*, December 6, p. D1.

Popple, P. (1981). Social work practice in business and industry. *Social Service Review, 55*, 257–269.

Reddin, N. (2007). Handling work in the face of adversity. *Des Moines Business Record*, December 3, p. 38.

Rubin, L. B. (1994). *Families on the faultline*. New York: HarperCollins.

Ryan, J. (2001). Unsafe for mice or men. *San Francisco Chronicle*, March 27, p. A17.

SAMHSA. (1999). *Mental health United States 1998*. Rockville, MD: Author.

Sanchez, M. (2001). Trading protest lines for boardroom battles: Civil rights leaders gain ground through company bargaining. *Kansas City Star*, January 8, p. A1.

Schoeff, M. (2007). Study cites gap in women's pay, ignites debate. *Workforce Management*, May 7, p. 9.

Sklar, H. (1995). *Chaos or community: Seeking solutions, not scapegoats for bad economics*. Boston: South End Press.

Solis, D. (2006). Racial horror stories keep EEOC busy. *Dallas Morning News*, July 30, p. 7.

Spake, A. (2000). Rocked to its roots by managed care, social work struggles to retool. *U.S. News and World Report*, November 6, p. 22.

Teicher, S. A. (2003). When social ills arrive at work. *Christian Science Monitor*, May 19, p. 14.

Thompson, J., & Chapman, J. (2006). *The economic impact of local living wages: EPI Briefing Paper #170*. Washington, DC: Economic Policy Institute.

Turkel, T. (2006). Learning to face depression at work: Businesses and mental-health experts take on the overlooked costs of the condition. *Portland Press Herald*, February 25, p. C.1.

Turner, T. (2008). Layoffs hit more older workers. *Columbus Dispatch,* January 13, p. 01.D.

U.S. Census Bureau. (2006). *2006 American community survey.* Washington, DC: Author.

U.S. Department of Labor. (2008a). *Employment situation summary.* Washington, DC: Author.

U.S. Department of Labor. (2008b). *Union members survey.* Washington, DC: Author.

U.S. Newswire. (2007). American Diabetes Association urges Congress to pass ADA Restoration Act, help end employment discrimination against Americans with disabilities. Retrieved on May 15, 2008, from http://proquest.umi.com/pqdweb?did=1353815831& Fmt=3&VInst=PROD&VType=PQD&RQT=309&VName=PQD&&cfc=1.

Vagins, D. J., & Engardio, J. P. (2007). Being LGBT shouldn't be a job hazard. *The Advocate,* October 9. p. 5

Vargas. D. J. (2001). Stressed out? *Houston Chronicle*, February 18, p. 1.

Vaughn, S. (2001). Career makeover: Burnout can strike anyone. *Los Angeles Times,* March 25, p. 1.

Viollis, P. (2005). Most workplace violence is avoidable. *Business Insurance*, April 11, p. 10.

Wickizer, T. , Kopjar, B. , Franklin, G. , & Joesch, J. (2004). Do drug-free workplace programs prevent occupational injuries? Evidence from Washington State. *Health Services Research*, *39,* 91–110.

Wilkinson, J., (2007). *Mental health: Indications of public health in the English regions.* London: Northeast Public Health Observatory.

Substance Abuse

CHAPTER 13

Gordo25/istockphoto.com

The following episodes highlight the devastating toll of alcohol and other drugs (AOD):

CASE EXAMPLE: Brian Hall started taking prescription drugs, for two to three dollars a pill, when he was only 12 years old. When he was 15 years old, he overdosed on Coricidin, a powerful, prescription-only antihistamine commonly called Triple-C. By age 17, Brian was in court-ordered drug rehabilitation. Teens are now more likely to have experimented with a prescription drug to get high, than with illegal drugs. Brian claims that prescription drugs are cheaper and easier to get than are illegal drugs (Weaver & Quan, 2005).

One in every five students reports having abused inhalants by the eighth grade, second only to the use of marijuana. There are more than 1,400 readily available, inexpensive products kids can use to sniff. The consequences are often deadly and can cause permanent damage to the brain, heart, kidneys, and lungs (Vedantum, 2005).

CASE EXAMPLE: Within a five-month period, two New Mexico State University students died after binge drinking. Christopher Berry, 22, died in March 2005 and Steve Judd, 21, died in December 2004 of alcohol poisoning. Approximately 43 percent of college students say they are binge drinkers and 21 percent say they do it frequently. Binge drinking accounts for almost half of the 75,000 alcohol-related deaths in the United States every year. As many as 360,000 of the nation's 12 million undergraduates will ultimately die from alcohol-related causes (*U.S. Federal News,* 2005).

CASE EXAMPLE: Louise Roux was not surprised that her son, Tom Desaulniers (age 22), died young. He was, after all, a soldier that had fought in Afghanistan. It is how he died that left her with so many aching questions. In August 2006, fresh from a tour of duty in Afghanistan, Tom was killed in a head-on collision with a drunk driver. He had survived Afghanistan only to be killed on the roadways of his own peaceful country (Harrold, 2007).

Each year close to 150,000 people die as a consequence of AOD problems, many of them in traffic accidents. According to the National Survey on Drug Use and Health (2006), in 2005 and 2006, illicit drug use among the nation's adolescents declined slightly. The level of marijuana use among youth ages 12 to 17 declined significantly from 8.2 percent in 2002 to 6.7 percent in 2006. The use of cigarettes decreased from 2002 to 2006 for people ages 18 to 25. However, the level of underage drinking, ages 12 to 20, remained unchanged since 2002, at 28.3 percent in 2006. One area of concern is the nonmedical use of prescription drugs among young adults. It increased from 5.4 percent in 2002 to 6.4 percent in 2006, due largely to an increase in the nonprescription use of pain relievers such as vicodin and oxycontin.

Substance abuse should be considered in the context of the general addictive nature of U.S. society. According to Fish (2007) the overwhelming prevalence of addiction in our society "indicates that the addict is our cultural canary-in-the-coal-mine warning us that something is undoubtedly amiss." While the disease model of addiction is commonly accepted among helping professionals, social workers must still approach the problem of addiction from a person-in-environment perspective and take into consideration the impact of the hedonistic and materialistic culture that we live in. Television, which provides us with vicarious pleasures, and other escapist technologies like the Internet, encourages our separation from the natural world and from each other, leaving us feeling alienated and isolated. It is in this environment that addiction to drugs, gambling, sex, shopping, plastic surgery, video games, Web surfing, sugar and caffeine, food, and many other things are nurtured and thrive.

It is not hard to understand why AOD problems are a major public health concern. The annual economic costs exceed the conservative estimate of $185 billion and include 500 million lost workdays. Other expense factors include the costs of health consequences to users, treatment, expected life earnings of those who die of AOD-related causes, criminal behavior, prosecution, jail time, job loss, financial destitution, and subsequent reliance on social welfare programs (National Institute on Alcohol Abuse and Alcoholism, 2007).

In 2006, approximately 595,000 social workers were employed in the United States, of those, at least 122,000 were in mental health or substance abuse settings (U.S. Department of Labor, 2006). Regardless of their practice setting, all social workers deal with the consequences of substance abuse. In fact, they are often the first service workers that people with AOD problems meet when they enter social service delivery agencies. Most often, a client's identified presenting problem is not alcohol or drug related. Therefore, all social workers need a working knowledge of AOD-related issues and must be able to recognize the signs and symptoms of AOD problems.

Terms used in the AOD field can be confusing because they can be used interchangeably or defined differently, depending on the context. In this chapter **drugs** are any chemical substances taken internally that alter the body's functioning, and **drug use** is a general term for all drug taking. **Drug misuse** refers to the inappropriate use of medications or prescribed drugs. **Substance abuse** is the continued use of alcohol or other drugs (legal or illegal) in spite of adverse consequences. **Addiction** is a compulsion toward a specific behavior, such as the use of alcohol or other drugs, despite negative consequences, and a psychological or physical dependence on the behavior or substance being abused (Fisher & Harrison, 2000). **Chemical dependency** describes addiction to alcohol or other drugs in contrast to nonchemical addictions like gambling (Fisher & Harrison, 2000).

SUBSTANCE ABUSE AND HUMAN DEVELOPMENT

CASE EXAMPLE: Terry is a 27-year-old Caucasian male and the youngest of five children. He grew up in a middle-class household. His parents were practicing Catholics, though Terry stopped going to church in his early teens. Terry started experimenting with drugs when he was in high school. He smoked pot, occasionally took cocaine, and started drinking, mainly on the weekends. His experimentation continued through young adulthood. He tried heroin, LSD, and other hallucinogens. Terry's drinking problem began to escalate when he was 20. By the time he was 23, he was stealing money to support his alcohol, pot, and cocaine habits. When he turned 26, he hit bottom. He went into a 90-day rehabilitation program and has been sober for one year. One of Terry's older brothers is also a recovering alcoholic. Terry's grandmother was an alcoholic, as were two of her brothers.

Why did Terry become an alcoholic and drug addict? Some religious groups would call him a sinner and say that his behavior was caused by his moral failings (Miller & Hester, 1995). The American Medical Association (AMA) and the American Psychiatric Association (APA) have stated that alcoholism and addiction are diseases that are treated by abstinence from alcohol and other drugs (see "More About ... Alcoholism").

| BOX 13.1 | MORE ABOUT ... ALCOHOLISM |

Alcoholism is the third leading cause of preventable mortality and morbidity in the United States (after smoking and obesity). The AMA defines alcoholism as "a primary, chronic disease [not a symptom] with genetic, psychosocial, and environmental factors influencing its development and manifestations. It is characterized by continuous or periodic impaired control over drinking, preoccupation with the drug alcohol, use of alcohol despite adverse consequences, and distortion in thinking, most notably denial" (Flavin & Morse, 2001, p. 267).

Benshoff and Janikowski (2000) suggest that replacing *alcoholism* with *addiction* and *drinking* with *drug use* would give an accurate definition of *addiction*. The disease, whether alcoholism or addiction, is progressive and can be fatal.

TYPES OF DRUGS

Lawmakers developed a system that classifies drugs on the basis of their medical use and potential for abuse during the early 1970s (Gray, 2001). Table 13.1 outlines the categories. Because the classification system is politically based and was not developed by pharmacologists, it has some problems. For example, many people believe that marijuana should not be a Schedule I drug because it is not as addictive as the other Schedule I drugs and has a number of beneficial medicinal uses. However, politicians do not want to downgrade marijuana because they fear that such a step would be perceived as a promarijuana position. In addition, some Schedule IV drugs, such as Valium, actually have a much higher potential for abuse than some Schedule I drugs like marijuana.

Table 13.2 provides an overview of some commonly used recreational drugs and their effects. The drugs are categorized as stimulants, hallucinogens, and depressants. **Stimulants** increase alertness, wakefulness, and energy. Psychostimulants or **amphetamines**, commonly called speed, stimulate the central nervous system.

TABLE 13.1 | U.S. GOVERNMENT DRUG CLASSIFICATION SYSTEM

Schedule I	Schedule II	Schedule III	Schedule IV	Schedule V
No current medical use in the United States	Restricted medical use, prescription only	Medical use, prescription only	Medical use, prescription only	Over-the-counter medications
High abuse potential	High abuse potential and can lead to physical and psychological dependence	Low risk for physiological dependence but a high risk for psychological dependence	Low abuse potential and limited risk of addiction	Contain codeine or other drugs with limited dependence-causing potential
E.g., heroin, marijuana	E.g., cocaine, morphine	E.g., anabolic steroids, codeine	E.g., valium, xanax	

TABLE 13.2 | COMMONLY USED RECREATIONAL DRUGS AND THEIR EFFECTS

	Street Name	Use	Effects	Health Risks
Stimulants Tobacco/ Nicotine	Cigars, cigarettes, spit, snuff, chew	45.3 million adults reported smoking in 2006. Tobacco use is the leading cause of preventable death, over 400,000 a year.	Nicotine is both a stimulant and a sedative. Immediately after exposure one may experience a kick caused by stimulation of the adrenal glands and resulting in a discharge of adrenaline. It also indirectly causes a release of dopamine in the brain region that controls pleasure and motivation.	Tobacco use accounts for 1/3 of all cancers (including mouth, stomach, pancreas, cervix, kidney, and bladder cancer). Cigarette smoking has been linked to about 90% of all lung cancer patients. Lung cancer is the number one cancer killer among men and women. Smoking also causes chronic bronchitis and emphysema, and aggravates asthma. Smoking increases the risk of heart disease, stroke, vascular disease, and aneurysm.
Cocaine	Coke, blow, crack, snow, toot, candy	Cocaine is presently the most abused major stimulant in the United States. Approximately 10% of recreational users develop a serious and heavy addiction to cocaine.	Cocaine is a central nervous system stimulant that can result in a high level of alertness, a rush of self-confidence, and a sense of euphoria. A coke crash is characterized by depression, irritability, paranoia, anxiety, and an intense craving for more drug. The onset of addiction is very rapid and severe.	Heart attacks, strokes, seizures, and respiratory depression can all result from cocaine use. Cocaine is highly addictive, and chronic use can result in serious medical problems as well as serious life problems (e.g., severe debt from supporting the habit). Pregnant women using cocaine risk miscarriage, premature birth, severe hemorrhaging, and stillbirth.
Stimulants/ Amphetamines Methylenedi- oxymetham- phetamine (MDMA)	Ecstasy, Adam, E, X, XTC, hug drug	At least 1 in every 10 teens has experimented with the drug.	Used as a stimulant and for psychedelic effects. Produces feelings of empathy for others, reduces anxiety and induces extreme relaxation. Can also cause confusion, depression, sleep problems, anxiety, and paranoia.	The most serious health effects include severe dehyrdration, heat stroke (the body temperature may go as high as 107 degrees), hypertension, heart or kidney failure, strokes or seizures. Chronic use can lead to memory impairment and permanent brain damage.

(Continued)

TABLE 13.2 | COMMONLY USED RECREATIONAL DRUGS AND THEIR EFFECTS *Continued*

	Street Name	Use	Effects	Health Risks
Benzedrine, dexedrine, methadrine, ritalin	Speed, ice, sulph, whizz, crank, crystal	About 5% of high school seniors have tried some type of speed.	Prevents sleep and feelings of fatigue, reduces appetite, speeds up breathing and heart rate and widens the pupils. The user feels more energetic, powerful, cheerful and confident, and because of these effects there is a high risk of psychological dependence.	High doses, especially if frequently repeated over several days, in some cases can produce delirium, panic, hallucinations and feelings of paranoia and depression. Heavy users also risk damaging blood vessels or heart failure, especially among people with existing high blood pressure, heart trouble or amongst people who exercise strenuously while using the drug.
Hallucinogens Marijauna	Pot, reefer, dope, joint, Mary Jane, weed, grass	It is the most widely used illegal drug in the United States.	Marijuana is an hallucinogen, not a narcotic. Marijuana creates a sense of euphoria and relaxes inhibitions. It also acts as a sedative, distorting perception and slowing reaction time. Marijuana use lowers blood glucose levels, increasing the appetite. It has been used medically to combat weight loss and reduce nausea in patients receiving chemotherapy.	Chronic use of marijuana may result in some adverse effects on the lungs, brain, reproductive system, attention, and memory. The greatest danger associated with marijuana use is while driving a vehicle. Because the drug slows reaction time and distorts perception, many accidents are caused by people who drive when they are high on pot.
LSD	Acid, cubes, microdot, yellow sunshine	Approximately 13% of high school seniors have experimented with LSD at least once.	Unlike cocaine and heroin, which have almost immediate effects, it takes 30 to 90 minutes to experience the effects of LSD. A "good" trip results in visual and sensory perception distortions that enable the user to exist in a psychedelic fantasy world of euphoria. A "bad trip" may result in panic, confusion, and anxiety.	Flashbacks of bad trips can occur even after one stops using the drug. Psychosis, convulsions, and death may result from an overdose. Unlike cocaine and heroin, LSD does not produce the same compulsive, drug-induced behavior. Therefore, most LSD users voluntarily stop taking the drug over time.

Drug	Street Names	Usage	Effects	Health/Social Consequences
PCP	Angel dust, hog, love boat	Approximately, 0.7% of high school seniors have used PCP at least once.	PCP, like LSD, distorts perception of time and results in hallucinations and illusions. Instills a sense of exhilaration.	Chronic use may result in depression, anxiety, and paranoid psychosis. Accidents, injuries, and violence are associated with the use of the drug. A large dose of the drug can lead to panic reactions and psychosis.
Psilocybin	Magic mushrooms, purple passion	Mushrooms are not as popular as the synthetic club drugs; however, the drug has been found on many college campuses.	Mushrooms induce a sense of profound relaxation and no desire to move. Colors appear brighter, and users feel detached from their bodies but at one with their surroundings. Side effects include nausea, dizziness, dry mouth, and diarrhea.	
Depressants Alcohol	Booze	61% of Americans reported alcohol use in 2006.	Alcohol is a central nervous system depressant and at low doses can produce feelings of relaxation and reduced anxiety and inhibition. Higher doses result in slurred speech, vomiting, extreme disinhibition, and blackouts.	Rapid ingestion of large doses can result in coma or death. Chronic use results in liver damage, high blood pressure, and a weakened heart. Family and work problems are also correlated with chronic use. Alcohol consumption is the cause of many traffic accidents and deaths.
Heroin Other opiates in the same category: codeine and morphine	H, horse, smack, skag, brown sugar, cheese	Estimates of heroin use vary widely. Perhaps as many as 2.4 million people have used heroin at some point in their lives. However, it is estimated that each year 150,000 people use heroin for the first time.	The short-term effects include a rush feeling, accompanied by a warm flushing of the skin. It also causes clouded mental functioning, a brief suppression of pain, and nausea.	Because, like cocaine, heroin is highly addictive, the social consequences of use can be devastating. The addict spends more and more time and energy finding and buying the drug, going deeper into debt. Addicts are likely to lose their livelihood. Many heroin addicts inject the drug putting themselves at increased risk for highly infectious diseases such as HIV/AIDS and hepatitis. The lining of the heart is damaged by chronic use. Liver and kidney problems may also result from blood clogging in the vessels. Arthritis may also occur.

(Continued)

TABLE 13.2 | COMMONLY USED RECREATIONAL DRUGS AND THEIR EFFECTS *Continued*

	Street Name	Use	Effects	Health Risks
Rohypnol	Roofies, rophies, forget-me pill	It is very difficult to track the useage of club drugs like rohypnol. The drug has been found in every major metropolitan area.	The use of rohypnol can result in anteretrograde amnesia. This effect has led some men to use the drug on unsuspecting women in order to rape them.	Users of the drug say it is similar to a feeling of intoxication, but there is no hangover effect.
Gamma Hydroxybu-trate (GHB) Chemicals commonly used as degreasers or floor strippers	Liquid ecstasy, soap, easy, liquid X, goop	There were 60 reported deaths from GHB between 1998 and 2001.	GHB generates feelings of euphoria and intoxication. It is often used to counter the effects of the stimulant MDMA. It can cause drowsiness, dizziness, and visual disturbances. It is considered a date rape drug because it has been used to render rape victims incapable of resisting and the victim may not be able to remember the rape clearly. The drug is easily masked when poured in a drink.	Use can result in unconsciousness, seizures, severe respiratory depression, and coma.
Ketamine Marketed as a general anesthetic for human and veterinary use	K, cat, valiums, vitamin K	Reports of the drug being stolen from veterinary clinics increased substantially in the early 2000s.	The effects are similar to PCP or LSD. Low doses produce an experience referred to as K-land, a mellow and wonderful world. Higher doses have the effect of an out-of-body or near-death experience.	The use of K can cause depression, delirium, amnesia, and fatal respiratory problems.
Benzodiazepine E.g., xanax, valium, klonopin	Downers, Roofies, tranks	Benzodiazepines are the most commonly prescribed group of drugs in the United States. 13% of the U.S. population have been on a benzodiazepine at some time in their	These drugs are prescribed for their ability to reduce anxiety and induce sleep. They can cause loss of coordination, disorientation, and slurred speech.	An overdose may result in a loss of concentration, unconsciousness, or death.

		life. 90% of the people who take the drug do so for 2 to 4 weeks. However, 30% of the people who take the drug for longer than six months become addicted.	
Depressants/ Inhalants Paint solvents, glues, motor fuels, cleaning agents, aerosol sprays, anesthetic gases	Poppers, zoom, rush, bolt, Whippets	After alcohol and tobacco, inhalants are the most commonly used drug by adolescents.	Inhalants, like alcohol are central nervous system depressants and induce relaxation, lightheadedness, giddiness, and reduced inhibitions. High doses can cause the user to lose consciousness and lapse into a coma. Suffocation can occur from inhaling vapors in plastic bags. Long-term use can cause the break down of myelin, the protective covering around brain cells. If myelin breaks down, the nerve cells may not be able to transmit messages. Paralysis or chronic pain may result.
Depressants/ Barbiturates Amytal, Butisol, Nembutal, Luminal, Seconal	Barbs, downers, goofballs, ludes, sleeping pills	Barbiturates are commonly and heavily used by heroin addicts. 3% of high school students report using prescribed barbiturates.	Induce feelings of relaxation, peacefulness, sleepiness, pleasurable intoxication, dizziness, inactivity, and withdrawal. Also interrupt thought processes and cause mood swings, hostility, depression, and anxiety. Long-term use causes depression of respiratory system and control centers of the brain. Barbiturates have the most life-threatening complications; e.g., death can come from stopped breathing. Reduce sex drive. There are severe withdrawal symptoms.

Sources: NHSDA, 2005; PRIDE Surveys 2008; Abbott, 2000; Benshoff & Janikowski, 2000.

They speed up the messages going to and from the brain and the body. Both stimulants and amphetamines are associated with euphoric feelings. They can be sniffed, snorted, smoked, injected, or swallowed.

Hallucinogens distort visual and sensory perception, often creating prolonged episodes of emotionality that can resemble psychotic states. **Psychoactive drugs,** or mood-altering drugs, are hallucinogens that alter sensory perceptions, mood, thought processes, or behavior by acting on the nervous system, especially the central nervous system (Gray, 1995). Examples of psychoactive drugs are LSD and PCP. Hallucinogens and psychoactive drugs can be taken in the form of eye drops, smoked, swallowed, licked off paper, chewed, or inhaled.

Depressants are drugs that cause disinhibition, reduce anxiety, and depress the central nervous system. Depressants include **inhalants** and **barbiturates.** Depressants can be swallowed, inhaled, or injected. Cheese is a depressant that first emerged in 2005. Cheese is a combination of heroin (2 to 8 percent) and over the counter crushed tablets of cold medicines like Tylenol pm or Benadryll. Finally, **club drugs** are illegal drugs used by young adults at all-night dance parties such as raves or trances and in dance clubs or bars. They are primarily synthetic and include MDMA, Ketamine, GHB, Rohypnol, LSD, and PCP. For the last decade, crystal meth, known as crank, crissy, champagne, and other slang names on the street, has decimated communities in the Midwest and on the West Coast.

DEPENDENCE AND ADDICTION

Variations in the effects of the drugs described in Table 13.2 can be explained by physiological, psychological, and social factors, including body weight, gender, age, ethnicity, genetics, and emotional and physical health (Lewis, Dana, & Blevins, 1994). For example, about 50 percent of people of Asian descent carry a gene that leads to an unusual increase in heart rate, facial flushing, sweating, and nausea when they consume alcohol (Ray & Kasir, 1999). These symptoms are not as prevalent or as intense in other ethnic groups. Women tend to develop higher blood alcohol levels than men who drink the same amount because women have a lower percentage of body water and a higher percentage of body fat, which causes alcohol to be metabolized faster. As a result, women have more AOD health-related problems and deaths (National Center for Health Statistics, 2008).

The variability of drug effects may leave some individuals more vulnerable to developing an addiction to or a **dependence** on a substance than others, and some may be able to use the same substance with no problematic effects. Dependence can be psychological or physical. In psychological dependence the habit of using drugs or alcohol is motivated by emotional reasons, whereas in physical dependence the body needs the drug to function normally. If the drug is withdrawn, the physically addicted person will experience physical symptoms or illness (Fisher & Harrison, 2000).

Not all people who use drugs will develop dependence or addiction. The criteria for determining whether an individual has developed dependence on or is abusing drugs are outlined in More About … Drug Dependence. These criteria were developed by the American Psychiatric Association (1999) in its *Diagnostic and Statistical Manual of Mental Disorders* (DSM-IV-TR), which was discussed in Chapter 10.

SUGAR AND CAFFEINE ADDICTION

In addition to the drugs described above, a case can be made that Americans also struggle with what might be termed addictions to sugar and caffeine. The average American consumes 32 teaspoons of sugar a day, or 12 pounds a month (Jones, 2008). Researchers do not all agree on whether sugar is addictive; however, several recent studies have produced evidence of sugar addiction (Avena, Rada, & Hoebel, 2008). At a minimum, everyone can agree that many people crave sugar.

Whereas refined sugar is a chemical and has a biochemical makeup very similar to alcohol, sugar addiction is defined as eating a large amount of high-sugar foods each day and feeling tired or irritable after going without a hit for a few hours. The addiction or craving occurs because the body becomes used to the energy rush and the brain becomes hooked on the releases of opioids and dopamine.

Withdrawal from white sugar can include tremors, flu like symptoms, headaches, and intense mood swings. The health consequences can be very severe and may include: depression, mood swings, irritability, depletion of mineral levels, hyperactivity, anxiety, panic attacks, chromium deficiency, depletion of the adrenal glands, type II diabetes, hypoglycemia, candida overgrowth, and raised levels of cholesterol.

Approximately 87 percent of adults and 76 percent of children regularly consume caffeine in their diets. Most researchers agree that regular caffeine use triggers a physical dependence or a mild form of addiction (Reid, 2005). Heavy caffeine users who go for a few hours without it may grow irritable, get headaches, or feel lethargic. In a University of Toronto study, researchers stopped short of using the term *caffeine addiction* but reported that men who possess certain dopamine-receptor genes experience an elevated mood after consuming a caffeinated beverage.

BOX 13.2 | **MORE ABOUT ... DRUG DEPENDENCE**
DSM-IV-TR CRITERIA FOR DEPENDENCE

Within a twelve-month period, the client must have manifested three or more of the following.

1. **Tolerance** is the process by which receptors in the brain become habituated to the use of a particular drug. When tolerance is reached, more of the drug is required to achieve the same effect. **Withdrawal** occurs either through the development of tolerance without an increase in dosage or through a decrease in dosage below the "tolerance point."
2. The client is taking the substance in larger amounts or over a longer period than was intended.
3. The client's efforts to cut down or control use are unsuccessful.
4. The client spends a great deal of time trying to obtain the substance, use the substance, or get over the effects of the substance.
5. Important social, occupational, or recreational activities are given up or reduced because of the substance use.
6. The client continues use despite knowledge of the negative effects; for example, the client continues to use cocaine despite recognition of cocaine-induced depression.

Source: American Psychiatric Association, 2000, p. 199

The men continued to seek out caffeine in order to feel a sense of elation. The same genetic link has not yet been found in women (*National Edition*, 2007).

CAUSES OF DEPENDENCE AND ADDICTION

The social work profession has rejected the moral failing explanation for Terry's behavior. Although most social workers have cautiously embraced the disease model, others reject it because it is not consistent with social work's strengths perspective. Even some social workers in settings that accept the medical explanation of alcoholism view the disease model as only one part of the equation because of its emphasis on pathology. From a biopsychosocial, or person-in-environment, approach, the etiology (origin) of alcoholism or addiction includes environmental, social, psychological, and genetic variables.

The fact that 30 percent of children with alcoholic parents develop alcoholism themselves, while only 10 percent of children with nonalcoholic parents develop alcoholism, suggests that both environmental and genetic variables are in play (Zucker, 2006). For example, children from disengaged, rigid families who repress emotions and have a lot of conflict and children from rigid, moralistic families are more likely to have AOD problems as adolescents. Without treatment, they continue to have AOD problems as adults (Tolan, Szapocznik, & Sambrano, 2007).

Many human service workers argue that AOD problems are secondary symptoms of emotional pain or mental health problems, rather than a primary disease (Erhmin, 2002; Hopwood, Baker, & Morey, 2008). For example, in a recent study 69 percent of the women who reported substance abuse also reported exposure to childhood physical, sexual, or emotional abuse; the majority reported multiple forms of abuse (Sacks, McKendricks, & Banks, 2008). The findings suggest the importance of adapting models of residential substance abuse treatment to address concurrent issues related to trauma history. Perhaps these women self-medicate with alcohol or other drugs to deal with clinical depression or suppress emotional pain. Some people may use alcohol and other drugs to help control anxiety. Addicts may use them to cope with (or avoid coping with) unemployment, legal conflicts, mental health problems such as bipolar disorder, or family problems. This theory of addiction is not accepted by groups like Alcoholics Anonymous (AA).

The way the problem is defined and assessed is critical because problem definition determines the type of intervention that will be used. For example, if AOD is defined as a moral failing, the intervention might be spiritual or moral counsel. If the problem is defined as a disease, the intervention will be geared toward legitimate medical treatment and the goal of abstinence. If the problem is defined as an adaptive response to a difficult situation, the goal of treatment will be to help the addict unlearn the adaptive response and replace it with a more functional response (Wood & Dunn, 2000).

People with AOD problems come from every socioeconomic category and every racial and ethnic background. They have varying degrees of dependence and respond differently to various types of treatment. Alcoholics Anonymous relies heavily on the disease model, in which blame is placed on the physiological incapacity to control alcohol consumption. This model seems to work well for people who have a severe dependence on alcohol, but it is not as effective with the largest group of alcohol abusers—those who do not progress to severe dependence (Connors, Walitzer, & Dermen, 2002).

The person-in-environment, or biopsychosocial, framework is the foundation on which social workers base successful diagnosis, assessment, and treatment of AOD problems. Social workers using this model evaluate each individual on the basis of his or her unique circumstances. According to this approach, the reasons for addiction may include biological (e.g., dependence, physical illness), psychological (e.g., depression, anxiety), and social (e.g., family, employment, community) factors (Burman, 2000). The biopsychosocial framework explains why people respond differently to treatment and helps identify the treatment interventions that might work best for a particular client.

To successfully use the biopsychosocial approach, social workers must be knowledgeable in several areas. These include social learning theory; various cognitive and behavioral treatment approaches; co-occurring mental health problems, including depression, bipolar disorder, and psychosis; cultural and economic factors; pharmacology and the use of medications such as methadone and naltrexone opiate to treat AOD problems; and fetal alcohol syndrome. **Fetal alcohol syndrome (FAS)** is a pattern of mental and physical defects that develops in some fetuses when the mother drinks too much alcohol during pregnancy. The alcohol circulates through the pregnant woman's bloodstream and crosses the placenta to the fetus. The alcohol interferes with the ability of the fetus to receive sufficient oxygen and nourishment. It is estimated that FAS is involved in 33 of every 1,000 live births (Floyd, O'Connor, Bertrand, & Sokol, 2006). A baby born with FAS may be seriously handicapped and require a lifetime of special care.

SUBSTANCE ABUSE TREATMENT AND PREVENTION

Social workers have often been at the forefront of substance abuse treatment and prevention efforts. However, until recently they were more likely to have used a medical or disease model to plan intervention and prevention programs. This section reviews the disease model and shows how social workers have slowly begun to move away from it in favor of the strengths model.

HISTORICAL BACKGROUND

Benshoff and Janikowski (2000) summarized the main developments in the history of drug and alcohol use, abuse, dependency, and treatment in the United States. Alcohol use did not become a social issue until the early nineteenth century. During the 1830s and 1840s, religious groups began to express opposition to alcoholic inebriation. Their efforts became known as the temperance movement. Proponents of the temperance movement developed and promoted the moral model of addiction, the belief that drunkenness was a sinful behavior and a moral failing. Public and private inebriate asylums were started, and a variety of cures for alcoholism were explored. In the 1870s doctors first suggested that alcoholism might be inherited or caused by developmental and environmental factors.

During the late 1800s the temperance movement began to give way to the prohibitionist movement, the focus of which was to criminalize drug taking. Cocaine and opium were legal and were used for medicinal purposes, but there was a growing awareness of the potential for abuse. In 1906 the Pure Food and Drug Act established the Food and Drug Administration, and all drugs were required to carry labels listing ingredients, including opium or cocaine.

In 1919 the prohibitionists claimed victory with the passage of the Eighteenth Amendment (also called the Volstead Act), which banned the manufacture and sale of beverages containing alcohol. As a result of the criminalization of alcohol distribution and use, many hospitals that attempted to treat alcohol-related problems closed. Despite the ban, many people consumed home-brewed or illegally obtained alcoholic beverages, got drunk, had accidents, and died. Criminal elements illegally imported and sold hard liquor. Marijuana was also popularized and was not made illegal until 1937. In 1933 the Twenty-first Amendment repealed the Eighteenth Amendment and ended prohibition.

In 1935 Alcoholics Anonymous was founded, and new research began on alcohol- and drug-related problems. In 1947 Jellinek published the seminal article on alcoholism viewed as a disease. However, it was not until 1956 that the AMA declared alcoholism a disease.

During the 1960s marijuana reemerged as a recreational drug, and the so-called drug culture began. Although LSD was not as widely used as marijuana, many experimented with it, and the word *psychedelic* was created to describe its effects. Heroin was the opiate of choice during the 1960s. The Community Mental Health Center Act, passed in 1963, funded some of the first AOD-dependent treatment programs.

The Comprehensive Alcohol Abuse and Alcoholism Prevention, Treatment and Rehabilitation Act of 1970 created the National Institute of Alcoholism and Alcohol Abuse, which funds research, prevention, and treatment efforts. The Comprehensive Drug Abuse Prevention and Control Act of 1971 (CDAPC) expanded funding for drug-treatment services in public hospitals and community mental health centers, established the Commission on Marijuana and Drug Abuse to study the effects of drugs besides alcohol, and created the drug schedule (see Table 13.1) that is still used today. The National Institute on Drug Abuse (NIDA) was also created through federal legislation in 1971. NIDA researchers have become important advisers to presidents. Methadone was a successful treatment tool for heroin addiction, but there was concern that it would become a street drug if not tightly controlled. The Methadone Control Act of 1972 established the controls. In 1973 the Alcohol Drug Abuse and Mental Health Administration (ADAMHA) was created under the auspices of the Department of Health, Education and Welfare. By 1974 there were over 900 federally funded drug programs.

Alcohol consumption reached an all-time high during the 1980s, and several grassroots movements were initiated to address the problem. One of them was Mothers Against Drunk Drivers (MADD), which supported stiffer drunk-driving penalties. Parent Resources Institute on Drug Education (PRIDE) addressed the emerging adolescent drug problem. In 1986 the Partnership for a Drug-Free America launched a comprehensive media campaign against alcohol and drug use. The demand for substance abuse treatment programs far exceeded the supply, and the private sector responded with a proliferation of grant-funded private nonprofit and, later, for-profit treatment centers. Employers were losing billions of dollars a year in productivity due to drug- and alcohol-related absenteeism, injuries, and death, and employee assistance programs (EAPs) began to provide substance abuse services (see Chapter 12).

In 1990 the Americans with Disabilities Act formally recognized substance abuse and dependence as a disability (with some restrictions). In 1992 the ADAMHA was reorganized as part of the Substance Abuse and Mental Health Services Administration (SAMHSA) in the Department of Health and Human Services.

CURRENT CONTEXT

Today, with over 11,000 specialized drug treatment facilities and programs in the United States, there is still a shortage. In some metropolitan areas people seeking AOD treatment can wait up to six months, especially for treatment of addiction to heroin and other hard drugs.

Treatment programs are funded by local, state, and federal governments as well as by private insurance plans. A program is likely to have an interdisciplinary staff that includes social workers, certified substance abuse counselors, psychiatrists, psychologists, physicians, nurses, and peer counselors, among others, many of whom are recovering addicts. Drug treatment services provided by social workers include prevention, rehabilitation, individual and group therapy, behavioral therapy, medication management assistance, and case management. Substance abuse treatment settings that employ social workers include detoxification units, inpatient or residential facilities, and outpatient settings in hospitals, prisons and juvenile justice agencies, schools, courts, welfare agencies, psychiatric facilities, and vocational rehabilitation centers.

The decision about where to place a client for treatment is most often determined by the client's insurance coverage and the availability of treatment programs rather than the client's medical condition, motivation, ability to discontinue use, past treatment history, and social support network (Benshoff & Janikowski, 2000). Many managed care organizations have eliminated or placed a cap on treatment for AOD problems. Social workers need to advocate for parity in health, mental health, and substance abuse coverage. Until parity is obtained, social workers should question the diagnosis and assessment protocol of clients' managed care organizations and advocate for appropriate placement and treatment.

A public policy statement by the National Association of Social Workers (1997) affirmed that abuse of alcohol; tobacco; and illicit, over-the-counter, and prescription drugs is a significant health problem and that the profession should focus on prevention efforts in addition to treatment. The NASW statement also indicated that social, economic, and environmental factors contribute to substance abuse problems and that social workers should therefore initiate interventions that include strengthening communities and individuals through empowerment and economic development, as well as engage in group, family, and individual treatment.

Additionally, it should be noted that AOD issues commonly occur in combination with other mental health challenges. Comorbidity between drug addiction and mental illness, also referred to as co-occurring disorders or dual diagnosis, is very common. For example, adolescents with substance use disorders have higher rates of depression (15 to 24 percent) than adolescents in the general population (Riggs, 2007); and 50 to 70 percent of psychiatric inpatients with bipolar disorder also have a substance use disorder. Addicts with a dual diagnosis are often successfully treated with behavioral interventions and medications, which may include antianxiety drugs, mood stabilizers, or antidepressants. Co-occurring disorders are discussed in greater detail in Chapter 10.

THE ROLE OF THE SOCIAL WORKER

AOD treatment interventions are individualized and have traditionally addressed the client's associated medical, psychological, social, vocational, and legal problems. This is due in part to the prevailing use of the medical model. However, the strengths perspective, which has only recently and often reluctantly been applied to clients with substance abuse issues, requires social workers to deemphasize problem areas and emphasize client strengths (Gruenert, Ratnam, & Tsantefski, 2006; Rapp et al., 2008). For example, if a client has had long periods of abstinence, the social worker should help the client determine what skills, strategies, resources, and assets served him or her and how they can again be invoked.

Denial occurs when the client does not recognize or admit that there is a connection between his or her life problems and the abuse of alcohol or another substance. Therefore, a significant part of treatment is dedicated to helping clients confront the problem and break through denial. Social workers who use the strengths perspective or solution-focused approach have suggested that the assumption that the client will be in denial and resistant to treatment may have adverse effects. The strong expectation that the client must break through denial could dominate the social worker's interactions with a drug abuser, making the intervention less sensitive to the client's actual situation and needs.

The social worker often acts as a case manager, networking with and monitoring family services, vocational services, mental health services, child-care services, medical and pharmacotherapy services, legal services, and behavioral therapy and counseling services. The strengths perspective requires the case management process to be driven by client-identified goals. Clients should be asked what they need and want to accomplish in terms of life skills, finance, leisure, relationships, living arrangements, occupation, education, health, internal resources, and recovery. The answers may be general, such as improving opportunities. The social worker must help the client break the general goal into specific objectives, for example, visit a local employment office to check out available opportunities (Rapp et al., 2008). The social worker may also be the actual provider of the clinical or counseling services.

Drug treatment interventions can reduce drug use by 40 to 60 percent, a success rate as high as treatment for chronic diseases like diabetes and hypertension (Fisher & Harrison, 2000). Treatment programs are also cost effective. For every dollar invested in treatment, the government saves four to seven dollars in drug-related health costs, crime, and criminal justice costs (NIDA, 2000).

The stages of treatment include stabilization, rehabilitation, and maintenance. During stabilization, the client often needs to be forcefully confronted about the addiction and the need for treatment. In the Johnson model of intervention, family and friends, with the help of a trained facilitator, confront the addict about the negative personal and financial consequences of his or her behavior (Fisher & Harrison, 2000). The stabilization period includes detoxification and abstinence from drugs and alcohol, acceptance of the problem, and a commitment to permanently overcome the addiction.

The rehabilitation phase involves intense therapeutic services. Stabilization and rehabilitation generally take at least three months and include both inpatient and outpatient services. Cognitive behavioral therapy has proven to be effective in the rehabilitation stage. The client learns to identify maladaptive behavior and thought patterns and to replace those patterns and behaviors with more positive thoughts and actions. Clients are taught to self-monitor in order to recognize drug cravings early and develop coping strategies (Carroll, Rounsaville, & Keller, 1991). During the maintenance stage, the priority is to engage the client in therapy and skill building focused on relapse prevention (NIDA, 2000). Other interventions utilized during the rehabilitation and maintenance phases include self-help groups such as Alcoholics Anonymous, aversion therapy, social skills training, and therapeutic community programs (Burnam, 2000).

In addition to providing treatment interventions, social workers should also be on the forefront of substance abuse prevention programs. Several studies sponsored have supported the hypothesis that prevention programs reduce substance abuse (Burrow-Sanchez & Hawken, 2007; Center for Substance Abuse Prevention, 2000). Evidence-based practice indicates that there are four important protective factors that need to be addressed in early intervention prevention programs: 1) parental investment in the child-adolescent, 2) child-adolescent social competence, 3) child-adolescent self-regulation, and 4) child-adolescent school bonding and academic achievement (Tolan et al., 2008).

Social workers have a responsibility to advocate for more funding for prevention and treatment programs and to evaluate prevention programs in order to demonstrate their effectiveness. The war on drugs will not be won by trying to prevent illegal drugs from entering the country or by putting drug users in jail. It can be won through prevention and treatment programs that effectively address the underlying reasons that lead people to abuse drugs (see "From the Field ... The Case of Twyla").

DIVERSITY ISSUES AND POPULATIONS AT RISK

The prevalence of substance abuse issues among nondominant groups and populations at risk may be explained in part by such societal factors as social isolation, institutional racism, and poverty. This section discusses substance abuse issues relevant to various nondominant groups and populations at risk. For example, alcohol abuse by older adults is difficult to detect because of their isolation and is believed to be symptomatic of other chronic and mental health conditions. Alcoholism is more prevalent among older African Americans, Latino men, and men in general. There is little research available on the effectiveness of substance abuse interventions among the elderly.

WOMEN

CASE EXAMPLE: Tina was 34 when she was murdered in Omaha in September 2000. She was a crack addict and worked as a prostitute to support her drug addiction. There were many points in Tina's life where early intervention might have helped. She was five when her parents divorced and she began to shuttle between her father's house and her grandmother's house. As a teenager she was often in trouble at school and with the law. She fell in with the wrong crowd, began staying out past her curfew, and ran away several times before she reached 16. By the time she was 18, she had spent time in adult prison. In her early 20s she became consumed by her crack addiction. Tina is buried in an unmarked grave (Spencer, 2000).

BOX 13.3	FROM THE FIELD ... THE CASE OF TWYLA
	Paul Rock Krech, MSW, CISW, CSAC

There are times in working with a chemically dependent client that we must call on nearly all of our resources and skills as social workers. The case of Twyla illustrates the varying levels of social work interventions necessary to bring about a positive outcome.

Twyla was a 38-year-old indigenous homemaker who had four school-aged children and a common-law husband of two years living with her. Her common-law husband was nearly 12 years her junior and was the family's breadwinner. Twyla came to our agency seeking help in attending a program for detoxification and treatment of substance dependence. She had become physically dependent on a prescription narcotic painkiller following a workplace injury 18 months earlier. She had built a massive tolerance to the drug and was taking nearly twenty 325-milligram tablets daily "just to feel normal" and avoid the pain of withdrawal. In order to maintain her dosage, she was "playing" ten physicians to get them to write prescriptions. She said, "I am just tired of all the lying, games, and feeling sick all of the time. I really want to be a better mother to my children."

About three years earlier, Twyla had been diagnosed with panic disorder, major depression, and post-traumatic stress disorder, and she took a physically addictive prescription medication to treat her anxiety. Her marriage to the children's father had involved escalating and unspeakable physical and emotional abuse. She had escaped the marriage, and her estranged husband had since abandoned the family and moved back to Mexico.

The agency was able to help Twyla obtain placement in a 30-day residential rehabilitation facility where she would be medically supervised during withdrawal from the narcotic drug. She would eventually undergo group and individual therapy, drug and alcohol education, and family therapy. Twyla expressed concern that other people might label her a common drug addict.

Part of the initial therapeutic approach was to gently remind Twyla that although her addiction was not the result of recreational drug use, it was nonetheless an important medical problem. The route to becoming addicted matters little, and the path to recovery is often difficult, involving false starts, slips, and possibly disillusionment.

Twyla's family spent the final week of treatment with her, receiving education and support from the professional staff at the facility. She was surprised that her children knew more about her condition than she had realized. She was also relieved that her entire family was supportive of her recovery process.

Twyla remained engaged in outpatient aftercare group therapy for nearly a year after completing the rehabilitation program. She became stabilized on medication and maintained medication checks with a psychiatrist. She was also referred to a therapist to help her work through some of the fear, resentment, and self-doubt brought about by years of spousal abuse and a genetic predisposition to mental illness.

Today, Twyla is happily married and attending community college full time. She hopes to become an elementary school teacher. She still has panic attacks some mornings, and she continues to feel the effects of depression, but she now has tools to help her cope. She volunteers at the agency as a peer supporter and sees herself as an important community member in the recovery effort.

Alcohol and drug addiction can destroy the lives of women. Twelve to 15 percent of women are heavy drinkers, and women are the largest group to abuse benzodiazepines or tranquilizers. Traditionally, women have been doubly stigmatized by AOD problems (Benshoff & Janikowski, 2000). Women with substance abuse problems are often viewed as promiscuous or as unfit mothers. In ancient Rome, women who were caught drinking wine were put to death (Abadinsky, 1997).

CASE EXAMPLE: Caroline Knapp worked as a newspaper columnist. She came from an upper-class Boston family of alcoholics, and she was herself a recovering alcoholic. "I loved the rituals, the camaraderie of drinking with others, the warming, melting feeling of ease and courage it gave me." But she dreaded the thought of anyone seeing her with a hangover. "It's such an instinctual and deeply rooted thing for women to maintain the appearance that they are doing well.... The more successful women are the more difficult it is to seek treatment" (Knapp, 1997).

Because of the stigma, women are less likely than men to seek treatment. In particular, women from the middle and upper socioeconomic classes like Caroline Knapp are less likely to be referred to treatment because their addictions occur largely in the privacy of their own homes (NIH, 2008).

There is a strong correlation between sexual or domestic violence and substance abuse in women. This correlation seems to indicate that women have more of a problem with shame than with guilt, which is the focus of many male-driven rehabilitation programs. Most rehabilitation programs do not emphasize women's developmental needs and the importance of healthy relationships in their lives (Burman, 2000). Bassuk, Dawson, and Huntington (2006) contend that the absence of these relationships often results in low self-esteem and feelings of powerlessness that can contribute to serious AOD problems. Also, programs often do not accommodate a woman's need to arrange for child care before entering treatment. Some of these issues are being addressed in newer treatment programs that emphasize women's development and empowerment through positive and mutually enhancing relationships (Rabinovitch & Strega, (2004).

AFRICAN AMERICANS

Alcohol abuse rates among African Americans and whites are approximately the same. However, research indicates that African American males have suffered more severe health consequences and a higher mortality rate from AOD-related problems than whites and African American women (Gil, Wagner, & Tubman, 2004). Patterns of alcohol use within the African American community also differ from patterns within the white community. The majority of the African American population abstains from alcohol, and heavy drinking occurs among a small subgroup. The extent of drug use in the African American community is difficult to gauge. Most data about the use of illegal drugs come from national surveys in which African Americans have been underrepresented (Gray, 2001). Available research suggests that marijuana is the most commonly used drug and that rates of cocaine and heroine use within the African American community are higher than rates among whites.

Like women, African Americans have been doubly stigmatized by AOD-related problems. In colonial America, anyone caught selling or giving alcohol to a Negro had to pay a heavy fine. There was fear that intoxicated slaves would foment rebellion (Fisher & Harrison, 2000). African Americans themselves viewed alcohol consumption as equivalent to promoting slavery. In the early twentieth century, African Americans who used alcohol were perceived as sexual predators (Wallace et al., 1999).

Racism explains these stereotypes. Racism also contributes to the fact that African Americans are six more times likely than whites to be arrested for AOD-related crimes. Inner-city areas are often targeted by the police, and offenses involving crack cocaine, which is more likely to be used in inner-city poverty areas among people of color, carry stiffer penalties than offenses involving powder cocaine, which is more likely to be used by wealthier, usually white, individuals (Gil et al., 2004). The African American community has been particularly hard hit by the federal government's war on drugs.

Robbins (2008) found that substance abuse in the African American population was related to economic deprivation, racism, and stress. High rates of poverty and the experience of racism cause added stress and pain in the lives of many African Americans. Additionally, many African Americans struggle to maintain their cultural identity and at the same time respond to the expectations of the dominant culture. Alcohol and drugs serve to medicate the emotional pain. Easy access to alcohol and drugs has also been a reason for AOD use. In high-poverty areas in which many African Americans live, liquor stores are often the most common businesses, and selling drugs is one of few income-producing activities.

Prevention programs that have been particularly effective among African American youth are based on the values of the traditional African American community, which emphasize extended community involvement and spirituality. To be effective, treatment programs must account for historical, social, and economic disparities when developing assessment and treatment protocols. They must also consider ways to involve kin, as well as members of the person's church (Burman, 2000). Social workers must advocate for more culturally appropriate treatment programs in African American communities because access to treatment has been inequitable (Robbins, 2008).

LATINO POPULATIONS

Research suggests that Latino adolescents have an early onset of AOD use, in particular the use of low-cost inhalants (Benshoff & Janikowski, 2000). Several factors account for the early drug use in this population, including acculturative stress, language barriers, and poverty. Poverty contributes to low self-esteem, gang involvement, and higher than average teen pregnancy, substance abuse, and dropout rates (Gil et al., 2004).

Latino men who have left their families behind when they legally or illegally immigrated to the United States constitute another high-risk group. Forced separation from family results in a higher risk of intravenous drug abuse and unsafe sex practices, both of which can result in contraction of HIV/AIDS. This may be one reason why Latino men are overrepresented in the HIV/AIDS population (Benshoff & Janikowski, 2000).

Drinking and driving is a serious problem among males in the Mexican American or Chicano community. When compared with Puerto Ricans, Cubans, and whites, Mexican Americans are more likely to be arrested for driving while intoxicated and they are more likely to die in car accidents while intoxicated (65 percent compared to 46 percent among whites). Mexican American men tend to overestimate the number of drinks it takes to become an unsafe driver. In one survey, Mexican American men estimated that it takes an average of eight to ten drinks to impair driving ability. The average answer among white men was four to five. The average male who weighs 170 pounds can only have about four drinks and still be considered sober enough to drive (Worby & Organisat, 2007). The machismo tradition, which emphasizes honor, dependability, and responsibility, can be used to encourage responsible drinking (Benshoff & Janikowski, 2000).

Latino populations are heterogeneous. However, family is important to all groups. Therefore, interventions designed for use with Latinos should allow clients to remain fully involved and engaged with their families whenever appropriate. Religion should also be incorporated in treatment. Many prevention and intervention programs in Latino communities are sponsored by the Catholic Church or other religious organizations. For example, the Teen Institute in New Orleans is designed to empower Latino high school students to embrace a lifestyle free of drugs, tobacco, and alcohol. The program includes workshops on conflict resolution and drug pharmacology, and information about the consequences of drug and alcohol use (Gershanik, 2000). For Latino men who are isolated from their families, group interventions tend to be successful because they allow the men to establish contacts, develop mutual support relationships, and receive validation of their experiences (Lyter & Lyter, 2000). Natural support networks among family and friends in Latino communities, often referred to as *personalismo,* are very common. Mutual-aid groups designed to support isolated Latino men who have AOD-related problems would be viewed as a natural way to build *personalismo.* Outreach is another essential component for this community, especially because of cultural isolation and language barriers.

INDIGENOUS PEOPLE

CASE EXAMPLE: In September 2000 the Yakama Nation in central Washington adopted a comprehensive alcohol ban. As far back as 1982, tribal leaders became concerned about the alarmingly high rate of fetal alcohol syndrome on the reservation. Other indigenous communities have had alcohol bans in place for several years (Murphy, 2000).

CASE EXAMPLE: In November 2000 Nathan Phillips, who is a member of Nebraska's Omaha tribe, set up three tepees on the National Mall in Washington, D.C. Accompanied by his partner and their two children, he held a month-long prayer vigil to raise awareness of centuries-long religious, economic, and cultural oppression. Mr. Phillips spent his childhood in and out of foster homes, and although he has been sober for sixteen years, he battled alcoholism for many years (Murphy, 2000).

Alcoholism rates in First Nation communities are higher than those in the general population. In fact, many of the leading causes of death among Indigenous Peoples, including liver disease, diabetes, hypertension, and auto accidents, are complicated by or attributable to AOD-related problems (Benshoff & Janikowski, 2000). As with other populations of color, racism and other historical, economic, and cultural factors help explain the AOD problems experienced by indigenous communities. The Bureau of Indian Affairs (BIA) acknowledged that high rates of alcoholism, suicide, and violence in indigenous communities stem from a legacy of racism and inhumanity toward First Nation peoples (Jackson, 2000).

The stereotype of the drunken Indian and the myths associated with it are powerful in indigenous communities and the general American society. One myth that has been internalized by Indigenous Peoples is that they have a genetic predisposition or physiological weakness toward alcohol and alcoholism. Research suggests that this is not the case (Sage & Burns, 1993).

Patterns of alcohol use in Indigenous communities are similar to patterns in the general population. The primary problem is with AOD-abusing clusters of young people who do not do well in school, do not strongly identify with either their indigenous culture or Western culture, and come from families who abuse alcohol, similarly to other groups. However, the disproportionate number of young indigenous males who meet these criteria is explained by the higher rates of poverty and joblessness in native communities (Benshoff & Janikowski, 2000). AOD-related problems also seem disproportionately high among unmarried, isolated individuals who drink alone. This is also similar to the pattern in the general population.

First-Nations people have a long tradition of noninterference in individuals' life choices. This tradition may partly explain why some tribal elders, many of whom abstain from alcohol use, have sometimes been reluctant to interfere in the alcohol abuse of other people (Benshoff & Janikowski, 2000). Because of the heterogeneity among indigenous tribal peoples, it is difficult to generalize about specific interventions for AOD-related problems. Any intervention in an indigenous community should take cultural and spiritual traditions and tribal languages into consideration. Indigenous youth who identify with their culture are less likely to use alcohol. Successful prevention and intervention efforts have incorporated cultural components, including the display of indigenous handicrafts and artifacts, practices such as sweats or praying with a sacred pipe, and the participation of traditional healers (Moran & May, 1997).

THE LGBT COMMUNITY

The extent of AOD problems in the LGBT community is difficult to determine. Research on alcohol and drug use among members of this community is particularly challenging because many people are not comfortable admitting their sexual orientation, nor are they willing to admit abuse of alcohol and/or drugs. Obtaining accurate information from two hidden populations is difficult. However, various research studies suggest that rates of AOD problems within the LGBT community range from 20 to 25 percent, compared to 3 to 10 percent of the heterosexual population (Weber, 2008).

There are a number of possible explanations for the higher rates of alcohol and drug use in the LGBT community. It is difficult to live in a homophobic society that condemns and rejects lesbians, bisexuals, gay men, and transgendered people without taking on some degree of self-hatred or **internalized homophobia**, including feelings of shame. Shame has been found to be closely related to AOD abuse (Holmes & Hodge, 1997). Those LGBT individuals who do not disclose their sexual orientation to family, friends, or coworkers often experience intense feelings of depression, anxiety, low self-esteem, and even suicidal despair. Without alternative coping skills, drugs and alcohol can be very tempting.

Gay and lesbian bars have been the central meeting places in many LGBT communities, largely because there are few other places members of the community can congregate without the fear of rejection, ridicule, or violence. Members of other oppressed groups, such as people of color, have historically been able to find safe havens within their communities and families of origin, but for LGBT people, the family of origin may not be a safe haven from bias. Bars have also been the sites of fundraising activities and political work. Spending a great deal of time in bars increases access to alcohol and social pressure to drink. Research suggests that it also increases the pressure to use other drugs (Halkitis, Palamar, & Mukherjee, 2007).

Awareness of the role of bar culture is essential for AOD prevention and intervention. Within the heterosexual community, people undergoing treatment for AOD abuse are usually encouraged to stay away from bars and other settings that encourage drug and alcohol consumption. If the bar is the only social outlet for the LGBT community in a town, encouraging them to stay out of it is essentially telling them to have no social connection. This may be unrealistic. Lesbian and gay bars can be used as sites to recruit participants and conduct programs to reduce internalized homophobia, increase social support, and improve self-esteem.

Many LGBT people may be reluctant to enter treatment because few programs are sensitive to their issues. Members of the LGBT community have reported overt homophobia from service providers and other program participants. For programs to be effective, service providers must be truly accepting of their LGBT clients. Awareness and sensitivity training can help achieve that goal. Specialized programs that offer members of this population a safe space to explore difficult issues have been developed in many communities, and more are needed.

SOCIAL WORK VALUES AND ETHICS

In addition to monitoring their own behavior as direct practitioners, the broad social work focus requires social workers to work toward the passage of ethical policies and to encourage agency administrators to act ethically. As in other types of ethical decision making, there is not necessarily one "right" answer to ethical dilemmas, but the social work Code of Ethics can provide guidance. One approach to making difficult choices is to ask which course of action would most effectively reduce harm and would cause the least harm or produce the most good. Keep these questions in mind while exploring substance abuse-related issues.

SHOULD DRUG USE DURING PREGNANCY BE PROSECUTED?

CASE EXAMPLE: Shortly after Lorenzo Kimbrough was born in July 1998, nurses noticed that he was jittery. When urine tests revealed he and his mother had cocaine in their systems, Lorenzo was immediately removed from his mother's custody. Ms. Kimbrough's custody case was eventually argued before the Ohio Supreme Court. The court held that, under state law, "an abused child is any child who—because of his parents—suffers physical or mental injury that harms or threatens the child's health or welfare" and that Ms. Kimbrough's use of crack cocaine during her pregnancy had caused injury to Lorenzo both before and after birth. Ms. Kimbrough was denied custody of her son (Candisky, 2000).

BOX 13.4	WHAT DO YOU THINK?

Should women who use illegal drugs or alcohol during a pregnancy be prosecuted for child abuse? Why?

If your pregnant client disclosed that she had been drinking alcohol, what would you do?

CASE EXAMPLE: In 1989 Charleston Medical University of South Carolina instituted a policy of testing pregnant women for cocaine without their knowledge or consent. When a woman had one positive drug test, the local police were informed and the woman was arrested. Of 30 women arrested during a five-year period, 29 were African American. Some were taken to jail during their eighth month of pregnancy; others when they were still bleeding from childbirth. Ten women sued the hospital, and the case, *Ferguson* v. *City of Charleston, S.C.*, went before the Supreme Court in 2001 (Daniels, 2000). In a 6 to 3 decision, the Court ruled that hospital workers cannot test maternity patients for illegal drug use without their consent if the purpose is to alert the police to a crime.

Whose rights—the mother's or the unborn infant's—are primary in this situation? Cases like these present social workers with difficult decisions (Abbott, 2000), and strong arguments can be made on both sides. Some social workers who have seen the effects of prenatal drug addiction contend that jailing pregnant drug users is the only way to ensure that they will not continue to use drugs and harm their unborn children. Other social workers argue that treatment and positive intervention are more effective than jail. They assert that when social workers turn clients in for their drug use, others will not come in for services, thus increasing the risk to their unborn children.

In 2000 the National Association of Social Workers (NASW) filed a friend-of-the-court brief in *Ferguson* v. *City of Charleston, S.C.* (Vallianatos, 2000). NASW took the position that professional doctors, nurses, and social workers should not be asked to assist in a campaign to arrest and prosecute their patients and clients and that drug testing without prior consent is invasive and interferes with the trust relationship between the professional and the patient. The Supreme Court decision was in agreement with NASW's position. Therefore, the best solution is to provide high-risk pregnant women with increased access to prenatal drug treatment centers. Prospective mothers will be more likely to patronize a place in which they can receive treatment without fearing arrest.

ARE NEEDLE EXCHANGE PROGRAMS ETHICAL?

CASE EXAMPLE: In spring 2000 Ventura County, California, supervisors began a needle exchange program for intravenous drug users. Half the intravenous drug users in the county had hepatitis B or C, and many had HIV/AIDS. The disease was traced back to intravenous drug use in 19 percent of all cases and in 45 percent of cases involving women. One supervisor who voted in favor of the program said, "It's easy to say no, because we don't believe in illegal drug use ... [but] people addicted to drugs will use them with dirty needles or not.... If we protect the spouse or children of users from the spread of the disease, then we are doing the right thing" (Kelly, 2000).

The evidence suggests that needle exchange programs save lives and reduce the amount of money spent on treating AIDS and hepatitis (Kelly, 2000). The primary argument of people who oppose such programs is that making needles more available will inevitably increase drug use and will send the message that using drugs is acceptable (Abbott, 2000). There is merit on both sides of the argument, and social workers must keep up with research and practice that support both sides. As with most ethical issues, the primary concern is protecting life, but it is not always clear how best to do so.

Should Some Drugs Be Legalized?

CASE EXAMPLES: In August 2005, Joseph Anthony Spano shot two parole officers and kidnapped a toddler while taking a get-away car, all to avoid arrest. His arrest was based on a warrant that was issued after Spano tested positive for amphetamines. The standoff concluded when Spano shot himself (Bittner & Gillum, 2005).

On May 12, 2007 in the District Heights neighborhood of Washington, D.C., seven young men and boys were wounded in a drive-by shooting that was drug related. The boys and young men ranged in age from 12 to 22, and they were treated at hospitals for gunshots in their feet and legs. Witnesses said the shootings abruptly ended a quiet afternoon in which many residents were outside enjoying the spring weather. One witness said, "They shot little kids. It was like what you see on TV. People were on the ground. Bullets in them" (Wagner, 2007).

Proponents of legalizing drugs might say that the Spano and District Heights shootings were the result of laws prohibiting the possession and use of certain substances. If drugs were legalized, fewer people would be arrested for drug trafficking crimes, and the violence associated with turf protection would be reduced. Additionally, the government could regulate the quality and sale of legalized drugs as they do the sale of alcohol and tobacco. This would mean a reduction in the harm caused by drugs that are mixed with dangerous substances, and it would bring in more tax revenues. The money from drug taxes could support drug prevention and treatment efforts. Opponents of legalization counter that most drug-related violence is not perpetrated by drug traffickers in low-income neighborhoods, but rather by people who are under the influence of drugs. Legalizing drugs would increase the number of people using them, thereby increasing drug-related violence. Both sides can cite research evidence to support their claims.

For social workers, the question is whether the drug prohibition laws cause more violence or less violence than drug use. In other words, how effective are laws in preventing damage from drugs, compared with the amount of injury caused by the laws themselves? The goal of social work is to reduce harm, and social workers need to advocate for actions that reduce harm most effectively. The profession remains open to a definitive answer.

BOX 13.5 | **What Do You Think?**

Should marijuana use be legalized? Why?

Marijuana can reduce nausea for chemotherapy patients and people with AIDS. Thus, some advocates support categorizing marijuana as a medicine. If you think it should remain illegal, how do you feel about its use in medical treatment?

EMERGING ISSUES AND FUTURE CONCERNS

The struggle against AOD-related problems takes place on three main fronts—the elimination of AOD from the workplace, the prevention of HIV/AIDS, and the decriminalization of addiction. The abuse of steroids and human growth hormone has received extensive press in the United States in the last five years, but these are also global problems in the developed world. Social workers must engage in these struggles on each front.

AOD PROBLEMS IN THE WORKPLACE

According to a survey by the Substance Abuse and Mental Health Services Administration, 70 percent of illicit drug users and 77 percent of heavy drinkers hold full-time jobs (Maynard, 2000). Employees who abuse drugs and alcohol cost their employers about twice as much in medical and workers compensation claims as their drug-free coworkers. Drug and alcohol use is associated with the majority of injuries and fatalities that occur in the workplace. Workers' AOD problems cost employers over billions of dollars each year in added workers compensation claims, sick days, injuries, and overall lost productivity (Miller, Zaloshnja, & Spicer, 2007).

Detection of drug and alcohol use in the workplace has been a subject of much debate in recent years. Some employers require a drug test as part of a physical examination before they will hire a new employee. A positive test can mean that the applicant will not be hired or will be hired on a probationary basis, with the agreement that regular drug screening will follow. People who test positive are usually referred for some type of treatment. Screening of established employees is conducted on either a scheduled or a random basis. Proponents of screening argue that drug testing identifies employees who are potentially hurting productivity and posing a risk to themselves and coworkers. Opponents argue that drug tests are an invasion of privacy and should be conducted only if there is reason to believe that an employee has an AOD problem.

The damage from AOD use in the workplace highlights the importance of effective employee assistance programs with well-defined drug and alcohol policies. AOD prevention efforts are effective in the workplace for several reasons. The vast majority of American adults work, so large numbers of people can be reached. Receiving a paycheck is an economic incentive for not using AOD. Prevention programs in the workplace are usually cost effective for employers. Research suggests that for every dollar an employer invests in an EAP, between 5 and 16 dollars can be saved in increased productivity and decreased medical claims and absenteeism (OSHA, 2004–2005).

Social workers can help employers address AOD problems. They can help shape and implement creative alcohol-free and drug-free workplace policies. They can assist in educating employees about the individual and the business costs of drug and alcohol abuse. They can train managers and supervisors to detect and prevent AOD abuse and to encourage employees to seek help. Social workers can also help employers develop prevention programs not only for employees but also for their families and the larger community.

DRUGS AND HIV/AIDS

Lisa Mysnyk contracted HIV from a man who could not stay out of jail and off drugs. Sometimes they used condoms. Sometimes they did not. Ms. Mysnyk, who is black, now knows that *'sometimes'* can be a very dangerous word. When the doctor told her she had HIV, Ms. Mysnyk started to cry. Her doctor cried with her. A few days later, she taught her younger son, who was seven at the time, how to use a condom. She had a no-nonsense conversation with her 14-year-old about sexually transmitted diseases. "I didn't want him to ever have to be afraid," she said. Ms. Mysnyk takes six pills a day, her virus level is undetectable, and her immune system continues to be strong. She thinks she could live 30 or 40 more years as long as the drugs keep working. She imagines that having the virus is a lot like having any other chronic disease. But unlike most other diseases, she knows, HIV can almost always be avoided. AIDS has become a disease that hits African Americans with particular force. Recent data suggest that blacks, who represent 13 percent of the country's population, compose half of those living with HIV in the United States (Goodman, 2007).

In the United States, most women, like Lisa Msynyk, are infected with HIV during sex with an HIV-infected man or while using HIV-contaminated syringes for the injection of drugs such as heroin, cocaine, or amphetamines. Of the new HIV infections diagnosed among women in the United States in 2004, CDC estimated 70 percent were attributed to heterosexual contact and 28 percent to injection drug use (NIAID, 2006). Intravenous drug users who do not enter treatment are six times more likely to become infected with HIV/AIDS than those who do enter treatment. Persons who are addicted to alcohol or other noninjected drugs also have an increased risk of contracting HIV. AOD use impairs judgment and often leads users to engage in risky sexual behavior. The immune-suppressing side effects of many drugs further the progression of HIV and leave users vulnerable to opportunistic infections (Moreno, El-Bassel, & Morrill, 2007).

Throughout the world AIDS hotspots include well known parts of Africa, but also lesser-known large urban areas within China and Russia. Due to drug users sharing dirty needles, infection rates have spiked to 50 percent from 2 percent in just two years in urban areas of China and Russia. HIV is steadily spreading among intravenous drug users, their sexual partners, and their offspring, who account for one-third of new cases. Whereas China's HIV infection rate is still relatively low, at about 0.1 per cent, the virus is spreading fast because of a lack of comprehensive education/prevention programs (United Nations, 2008).

The number of women with HIV infection and AIDS has increased steadily worldwide. By the end of 2005, according to the World Health Organization (WHO), 17.5 million women worldwide were infected with HIV. Most contracted the virus from intravenous drug use or from sexual partners who were intravenous drug users (NIAID, 2006). These women come from predominantly poor neighborhoods with limited access to medical and prevention services and limited information about unsafe sex practices.

Social workers have a special obligation to help educate people of color living in poverty areas about the risks of contracting the disease and preventive measures. Outreach programs that are gender specific and culture specific and include empowerment as a theme have been effective in many communities of color (U.N.

Report, 2008). Finally, social workers must advocate for better access to and more affordable medications worldwide.

CRIMINALIZATION OR TREATMENT

During the early 1970s the Nixon administration began a war on drugs. That war dramatically expanded during the 1980s and 1990s. Its focus has been to stop the flow of drugs into the United States and to impose stiffer penalties for drug offenses. These approaches address the supply side of the drug problem, meaning that they attempt to decrease the supply of available drugs. The assumption is that reduced availability will result in less use. Treatment and prevention programs address the demand side of the drug problem; they are based on the assumption that lower demand will cause fewer drugs to be manufactured, imported, and sold. Nearly the entire U.S. drug control budget during the 1980s and 1990s was spent on the law enforcement or supply side. Little was spent on treatment and prevention. By 2007, the United States spent over $13.7 billion for drug control, of which about 66 percent went toward incarceration, border control, international production reduction, and other supply-side activities and 32 percent went to prevention and treatment (Office of National Drug Control Policy, 2008).

The effectiveness of current efforts is questionable. Past experience suggests that it is not possible to keep drugs from being brought into the United States or to stop the sale of drugs within the United States. As long as there is strong demand, there is likely to be a supply. The prisons are overcrowded in large part because so many people have been locked up for drug offenses. It is estimated that as many as 70 percent of the people in prison are there for drug-related offenses (Petteruti & Walsh, 2008).

Many people favor a shift in focus away from punishment and toward prevention and treatment. They contend that this would not only be more effective, but would also be less expensive. Petteruti & Walsh (2008, pp. 26–27) outlined the following:

1. Treating cocaine users reduces serious crime 15 times more effectively than incarceration.
2. Treatment programs reduce substance abuse, crime, and homelessness, while increasing employment.
3. Drug treatment not only provided $10,054 in benefits per participant after deducting costs of treatment but also lowered the chance that a person will commit crimes in the future by 9.3 percent.
4. Diverting nonviolent offenders, particularly drug offenders, into communities relieved the stress on overcrowded facilities, saved money, and provided space for people charged with more serious, violent crimes.

By allowing people convicted of nonviolent offenses to return to the community, they will be less likely to commit crimes in the future and more likely to return to work, family, and community obligations.

One treatment model being implemented nationwide is the use of drug courts, in which people arrested for drug-related offenses can choose treatment rather than incarceration. Participants must agree to plead guilty and to undergo regular drug testing after they complete treatment. The number of drug courts grew dramatically

BOX 13.6 | **ETHICAL PRACTICE ... PUNISHMENT OR TREATMENT?**

You are working with a neighborhood association as part of your job at a community center. You get a call from a representative of the association to discuss their concerns about drug use and related violence in the neighborhood. Members of the group feel that the drug culture of the area is having a negative effect on their children and putting all those in the neighborhood at risk. The group is asking for your help to promote a bill that would require those caught using or selling drugs to be sentenced to jail time. The proposed bill would take money away from drug treatment and prevention and put it into enforcement. While you respect the community's concerns, you know that the profession of social work places a greater emphasis on prevention and treatment. How would you respond to the request from the community?

in the 1990s in part because of support and funding from the Clinton administration. The drug court participant undergoes an intensive regimen of substance abuse treatment, case management, drug testing, supervision and monitoring, and immediate sanctions and incentives while reporting to regularly scheduled status hearings before a judge with expertise in the drug court model. In addition, drug courts increase the probability of participants' success by providing ancillary services such as mental health treatment, trauma and family therapy, and job skills training. Studies have found the courts to be extremely effective (Marlowe, DeMatteo, & Festinger, 2003; Worcel, Green, Furrer, Burrus, & Finigan, 2007).

STEROIDS AND HUMAN GROWTH HORMONE

Recent performance-enhancing drug investigations into famous athletes, like baseball players Barry Bonds and Roger Clemens, and track star Marion Jones, have put **steroids** and **human growth hormone (HGH)** abuse in the headlines. The problem is not limited to the United States. International investigations have also uncovered the illicit trade of performance-enhancing drugs. Sadly, interscholastic investigations in colleges and high schools have underscored the seriousness of the problem and the young age at which many people begin abusing anabolic steroids. In 2007, it was estimated that 1.5 percent of twelfth graders had used steroids in the previous year (NIDA, 2007).

The nonprescription use of anabolic androgenic steroids has been linked to changes in behavior such as depression, hypomania, hostility and aggressiveness, suicide, and violent antisocial or impulsive acts (*Drug Week*, 2006). An extreme example can be found in the life of the World Federation wrestler, David Benoit, a known user of steroids and HGH, who murdered his wife and son and then killed himself. Public awareness has grown, but the use of steroids and HGH continues. Social workers have an obligation to participate in prevention and treatment of steroid and HGH abuse, particularly with young people.

CONCLUSION

Abuse of alcohol and other drugs continues to be a major concern for society in general and for social workers and other social service providers in particular. Addiction thrives where poverty and racism are most prevalent. Substance abuse exacerbates the original problems in a vicious cycle that prematurely ends far too many lives and irreparably damages others.

Present efforts to control AOD problems lean toward punishment, a bias that has had mixed results, some of them profoundly negative. Even when our national policies follow the drug sources internationally, the efforts at eradication lean toward punishment (see the box "Becoming a Change Agent"). There are a number of alternative strategies, and for many decades social work has been at the forefront in exploring and using them. The practical experience of service providers who fight addiction in the trenches suggests that a shift in focus and funding toward prevention and treatment could go a long way toward reducing the incidence of drug and alcohol abuse.

BOX 13.7   **BECOMING A CHANGE AGENT**

The United States has long tried to address its drug problems by eliminating the growth in other countries of plants that are used to produce drugs. The activities the U.S. government has been engaged in to reduce drugs coming into this country include fumigating drug crops in Columbia and funding and training the Columbian army to more effectively police drug plant growth and drug production. In Columbia, for the past seven years the United States has been spraying defoliants (products that kill plants) on fields where they suspect coca is grown. Coca is a central ingredient in the production of cocaine, and is grown primarily in Peru, Bolivia and Columbia. The spraying has wiped out many fields of coca, but it has also destroyed fields of legal crops, such as bananas. Critics of U.S. drug actions in Central and South America point out that after seven years and more than $5.4 billion, there is as much coca being grown in Columbia as there was when the effort started. They note that without legal options for making a living, people will continue to find ways to grow profitable coca crops. Supporters of the U.S. effort to stem the drug trade by eliminating the drugs at their source argue that the program is working. They stress the importance of reducing both supply and demand if we are to be successful in reducing drug use.

Analyzing the Situation

The United States has been actively involved in trying to control coca production in Bolivia and Peru, in addition to Columbia. Try to learn more about U.S.

drug policy that focuses on controlling drug production in these countries by conducting an Internet search and by looking for articles on the subject in the library. How effective has this approach been in reducing the production of illegal drugs and reducing their use in the United States? What has the impact been on the people living in Bolivia, Peru, and Columbia? Given what you learn about what is being done and how effective it is, does this seem to be a good approach to addressing the U.S. drug problem? What are the pros and what are the cons to this approach? Do any of the social work values and ethics provide any guidance about whether this is a good approach to take?

What Can Social Workers Do?

Given your analysis, what might social workers do to promote continuance of this policy or to promote a change in U.S. drug policy? Does the social work community have an obligation to intervene in U.S. policies that are directed toward other countries or only in policies that are directed toward the United States? What approaches to controlling U.S. substance abuse do you think would be more effective for social workers to support and engage in?

What Can You Do?

What one step might you take now, alone or working with others, to address the problem of substance abuse or to try to shape U.S. drug policy? What are the barriers that might keep you from taking this step? What could you do to reduce those barriers?

Social workers have long been key providers for those who seek help for drug- and alcohol-related problems. They are involved in all stages of recovery, from creating prevention programs in schools and preschools, to urging safer practices among addicts, to assisting and supporting people in recovery. In addition, social workers can connect populations affected by substance abuse with the mainstream culture, helping each side understand the aims and objectives of the other, and informing attempts to reduce the damage caused by addictive chemicals. In all these ways, social workers provide hope to the millions of people whose lives are affected by drug and alcohol abuse.

Key Terms

addiction, (p. 359)
amphetamines, (p. 360)
barbiturates, (p. 366)
chemical dependency, (p. 359)
club drugs, (p. 366)
denial, (p. 372)
dependence, (p. 366)
depressants, (p. 366)
drug misuse, (p. 359)
drugs, (p. 359)
drug use, (p. 359)

fetal alcohol syndrome (FAS), (p. 369)
hallucinogens, (p. 366)
human growth hormone (HGH), (p. 385)
inhalants, (p. 366)
internalized homophobia, (p. 378)
psychoactive drugs, (p. 366)
steroids, (p. 385)
stimulants, (p. 360)
substance abuse, (p. 359)
tolerance, (p. 369)
withdrawal, (p. 369)

Questions for Discussion

1. Discuss the key elements in the historical development of Americans' attitudes toward drug and alcohol use, abuse, dependency, and treatment.
2. Describe the system used to classify drugs in the United States, and explain why it may not accurately classify some drugs in terms of their true level of risk.
3. Discuss some ways gender, race or ethnicity, and sexual orientation can affect drug and alcohol use. How might these factors influence the type of treatment social workers would use with each population?
4. Compare the criminalization and treatment approaches to drug abuse. Which approach do you think is more effective, and why?
5. Discuss the pros and cons of legalization of some or all drugs as a method of addressing drug abuse in the United States.
6. Explain why the strengths perspective has not been completely embraced by social workers in substance abuse settings.

How to Become a Change Agent

Working with others in your class, find out who in your community is providing prevention or treatment services in the area of substance abuse. Contact one organization and ask how their programs are funded. Determine if you could participate in any fundraising efforts that are currently underway. If that is not possible, brainstorm with others in your class about how you could raise money for the organization (or another organization of interest to you).

Chapter Exercises

1. **Addressing Substance Abuse**

   There are two distinct views on how to address drug use in the United States. Some people see drugs as a personal failing and hence a crime problem. Describe how they believe the United States should deal with drug abuse.

   Drug use is a personal failure and should be treated as a crime because:

   Other people see drug use as a disease. Describe how they believe the United States should deal with drug abuse.

   Drug use is a disease and should be treated as an illness because:

   Which view do you support? Why?

2. **Community Assessment**

   What types of substance abuse prevention programs exist in your community?

   How are they funded?

   Does your community have a needle exchange program?

   If not, why do you think it does not have one?

   What could your community do differently in preventing and treating substance abuse?

3. **Substance Abuse and Diversity**

   In a small group, brainstorm the factors that contribute to the double stigmatization of women and members of nondominant groups in the context of substance abuse.

   Factors:

   For each factor, suggest how social workers could intervene to diminish the effect of the double stigma.

4. **Imaging**

   Think about the term *drug abuser*. What images come to mind?

   How do these images and thoughts compare with the data on people who abuse drugs presented in the chapter?

5. **Media Portrayals**

   How do the news and entertainment media portray drug use and drug abuse?

   Provide examples from books, movies, television shows, websites, or news programs to support your view.

   Do these media support drug use, condemn it, or give mixed messages?

References

Abadinsky, H. (1997). *Drug abuse: An introduction*. Chicago, ILL: Nelson-Hall.

Abbott, A. A. (2000). Values, ethics, and ethical dilemmas in ATOD practice. In Abbott, A. A. (ed.), *Alcohol, tobacco, and other drugs*. Washington, DC: NASW Press.

American Psychiatric Association. (2000). *Diagnostic and statistical manual for the diagnosis of mental disorder* (4th ed.). Washington, DC: Author.

Avena, N. M., Rada, P., Hoebel B. G. (2008). Evidence for sugar addiction: Behavioral and neurochemical effects of intermittent, excessive sugar intake. *Neuroscience and Biobehavioral Reviews, 32,* 1, 20–39.

Bassuk, E., Dawson, R., & Huntington, N. (2006). Intimate partner violence in extremely poor women: Longitudinal patterns and risk markers. *Journal of Family Violence, 21,* 6, 387–399.

Benshoff, J. J., & Janikowski, T. P. (2000). *The rehabilitation model of substance abuse counseling.* Pacific Grove, CA: Brooks/Cole.

Bittner, E. & Gillum, J. (2005). Man shoots officers, self. *Arizona Republic,* August 4, p. B1,2.

Burman, S. (2000). Strategies for intervention with individuals. In Abbot, A. A. (ed.), *Alcohol, tobacco and other drugs.* Washington, DC: NASW Press.

Burrow-Sanchez, J. J. & Hawken, L. S. (2007). *Effective practices for prevention and intervention.* New York: Guilford Press.

Candisky, C. (2000). Drug use can equal child abuse. *Columbus Dispatch,* October 26, p. 1C.

Carroll, K., Rounsaville, B., & Keller, D. (1991). Relapse prevention strategies for the treatment of cocaine abuse. *American Journal of Drug and Alcohol Abuse, 17,* 3, 249–265.

Center for Substance Abuse Prevention. (2000). *Model programs.* Retrieved on January 25, 2000, from www.prevention.samhsa.gov/Progs/.

Connors, G. J., Walitzer, K. S., & Dermen, K. H. (2002). Preparing clients for alcoholism treatment: Effects on treatment participation and outcomes. *Journal of Consulting and Clinical Psychology, 70,* 5, 1161–1169.

Congress on Alcohol and Health: Highlights from Current Research. Washington, DC: Author.

Daniels, C. (2000). Doctors should not police pregnant women's actions. *San Francisco Chronicle,* November 15, p. A23.

Drug Week. (2006). Steroids may be associated with an antisocial lifestyle. *Drug Week,* December 1, p. 276.

Ehrmin, J. T. (2002). "That feeling of not feeling": Numbing the pain for substance-dependent African American women. *Qualitative Health Research, 12,* 6, 780–791.

Fish, L. (2007). Nature, culture, and abnormal appetites: An ecopsychological analysis of addiction. *Dissertation Abstracts International,* Section B: The Sciences and Engineering, *67,* 9–B, 53–99.

Fisher, G. L., & Harrison, T. C. (2000). *Substance abuse: Information for school counselors, social workers, therapists, and counselors.* Upper Saddle River, N.J.: Allyn and Bacon.

Flavin, D. K., & Morse, R. M. (2001). What is alcoholism? Current definitions and diagnostic criteria and their implications for treatment. *Alcohol, Health and Research World, 15,* 4, 266–271.

Floyd, R. L., O'Connor, M. J., Bertrand, J., & Sokol, R. (2006). Reducing adverse outcomes from prenatal alcohol exposure: A clinical plan of action. *Alcoholism, Clinical, and Experimental Research, 30,* 8, 1271–1275.

Gershanik, A. (2000). Substance abuse target of council. *Times-Picayune,* July 20, p. 3A1.

Gil, A. G., Wagner, E. F., & Tubman, J. G. (2004). Culturally sensitive substance abuse intervention for Hispanic and African American adolescents: Empirical examples from the alcohol treatment targeting adolescents in need program. *Addiction, 99,* 2, 140–150.

Goodman, B. (2007). The state of AIDS. *New York Times,* June 5, Section A, p.16.

Gray, J. P. (2001). *Why our drug laws have failed and what we can do about it: A judicial indictment of the war on drugs.* Philadelphia: Temple University Press.

Gray, M. C. (1995). Drug abuse. In *Encyclopedia of social work* (19th ed.). Washington, DC: NASW.

Gruenert, S. M., Ratnam, S. S., & Tsantefski, M. (2006). Identifying children's needs when parents access drug treatment: the utility of a brief screening measure. *Journal of Social Work Practice in the Addictions, 6,* 1/2, 139–154.

Halkitis, P. N., Palamer, J. J., & Mukherjee, P. P. (2007). Poly-club-drug use among gay and bisexual men: A longitudinal analysis. *Drug and Alcohol Dependence, 89,* 2/3, 153–160.

Harrold, M. (2007). Drunk driving charges laid a year after death: As grieving mother waits for justice, National Assembly will weigh stiffer penalties for impaired drivers. *Gazette,* October 21, p. A1.

Holmes, K. A. & Hodge, R. H. (1997). Gay and lesbian people. In J. Philleo & F. L. Brisbane, (eds.), *Cultural competence in substance abuse prevention.* Washington, DC: NASW Press.

Hopwood, C. J, Baker, K. L., & Morey, L. C. (2008). Personality and drugs of choice. *Personality and Individual Differences* 44(6), 1413–1421.

Jackson, B. (2000). Head of Indian bureau offers apology. *Denver Rocky Mountain News,* November 20, p. 45A.

Jellinek, E. M. (1947). Phases in drinking history of alcoholics: Analysis of a survey. *Memoirs of the Laboratory of Applied Physiology, 5,* 88.

Jones, C. (2008). Are you a sugar addict? *Express,* April 22, p. 32.

Kelly, D. (2000). Supervisors OK needle exchange program. *Los Angeles Times,* December 20, p. 1B.

Knapp, C. (1997). *Drinking: A love story.* New York: Dial Press.

Lewis, J. A. Dana, R. Q., & Blevins, G. A. (1994). *Substance abuse counseling.* Pacific Grove, CA: Brooks/Cole.

Lyter, S. C., & Lyter, L. L. (2000). Intervention with groups. In Abbott, A. A. (ed.), *Alcohol, tobacco, and other drugs.* Washington, D.C: NASW Press.

Marlowe, D. B., DeMatteo, D. S., & Festinger, D. S. (2003). A sober assessment of drug courts. *Federal Sentencing Reporter, 16,* 1, 113–128.

Maynard, J. (2000). Growing new roots. *EAPA Exchange, 30,* 6, 2.

Miller, T., Zaloshnja, E., & Spicer, R. S. (2007). *Accident Analysis & Prevention, 39,* 3, 565–573.

Miller, W. R., & Hester, R. K. (1995). Treatment for alcohol problems: Toward an informed eclecticism. In Hester, R. K., & Miller, W. R. (eds.), *Handbook of alcoholism treatment approaches: Effective alternatives.* Boston: Allyn & Bacon.

Moran, J. R., & May, P. A. (1997). American Indians. In Brisbane, L., & Epstein, L. (eds.), *Cultural competence in substance abuse prevention.* Washington, DC: NASW Press.

Moreno, C. L., El-Bassel, N., & Morrill, A. C. (2007). Heterosexual women of color and HIV risk: Sexual risk factors for HIV among Latina and African American women. *Women & Health, 45,* 3, 1–15.

Murphy, K. (2000). Yakama ban alcohol on reservation. *Milwaukee Journal Sentinel,* October 15, p. 2A.

NIAID, (2006). *HIV infection in women.* Washington, D. C.: National Institute of Allergies and Infectious Disease.

National Association of Social Workers. (1997). Alcohol, tobacco and other substance abuse. In *Social work speaks: NASW policy statements* (4th ed.) (pp. 31–38). Washington, DC: NASW Press.

National Center for Health Statistics. (2008). *Health, United States 2007 with Chartbook on Trends in the Health of Americans.* Hyattsville, MD: Centers for Disease Control and Prevention, National Center for Health Statistics.

National Edition. (2007). Some men genetically predisposed to caffeine's kick, U of T study finds. *National Edition,* June 11, p. A3.

National Institute on Alcohol Abuse and Alcoholism (2007). *10th Special Report to the U.S.* Washington, DC: Author.

National Survey on Drug Use and Health. (2006). *Overview of the findings from the 2006 national survey on drug use and health.* Washington, DC: Department of Health and Human Services.

NHSDA. (2005). *The national household survey on drug abuse.* Washington, DC: Substance Abuse and Mental Health Services Administration.

NIDA. (2000). The next step in disseminating proven prevention programs. *NIDA Notes,* 14, 6, 1–2.

NIH. (2008). *Alcohol: A women's health issue.* Washington, DC: National Institute of Health.

Office of National Drug Control Policy. (2008). *National drug control strategy budget summary.* Washington, DC: Whitehouse.

OSHA Report. (2004–2005). *Drug free workplace alliance annual report.* Washington, DC: Occupational Safety and Health Administration.

Petteruti, A., & Walsh, N. (2008). *Jailing communities: The impact of jail expansion and effective public safety strategies.* Washington, DC: Justice Policy Institute.

PRIDE Surveys. (2008). *2006–2007 national summary.* Retrieved on April 23, 2008, from http:\\www.pridesurveys.com.

Rabinovitch, J., & Strega, S. (2004). The PEERS story: Effective services sidestep the controversies. *Violence Against Women,* 10(2), 140–159

Rapp, R. C., Otto, A. L., Lane, D. T., Redko, C., McGatha, S., & Carlson, R. G. (2008). Improving linkage with substance abuse treatment using brief case management and motivational interviewing. *Drug and Alcohol Dependence,* 94, 1–3, 172–182.

Ray, O., & Kasir, C. (1999). *Drugs, society and human behavior.* Boston: WGB/McGraw-Hill.

Reid, T. R. (2005). Slurped in black coffee or sipped in green tea, gulped down in a soda or knocked back in a headache pill, caffeine is the world's most popular psychoactive drug. *National Geographic,* January., p. 22

Riggs, P. (2007). Depression: Behavior therapy plus medication may help teens with depression and substance abuse disorders. *Biotech Business Week,* November 19, p. 1973.

Robbins, M. S. (2008). The efficacy of structural ecosystems therapy with drug-abusing/dependent African American and Hispanic American adolescents. *Journal of Family Psychology, 22,* 1, 51–61.

Sacks, J. Y., McKendrick, K., & Banks, S. (2008). The impact of early trauma and abuse on residential substance treatment outcomes for women. *Journal of Substance Abuse Treatment, 34,* 1, 90–100.

Sage, G. P., & Burns, G. L. (1993). Attributional antecedents of alcohol use in American Indian and Euroamerican adolescents. *American Indian and Native Alaskan Mental Health Research, 5,* 2, 46–56.

Spencer, K. (2000). Drugs, prostitution defined slaying victim's life of prostitution in Omaha. *Omaha World-Herald,* November 23, p. 1.

Tolan, P., Szapocznik, J., & Sambrano, S. (2006). *Preventing youth substance abuse: Science-based programs for children and adolescents.* New York: Sage Publications.

U.S. Department of Labor (2006). *Social workers.* Washington, DC: U.S. Department of Labor.

U.S. Federal News. (2005). Attorney general Madrid bringing statewide effort to fight underage, binge drinking in New Mexico to New Mexico State University. *U.S. Federal News,* April 19, 2005.

Vallianatos, C. (2000). Arrests for drug use in pregnancy opposed. *NASW News,* November, p. 5.

Vendantum, S, (2005). Inhalant abuse on the rise among children. *Washington Post,* January 24, p. A6.

Wagner, A. (2007). Drive-by riles neighbors. *Washington Times,* May 14, p. B1.

Wallace, Jr., F. M., Forman, T. A., Guthrie, B. J., Bachman, J. G., O'Malley, P. M., & Johnston, L. D. (1999). The epidemiology of alcohol, tobacco and other drug use among black youth. *Journal of Studies on Alcohol, 60,* 6, 800–809.

Weber, G. (2008). Using to numb the pain: Substance use and abuse among lesbian, gay, and bisexual individuals. *Journal of Mental Health Counseling, 30,* 1, 31–48.

Wood, K. M., & Dunn, P. C. (2000). Criteria for selecting theories and models of ATOD practice. In Abbot, A. A. (ed.), *Alcohol, tobacco, and other drugs.* Washington, DC: NASW Press.

Worby, P. A., & Organisat, K. C. (2007). Alcohol Use and Problem Drinking Among Male Mexican and Central American Im/migrant Laborers: A Review of the Literature, *Hispanic Journal of Behavioral Sciences, 29*(4), 413–455.

Worcel, S. D., Green, B. L., Furrer, C. J., Burrus, S. W., & Finigan, M. W. (2007). *Family treatment drug court evaluation final report.* Portland, OR: NPC Research.

Zucker R. A. (2006) Alcohol use and alcohol use disorders: A developmental-biopsychosocial systems formulation covering the life course. In Cicchetti, D., & Cohen, D. J. (eds.), *Developmental Psychopathology,* Vol. 3, *Risk, Disorder and Adaptation* (pp. 620–656). Hoboken, NJ: Wiley & Sons.

VIOLENCE, VICTIMS, AND CRIMINAL JUSTICE

Social workers respond to all kinds of social problems. Violence, criminal behavior, and victims of crime can be the concerns of social workers across many domains. For example, as discussed in the previous chapter, substance abuse can go hand in hand with crime. Survivors often have major emotional and mental health problems after becoming victims of crime or violence. This chapter explores these concerns, and highlights the ways that social workers interact with the criminal justice system.

VIOLENCE, CRIME, AND PUNISHMENT IN THE UNITED STATES

In 2008, the United States had 2.3 million criminals behind bars, 1 in every 100 American adults, which is more than any other nation (Liptak, 2008). In per capita terms, Russia was next with 627 prisoners for every 100,000 people. China has four times the population of the United States and only 1.6 million people in prison. There are several factors that help explain why the United States is the leading producer of prisoners, including higher levels of violent crime, easy access to guns, laws that require longer sentences, institutional racism, America's deeply held values of individualism and personal responsibility, the war on drugs, and the lack of an effective social safety net.

Between 2003 and 2008, there was a decline in the murder rate in the United States (Uniform Crime Report, 2007), but the United States still has about four times the murder rate of countries in western Europe. Although the United States has relatively low rates of nonviolent crime, offenders in the United States are more likely to go to jail and have longer sentences than offenders in other countries. The growing disparity in the number of prisoners in the United States compared to those of the rest of the world did not really begin until the 1980s. During this time period the war on drugs began, and it exponentially increased the number of drug-related offenders in prison from 40,000 to over 500,000 in 2008 (Pew Report, 2008).

Since the 1980s, there has been a somewhat uneven (there have been spikes from time to time) downward trend in crime. The Federal Bureau of Investigation's Uniform Crime Report (2006–2007) identified 5.7 murders per 100,000 inhabitants in 2006, and a slight increase in that number in the first half of 2007. Almost half of murder victims are African American. There were 92,455 rapes reported in 2006, with a slight decrease in that number in the first part of 2007. Overall, there was a decrease of 1.8 percent in the number of violent crimes (murder, rape, robbery, and aggravated assault).

While the overall rate of violent crime in the United States has dropped slightly in the last few years, Americans are still the victims of seemingly random spectacular gun deaths, including drive-by gang shootings or mass murder in shopping malls, schools, or other public places. The most recent well-known event took place on the Virginia Tech University campus in Blacksburg, Virginia in April 2007. Cho Seung Hui, 23, a senior English major and South Korean national, murdered 32 of his fellow students and then killed himself.

As alarming as this massacre was, it may be even more alarming to learn that every day eight children and teenagers are killed by gun violence. That is the equivalent of a Virginia Tech massacre about every four days. American children are more at risk from firearms than the children of any other industrialized nation, with a death rate 500 percent higher than anywhere in Europe and Japan. Since the murders of Robert Kennedy and the Reverend Martin Luther King Jr. in 1968, well over a million Americans have been killed by firearms in the United States. That's more than the combined U.S. combat deaths in all the wars in all of U.S. history (Herbert, 2007). Herbert (2007, p.6) declared that "Americans are addicted to violence, specifically gun violence. We profess to be appalled at every gruesome outbreak of mass murder (it's no big deal when just two, three or four people are killed at a time), but there's no evidence that we have the will to pull the guns out of circulation, or even to register the weapons and properly screen and train their owners."

The extent of violence, crime, and victimization is significant, and social workers are often faced with the consequences of these problems. Some social workers do so as formal participants in law enforcement and legal justice systems, and some work directly with victims. Because violence and crime are part of American society, they are also part of social work practice.

THE CRIMINAL JUSTICE SYSTEM

The primary goals of the criminal justice system are to maintain public safety and punish lawbreakers by confining or controlling them (Miller, 1995). With this emphasis on control and punishment, is the criminal justice system a place for social workers? Some of the most dedicated and idealistic social workers answer this question with an impassioned yes!

Social work in a criminal justice setting covers an enormous amount of territory. Social workers specialize in juvenile corrections, rehabilitation in the adult correctional system, case management and counseling services in probation and parole, police social work, and victim assistance services. They are most often employed by federal, state, and local governments and nonprofit victim assistance agencies or lobbies. Regardless of setting, criminal justice social workers advocate for public policies that address poverty, unemployment, and hopelessness.

The prevalence of criminal behavior is closely watched by ordinary citizens, policy makers, and social workers alike. Many theories have been proposed to explain the causes and varieties of crime, and several of those theories, from all fields of social science, can help inform social workers who deal directly with crime and its effects.

THE EXTENT AND VARIETY OF CRIME IN THE UNITED STATES

The extent of crime in the United States is measured by the annual National Crime Victimization Survey (NCVS), sponsored by the U.S. Justice Department, Bureau of Justice Statistics, and the annual FBI Uniform Crime Report (UCR). Neither measurement is entirely accurate. The NCVS survey, which makes use of statistical sampling, polls about 76,000 people every six months. It includes reported and unreported crimes and relies on peoples' memories. The UCR is based on data that are systematically collected from police department reports. It does not include unreported crimes. This is a substantial omission, since victims report only half of all violent crimes and one-third of property crimes to the police (Pew Report, 2008).

In 2005, U.S. residents age 12 or older experienced approximately 23 million crimes, according to findings from the National Crime Victimization Survey (2006). Seventy-seven percent were property crimes, 22 percent were violent crimes, and 1 percent were personal thefts. In 2005, for every 1,000 people there was 1 rape or sexual assault, 1 assault with injury, and 3 robberies. Overall, one in six American women has been the victim of some kind of sexual assault. Despite trends indicating that crime is decreasing, the basic facts of crime and punishment are dauntingly grim and the statistics do not begin to do justice to the toll crime takes on its victims.

To begin with, victims of crime who live in poor areas, with few social supports, sometimes end their journey of victimization by becoming criminals themselves. One study (Bennett, 2007) identified three pathways to explain how the cycle of violence can be perpetuated or victimization can lead to offending: retaliatory violence toward the perpetrator, the victim lashing out indiscriminately out of frustration and anger, or the victim befriending his or her attackers. This is evidence of why crime victims, especially children, adolescents, and young adults, need social work assistance.

And as the cycle of violence continues, criminals are increasingly becoming victims themselves. In Baltimore, about 91 percent of murder victims in 2006 had criminal records. In Philadelphia, 75 percent of murder victims had a criminal past, and in Newark it was 86 percent. Finally, in Milwaukee, they found that 77 percent of homicide victims had an average of nearly 12 arrests. Although it has been known for some time that many murder victims have criminal records, the current levels are surprising even to analysts who study homicides (Johnson, 2007). The fact that most murder victims in large cities are criminals has remained largely off the radar. However, the impact in many of these cities has been mind numbing to the point that the slaying of truly innocent victims gets very little reaction because people are so anesthetized to murder.

THEORIES OF CRIMINAL BEHAVIOR RELEVANT TO SOCIAL WORK

In his best-selling book, *The Gift of Fear*, the security specialist Gavin DeBecker wrote:

> Though our experiences as children will affect much of what we do, a violent history does not ensure a violent future.... The boy who suffers violence ... might grow up to help people avoid violence.... The boy whose father is killed by robbers might grow up to be a Secret Service agent.... Unfortunately, many children of violence will contribute something else to our nation: more violence—against their children, against their wives, against you or me.... When you can find no other common ground ... remember that the vast majority of violent people started as you did, felt what you felt, wanted what you wanted. (1997, pp. 52–53)

DeBecker's insights raise an age-old question: Why do some people commit crimes, whereas others do not? Social workers need to be familiar with the various answers to this question. The reason that is most accepted by society at a given time inevitably determines how the criminal justice system treats offenders.

Individualistic Theories   Table 14.1 summarizes some of the theories that have been proposed to explain criminal behavior. Individualistic theories tend to be the most popular. They see criminals not as societal victims but instead as responsible individuals who must be punished. Individualistic theories require society to do very little and to change nothing. **Deterrence theory,** using punishment to discourage people from committing crimes, and biological determinism are more punitive than behaviorist theories and psychological determinism, but all four locate the root cause of criminal behavior within the perpetrator of the crime.

TABLE 14.1	THEORIES ABOUT WHY SOME PEOPLE COMMIT CRIMES AND OTHERS DO NOT
Theory	**Action Implication**
Individualistic Theories	
<u>Deterrence Theory</u> First proposed by Cesare Beccaria, the father of criminology, in the late 1700s.	Swift and severe punishment must be exacted, even for minor crimes.
People who do not associate certain, swift, and severe punishment with criminal activity will choose crime.	Example: In some countries where lawmakers apparently accept deterrence theory, legal authorities cut off the hand of a person caught stealing.
Underlying assumption: We all have a free will and are responsible for our actions.	
Major Point: Criminals willfully choose crime.	
<u>Biological Determinism</u> First proposed by Cesare Lombroso in 1876.	Lock them up indefinitely. Rehabilitation is not possible.
Criminals are genetic misfits or throwbacks to a more primitive, violent time. They may have extremely low IQs or a biochemical imbalance.	
Underlying assumption: Criminal tendencies are atavistic and inborn.	
Major Point: Criminals cannot help themselves, they are destined to be violent and commit crimes.	
<u>Psychological Determinism</u> First popularized in the 1920s. Defects of the mind are the cause of all misbehavior including crime.	Criminal offenders should be housed in secure mental health facilities, some for life, others for whatever length of time necessary for them to be rehabilitated through therapy.
Underlying assumption: Internal forces, beyond the offender's control, determine destiny.	
Major Point: Criminals either have a mental illness or they are psychopaths, or in Freudian terms, their superegos/conscience failed to develop.	
<u>Behaviorism</u> Popularized in the 1970s and 1980s. Deviant and criminal behaviors are inappropriate learned responses.	Behavior modification programs like "token economies" should be used in prisons. Prisoners are rewarded for good behavior and punished for bad behavior. Reality therapy should be used to hold offenders accountable for their actions.
Underlying Assumption: Criminal acts that are followed by small but immediate gratification tend to be repeated, even if there are delayed, painful long-term consequences.	

TABLE 14.1 | THEORIES ABOUT WHY SOME PEOPLE COMMIT CRIMES AND OTHERS DO NOT (*CONTINUED*)

Theory	Action Implication
Major Point: Criminals must be shown the error of their ways and change their behaviors.	*Reality therapy* is based in behaviorism and is often used with juveniles and adults in the correctional system. Rewards and punishments are used to help the client learn and adopt the moral standards of society.
Sociological Theories Social Disorganization, The Subcultural Hypothesis, and Cultural Transmission The roots of these theories come from the nineteenth century French sociologist/philosopher Emile Durkheim. Criminals emerge from poverty-stricken, deviant, and delinquent subcultures that have rejected the values of mainstream society. Criminal values and actions are passed from one generation to the next. *Underlying assumptions*: The poverty conditions of a geographic area, not the people who live there, are responsible for crime. However, if people live there long enough they begin to share similar values, such as using violence as an accepted means to solve problems. Criminal behavior is learned. *Major Point*: Change the conditions of the geographic area and people will have no reason to turn to crime. Otherwise, people living in poverty must either accept their fate and work hard to gain little, or reject a classist society's values and resort to crime.	Eliminate poverty. Prisons and prison personnel must model a positive and supportive environment for prisoners. Offer legitimate educational opportunities and job skills to offenders so that when they return to the outside world they will have the means to access mainstream society's reward system.

Sociological Theories   By contrast, sociological explanations of criminal behavior hold individuals accountable but also suggest that society and prison environments need to change. Structural problems such as poverty, inequality, constrained residential patterns, and institutionalized racism (discussed in Chapters 3 and 4), rather than personal, psychological, or biological problems, are viewed as the root causes of criminal behavior (DeCoster, Heimer, & Wittrock, 2006). The findings from the DeCoster et al. study (p. 751) suggest that "violent delinquency is largely a product of family disadvantage, community disadvantage, weakened family bonds, and exposure to some elements of a criminogenic street milieu." In other words, the evidence suggested that minorities and disadvantaged families have fewer residential choices and are more likely to live in neighborhoods that provide opportunities for, and even encourage, youth to commit acts of violence.

BOX 14.1 | **WHAT DO YOU THINK?**

Do you believe that institutionalized racism and poverty may be root causes of criminal behavior? Why?

In a Texas study, violent female prisoners were more likely than nonviolent female prisoners to be African American, come from single-parent households, and to have been the victims of sexual abuse (Pollock, Mullings, & Crouch, 2006). Perhaps the most telling example of racism in the criminal justice system is the fact that police response time is faster, effort exerted stronger, and follow-up more rigorous when the crime victims are white (Howerton, 2007). Studies such as these provide compelling evidence that institutionalized racism, poverty, and economic inequality breed criminals. There is a need for programs in low-income neighborhoods to help children stay in school and provide parents with economic opportunities and jobs.

At the end of the twentieth century, James Q. Wilson and George Kelling proposed the broken window theory, which views criminal behavior as a function of social context (Gladwell, 2000). The idea is that the level of crime committed in an urban area is correlated with the number of broken windows. The theory suggests that neighborhoods in which police tolerate misdemeanors are most likely to have high rates of felony-level crimes. A **misdemeanor** is the least serious type of crime, usually punishable by a fine or a combination of a fine and less than one year of incarceration. According to the broken window theory, changing the context will eliminate or radically reduce the criminal behavior. It suggests that focusing on little things in the environment is more effective than trying to directly fix the problems of institutionalized racism and poverty.

To test the broken window theory, Kelling and Sousa (2001) isolated four variables—unemployment, population of male teenagers, usage of crack cocaine, and enforcement of laws related to minor crimes or misdemeanors—in order to determine whether they were associated with the 60 percent decrease in crime in 78 New York City precincts during the 1990s. Their only consistent and significant finding was a strong negative correlation between the enforcement of laws against minor crimes and the overall crime rate, including the most violent crimes such as murder and rape. In other words, in places where minor laws were being enforced, the overall crime rate was lower. Surprisingly, in the 78 precincts studied there was no association between the crime rate and unemployment, a large population of male teenagers, or the use of crack cocaine. In fact, crime decreased the most in some of the precincts with the highest unemployment rates.

When Rudolph Giuliani was elected mayor of New York in 1994, he used the broken window theory to implement a crime prevention strategy. Police officers and prosecutors were required to aggressively enforce misdemeanor laws against defacing property with graffiti, approaching cars and demanding money for washing windshields, turnstile jumping in subways, urinating in the street, and engaging in other petty street crimes. The Kelling and Sousa study is at least partial evidence that Giuliani's crime prevention strategy may have contributed to a substantial decrease in crime during the 1990s.

Theories and Social Work   The person-in-environment and systems theory frameworks require social workers to consider both individual and sociological factors. Some criminals are sociopaths or psychopaths; some have mental illnesses; and some have grown up in areas of extreme poverty and rampant violence. Others meet none of these criteria. Social workers must remain open to all explanations that seem applicable.

At the micro level, social work values require treating each offender as a unique individual and developing a specific plan of action to meet the person's needs. From a systems theory perspective, social workers must campaign vigorously for policies that promote social and economic justice. Combining the elimination of injustice with the broken window strategy is probably most likely to significantly reduce crime. Society has tried many forms of deterrence and imprisonment, but crimes continue to be committed and the prisons are overflowing. On the other hand, society has not substantially invested in prevention and treatment programs or education and job skills training. Nor have large-scale, nonpunitive ways to eliminate poverty been instituted. Prevention, treatment, and training all require a strengths perspective to be successful.

The social work profession supports

- Using the political system to eliminate poverty and make society's rewards accessible to all
- Making prisons humane and safe environments in which inmates can learn from the modeling behaviors of prison personnel
- Giving inmates access to effective therapy, educational opportunities, and job skills training
- Removing offenders who have diagnosed mental illnesses or substance abuse problems from prisons and providing treatment in secure environments
- Accepting that violent career criminals, sociopaths, serial killers, and psychopaths will probably never change and are a continuing danger to themselves and others and isolating them in maximum-security prisons.

THE CRIMINAL JUSTICE SYSTEM

Social workers have not always been comfortable working within institutionalized structures created to deal with crime. These structures have been called "an authoritarian system that dehumanizes, discriminates, and focuses on custody instead of rehabilitation" (van Wormer, 1999, p. 82). The social work profession's reliance on the strengths perspective is in direct conflict with the criminal justice system's goals of social control and punishment. If a strengths perspective were utilized, the primary goals of the system would be prevention, treatment, and rehabilitation.

As mentioned previously, there are over 2 million persons incarcerated in the United States' jails and prisons, an all-time high. Society's response to overcrowded prisons and juvenile facilities has been to call for more prisons, to put more people in them, and to refer more juveniles to the adult criminal justice system. In stark contrast, the social work profession's response has been to argue that convicted criminals can be rehabilitated, that more funds should be spent on juvenile prevention and treatment programs, and that all victims should receive assistance. Even more fundamentally, the profession has argued for more funds to prevent crime by alleviating poverty and healing people's emotional wounds. Unfortunately, as long as mainstream society embraces individualistic theories of criminal behavior, punishment will win out over rehabilitation. As a result, a discouragingly small percentage of criminals are successfully rehabilitated in the U.S. criminal justice system.

RACIAL IMBALANCE

Both the juvenile justice and adult criminal justice systems have long been plagued by charges of racism, largely because of the disproportionate number of nondominant group members in them. For example, in the society as a whole, about 16 percent of juveniles are African American but they account for 29 percent of the juvenile delinquency caseload. While white youth account for the largest number of delinquency cases involving detention, they are the least likely to be detained (Office of Justice Programs, 2006). Harrington and Spohn (2007) found black males were significantly less likely than white males, white females, and black females to be placed on probation rather than sentenced to jail. Schanzenbacj & Yaeger (2006) found, when controlling for as many relevant characteristics as possible, blacks and Latinos received longer prison sentences than whites for white-collar crimes.

More than 60 percent of prisoners are members of nondominant groups (estimated at 44 percent black, 35 percent white, 19 percent Latino, and 2 percent other races). Blacks in the United States are imprisoned at more than five times the rate of whites, and Latinos are locked up at nearly double the white rate (Pew Report, 2008; Sentencing Project, 2007). This is especially egregious in light of the fact that African Americans constitute only 12 percent of the general population, and Latinos only 13 percent. States in the Midwest and Northeast have the greatest black-to-white disparity in incarceration. Iowa had the widest disparity in the nation, imprisoning blacks at more than 13 times the rate of whites. Less than one year after the Sentencing Project report came out, the governor of Iowa, Chet Culver, signed legislation in 2008 requiring examination of the racial and ethnic impact of all new sentencing laws prior to passage.

While many different theories have been put forth to explain racial differences in the correctional system, institutionalized racism and racial bias in sentencing are two of the most likely culprits (Sentencing Project, 2007). The Pew Report (2008) found that African American drug offenders generally receive longer sentences than white drug offenders. In addition, even after controlling for prior criminal record and the type of offense, African Americans were twice as likely as whites to receive habitual offender sentences. Part of this discrepancy is explained by federal legislation that passed during the 1980s and was designed to address the growing concern about crack cocaine in urban areas. Under federal law a small-time drug addict caught with one-fifth of an ounce of crack (the less expensive form of cocaine prevalent in poor, urban African American areas) received an automatic five-year sentence, whereas someone caught with the identical amount of cocaine (more typically used by dominant group people) had only committed a misdemeanor and was less likely to go to jail. In addition, four out of five defendants in federal crack cases are black (Hensley, 2008). In order to address this bias, new federal legislation was passed in April 2008 that brought the punishment for selling crack cocaine more in line with selling powder cocaine. As a result of the legislation, more than 20,000 inmates (mostly black) nationwide were eligible to have their sentences reduced. In fact, most experts agree that one way to reduce racial disparities sentencing is to review all federal drug laws and give judges more discretion to decide sentences rather than imposing mandatory minimum prison terms (Hensley, 2008).

The correctional system reflects society's racial tensions and problems. Until society is able to effectively deal with racism, especially institutional racism, people of color will continue to be overrepresented in the criminal justice system. The tension that results from this imbalance will also continue.

WOMEN

Women make up about 7 to 8 percent of the prison population (Pew Report, 2008). During the last 30 years, there has been a huge increase in the number of women inmates serving sentences of more than a year. Between 1977 and 2004, there was a 574 percent increase, nearly twice the 388 percent increase for men (Women's Prison Association, 2006). The increase is largely due to mandatory drug sentencing, with women (one out of three) more likely than men to be in jail for a drug offense (Staton-Tindall et al., 2007). Although the surge occurred nationwide, it was most notable in the mountain states, where the number of incarcerated women soared by 1,600 percent. Almost half of female convicts are survivors of physical or sexual abuse. Two-thirds are unmarried and have children under the age of 18; over 59,000 children have mothers in prison (King, 2006). Women in prison are more likely than men to test positive for HIV/AIDS (Staton-Tindall et al., 2007). As in the male population, African Americans and Latinos are disproportionately represented in the female inmate population (Sentencing Project, 2007).

The needs of women offenders are different than those of men because of their disproportionate victimization from sexual or physical abuse and their responsibilities to their children. They are also more likely to be addicted to drugs or have mental illnesses than male inmates. When cut off from their children, families, and friends, female inmates are far more likely than male inmates to experience feelings of helplessness, powerlessness, and despair (Women's Prison Association, 2006).

Among the key elements of successful programs for women offenders are the following:

- Program staff should include women who are former addicts and former offenders to serve as role models.
- Inmates must help run the program.
- The program should address issues of self-esteem, domestic violence, empowerment, and self-sufficiency.
- Participants need to acquire marketable job skills, parenting skills, and anger management techniques (Pollack, 2005).

Successful programs address the special needs, both emotional and medical, of women inmates. They also help them return home to their children and lead productive lives. For example, the Bedford Hills Correctional Facility in New York State houses a nursery in which inmates' infants under 18 months old are cared for. The purpose of the program is to address the mental health needs of inmates and help them learn to be mothers (Farmer, 2007).

BOX 14.2	WHAT DO YOU THINK?

Should rehabilitation programs for women differ from rehabilitation programs for men? Why or why not, and if so, how?

INMATES WITH DISABILITIES

Under the Americans with Disabilities Act (ADA), correctional facilities must provide programs, services, and activities for inmates and employees with disabilities (Rubin & McCampbell, 1995). For example, mental health screening, evaluation, and treatment must be provided to the estimated 30 percent of offenders who have mental disabilities (Pollack, 2005).

According to Rubin and McCampbell (1995), there are several ways for correctional facilities to accommodate inmates with disabilities, including providing specialized housing units and diverting inmates to more specialized facilities. Under the ADA, inmates who are hearing or speech impaired must be provided with auxiliary aids, including listening devices, taped texts, and other telecommunications devices. In some cases, inmates with developmental disabilities must be allowed alternative visiting procedures if traditional procedures are inadequate for effective communication.

INMATES WITH CHRONIC HEALTH PROBLEMS

Almost 3 percent of all female prison inmates and 1.9 percent of male inmates are HIV positive (Staton-Tindall et al., 2007). The overall rate of confirmed AIDS cases (of about 0.5%) is three and one half times larger than in the general population (Bureau of Justice Statistics, 2005). Public health experts estimate that 17 percent of prison inmates are infected with hepatitis C (HCV), a virus that damages the liver. The nation's prisons could be characterized as incubators for such infectious diseases as HIV, tuberculosis, syphilis, and HCV.

Most prisons now offer medical treatment for many of these diseases, but many do not provide treatment for hepatitis C because it costs about $10,000 a year to treat a person who has the virus, only 30 percent of treated patients get better, and no one knows how long they will stay healthy. About 85 percent of people who contract HCV suffer from chronic infection and die from liver failure 10 to 40 years later.

Social workers must advocate for the protection and rights of inmates who have been diagnosed with infectious diseases. Currently, the Alabama, Mississippi, and South Carolina prison systems segregate HIV-positive inmates from the general population. As recently as January 19, 2000, the Supreme Court upheld Alabama's right to segregate these prisoners, stating that prison officials should be allowed to make judgments about the difficulty of controlling prisoners in various settings and programs (Greenhouse, 2000). Though Alabama officials claim that they have been more successful than most states in preventing the spread of HIV in the prison population, HIV-positive inmates are excluded from 70 different programs, including job training, educational, and work-release programs. They are offered some alternative programs, but these are more limited and appear to be less effective than the programs provided to the general population. Most states have not found it necessary to segregate infected prisoners. If they are to be segregated, they should have the right to programs of the same quality.

UNDOCUMENTED IMMIGRANTS AND CRIME

In 2006 it was estimated that there were 11.5 to 12 million unauthorized people living in the United States, of whom more than half (56 percent) were thought to be from Mexico and 22 percent from the rest of Latin America (Passel, 2006). The most prevalent occurrence of undocumented people has been found in the states that border Mexico, as this has been the transit route for migrants from Mexico and the rest of Latin America. However, people who lack legal documentation can be found living throughout the United States.

Although immigration is not new for this country, in recent years attention has focused on the danger that is posed by the surge in immigrants who either overstay their visas or permits to visit or sneak over the border. Since 2005, the Department of Homeland Security (DHS) has increased efforts to detain undocumented immigrants and remove them from the United States (National Immigration Law Center, 2007). These efforts have been accompanied by increased state and local enforcement of immigration law. Although the initial impetus was in response to the illegal entry of the terrorists from the 9/11 attacks on the World Trade Center, it has become focused primarily on Latino undocumented immigrants. Enforcement of immigration laws was minimal prior to 2000. From 1996 to 2000, fewer than 12,000 people had been deported and barred from reentry; in 2006 alone, more than 13,000 people were barred from reentering the United States for 10 years (Gonzalez, 2008). The difference is not in the laws on the books, which have not been changed, but in the enforcement of those laws.

Immigration detainees are held under civil law, not criminal law. As such, they are legally entitled to better living conditions than convicted prisoners or pretrial detainees (American Civil Liberties Union, 2007). Civil law covers issues such as property rights, child custody, divorce, contracts, and agreements and are not considered crimes. Therefore, under law, undocumented people are to be tried for a breach of contract, not for committing a crime. However, the reality of detaining thousands of undocumented people in recent years has led to the accusation of abuses of their rights.

The DHS detainee population exceeds 261,000 annually (Nugent, 2007). The detention is civil and not punitive, yet the vast majority are held in prisons, housed with criminal convicts. Other than entering or staying in the country illegally, the detainees have not committed any other crime.

The surge in immigration law enforcement has affected the criminal justice system and social workers in numerous ways. The numbers of undocumented people in prisons and requiring legal authorities' attention has grown dramatically, particularly in the border states of California, Arizona, and Texas. The cost for the increase in incarceration is growing, and the extra efforts at border control are costly.

One of the rationales for this increase in enforcement is to combat crime. This is a controversial issue. Do immigrants, particularly undocumented immigrants, cause more crime? Although there may be a public perception as such, studies indicate that may not be true. Research indicates that the opposite may be the case, that crime decreases with growth in immigrant populations (Press, 2006). Immigrant communities are often tight knit, and there is an informal system of social control.

The challenge to social workers is to address public perceptions of immigrants, while at the same time serving immigrant populations. People who are undocumented are fearful of accessing social or public services. Fear of becoming known to authorities and potentially detained or deported holds people back. This fear includes reluctance to report crimes or make oneself known to school authorities. Undocumented immigrants, already marginalized due to language and economic barriers, are now even more marginalized due to fear of all authorities. This means that social workers have an even greater task of helping families who are undocumented access services such as health care, education, and protection from becoming victims of crimes.

SOCIAL WORK ROLES AND SKILLS

Social workers have played a role in forming many aspects of our current judicial system. They have contributed to significant changes in the way society handles crime and punishment, working to make the system more fair and beneficial to both convicted criminals and their victims. Social workers are also called to respond to violent events to aid survivors in dealing with the aftermath.

HISTORICAL BACKGROUND

In Great Britain during the 1740s a sheriff named John Howard and an ordinary citizen, Elizabeth Gurney Fry, began to create prisoner assistance programs (Fox, 1997). Sheriff Howard focused on improving prison conditions, while Fry provided direct aid to prisoners. By the late 1800s Americans in Massachusetts, Maryland, and New York were attempting to duplicate Howard's and Fry's prison reform efforts. The foundation of criminal justice social work had been laid. The prevailing belief among social workers of the time (a view still held by some today) was that they could not help people help themselves in an authoritarian prison context, and the profession largely avoided work with adult criminal offenders until the 1920s (Roberts, 1997a).

In 1841 John Augustus, a Boston philanthropist, became the first unofficial probation officer when he convinced the Boston courts to release people convicted of alcohol-related offenses to his care so that he could help with rehabilitation efforts (Allen, 1995). In today's world, **probation** is a sentence that does not, at least initially, require incarceration. It may involve a fine, supervision, community service, restitution, or home confinement. The goal of probation is to reintegrate offenders into the community. In many cases, if the conditions of probation are not met, the person who was convicted can be incarcerated. The concept of parole was officially introduced into the U.S. criminal justice system in 1884. **Parole** is the conditional release of a prisoner from incarceration to supervision after part of his or her sentence has been completed (Allen, 1995).

Prior to the twentieth century, juveniles were treated in about the same way as adult criminals. In 1897 social workers began advocating for **delinquent youth—** children under the age of 18 years who have violated a local, state, or federal law for which an adult can be prosecuted—and began fighting for a separate court system to serve them (Ezell, 1995). The first official juvenile court was established in Chicago in 1899 (Office of Juvenile Justice and Delinquency Prevention, 1999), paving the way for the creation of the juvenile justice system.

Jane Addams and other social workers played an important role in developing the first juvenile courts and promoting juvenile reform measures. By the early 1900s the entire juvenile court system had acquired a social work emphasis. The goal was to provide treatment and rehabilitation for youth. Thanks in part to the efforts of social workers, **due process** was introduced into the juvenile system during the 1960s. Due process includes the right to a fair trial, the right to be present at the trial, the right to an impartial jury trial, and the right to be heard in one's own defense. Previously, only adults had these constitutional rights. By the 1980s the perceived failure of juvenile rehabilitation to control delinquency would lead to a shift toward the control and punishment philosophy that dominated the adult corrections system. The social work profession's influence on juvenile courts was largely lost, and the juvenile court system began to once again mimic the worst of the adult system (Miller, 1995).

During the early 1900s social workers in many large cities initiated programs to do protective and preventive work with female and juvenile prisoners (Roberts, 1997b). These programs, originally called women's bureaus, were the first examples of **police social work**, which evolved into a specialization that provides social work services to victims and offenders who are referred by the police (Treger, 1995). By the 1940s social workers had begun to interact regularly with adult offenders in the court system, and police social workers were routinely engaged in counseling women and troubled children (Roberts, 1997a). Police social work experienced a resurgence during the 1980s, when many social workers were hired with funds from a federal grant program, the Law Enforcement Assistance Administration. When the grants ran out in the mid-1980s, many police social workers lost their jobs (Roberts, 1997a).

During the 1960s rehabilitation had become the focus of adult corrections in the U.S. legal system. **Rehabilitation** is treatment that helps criminal offenders change their antisocial styles of thinking, feeling, and acting (Gendreau, 1995). Because rehabilitation requires employees to understand human behavior and have the skills to make successful interventions, more social workers than ever before began working with adult prisoners. Judges began to rely on social workers to provide information on family history, social environment, attitudes, and motivation before making sentencing recommendations (Treger & Allen, 1997).

In the late 1960s reformers introduced the practice of offering diversion as part of criminal rehabilitation. **Diversion** involves officially suspending criminal or juvenile proceedings so as to allow defendants to meet specified conditions, such as completing treatment, community service, or an educational program. On successful fulfillment of the conditions, the charges may be dismissed. Diversions are now being used more frequently, particularly for minor first offenses in the juvenile justice system. During the 1970s social workers also began to assist in **reintegration** services, providing a bridge to the community for adults released from prison (Mays & Winfree, 1998).

During the 1970s victim assistance programs were a rarity. In 1982, perhaps because the number of people victimized by crime had reached an all-time high, the federal government organized the first President's Task Force on Victims of Crime. The task force focused attention on the psychological trauma suffered by victims of violent crime. The Office for Victims of Crime (OVC) was instituted by the Department of Justice in 1983, and the federal Victim of Crime Act (VOCA) was enacted in 1984. Both provide federal funds to support victim assistance programs and advocate for the fair treatment of crime victims (U.S. Department of Justice, 1998). The Office of Victim Assistance also provides direct services, including crisis counseling and temporary shelter, on tribal and federal lands and sponsors a training program for multidisciplinary teams that handle child sexual abuse cases and comprehensive victim services on tribal lands. The OVC is partially funded by fines and penalties paid by federal crime offenders.

The Academy of Forensic Social Work was started in 1985. Many certified members of the academy also belong to the National Organization of Forensic Social Workers (NOFSW), which is a clearinghouse for information regarding forensic social work and provides a forum for professional networking. **Forensic social work** is the application of social work to questions and issues relating to law and the legal system (NOFSW, 1998), which essentially covers the entire criminal justice system as well as civil family matters such as divorce and custody issues. Certification as a diplomate in forensic social work by the National Organization of Forensic Social Work is required by many employers in correctional facilities, courts, and police departments.

Social work's effect on the criminal justice system has been uneven. Over time, the system has become increasingly punitive. It has almost never provided criminals with appropriate access to effective treatment and rehabilitation programs (Pew Report, 2008). Instead, the correction system emphasizes containment and punishment. While it is difficult to advocate for criminal offenders in a system and a society that promote punishment over rehabilitation, social workers continue to strive to improve the criminal justice system.

PRACTICE SETTINGS

Forensic social workers practice in a variety of legal settings, from juvenile and family courts to adult corrections, probation, parole, and victim assistance. Their presence helps monitor and modify legal processes to ensure fair treatment for all concerned.

Juvenile and Family Courts   The juvenile and family court system is the organizational and policy context for social work practice with children, youth, and families.

CASE EXAMPLE: Andie was 16 when she was arrested for shoplifting in a Minneapolis mall. Since this was her first offense, she was sent to the juvenile diversion program, which worked with first-time offenders, their families, and their schools. The purpose of the program is to keep young people out of the court system and prevent them from committing other crimes. Sheila, Andie's social worker, required her to attend shoplifting prevention classes. "I didn't want to go," Andie said. "[Sheila] forced me to go. Well, she pushed me; she encouraged me." Because shoplifting is often a sign of problems at home, including abuse, Sheila also worked with Andie's family. Two years after successfully completing the program, Andie was working in a nursing home and had her own apartment. She said, "I owe at least half of my success to Sheila" (O'Connor, 1995).

The juvenile and family court system is intended to (1) prevent delinquency, (2) protect society by reeducating children who break the law, (3) prevent abuse and neglect, (4) protect children who are being abused and neglected, and (5) preserve and strengthen families (Ezell, 1995). The system deals with two kinds of offenses: delinquent youth offenses and status offenses. Delinquent youth offenses are violations of the law for which an adult can also be prosecuted. **Status offenses,** on the other hand, are illegal only for people young enough to be considered minors. Missing school and running away from home, for example, are not crimes when carried out by a person over 18 years of age (Ezell, 1995).

The functions of social workers in the court system can include making psychosocial assessments, conducting court investigations, giving courtroom testimony, supervising probation, and fulfilling court-assigned social services (Needleman & Needleman, 1997). When social workers investigate reports of abuse, perform custody evaluations, or find shelter for runaway youths, they are acting as agents of the court, and the powers and protections of the court allow them to intervene (Ezell, 1995). There is no consistency in the way juvenile and family courts operate from state to state, so social work functions may vary according to location.

Social workers can and have made important contributions to juvenile delinquency prevention programs, including parent training interventions, early intervention, child abuse prevention, violence prevention, substance abuse prevention, gang prevention, conflict resolution, and truancy reduction. These programs are best situated in family, school, or community settings. The evidence suggests that a comprehensive program that includes components drawn from virtually all theories of criminal behavior best prevents juvenile delinquency (Welsh & Farrington, 2007).

Juvenile Corrections   Juvenile corrections encompass a wide range of interventions for young people who have broken the law. Juvenile corrections social workers play major roles in the system as caseworkers, counselors, administrators, policy analysts, program evaluators, and advocates.

CASE EXAMPLE: Ten-year-old Eric was brought before a Tampa judge on arson and theft charges. He had been in trouble with the law before, and so had his siblings. When the judge asked Eric's father what he thought about his son's actions, the father dispassionately replied, "Boys will be boys." Jeanene Janes, Eric's social worker, intervened, asking the judge to consider sending the boy to an Outward Bound wilderness program rather than to a state training school. The judge agreed, and Jeanene had to help Eric prepare and also drove him to the site. Thirty years later, after Eric was a successful adult, Ms. Janes said, "His dad was not a good role model. I just couldn't see this kid going off to reform school. From that day forward, [I] understood the power of someone in [my] chosen career to help shape the life of a child, particularly if that child came from an uncaring family" (Bettendorf, 1999).

Adjudication is the process of formal accusation, trial, and sentencing. Most adjudicated juveniles are sent to training schools. Typically, training schools are physically similar to maximum-security prisons, although some are more like secured communities of houses or cottages (Mays & Winfree, 1998).

After a juvenile has been adjudicated, a comprehensive assessment is completed, and the corrections system attempts to recommend effective treatment programs that can utilize the offender's strengths to address the needs identified in assessment. Seven components are key in making juvenile treatment programs effective.

1. Programs should be holistic in their approach to placement and treatment of juvenile offenders.
2. Treatment must be family centered, instead of working only with the identified juvenile client.
3. The needs of the youth should take priority over the institutional needs of the placement agencies and services.
4. Ethnically and culturally appropriate programs should receive priority funding.
5. Administrators must be willing to think "outside the box" to create placement and treatment options that are best suited to the individual needs of the client.
6. Each state should determine priorities and hold treatment providers accountable.
7. Community-based programs are more effective than incarceration (NASW, 1997, p. 195).

Although the vast majority of violent crimes and felonies committed by juveniles can be traced to male offenders, the crime rate among female juveniles is actually increasing faster (Grascia, 2006). This has created a problem for juvenile correctional facilities that were developed with boys in mind. Juvenile corrections programs have traditionally used sports and team-oriented tasks and games to keep boys busy, and there is a significant gender gap in services (van Wormer & Kaplan, 2006).

For girls, the first step toward becoming an offender is being physically, sexually, and emotionally victimized (Belknap & Holsinger, 1998). A female offender needs and wants to process her experience of victimization and determine how it has affected her life. In addition, girls mature differently than boys do, so developmentally appropriate services are crucial, particularly for 8- to 11-year-olds (van Wormer & Kaplan, 2006).

The Maryland Department of Justice developed a female intervention team to assess the needs of female offenders and to develop gender-specific services for them. The team was staffed in large part by social workers. Two years after it began work in Baltimore, 50 percent fewer females were committed to Maryland's secure commitment facility. By its third year of operation, commitments to the secure facility were down 95 percent (Daniel, 1999). The social workers on the team served as case managers, advocates, and counselors. Perhaps even more important is protecting young girls from violence and abuse both inside and outside the juvenile justice system.

Despite the development of innovative programs for male and female juvenile offenders, most continue to be punished rather than treated. The Coalition for Juvenile Justice, which is mandated by federal law to examine the juvenile justice system, found that research indicates that there is still limited access to effective treatment or rehabilitation services (Kupchik, 2007).

Adult Corrections   Imagine walking into a dark concrete tunnel, hearing bars close behind you, and being surrounded by violent men. If this scenario disturbs you, adult criminal justice probably is not the context in which you want to practice social work. On the other hand, it may present precisely the kind of challenge you would like to take on.

CASE EXAMPLE: In 1984 Robert Thiret kidnapped a three-year-old girl, took her to the Colorado mountains, sexually molested her, and left her in a toilet. Some tourists happened to stumble upon the girl and saved her life. When Thiret's 10-year sentence was near completion, a social worker recommended transferring him to a community corrections program that offered sex-offender treatment and intense supervision. There was a public outcry against the transfer, and Thiret completed his sentence in prison. Eight months after the proposed transfer, he was released into the community without parole supervision or reporting requirements. He was not required to undergo treatment because he had served his full sentence (Williams, 1999).

Social workers in correctional facilities similar to the one where Thiret resided evaluate inmates' behavior, write comprehensive psychosocial histories, and prepare reports for parole boards. They may administer treatment programs to sex offenders, alcoholics, and addicts. They might spend most of their time conducting individual and group therapy, teaching life skills, or advocating for prisoners' rights.

Every day, thousands of prisoners—some illiterate, some mentally ill, many addicted to drugs—are released throughout the United States. They often lack the job skills or education they need to become successful, law-abiding citizens. The conditions they experienced in prison, including the withholding of human contact and basic rights, may have impaired their ability to function peacefully and productively in society. Two out of three eventually return to prison (Pew Report, 2008).

In 2008, President George W. Bush signed the Second Chance Act (SCA). This policy is designed to help reduce the recidivism rate. Newly released inmates are often driven right back to prison by difficulty in obtaining jobs, education, and housing, as well as by the social stigma that comes from having been in prison. In addition, many of these people suffer from mental illnesses but have no access to treatment. Some states have begun offering assistance in these areas, but much more needs to be done. The SCA established a federal reentry task force, along with a national resource center to collect and disseminate information about proven programs. It also broadened access to high-quality drug treatment and encourages states to work harder at reuniting families, which are often torn apart when a parent goes to prison.

The social work value of self-determination and the strengths perspective emphasize the need to educate the public, political leaders, and prison officials about the cost-effectiveness of sound rehabilitation programs as compared to simply building more prisons. According to some analysts, the few prisons that offer inmate work and education, in-prison drug treatment, and community aftercare programs have reduced the recidivism rate by as much as 50 percent (Arax, 1999). **Recidivism** refers to a criminal offender's return to criminal behavior after a period of correctional treatment.

PROBATION, PAROLE, AND COMMUNITY CORRECTIONS

CASE EXAMPLE: Sixteen-year-old Daniel is on probation for breaking gumball machines outside stores and stealing the change. Daniel has a developmental disability; his IQ of 70 puts him in the category of mildly mentally retarded. He lives with his grandparents, who are elderly and have needed a lot of support in raising Daniel.

CASE EXAMPLE: Rolanda is 28 years old and has been diagnosed with bipolar disorder. She is on parole after serving a six-month sentence for writing bad checks. Rolanda was homeless before she was arrested. Her eight-year-old daughter lives with Rolanda's mother.

CASE EXAMPLE: Franklin is 40 years old and is on probation for possession of cocaine. As part of his probation agreement, he is currently staying in a halfway house that provides drug treatment services. Franklin had been unemployed for two years before his latest drug arrest. He has a wife and three children. He also has a prior conviction for spouse abuse.

Case management and counseling are the primary services provided by social workers to people like Daniel, Rolanda, and Franklin who are on probation or parole or are participating in community corrections programs. Social workers may be hired by a state or county government as probation or parole officers, or they may be assigned to work in conjunction with probation or parole officers. The term **community corrections** refers to punishments or sanctions that occur outside of secure correctional facilities in halfway houses, treatment programs, work or educational release programs, community service programs, and diversion programs (particularly for juvenile offenders) or when offenders are on furlough or under house arrest. Community corrections allow offenders to work and support their families while paying restitution and defraying program costs (Mays & Winfree, 1998).

The social worker/case manager who deals with probationers and parolees has ten primary responsibilities.

Engage the client in the helping process: The social worker must be able to establish rapport with possibly resistant clients who come from diverse backgrounds and circumstances.

Assess the needs of the client: Daniel needs developmental disability services, educational and job resources, and independent living skills. Rolanda needs a place to live, access to medication for her bipolar disorder, and appropriate psychiatric treatment. Franklin needs job skills, employment resources, and perhaps some assistance in resolving family issues and problems.

Develop a service plan: The service plan must identify the strengths of the client and capitalize on them to help the client succeed. For example, Rolanda is bright but has little formal education. Her service plan might encourage and support attendance at an educational institutional.

Link the client with appropriate services: The services needed in the above cases include batterer intervention, mental health treatment, employment services, substance abuse treatment, and developmental disability services.

Coordinate with other case managers and helping professionals involved in the client's service plan: Franklin's probation officer/case manager brokers services and provides court liaison, informal counseling, and guidance. The probation officer/case manager also coordinates the efforts of a substance abuse treatment case manager, a batterer's intervention case manager, and Franklin's therapist.

Monitor the progress of the client: The purpose of monitoring is to ensure that services are delivered and that the service plan is effectively implemented.

Intervene with sanctions when necessary: Sanctions can range from probation or parole revocation, to more intense supervision and restrictions on travel, to random drug testing (Healey, 1999).

Advocate for the client when necessary: Sometimes it is necessary to advocate for the client to the courts or to the client's employer. For example, Daniel was accused of stealing supplies at his new job as a janitor for a local school. His probation could have been revoked, but the case manager intervened on his behalf and helped sort out the situation with Daniel's employer and the police. It turned out that Daniel did not steal the supplies, but instead gave them to an unauthorized person who took advantage of his inexperience.

Provide counseling and informal guidance: Case managers are generally not expected to do therapy with their clients, but they do need well-developed clinical skills. Rolanda often discusses her feelings and thoughts with her case manager, who uses reflective listening and cognitive restructuring techniques to help Rolanda expand her self-awareness and enhance her decision-making ability.

Evaluate the effectiveness of the service: The case manager must be able to determine whether Daniel, Rolanda, and Franklin are experiencing positive outcomes from their service plans. If not, alternative plans need to be developed (Martin & Inciardi, 1993).

The goals of probation, parole, and community-based corrections are protection of the community and reintegration of the offender. Both goals have become increasingly difficult to accomplish in recent years because caseloads have increased dramatically. A single case manager may work with as many as 300 probationers or parolees (American Correctional Association, 2007). In addition, because of the overcrowding in prisons, many violent criminals are being released early. The social work case manager must find a balance between support for the client's successful re-entry into the community and a level of supervision that protects the community.

VICTIM ASSISTANCE SERVICES

In addition to working with offenders, social workers also assist victims of crime. A **victim** is not only the person against whom a criminal offense has been committed but also, if that person has been killed or incapacitated, his or her spouse, parent, child, family, or other lawful representative.

CASE EXAMPLE: Less than 24 hours after the school shooting at Columbine High School in Colorado (see Chapter 11), American Red Cross social workers and other mental health professionals from California to Utah were en route. All were certified to provide services to victims of traumatic events. Their immediate goal was to provide crisis intervention services to the students, teachers, and parents, who were all victims. Their longer-term objectives were to reassure the victims of their safety and to help them express their thoughts, feelings, and reactions. The social workers hoped to provide victims with information and assistance that would help them deal with the aftermath of the tragedy.

Criminal victimization is physically, psychologically, and financially devastating. Victims may develop emotional problems, including intense anger, fear, isolation, low

BOX 14.3	MORE ABOUT ... VICTIM ASSISTANCE

Social workers are on call at the Rape Treatment Center at Santa Monica-UCLA Medical Center 24 hours a day, seven days a week. They provide long-term counseling, information, and referrals for rape victims and their families. They also help educate medical, law enforcement, criminal justice, judiciary, school, and other personnel about the particular traumas associated with rape. Social workers support victims throughout the investigation of the crime and the prosecution of the perpetrator.

self-esteem, depression, and helplessness (Kopiec, Finkelhor, & Wolak, 2004). The financial effects often include missing work as a result of physical and psychological injuries, paying for expensive medical treatment, having to replace or repair property, and paying for therapy. Survivors of prolonged or repeated criminal victimization, such as battered women and abused children, often suffer from debilitating emotional distress. When these crime victims seek help, they are often revictimized or stigmatized by the criminal justice system, and sometimes even by friends and family members who are overwhelmed by their own anger, guilt, and fear (Davis, Taylor, & Bench, 1994). This has been particularly true for rape victims (see "More About ... Victim Assistance").

Social workers in victim assistance are advocates and counselors. They need to be skilled in advocacy, negotiation, mediation, and crisis intervention (Roberts, 1995). They must know how to prepare victim impact statements, victim compensation forms, and applications for emergency monetary assistance for food and shelter. They must also be able to facilitate victim-offender mediation. Most victim assistance programs are housed in prosecutors' offices, hospitals, police and fire departments, sheriffs' offices, and nonprofit organizations.

Crisis intervention skills are critical for social workers in criminal justice contexts. Social workers respond to all kinds of emergencies, including rape, homicide, suicide, and death notification, to name a few. Crisis intervention—the mobilization of needed resources in emergency situations—can help prevent further disruption at the crime scene and help victims immediately begin to deal with the trauma (Hendricks & Byers, 1996).

After the immediate effect of the crisis has been dealt with, the client needs ongoing support. Eventually, referral for longer-term counseling services may be necessary. This is particularly true when children are victims of crime and experience traumatic crisis. They are the primary victims in cases of child abuse and gang violence, and they can also be secondary victims. For example, children may be traumatized if they witness spousal abuse or see their parents abusing drugs. Children who witness violent acts are at risk to become violent themselves as they grow older (Frank, 2000); this makes early intervention even more critical.

For social workers to effectively intervene in a crisis situation with a child, they must understand how children think and develop. Social workers use play therapy, puppets, dolls, and drawings to help children tell their stories and express their emotions. For example, after a four-year-old witnessed her mother's murder in a shopping mall parking lot, she was unable to say more than that a man killed her mother.

However, the child was able to use a toy shopping mall, a toy parking lot, and dolls to reenact the events that led up to and followed the murder (Goodman, 1984).

POLICY ISSUES

The social work profession's goal in dealing with criminal justice is to serve the public interest by developing, advocating for, and implementing effective public policies. This section identifies some of the most critical policy issues that criminal justice social workers are confronting in the early twenty-first century.

JUVENILE OFFENDERS

During the 1960s the Supreme Court required juvenile courts to become more like adult criminal courts by giving defendants protection against self-incrimination, the right to question and present witnesses, the right to an attorney, and the right to due process—a standard of proof that is "beyond a reasonable doubt" rather than merely a "preponderance of evidence" (*Kent* v. *U.S.*, 383 U.S. 541, 86 S.Ct. 1045, 1966; *In re Gault*, 387 U.S. 1, 87 S.Ct. 1428, 1967). These changes eventually led to the Juvenile Justice and Delinquency Prevention Act of 1974, which required states to deinstitutionalize or decriminalize status offenders and to separate juvenile delinquents from adult offenders. In 1980 the act was amended to require states to remove juveniles from adult jails (Synder & Sickmund, 1999). The act also established the Office of Juvenile Justice and Delinquency Prevention (OJJDP) to provide national leadership, coordination, and resources to prevent and respond to child victimization and juvenile delinquency.

Increases in the number of juvenile crimes during the 1980s caused many states to change their juvenile justice laws. In some states certain classes of juvenile offenders were automatically remanded to the adult criminal court system. Other states treated the youths as criminals in juvenile court. For the first time, many juveniles were facing mandatory sentences (Allard & Young, 2002). State laws have made it easier to move juveniles to adult criminal courts and adult correctional facilities. The oldest age for juvenile court was lowered in some states to 15 (Szymanski, 1998). Confidentiality laws were modified or eliminated in some cases, and judges were given expanded sentencing options that included blended sentences—sentencing a juvenile to serve time in a juvenile correctional facility and to be transferred to an adult facility at the age of 18 or 21 (Allard & Young, 2002).

Between 1985 and 1997 the number of juveniles sentenced to adult prisons doubled. Of juveniles sentenced to adult prison, 58 percent were African American; 25 percent were white; 15 percent were Latino; and 2 percent were Asian American.

BOX 14.4 | **WHAT DO YOU THINK?**

Should violent juvenile offenders be transferred to criminal court and tried as adults?

Sixty-one percent were convicted of violent offenses, including rape, robbery, and murder. On any given day, there are about 7,000 children in adult prisons (Campaign for Youth Justice, 2007).

People who propose transferring violent juveniles to criminal court argue that doing so will reduce recidivism. This line of reasoning assumes that young people will be sobered by their experiences in the adult criminal system and will not commit further crimes. However, Bishop, Frazier, Lanza-Kaduce, and Winner (1996) found that juveniles who were transferred to criminal court reoffended more times and more quickly than those who were tried in juvenile court. It is not known whether the juveniles who were transferred were more serious offenders because there were no data available on weapon use, victim injury, gang involvement, or drug use history (Campaign for Youth Justice, 2007). Thus, the jury is still out on the recidivism argument, but initial evidence suggests that transferring juveniles to adult court may not have the intended effect of reducing the reoffense rate.

Roush and Dunlap argue that the adult correctional system is "overworked, overcrowded and overwhelmed, and there is not evidence that it can rehabilitate juveniles" (1997, p. 2). Youths who are currently in the adult system have higher rates of recidivism than those who are in juvenile facilities for the same offenses. Juveniles in adult facilities are more likely to be sexually assaulted and beaten than their counterparts in juvenile corrections. Social workers must protect the rights and needs of juveniles who are placed in the adult criminal justice system, and advocate for more funds and policies that emphasize rehabilitation and treatment for both adult and juvenile correctional facilities. If state laws require some young people to be placed in adult facilities, social workers should argue for the separation of adults and juveniles within those facilities.

DOMESTIC VIOLENCE

Domestic violence is a pattern of assaultive behaviors, including physical, sexual, and psychological attacks and economic coercion, by adults and juveniles against their families or intimate partner or both. Family violence, particularly violence between spouses, gained recognition as a social problem during the 1970s when the women's movement pushed for examination of conditions for battered women, women who were physically abused by their intimates. Although the incidence of domestic violence is difficult to measure because some victims are reluctant to report it, domestic violence is estimated to represent 9 percent of all violent crime. In 2005, approximately 389,100 women and 78,180 men were victimized by an intimate partner. The majority of victims are female (85 percent) and females who are 20 to 24 years of age are at the greatest risk for intimate partner violence (Catalano, 2006). Beginning in 1993, there was a slow downward trend in domestic violence incidences. Part of reason for the decline in domestic violence may be the increase in attention and services for victims and potential victims.

The Violence Against Women Act, enacted in 1994, made available $1.6 billion in support of programs that research domestic violence and sexual assault. One of the funded efforts is the Violence Against Women Grants Office (VAWGO), which was designed to respond to the needs and concerns of victims and potential victims of domestic violence. The first national response to the problem of domestic violence, the Violence Against Women Act may have contributed to the decline in incidents from 1993 to 2002. With greater attention to and funding of support for victims of intimate violence, the role of social work practitioners in the treatment and prevention of domestic violence will continue to be important (see "From the Field…An Unexpected Journey").

In April 2008, the International Violence Against Women Act (IVAWA), was presented to Congress. This unprecedented legislation would make the global crisis of violence against women a top U.S. foreign policy priority. The bill would authorize U.S. aid to promote international violence prevention programs. It would support health care and other services for survivors, promote access to education and economic opportunity, and better address violence against women in humanitarian crises. The crisis of rape in the Democratic Republic of Congo illustrates the urgent worldwide need for pragmatic ways to prevent violence against women.

BOX 14.5   **FROM THE FIELD … AN UNEXPECTED JOURNEY**
Sharon Murphy MSW, PhD

I chose a career in social work because I wanted to help adults who suffered from various forms of mental illness. After a few years of clinical practice, I discovered that the majority of the people with whom I worked were victims of family or domestic violence. From that time forward, clients affected by family violence have become the focus of my practice, and for the past 17 years, I have concentrated on assisting women who have survived domestic violence, most recently First Nations women survivors.

Approximately six years ago I began working as a domestic violence consultant to a First Nations agency. The public defender's office was looking for someone to provide expert testimony in the case of an indigenous woman who had admitted to killing her partner and was charged with second-degree murder. The defense believed that the defendant was a victim of domestic violence and had acted in self-defense. I accepted the case and began a new phase of my career.

My social work education and practice experience were invaluable during the interview and assessment process. I drew on all the fundamental tools from the first-year practice course: reflective listening, paraphrasing, assessment, and conducting culturally appropriate interviews. The defendant was initially hesitant to tell me her story, but she became more comfortable over time. Eventually she was able to describe a 19-year history of domestic violence victimization by the

father of her children. My task was to reconstruct her life story and that of her children in the context of her culture and to present them to the jury.

The defendant was convicted of negligent homicide and received the minimum sentence of four years, with a recommendation from the judge for clemency. At the most recent clemency hearing, three of the five members of the clemency review board voted in favor of clemency. Because it was not a unanimous vote, the governor did not have to review the findings of the board within a certain period of time, and the defendant could complete her prison sentence without the governor's review.

We all could give up at this point, say that we did our best, and walk away. But my social work training and practice experience have taught me to move forward. We will continue to fight for the defendant's right to protect herself.

I became a part of this criminal proceeding four years ago. Since then I have served as a consultant to numerous attorneys during their trial preparation in domestic violence cases, have assessed women in jail, and am currently preparing for another trial. Social work education prepares students for this work, but it is often overlooked as a career opportunity. The combination of interview and assessment, the strengths perspective, and the person-in-environment framework is perfect preparation for working within the criminal justice system.

This legislation offers just that and should be passed with broad congressional support.

CRIME AND MENTAL ILLNESS

CASE EXAMPLE: On June 20, 2001, in Houston, Texas, 37-year-old Andrea Yates drowned her five children, who ranged in age from six months to seven years, in the bathtub. She told the police that she knew killing her children was against the law but that killing them was the only way to save them from the fires of hell and keep Satan from tormenting them. Mrs. Yates's attorneys entered a plea of innocent by reason of insanity and presented evidence that she suffered from a severe form of postpartum depression complicated by schizophrenia. Nevertheless, she was convicted on two counts of capital murder and sentenced to 40 years in prison without the possibility of parole. However, in 2006 on appeal she won a re-trial and was eventually acquitted by reason of insanity. Texas has found a middle ground that allowed defendants like Yates who are truly sick to use the defense, while blocking sane criminals from trying to getting off the hook by claiming temporary insanity.

It is likely that Mrs. Yates will now spend a significant amount of time in a se-cure mental health treatment facility, and the judge will have to reevaluate her case every year. Texas law requires more than mental illness to involuntarily hospitalize someone. The person must also be considered a danger to himself or herself or others. Currently, juries in most states can find a person guilty but mentally ill, but the finding does not mandate treatment, and the defendant is typically sent to prison.

Mrs. Yates is not the only prisoner who suffered from mental illness while incar-cerated. Research indicates that as many as 20 percent of inmates in jail or prison are in need of psychiatric care, frequently because of a serious mental disorder (Metzner, 2007). James & Glaze (2007) found that over 70 percent of inmates who had a mental health problem met criteria for substance dependence or abuse; jail in-mates who had a mental health problem were three times as likely as those who did not to report being physically or sexually abused in the past; and women had higher rates of mental health problems than men.

Mrs. Yates has not been the only imprisoned person who suffers from mental illness. It is estimated that as many as 70 percent of juvenile offenders suffer from mental disorders, and 20 percent of them are suicidal. Another 20 percent suffer from such serious mental illnesses as schizophrenia, major depression, and bipolar disorder. Over half of them suffer from conduct disorders, attention deficit hyper-activity disorder, or substance abuse problems (Mears, 2002).

Juvenile offenders who are mentally ill rarely receive proper treatment and are often abused and neglected by corrections officers. Some have been restrained with shackles, placed in isolation for long periods of time, and harshly punished. Be-cause mental illness is believed to be rare in the general population as well as in the prison population, social workers advocate for the right of seriously mentally ill prisoners to receive mental health treatment and for juveniles and adult prisoners to have access to rehabilitative services.

OVERCRIMINALIZATION AND OVERCROWDING

Perhaps one of the toughest challenges facing both the juvenile and adult correctional systems is overcrowding of jails and prisons. In 2001, the nation's prison population rose above 2 million for the first time, and by 2008, it was over 2.3 million (Pew Report, 2008). One reason for overcrowding is that legislators across the country have increased the number of offenses considered criminal and the severity of punishment. Some nonviolent drug addicts have been sentenced to more prison time than some murderers (Cose, 2000). Another reason for overcrowding is get-tough laws that require longer mandatory sentencing (Lloyd, 1999).

During the 1990s many states tried to deal with overcrowding by building more prisons (Coughlin, 1996). In most jurisdictions this strategy has failed to alleviate the intense pressure on the correctional system and has not reduced crime. However, Morgan Reynolds (2000), a professor of economics at Texas A&M University, put forward an argument in defense of building more prisons. In 1990 Texas inmates were serving only 16 percent of their sentences because of prison overcrowding. During the next 10 years, Texas tripled prison capacity, and most inmates now serve 48 percent of their sentences, whereas violent offenders serve 90 percent. Time served in Texas prisons was three times the national average during 1998 and 1999. Murder, rape, robbery, aggravated assault, and burglary dropped 33 percent in Texas, compared to a 27 percent decline nationwide.

Reynolds (2000) is quick to point out that while long sentences seem to be working in Texas, the Texas Department of Criminal Justice still needs to focus on more and better prevention and rehabilitation programs. Crime can be decreased significantly if the recidivism rate among offenders can be reduced through rehabilitation. In the end, no matter how many prisons or jails are built, if inmates are not rehabilitated, the rate of crime will not appreciably decline.

THE DEATH PENALTY

CASE EXAMPLE: Ray Krone was released from an Arizona prison in April 2002, after having been on death row for 10 years. Krone was the 100th inmate released from death row in the last 25 years. At least 14 of them, including Krone, were released after DNA evidence exonerated them and implicated another person in the crime.

The death penalty is very controversial (see "The Case of Cameron Todd Willingham"). Those who are against it point to the lack of reliable evidence that it decreases murder rates (*Economist,* 2007). In addition, carrying out the death penalty costs taxpayers three times more than keeping an offender in a maximum-security prison for 40 years (Logan, 2008). The United States is the only industrialized nation that still employs the death penalty.

Thirteen states—Alaska, Hawaii, Iowa, Maine, Massachusetts, Michigan, Minnesota, North Dakota, Rhode Island, Vermont, West Virginia, and Wisconsin— and the District of Columbia do not have the death penalty. However, several other states, including Illinois, Maryland, and Missouri, have moratoriums on the death penalty until the fairness of the process, racial disparities, and the quality

| BOX 14.6 | THE CASE OF CAMERON TODD WILLINGHAM: IS THE SYSTEM TOO FALLIBLE? |

In 2007, there were 42 executions in the United States. Twenty-six, or 60 percent, were carried out in the state of Texas. Texas has executed over 400 people since 1976. But the most controversial execution in Texas may have occurred in 2004 when Cameron Todd Willingham was the first and only man executed in the United States for suspected arson after his three children were killed in a fire. His children were all under the age of three. They burned to death at their home in Corsicana, Texas, in December 1991. When Mr. Willingham was executed in 2004 his final words were: "The only statement I want to make is that I am an innocent man, convicted of a crime I did not commit," he said. "I have been persecuted for 12 years for something I did not do."

Willingham testified at his trial that he narrowly escaped the fire himself, that he tried and failed to rescue his children, and that he then made repeated attempts to call for help and reenter the building, at one point smashing a window with a pool cue in the hope of reaching the children's bedrooms. Mr. Willingham was convicted primarily on the testimony of the Deputy State Fire Marshall, Manuel Vasquez: "The fire tells a story, I am just the interpreter. I am looking at the fire, and I am interpreting the fire. That is what I know. That is what I do best. And the fire does not lie. It tells the truth." Mr. Vasquez went on to testify that the fire was intentionally started.

In 2004, Project Innocence commissioned a report completed by four nationally known arson experts who used all the most recent advances in the understanding of arson evidence. Their conclusion in December 2004 (about 10 months after the execution): Willingham's conviction was based on bad science, and none of the evidence should have ever led investigators to believe the fire was set deliberately. "While we have no doubt that … witnesses believed what they were saying, each and every one of the indicators relied upon have since been scientifically proven to be invalid," the report says. In other words, Willingham likely did not commit a crime, and his execution was just one more ghastly element in an unspeakable family tragedy.

The Innocence Project claimed that the release of their report "marked the first time in the nation that scientific evidence showing an innocent person was executed." Perhaps most poignant for Willingham's surviving relatives is that, at the time of his execution, a similar case was going through the Texas legal system, that of Ernest Willis, who had been sentenced to death for his alleged role in setting a fatal fire in West Texas in 1987. One of the arson experts examined his case, too, found the forensic evidence similarly flawed, and said he saw no evidence of arson. Willis was able to have his case reopened and dismissed. He walked out of death row a free man seven months after Willingham's execution.

The Project Innocence lawyers have been instrumental in forcing courts to take new DNA-testing technology into account when reviewing convictions. Since 1992, when the Innocence Project first began, over 216 prisoners have been exonerated, including 16 who spent time on death row. Texas continues to lead the nation in executions (Gumbel, 2006).

of representation and evidence have all been reviewed (Logan, 2008). The moratoriums are explained in part by the fact that 214 people on death row were exonerated, one-third by new DNA evidence (Barksdale, 2008).

The death penalty was briefly suspended nationwide during part of 2007 and 2008, while the Supreme Court considered whether lethal injection was cruel and unusual punishment (*Baze* v. *Rees*). The case was based on a death row inmate in Kentucky whose lawyers argued that lethal injection was contrary to the Eighth Amendment. In April 2008, in a 7 to 2 decision, the court decided that as long as lethal injection was implemented properly it was not cruel and unusual. The decision lifted the temporary nationwide ban on the death penalty.

The moratorium on executions in Illinois, which was initiated in 2000, is still in place. In Illinois, the moratorium was imposed because more people on death row had been exonerated (13) than executed (12) since 1976 (Cole, 2000). DNA evidence was increasingly being used to acquit many death row inmates, and the governor, who favored the use of the death penalty, wanted to "be sure with moral certainty" that no more innocent people were headed for execution. Before he left office in 2003, Governor Ryan commuted the sentences of everyone (167 persons) on Illinois's death row to life in prison. In 2001, New Jersey, Indiana, Kentucky, and Pennsylvania instituted studies on whether to place a moratorium on the death penalty. New Jersey has not executed anyone since 1963; and in 2007, Governor John Corzine abolished the death penalty. Pennsylvania has only executed three people since 1978 (all three asked to be executed). The results of the Pennsylvania study were similar to findings in the other states. Pennsylvania must work to reduce the likelihood of false confessions, crime-lab errors, witness misidentification, and racial disparities (Shiffman & Couloumbis, 2007). The death penalty remains legal in Pennsylvania. It is important to note that in June 2002, in a 6 to 3 Supreme Court decision (*Atkins* v. *Virginia*), the death penalty was deemed to be cruel and unusual punishment for a person with mental retardation (Kaminer, 2002). In *Ring* v. *Arizona*, also in June 2002, the Supreme Court, ruled that only juries, not judges, could impose the death penalty. *Ring* v. *Arizona* overturned more than 100 pending death penalty cases in Arizona alone. Finally, in 2005, the U.S. Supreme Court abolished the use of the death penalty for persons who were under the age of 18 when the crime was committed.

Policy change to influence the ways we view and treat criminals can be daunting. Factors such as race and class play significant parts in our public response to crime. The box "Becoming a Change Agent" asks you to consider how you might advocate for change in the criminal justice system.

VICTIMS' RIGHTS

In 1982, Ronald Reagan established the President's Task Force on Victims of Crime. Tobolowsky's (1999) evaluation of the impact of the Task Force's Final Report indicates there was a surge in federal and state legislative and judicial action on behalf of crime victims. As a result of the task force's recommendations, "the federal government and the majority of the states have constitutional or legislative provisions (or both) which require victim notification of important events and actions in the criminal justice process and allow, to varying degrees, crime victim presence and hearing at critical stages of the criminal justice process" (p. 25). The most recent federal legislation addressing victims' rights is the Justice for All Act: Crime Victims' Rights (2004). This law and other state laws or constitutional amendments give crime victims in most states the following rights:

Victims must receive timely notice of any release, escape, and public proceeding involving the crime.

Victims must not be excluded from such proceedings.

Victims can consult with the prosecutor about important decisions in the prosecution and are to be heard at release, plea, sentencing, commutation, and pardon proceedings.

Victims are not to be subjected to undue delay or to decisions that disregard their safety or their just claims to restitution.

| **BOX 14.7** | **BECOMING A CHANGE AGENT** |

Are some victims of crime more important than others? School shootings have become increasingly common events and many receive a great deal of media attention. Some incidents of violence become national news stories and are discussed nationwide for weeks or months after they occur. But shootings occur at schools on a regular basis that we rarely hear about. When low-income students of color are shot at school, the events often receive limited local coverage and no national coverage. For example, in the first two months of 2008, there were three school shootings in Memphis, Tennessee, at Mitchell High School, Manassas High School, and Hamilton High School. The victims in all three were African American, and none of the three received much media attention.

The victims in the vast majority of school homicides are African American, and most of these are not widely reported (Finkelhor & Ormrod, 2001). Looking at the situation another way, some argue that the intense attention to where children are shot, at school, poses a problem. School shootings garner media attention while homicides of children that take place away from school do not receive the same attention. Between 1992 and 2002, 261 youth ages 5 to 19 were victims of homicide at school. During this same time period, 28,500 youth ages 5 to 19 were homicide victims away from school (DeVoe et al., 2004).

Similar concerns can be raised about media attention paid to cases of kidnapped children and victims of domestic violence. Many people around the country know the name Laci Peterson, a missing pregnant woman whose husband was later accused and convicted of the crime. It was difficult to turn on the news after her disappearance and during her husband's trial without hearing about the case. Laci Peterson was white. Statistics tell us that most pregnant homicide victims are young and African American (Goldwert, 2008). Yet few if any of these cases receive any media attention, much less the massive media attention given to the Peterson case.

Analyzing the Situation

- Conduct research on youth homicides at school or kidnapped children. Have you heard about most of the cases where the victims were white? Have you heard about most of the cases where the victims were children of color? If you see a disparity, why do you think that disparity occurs?
- Does media coverage matter? Does broad coverage say something about the importance or worth of the victims or does it shape how we see and understand crime and violence and our fears about crime and violence?
- What makes something worthy of news coverage? Is it the event, the types of people involved, the location, or something else?

What Can Social Workers Do?

Given your analysis, what might social workers do to influence what and who the media decides is newsworthy? Can you think of possible approaches to shape media coverage that involve the use of community practice or legislative advocacy?

What Can You Do?

What one step might you take now, alone or working with others, to influence media coverage about an issue that matters to you? What are the barriers that might keep you from taking this step? What could you do to reduce those barriers?

Victims may be eligible for cash or in-kind assistance from victim compensation funds.

Perhaps the most important victims' right is that victims must be given notice of the existence of their participatory rights. Law enforcement officers, prosecutors, and victim services personnel, including social workers, all share notification responsibility.

The victim rights movement does have some limitations. For example, many states only apply victims' rights to felony cases or cases involving physical or sexual violence or injury. Unfortunately, there is evidence to suggest that some law enforcement officers do not always notify victims of the availability of compensation funds (Fritsch, Caeti, Tobolowsky, & Taylor, 2004). Finally, it is not always clear what the remedies are if victims' rights are violated or ignored. Therefore, one of the most important roles social workers have when working in victim assistance programs is to be knowledgeable about victims' rights in the state in which they are practicing. Most importantly, they must continue to advocate for the expansion and more effective enforcement and implementation of victims' rights.

ETHICS AND VALUES

Supporters of the death penalty argue that, as the ultimate punishment, it deters crime. Some feel that keeping perpetrators of especially heinous crimes alive sends the message that society condones their acts. This presents an ideological dilemma for social workers.

Social workers have a professional commitment to ensure the right of all people to receive treatment. In addition, the profession is based on the belief that, with intervention, people can be rehabilitated. The decision that a criminal is not worthy of living and cannot be changed is subjective. Who is qualified to decide that an act is evidence of inability to change? Are all people who commit murder incapable of change or remorse? Is that true of only some murderers? How do people know who can change?

Probably the most profound practice challenge and value dilemma faced by social workers in adult and juvenile corrections is how to use the strengths perspective in a system that promotes punishment over rehabilitation. Some social workers have left their jobs in criminal justice settings because of this dilemma, whereas others have chosen to stay and advocate for change. Social workers need to provide empirical evidence that rehabilitation programs can and do work to politicians and prison officials. Although treatment programs may be more expensive in the short term, over the long haul they are cost effective because they reduce recidivism rates.

BOX 14.8	ETHICAL PRACTICE ... REHABILITATION OR PUNISHMENT?

In your work with juvenile probation, one of your jobs is to write reports for the court. In these reports you provide an assessment for the juvenile court judge about the behavior of those on probation. One of your clients, Michele, lives in a group home and left for a weekend. You find out she went to help her younger brother resolve a problem. When it is time to write the report, you find yourself struggling. You believe that Michele was fulfilling a familial obligation when she went to help her brother, and you were impressed that she came back. You know that the judge to whom you will give the report is extremely strict and will probably be harsh on Michele if he finds out that the she left the home for the weekend. Other than this incident Michele has been doing extremely well, and you believe it is in her best interest to have a positive report to the judge. Would you include the weekend incident in the report? Why or why not?

CONCLUSION

The three major areas of concern for social workers involved with the justice system are improved prevention efforts, better assessment of needs, and the institution of effective rehabilitation interventions. In all these areas, social work has experienced a slow and pendular evolution, and the system has moved back and forth between prevention and punishment. Social workers who choose to focus on the criminal justice system are likely to encounter some of the most intense experiences, both positive and negative, that the profession has to offer. While social work practice in juvenile and criminal justice settings can be demanding and at times overwhelming, it provides a valued contribution to promoting a socially just society.

Key Terms

adjudication, (p. 408)

community corrections, (p. 411)

delinquent youth, (p. 405)

deterrence theory, (p. 396)

diversion, (p. 406)

domestic violence, (p. 415)

due process, (p. 406)

forensic social work, (p. 407)

juvenile corrections, (p. 408)

misdemeanor, (p. 399)

parole, (p. 405)

police social work, (p. 406)

probation, (p. 405)

recidivism, (p. 410)

rehabilitation, (p. 406)

reintegration, (p. 406)

status offenses, (p. 408)

victim, (p. 412)

Questions for Discussion

1. What is the primary goal of the criminal justice system? Do you agree with the goal? Why?
2. Compare the following theories about why people commit crimes: deterrence, biological determinism, psychological determinism, behaviorism, social disorganization, and broken window.
3. What is the difference between rehabilitation and diversion programs?
4. Describe the characteristics of successful treatment programs for juvenile offenders.
5. What is the difference between probation and parole?

Change Agent Exercise

Voting is an important right that Americans enjoy. The officials we choose to elect have a major impact on the funding that is available for social services and the policies that shape many areas of our lives. Before people can vote they must be registered to vote. Find out how people in your state can register to vote. Is everyone afforded the right to vote? What about prisoners or people who have committed a crime? Find out whether they have the right to vote. What do you think of these policies? Make sure you are registered to vote, and help others to register to vote.

Chapter Exercises

1. **Theories of Criminal Behavior**

   Describe the central theories used to explain why people commit crimes.

   Choose one theory or a combination of theories that make the most sense to you. Discuss why the theory or theories you've chosen explain criminal behavior better than the other theories.

   Using your theory as the underlying framework, describe a policy that could be implemented to reduce crime.

2. **The Death Penalty**

   Should the United States continue to use the death penalty in cases of violent crime?

   Do research on arguments on both sides of the issue.

   Describe why the death penalty is a controversial issue.

   - Is there adequate evidence to resolve the issue?
   - Is the current evidence contradictory?
   - What are the underlying values on each side of the issue?
   - Examine your personal beliefs on this issue. Does the death penalty affect your life? If so, how? Have you had personal experiences related to the death penalty?
   - Choose one side. Brainstorm arguments that support your side. List and explain the strongest arguments.
   - Do the same for the arguments on the other side.
   - What gaps do you see in the information? What would you need to know to help convince you to favor one side or the other? Where might you find this information?
   - Which side do you favor? What specifically convinces you that this is the right side? Is this the same position or a different position than you had before researching this topic?

3. **Current Issues in Criminal Justice**

   Find at least one article about the criminal justice system in a newspaper or a newsmagazine.

   Describe the article:

   How is the information in the article relevant to social work practice in criminal justice settings?

   What questions does the article raise for you?

   What would you like to know about the topic, and how could you find the information you seek?

   Does the article make you more or less interested in working in criminal justice social work? Why?

4. **Interpreting Data from the Criminal Justice System**
   Examine the data below and answer the questions that follow.

   Ethnicity of Juveniles in the Juvenile Justice System

White	33%
African American	41%
Latino	24%
Other	2%

   Ethnicity of Adults in the Criminal Justice System

White	37%
African American	35%
Latino	25%
Other	3%

   Ethnicity in the General Population

White	73%
African American	13%
Latino	11%
Other	3%

   How would you describe the differences between ethnicity in the general population and ethnicity in the juvenile and criminal justice systems?

   What do you think accounts for the differences between ethnicity in the general population and ethnicity in the juvenile and criminal justice systems?

   Identify two social policies that might eliminate the differences between ethnicity in the general population and ethnicity in the juvenile and criminal justice systems.

   1.

   2.

   Explain how these policies would make a difference.

5. **Dialogues with People with Differing Points of View**
   Interview a public official who believes that youth who commit serious crimes should be prosecuted and sentenced as adults. Interview an official who believes that they should remain in the juvenile justice system. Summarize each person's main points.

   Which position do you agree with the most? Why?

References

Allard, P. & Young, M. (2002). *Prosecuting juveniles in adult court: Perspectives for policymakers and practitioners*. Washington DC: Sentencing Project.

Allen, G. F. (1995). Probation and parole. *Encyclopedia of social work* (19th ed.). Washington, DC: NASW Press.

American Civil Liberties Union. (2007, January 24). *ACLU sues immigration officials and for-profit corrections corporation over dangerous and inhumane housing of detainees.* New York: Author.

American Correctional Association. (2007). *ACA directory: Juvenile and adult correctional departments, institutions, agencies and paroling authorities.* College Park, MD: Correctional Association.

Arax, M. (1999). A return to the goal of reforming inmates: Officials reconsider the discredited idea of rehabilitation as two out of three California parolees are back in prison within two years. *Los Angeles Times*, June 1, Metro, p. 1.

Barksdale, T. (2008). Other issues block North Carolina executions. *Charlotte Observer*, April 17, p. 1.

Belknap, J., & Holsinger, K. (1998). An overview of delinquent girls: How theory and practice failed and the need for innovative changes. In Zaplin, R. T. (ed.), *Female offenders: Critical perspectives and effective interventions.* Gaithersburg, MD: Aspen Publisher.

Bennett, A. (2007). Retaliation is the main driver of children's offenses. *Children Now*, October 10, p. 17.

Bettendorf, E. (1999). Gift to help teach social workers. *Tampa Tribune*, August 10, Metro, p. 1.

Bishop, D., Frazier, C., Lanza-Kaduce, L., & Winner, L. (1996). The transfer of juveniles to criminal court: Does it make a difference? *Crime and Delinquency, 42*, 171–191.

Bureau of Justice Statistics. (2005). *HIV in prisons and jails, 2002.* Washington, DC: U.S. Department of Justice, Office of Justice Programs.

Campaign for Youth Justice. (2007). *The consequences aren't minor: The impact of trying youth as adults and strategies for reform.* Washington, DC: Campaign for Youth Justice.

Catalano, S. M. (2006). *Criminal victimization.* Washington, DC: Bureau of Justice Statistics.

Cole, W. (2000). Death takes a holiday. *Time, 155*, 6, 24.

Cose, E. (2000). Locked away and forgotten. *Newsweek*, February 28, p. 54.

Coughlin, E. K. (1996). Throwing away the key. *Chronicle of Higher Education*, April 26, p. A8.

Daniel, M. D. (1999). The female intervention team. *Juvenile Justice Journal*, 6, 1, 14–20.

Davis, R., Taylor, B., & Bench, S. (1994). *The impact of sexual and non-sexual assault on secondary victims.* New York: Victim Services.

DeCoster, S., Heimer, K., & Wittrock, S. M. (2006). Neighborhood disadvantage, social capital, street context, and youth violence. *Sociological Quarterly, 47*, 4, 723–753.

Economist. (2007). Capital punishment in America: Revenge begins to seem less sweet. *Economist*, August 7, p. 10.

DeVoe, J. F., Peter, K., Kaufman, P., Miller, A., Noonan, M., Snyder, T. D., & Baum, K. (2004). *Indicators of school crime and safety: 2004* (NCES 2005-002/NCJ 205290). Washington, DC: U.S. Departments of Education and Justice.

Ezell, M. (1995). Juvenile and family courts. *Encyclopedia of social work* (19th ed.). Washington, DC: NASW Press.

Farmer, A. (2007). Going off to summer camp behind the fence of a prison. *New York Times*, August 22, p. B3.

Finkelhor, D., & Ormrod, R. (2001). Homicides of children and youth. *Juvenile Justice Bulletin*. Washington, DC: U.S. Government Printing Office.

Fox, V. (1997). Foreword to the first edition. In Roberts, A. R. (ed.), *Social work in juvenile and criminal justice settings*. Springfield, IL: Charles C. Thomas.

Frank, C. (2000). Betsy Groves: Helping children in a violent world. *Biography*, January, pp. 89–91.

Fritsch, E. J., Caeti, T. J., Tobolowsky, P. M., & Taylor, R. W. (2004). Police referrals of crime victims to compensation sources: An empirical analysis of attitudinal and structural impediments. *Police Quarterly, 7,* 3, 372–393.

Gendreau, P. (1995). Rehabilitation of criminal offenders. *Encyclopedia of social work* (19th ed.). Washington, DC: NASW Press.

Gladwell, M. (2000). *The tipping point: How little things can make a big difference*. Boston: Little, Brown.

Goldwert, L. (2008). *Murdered pregnant women: The racial divide*. CBSnews.com Report. http://www.cbsnews.com/stories/2008/04/11/national/main4009249.shtml.

Goodman, G. (1984). The child witness: An introduction. *Journal of Social Issues, 40,* 2, 1–9.

Gonzalez, D. (2008). U.S. immigration law drives husband, wife apart. *Arizona Republic*, February 17, pp. A1, A 18.

Grascia, A. M. (2006). Girls, gangs and crime: Profile of the young female offender. *Journal of Gang Research, 13,* 2, 37–49.

Greenhouse, L. (2000). Justices allow segregation of inmates with HIV. *New York Times*, January 19, p. 19A.

Gumbel, A. (2006). Guilty until proven innocent: Capital punishment in the US is under the microscope. *Independent*, May 4, p. 1.

Harrington, M. P., & Spohn, C. (2007). Defining sentence type: Further evidence against use of the total incarceration variable. *Journal of Research in Crime and Delinquency*. 44(1), Feb 2007, 36–63.

Healey, K. M. (1999). Case management in the criminal justice system. *National Institute of Justice Research in Action*. Washington, DC: U.S. Department of Justice.

Hendricks, J. E., & Byers, B. (1996). *Crisis intervention in criminal justice/social service*. Springfield, IL: Charles C. Thomas.

Herbert, B. (2007). An American addiction. *New York Times,* April 27, p. 6.

Hensley, J. J. (2008). Cocaine, prison, racial bias, reform. *Arizona Republic*, April 6, p. A1.

Howerton, A. (2007). Police response to crime: Differences in the application of law by race. *Ethnicity in Criminal Justice, 4,* 3, 51–66.

James, D. J., & Glaze, L. E. (2007). Mental health problems of prison and jail inmates. Retrieved on April 24, 2008, from http://www.ojp.usdoj.gov.bjs/abstract/mjppji.htm.2008.

Johnson, K. (2007). Criminals target one another, trend shows; Links to drugs, gangs suggested by slayings. *USA Today*, August 31, p. 1A.

Kaminer, W. (2002). The way we live now. *New York Times*, July 7, pp. 6, 7.

Kelling, G. L., & Sousa, W. H. (2001). *Do police matter? An analysis of the impact of New York City's police reforms*. New York: Manhattan Institute for Policy Research.

King, R. S. (2007). Moving toward a gender-appropriate response in the criminal justice system. *Journal on Criminology and Civil Confinement, 33,* 3, 3–12.

Kopiec, K., Finkelhor, D., & Wolak, J. (2004). Which juvenile crime victims get mental health treatment? *Child Abuse & Neglect, 28,* 1, 45–59.

Kupchik, A. (2007). The correctional experiences of youth in adult and juvenile prisons. *Justice Quarterly, 24,* 2, 247–270.

Liptak, A. (2008). American exception: Inmate count in American prison dwarfs other nations. *New York Times,* April 23, p.1.

Lloyd, J. (1999). Outdated rural jails are packed, troubled. *USA Today,* December 24, p. 2.

Logan, L. (2008). Measure calls for freeze on executions in Missouri Senate bill also would set up a commission to study fairness of death penalty process. *St. Louis Dispatch,* April 2, p.1.

Martin, S. S., & Inciardi, J. A. (1993). Case management approaches for the criminal justice client. In Inciardi, J. A. (ed.), *Drug treatment and criminal justice.* Thousand Oaks, CA: Sage Publications, pp.46–58.

Mays, G. L. & Winfree, L. T. (1998). *Contemporary corrections.* Belmont, CA: Wadsworth.

Mears, D. P. (2002). Treat mental illness of juvenile offenders. *Baltimore Sun,* April 22, p. 11A.

Metzner, J. L. (2007). Evolving issues in correctional psychiatry. *Psychiatric Times,* September 1, p. 9.

Miller, J. G. (1995). Criminal justice: Social work roles. *Encyclopedia of social work* (19th ed.). Washington, DC: NASW Press.

NASW. (1997). *NASW speaks.* Washington, DC: National Association of Social Workers.

National Immigration Law Center. (2007). *Overview of key immigration issues facing the immigrants' rights movement.* Washington, DC: Low-Income Immigrant Rights Conference.

Needleman, C., & Needleman, M. L. (1997). Social work with juvenile offenders. In Roberts, A. R. (ed.), *Social work in juvenile and criminal justice settings.* Springfield, IL: Charles C. Thomas.

NOFSW. (1998). *National Organization of Forensic Social Work.* http://www.nofsw.org.

Nugent, C. (2007). Testimony before the Subcommittee on Immigration, Citizenship, Refugees, Border Security, and International Law, November 8, *H.R. 750, the Save America Comprehensive Immigration Act of 2007.* Washington, DC: House Committee on the Judiciary.

O'Connor, A. (1995). Successful city youth program faces ax. *Star Tribune,* September 18, p. 1B. Office of Justice Programs. (2006). *Juvenile offenders and victims: 2006 national report.* Washington, DC: U.S. Department of Justice.

Office of Juvenile Justice and Delinquency Prevention. (1999). *Fact sheet: Juvenile court processing of delinquency cases, 1986–1995.* Washington, DC: Office of Juvenile Justice and Delinquency Prevention.

Passel, J. S. (2006). *The size and characteristics of the unauthorized migrant population in the US.* Washington, DC: Pew Hispanic Center.

Pew Report. (2008). *One in 100: Behind bars in America.* Washington, DC: Pew Center on the States.

Pollack, S. (2005). Taming the shrew: Regulating prisoners through women-centered mental health programming. *Critical Criminology, 13,* 1, 612–616.

Pollock, J. M., Mullings, J. L., & Crouch, B. M. (2006). Violent women: Findings from the Texas women inmates study. *Journal of Interpersonal Violence, 21*(4), 485–502.

Press, E. (2006). Do immigrants make us safer? *New York Times Magazine*, December 3. http://www.nytimes.com/2006/12/03/magazine/03wwln_idealab.html.

Reynolds, M. (2000). The Texas experience shows that prisons work. *Houston Chronicle*, January 23, p. 1.

Roberts, A. R. (1995). Victim assistance and victim/witness assistance programs. *Encyclopedia of social work* (19th ed.). Washington, DC: NASW Press.

Roberts, A. R. (1997a). Introduction and overview. In Roberts, A. R. (ed.), *Social work in juvenile and criminal justice settings*. Springfield, IL: Charles C. Thomas.

Roberts, A. R. (1997b). Police social work: Bridging the past to the present. In Roberts, A. R. (ed.), *Social work in juvenile and criminal justice settings*. Springfield, IL: Charles C. Thomas.

Roush, D., & Dunlap, E. (1997). *Juveniles in adult prison: A very bad idea*. Washington, DC: American Correctional Association.

Rubin, P. N., & McCampbell, S. W. (1995). *The Americans with Disabilities Act and criminal justice: Mental disabilities and corrections*. Washington, DC: U.S. Department of Justice, National Institute of Justice.

Schanzenbacj, M., & Yaeger, M. L. (2006). Prison time, fines, and federal white-collar criminals: The anatomy of a racial disparity. *Journal of Criminal Law and Criminology*, *96*, 2, 757–793.

Sentencing Project (2007). Racial disparities report. Retrieved on April 22, 2008, from http://www.sentencingproject.org/IssueAreaHome.aspx?IssueID=3.

Shiffman, J., & Couloumbis, A. (2007). Report: Flaws risk wrong execution. *Philadelphia Inquirer,* October 10, p. B1.

Staton-Tindall, M., Leukefeld, C., Palmer, J., Oser, C., Kaplan, A., Krietmeyer, J., Saum, C., & Surratt, H. L. (2007). Relationships and HIV risk among incarcerated women. *Prison Journal, 87,* 1, 143–165.

Snyder, H. & Sickmund, M. (1999). Juvenile offenders and victims: 1999 National report. Washington, DC: National Center for Juvenile Justice and the Office of Juvenile Justice and Delinquency Prevention.

Szymanski, L. (1998). Oldest age juvenile court may retain jurisdiction in delinquency matters. *NCJJ Snapshot, 3,* 9. Pittsburgh, PA: National Center for Juvenile Justice.

Tobolowsky, P. (1999). Victim participation in the criminal justice process: Fifteen years after the President's Task Force on Victims of Crime. *New England Journal on Criminal and Civil Confinement, 25,* 1, 21–105.

Treger, H. (1995). Police social work. *Encyclopedia of social work* (19th ed.). Washington, DC: NASW Press.

Treger, H., & Allen, G. F. (1997). Social work in the justice system: An overview. In Roberts, A. R. (ed.), *Social work in juvenile and criminal justice settings*. Springfield, IL: Charles C. Thomas.

Uniform Crime Report. (2007). Washington, D.C.: Federal Bureau of Investigation.

U.S. Department of Justice. (1998). New directions for the victim assistance community. In *New directions from the field: Victims rights and services in the 21st century*. Washington, DC: Office of Justice Programs and Office for Victims of Crime.

van Wormer, K. (1999). Book review: Social work in juvenile and criminal justice (2d ed.). *Social Work, 44,* 1, 82.

van Wormer, K., & Kaplan, L. (2006). Results of a national survey of wardens in women's prisons: The case for gender-specific treatment. *Women & Therapy, 29,* 1/2, 133–151.

Viewpoints. (2002). Time to bury the death penalty? *Arizona Republic,* May 12, pp. 1–2.

Welsh, B. C., & Farrington, D. P. (2007). Scientific support for early prevention of delinquency and later offending. *Victims & Offenders, 2,* 2, 125–140.

Williams, C. (1999). Re-entering society: Community corrections paves way. *Denver Post,* September 12, p. K-01.

CRISIS, TRAUMA, AND DISASTERS

CHAPTER **15**

Elhenyo/istockphoto.com

The previous 14 chapters demonstrate that social workers are found in every area of human services. Some are in unexpected places such as employee assistance programs, legislative advisers in state capitols, even mortgage lenders working with community banks, and many are in social service settings. What all these positions have in common is the need for social work practitioners with knowledge and understanding of human behavior and a skill set that enables them to help empower clients. There are social and behavioral concerns that cut across all areas of social work. For example, Chapters 13 and 14 discussed substance abuse and violence, two problems that can be found in every social work practice setting. This chapter covers another problem that is found in all fields of social work practice—dealing with the effects of trauma. Nothing calls for social work skills and abilities more than the need to help empower people and communities who have been victimized by crises, traumas, or disasters. This chapter explores a variety of contexts in which trauma can occur, including natural and human-made disasters; and provides an overview of the roles social workers play in these situations.

WHAT DO WE MEAN BY CRISIS, TRAUMA, AND DISASTER?

Chapter 5 discussed the role of social workers in crisis intervention. As a practice method, it emphasizes assisting victims and survivors to return to precrisis levels of functioning. Therefore, a **crisis** is an event that disrupts a person's equilibrium, the person's usual ways of coping fail, and there is evidence of distress and impairment of functioning (Roberts, 2005). Personal crises can result from life events such as divorce or death of a loved one. Community crises can result from violent acts or natural disasters such as hurricanes or floods. "The main cause of a crisis is an intensely stressful, traumatic, or hazardous event" (Roberts, 2008, p. 485). In many ways, crisis is the overall framework under which several types of events fall: stress, traumas, and disasters. All of these can be regarded as crises.

A **trauma** can be defined as "an injury to the body or psyche by some type of shock, violence, or unanticipated situation" (Barker, 2003, p. 441). And a **disaster** is "an extraordinary event, either natural or human-made, concentrated in time and space, that often results in damage to property and harm to human life or health and that is disruptive of the ability of some social institutions to continue fulfilling their essential functions" (Barker, 2003, p. 122). **Stress** is typically part of all of these events, is characterized by a physiological response to a real or perceived threat, and leads to anxiety, which is the physical discomfort experienced because of the increased production of stress hormones (Scaer, 2005).

It is difficult to separate these types of events. For example, consider a soldier returning from the war in Iraq. After serving months and months in a hostile region of the world where every move could end in injury or death, the soldier returns to the United States where life is relatively peaceful and safe. It is very difficult to simply turn off the state of readiness and alarm that the soldier has been living under for the previous year. First, the soldier served in a very traumatic environment, with crises or unexpected hazardous events occurring regularly. Second, over time, the pressure caused continuous levels of stress. Third, in some ways the destruction and turmoil reflects a disaster, albeit human-made as opposed to natural. The end result

BOX 15.1 | **WHAT DO YOU THINK?**

Imagine if you were a social worker meeting with Sergeant Twiggs's wife. How might you respond to her comment that medications were not what he needed, that "he needed help"? What kind of help might social workers offer in this case?

is that the returning soldier is experiencing stress because of crisis, trauma, and disaster.

> On May 14, 2008, Sergeant Travis N. Twiggs, 36 years old, led police on a 130-mile vehicle pursuit and, in the end, killed his brother who was traveling with him and turned the gun on himself and committed suicide. Sergeant Twiggs, a Marine, had served four tours of duty in Iraq and Afghanistan. He was placed on several medications after he developed post-traumatic stress disorder. He wrote about his struggles in "PTSD: The War Within" in the *Marine Corps Gazette*. His wife described him as a great father and husband who needed help, not just medication. (Galvin, 2008)

It is estimated that 300,000 U.S. soldiers who served in Iraq, or 20 percent of those who were deployed between 2003 and 2008, are suffering from major depression or post-traumatic stress syndrome, and only half have sought treatment (Rand Report, 2008). This growing need and other areas of crisis are discussed throughout this chapter.

STRESS

Not all stress is the same. The National Scientific Council on the Developing Child (2005) identified three types of stress—positive, tolerable, and toxic. Although the council directed its report specifically toward children and their development, they described the types of stress we all face.

1. *Positive stress:* Stress generated by short-lived adverse experiences that result from events such as starting a new job, meeting new people, or seeing a doctor for routine medical care.
2. *Tolerable stress:* Stress generated by adverse experiences that are more intense, but still of relatively short duration such as the death of a loved one, an accident, divorce or separation; this stress can become positive and help people emotionally or psychologically develop, or it can become more severe and lead to the toxic level.
3. *Toxic stress:* Stress generated by intense adverse experiences sustained over a long period of time, such as by abuse or exposure to violence, which place the body under a prolonged physiological and psychological response.

High levels of stress, particularly over prolonged periods of time, mean the body emits high levels of stress hormones such as cortisol, which have severely negative effects on people's health. In children, toxic stress can impair brain development, as well as suppress immunity to infections, and do permanent damage that affects learning and memory (Centers for Disease Control and Prevention, 2008). The link between stress in childhood and adult health is significant. Studies have found that adverse childhood experiences are common among people in the United States, and the consequence is distressing. The Adverse Childhood Experiences (ACE) Study (Centers for Disease Control and Prevention, 2006) focused on the occurrence and impact of 10 adverse events: emotional abuse, physical abuse, sexual abuse, emotional neglect, physical neglect, household dysfunctions of mother treated violently, household substance abuse, household mental illness, parental separation or divorce, and incarcerated household member. On the basis of responses of over 17,000 adults, the ACE Study found that almost 66 percent reported at least one experience and 25.5 percent reported three or more adverse experiences. The study further documented that as the number of adverse experiences increased, the risk for negative health outcomes increased. These negative outcomes include alcoholism and alcohol abuse, depression, illicit drug use, heart disease, sexually transmitted diseases, smoking, and suicide attempts. This interrelationship of stress and trauma with mental well-being make the understanding of crises and intervention key concerns for social workers.

Stress in the United States is now a major health problem (American Psychological Association, 2007). The APA annual nationwide survey found that one-third of people in this country live with extreme stress, and 48 percent report that they have experienced increased stress over the past five years. The result of this stress hits on the personal as well as societal levels. For individuals, there are declines in health and poor relationships, and for society there is a decrease in work productivity and social interactions. Stress increases with major events and conditions in our society. For example, the economic downturn of the housing market impacts people. The 2007 survey found that 51 percent of respondents reported rent or mortgage costs as sources of stress, and overall three-fourths cited money and work as the leading causes of stress. That was almost a 30 percent increase over the previous year.

Social workers face the impact and consequences of stress on people all the time. It covers many groups and circumstances in society. However, there are some groups who are more prone to stress and its debilitating effects. Many years of research indicate that people in subordinate or marginalized groups have additional stressors in their lives that often have a negative impact on mental and physical health. When asked about some of the symptoms of stress, particularly nervousness and restlessness, adults in poor families and those with low educational achievement were more likely than adults in nonpoor families and adults with bachelor's degrees or higher to report those feelings (Centers on Disease Control and Prevention, 2007).

As was discussed in Chapter 9, health disparities between those living in poverty and those with more financial resources have been noted for many years. Although a number of causes for health disparities have been suggested, ongoing stress from structural causes, such as poverty and oppression, must be noted among them. This type of stress is often chronic, meaning it recurs over long periods of time. Research demonstrates that stress from living in poverty or being a member of an oppressed group has a negative impact on health and well-being across the life span, including compromised health in later life (Pearlin, Schieman, Fazio, & Meersman, 2005). Similarly, as discussed in Chapter 10, structural or societal issues can increase the risk of mental illness, including stress experienced due to poverty and oppression. Being oppressed and living in poverty mean extreme exposure to a variety of social stressors (Aneshensel & Phelan, 1999; Thoits, 1999). There are ongoing societal conditions, viewed by many as "normal," that cause ongoing stress for members of oppressed groups. These include living in high-crime neighborhoods, lack of adequate preventative health care, unequal access to education, and discrimination in housing, employment, and other realms. This chronic stress offers one explanation for higher levels of mental illness among people of lower socioeconomic status. Stress is a critical area that warrants social work attention. One specific form of stress that has received public attention and may be on the increase is post-traumatic stress. This problem is discussed following the next section.

TRAUMA

Trauma is categorized by the DSM-IV-TR as witnessing or experiencing an event that involves actual or the threat of injury, death, or serious physical danger. Trauma often precipitates stress, as discussed above. Although there is clearly overlap in the occurrence of stress, disasters, and trauma, the key variable in understanding trauma is that it is the tendency for traumatic events to have a deep impact that is a threat or feels like a threat to one's survival.

People experience many types of trauma in their lives. Some trauma is confined to a single individual or family. Examples of this could be a house fire that threatens the lives of a family, a serious car accident, domestic violence, or a robbery where a person or group of people is threatened at gunpoint. Other traumas affect larger groups of people. Thousands of people are traumatized during natural disasters such as hurricanes, cyclones, or earthquakes. Similarly, large numbers of soldiers and civilians experience trauma during wars. Many members of communities around the United States experience trauma from persistent violence in their communities.

The extent of trauma in society is difficult to gauge. A national study (National Comorbidity Study, 2007) found that the indicator of severe stress, which is the diagnosis of post-traumatic stress disorder, affects almost 7 percent of the population. Women are more likely than men to experience severe trauma, almost 10 percent compared to 4 percent for men. Overall exposure to trauma is much greater, with a number of life events that could be witnessed or experienced by people. Traumatic events include seeing someone injured or killed, being involved in a disaster, physical attack, rape, sexual molestation, and physical abuse or neglect. Estimates place the exposure to trauma at 50 to 60 percent of the population (National Comorbidity Study, 2007).

With so many people exposed to trauma, the likelihood of impact and long-term consequences are major concerns for social workers. Recent research suggests that there may be physical impacts that last long after the trauma (Ganzel, Casey, Glover, Voss, & Temple, 2007) and, although not severe enough to be diagnosed as a stress-related disorder, can affect people's behavior. There appears to be a slow recovery of our stress-response system after exposure to trauma, and especially the deeper or closer to the trauma a person has been. This may lead to a greater sensitivity to new fearful events and provide a quicker pathway to stress. Therefore, the potential for needing more mental health treatment for exposure to trauma is significant for a large portion of our population. The most severe mental health diagnosis of the fallout from exposure to trauma is post-traumatic stress disorder.

BOX 15.2 | MORE ABOUT ... TRAUMA
A UNIQUE APPROACH TO RECOVERY FROM TRAUMA

Trauma can affect entire communities or nations. Legalized racial segregation, known as apartheid, was the practice in South Africa from 1948 to 1994. Under the early apartheid system, South Africans were classified into three racial groups, black, white, and coloured (people of mixed race), and racial discrimination was institutionalized. Whites held all the official power under the apartheid system, and they created a series of race laws that touched every aspect of a person's life. These laws banned interracial marriage, created white-only jobs, and formed the foundation of a separate and very unequal education system for black and coloured residents. In the early 1950s, the apartheid government created a series of homelands. All black South Africans were assigned to a homeland, where they had voting rights. After being assigned to a homeland, they were stripped of their South African citizenship. Although the government said that the homelands were independent states, the white South African government sill maintained the ultimate authority over what happened there. The homelands were in the most barren and resource-poor parts of the country. Nine million South Africans were assigned to homelands, and thus lost most of their rights in South African society. Those fighting against the apartheid system were treated harshly. Killings, long prison terms, rape, and torture became common, and mistreatment of the black population increased over the years as the government fought to maintain power.

Forty-six years of the brutal apartheid system created community-wide trauma in South African society. The first truly free elections were held in 1994, and the majority black population elected a National Unity Government with the country's first black president. One of the early decisions made by the new government was to establish the Truth and Reconciliation Commission (TRC). The government noted that extreme human rights violations had been committed by people on all sides of the conflict during apartheid. If the country were to move forward in a unified way and avoid repeating the violence and abuses that had occurred, the trauma that many had experienced needed to be addressed in an official way, which is the goal of **truth and reconciliation** interventions. The TRC gave the many victims of trauma an opportunity to face those who had harmed them and talk about what had happened to them. The belief was that remembering what happened was important and that truth was the path to healing, reconciliation, and possibly even forgiveness. This approach may offer interesting insight to social workers and others who deal with the aftermath of trauma and attempt to avoid additional trauma in the future. As one of the staff members of the commission stated:

> South Africans face the challenge of how to embrace the past without being swallowed by the tide of vengeful thinking. The Truth and Reconciliation Commission was a strategy not only for breaking the cycle of politically motivated violence but also for teaching important lessons about how the human spirit can prevail even as victims remember the cruelty visited upon them in the past. If memory is kept alive in order to cultivate old hatreds and resentments, it is likely to culminate in vengeance, and in a repetition of violence. But if memory is kept alive in order to transcend hateful emotions, then remembering can be healing. (Gobodo-Madikizela, 2003)

POST-TRAUMATIC STRESS DISORDER

The longer-term impact of trauma can be the development of severe stress. Post-Traumatic Stress Disorder (PTSD) is included in the category of anxiety disorders from the Diagnostic and Statistical Manual of the American Psychiatric Association

(DSM-IV-TR) (American Psychological Association, 2000). Although stress can be a common occurrence of daily living, when the situation is severe and typically perceived as life threatening, the reactions are more intense and considered to have the potential to lead to PTSD (Van Der Kolk, Weisaeth, & McFarlane, 1996).

PTSD was first recognized in relation to war veterans, particularly of the Vietnam War, which occurred during the late 1960s and early 1970s. However, we now know that a variety of traumatic events, such as rape, natural disasters, car or plane accidents, and many other stressful experiences can lead to PTSD. Symptoms, which generally begin within three months of the event, can include emotional numbness or disassociation, depression, heightened startle response, irritability, aggression, and sometimes violence (DSM-IV-TR). The symptoms must be experienced for at least a month before the diagnosis applies. Victims often relive the trauma event in their thoughts during the day and in their dreams at night. Sufferers of PTSD tend to avoid distressing reminders of their traumatic experience because these triggers can lead to dramatic flashbacks that can be accompanied by the same smells, sounds, and feelings that surrounded the initial events. Anniversary dates can be especially stressful. The course of the illness varies. Some people recover within six months, while others have symptoms that last much longer. In some people, the condition becomes chronic. See the box "More About ... PTSD."

The wars in Iraq and Afghanistan have caused increased attention to the connection between armed conflict and PTSD and the high fiscal and human mental health costs caused by war. Estimates are that as many as 20 percent of soldiers returning from Iraq have PTSD (Zoroya, 2008). Soldiers most likely to experience PTSD are those who experienced more frequent combat, including those who were shot at, handled dead bodies, knew someone who was killed, or killed someone else

---

BOX 15.3　　| 　**MORE ABOUT ... PTSD**

According to the National Center for PTSD, when the following conditions accompany exposure to trauma, people are more likely to experience long-term PTSD:

- Threat to life
- Physical harm
- Witnessing death, bodily injury, or dead or maimed bodies
- Extreme environmental destruction
- Witnessing extreme human violence
- Losing one's home, valued possessions, neighborhood, or community
- Experiencing fatigue, weather exposure, hunger, or sleep deprivation
- Long-term or continued exposure to danger, loss, or stress

- Prior exposure to trauma
- Chronic poverty
- Prior incidence of a psychological disorder (Young, Ford, & Watson, 2007)

Although most survivors return to normal, for some the brain engages a survival mechanism that does not recede, and so the automatic reactions increase over time. Other problems to watch for include

- Depression
- Alcohol and drug abuse
- Memory problems
- Worsening intimate relationships
- Difficulty in performing daily living and work activities (Priest & Hull, 2007)

(Hoge et al., 2004). Evidence suggests that sexual assault and sexual harassment increase for soldiers during war times, and both are causes of stress and PTSD (Litz, 2007). The care for returning soldiers is escalating. Between 1999 and 2004, Veterans Affairs disability pay for PTSD jumped 150 percent, costing $4.2 billion, in spite of the fact that many veterans return and receive no monitoring or care (Priest & Hull, 2007). And the need will only increase with the time at war and number of missions served growing.

There is also evidence of a strong relationship between domestic violence and PTSD. Studies have shown that somewhere between 45 and 56 percent of women who had been in abusive relationships were experiencing PTSD (Vitanza, Vogel, & Marshall, 1995; Mertin & Mohr, 2000) This research also suggests that PTSD is common, regardless of whether there was only psychological abuse, moderate violence, or severe violence. Additionally, women who experienced abuse as children are more likely to develop PTSD following intimate partner abuse (Leahy, 2007). Thus, it is not enough to help women leave violent relationships, but care must be paid to addressing the results of relationship trauma.

The 9/11 attacks demonstrated that PTSD is not only associated with war, rape, and violent crime. Following the attacks, clinicians noted that thousands if not millions of Americans experienced high levels of stress and were potentially at risk for developing PTSD (Arehart-Treichel, 2001). The attacks were certainly a national trauma, and even years later we are still learning about their effects. While political violence and terrorism have been common in other countries, Americans had been relatively isolated from them prior to 9/11. Social workers and others are still learning about how this large-scale trauma has changed individuals and the society as a whole.

DISASTERS—NATURAL AND HUMAN MADE

Harding (2008) defines human-created disasters as processes or events that facilitate the breakdown of families and communities. Human-made disasters are caused both by unintended consequences from state policies and by deliberate decisions by governments or individuals. They can include, but are not limited to, drug infiltration in African American communities (Stevens & Capitman, 2005), chronic poverty and dislocation and violence against women (Lohokare & Davar, 2000), wars, repressive regimes, and the failure to halt preventable diseases. Sometimes the natural and human-made disasters can converge as in human error in response to a natural disaster, which compounds the impact and makes the disaster worse.

Recent examples of national and international crises include the human-created disasters of the terrorist attack in New York on September 11, 2001, the ensuing Afghanistan and Iraq wars, and college and high school shootings, as well as natural disasters such as the 2004 Indian Ocean tsunami, 2005 Hurricane Katrina, the 2008 Myanmar cyclone, and the 2008 Sichuan, China, earthquake. Although there is a dearth of literature on psychological trauma caused by catastrophic disasters such as these, we do know that appropriate treatment can mitigate the effects of these disasters (Schein, 2006).

Human-made disasters are often more devastating over the long term than natural disasters. For example, between 1990 and 2003 there were over 59 armed conflicts in the world that displaced millions and killed over 1.5 million children (UNICEF, 2004). Women, children, older people, people with disabilities, people living in poverty, and nondominant groups are most vulnerable to these events. The unchecked global spread of HIV/AIDS had killed over 20 million people by 2003 and left an estimated 15 million orphans. A sense of urgency motivated millions of donors worldwide during the 2004 Indian Ocean tsunami; however, this sense of urgency often does not translate to plodding human-made disasters such as AIDS, pervasive poverty, and war-torn areas (Harding, 2008).

Social workers have a significant international, national, and local role to play in policies that are designed to ameliorate the effects of such disasters (Harding, 2008; Zakour, 2006). Our core values of social justice and the elimination of discrimination and inequality demand that we develop and promote strategies to prevent human-created disasters. In addition, in the case of both human-made and natural disasters, we have put forward effective mental health and social service interventions as well as postdisaster strategies for reconstruction and development. After first responders (e.g., EMTs, police, firemen), social workers are the major professionals involved in helping victim-survivors in the immediate aftermath of a crisis or disaster (Dominelli, 2008)

TERRORIST ATTACKS ON AMERICAN SOIL—SEPTEMBER 11, 2001

Almost all people in the United States and many around the world are familiar with the events of September 11, 2001. By most accounts these events fit the criteria of a disaster. The planes that crashed into the World Trade Center, the Pentagon, and the field in Pennsylvania killed more than 3,000 people. As discussed above, the events also caused tremendous trauma for many people. Individuals and families directly affected by the attacks included all those killed and injured on the planes and in the World Trade Center and the Pentagon and their families and friends. Rescue workers and emergency responders had to deal directly with the aftermath of the attacks. Many have experienced mental and physical health problems in the ensuing years. These problems include respiratory symptoms, increased rates of cancer, and PTSD (Mauer, Cummings, & Carlson, 2007). Family members of those helping victims after the attacks have also been found to be experiencing trauma even several years later (Linkh, 2006). Additionally, the September 11th attacks had an impact on the general public as a whole. Estimates are that 10 percent of people in Manhattan and 4 percent of U.S. residents experienced serious emotional reactions post-9/11 (Hajer & Walsh, 2005). Research found that anxiety-related visits to emergency rooms within 50 miles of the World Trade Center increased in the months after the attacks (Adinaro, Allegra, Cochrane & Cable, 2008). Nationally, people who reported acute stress following 9/11 were 53 percent more likely to have cardiovascular ailments during the three-year period following the attacks (Holman et al., 2008).

The ramifications of September 11th are not limited to individuals and communities experiencing loss, stress, and trauma. The wars in Afghanistan and Iraq were directly related to the 9/11 attacks. These conflicts have had a large impact on the United States economically and socially. As of early 2008, the two wars have cost U.S. taxpayers over $845 billion. As war costs continue to rise, it is estimated that during 2008, the cost of both operations will be approximately $16 billion per month. It is estimated that the two conflicts will likely end up costing more than $3 trillion (Bilmes & Stiglitz, 2008). Money that is being spent on the wars is money that is not available for domestic uses such as education and social services. As discussed in Chapter 3, fear of more terrorist attacks prompted legislation that has limited the civil rights of all Americans. The attacks have also been introduced into the immigration debate, providing anti-immigration forces with an argument that immigrants, and particularly those in the country illegally, pose a threat to national security and that further measures should be taken to secure the borders.

HURRICANE KATRINA

Hurricane Katrina came ashore on August 29, 2005. It ripped through the Gulf coasts of Louisiana, Mississippi, and Alabama creating the largest natural disaster in U.S. history. The storm was responsible for the deaths of 1,836 people, and it caused over $80 billion worth of damage. It also resulted in the dislocation of more than a million people from their homes and the separation of family members and social networks. Many thousands of people lost their homes and all of their belongings. They were relocated to other cities and states into temporary housing, where many are still living three years later. Hundreds of thousands of people left their lives, family, friends, and jobs to live in states all over the United States, often where they knew no one and where the culture was quite different from what they were used to. The suffering caused by the storm was magnified by an inadequate government response to the disaster. Charges have been levied by many that the government response was both slow and inadequate because most of those affected were African American and low-income people. Three years after the storm hit, the devastation was still evident. Much needed aid had not materialized. Many neighborhoods in New Orleans remain uninhabitable, particularly those that had been home to low-income and African American residents. As of the writing of this text, it is still not known whether thousands of former Gulf Coast residents will be able to return to their former homes and lives. Citizens throughout the region continue to struggle with a variety of challenges. Three years after Katrina hit, more than half of the residents of Louisiana and Mississippi who were affected by the storm continued to experience significant mental health problems (Abramson, Stehling-Ariza, Garfield, & Redlener, 2008).

The storm exposed vast racial and class differences. A study by the Kaiser Family Foundation conducted in New Orleans a year after the storm found large disparities along racial lines. Fifty-nine percent of African American respondents, as opposed to only 29 percent of white respondents, stated that their lives were still disrupted. Larger numbers of African American residents reported continuing financial and housing difficulties, and 72 percent of African Americans reported storm-related health care problems, while only 32 percent of white residents reported health-related concerns (Kaiser Family Foundation, 2007). As noted above, rebuilding in low-income and primarily African American parts of New Orleans has been particularly slow.

Social workers have been effective in advocating for the most marginalized citizens who were displaced after the New Orleans disaster. These people faced multiple barriers after the disaster including finding safe, affordable housing and living-wage

BOX 15.4	BECOMING A CHANGE AGENT

While it is clear that Hurricane Katrina represents an immense natural disaster, some people argue that it is also a human-made disaster. Scientists and nonscientists have suggested that increasingly frequent and increasingly strong hurricanes may be the result of human-made climate change. Those who support this belief point to the fact that four hurricanes hit Florida in 2004, something that has never happened before. That same year 10 cyclones or typhoons hit Japan. The previous record was six in one season. Two studies found a roughly 80 percent increase in powerful cyclones and hurricanes over the past 35 years (Kerr, 2005). One recent study published in the journal *Science* found that a compilation of available data supported the contention that human activity is likely affecting hurricane intensity but that the current available data are not clear of the effect on the number of storms (Trenberth, 2005). Other scientists argue that we do not yet have the data to know if human activity is contributing to either the number or the intensity of storms. Whether or not human activity and climate change played a role in Katrina's intensity, it is clear that a number of policy decisions and the government's response before and after Katrina hit impacted the scale of the devastation and human suffering.

Analyzing the Situation

Research the basic science of climate change and its impact on major storms. Do the data support a human connection? Given what you have learned about the human cost of Hurricane Katrina from news reports and in various chapters in this text, is the issue of climate change and possible related disasters something that social workers should be involved in? How does it fit with the profession's values and ethics? What can you learn about the policy decisions made both before and after the storm that had an impact on the scope and scale of this disaster?

What Can Social Workers Do?

Given your analysis, what can social workers do to help reduce the human suffering that comes from natural disasters? What type of prevention seems possible? What types of interventions at the individual and family levels? What could be done at the community and policy levels?

What Can You Do?

What one step might you take now, alone or working with others, to reduce suffering caused by a recent natural or human-caused disaster? What are the barriers that might keep you from taking this step? What could you do to reduce those barriers?

jobs (Pyles, 2008). The key to effective intervention has been to help survivors deal with the psychological fallout, and then to organize grassroots efforts by the citizens to press for change. Social workers have also been involved in developing policies (e.g., about housing) and utilizing the local political process to get them implemented.

INTERNATIONAL EVENTS

Even after the 9/11 terrorist attacks, Americans are still relatively sheltered from the level of devastation and trauma experienced by people around the world. As this book went to press, two large international disasters had recently occurred. The 2008 Myanmar (formerly known as Burma) cyclone killed over 150,000 people and displaced millions more. The 2008 Sichuan, China, earthquake killed approximately 80,000 people with 5 million people left homeless. Although China was accepting some international aid, Myanmar is a closed country and therefore was very reluctant to accept international aid or allow international aid workers into the country. It will be several years before we know the full impact of these two events.

However, another example may give us insight into the kinds of activities aid workers and social workers undertook in Myanmar and China. In December 2003, a devastating earthquake hit in Bam, Iran. Social workers were among the professionals who joined the rescue efforts. Javadian (2008) describes the activities of social workers in Bam. They helped those who survived find their family members; consoled victims by helping them to deal with feelings of anger, loss, fear, and grief; helped set up makeshift shelters and find transportation; and collected and distributed food and supplies. And they linked survivors with resources (Cronin, Ryan, & Brier, 2008).

In addition to these natural disasters, human-made disasters continue to have astonishingly devastating effects on people in other countries. A war in Sudan between black Africans and Arabs, that many believe constitutes the genocide of non-Muslims living in Sudan, has resulted in 400,000 deaths and more than 3 million people being displaced from their homes (Cotler, 2008). Millions more have been victims of rape, torture, and violence. The sheer numbers of people affected by just this one conflict are difficult to comprehend, and there are multiple conflicts happening at any given time worldwide.

The Iraq War   The devastating impact of the Iraq war and the preceding events and circumstances on the Iraqi people has not received much attention even though it is among one of the most destructive human-made disasters in recent history. Harding (2008) summarizes the events prior to the 2003 war and the effects of the war itself. During the 1980s the Reagan administration, the Soviet Union, and France, among others, implemented foreign policies in Iraq that condoned and supported, through trade agreements and military support, the repressive regime of Saddam Hussein, a regime that committed unconscionable human rights violations on its own people. Some people argue that the economic and strategic interests of the United States and other countries were the focus, not human rights.

In the early 1990s, the United Nations imposed economic sanctions on Iraq for its invasion of Kuwait which caused severe hardship on the Iraqi people. The Iraqi infrastructure was destroyed during the U.S. bombing in the 1991 Gulf War. As a result of these events and the repressive regime, by 2003 (before the Iraq war) the Iraqi health care system, which had been one of the best in the region, was almost nonexistent. In addition, child malnutrition, disease, and infant mortality skyrocketed, long-standing family networks were destroyed, one-fifth of the Iraqi population was living in poverty, and emotional and psychological stress was pervasive. In the 1990s alone, it is estimated that 300,000 to 500,000 Iraqis lost their lives due to economic sanctions and the effects of the Kuwait war.

The U.S.-led war in 2003 produced a deepening disaster for the Iraqi people. The war created more than 3 million refugees. The Iraqi government estimates the war has been responsible for over 300,000 civilian deaths, with more than 100,000 deaths caused directly by U.S. troop actions; and water, sewer, and electricity systems are unreliable generating even more health problems. Unemployment is as high as 40 percent. Violence has become normalized as sectarian violence and retaliatory killings have destroyed entire neighborhoods.

Since October 2001, approximately 1.64 million U.S. troops have been deployed in Afghanistan and Iraq. A recent Rand report (2008) indicates that prolonged exposure to combat-related stress over multiple rotations has taken a devastating psychological toll on the men and women in uniform. In fact, the psychological effects may be disproportionately high compared with the physical injuries of combat. The two most debilitating combat-related injuries are post-traumatic stress disorder and traumatic brain injury.

In order for social workers to be prepared to practice effectively in the face of devastating natural and human-made disaster situations, they must have a wide range of knowledge including awareness of cultural, religious, and ethnic differences related to the prevention, diagnosis, and treatment of traumatic grief and retraumatization (Schein, 2006). Both in Iraq and with those who have served in the region, there is tremendous work to be done to mitigate the impact of trauma and disaster.

SECONDARY TRAUMATIC STRESS

Workers who feel emotionally spent or drained are considered to suffer from burnout and can be found in high-stress areas of social work such as child protective or domestic violence services. Working with victims of trauma and disasters is draining, but the fallout has recently been identified as something different from burnout. Pryce, Shackelford & Pryce (2007) differentiate **secondary traumatic stress (STS)** from burnout. Burnout occurs in jobs where there is some combination of insufficient support, long hours, high caseloads, burdensome paperwork, and a long-term degradation of energy and spirit. STS is the second-hand exposure to traumatic events. For example, social workers involved in the care of survivors and family members of survivors of the 9/11 attacks reported that "they felt as if they were re-experiencing the trauma of 9/11 when their clients discussed their own stories. They also reported experiencing flashbacks of their clients' stories" (Pulido, 2007, p. 280). These reports reflected the symptoms of trauma—intrusive thoughts, avoidance, and feelings of anger and irritability. They were secondary because the social workers were reacting to the reports of their clients, although not themselves having experienced the trauma directly. And in cases of disasters, some of the social workers are local and have their own experiences related to the trauma, but not as directly as the clients.

Figley (1995) coined the term *compassion stress* to describe the natural and not pathological outcome of prolonged exposure of helping professionals to stressful situations. Cronin, Ryan, & Brier (2008) describe the symptoms of compassion fatigue as feelings of helplessness, confusion, and isolation. Long-term exposure to stressful situations causes physical, mental, and emotional exhaustion and mild, normal stress reactions in most cases. However, one out of three disaster workers will experience severe stress symptoms (Fullerton, Ursano, & Wang, 2004).

The importance of self-care and preventative measures for relief workers cannot be stressed enough. It is akin to the metaphor of being on an airplane and being told, in case of emergency, put on your own oxygen mask first and only help others, even your own children, with their masks after. Obviously, the message is that if you do not take care of yourself first, you cannot continue to effectively help others. Awareness is important, and thus recognizing secondary traumatic stress is the first step in dealing with it. Other ways to address it include basic care such as sufficient sleep, exercise, and eating well; social support; asking for and receiving supervision and guidance on the job; and understanding your own history of trauma (Stoesen,

2007). Social workers will continue to be among the frontline workers providing care to disaster survivors and their families. In addition to having the knowledge and skills to deal with people in crisis, social workers must be aware of their own feelings and of the possibility of experiencing secondhand the trauma.

SOCIAL WORK PRACTICE

As discussed earlier, stress and trauma can be experienced by individuals, families, small groups, and entire communities. Social workers have opportunities to intervene to prevent crises, trauma, and disasters at all of these levels and to provide a variety of interventions to help reduce stress and assist in healing at all levels after traumatic events have occurred. Part of social work practice is the unexpected nature of trauma and disasters. Consider the experience of one social worker addressing the stress of divorce for a family and investigation of child abuse when suddenly the family faces the disaster of a fire and the loss of their home and all their belongings. See "From the Field ... We Didn't Start the Fire."

BOX 15.5 | **FROM THE FIELD ... WE DIDN'T START THE FIRE**
Jennifer L. Mullins, MSW

I still can never imagine what it would be like to lose everything. Your favorite things, your pets, your home, your sense of safety and comfort, or your family can all be gone with a matter of hours. A disaster, an event, no matter how little or big can change your life forever, and how you react immediately to help can make all the difference.

Samantha, Nick, and Amy grew up in a normal family, at least to them. Their mother and father fought a lot and sometimes the police came to the house, but the kids always thought it would work out. Their parents started getting divorced a few years ago, and a nasty custody battle ensued. The father, Michael, worked many jobs over the years, and the mother, Tina, stayed at home with the kids. When they decided to get divorced, the kids stayed in the home with Tina and Michael moved into an apartment. At first, the visitation worked out. Then came the fights about money and time with the kids. They brought out the worst in court about drug use, taking the kids out of state, and hitting the kids.

One day, Tina was cooking dinner for the kids, their favorite—corn dogs in grease in a frying pan on the stove. She thought she had enough for all three kids but decided to run down the street to the grocery store to get some chips and more corn dogs. She left nine-year-old Samantha in charge. Samantha was

mature for her age and responsible. When Tina was walking back, there were two fire trucks in front of the house, police cars, news vans, and a group of people watching her house burn. She began running frantically, screaming the children's names. She spotted them clutching their neighbor Angie while holding the family cat and dog. The kids were in shock. Tina grabbed them while news reporters tried to ask her questions about the fire. "What happened? Where were you? Why were the kids alone?" When the police came over and questioned her, she could not speak. She was so distraught. The police called Child Protective Services to investigate the case, because it appeared as though the kids were alone during the fire. We workers at the CPS office were familiar with this family. There had been reports before. We talked to the kids, the parents, and others that knew the family. I stood with the family and watched as firefighters tried to save the home and its contents. Although this was the main concern at the time, I had to also focus on the safety of the kids. The kids were concerned about their toys and schoolwork. I can only imagine the desperation and feeling of powerlessness of watching your home engulfed in flames, not knowing where you would sleep that night. All the things you had worked so hard to buy were gone.

BOX 15.5   FROM THE FIELD ... WE DIDN'T START THE FIRE *continued*

There are the short-term effects of a crisis, the physiological response, the emotional response, the physical consequences, the panic and hopelessness. Most people cannot be prepared for a crisis or disaster to occur. And even when you feel as though you are prepared for a storm or a death, you still cannot be completely prepared for how you will feel or deal with the aftermath. Social workers have always been an essential part of an emergency response team, whether it be a crisis intervention team that works with police and fire crews or one that works on a larger scale with natural disasters, school shootings, or terrorist acts. Social workers work with people on an individual level to attend to the immediate emotional and psychological shock, to calm and reassure while providing follow-up and resources to ensure safety after the event.

Following such an event, a fire or a tornado, there are long-term effects that can affect an individual or family. There are stressors put on a family such as the financial consequences of an event. There could be a loss of job or income, the loss of a home and dealing with insurance, and paying bills on time. Dealing with these unexpected losses is much more difficult when your emotional stability is compromised. Many individuals that lived through events such as 9/11 in New York or Hurricane Katrina in Louisiana developed post-traumatic stress disorder and deal with the emotional aspects of the disaster every day. Our team would have to help this family secure a new home, furnishings, and clothes for the kids and address the psychological needs of the family. All this on top of the work we had been doing to help the family deal with the divorce.

What about the children involved in the fire? Fortunately, nobody was injured and required medical attention. However, they were already in a state of shock, trying to recover from the initial panic and danger of the fire and trying to get out alive. But then they were told by a stranger that they would be staying somewhere new tonight and that things would be alright. They had nothing but the clothes they were wearing during the fire. Samantha worried about school and her mom. Was her mom going to jail? What about her cat? What about her toys and clothes? When could she go to school?

Three days later, we came back and Samantha put on her coat to leave. We talked some more, and I asked about what happened. She was in charge while her mom went to the store, and a small fire started with the grease on the stove. She said they tried to put it out, but then it just went everywhere. She said her brother got her little sister and she got the cat and dog out and ran to the neighbor's house to call 911. She wanted to know when she could go home and if her stuff was still there. She kept apologizing about the fire. She felt a lot of guilt about what had happened.

In such complex cases, we can only imagine the trauma and feelings of loss and worry that these children experience. Samantha felt a tremendous amount of guilt for the fire but also a great sense of loss for her favorite movies, photo album, and flute. There is the immediate panic and fear and the subsequent feelings when removed from your parents and placed in a strange environment. Samantha's father was really upset with her mother for letting this happen and blamed her for the fire. As social workers who work with victims of disasters, we have to act quickly but calmly and somehow manage to not have the situation affect us, which is nearly impossible for a human. We have to be prepared, supportive, and able to create a more calming and safe situation among the chaos. Even though my purpose for being at the home was to investigate the allegations of child neglect, I had to also consider the current situation and the effects on the children and family.

Such an event can be devastating in all aspects of life, but it can also be an opportunity to change. In the Japanese language, the characters meaning crisis are "danger" and "opportunity." Many people that have experienced natural disasters use the act of rebuilding as a means of healing. A crisis situation has also been shown to bring families and communities closer together.

Samantha and her family were reunited after some help from a team of social workers, counselors, and family service agency staff. They received an insurance settlement and were able to move into a new home and replace some of the things lost in the fire. Michael and Tina divorced and are working to coparent their children. I have learned that you cannot take anything for granted because you can lose everything in the blink of an eye.

Intervention following disasters includes micro- and macropractices. On the micro level, social workers intervene with the individual, and on the macro level, social workers engage in rebuilding communities. These two tasks are interrelated and, although we discuss them separately, should be simultaneous in application. Although in the cases of large natural disasters the immediacy of macro support such as providing food, water, and shelter may take precedence, individual attention must also be addressed.

MICRO-LEVEL INTERVENTIONS

Disaster aid is not included in most social work curricula; however, crisis intervention and generalist social work knowledge and skills can be easily applied to disaster situations. In fact, social workers are uniquely prepared to deal with the complex situations following disasters because of the extended networks they develop in the communities in which they work and their expertise in information and referral. These skills can help social workers reduce chaos in the aftermath by quickly identifying resources and helping to create access to those resources, especially for vulnerable populations like children, older people, disabled people, and those living in poverty before the disaster. Social workers have been effective working with children after disasters and trauma by encouraging them to draw pictures of their experiences, support each other by telling their stories in a group, and playing music that will help them to discuss their feelings (Javadian, 2008).

Yueh (2003) identified the key social work functions after a disaster as providing emotional support to individuals and families by consoling them and offering grief counseling and debriefing services and as linking people with needed resources. Debriefing is one way that victims can describe their personal experience, express feelings of grief and loss, and create a narrative that in retelling can help prevent stress and PTSD. Consoling and debriefing in small groups can help victims gain support from each other. Once participants have had a chance to share their grief and tell their stories, they should be encouraged to identify their strengths, promote hopefulness among themselves, and mobilize to take action. This will help victims becomes survivors.

Ehrenreich (2001) outlines a number of principles that should guide our practice in response to disasters. The first principle is that first and foremost both victims and relief workers must be assured of their safety and security. This prioritizes access to food, water, and shelter, as well as security from dangers such as assault, theft, or victimization. The second principle stresses the awareness that initial emotional responses that reflect trauma are expected, and workers need to assure people that experiencing those symptoms is common. This can destigmatize people and leave them more receptive to mental health interventions. Additional principles to guide practice include taking into account people's culture, traditions, and spiritual beliefs, as well as possible differences between men and women in response to trauma.

Young, Ford, and Watson (2007) suggest that there are a number of roles for mental health providers including

Protection—Helping to preserve people's safety, privacy, health, and self-esteem
Direction—Getting people to where they belong

Connection—Helping people to communicate with family, friends, and service providers

Detection—Screening for risk of deeper problems, identifying need, and providing crisis care

Referral—Connecting people to health, mental health, social, support, and financial services

Validation—Providing formal and informal education to affirm the normalcy and value of each person's reactions, concerns, and ways of coping

TECHNIQUES FOR REDUCING STRESS

A very effective way to respond to trauma and disaster is to deal with the stress that has built up within a person. There are a number of stress reduction approaches, some involving medication, others using mind-body work, and some combining both. Approaches that combine interventions that address both the mind and body are advantageous. The risks involved are minimal, and the interventions can be taught easily. Research suggests that mind-body interventions improve psychological functioning and can help people cope with chronic conditions (National Center for Complementary and Alternative Medicine, 2007).

Mindfulness and Stress   One approach that is often successful in reducing stress is the application of **mindfulness**, the state of being aware of everything in the present moment, and to do so without judgment or analysis. Our bodies are hard wired to respond to stress with an immediate sense of urgency and alert, and this can act to save us from danger. However, once the emergency is past, bringing down this level of alert from the acute state is difficult. In order to do so, a person might use some of the following techniques:

- Becoming aware of your thoughts, feelings, and fears
- Breathing slowly to reduce the state of arousal
- Reframing the event to calm yourself
- Seeing options and alternative behaviors (Napoli, 2007)

The goal of mindfulness and using the above techniques is to take action to reduce stress and deescalate the body's pattern of responding in a hyperstate of readiness and stress. When a person is in a state of distress, mindfulness training can offer an alternative that once learned, can be practiced by the individual in any setting at any time that symptoms emerge.

Cognitive Behavioral Therapy   Cognitive behavioral therapies (CBTs) are among the most researched and most used treatments for stress and trauma, including PTSD (Dobson, 2002). For example, a recent study demonstrated the efficacy of CBT in alleviating post-traumatic stress symptoms among adolescents after a catastrophic disaster (Shooshtary, Panaghi, & Moghadam, 2008). According to the National Association of Cognitive Behavioral Therapists, CBT is not a distinct therapeutic technique but instead a group of therapies that share certain common elements. The central premise of CBT is that thoughts, rather than the external environment, cause emotions and behaviors. The logic is that if we change our thoughts, we can change our emotions and actions. CBT therapies are relatively brief in duration; they usually involve the client practicing outside of sessions what he or she has learned, and the therapist usually has a structured agenda for each session. The discussions of CBT and crisis intervention in Chapter 5 reflect these approaches from a general practice standpoint. These forms of intervention provide social workers with excellent treatment choices to use with people exposed to significant stress and trauma.

Eye Movement Desensitization and Reprocessing   Eye movement desensitization and reprocessing (EMDR) was developed by Francine Shapiro in 1987 and is increasingly used to treat stress and trauma. It incorporates components of several therapeutic techniques, including cognitive behavioral, psychodynamic, and body therapies. EMDR involves paying attention to past and current experiences while simultaneously focusing on an external stimulus. During the treatment, clients focus on troubling memories, images, or feelings while they follow an external stimulus, usually the therapist's fingers, with their eyes. They also identify alternative positive beliefs. Adding eye movement to other therapeutic techniques has been found to be effective in reducing stress and increasing confidence in positive beliefs in a relatively short period of time. Studies suggest that EMDR is an effective intensive and brief therapy that can dramatically reduce PTSD symptoms for many people in as few as two sessions (Hogberg, et al., 2007; Korn & Leeds, 2002).

Emerging Techniques—Energy Psychology and Trauma-Releasing Exercises
Energy psychology includes several therapeutic techniques that focus on recalling past trauma combined with physical stimulation. The therapies include thought field therapy (TFT), emotional freedom techniques (EFT), and Tapas acupressure technique (TAT). Each of these therapies is relatively new and continued research is needed to determine their effectiveness to address stress, including PTSD. However, some of the early research suggests that they may provide promising alternatives to more conventional treatments. One study examining the effectiveness of EFT on people with PTSD found it to be 33 percent more effective than using cognitive behavioral therapy combined with antianxiety drugs (Rowe, 2005). All of the techniques claim to reduce trauma symptoms in a shorter period of time than traditional therapies, and they are structured in such a way that they can be taught to groups of people suffering from the effects of trauma, and then can be continued without the need for a professional to be present. This can be important in situations where there is mass trauma and not enough trained practitioners to address it all.

Trauma-releasing exercises (TRE) were developed by David Berceli (2007), a social worker who worked with people suffering from trauma-related stress and PTSD around the world. TRE is a set of exercises premised on the understanding that healing from PTSD requires involvement of both the mind and the body. The technique is based on the fact that humans seem to react similarly to other mammals following trauma. After a traumatic experience, mammals tend to shake or shiver. It is common to see pets shake after an event that frightens them. One theory is that this shaking allows the animal to release the trauma from its muscles. TRE uses a set of exercises that cause slight fatigue in the leg and pelvic muscles. Following the exercises, clients experience tremors that allow the body to release stress from the traumatic event, thus relieving symptoms of PTSD. Like the energy psychology techniques described above, TRE can be taught to large groups of people who can do the exercises on their own and reduce problems associated with PTSD without ongoing need of a therapist.

PHARMACOLOGICAL TREATMENT

Most people who live through a trauma or disaster experience stress and anxiety. As noted previously, more than half the population will likely be exposed to trauma, while about 8 percent will experience stress that is severe enough to be diagnosed as clinical PTSD. Pharmacological intervention can be an option for treatment in cases of severe stress, particularly when the person is extremely agitated, dangerous, or psychotic (National Center on PTSD, 2008). A persistent state of anxiety, panic, irritability, and hypervigilance that may follow surviving a disaster means there is higher risk for PTSD. This higher risk might suggest that in addition to psychotherapy and relaxation and breathing, survivors would benefit from antianxiety medications. The co-occurrence of depression is also a possibility for trauma and disaster survivors and is another aspect to assess that may lead practitioners to consider medication as a possible intervention.

The American Red Cross's Disaster Mental Health (DMH) program currently has tens of thousands of mental health volunteers who can respond to an emergency situation anywhere in the country. The volunteers are all licensed mental health practitioners, 40 percent are social workers, 22 percent are psychologists, and only 1 percent are psychiatrists. Although the psychiatrists and some psychologists are the only ones who can prescribe medication, social workers can play a critical role in identifying victims that may need pharmacological intervention (Cronin et al., 2008).

MACRO-LEVEL INTERVENTIONS

Disasters such as Hurricane Katrina or the attacks of 9/11 clearly cause community-wide trauma. However, ongoing community conditions such as gang violence or large numbers of deaths from AIDS, can also produce trauma and cause residents of an area to lose their sense of safety and feel tremendous fear and grief. The ramifications of community-wide trauma can affect a community for years or even generations. As the trauma specialist Dr. Richard Ornstein notes, "The South Asia tsunami recovery will not be measured in days, weeks, months, years or even decades, but will take generations. The impact will remain within the affected nations' legacies for possibly centuries" (Hajer & Walsh, 2005, p. 8).

Social workers can provide support and counseling for groups and entire communities after traumatic events. This is a common practice after school shootings and other events that produce large-scale trauma. We often see communities pulling together to provide assistance after disasters. Social workers can use community-building techniques to help strengthen communities so that they can work effectively together to help each other recover from trauma. Neighborhoods can be organized and encouraged to think about what their needs may be after a disaster and how they can best prepare and work together to meet those needs. Community workers can assist neighborhood residents to think about issues such as how the culture of residents affects their experience with trauma, how the diverse people living in the area can best work together, and how to recruit and maintain volunteers so that the area is ready if a disaster should strike. Social workers can use lobbying and public education skills to encourage governments to develop and fund plans to address community-wide trauma. These plans should include having adequate mental health practitioners and community organizers available to address needs that arise from various types of crises and disasters.

CASE EXAMPLE: Tulsa, Oklahoma, includes plans to address community-wide trauma in their disaster response program. When large numbers of families in the area experienced extreme stress during the Gulf War in 1991, the city formed the Tulsa Human Response Coalition (THRC) to coordinate the city's response to community-wide trauma. The coalition now has a rapid response team that is ready to respond as needed to local crises and disasters. The team is made up of mental health professionals who have additional critical incident stress training (Hajer & Walsh, 2005).

CASE EXAMPLE: Berkeley, California, has been offering training to neighborhood residents to help them be prepared to address community-wide traumatic events. The city developed a training program in 1983 and has been offering it to the community since then. They increased these efforts after 9/11 when they found that their mental health teams were struggling to keep up with the need (Hajer & Walsh, 2005).

Social workers can also organize community residents to lobby for needed policies and funding to prevent or decrease community-wide trauma. For example, residents of an area with a high violent crime rate may be experiencing a great deal of stress and fear related to the trauma caused by ongoing violence. Social workers can assist local residents to become a unified voice to call for funding for youth programs and additional police resources to reduce the violence.

Using the strengths perspective with communities can be helpful in responding to crises, trauma, and disasters. Identify the strengths and assets that are already there. Restoring people's sense of ownership and belonging to the community can be achieved through quickly rebuilding schools, businesses, religious institutions, and social service organizations; ensuring police and fire protection; and facilitating social networks (Ehrenreich, 2001). The challenge for social workers, as aptly demonstrated in New Orleans, is that rebuilding is more difficult to accomplish when communities are poor before the disaster. Therefore, part of macro intervention needs to be efforts directed toward prevention so that the limited resources of a community are not overtaxed with a crisis.

PREVENTION

Of course the best course of action with crises, traumas, and disasters is that they would never happen (Tsuchiya & Shuto, 2007). As cited in several places in this chapter, the incidence of traumas and stress is significant and crosses through many facets of American lives. Prevention of any such events is beneficial to individuals as well as society. The cost of treatment, in financial measures as well as personal emotional aspects, is expensive and the lasting effects of experiencing trauma can compromise a person's quality of life.

Prevention can be directed at predictable problems as well as unpredictable events. There are several areas of prevention that that affect the incidence of crises, trauma, and disasters (Harding, 2008). There is the category of **risk prevention**, for example taking measures to prevent or minimize financial loss or health problems. There is **hazard prevention**, which can include preparation for a possible natural disaster or efforts to protect from a natural disaster. An example of the break down of both these strategies was the case of Hurricane Katrina. Authorities were unprepared to address the destruction from the storm and also care for the numbers of people displaced and in need. In addition, postdisaster analysis of the levees that were designed to keep the city from being flooded revealed that they were insufficient to control the water from that category of storm. Other forms of prevention include **crime prevention**, which strives to stop criminal behaviors from happening, and **preventive medicine**, which emphasizes behaviors that promote healthy living and the prevention of illness and disease (Nafziger, 2002).

Legislation and regulation can serve as preventive measures. For example, vehicle accidents and misuse of firearms have been addressed through laws. Mandatory seatbelt laws are designed to mitigate injury in the event of an accident, and regulations of the sale of firearms are passed with the intent to minimize the misuse and illegal distribution of handguns. Individuals practice prevention when they do not engage in risky behaviors that might be dangerous. Smoking-cessation campaigns advocate lowering a person's health risks by the promotion of not smoking. Communities address prevention through efforts to anticipate potential disasters such as weather emergency warnings that keep people in safe locations during storms or educational campaigns advertising healthy behaviors. Social workers can be involved in all these prevention efforts.

SOCIAL WORK VALUES AND ETHICS

Terrorism and other types of human-made and natural disasters can impact social workers' lives in much the same way they affect other people. Social workers are at risk of being victims of terrorism or of natural disasters to the same degree that other people are at risk. Social workers experience fear and anger, as others do. When a disaster hits an area, how do social workers respond as professionals rather than as members of the community who are being affected by what is going on around them? If a social worker's home is destroyed in a flood, how does he or she put the trauma aside, at least for a while, to be fully present to address the needs of clients?

Living in the post-9/11 world challenges social workers to examine their personal values and ethics and how social work values and ethics fit into this changing world (Ellis, 2006). Social work has taken a leading role in helping victims of the terrorist attacks and other human-made disasters, but what about the perpetrators? This issue comes up in a number of social work practice areas, but it may be particularly acute when addressing something as large and devastating as the 9/11 attacks.

Since 9/11, there has been a good deal of discussion about profiling and whether it is discrimination. Profiling involves giving added scrutiny to certain populations on the basis of a group characteristic that they share. All of the assailants on 9/11 were Muslim men from Middle Eastern countries. Faces similar to theirs have become the faces of terrorism that many Americans fear. Many law enforcement efforts, from airport screenings to general surveillance, are now focused on members of this population. The NASW Code of Ethics notes the value social workers should place on safety and the preservation of human life. Going from this, one could argue that profiling is good, as it may have the effect of stopping another terrorist attack, thus increasing safety and preserving human life. The Code of Ethics also talks about social justice, equality, and nondiscrimination. Although the 9/11 assailants were all Middle Eastern Muslim men, clearly the vast majority of Middle Eastern Muslim men are not terrorists and pose no threat. Is it acceptable to target people just because some like them are involved in terrorist activities? Is that justice or equality?

Little research has been conducted on how social workers have responded to the 9/11 attacks and the threat of future terrorism. While waiting for more formal research, some anecdotal information is emerging. A social worker in New York who has long been involved in trauma services reported seeing changes in attitudes, including her own. She admitted having a different attitude toward Arab-looking men post-9/11 and struggling with her biases (Ellis, 2006). Are there circumstances where social workers should remove themselves from a case if they are not able to control their fear or prejudice? Can social workers treat each person with respect and dignity if they are experiencing the fear that is shared by other Americans in the post-9/11 United States?

CONCLUSION

With societies' propensity for conflict and war, stressful living conditions, and periodic natural disasters, the need for prevention and intervention in the areas of crisis, disasters, and trauma will be ongoing. Social workers will face situations and clients with needs related to immediate crises or with the lingering effects of earlier traumatic events. The incidence of such needs cuts across all areas of social work. Awareness of the signs of PTSD and secondary traumatic stress, as well as understanding the sense of loss and powerlessness that survivors feel, are necessary for all of today's social workers.

Key Terms

cognitive behavioral therapies (CBTs), (p. 447)

crime prevention, (p. 451)

crisis, (p. 432)

disaster, (p. 432)

eye movement desensitization and reprocessing (EMDR), (p. 448)

hazard prevention, (p. 451)

mindfulness, (p. 447)

preventive medicine, (p. 451)

risk prevention, (p. 451)

secondary traumatic stress (STS), (p. 443)

stress, (p. 432)

trauma, (p. 432)

truth and reconciliation, (p. 436)

Questions for Discussion

1. Looking at natural and human-caused disasters around the world, it is clear that the magnitude of destruction of property and loss of life is much greater in developing nations than it is in the United States. Why do you think that is the case?
2. When discussing the war in Sudan in the chapter, the word *genocide* is used. There is debate as to whether what is going on in the Sudan is actually genocide. Given the situation that was described, what do you think? Why?
3. The attacks of September 11, 2001, prompted a great deal of anxiety and stress among the American people and increased limitations on civil rights. Where is the balance between safety and the protection of civil rights?
4. What distinguishes a natural disaster from a human-made disaster? Is it possible for social workers to intervene to prevent both?
5. What distinguishes post-traumatic stress disorder from other types of stress reactions that people have?

Change Agent Exercise

Read your local newspaper or conduct an Internet search to find out where disasters have happened recently throughout the world or where a population is experiencing a great deal of trauma. Learn what you can about the struggles that people are facing who live in the disaster area. Try to find out what groups in your area are doing to assist with disaster relief. What are others around the country or around the world doing to help relieve the suffering in the disaster area or prevent future trauma? Work with other people in your class to find a way to get involved in a disaster relief effort.

Chapter Exercises

1. **Contemporary Issues Journal**

   Find at least one newspaper article that relates to crisis, disaster, or trauma. Describe the central points from the article. Which of the three or what combination of the three does it relate to?

   What questions or concerns does it raise for you?

   What else would you like to know about the topic, and how might you find the information?

   Discuss how social workers could be involved to help those suffering from the event in your article. Would any type of social work intervention have been possible to prevent this crisis, disaster, or trauma?

2. **Ethical Concerns**

   What are the primary ethical concerns for social workers who work in the area of crisis and trauma?

   Social workers often work with trauma victims. Is the decision of whether to work with those who cause trauma by harming others an ethical concern? Get into pairs or small groups and discuss your thoughts on working with those who have caused trauma to others.

3. **Intervention Versus Prevention Debate**

There is limited money available to address the various challenges that social workers address, including issues related to crises, disasters, and traumas. Strong cases can be made about whether the bulk of the resources should go into interventions designed to help people who have experienced a crisis, disaster, or trauma or resources are better spent trying to prevent future crises, disasters, and trauma from happening.

Research arguments on both sides of the issue.

Meet with classmates and discuss the pros and cons of using resources for interventions to treat people experiencing trauma, and the pros and cons of using resources for trauma prevention.

Divide into teams and debate the issue. After the debate, discuss what you have learned and see if your group can reach agreement about how resources are best used in the areas of crisis, disaster, and trauma.

4. **Crisis Intervention Social Work Interview**

Identify agencies or organizations in your area that provide crisis intervention services. Try to learn who receives these services.

Arrange an interview with a social worker who provides crisis intervention services. Find out what is rewarding, challenging, and unique about this type of work. Does he or she have thoughts about what type of person is best suited to crisis intervention work?

Reflect on your interests, strengths, and areas for growth. Given what you know about the field of crisis intervention and about yourself, do you believe this would be a good fit for you? Why or why not?

5. **Trauma and Diversity**

People deal with stress, crises, disasters, and traumas in different ways. Some part of how we view these events and how we cope with them and heal from them is shaped by the culture we were raised in or currently live in. Think about what you learned from your family and cultural background that might shape how you cope with stress or traumatic events.

Meet in small groups to share your thoughts on the relationship between your cultural background and coping with stress and trauma.

Trauma can also be caused by societal conditions such as discrimination and oppression. Discuss some of the ways that experiencing discrimination or oppression can be traumatic for members of oppressed groups. What is social work's role in preventing or reducing the trauma caused by social injustice?

References

Abramson, D., Stehling-Ariza, T., Garfield, R., & Redlener, I. (2008). Distress post-Katrina: Findings from the Gulf Coast Child and Family Heath Study. *Prevalence and Predictors of Mental Health, 2,* 77–86.

Adinaro, D. J., Allegra, J. R., Cochrane, D. G., & Cable, G. (2008). Anxiety-related visits to New Jersey emergency departments after September 11, 2001. *Journal of Emergency Medicine, 34,* 311–314.

American Psychological Association. (2000). *Diagnostic and Statistical Manual of Mental Disorders DSM-IV-TR*. Washington, DC: Author.

American Psychological Association. (2007). *Stress in America*. Washington, DC: Author.

Aneshensel, C. S., & Phelan, J. C. (1999). *Handbook of the Sociology of Mental Health*. New York: Kluwer Academic/Plenum.

Arehart-Treichel, J. (2001). Data back cognitive behavior therapy for PTSD treatment. *Psychiatric News*, 36, 21.

Barker, R. I. (2003). *The social work dictionary*. Washington, DC: NASW Press.

Berceli, D. (2007). *Evaluating the effects of stress reduction exercises*. Unpublished PhD dissertation, Arizona State University.

Bilmes, L. J., & Stiglitz, J. E. (2008). The Iraq conflict will raid our wallets for years to come, with California taking a huge hit. *Los Angeles Times*, March 16, p. M1.

Centers for Disease Control and Prevention. (2006). *Adverse childhood experience study*. Atlanta, GA: Author.

Centers for Disease Control and Prevention. (2007). *Summary health statistics for adults: National health survey*. Atlanta, GA: Author.

Centers for Disease Control and Prevention. (2008). *The effects of childhood stress on health across the lifespan*. Atlanta, GA: Author.

Cotler, I. (2008). Saving Sudan: If not now, when? [Canada] *National Post*, April 12, p. 22.

Cronin, M. S., Ryan, D. M., & Brier, D. (2008). Support for staff working in disaster situations. *International Social Work, 50*, 3, 370–382.

Dobson, K. (2002*). The handbook of cognitive-behavioral therapies*. New York: Guilford Press.

Dominelli, L. (2008). Editorial. *International Social Work, 50*, 3, 291–294.

Ehrenreich, J. H. (2001). *Coping with disasters: A guidebook to psychosocial intervention*. New York: Center for Psychology and Society, State University of New York.

Ellis, D. (2006). Can we be fair? Balancing the personal with the professional response to terrorism. *Journal of Social Work Values and Ethics*, 3, na.

Figley, C. R. (ed.). (1995). *Compassion fatigue: Coping with secondary traumatic stress disorder in those who treat the traumatized*. New York: Bruner/Mazel.

Fullerton, C. S., Ursano, R. J., & Wang, M. S. (2004). Acute stress disorder, post-traumatic stress disorder, and depression in disaster or rescue workers. *American Journal of Psychiatry, 161*, 8, 1370–1376.

Galvin, A. (2008). Murder-suicide gunman had a stress disorder. *Arizona Republic*, May 18, pp. B1, B6.

Ganzel, B., Casey, B. J., Glover, G., Voss, H. U., & Temple, E. (2007). The aftermath of 9/11: Effect of intensity and recency of trauma on outcome. *Emotion*, 7, 2, 227–238.

Gobodo-Madikizela, P. (2003). *A human being died that night*. New York: Houghton Mifflin.

Hajer, M., & Walsh, M. (2005). Coping with community trauma. *Public Management*, 87, 8–11.

Harding, S. (2008). Man-made disaster and development. *International Social Work, 50*, 3, 295–306.

Hogberg, G., Pagani, M., Sundin, O., Soares, J., Aberg-Wistedt, A., et al. (2007). On treatment with eye movement desensitization and reprocessing of chronic post-traumatic stress disorder in public transportation workers—A randomized controlled trial. *Nordic Journal of Psychiatry, 61*, 1, 54–61.

Hoge, C. W., Castro, C. A., Messer, S. C., McGurk, D., Cotting, D. I., & Koffman, R. L. (2004). Combat duty in Iraq and Afghanistan, mental health problems and barriers to care. *New England Journal of Medicine, 351*, 13–22.

Holman E. A., Silver R. C., Poulin M., Andersen, J., Gil-Rivas V., McIntosh, D. N. (2008). Terrorism, acute stress, and cardiovascular health: A 3-year national study following the September 11th attacks. *Archives of General Psychiatry, 65*, 73–80.

Javadian, R. (2008). Social work responses to earthquake disasters. *International Social Work, 50*, 3, 335–346.

Kaiser Family Foundation. (2007). *Giving voice to the people of New Orleans*. Washington, DC: Author.

Kerr, R. A. (2005). Atmospheric science: Is Katrina a harbinger of still more powerful hurricanes? *Science, 309*, 1807.

Korn, D. L., & Leeds, A. M. (2002). Preliminary evidence of efficacy for EMDR resource development and installation in the stabilization phase of treatment of complex posttraumatic stress disorder. *Journal of Clinical Psychology, 58*, 1465–1487.

Leahy, K. (2007). Complex posttraumatic stress symptoms among a community sample of battered women. PhD Dissertation, Michigan State University. *Proquest Dissertation and Theses, AAT 3298071.*

Linkh, D. J. (2006). Fire from a cloudless sky: A qualitative study of loss, trauma and resilience in the families of surviving New York City firefighters in the wake of the terrorist attacks of September 11th 2001. PhD Dissertation. *Dissertation Abstracts International, 46.*

Litz, B. T. (2007). A brief primer on the mental health impact of wars in Afghanistan and Iraq. *National Center for PTSD fact sheet*. Washington, DC: U.S. Department of Veterans Affairs.

Lohokare, M. & Davar, B. V. (2000). Women in disasters and mental health. *Indian Journal of Social Work, 61*, 4, pp. 565–580.

Mauer, M. P., Cummings, K. R., & Carlson, G. A. (2007). Health effects in New York State personnel who responded to the World Trade Center disaster. *Journal of Occupational and Environmental Medicine, 49*, 1197–1205.

Mertin, P., & Mohr, P. B. (2000). Incidence and correlates of posttraumatic stress disorder in Australian victims of domestic violence. *Journal of Family Violence, 15*, 411–422.

Nafziger, E. W. (2002). *The prevention of humanitarian emergencies*. New York: Palgrave Macmillan.

Napoli, M. (2007). *Tools for balanced living: A mindfulness practice workbook*. Phoenix, AZ: Performance Press.

National Center for Complementary and Alternative Medicine. (2007). *Mind-body medicine: An overview*. NCCAM Publication No. D239. Bethesda, MD: National Institute of Health.

National Center for PTSD. (2008). *Pharmacological treatment of acute stress reactions and PTSD: A fact sheet for providers*. Bethesda, MD: Author.

National Comorbidity Study. (2007). *Lifetime prevalence*. Retrieved on May 24, 2008, from http://www.hcp.med.harvard.edu/ncs/index.php.

National Scientific Council on the Developing Child. (2005). *Excessive stress disrupts the architecture of the developing brain*. Cambridge, MA: Author.

Pearlin, L., Schieman, S., Fazio, E. , Meersman, S. (2005). Stress, health, and the life course: Some conceptual perspectives. *Journal of Health & Social Behavior, 46*, 205–219.

Priest, D., & Hull, A. (2007). The war inside: Veterans encounter a mental-health system that makes healing difficult. *Washington Post National Weekly Edition, 24* (36 & 37), pp. 6–8.

Pulido, M. L. (2007). In their words: Secondary traumatic stress in social workers responding to the 9/11 terrorist attacks in New York City. *Social Work, 52,* 3, 279–281.

Pyles, L. (2008). Community organizing for post disaster social development.

International Social Work, 50, 3, 322–333.

Rand Report. (2008). *Invisible wounds of war: Psychological and cognitive injuries, their consequences and services to assist recovery.* Santa Monica, CA: Rand Corporation.

Roberts, A. R. (2005). *Crisis intervention handbook: Assessment, treatment and research* (3d ed.). New York: Oxford University Press.

Roberts, A. R. (2008). Crisis interventions. In *Encyclopedia of social work* (pp. 484–487). Washington, DC: NASW Press.

Rowe, J. E. (2005). The effects of EFT on long-term psychological symptoms. *Counseling and Clinical Psychology Journal, 2,* 3, 104–111.

Scaer, R. (2005). *The trauma spectrum: Hidden wounds and human resiliency.* New York: W. W. Norton.

Schein, L. A. (2006). *Psychological effects of catastrophic disasters: Group approaches to treatment.* Binghamton, NY: Haworth Press.

Shooshtary, M. H., Panaghi, L., & Moghadam, J. A. (2008). Outcome of cognitive behavioral therapy in adolescents after natural disaster. *Journal of Adolescent Health, 42,* 5, 466–472.

Stoesen, L. (2007). Recognizing secondary traumatic stress. *NASW News, 52,* 6, 4.

Stevens, J. W., & Capitman, J. A. (2005). Disaster and loss: Drug research in an urban community. *Families in Society, 86*(2), 279–286.

Thoits, P. (1999). Sociological approaches to mental illness. In Horwitz, A. V., & Scheid, T. L. (eds.). *A handbook for the study of mental health: Social contexts, theories and systems* (pp. 121–138). Cambridge, UK: Cambridge University Press.

Trenberth, K. (2005). Climate: Uncertainty in hurricanes and global warming. *Science, 309,* 1753–1754.

Tsuchiya, Y., & Shuto, N. (2007). *Tsunami: Progress in prediction, disaster prevention and warning.* New York: Springer.

United Nations Children's Fund (UNICEF). (2004). *The State of the World's Children 2005: Childhood Under Threat.* New York: UNICEF.

Van Der Kolk, B., Weisaeth, L., & McFarlane, A. (1996). *Traumatic stress: The effects of overwhelming experience on mind, body, and society.* New York: Guildford Press.

Vitanza, S., Vogel, L. C., & Marshall, L. L. (1995). Distress and symptoms of posttraumatic stress disorder in abused women. *Violence and Victims, 10,* 23–34.

Young, B. H., Ford, J. D., & Watson, P. J. (2007). *Fact sheet: Helping survivors in the wake of disaster.* Bethesda, MD: National Center on PTSD.

Yueh, C. C. (2003). Social work's involvement in Taiwan's 1999 earthquake disaster aid. *Online Journal of Social Work and Society, 1,* 1, 1–22.

Zakour, M. J. (2006). Social work and disasters. In McEntire, D. (ed.), *Disciplines, disasters and emergency management: The convergence and divergence of concepts, issues and trends from the research literature* (chap. 9). Washington, DC: Federal Emergency Management Agency.

Zoroya, G. (2008). A fifth of soldiers at PTSD risk: Rate rises with tours, army says. *USA Today,* March 7, p. 11A.

NASW CODE OF ETHICS

APPENDIX **A**

Approved by the 1996 NASW Delegate Assembly and
revised by the 2008 NASW Delegate Assembly

PREAMBLE

The primary mission of the social work profession is to enhance human well-being
and help meet the basic human needs of all people, with particular attention to the
needs and empowerment of people who are vulnerable, oppressed, and living in poverty. A historic and defining feature of social work is the profession's focus on individual well-being in a social context and the well-being of society. Fundamental to
social work is attention to the environmental forces that create, contribute to, and
address problems in living.

Social workers promote social justice and social change with and on behalf of
clients. "Clients" is used inclusively to refer to individuals, families, groups, organizations, and communities. Social workers are sensitive to cultural and ethnic diversity and strive to end discrimination, oppression, poverty, and other forms of social
injustice. These activities may be in the form of direct practice, community organizing, supervision, consultation, administration, advocacy, social and political action,
policy development and implementation, education, and research and evaluation.
Social workers seek to enhance the capacity of people to address their own needs.
Social workers also seek to promote the responsiveness of organizations, communities, and other social institutions to individuals' needs and social problems.

The mission of the social work profession is rooted in a set of core values.
These core values, embraced by social workers throughout the profession's history,
are the foundation of social work's unique purpose and perspective:

- service
- social justice
- dignity and worth of the person
- importance of human relationships
- integrity
- competence.

This constellation of core values reflects what is unique to the social work profession. Core values, and the principles that flow from them, must be balanced within the context and complexity of the human experience.

PURPOSE OF THE NASW CODE OF ETHICS

Professional ethics are at the core of social work. The profession has an obligation to articulate its basic values, ethical principles, and ethical standards. The NASW Code of Ethics sets forth these values, principles, and standards to guide social workers' conduct. The Code is relevant to all social workers and social work students, regardless of their professional functions, the settings in which they work, or the populations they serve.

THE NASW CODE OF ETHICS SERVES SIX PURPOSES:

1. The Code identifies core values on which social work's mission is based.
2. The Code summarizes broad ethical principles that reflect the profession's core values and establishes a set of specific ethical standards that should be used to guide social work practice.
3. The Code is designed to help social workers identify relevant considerations when professional obligations conflict or ethical uncertainties arise.
4. The Code provides ethical standards to which the general public can hold the social work profession accountable.
5. The Code socializes practitioners new to the field to social work's mission, values, ethical principles, and ethical standards.
6. The Code articulates standards that the social work profession itself can use to assess whether social workers have engaged in unethical conduct. NASW has formal procedures to adjudicate ethics complaints filed against its members.

In subscribing to this Code, social workers are required to cooperate in its implementation, participate in NASW adjudication proceedings, and abide by any NASW disciplinary rulings or sanctions based on it.

The Code offers a set of values, principles, and standards to guide decision making and conduct when ethical issues arise. It does not provide a set of rules that prescribe how social workers should act in all situations. Specific applications of the Code must take into account the context in which it is being considered and the possibility of conflicts among the Code's values, principles, and standards. Ethical responsibilities flow from all human relationships, from the personal and familial to the social and professional.

Further, the NASW Code of Ethics does not specify which values, principles, and standards are most important and ought to outweigh others in instances when they conflict. Reasonable differences of opinion can and do exist among social workers with respect to the ways in which values, ethical principles, and ethical standards should be rank ordered when they conflict. Ethical decision making in a given situation must apply the informed judgment of the individual social worker and should also consider how the issues would be judged in a peer review process where the ethical standards of the profession would be applied.

Ethical decision making is a process. There are many instances in social work where simple answers are not available to resolve complex ethical issues. Social workers should take into consideration all the values, principles, and standards in this Code that are relevant to any situation in which ethical judgment is warranted. Social workers' decisions and actions should be consistent with the spirit as well as the letter of this Code.

In addition to this Code, there are many other sources of information about ethical thinking that may be useful. Social workers should consider ethical theory and principles generally, social work theory and research, laws, regulations, agency policies, and other relevant codes of ethics, recognizing that among codes of ethics social workers should consider the NASW Code of Ethics as their primary source. Social workers also should be aware of the impact on ethical decision making of their clients' and their own personal values and cultural and religious beliefs and practices. They should be aware of any conflicts between personal and professional values and deal with them responsibly. For additional guidance social workers should consult the relevant literature on professional ethics and ethical decision making and seek appropriate consultation when faced with ethical dilemmas. This may involve consultation with an agency-based or social work organization's ethics committee, a regulatory body, knowledgeable colleagues, supervisors, or legal counsel.

Instances may arise when social workers' ethical obligations conflict with agency policies or relevant laws or regulations. When such conflicts occur, social workers must make a responsible effort to resolve the conflict in a manner that is consistent with the values, principles, and standards expressed in this Code. If a reasonable resolution of the conflict does not appear possible, social workers should seek proper consultation before making a decision.

The NASW Code of Ethics is to be used by NASW and by individuals, agencies, organizations, and bodies (such as licensing and regulatory boards, professional liability insurance providers, courts of law, agency boards of directors, government agencies, and other professional groups) that choose to adopt it or use it as a frame of reference. Violation of standards in this Code does not automatically imply legal liability or violation of the law. Such determination can only be made in the context of legal and judicial proceedings. Alleged violations of the Code would be subject to a peer review process. Such processes are generally separate from legal or administrative procedures and insulated from legal review or proceedings to allow the profession to counsel and discipline its own members.

A code of ethics cannot guarantee ethical behavior. Moreover, a code of ethics cannot resolve all ethical issues or disputes or capture the richness and complexity involved in striving to make responsible choices within a moral community. Rather, a code of ethics sets forth values, ethical principles, and ethical standards to which professionals aspire and by which their actions can be judged. Social workers' ethical behavior should result from their personal commitment to engage in ethical practice. The NASW Code of Ethics reflects the commitment of all social workers to uphold the profession's values and to act ethically. Principles and standards must be applied by individuals of good character who discern moral questions and, in good faith, seek to make reliable ethical judgments.

ETHICAL PRINCIPLES

The following broad ethical principles are based on social work's core values of service, social justice, dignity and worth of the person, importance of human relationships, integrity, and competence. These principles set forth ideals to which all social workers should aspire.

Value: Service

Ethical Principle: Social workers' primary goal is to help people in need and to address social problems.

Social workers elevate service to others above self-interest. Social workers draw on their knowledge, values, and skills to help people in need and to address social problems. Social workers are encouraged to volunteer some portion of their professional skills with no expectation of significant financial return (pro bono service).

Value: Social Justice

Ethical Principle: Social workers challenge social injustice.

Social workers pursue social change, particularly with and on behalf of vulnerable and oppressed individuals and groups of people. Social workers' social change efforts are focused primarily on issues of poverty, unemployment, discrimination, and other forms of social injustice. These activities seek to promote sensitivity to and knowledge about, oppression and cultural and ethnic diversity. Social workers strive to ensure access to needed information, services, and resources; equality of opportunity; and meaningful participation in decision making for all people.

Value: Dignity and Worth of the Person

Ethical Principle: Social workers respect the inherent dignity and worth of the person.

Social workers treat each person in a caring and respectful fashion, mindful of individual differences and cultural and ethnic diversity. Social workers promote clients' socially responsible self-determination. Social workers seek to enhance clients' capacity and opportunity to change and to address their own needs. Social workers are cognizant of their dual responsibility to clients and to the broader society. They seek to resolve conflicts between clients' interests and the broader society's interests in a socially responsible manner consistent with the values, ethical principles, and ethical standards of the profession.

Value: Importance of Human Relationships

Ethical Principle: Social workers recognize the central importance of human relationships.

Social workers understand that relationships between and among people are an important vehicle for change. Social workers engage people as partners in the helping process. Social workers seek to strengthen relationships among people in a purposeful effort to promote, restore, maintain, and enhance the well-being of individuals, families, social groups, organizations, and communities.

Value: Integrity

Ethical Principle: Social workers behave in a trustworthy manner.

Social workers are continually aware of the profession's mission, values, ethical principles, and ethical standards and practice in a manner consistent with them. Social workers act honestly and responsibly and promote ethical practices on the part of the organizations with which they are affiliated.

Value: Competence

Ethical Principle: Social workers practice within their areas of competence and develop and enhance their professional expertise.

Social workers continually strive to increase their professional knowledge and skills and to apply them in practice. Social workers should aspire to contribute to the knowledge base of the profession.

ETHICAL STANDARDS

The following ethical standards are relevant to the professional activities of all social workers. These standards concern (1) social workers' ethical responsibilities to clients, (2) social workers' ethical responsibilities to colleagues, (3) social workers' ethical responsibilities in practice settings, (4) social workers' ethical responsibilities as professionals, (5) social workers' ethical responsibilities to the social work profession, and (6) social workers' ethical responsibilities to the broader society.

Some of the standards that follow are enforceable guidelines for professional conduct, and some are aspirational. The extent to which each standard is enforceable is a matter of professional judgment to be exercised by those responsible for reviewing alleged violations of ethical standards.

1. SOCIAL WORKERS' ETHICAL RESPONSIBILITIES TO CLIENTS

1.01 COMMITMENT TO CLIENTS

Social workers' primary responsibility is to promote the well-being of clients. In general, clients' interests are primary. However, social workers' responsibility to the larger society or specific legal obligations may on limited occasions supersede the loyalty owed clients, and clients should be so advised. (Examples include when a social worker is required by law to report that a client has abused a child or has threatened to harm self or others.)

1.02 SELF-DETERMINATION

Social workers respect and promote the right of clients to self-determination and assist clients in their efforts to identify and clarify their goals. Social workers may limit clients' right to self-determination when, in the social workers' professional judgment, clients' actions or potential actions pose a serious, foreseeable, and imminent risk to themselves or others.

1.03 INFORMED CONSENT

a. Social workers should provide services to clients only in the context of a professional relationship based, when appropriate, on valid informed consent. Social workers should use clear and understandable language to inform clients of the purpose of the services, risks related to the services, limits to services because of the requirements of a third-party payer, relevant costs, reasonable alternatives, clients' right to refuse or withdraw consent, and the time frame covered by the consent. Social workers should provide clients with an opportunity to ask questions.

b. In instances when clients are not literate or have difficulty understanding the primary language used in the practice setting, social workers should take steps to ensure clients' comprehension. This may include providing clients with a detailed verbal explanation or arranging for a qualified interpreter or translator whenever possible.

c. In instances when clients lack the capacity to provide informed consent, social workers should protect clients' interests by seeking permission from an appropriate third party, informing clients consistent with the clients' level of understanding. In such instances social workers should seek to ensure that the third party acts in a manner consistent with clients' wishes and interests. Social workers should take reasonable steps to enhance such clients' ability to give informed consent.

d. In instances when clients are receiving services involuntarily, social workers should provide information about the nature and extent of services and about the extent of clients' right to refuse service.

e. Social workers who provide services via electronic media (such as computer, telephone, radio, and television) should inform recipients of the limitations and risks associated with such services.

f. Social workers should obtain clients' informed consent before audiotaping or videotaping clients or permitting observation of services to clients by a third party.

1.04 COMPETENCE

a. Social workers should provide services and represent themselves as competent only within the boundaries of their education, training, license, certification, consultation received, supervised experience, or other relevant professional experience.

b. Social workers should provide services in substantive areas or use intervention techniques or approaches that are new to them only after engaging in appropriate study, training, consultation, and supervision from people who are competent in those interventions or techniques.

c. When generally recognized standards do not exist with respect to an emerging area of practice, social workers should exercise careful judgment and take responsible steps (including appropriate education, research, training, consultation, and supervision) to ensure the competence of their work and to protect clients from harm.

1.05 CULTURAL COMPETENCE AND SOCIAL DIVERSITY

a. Social workers should understand culture and its function in human behavior and society, recognizing the strengths that exist in all cultures.

b. Social workers should have a knowledge base of their clients' cultures and be able to demonstrate competence in the provision of services that are sensitive to clients' cultures and to differences among people and cultural groups.

c. Social workers should obtain education about and seek to understand the nature of social diversity and oppression with respect to race, ethnicity, national origin, color, sex, sexual orientation, gender identity or expression, age, marital status, political belief, religion, and mental or physical disability.

1.06 CONFLICTS OF INTEREST

a. Social workers should be alert to and avoid conflicts of interest that interfere with the exercise of professional discretion and impartial judgment. Social workers should inform clients when a real or potential conflict of interest arises and take reasonable steps to resolve the issue in a manner that makes the clients' interests primary and protects clients' interests to the greatest extent possible. In some cases, protecting clients' interests may require termination of the professional relationship with proper referral of the client.

b. Social workers should not take unfair advantage of any professional relationship or exploit others to further their personal, religious, political, or business interests.

c. Social workers should not engage in dual or multiple relationships with clients or former clients in which there is a risk of exploitation or potential harm to the client. In instances when dual or multiple relationships are unavoidable, social workers should take steps to protect clients and are responsible for setting clear, appropriate, and culturally sensitive boundaries. (Dual or multiple relationships occur when social workers relate to clients in more than one relationship, whether professional, social, or business. Dual or multiple relationships can occur simultaneously or consecutively.)

d. When social workers provide services to two or more people who have a relationship with each other (for example, couples, family members), social workers should clarify with all parties which individuals will be considered clients and the nature of social workers' professional obligations to the various individuals who are receiving services. Social workers who anticipate a conflict of interest among the individuals receiving services or who anticipate having to perform in potentially conflicting roles (for example, when a social worker is asked to testify in a child custody dispute or divorce proceedings involving clients) should clarify their role with the parties involved and take appropriate action to minimize any conflict of interest.

1.07 PRIVACY AND CONFIDENTIALITY

a. Social workers should respect clients' right to privacy. Social workers should not solicit private information from clients unless it is essential to providing services or conducting social work evaluation or research. Once private information is shared, standards of confidentiality apply.

b. Social workers may disclose confidential information when appropriate with valid consent from a client or a person legally authorized to consent on behalf of a client.

c. Social workers should protect the confidentiality of all information obtained in the course of professional service, except for compelling professional reasons. The general expectation that social workers will keep information confidential does not apply when disclosure is necessary to prevent serious, foreseeable, and imminent harm to a client or other identifiable person. In all instances, social workers should disclose the least amount of confidential information necessary to achieve the desired purpose; only information that is directly relevant to the purpose for which the disclosure is made should be revealed.

d. Social workers should inform clients, to the extent possible, about the disclosure of confidential information and the potential consequences, when feasible before the disclosure is made. This applies whether social workers disclose confidential information on the basis of a legal requirement or client consent.

e. Social workers should discuss with clients and other interested parties the nature of confidentiality and limitations of clients' right to confidentiality. Social workers should review with clients circumstances where confidential information may be requested and where disclosure of confidential information may be legally required. This discussion should occur as soon as possible in the social worker-client relationship and as needed throughout the course of the relationship.

f. When social workers provide counseling services to families, couples, or groups, social workers should seek agreement among the parties involved concerning each individual's right to confidentiality and obligation to preserve the confidentiality of information shared by others. Social workers should inform participants in family, couples, or group counseling that social workers cannot guarantee that all participants will honor such agreements.

g. Social workers should inform clients involved in family, couples, marital, or group counseling of the social worker's, employer's, and agency's policy concerning the social worker's disclosure of confidential information among the parties involved in the counseling.

h. Social workers should not disclose confidential information to third-party payers unless clients have authorized such disclosure.

i. Social workers should not discuss confidential information in any setting unless privacy can be ensured. Social workers should not discuss confidential information in public or semipublic areas such as hallways, waiting rooms, elevators, and restaurants.

j. Social workers should protect the confidentiality of clients during legal proceedings to the extent permitted by law. When a court of law or other legally authorized body orders social workers to disclose confidential or privileged information without a client's consent and such disclosure could cause harm to the client, social workers should request that the court withdraw the order or limit the order as narrowly as possible or maintain the records under seal, unavailable for public inspection.

k. Social workers should protect the confidentiality of clients when responding to requests from members of the media.

l. Social workers should protect the confidentiality of clients' written and electronic records and other sensitive information. Social workers should take reasonable steps to ensure that clients' records are stored in a secure location and that clients' records are not available to others who are not authorized to have access.

m. Social workers should take precautions to ensure and maintain the confidentiality of information transmitted to other parties through the use of computers, electronic mail, facsimile machines, telephones and telephone answering machines, and other electronic or computer technology. Disclosure of identifying information should be avoided whenever possible.

n. Social workers should transfer or dispose of clients' records in a manner that protects clients' confidentiality and is consistent with state statutes governing records and social work licensure.

o. Social workers should take reasonable precautions to protect client confidentiality in the event of the social worker's termination of practice, incapacitation, or death.

p. Social workers should not disclose identifying information when discussing clients for teaching or training purposes unless the client has consented to disclosure of confidential information.

q. Social workers should not disclose identifying information when discussing clients with consultants unless the client has consented to disclosure of confidential information or there is a compelling need for such disclosure.

r. Social workers should protect the confidentiality of deceased clients consistent with the preceding standards.

1.08 ACCESS TO RECORDS

a. Social workers should provide clients with reasonable access to records concerning the clients. Social workers who are concerned that clients' access to their records could cause serious misunderstanding or harm to the client should provide assistance in interpreting the records and consultation with the client regarding the records. Social workers should limit clients' access to their records, or portions of their records, only in exceptional circumstances when there is compelling evidence that such access would cause serious harm to the client. Both clients' requests and the rationale for withholding some or all of the record should be documented in clients' files.

b. When providing clients with access to their records, social workers should take steps to protect the confidentiality of other individuals identified or discussed in such records.

1.09 SEXUAL RELATIONSHIPS

    a. Social workers should under no circumstances engage in sexual activities or sexual contact with current clients, whether such contact is consensual or forced.

    b. Social workers should not engage in sexual activities or sexual contact with clients' relatives or other individuals with whom clients maintain a close personal relationship when there is a risk of exploitation or potential harm to the client. Sexual activity or sexual contact with clients' relatives or other individuals with whom clients maintain a personal relationship has the potential to be harmful to the client and may make it difficult for the social worker and client to maintain appropriate professional boundaries. Social workers—not their clients, their clients' relatives, or other individuals with whom the client maintains a personal relationship—assume the full burden for setting clear, appropriate, and culturally sensitive boundaries.

    c. Social workers should not engage in sexual activities or sexual contact with former clients because of the potential for harm to the client. If social workers engage in conduct contrary to this prohibition or claim that an exception to this prohibition is warranted because of extraordinary circumstances, it is social workers—not their clients—who assume the full burden of demonstrating that the former client has not been exploited, coerced, or manipulated, intentionally or unintentionally.

    d. Social workers should not provide clinical services to individuals with whom they have had a prior sexual relationship. Providing clinical services to a former sexual partner has the potential to be harmful to the individual and is likely to make it difficult for the social worker and individual to maintain appropriate professional boundaries.

1.10 PHYSICAL CONTACT

Social workers should not engage in physical contact with clients when there is a possibility of psychological harm to the client as a result of the contact (such as cradling or caressing clients). Social workers who engage in appropriate physical contact with clients are responsible for setting clear, appropriate, and culturally sensitive boundaries that govern such physical contact.

1.11 SEXUAL HARASSMENT

Social workers should not sexually harass clients. Sexual harassment includes sexual advances, sexual solicitation, requests for sexual favors, and other verbal or physical conduct of a sexual nature.

1.12 DEROGATORY LANGUAGE

Social workers should not use derogatory language in their written or verbal communications to or about clients. Social workers should use accurate and respectful language in all communications to and about clients.

1.13 PAYMENT FOR SERVICES

a. When setting fees, social workers should ensure that the fees are fair, reasonable, and commensurate with the services performed. Consideration should be given to clients' ability to pay.

b. Social workers should avoid accepting goods or services from clients as payment for professional services. Bartering arrangements, particularly involving services, create the potential for conflicts of interest, exploitation, and inappropriate boundaries in social workers' relationships with clients. Social workers should explore and may participate in bartering only in very limited circumstances when it can be demonstrated that such arrangements are an accepted practice among professionals in the local community, considered to be essential for the provision of services, negotiated without coercion, and entered into at the client's initiative and with the client's informed consent. Social workers who accept goods or services from clients as payment for professional services assume the full burden of demonstrating that this arrangement will not be detrimental to the client or the professional relationship.

c. Social workers should not solicit a private fee or other remuneration for providing services to clients who are entitled to such available services through the social workers' employer or agency.

1.14 CLIENTS WHO LACK DECISION-MAKING CAPACITY

When social workers act on behalf of clients who lack the capacity to make informed decisions, social workers should take reasonable steps to safeguard the interests and rights of those clients.

1.15 INTERRUPTION OF SERVICES

Social workers should make reasonable efforts to ensure continuity of services in the event that services are interrupted by factors such as unavailability, relocation, illness, disability, or death.

1.16 TERMINATION OF SERVICES

a. Social workers should terminate services to clients and professional relationships with them when such services and relationships are no longer required or no longer serve the clients' needs or interests.

b. Social workers should take reasonable steps to avoid abandoning clients who are still in need of services. Social workers should withdraw services precipitously only under unusual circumstances, giving careful consideration to all factors in the situation and taking care to minimize possible adverse effects. Social workers should assist in making appropriate arrangements for continuation of services when necessary.

c. Social workers in fee-for-service settings may terminate services to clients who are not paying an overdue balance if the financial contractual arrangements have been made clear to the client, if the client does not pose an imminent danger to self or others, and if the clinical and other consequences of the current nonpayment have been addressed and discussed with the client.

d.   Social workers should not terminate services to pursue a social, financial, or sexual relationship with a client.

e.   Social workers who anticipate the termination or interruption of services to clients should notify clients promptly and seek the transfer, referral, or continuation of services in relation to the clients' needs and preferences.

f.   Social workers who are leaving an employment setting should inform clients of appropriate options for the continuation of services and of the benefits and risks of the options.

2. SOCIAL WORKERS' ETHICAL RESPONSIBILITIES TO COLLEAGUES

2.01 RESPECT

a.   Social workers should treat colleagues with respect and should represent accurately and fairly the qualifications, views, and obligations of colleagues.

b.   Social workers should avoid unwarranted negative criticism of colleagues in communications with clients or with other professionals. Unwarranted negative criticism may include demeaning comments that refer to colleagues' level of competence or to individuals' attributes such as race, ethnicity, national origin, color, sex, sexual orientation, gender identity or expression, age, marital status, political belief, religion, and mental or physical disability.

c.   Social workers should cooperate with social work colleagues and with colleagues of other professions when such cooperation serves the well-being of clients.

2.02 CONFIDENTIALITY

Social workers should respect confidential information shared by colleagues in the course of their professional relationships and transactions. Social workers should ensure that such colleagues understand social workers' obligation to respect confidentiality and any exceptions related to it.

2.03 INTERDISCIPLINARY COLLABORATION

a.   Social workers who are members of an interdisciplinary team should participate in and contribute to decisions that affect the well-being of clients by drawing on the perspectives, values, and experiences of the social work profession. Professional and ethical obligations of the interdisciplinary team as a whole and of its individual members should be clearly established.

b.   Social workers for whom a team decision raises ethical concerns should attempt to resolve the disagreement through appropriate channels. If the disagreement cannot be resolved, social workers should pursue other avenues to address their concerns consistent with client well-being.

2.04 DISPUTES INVOLVING COLLEAGUES

    a.   Social workers should not take advantage of a dispute between a colleague and an employer to obtain a position or otherwise advance the social workers' own interests.

    b.   Social workers should not exploit clients in disputes with colleagues or engage clients in any inappropriate discussion of conflicts between social workers and their colleagues.

2.05 CONSULTATION

    a.   Social workers should seek the advice and counsel of colleagues whenever such consultation is in the best interests of clients.

    b.   Social workers should keep themselves informed about colleagues' areas of expertise and competencies. Social workers should seek consultation only from colleagues who have demonstrated knowledge, expertise, and competence related to the subject of the consultation.

    c.   When consulting with colleagues about clients, social workers should disclose the least amount of information necessary to achieve the purposes of the consultation.

2.06 REFERRAL FOR SERVICES

    a.   Social workers should refer clients to other professionals when the other professionals' specialized knowledge or expertise is needed to serve clients fully or when social workers believe that they are not being effective or making reasonable progress with clients and that additional service is required.

    b.   Social workers who refer clients to other professionals should take appropriate steps to facilitate an orderly transfer of responsibility. Social workers who refer clients to other professionals should disclose, with clients' consent, all pertinent information to the new service providers.

    c.   Social workers are prohibited from giving or receiving payment for a referral when no professional service is provided by the referring social worker.

2.07 SEXUAL RELATIONSHIPS

    a.   Social workers who function as supervisors or educators should not engage in sexual activities or contact with supervisees, students, trainees, or other colleagues over whom they exercise professional authority.

    b.   Social workers should avoid engaging in sexual relationships with colleagues when there is potential for a conflict of interest. Social workers who become involved in, or anticipate becoming involved in, a sexual relationship with a colleague have a duty to transfer professional responsibilities, when necessary, to avoid a conflict of interest.

2.08 SEXUAL HARASSMENT

Social workers should not sexually harass supervisees, students, trainees, or colleagues. Sexual harassment includes sexual advances, sexual solicitation, requests for sexual favors, and other verbal or physical conduct of a sexual nature.

2.09 IMPAIRMENT OF COLLEAGUES

a.   Social workers who have direct knowledge of a social work colleague's impairment that is due to personal problems, psychosocial distress, substance abuse, or mental health difficulties and that interferes with practice effectiveness should consult with that colleague when feasible and assist the colleague in taking remedial action.

b.   Social workers who believe that a social work colleague's impairment interferes with practice effectiveness and that the colleague has not taken adequate steps to address the impairment should take action through appropriate channels established by employers, agencies, NASW, licensing and regulatory bodies, and other professional organizations.

2.10 INCOMPETENCE OF COLLEAGUES

a.   Social workers who have direct knowledge of a social work colleague's incompetence should consult with that colleague when feasible and assist the colleague in taking remedial action.

b.   Social workers who believe that a social work colleague is incompetent and has not taken adequate steps to address the incompetence should take action through appropriate channels established by employers, agencies, NASW, licensing and regulatory bodies, and other professional organizations.

2.11 UNETHICAL CONDUCT OF COLLEAGUES

a.   Social workers should take adequate measures to discourage, prevent, expose, and correct the unethical conduct of colleagues.

b.   Social workers should be knowledgeable about established policies and procedures for handling concerns about colleagues' unethical behavior. Social workers should be familiar with national, state, and local procedures for handling ethics complaints. These include policies and procedures created by NASW, licensing and regulatory bodies, employers, agencies, and other professional organizations.

c.   Social workers who believe that a colleague has acted unethically should seek resolution by discussing their concerns with the colleague when feasible and when such discussion is likely to be productive.

d.   When necessary, social workers who believe that a colleague has acted unethically should take action through appropriate formal channels (such as contacting a state licensing board or regulatory body, an NASW committee on inquiry, or other professional ethics committees).

e.   Social workers should defend and assist colleagues who are unjustly charged with unethical conduct.

3. SOCIAL WORKERS' ETHICAL RESPONSIBILITIES IN PRACTICE SETTINGS

3.01 SUPERVISION AND CONSULTATION

a.   Social workers who provide supervision or consultation should have the necessary knowledge and skill to supervise or consult appropriately and should do so only within their areas of knowledge and competence.

b.   Social workers who provide supervision or consultation are responsible for setting clear, appropriate, and culturally sensitive boundaries.

c.   Social workers should not engage in any dual or multiple relationships with supervisees in which there is a risk of exploitation of or potential harm to the supervisee.

d.   Social workers who provide supervision should evaluate supervisees' performance in a manner that is fair and respectful.

3.02 EDUCATION AND TRAINING

a.   Social workers who function as educators, field instructors for students, or trainers should provide instruction only within their areas of knowledge and competence and should provide instruction based on the most current information and knowledge available in the profession.

b.   Social workers who function as educators or field instructors for students should evaluate students' performance in a manner that is fair and respectful.

c.   Social workers who function as educators or field instructors for students should take reasonable steps to ensure that clients are routinely informed when services are being provided by students.

d.   Social workers who function as educators or field instructors for students should not engage in any dual or multiple relationships with students in which there is a risk of exploitation or potential harm to the student. Social work educators and field instructors are responsible for setting clear, appropriate, and culturally sensitive boundaries.

3.03 PERFORMANCE EVALUATION

Social workers who have responsibility for evaluating the performance of others should fulfill such responsibility in a fair and considerate manner and on the basis of clearly stated criteria.

3.04 CLIENT RECORDS

a.   Social workers should take reasonable steps to ensure that documentation in records is accurate and reflects the services provided.

b. Social workers should include sufficient and timely documentation in records to facilitate the delivery of services and to ensure continuity of services provided to clients in the future.

c. Social workers' documentation should protect clients' privacy to the extent that is possible and appropriate and should include only information that is directly relevant to the delivery of services.

d. Social workers should store records following the termination of services to ensure reasonable future access. Records should be maintained for the number of years required by state statutes or relevant contracts.

3.05 BILLING

Social workers should establish and maintain billing practices that accurately reflect the nature and extent of services provided and that identify who provided the service in the practice setting.

3.06 CLIENT TRANSFER

a. When an individual who is receiving services from another agency or colleague contacts a social worker for services, the social worker should carefully consider the client's needs before agreeing to provide services. To minimize possible confusion and conflict, social workers should discuss with potential clients the nature of the clients' current relationship with other service providers and the implications, including possible benefits or risks, of entering into a relationship with a new service provider.

b. If a new client has been served by another agency or colleague, social workers should discuss with the client whether consultation with the previous service provider is in the client's best interest.

3.07 ADMINISTRATION

a. Social work administrators should advocate within and outside their agencies for adequate resources to meet clients' needs.

b. Social workers should advocate for resource allocation procedures that are open and fair. When not all clients' needs can be met, an allocation procedure should be developed that is nondiscriminatory and based on appropriate and consistently applied principles.

c. Social workers who are administrators should take reasonable steps to ensure that adequate agency or organizational resources are available to provide appropriate staff supervision.

d. Social work administrators should take reasonable steps to ensure that the working environment for which they are responsible is consistent with and encourages compliance with the NASW Code of Ethics. Social work administrators should take reasonable steps to eliminate any conditions in their organizations that violate, interfere with, or discourage compliance with the Code.

3.08 CONTINUING EDUCATION AND STAFF DEVELOPMENT

Social work administrators and supervisors should take reasonable steps to provide or arrange for continuing education and staff development for all staff for whom they are responsible. Continuing education and staff development should address current knowledge and emerging developments related to social work practice and ethics.

3.09 COMMITMENTS TO EMPLOYERS

a. Social workers generally should adhere to commitments made to employers and employing organizations.
b. Social workers should work to improve employing agencies' policies and procedures and the efficiency and effectiveness of their services.
c. Social workers should take reasonable steps to ensure that employers are aware of social workers' ethical obligations as set forth in the NASW Code of Ethics and of the implications of those obligations for social work practice.
d. Social workers should not allow an employing organization's policies, procedures, regulations, or administrative orders to interfere with their ethical practice of social work. Social workers should take reasonable steps to ensure that their employing organizations' practices are consistent with the NASW Code of Ethics.
e. Social workers should act to prevent and eliminate discrimination in the employing organization's work assignments and in its employment policies and practices.
f. Social workers should accept employment or arrange student field placements only in organizations that exercise fair personnel practices.
g. Social workers should be diligent stewards of the resources of their employing organizations, wisely conserving funds where appropriate and never misappropriating funds or using them for unintended purposes.

3.10 LABOR-MANAGEMENT DISPUTES

a. Social workers may engage in organized action, including the formation of and participation in labor unions, to improve services to clients and working conditions.
b. The actions of social workers who are involved in labor-management disputes, job actions, or labor strikes should be guided by the profession's values, ethical principles, and ethical standards. Reasonable differences of opinion exist among social workers concerning their primary obligation as professionals during an actual or threatened labor strike or job action. Social workers

should carefully examine relevant issues and their possible impact on clients before deciding on a course of action.

4. SOCIAL WORKERS' ETHICAL RESPONSIBILITIES AS PROFESSIONALS

4.01 COMPETENCE

a. Social workers should accept responsibility or employment only on the basis of existing competence or the intention to acquire the necessary competence.

b. Social workers should strive to become and remain proficient in professional practice and the performance of professional functions. Social workers should critically examine and keep current with emerging knowledge relevant to social work. Social workers should routinely review the professional literature and participate in continuing education relevant to social work practice and social work ethics.

c. Social workers should base practice on recognized knowledge, including empirically based knowledge, relevant to social work and social work ethics.

4.02 DISCRIMINATION

Social workers should not practice, condone, facilitate, or collaborate with any form of discrimination on the basis of race, ethnicity, national origin, color, sex, sexual orientation, gender identity or expression, age, marital status, political belief, religion, or mental or physical disability.

4.03 PRIVATE CONDUCT

Social workers should not permit their private conduct to interfere with their ability to fulfill their professional responsibilities.

4.04 DISHONESTY, FRAUD, AND DECEPTION

Social workers should not participate in, condone, or be associated with dishonesty, fraud, or deception.

4.05 IMPAIRMENT

a. Social workers should not allow their own personal problems, psychosocial distress, legal problems, substance abuse, or mental health difficulties to interfere with their professional judgment and performance or to jeopardize the best interests of people for whom they have a professional responsibility.

b. Social workers whose personal problems, psychosocial distress, legal problems, substance abuse, or mental health difficulties interfere with their professional judgment and performance should immediately seek consultation and take appropriate remedial action by seeking professional help, making adjustments in workload, terminating practice, or taking any other steps necessary to protect clients and others.

4.06 MISREPRESENTATION

a. Social workers should make clear distinctions between statements made and actions engaged in as a private individual and as a representative of the social work profession, a professional social work organization, or the social worker's employing agency.

b. Social workers who speak on behalf of professional social work organizations should accurately represent the official and authorized positions of the organizations.

c. Social workers should ensure that their representations to clients, agencies, and the public of professional qualifications, credentials, education, competence, affiliations, services provided, or results to be achieved are accurate. Social workers should claim only those relevant professional credentials they actually possess and take steps to correct any inaccuracies or misrepresentations of their credentials by others.

4.07 SOLICITATIONS

a. Social workers should not engage in uninvited solicitation of potential clients who, because of their circumstances, are vulnerable to undue influence, manipulation, or coercion.

b. Social workers should not engage in solicitation of testimonial endorsements (including solicitation of consent to use a client's prior statement as a testimonial endorsement) from current clients or from other people who, because of their particular circumstances, are vulnerable to undue influence.

4.08 ACKNOWLEDGING CREDIT

a. Social workers should take responsibility and credit, including authorship credit, only for work they have actually performed and to which they have contributed.

b. Social workers should honestly acknowledge the work of and the contributions made by others.

5. SOCIAL WORKERS' ETHICAL RESPONSIBILITIES TO THE SOCIAL WORK PROFESSION

5.01 INTEGRITY OF THE PROFESSION

a. Social workers should work toward the maintenance and promotion of high standards of practice.

b. Social workers should uphold and advance the values, ethics, knowledge, and mission of the profession. Social workers should protect, enhance, and improve the integrity of the profession through appropriate study and research, active discussion, and responsible criticism of the profession.

c. Social workers should contribute time and professional expertise to activities that promote respect for the value, integrity, and competence of the social work profession. These activities may include teaching, research, consultation, service, legislative testimony, presentations in the community, and participation in their professional organizations.

d. Social workers should contribute to the knowledge base of social work and share with colleagues their knowledge related to practice, research, and ethics. Social workers should seek to contribute to the profession's literature and to share their knowledge at professional meetings and conferences.

e. Social workers should act to prevent the unauthorized and unqualified practice of social work.

5.02 EVALUATION AND RESEARCH

a. Social workers should monitor and evaluate policies, the implementation of programs, and practice interventions.

b. Social workers should promote and facilitate evaluation and research to contribute to the development of knowledge.

c. Social workers should critically examine and keep current with emerging knowledge relevant to social work and fully use evaluation and research evidence in their professional practice.

d. Social workers engaged in evaluation or research should carefully consider possible consequences and should follow guidelines developed for the protection of evaluation and research participants. Appropriate institutional review boards should be consulted.

e. Social workers engaged in evaluation or research should obtain voluntary and written informed consent from participants, when appropriate, without any implied or actual deprivation or penalty for refusal to participate; without undue inducement to participate; and with due regard for participants' well-being, privacy, and dignity. Informed consent should include information about the nature, extent, and duration of the participation requested and disclosure of the risks and benefits of participation in the research.

f. When evaluation or research participants are incapable of giving informed consent, social workers should provide an appropriate explanation to the participants, obtain the participants' assent to the extent they are able, and obtain written consent from an appropriate proxy.

g. Social workers should never design or conduct evaluation or research that does not use consent procedures, such as certain forms of naturalistic observation and archival research, unless rigorous and responsible review of the research has found it to be justified because of its prospective scientific, educational, or applied value and unless equally effective alternative procedures that do not involve waiver of consent are not feasible.

h. Social workers should inform participants of their right to withdraw from evaluation and research at any time without penalty.

i. Social workers should take appropriate steps to ensure that participants in evaluation and research have access to appropriate supportive services.

j. Social workers engaged in evaluation or research should protect participants from unwarranted physical or mental distress, harm, danger, or deprivation.

k. Social workers engaged in the evaluation of services should discuss collected information only for professional purposes and only with people professionally concerned with this information.

l. Social workers engaged in evaluation or research should ensure the anonymity or confidentiality of participants and of the data obtained from them. Social workers should inform participants of any limits of confidentiality, the measures that will be taken to ensure confidentiality, and when any records containing research data will be destroyed.

m. Social workers who report evaluation and research results should protect participants' confidentiality by omitting identifying information unless proper consent has been obtained authorizing disclosure.

n. Social workers should report evaluation and research findings accurately. They should not fabricate or falsify results and should take steps to correct any errors later found in published data using standard publication methods.

o. Social workers engaged in evaluation or research should be alert to and avoid conflicts of interest and dual relationships with participants, should inform participants when a real or potential conflict of interest arises, and should take steps to resolve the issue in a manner that makes participants' interests primary.

p. Social workers should educate themselves, their students, and their colleagues about responsible research practices.

6. SOCIAL WORKERS' ETHICAL RESPONSIBILITIES TO THE BROADER SOCIETY

6.01 SOCIAL WELFARE

Social workers should promote the general welfare of society, from local to global levels, and the development of people, their communities, and their environments. Social workers should advocate for living conditions conducive to the fulfillment of basic human needs and should promote social, economic, political, and cultural values and institutions that are compatible with the realization of social justice.

6.02 PUBLIC PARTICIPATION

Social workers should facilitate informed participation by the public in shaping social policies and institutions.

6.03 PUBLIC EMERGENCIES

Social workers should provide appropriate professional services in public emergencies to the greatest extent possible.

6.04 SOCIAL AND POLITICAL ACTION

a. Social workers should engage in social and political action that seeks to ensure that all people have equal access to the resources, employment, services, and opportunities they require to meet their basic human needs and to develop fully. Social workers should be aware of the impact of the political arena on practice and should advocate for changes in policy and legislation to improve social conditions in order to meet basic human needs and promote social justice.

b. Social workers should act to expand choice and opportunity for all people, with special regard for vulnerable, disadvantaged, oppressed, and exploited people and groups.

c. Social workers should promote conditions that encourage respect for cultural and social diversity within the United States and globally. Social workers should promote policies and practices that demonstrate respect for difference, support the expansion of cultural knowledge and resources, advocate for programs and institutions that demonstrate cultural competence, and promote policies that safeguard the rights of and confirm equity and social justice for all people.

d. Social workers should act to prevent and eliminate domination of, exploitation of, and discrimination against any person, group, or class on the basis of race, ethnicity, national origin, color, sex, sexual orientation, gender identity or expression, age, marital status, political belief, religion, or mental or physical disability.

National Association of Social Workers
750 First Street NE, Suite 700
Washington, DC 20002-4241
202-408-8600 | 800-638-8799

WEB RESOURCES

Note: URLs (Web addresses) may change frequently, or sites may shut down.

CHILDREN AND FAMILIES

- Child Abuse Prevention Network [http://www.child.cornell.edu]
- Child Welfare Resource Centre [http://www.childwelfare.ca]
- Childwatch International Research Network [http://www.childwatch.uio.no]
- National Parent Information Network [http://www.npin.org]
- Pregnancy and Parenting [http://www.parenting.ivillage.com/]
- Children's Defense Fund [http://www.childrensdefense.org]
- Connect for Kids [http://www.usakids.org]

CRIMINAL JUSTICE

- Bureau of Justice Statistics [http://www.ojp.usdoj.gov/bjs]
- Center on Juvenile and Criminal Justice [http://www.cjcj.org]
- Criminal Justice Policy Foundation [http://www.cjpf.org]
- National Criminal Justice Association [http://www.ncja.org]
- Sourcebook of Criminal Justice Statistics [http://www.albany.edu/sourcebook]

DISABILITY RIGHTS, CULTURE, AND INFORMATION

- Alliance for Technology Access [http://www.ataccess.org]
- The Disability Rights Advocate [http://www.disrights.org]
- Disability Rights Education and Defense Fund [http://www.dredf.org]
- Federation for Children with Special Needs [http://www.fcsn.org]
- National Parent Network on Disabilities [http://www.npnd.org]
- New Mobility [http://www.newmobility.com]
- Reach Out Magazine [http://www.reachoutmag.com]

DIVERSITY AND CULTURE, AFRICAN AMERICANS

- Job and Volunteer Links [http://www.igc.org/jobs.html]
- African American Planning Commission Inc. [http://www.aapci.org]
- African Village [http://www.africanvillage.com]
- National Association for the Advancement of Colored People [http://www.naacp.org]
- National Congress of Black Women [http://www.npcbw.org]
- National Urban League [http://www.nul.org]

DIVERSITY AND CULTURE, ASIAN AMERICANS

- Asian American Net [http://www.asianamerican.net]
- Asian Pacific Policy and Planning Council [http://www.a3pcon.org]
- Coalition for Asian American Children and Families [http://www.cacf.org]
- Japanese American Citizens League [http://www.jacl.org]
- National Asian Pacific American Legal Consortium [http://www.napalc.org]
- Southeast Asia Resource Action Center [http://www.searac.org]

DIVERSITY AND CULTURE, FIRST NATIONS AND INDIGENOUS PEOPLE

- American Indian Movement [http://www.horizons.k12.mi.us/~aim/index.html]
- American Indian Policy Center [http://www.airpi.org]
- Center for World Indigenous Studies [http://www.cwis.org]
- The Village of First Nations [http://www.firstnations.com]
- National Congress of American Indians [http://www.198.104.130.237/ncai/index.jsp]
- Native American Rights Fund [http://www.narf.org]
- Native Web [http://www.nativeweb.org]

DIVERSITY AND CULTURE, GAY/LESBIAN/BISEXUAL/TRANSGENDER

- Gay and Lesbian Alliance Against Defamation [http://www.glaad.org]
- Bi.Org: Serving the world bisexual community [http://www.bi.org]
- Children of Lesbians and Gays Everywhere [http://www.colage.org]
- Deaf Queer Resource Center [http://www.deafqueer.org]
- Human Rights Campaign [http://www.hrc.org]
- Lambda Legal [http://www.lambdalegal.org/cgi-bin/iowa/index.html]

DIVERSITY AND CULTURE, LATINO AND LATINA

- The Borderlands Encyclopedia ("Enciclopedia de la Frontera") [http://www.utep.edu/border]
- Congressional Hispanic Caucus [http://www.rodriguez.house.gov/chc/index.asp]

- Council of Latino Agencies [http://www.consejo.org]
- Latino Issues Forum [http://www.lif.org]
- Latinolink [http://www.latinolink.com]
- Latino Web [http://www.latinoweb.com]
- Mexican American Legal Defense and Educational Fund [http://www.maldef.org]
- National Latino Research Center [http://www.csusm.edu/nlrc]

DIVERSITY AND CULTURE, WOMEN

- Feminist Majority Foundation Online [http://www.feminist.org]
- League of Women Voters [http://www.lwv.org]
- Madre: Demanding Human Rights for Women and Families Around the World [http://www.madre.org]
- National Organization for Women [http://www.now.org]
- National Coalition Against Domestic Violence [http://www.ncadv.org]
- National Partnership for Women and Families [http://www.nationalpartnership.org]
- National Women's Political Caucus [http://www.nwpc.org]
- Third Wave Foundation [http://www.thirdwavefoundation.org]
- United Nations WomenWatch [http://www.un.org/womenwatch]
- Women in America [http://xroads.virginia.edu/~HYPER/DETOC/FEM/topic.htm]

ELDERLY PEOPLE

- Administration on Aging [http://www.aoa.gov]
- Alliance for Retired Americans [http://www.retiredamericans.org]
- American Association of Retired Persons [http://www.aarp.org]
- FirstGov for Seniors [http://www.firstgov.gov/topics.seniors.shtml]
- Senior Law Home Page [http://www.seniorlaw.com]
- SeniorNet [http://www.seniornet.org/php/default.php]

HEALTH

- American Public Health Association [http://www.apha.org]
- Centers for Disease Control and Prevention [http://www.cdc.gov]
- The HIV/AIDS Surveillance Report [http://www.cdc.gov/hiv/stats/hasrlink.htm]
- Clinical Tools [http://www1.clinicaltools.com/topicreq?]
- Health Resources and Services Administration [http://www.hrsa.gov]
- JAMA and Archives Journals [http://pubs.ama-assn.org/]
- National Center for Health Statistics [http://www.cdc.gov/nchswww]
- National Health Information Center [http://www.health.gov/nhic]

- National Institutes of Health [http://www.nih.gov]
- U.S. Department of Health and Human Services [http://www.hhs.gov]
- World Health Organization [http://www.who.int/en/]

INFORMATION AND REFERRAL

- Community Information and Referral (CIR) [http://www.cir.org]

MENTAL HEALTH

- Children and Adults with Attention Deficit Hyperactivity Disorder [http://www.chadd.org]
- Ending Discrimination in Health Insurance [http://www.apa.org/practice/paper]
- Mental Health, Self-Help, and Psychology Information and Resources [http://www.mental-health-matters.com]
- Mental Health Resources [http://www.mentalhealth.about.com]
- Mental Help Net [http://www.mentalhelp.net]
- National Institutes of Mental Health [http://www.nimh.nih.gov]
- National Mental Health Association [http://www.mnha.org]

NEWSPAPERS AND NEWS MEDIA

- Christian Science Monitor [http://www.csmonitor.com]
- CNN [http://www.cnn.com]
- National Public Radio–NPR Online [http://www.npr.org]
- Washington Post [http://www.washingtonpost.com]
- New York Times [http://www.nytimes.com]

POPULATION

- Population and Household Economic Topics [http://www.census.gov/ftp/pub/population/www]
- U.S. POPClock Projection [http://www.census.gov/population/www/popclockus.html]
- World POPClock Projection [http://www.census.gov/ipc/www/popclockworld.html]
- Population Projections [http://www.census.gov/population/www/projections/popproj.html]
- Index of Population [http://www.census.gov/population]
- Urban and Rural Definitions and Data [http://www.census.gov/population/www/censusdata/ur-def.html]
- International Programs Center [http://www.census.gov/ipc/www]

POVERTY

- Center on Budget and Policy Priorities [http://www.cbpp.org]
- Center for Law and Social Policy [http://www.clasp.org]
- Food Research and Action Center [http://www.frac.org]
- Institute for Research on Poverty [http://www.irp.wisc.edu/]
- Poverty and Race Research Action Council [e-mail: prrac@aol.com]
- Southern Poverty Law Center [http://www.splcenter.org]
- Welfare Law Center [http://www.welfarelaw.org]

SCHOOL SOCIAL WORK

- School Social Work Association of America (SSWAA) [http://www.sswaa.org/]
- School Social Work National and State References [http://ideanet.doe.state.in.us/sservices/socwork.htm]
- International Network for School Social Work [http://internationalnetwork-schoolsocialwork.htmlplanet.com/]
- Illinois Association of School Social Workers [http://www.iassw.org/]

SOCIAL JUSTICE AND CIVIL RIGHTS

- American Civil Liberties Union [http://www.aclu.org]
- American Arab Anti-Discrimination Committee [http://www.adc.org]
- Anti-Defamation League [http://www.adl.org]
- Citizens Commission on Civil Rights [http://www.cccr.org]
- U.S. Equal Employment Opportunity Commission [http://www.eeoc.gov]
- Hatewatch [http://www.splcenter.org/intel/hatewatch/]
- Human Rights Watch [http://www.hrw.org]
- The People's Movement for Human Rights Education [http://www.pdhre.org]
- United Nations High Commissioner for Human Rights [http://www.ohchr.org/English/]
- U.S. Commission on Civil Rights [http://www.usccr.gov]

SOCIAL WORK PROFESSIONAL RESOURCES

- Association for Community Organization and Social Administration [http://www.acosa.org]
- Council on Social Work Education [http://www.cswe.org]
- The Julian Samora Research Institute [http://www.jsri.msu.edu]
- Latino Social Workers Organization [http://www.lswo.org]
- National Association of Social Workers [http://www.naswdc.org]
- The New Social Worker Online [http://www.socialworker.com/home/index.php]

SUBSTANCE ABUSE

- The National Center on Addiction and Substance Abuse at Columbia University [http://casacolumbia.org/absolutenm/templates/article.asp?articleid=287&zoneid=32]
- Join Together to Advance Effective Alcohol and Drug Policy, Prevention, and Treatment [http://www.jointogether.org/home/]
- National Clearinghouse for Alcohol and Drug Information [http://www.health.org]
- Substance Abuse and Mental Health Services Administration [http://www.samhsa.gov]
- Substance Abuse Policy Research Program [http://www.saprp.org]

WORKPLACE

- U.S. Department of Labor, Occupational Safety and Health Administration [http://www.osha.gov]
- Institute for a Drug-Free Workplace [http://www.drugfreeworkplace.org/]
- Office of Personnel Management: Dealing with Workplace Violence [http://www.opm.gov/workplac]
- Workplace Publications [http://www.health.org/workplace/]
- Workplace Resource Center [http://www.workplace.samhsa.gov/]
- Workplace Solutions: Conflict and Crisis Prevention [http://wps.org/]

GLOSSARY

ableism (p. 73) oppression of people with disabilities

absolute poverty (p. 90) level of poverty determined by a set dollar amount

acquired immune deficiency syndrome (AIDS) (p. 257) chronic disease that damages and destroys the immune system

active euthanasia (p. 217) doctor-administered cause of death of terminally ill patients

acute care (p. 247) medical attention to immediate problems

addiction (p. 359) compulsion toward a specific behavior or substance despite negative consequences and a psychological or physical dependence on the behavior or substance being abused

adjudication (p. 408) process of formal accusation, trial, and sentencing

adoption (p. 181) legally moving a child to an adoptive family

advance directive (p. 219) formal written statement that outlines the medical options and procedures a person may or may not want to prolong life

advocacy (p. 134) pleading the cause of another or speaking up and supporting what one believes in

affirmative action (p. 81) plans by employers and educational institutions to diversify workforces and student bodies by creating opportunities for women and people of color

Age Discrimination in Employment Act (ADEA) (p. 80) law that protects employees over 40 years old from age discrimination in their workplace

ageism (pp. 73, 204) belief in the superiority of youth over age and the systematic oppression of people because they are older

Alzheimer's disease (p. 224) most common form of dementia

ambulatory care (p. 249) outpatient, education, counseling, and community health services

Americans with Disabilities Act (p. 80) legislation that provides civil rights protections for people with disabilities

amphetamines (p. 360) drugs that stimulate the central nervous system

anti-Semitism (p. 73) systematic discrimination or oppression of Jews

Area Agencies on Aging (AAA) (p. 208) federally sponsored statewide offices designed to coordinate and fund social services for older people

assessment (pp. 116, 186) determination of the presenting concerns, details of others involved, the person's environment, personal history, and background in order to identify appropriate services

assisted living facilities (p. 250) places for congregate living for people who need some assistance with daily living skills and medical attention

attention deficit hyperactivity disorder (ADHD) (p. 305) repeated displays of distractibility, hyperactivity, and impulsivity for more than six months

baby boomers (p. 210) Americans born between 1946 and 1964

barbiturates (p. 366) depressant drugs

bilingual education (p. 165) school programs that allow children to learn course material in their native language while they develop skills in a second language, usually English

case management (p. 120) coordination and referral of services for a client

cash assistance (p. 54) provision of resources through financial transfers

change agent (p. 28) social worker or other helping professional or a group of helpers whose purpose is to facilitate improvement

Charity Organization Societies (COS) (p. 4) associations begun in the 1870s with the primary goals of learning what caused individual poverty and providing organized services to alleviate poverty, emphasis on serving individuals and their families

chemical dependency (p. 359) addiction to alcohol or other drugs

childhood (p. 175) first period of life that begins at birth and ends at age 18

child welfare (p. 180) activities, programs, interventions, or policies that are intended to improve the overall well-being of children

civil rights (p. 79) rights to which people are entitled because they are members of society, including legal protection from discrimination and oppression

Civil Rights Act of 1964 (pp. 46, 80) legislation that prohibits segregation and discrimination based on race

Civil Rights Act of 1968 (p. 80) legislation that prohibits discrimination in housing

classism (p. 73) institutional and cultural attitudes and behaviors that stigmatize the poor and place a higher value on wealthier people

club drugs (p. 366) illegal drugs used at all-night parties such as raves and in dance clubs and bars

cognitive-behavioral therapy (pp. 124, 447) practice interventions designed to weaken or lessen habitual reactions to troublesome situations in order to calm the mind and body so the person can think more clearly and make better decisions

cognitive development (p. 178) developmental stages that children must go through in order to progress to higher levels of thinking; thinking starts out basic and concrete in infancy and becomes more abstract and complicated

colonization (p. 152) settlement and occupation of a new country

community change (p. 133) desired outcome for improving social and economic conditions

community corrections (p. 411) punishments or sanctions that occur outside of secure correctional facilities in halfway houses, treatment programs, work, or educational release programs

community development (p. 133) process of helping individuals improve the conditions of their lives by increased involvement in the social and economic conditions of their communities

community organizing (p. 133) bringing people together to work for needed change

community planning (p. 133) collecting data, analyzing a situation, and developing strategies to move from a problem to a solution

community relations (p. 339) programs to help companies function better within their community settings

confidentiality (p. 289) situation in which all information remains with the therapist and is released only with the consent of the client

consumer (p. 274) term used by advocacy groups for a person who has received or is currently receiving services

contingent workers (p. 350) temporary, contract, and part-time employees

Council on Social Work Education (CSWE) (p. 6) nonprofit national association that represents over 3,000 individual members, 191 graduate programs, and 463 undergraduate programs of professional social work education; founded in 1952 and recognized by the Council for Higher Education Accreditation as the sole accrediting agency for social work education in the United States

crime prevention (p. 451) efforts to stop criminal behaviors from happening

crisis (p. 4) event that disrupts a person's equilibrium so that the person's usual ways of coping fail and from which there is evidence of distress and impairment of functioning

crisis intervention (p. 123) short-term social work practice that is designed to assist victims and survivors to return to their precrisis level of functioning

cultural competence (p. 157) understanding of how and why people are different and awareness of the effect of oppression and discrimination on people's lives

cultural pluralism (p. 78) people mixing socially and economically with other groups while retaining their unique cultural characteristics

culture-bound syndrome (p. 281) pattern of aberrant or problematic behavior unique to a local culture

culture of poverty (p. 93) belief that people learn to be poor from growing up in impoverished areas

deindustrialization (p. 331) late-twentieth-century economic shift from a manufacturing to an information-based economy

deinstitutionalization (p. 274) shift in the location of psychiatric care from inpatient facilities, particularly public mental hospitals, to the community

delinquency (p. 194) behavior that is illegal and could cause a child to become involved with the juvenile justice system

delinquent youth (p. 405) children under the age of 18 who have violated a local, state, or federal law for which an adult can be prosecuted

dementia (p. 224) condition of loss of intellectual and social abilities that is severe enough to interfere with daily functioning

denial (p. 372) person's not recognizing or admitting that there is a connection between his or her life problems and the abuse of alcohol or another substance

dependence (p. 366) addiction to a substance

depressants (p. 366) drugs that cause disinhibition, reduce anxiety, and depress the central nervous system

deterrence theory (p. 396) belief that the use of punishment will discourage people from committing crimes

developmental disability (pp. 251, 303) severe, chronic disability that is attributable to a mental or physical impairment that manifests itself before the age of 22 and is likely to continue indefinitely

devolution (p. 49) decreasing the federal government's role in social welfare and turning responsibility back to the local level

devolution of services (p. 103) movement of social programs from the federal level to the state level

digital divide (p. 331) the gap between those who have access and training to technology and those who do not have access

direct services (p. 119) social services provided by social workers

disability (p. 255) physical or mental impairment that substantially limits one or more major life activities

disaster (p. 432) extraordinary event, either natural or human made, concentrated in time and space, that often results in damage to property and harm to human life or health and is disruptive of the ability of some social institutions to continue fulfilling their essential functions

discharge planning (p. 248) arranging to help patients in acute care settings transition out of the facility and receive necessary care on leaving, included in the role of social workers

discouraged workers (p. 330) people not actively looking for work and not included in federal unemployment statistics

discrimination (p. 69) actions of treating people differently on the basis of their membership in a group, usually involving denial of something

diversion (p. 406) officially suspending criminal or juvenile proceedings so as to allow dependents to meet specified conditions, such as completing treatment, community service, or an educational program

diversity perspective (p. 14) theoretical framework that emphasizes the broad and varied differences of social workers and their clients and how these differences can enhance society

domestic violence (p. 415) pattern of assaultive behavior by adults and juveniles against their families or intimate partners

drug misuse (p. 359) inappropriate use of medications or prescribed drugs

drugs (p. 359) any chemical substances taken internally that alter the body's functioning

drug use (p. 359) general term for all drug taking

DSM-IV-TR (p. 277) manual that lists all currently recognized mental disorders and provides a detailed description of each diagnostic category and specific diagnostic criteria; published by the American Psychiatric Association

due process (p. 406) right to a fair trial, right to be present at the trial, right to an impartial jury trial, and right to be heard in one's own defense

ecological systems framework (p. 13) perspective with emphasis on understanding people, their environments, and their transactions; major concepts of this orientation include goodness of fit between people and the environment, reciprocity, and mutuality

educational groups (p. 129) groups that impart information and train people in needed skills

Education for All Handicapped Children Act (p. 299) mandate for educating every child, including children with disabilities

Education of Homeless Children and Youth (EHCY) (p. 311) provides grants to state and local educational agencies to ensure that homeless children have access to education

elder abuse (p. 221) maltreatment of older people

Elementary and Secondary Education Act (ESEA) (p. 311) law requiring federal assistance to poor schools and communities for educating children

Elizabethan Poor Laws (p. 41) first social welfare policy implemented in colonial America, which outlined the public's responsibility for people who were poor

employee assistance program (EAP) (p. 330) program set up by employees or unions to provide health and social services to employees and their families

Employment Non-Discrimination Act (ENDA) (p. 80) proposed legislation that would prohibit employers from discrimination based on sexual orientation

empowerment (p. 14) psychological state that reflects a sense of competence, control, and entitlement, allows one to pursue concrete activities aimed at becoming powerful, gives control over the environment, which makes it possible for people to improve their lives

entitlements (p. 54) guaranteed social support to all eligible persons through services or financial remuneration without time limits

e-therapy (p. 127) therapy or support delivered electronically

ethnic group (p. 150) group of people who share common cultural patterns or national origins

ethnopsychopharmacology (p. 284) area of study that looks at the way ethnic and cultural influences affect a client's response to medication

eye movement desensitization and reprocessing (EMDR) (p. 448) form of therapy that involves paying attention to past and current experiences while simultaneously focusing on an external stimulus

evidence-based practice (p. 269) use of the best scientific knowledge to guide professional interventions

family (p. 175) system of individuals who are interrelated and have significant relationships

Family and Medical Leave Act (p. 214) law that allows people unpaid time off from work to care for dependent parents or newborn children

family preservation services (p. 181) services to provide support to families so crises can be averted or to help families cope and stay together if crises do occur

fee-for-service (p. 242) health insurance coverage that allows the insured person to choose a doctor and receive services, while the insurance company pays all or part of the bill

feminization of poverty (p. 93) trend that poverty is more likely to happen to women

fetal alcohol syndrome (p. 369) pattern of mental and physical defects that develop in some fetuses when the mother drinks too much alcohol during pregnancy

Fifteenth Amendment (p. 79) constitutional amendment of 1870 that gave all men, regardless of race, the right to vote

Food Stamp Program (p. 105) food assistance program run by the Department of Agriculture

forensic social work (p. 407) application of social work to questions and issues related to law and the legal system

foster care (p. 181) social welfare program designed to care for children outside of their families

Fourteenth Amendment (p. 79) constitutional amendment of 1868 that offered early civil rights protections

generalist social work practice (p. 114) social work practice backed with broad range of training and primarily used to guide and coordinate service

general systems theory (p. 11) belief that the behavior of people and societies is explained by identifying the components of subsystems of the larger (or host) system and how those subsystems interact and impact on the larger system; holistic framework concerned with system boundaries, roles, relationships, and interactions between people in the system or its subsystems

gerontology (p. 205) study of the biological, psychological, and social aspects of aging

globalization (p. 332) increasing interconnection of the world's economy

hallucinogens (p. 366) drugs that distort visual and sensory perception

hate crimes (p. 66) illegal acts against people because of their race, ethnicity, religion, sexual orientation, ability, or gender

hazard prevention (p. 451) preparation for a possible natural disaster or efforts to protect from a natural disaster

health (p. 237) state of complete physical, mental, and social well-being

health maintenance organization (HMO) (p. 242) managed health care structure that requires referrals from a primary care physician

heterosexism (p. 71) institutionalized bias directed at gay men, lesbians, bisexuals, and people who are transgender

homophobia (p. 71) fear of homosexuality or fear of lesbians and gay men

hospice (p. 250) services for people with terminal illnesses who are expected to die within six months

human growth hormone (HGH) (p. 385) a protein hormone that stimulates growth and cell reproduction

human immunodeficiency virus (HIV) (p. 257) viral antibodies that lead to AIDS

human resource (HR) management (p. 339) workplace planning for staff needs, recruitment, training, labor relations, compensation and benefits, and evaluation of employee performance

immigration (p. 153) movement of people away from their native lands to become permanent residents of another country

inclusion (p. 309) making every effort to educate a child with a disability in his or her own neighborhood school and with his or her own peers

individualized education plan (IEP) (p. 300) outline for expected level of educational performance goals, objectives, and outcomes for a child with disabilities

Individuals with Disabilities Education Act (IDEA) (p. 309) law reauthorizing Education for All Handicapped Children Act; sets legal standards and requirements for education of children with disabilities

information and referral (I&R) (p. 117) providing information on availability, location, and eligibility to clients to enhance their access to services

inhalants (p. 366) depressant drugs that are inhaled

in-kind benefits (p. 54) aid in the form of tangible items

institutional (p. 39) preventive social welfare services built into the institutional structures of society

institutional discrimination (p. 69) discrimination built into the norms and institutions of society and enforced by those in power

intake (p. 116) form of assessment that is usually conducted through a formal interview with the client and includes provision of information on available services

internalized homophobia (p. 378) self-hatred by lesbians and gay men

juvenile corrections (p. 408) wide range of interventions for young people who have broken the law

juvenilization of poverty (p. 93) tendency for children to be disproportionately represented in the ranks of those who are poor

labor unions (p. 333) organizations representing workers through membership

learning disability (p. 303) significant difference between overall intelligence and ability to read and write, or do mathematical calculations

least restrictive environment (p. 301) educational environment that permits a child with disabilities the most freedom he or she can handle

living wage (p. 347) amount of earnings necessary for a person and his or her family to afford basic needs

living will (p. 218) formal statement written and signed while a person is mentally competent that specifies how the person wishes to have his or her own death handled in the event that the person cannot participate in the decision making

long-term care (pp. 215, 249) set of health and social services delivered over a sustained period of time at home or in a medical or nursing facility

macro practice (pp. 2, 115) work to change the larger social environment so that it benefits individuals and families

mainstreaming (p. 310) removing a child with a disability from special education classes and placing him or her in one or more regular education classes

maltreatment (p. 181) ways that children are hurt by the people who are expected to care for them; includes physical abuse, sexual abuse, emotional abuse, or neglect

managed care (pp. 242, 274) health care delivery system designed to screen out unnecessary and inappropriate care and thereby reduce costs

Medicaid (pp. 213, 241) federal- and state-funded needs-based health insurance program for people whose incomes and assets fall beneath a set amount

medical model (p. 238) approach to health care traditionally used by doctors that locates sickness in the patient, which a physician or medical expert has the authority to heal or cure

Medicare (pp. 213, 241) universal, federally funded compulsory health insurance program for older people, added to the Social Security Act in 1965

Medicare Prescription Drug Improvement and Modernization Act (MMA) (p. 209) legislation that provides prescription drug benefits for Medicare eligible seniors by implementing a Part D benefit to the Medicare program where members enroll with private companies to obtain prescription medications

mental disorders (p. 269) health conditions characterized by alterations in thinking, mood, or behavior associated with distress or impaired functioning

mental health (p.269) successful performance of mental function, resulting in productive activities, fulfilling relationships with other people, and the ability to adapt to change and cope with adversity

Mental Health Parity Act (p. 286) law that prohibits insurers from imposing lifetime and annual benefit limits on mental health services that differ from limits on physical health care

mental illness (p. 269) collective term for all diagnosable mental disorders

micro practice (pp. 2, 115) work to help individuals, families, and small groups function better within the larger environment

mindfulness (p. 447) state of being aware of everything in the present moment without judgment or analysis

misdemeanor (p. 399) least serious type of crime, usually punishable by a fine or a combination of a fine and less than one year of incarceration

morbidity (p. 239) rate of illness

mortality (p. 239) rate of death

multicultural education (p. 313) teaching that challenges and rejects racism and other forms of discrimination in schools and society

multiculturalism (p. 157) acknowledgement, appreciation, and understanding of cultural diversity

multiethnic or transracial adoption (p. 164) permanent placement of children of one ethnicity or race with parents of a different ethnicity or race

National Association of Social Workers (NASW) (p. 7) membership organization of professional social workers with more than 150,000 members; works to enhance the professional growth and development of its members, creates and maintains professional standards, and advances social policies

neglect (p. 221) not providing basic necessities such as food or medical attention

network linkages (p. 119) connections between social service systems for a client

Nineteenth Amendment (p. 80) constitutional amendment of 1920 that guaranteed women the right to vote

No Child Left Behind (p. 312) 2001 federal legislation that requires every child learn to read, write, and subtract at grade level; every state is required to set standards to achieve this goal, which is applied to all schools that receive Title I education funding

nursing home (p. 250) residential health care facility that provides medical care

occupational social work (p. 330) social work services to help people with job-related pressures or personal problems that affect the quality of their work and home lives

Older Americans Act (OAA) (p. 208) law that established the federal Administration on Aging (AOA)

ombudsman (p. 222) advocate for residents of nursing homes, board and care homes, and assisted living facilities

oppression (p. 69) systematic and pervasive mistreatment of people based on their membership in a certain group

organizational development (p. 340) efforts to improve organizational effectiveness and efficiency

parole (p. 405) conditional release of a prisoner from incarceration to supervision after part of his or her sentence has been completed

passive euthanasia (p. 217) intentional termination of one's own life with means provided by another person, such as a doctor

peer counselors (p. 277) consumers who themselves have recovered from disorders and who assist others facing the same disorder

permanency planning (p. 181) effort to achieve child welfare goal of placing children in the most stable and safe living situation

person-in-environment (p. 10) perspective used by social workers to understand clients experiencing difficulties with their roles, self-perceptions, and expectations in their interactions with others and in the context of their surrounding environment

police social work (p. 406) social work services provided to victims and offenders who are referred

poverty guidelines (p. 91) guidelines for use of Department of Health and Human Services poverty line to determine eligibility for social services

poverty threshold (p. 91) Census Bureau absolute measure of poverty, used for statistical purposes

preferred provider organization (PPO) (p. 242) form of managed care

prejudice (p. 68) attitude of judging or disliking groups and individuals based on myths and misconceptions

preventive medicine (p. 451) behaviors that promote healthy living and the prevention of illness and disease

primary care (p. 242) first medical care provided by professional in a managed care system

privilege (p. 74) social and economic advantages that are ascribed to members of dominant groups

probation (p. 405) legal sentence that does not require incarceration

problem-solving method (p. 122) pragmatic approach to social work direct practice that emphasizes identifying the client's present difficulties, which are a natural part of life, and providing knowledge and resources to help with them

Protestant work ethic (p. 331) early historic belief that everyone must work hard, not working was a sin, and leisure and free time were immoral

psychoactive drugs (p. 366) drugs that alter sensory perceptions, mood, thought processes, or behavior by acting on the nervous system

psychogeriatrics (p. 211) combination of psychiatric and mental health care and services for older people

psychosocial assessment (pp. 178, 248) investigation of psychological and social challenges faced by a client

psychosocial theory (p. 178) belief that human development progresses through a series of psychosocial crises that must be resolved

psychosocial treatment (p. 122) form of direct practice that emphasizes explanation of the internal determinants of people's behaviors, with focus on early life experiences and childhood memories

psychotropic drugs (p. 273) chemicals used to treat mental disorders

public assistance programs (p. 54) means-tested social welfare programs designed to alleviate poverty

pupil services team (p. 301) interdisciplinary team in schools

race (p. 150) umbrella term that includes multiple ethnic groups

racism (p. 70) systematic mistreatment of people based on their race

recidivism (p. 410) return of a criminal offender to criminal behavior after a period of correctional treatment

recovery (p. 290) symptom remission and improved functioning in life for people with serious mental illness, the desired outcome of treatment

referral (p. 185) request or demand by other professionals that social services be provided for a client

refugee (p. 154) person who is fleeing persecution from countries considered to be oppressive

rehabilitation (p. 406) treatment that helps criminal offenders change their antisocial style of thinking, feeling, and acting

reintegration (p. 406) services designed to provide a bridge to help with the transition to the community for adults released from prison

relative poverty (p. 90) state of being poor determined by comparisons

reparations (p. 164) payments made to redress past injustices

residual (p. 39) social welfare services designed to address an identified problem

risk prevention (p. 451) taking measures to prevent or minimize loss or problems

school social work (p. 298) services in educational settings by credentialed school social workers

secondary traumatic stress (p. 443) stress from secondhand exposure to traumatic events

self-determination (pp. 3, 190) client's making own choices, respect value of social workers

separatism (p. 78) situation in which social groups live in the same country, but do things as separately as possible

Settlement Movement (p. 5) organized social welfare efforts begun in the late 1880s to help people who were poor, particularly immigrants, included workers living within the community and providing services from their dwelling or settlement

sexism (p. 71) oppression that grows out of the belief that men are superior to women

single-payer plan (p. 236) health insurance coverage provided by one insurer, typically the federal government

social construction (p. 148) image of group's characteristics and value determined by people who have power in society

social insurance programs (p. 54) social welfare programs designed to prevent poverty that are based on shared contributions made while people are working to be used later to provide services and benefits

socialization groups (p. 129) groups designed to help participants learn how to behave in socially accepted ways so they can function effectively in their lives and communities

social justice (p. 67) level of fairness that exists in human relationships and overall in society

social learning theory (p. 178) belief that behavior is learned through socialization

Social Security Act of 1935 (p. 46) legislated federal policy that provides long-term protections through social insurance and aid to people in poverty through public assistance

social welfare system (p. 38) collection of programs, resources, and services available to help people

status offenses (p. 408) violations of the law only for people young enough to be considered minors

steroids (p. 385) natural or synthetic drugs that provide hormones to the body

stigma (p. 284) discredit that occurs when an individual's diagnosis or condition becomes an enduring label

stimulants (p. 360) drugs that increase alertness, wakefulness, and energy

strengths perspective (p. 13) view that emphasizes using clients' strengths, resources, support networks, and motivations to meet challenges; focus on clients' assets rather than problems or dysfunction

stress (p. 432) physiological response to a real or perceived threat that leads to anxiety, which is physical discomfort experienced because of the increased production of stress hormones

substance abuse (p. 359) continued use of alcohol or other drugs in spite of adverse consequences

Supplemental Security Income (SSI) (pp. 101, 213) cash assistance to people who are poor and older, or poor with disabilities

task-centered groups (p. 131) groups that are concerned with organizational and social change

task-centered social work (p. 123) short-term treatment focused on client-acknowledged problems

Temporary Assistance for Needy Families (TANF) (p. 102) cash assistance program for poor families

termination (p. 188) final stage of the problem-solving model for treatment

therapeutic groups (p. 130) groups focused on the use of psychological intervention to address internal concerns

tolerance (p. 369) process by which receptors in the brain become habituated to the use of a particular drug

trauma (p. 432) injury to the body or psyche by some type of shock, violence, or unanticipated situation

truth and reconciliation (p. 436) opportunities for victims of trauma to publicly face those who had harmed them and talk about what had happened to them

underemployed (p. 96) working but not earning a sufficient income

underemployment (p. 330) condition of people who are employed but are not working enough hours to earn an adequate income to meet financial need

unemployed (p. 96) physically able to work, but unable to find employment

unemployment (p. 330) condition of people who want jobs but do not have paid employment

universal health care (p. 236) health insurance coverage for all people, regardless of preexisting conditions and employment status

victim (p. 412) person against whom a criminal offense has been committed

Voting Rights Act (p. 48) legislation that prohibits denying people of color the right to vote

vulnerable (p. 175) needing special attention and advocacy; needing others to recognize and respond to one's needs

War on Poverty (p. 48) general term used to describe the social welfare policies and programs of the 1960s that were designed to alleviate poverty

wellness model (p. 238) view that authority and responsibility for health rests with each individual

withdrawal (p. 369) development of tolerance to a drug without an increase in dosage or through a decrease in dosage below a person's tolerance point

work (p. 330) what people do outside the home to earn money and inside the home to care for home and family

working poor (p. 96) employed, but earnings are not sufficient for meeting basic needs

INDEX